INTEGRATED PEST MANAGEMENT FOR

FLORICULTURE AND NURSERIES

INTEGRATED PEST MANAGEMENT FOR

FLORICULTURE AND NURSERIES

UNIVERSITY OF CALIFORNIA
STATEWIDE INTEGRATED PEST MANAGEMENT PROJECT

DIVISION OF AGRICULTURE AND NATURAL RESOURCES
PUBLICATION 3402
2001

PRECAUTIONS FOR USING PESTICIDES

Pesticides are poisonous and must be used with caution. READ THE LABEL BEFORE OPENING A PESTICIDE CONTAINER. Follow all label precautions and directions, including requirements for protective equipment. Pesticides used in greenhouses must list greenhouse on the label. Use a pesticide only on crops specified on the label or in published University of California recommendations. Apply pesticides at the rates specified on the label or at lower rates if suggested in this publication. In California, all agricultural uses of pesticides must be reported, including use in flower fields, greenhouses, and nurseries. Contact your county agricultural commissioner for further details. Laws, regulations, and information concerning pesticides change frequently, so be sure the publication you are using is up-to-date.

Legal Responsibility. The user is legally responsible for any damage due to misuse of pesticides. Responsibility extends to effects caused by drift, runoff, or residues.

Transportation. Do not ship or carry pesticides together with food or feed in a way that allows contamination of the edible items. Never transport pesticides in a closed passenger vehicle or in a closed cab.

Storage. Keep pesticides in original containers until used. Store them in a locked cabinet, building, or fenced area where they are not accessible to children, unauthorized persons, pets, or livestock. DO NOT store pesticides with foods, feed, fertilizers, or other materials that may become contaminated by the pesticides.

Container Disposal. Dispose of empty containers carefully. Never reuse them. Make sure empty containers are not accessible to children or animals. Never dispose of containers where they may contaminate water supplies or natural waterways. Consult your county agricultural commissioner for correct procedures for handling and disposal of large quantities of empty containers.

Protection of Nonpest Animals and Plants. Many pesticides are toxic to useful or desirable animals, including honey bees, natural enemies, fish, domestic animals, and birds. Certain rodenticides may pose a special hazard to animals that eat poisoned rodents. Crops and other plants may also be damaged by misapplied pesticides. Take precautions to protect nonpest species from direct exposure to pesticides and from contamination due to drift, runoff, or residues.

Posting Treated Fields, Greenhouses, and Nurseries. For some materials, reentry intervals are established to protect field workers. Keep workers out of fields, greenhouses, and nurseries for the required time after application, and, when required by regulations, post the treated areas with signs indicating the safe reentry date.

Harvest and Reentry Intervals. Some materials or rates cannot be used in certain crops within a specified time before harvest. Treated areas generally cannot be entered until completion of a time period after application called the reentry interval. Follow pesticide label instructions and allow the required time between application, harvest, and reentry.

Permit Requirements. Many pesticides require a permit from the county agricultural commissioner before possession or use.

Processed Crops. Some processors will not accept a crop treated with certain chemicals. If your crop is going to a processor, be sure to check with the processor before applying a pesticide.

Plant Injury. Certain chemicals may cause injury to plants (phytotoxicity) under certain conditions. Always consult the label for limitations. Before applying any pesticide, take into account the stage of plant development, the soil type and condition, the temperature, moisture, and wind. Injury may also result from the use of incompatible materials.

Personal Safety. Follow label directions carefully. Avoid splashing, spilling, leaks, spray drift, and contamination of clothing. NEVER eat, smoke, drink, or chew while using pesticides. Provide for emergency medical care IN ADVANCE as required by regulation.

Worker Protection Standards. Federal Worker Protection Standards require pesticide safety training for all employees working in fields, greenhouses, and nurseries that have been treated with pesticides, including pesticide training for employees who don't work directly with pesticides.

ORDERING

For information about ordering this publication, write to:

University of California
Agriculture and Natural Resources
Communication Services
6701 San Pablo Avenue, 2nd Floor
Oakland, California 94608-1239

Telephone (510) 642-2431
(800) 994-8849
FAX (510) 643-5470
E-mail danrcs@ucdavis.edu
http://anrcatalog.ucdavis.edu

Publication 3402

Other books in this series include:

ISBN 1-879906-46-5
Library of Congress Catalog Card No. 99-076566

3m-rep-5/05-ipm/ns

Contributors and Acknowledgments

Written by Steve H. Dreistadt
Photographs by Jack Kelly Clark
Mary Louise Flint, Technical Editor

Technical Coordinators

Heather Costa, Department of Entomology, UC Riverside
Dean R. Donaldson, Cooperative Extension, Napa County
Clyde L. Elmore, Weed Science Program, UC Davis
Richard Y. Evans, Environmental Horticulture
  Department, UC Davis
Marcella E. Grebus, Department of Plant Pathology,
  UC Riverside
John N. Kabashima, UC Cooperative Extension,
  Orange County
Ann I. King, UC Cooperative Extension,
  San Mateo County
Julie P. Newman, UC Cooperative Extension,
  Ventura and Santa Barbara Counties
Albert O. Paulus, Department of Plant Pathology,
  UC Riverside
Michael P. Parrella, Department of Entomology, UC Davis
Robert D. Raabe, Division of Environmental Science,
  Policy, and Management, UC Berkeley
Richard A. Redak, Department of Entomology,
  UC Riverside
Karen L. Robb, UC Cooperative Extension,
  San Diego County
Steven A. Tjosvold, UC Cooperative Extension,
  Santa Cruz and Monterey Counties
Diane E. Ullman, Department of Entomology, UC Davis
Cheryl A. Wilen, UC Cooperative Extension and
  UC Statewide IPM Project, San Diego County and
  Central Coast and Southern Region

Contributors

J. Ole Becker, Alison M. Berry, James A. Bethke, Robert L.
Bugg, Dave W. Burger, Christine Casey, David E. Chaney,
William E. Chaney, Heather Costa, Larry R. Costello,
Michael J. Costello, Richard Cowles, Dave W. Cudney,
Kent M. Daane, Donald L. Dahlsten, Jerry Davidson,
Linda Dodge, Dean R. Donaldson, Jim A. Downer,
Lester E. Ehler, Clyde L. Elmore, Richard Y. Evans,
Deborah Fisher, Paul Fisher, Rosser W. Garrison,
Pam Elam Geisel, D. Ken Giles, Deborah D. Giraud,
Elizabeth E. Grafton-Cardwell, David A. Grantz,
Marcella E. Grebus, David Headrick, Kevin M. Heinz,
Mike J. Henry, Gary W. Hickman, Mark S. Hoddle,
Chuck Ingels, John N. Kabashima, John F. Karlik,
Harry K. Kaya, Ann I. King, W. Thomas Lanini,
Heinrich J. Leith, Michelle LeStrange, Robert F. Luck,
James D. MacDonald, Jim J. Marois, Dennis Mayhew,
Michael V. McKenry, Richard H. Molinar, Carolyn A.
Napoli, Julie P. Newman, Nick Nisson, Pat Nolan, Patrick
J. O'Connor-Marer, Timothy D. Paine, Michael P. Parrella,
Albert O. Paulus, Edward J. Perry, Dennis R. Pittenger,
Antoon T. Ploeg, Robert D. Raabe, Nancy A. Rechcigl,
Richard A. Redak, Michael S. Reid, Richard E. Rice,
Karen L. Robb, Mike Rose, Robin L. Rosetta, Roy M.
Sachs, Ursula Schuch, Norman J. Smith, Richard Smith,
James J. Stapleton, Pavel Svihra, Steven A. Tjosvold,
Diane E. Ullman, Mark Van Horn, Baldo Villegas,
Doug E. Walker, Becky B. Westerdahl, Cheryl A. Wilen,
Frank G. Zalom

Production

Designed and production by: Seventeenth Street Studios
Drawings: Valerie Winemiller
Edited by: Stephen W. Barnett
Page composition: Bob Giles

Special Thanks

Joe C. Ball, Thomas S. Bellows, Glen Berger,
Matthew Blua, Kelly Brannigan, Gary Brothers,
Margaret A. Brush, Tom G. Byrne, Leslie Rickert Campbell,
John A. DeBenedictis, Ellen Davenport, Michael J.
Delwiche, Gwyn C. Dixon, Donna Duddy, Ron Entomoto,
Linda Farrar, Nancy Garrison, Raymond J. Gill, Pattie
Gouveia, Ian Greene, Bruce Hall, Jan Hall, Mark Hanzlik,
Jean Harris, Jenny Hing, Robert Hunter, Jason A. Joseph,
Christine Joshel, Sandra Kelley, Shawn King, Steven T.
Koike, Rich Kundy, Marvin G. Kimsey, John LaFlour,
Jill Lionvale, Steven Lock, Jacqueline L. Lockwood,
Mike Mellano, Valerie Mellano, Barbara L. P. Ohlendorf,
Loren R. Oki, Suzanne Paisley, Gretchen Platt, Keith Pratt,
Rosalind R. Rickard, Larry L. Strand, Michael W. Stimmann,
Will Suckow, Pat Thompson, Bill Weigle, Butch Yamashita,
Perry Yoshida, Cecilia Young, Ellen M. Zagory

This manual was produced under the auspices of
the University of California Statewide IPM Project,
Frank G. Zalom, Director, and prepared by IPM
Education and Publications of the Statewide IPM
Project at the University of California, Davis,
Mary Louise Flint, Director.

Contents

Integrated Pest Management for Floriculture and Nurseries

Floriculture and nursery managers are increasingly adopting integrated pest management (IPM) principles and practices in their operations. Reducing the use of pesticides, especially broad-spectrum, persistent pesticides, is one of the major benefits of integrated pest management because it helps maintain pesticide efficacy by delaying the development of pesticide resistance. Less spraying also reduces the disruptions of cultural practices that occur during applications and worker reentry intervals. Fewer applications can improve plant growth and quality by minimizing phytotoxicity and increase profit by reducing the costs of pesticide purchases, application labor, and regulatory compliance. Consumers are increasingly drawn to "environmentally friendly" or "organically grown" products, providing a public relations and marketing advantage to growers who adopt IPM.

Over $2.5 billion worth of flower, foliage, and nursery crops is produced in California each year. Most counties in

Much of California's floriculture and nursery industry is in urban coastal counties, growing areas that have a relatively mild climate year-round and are close to markets. Adopting IPM methods can reduce potential conflicts with neighbors concerned about pesticide drift and provide a public relations and marketing advantage to growers who adopt "environmentally friendly" IPM methods.

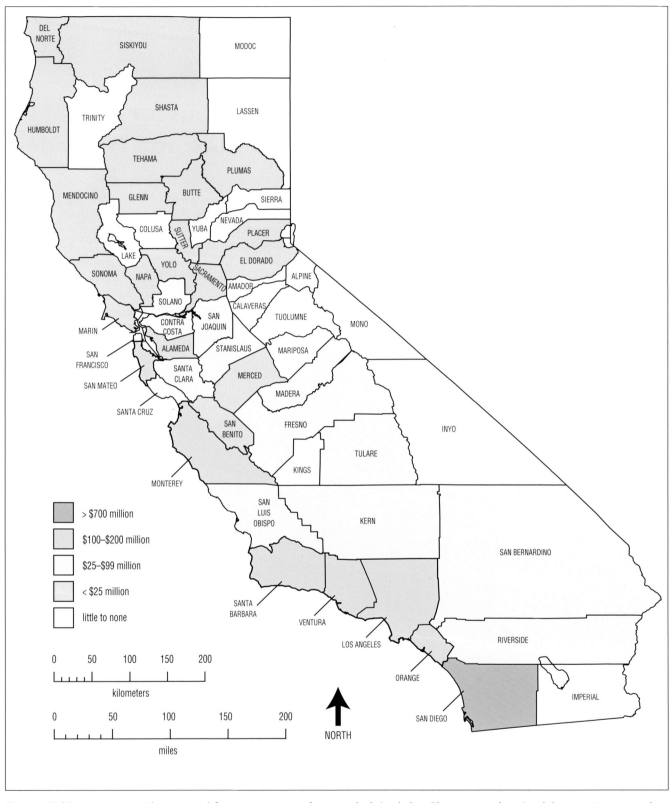

Figure 1. California counties with commercial flower or nursery production or both (excluding Christmas tree farms) and the approximate annual farm-level crop sales value during 1999.

the state have some commercial nursery or flower production (Fig. 1). The largest concentration of producers is in coastal counties, growing areas that have a relatively mild climate year-round and are close to urban markets. San Diego County is the largest flower- and nursery-crop-producing county in the world, with sales exceeding $700 million per year; Los Angeles, Monterey, Orange, San Mateo, Santa Barbara, and Ventura Counties produce over $100 million per year. Thirteen counties have $25 million to $99 million in annual production. Most of the counties with little or no production are mountainous and have Christmas tree nurseries that are not covered in this publication.

This manual will help you apply IPM principles to flower and nursery crops. It is written for growers, farm advisors, IPM scouts, pesticide applicators, and pest control advisers and students. This manual will help you recognize and prevent damage caused by abiotic disorders, insects, mites, nematodes, pathogens, and weeds in bulbs, cut flowers, potted flowering plants, foliage plants, bedding plants, and ornamental trees and shrubs grown in the field, greenhouse, and nursery. Following the recommendations in this manual will help create better crops, more profit, and a healthier environment.

The chapter "Managing Pests in Flower and Nursery Crops" shows how to establish an IPM program. Strategies include damage prevention, regular monitoring, accurate diagnosis of problems, and use of control action guidelines and effective management methods. Two key requirements for success are to take nonchemical preventive actions and to use a knowledgeable IPM scout, someone who monitors crops regularly, keeps good records, and prepares information summaries for pest management decision making. Based on this monitoring information, you can gradually modify pesticide use to reduce the number of applications, adjust intervals between applications, and switch to reduced-risk pesticides and more pest-specific control methods.

"Abiotic Disorders and Cultural Practices" discusses and illustrates preventable problems such as inappropriate irrigation, poor water quality, nutrient toxicity, excess humidity, and improper temperatures. The chapter also summarizes basic growing practices such as irrigation and fertilization. Detailed recommendations on cultural practices are, however, beyond the scope of this publication; refer to the suggested reading and literature cited at the back of this manual for more information on crop production.

The next chapter, "Diseases," provides background and management information on plant pathogenic fungi, bacteria, viruses, and phytoplasmas. Major problems include root and crown decays, vascular wilt diseases, and various pathogens infecting flowers and foliage; control techniques include sanitation, pasteurization, solarization, using disease-suppressive compost, managing humidity and ventilation, and using appropriate fungicides.

The "Insects, Mites, and Other Invertebrates" chapter helps growers identify and manage aphids, leafminers, thrips, whiteflies, mites, and related invertebrates by correct pest identification, excluding pests with screens, using monitoring tools such as yellow sticky traps, targeting the life stages most susceptible to selective insecticides, and using cultural and biological pest controls.

"Weeds" illustrates many of the common pest plants likely to be encountered in floriculture and nursery operations and discusses good site selection and preparation, starting with weed-free plants and media, effective sanitation and exclusion, and preventing weed emergence in crops. Integrated pest management practices for weeds include regular scouting, pasteurizing media, hand-weeding, cultivation, cover cropping, mowing, mulching, and using selective herbicides. The specific methods used will depend on the growing site (field, greenhouse, or nursery) and whether actions are taken before planting, around crop plants, or outside growing areas.

Foliar, root knot, lesion, and stem and bulb nematodes are discussed in the separate chapter on nematodes, which covers nematode biology, crop susceptibility, damage diagnosis, and soil sampling methods. Using pest-free or certified stock plants, pasteurizing media, preventing nematode spread, and rotating crops are among the recommended controls.

The chapter "Crop Tables" provides a symptom-based, crop-specific guide for diagnosing problems. The crop tables list damage symptoms, probable causes, and recommended controls for problems affecting over 120 major flower and foliage crop genera or species. Crops are presented alphabetically by common name. Because plants often have several common names, consult the index to identify the name under which your crop is listed. Most woody ornamental crops are not included in the crop tables. Producers of woody ornamentals should consult *Pests of Landscape Trees and Shrubs* (Dreistadt 1994), another University of California IPM publication, and use that publication in combination with this manual. Nursery growers of commercial or home garden fruit and vegetable crops should also consult other UC IPM publications for specific recommendations for their crops. These publications include *Pests of the Garden and Small Farm* (Flint 1998); UC IPM manuals for almonds, apples and pears, citrus, cole crops and lettuce, stone fruits, strawberries, tomatoes, and walnuts; and *UC IPM Pest Management Guidelines* for about 40 major crops. Refer to the suggested reading and literature cited sections at the end of this manual for more information on these publications. The manual is completed by a list of suppliers of IPM information and products and a detailed index.

To get the most from an IPM program, use this manual in combination with the pesticide recommendations in the latest *UC IPM Pest Management Guidelines: Floriculture and Ornamental Nurseries*. Pest management guidelines are regularly updated, for-sale publications from the University of California. They are also available free online from the UC Statewide IPM Project's World Wide Web site at www.ipm.ucdavis.edu.

Managing Pests in Flower and Nursery Crops

Integrated pest management is a strategy that avoids or prevents pest damage with minimum adverse impact on human health, the environment, and nontarget organisms. Pest damage may be caused by insects, mites, nematodes, pathogens, and weeds. The term *pests* is used when referring to more than one cause of problems, including diseases, undesirable insects and mites, and weeds. Crops may also be damaged by abiotic disorders caused by improper cultural practices or environmental conditions. In IPM programs, managers use knowledge of crop and pest biology to take actions that reduce the environment's suitability for pest establishment and population increase. IPM employs careful monitoring techniques and combinations of biological, cultural, mechanical, chemical, and physical (also called environmental) control. Pesticides are used only if monitoring reveals that they are needed. If pesticides are necessary, they are chosen and applied in a way that avoids disrupting other IPM practices.

Routine applications of broad-spectrum pesticides have traditionally been used to control pests affecting flower and nursery crops. These pesticides kill a wide range of organisms and often persist for a relatively long time, controlling pests for days or weeks after application. However, many of these pesticides can cause outbreaks of secondary pests such as leafminers and mites and can accelerate development of pesticide resistance. Often they are toxic to natural enemies and pose hazards to workers and the environment as well. If pesticide use is necessary, biological, pest-specific, and reduced-risk pesticides should be used whenever possible and broad-spectrum pesticides should be avoided.

The first steps in developing an IPM program are to take nonchemical preventive actions and to use regular monitoring. Next, gradually modify pesticide use to reduce the number of applications, adjust intervals between applications, and switch to more pest-specific pesticides. Successful IPM has five key components:

- prevent problems
- regularly monitor crops and growing areas
- accurately diagnose problems
- develop control action thresholds or guidelines
- use effective management methods

Crop production and IPM planning. Plan and prepare to implement an IPM program by educating yourself as much as

One of the first steps in developing an IPM program is to take nonchemical preventive actions, such as creating a pest-free growing area and providing environmental conditions that promote good plant growth.

possible before planting. Learn to recognize the problems to which your crops are susceptible and take steps to prevent these problems before they occur. Be aware of crops or cultivars that are highly susceptible to pests and be especially stringent about pest prevention for these crops, using as many of the methods discussed in the sections on sanitation, exclusion, environmental management, and cultural practices as possible.

Determine the objectives of your IPM program. These objectives may include saving money, improving crop quality, reducing pesticide applications, and switching from broad-spectrum to reduced-risk pesticides. All objectives may not be compatible with each other or with your operations; identifying your primary objectives can help determine the elements and practices of your IPM program.

Prepare a written summary of the IPM program for each crop. Assembling this information before problems occur will make decision making easier and quicker when action must be taken. The IPM summary should list each pest problem that could be encountered and the scouting and management methods that will be used. List the acceptable pesticides and application rates and identify alternative treatment options. Identify the pest control action thresholds, if known; if thresholds are not known, infer tentative thresholds from experience or records from previous crops and refine them through systematic experimentation (see the section on establishing thresholds, below). In addition to this manual, you may find it helpful to consult experts such as private consultants and Cooperative Extension personnel when developing an IPM program.

Pest Prevention

Most crop problems can be anticipated and avoided. In many cases, prevention is often the least expensive, most effective, and only control option available. By the time plants begin to appear unhealthy, many problems cannot be cured, and the crops may have already been seriously damaged. Key pest prevention techniques include

- planning your crop production and IPM program in advance
- using good sanitation and exclusion
- properly managing the environment and cultural practices

Sanitation and exclusion. Make the site as pest-free as possible before planting. Clean the growing area well by removing old plants, crop debris, and weeds. Disinfect benches, tools, and irrigation systems (see the chapter "Diseases"). Before planting, make containers, equipment, growing areas, and growing media (including field soil, container planting mixes, and substrates such as rock wool) as pest-free as possible. Always start with high-quality, pest-free planting stock. Keep pests out of growing areas by introducing only clean equipment and plants, by screening greenhouses, and by installing double doors at greenhouse entrances. Regularly inspect crops and growing areas throughout the production cycle and promptly eliminate any problems.

Environmental management and cultural practices. Cultural practices and the environment often determine whether pest or abiotic problems develop. Each crop needs specific growing conditions; drastic fluctuations from proper conditions predispose crops to damage. Use cultural practices (such as fertilization and irrigation), environmental controls (such as heating and lighting), and other management practices that favor the crop and discourage potential pests or problems. Before planting, check irrigation systems and environmental monitoring and control equipment to ensure that they work well and can provide the necessary growing requirements. Be sure that the growing media has the aeration, drainage, and salinity necessary for good crop growth (see the chapter "Abiotic Disorders and Cultural Practices").

Cultural practices such as using resistant cultivars, rotating crops, or changing irrigation or fertilization can prevent

Cultural practices and the environment often determine whether pest or abiotic problems develop. For example, the crop on the right side beneath this shade structure is exposed to direct light in the afternoon, causing most plants there to die or grow poorly.

An important part of an IPM program is properly preparing pest-free growing media, being careful not to contaminate the media during handling and storage.

many abiotic disorders and pest problems. Proper use of equipment such as fans, heaters, and lights to control humidity and temperature can avoid flower and foliage blights, gray mold, and powdery mildew. Prepare a written summary of the cultural practices and environmental conditions required by each crop and make certain that someone is responsible for seeing that these conditions are provided. Be sure that all people responsible for crop production and management are well-informed about the IPM program and will coordinate their efforts toward the goals of the program.

Monitoring

Monitoring, also called scouting, is the regular, systematic inspection of crops and growing areas. Scout each crop and the surrounding growing area at regular intervals using methods appropriate for the situation. Good sampling methods can be invaluable in conducting an IPM program. Sampling is quantitative monitoring that estimates an overall pest population. To conduct quantitative sampling, for example, remove one leaf from each of several plants and count (or closely estimate) the pests on that sample leaf. Then find the average number of pests on all sample leaves; this average can be used to estimate the pest density on all leaves of all the plants. Quantitative sampling can also be done by measuring the percentage of plants infested or recording the number of pest insects found in sticky traps (see the chapter "Insects, Mites, and Other Invertebrates"). Because of its relative accuracy and objectivity, sampling can be much more useful in decision making than qualitative monitoring descriptions.

Scouting benefits. The symptoms of pest damage and the numbers of the pests themselves can increase very rapidly. If problems are not detected early, crops may be severely damaged and management options may become limited. Dispos-

Drastic fluctuations from proper cultural and environmental conditions predispose crops to damage. Flower buds on this camellia became necrotic and aborted because plants experienced high temperatures and wide variations in soil moisture (alternately soggy then very dry) during the previous growing season.

ing of the plants may be the only option. Regular scouting helps you

- prevent problems or reduce the amount of damage and the cost of control by providing early warning that problems are developing
- determine the specific cause and severity of problems
- identify the locations that require treatment, so you can avoid control actions in areas where control is not needed
- determine the most effective and economical timing and method of treatment
- use slower-acting methods that are more environmentally friendly and safer for workers
- evaluate control efficacy

- build a pest problem history that is useful for predicting and avoiding future problems
- improve crop quality and sales revenue

Scouting costs and crop quality. The cost savings that result from expending less labor and materials on pesticides more than offset the cost of IPM scouting (Fig. 2). In comparison with routine application of pesticides, using IPM scouting to determine treatment need, method, and timing leads to production of equal or superior quality crops that also have less pest damage and less phytotoxicity from repeated sprayings. If your monitoring resources are limited, derive the best economic return by beginning your scouting program in crops that

- have a history of significant treatment costs
- generate substantially more revenue when crop quality is high
- are susceptible primarily to pests that are easy to scout and have well-established treatment thresholds

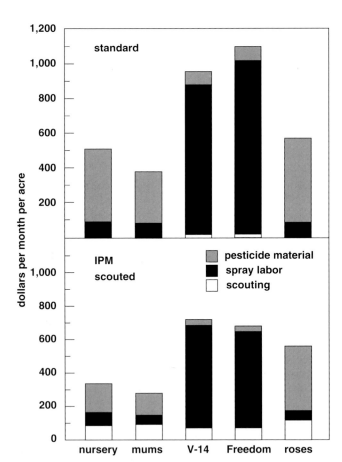

Figure 2. Monthly pest management costs (in dollars per acre) were less in IPM-scouted crops (bottom figure) than when those crops were managed using standard grower practices (top). Studies were conducted in five coastal California counties: San Diego, San Mateo, Santa Barbara, Santa Cruz, and Ventura. The crops were potted nursery plants (nursery), cut chrysanthemums (mums), the poinsettia cultivars 'V-14' and 'Freedom,' and cut roses. Adapted from Newman and Mayers 1997, Newman et al. unpublished.

Beginning a monitoring program. The best way to build an IPM program is to start with simple steps and adopt more involved practices as they are needed (Table 1). Begin a regular monitoring program to learn more about the extent and magnitude of pest problems. Once you have some background information, modify your monitoring and management program based on evaluation of this information. Develop a clear and concise plan that includes designating who is responsible for crop cultural practices, growing area environmental conditions, and pest management.

Start by inspecting growing sites and learning their layout before the crop is planted. Analyze each growing site to identify problems, such as weeds, water leaks, crop debris, and poor pest exclusion. Identify the previous crops and pest problems that were present at the site to learn about the pests that may already be present. Learn the history of spraying and other control actions.

Prepare a written monitoring plan that identifies the monitoring methods that will be used and how and when they will be implemented. Identify how samples will be chosen, how many samples will be taken, how often sampling will be done, where traps will be located, and how much time will be spent scouting. Develop scouting record-keeping forms and maps such as the ones in Figures 3 through 8. Use photocopies of each map and form to record information every time you monitor.

Once the scout and grower have agreed on the sampling plan, it is vital that crops be scouted the same way each week. Monitoring methods such as visual plant inspection and trapping insects are relative measures that over time tell you whether pest populations or damage are increasing, decreasing, or remaining about the same. You must sample

Table 1. Building an IPM Monitoring Program.

- **Start simple** and small when beginning a program.
- **Develop a clear, concise plan** that designates specifically what and how things will be done and who will do them.
- **Rely on careful inspection** of growing areas and plants, special tools that vary depending on the key pests (such as traps for monitoring insects), and ongoing knowledge of whether cultural practices and environmental conditions are appropriate for the crop.
- **Scout at least once every week** on a regular schedule, using a professional consultant or a well-trained employee.
- **Communicate weekly face-to-face.** The grower, scout, and applicator must work together as a team and be committed to basing pest management decisions on monitoring information.
- **Designate pest management units (PMUs),** contiguous areas of a similar crop for which pest management needs are similar and monitoring results are summarized.
- **Have a kit of necessary tools.**
- **Have some prior knowledge of the problems** likely to affect the crop (such as what the pests are and what their damage looks like), and be familiar with the biology of these problems.
- **Keep good written records** of scouting results and management actions.
- **Begin monitoring to learn** more about pest problems. Once background information is developed, modify the monitoring and management program based on evaluation of this information.

the same way every time to make the results comparable among sample dates.

The scout. An IPM scout is the individual responsible for collecting, recording, and summarizing monitoring data. At least once each week, the scout presents an information summary to the grower, pest control adviser, and possibly to others responsible for pest management, such as the applicator. Together, the grower, scout, and others evaluate the effectiveness of the IPM program and determine whether any control actions are needed.

The IPM scout can be the grower, an employee, or a professional consultant or pest control adviser. The grower or an employee scout are present daily and have the advantage of more thorough knowledge of the growing operation than an outside consultant. However, employee scouts may lack the necessary training, pest management expertise, and motivation to scout effectively. Scouting ability will improve with training and experience, but good scouts need to be observant, with "an eye for the pest." Employee scouts typically have many responsibilities, and monitoring can be neglected if the scout is diverted to other tasks. If an employee is used, the scout must have a defined time devoted solely to monitoring because it is vital that monitoring be conducted on a regular schedule.

A pest control adviser (PCA) or professional consultant is more likely to fulfill the critical requirement of monitoring at regular intervals and may be more efficient at monitoring. A PCA or consultant should have formal training, regular professional continuing education, and thorough knowledge of pests specific to the crops being grown. In California, PCAs must meet specific educational requirements and be licensed by the state Department of Pesticide Regulation. Outside consultants and PCAs also benefit from working with other growers, so they may recognize a new problem earlier. The cost of a good consultant frequently can be offset by the savings from reduced pesticide applications (Fig. 2).

Train all workers to recognize and report problems, regardless of whether the special monitoring is done by an employee or consultant. This combination of a professional weekly scouting and employees trained to be observant is often ideal. Training employees to recognize pests and unhealthy plants is especially critical for propagators and workers who handle incoming cuttings and other new stock.

Communication. The grower, scout, and applicator must have good communication and work together as a team. Everyone involved with pest management should meet face-to-face on a weekly basis to discuss monitoring results and make management decisions. When someone other than the scout is responsible for making decisions and conducting pest control, the decision maker and applicator must be committed to basing management decisions on monitoring information.

The scout must provide clear and timely summaries of monitoring results and should compare monitoring summaries with control action guidelines and thresholds. After discussing the monitoring information and deciding what

Regularly scouting crops and keeping good records are critical when diagnosing plant problems.

Successful IPM requires good face-to-face communication on a weekly basis between the grower and the scout or pest control adviser.

control actions to take, draw a map of areas to be treated and mark their locations with colored tape or flags. These records and markings allow you to clearly target control actions based on monitoring results, and they also identify where to revisit plants after treatment to assess control effectiveness.

Pest management units. Many growing areas are too large or diverse to allow recording of information on only one form. Within a field or greenhouse, a scout often must delineate sampling areas. The sampling area, or pest management unit (PMU), is a contiguous area for which monitoring results are recorded and summarized each time it is scouted. Each PMU is typically a crop area that has similar pest management requirements, such as the same or similar cultivars, plant growth stages, and cultural practices. By dividing the overall growing area into smaller units (PMUs), all areas can be efficiently monitored on a regular basis and scouting data is easier to manage and communicate. PMUs facilitate targeting of control actions, such as spot spraying, which can reduce overall pesticide use by limiting treatments only to areas that need it.

The scouting results from each PMU can be recorded on a separate sheet (Fig. 3). Each PMU should also have at least 1 sticky trap for monitoring insects. Mark PMU boundaries with stakes or flagging. Or, the size and layout of the PMUs may be dictated by the cropping pattern or growing structure: for example, a PMU may be one bay (the area underneath one peak of a greenhouse). Each PMU typically is about 2,000 to 10,000 square feet (180–900 sq m) of crop area. An entire 1-acre (0.4-ha) field with multiple

Foliage inspection record		Location GH 20, PMU 1			Date 20 July 2000	
Scout's name J. Doe		Time in 7:15			Time out 7:45	
	Number of pests					
Sample no.	Aphids	Mites	Powdery mildew	Thrips	*Botrytis*	Other
1	55	—	—			
2	—	—	—			
3	—	—	—			
4	—	—	—			
5	—	—	—			
6	22	~ 50	—			
7	—	—	—			
8	—	—	—			
9	—	—	—			
10						
11	—	—	—			
12	—	—	—			
13	—	12	1			
14	—	—	—			
15	~ 100	—	—			
16	—	—	—			yellowing
17	—	—	—			yellowing
18	—	—	—			
19	—	—	—			
20	—	—	3			
Pest total	~ 177	~ 62	4			
Average	~ 9	~ 3	0.2			

Comments — = none; ~ = approximate number, estimated
Investigate yellow plants for pathogens, nutrient, pH problem
Make spot applications of soap for aphids

Figure 3. Sample plant inspection record-keeping form. Use this form to record the numbers of pests on each sample. To record the proportion of plant parts infested (presence/absence sampling), substitute "Percentage infested" for "Number of pests."

crops is generally too large for a single PMU—sampling a large area well would generate too much information for a single data sheet, and it would be difficult to target spot sprays. The size of PMUs should increase as crop uniformity increases; PMUs in the field are usually larger than in greenhouses. Divide high-value and problem-prone crops into smaller PMUs, allowing a larger proportion of the crop to be sampled on each date. Larger PMUs may be adequate for lower-value crops or hardier crops not commonly subject to many problems.

How to monitor. Visually inspect plants and growing areas for pests, damaged crops, and conditions and practices that promote pest problems. Monitor environmental conditions and cultural practices to detect any deviations from conditions recommended for the crop. Effectively monitoring certain problems requires special tools, such as instruments for recording electrical conductivity (EC), pH, humidity, and temperature to assess abiotic disorders; on-site test kits for certain pathogens; and yellow sticky traps for invertebrates. Use additional monitoring methods where warranted (Tables 2 and 3).

How much to monitor. Monitoring once each week is adequate in many situations when using visual inspection. More frequent monitoring may be necessary for high-value crops, problem-prone cultivars, pest-infested areas, and plants that will soon be sold. Scout plug production areas at least every 3 to 4 days. Inspect incoming stock as soon as possible after it arrives and before plants are moved into production areas. Inspect propagation plants in the nursery before they are transplanted.

In most cases there are no specific guidelines for how many locations or plants should be monitored. The number of plants inspected will depend on factors such as crop value, extent of potential problems, size and type of the PMU, and resources available for sampling. The more plants or locations you inspect, the more likely it is you will detect problems sooner, when management is easier. In practice, scouting is a compromise between thoroughness (examining everything), efficiency (putting limited time to the best use), and cost (the value of improved management information).

One suggestion is to spend a predetermined amount of time per area of growing space, such as 3 or 10 minutes for each 1,000 square feet (90 sq m) of growing area. This could entail examining a fixed number of samples, for example, stopping at 10 locations and inspecting 1 plant or plug tray at each stop.

When quantitatively sampling plants, select a predetermined sample unit to inspect during each scouting stop. One sample unit can be an entire small plant, a fixed number of leaves and terminals per plant for large plants, or one-half of a flat. The appropriate sample unit depends on the crop, the anticipated pest problems, and the part of the plant where pests or injury symptoms occur.

Selecting plants for inspection. When deciding which plants to inspect, selecting plants at random is the best way to find unexpected new problems and 'hot spots' before pests or damage become obvious. Targeted scouting is the best way to assess problems that you anticipate or know to exist in the crop.

One approach is to use a combination of random and targeted scouting. Use each method to sample the same fixed number or proportion of plants every week in a PMU. For example, one-third of sample plants could be randomly selected from locations scattered throughout the PMU, while the other two-thirds of the samples are known or suspected to have problems. It is important to use a consistent method of

Table 2. Monitoring Methods and the Types of Pests They Detect.

	PEST PROBLEM				
	Pathogens	Abiotic disorders	Insects & mites	Nematodes	Weeds
visual inspection of crops	●	◐	●	◐	●
visual inspection of growing areas	●	●	●	●	●
environmental monitoring compared with optimal conditions	●	●	◐	○	○
cultural care compared with recommended practices	●	●	◐	◐	◐
on-site tools and tests (e.g., ELISA kits, traps, and water chemistry meters)	◐	●	●	○	○
off-site laboratory tests	●	●	◐	●	○
historic records compared with current scouting results	●	●	●	●	●

KEY: ● = very important method for that problem
◐ = somewhat important method
○ = not important method

Table 3. Tools for Monitoring and Diagnosing Pest Problems.

	Tool	Pathogens	Abiotic disorders	Insects & mites	Nematodes	Weeds	Tool use
	clipboard, record-keeping forms, pencils (not pens: ink runs when wet), waterproof marking pen	●	●	●	●	●	recording scouting information; labeling traps, samples, and pest management units
	calculator or portable computer	●	●	●	◐	◐	summarizing and analyzing scouting information
	flagging tape, measuring tape, and stakes	●	●	●	●	●	delineating scouting area boundaries (PMUs) and marking infestations
	hand lens (10×–20×) and a hands-free magnifier such as those mounted on an adjustable headband	◐	◐	●	○	○	examining invertebrates and damaged plants
	disposable gloves and disinfectant hand rinse	●	○	○	○	○	avoiding spread of pathogens during scouting after handling contaminated plants
	hand tools, including knife, trowel, and soil sampling tube	●	◐	●	●	●	examining roots, internal plant tissues, and collecting samples
	plastic bags, labels, small containers, ice chest, vials (empty and with alcohol), fine-tip brush, and aspirator	●	●	●	●	○	collecting and preserving samples
	pocketed apron, waist pouch, or fishing vest with pockets	●	●	●	●	●	keeping tools handy and hands free
	aspirator	○	○	●	○	○	collecting tiny insects
	moisture-sensitive paper	●	○	●	○	○	evaluating spray coverage
	spore collection plates	◐	○	○	○	○	detecting and sampling pathogens
	traps, including yellow sticky cards and possibly others, such as black light, pheromone, or potato	○	○	●	○	○	detecting insects; each trap type is selective for certain pests (see Table 51)

PEST PROBLEM

Tool	Pathogens	Abiotic disorders	Insects & mites	Nematodes	Weeds	Tool use
good quality 40×–60× dissecting microscope (stereomicroscope)	◑	○	●	●	○	identifying pest type and life stage
tally counter	○	○	●	○	◑	recording counts with hand clicker
indicator plants	●	○	●	○	○	detecting viruses, timing treatment, and evaluating efficacy
computerized systems	●	●	◑	○	○	monitoring and controlling environmental and cultural practices
tensiometer, lysimeter (container weight scale)	●	●	○	○	○	assessing irrigation need and frequency
light sensor	○	●	○	○	○	controlling automated shade curtain systems
ELISA test kits	●	○	◑	○	○	detecting and identifying pathogens
portable soluble-salt meter (EC meter)	●	●	○	○	○	measuring water salinity
ion-specific meters	●	●	○	○	○	measuring concentration of certain nutrients and minerals
pH meter or test papers	●	●	○	○	○	measuring acidity
humidity sensors, leaf wetness monitors, thermometers, thermocouples, digital or computerized temperature loggers	●	●	●	○	○	detecting disease-conducive conditions, assessing pasteurization efficacy, monitoring pest development rates, and timing treatments

KEY: ● = very important method for that problem
◑ = somewhat important method
○ = not important method

plant selection so that scouting results can be compared among monitoring dates. If both targeted and random plant selection are used, record and summarize targeted scouting information separately from that of random scouting.

In both targeted and random sampling, avoid sampling the same individual plants each week. For example, vary the number of steps between each random sample spot or enter fields at different locations to help ensure that different plants are sampled each week. In addition to randomly selecting plants, it can be helpful to flag an infested plant at one or more locations and reinspect those same plants each time you monitor, as discussed in the indicator plants section below.

Targeted plant selection. Begin targeted inspections by standing at the end of each PMU or walking through it and giving the area an overview. Identify any portions of the crop that look off-color, stunted, or otherwise unhealthy. Select some of those plants for inspection. Also target

- plants surrounding apparent problems, such as 'hot spots' discovered during random sampling. This helps you estimate the number of plants affected or the size of an infested area.

- pest-prone cultivars, highly susceptible crop species, or key plants where pests frequently occur or first appear each season.

- problem-prone areas where plants are more likely to be unhealthy than other plants of the same cultivar. Problem-prone areas could be due to variation in the growing environment (such as light, temperature, humidity, and ventilation), location (such as proximity to doors, vents, fans, weedy locations, and the edges and windward sides of fields and nurseries), or management (such as more or less irrigation water, nutrients, or pesticides).

Random plant selection. Begin at a major entrance, which is usually an introduction point for pests. Walk in a zigzag or snakelike pattern down each aisle or row, alternating between sample spots on your left and right side (Fig. 4). Randomly select one sample unit for inspection at each sample location. Make sure that samples are actually selected at random. For example, take a fixed number of steps between each sample point and examine the plant nearest your foot or elbow, or toss a brightly colored ping-pong ball into the air and select the plant nearest to where it lands.

Scout the entire PMU. Inspect plants that are closer to and farther from doors, vents, and fans. Examine plants on the border or edge of fields and nurseries as well as plants in the middle. Sample plants that are hanging, growing on the ground, and on benches. Where pests or damage are discovered, use targeted scouting to examine nearby plants to better define the extent of the problem.

How to examine plants. Examine plant parts in a systematic manner. For example, start with any buds or flowers, then inspect succulent new growth, younger leaves, older leaves, and finally basal stems. Examine leaf axils and the tops and bottoms of leaves. Many pests prefer the underside of leaves or inner, protected plant parts, so examine these locations carefully. Use a 10× to 20× hand lens to facilitate observation of smaller pests such as mites and thrips. If the plants are small, the sample unit may be an entire plant; for larger plants, the sample unit may be a set number of shoots and leaves, typically 2 to 6 per plant. When inspecting only a portion of the plant, begin by giving it an overview (you may have to lift small containers over your head to view leaf undersides).

If crops are prone to infestation by thrips and other invertebrates that can be dislodged, consider starting your inspection of each plant by striking or tapping foliage, terminal buds, or containers over a white sheet of paper or a paper plate. This dislodges many kinds of invertebrates onto the collecting surface, where you can observe and count them more easily (see the chapter "Insects, Mites, and Other Invertebrates"). Plant shaking or tapping may be undesirable when inspecting for pests that readily fly away, such as adult whiteflies that rest on leaf undersides.

For at least several plants in each PMU, uncover and examine roots. Inspecting roots is especially important if root decay, root-feeding insects, or root-damaging abiotic

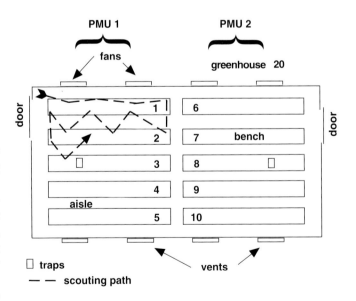

Figure 4. A growing area map showing major features such as benches, doors, sticky traps, and vents. The dotted line beginning near a door indicates the typical snakelike path an IPM scout might follow when randomly selecting plants to monitor. Each change in direction indicates a point where the scout stopped to inspect a plant. This greenhouse is divided into two pest management units (PMUs), each with one yellow sticky trap. The scout thoroughly monitors one PMU (benches 1–5) before moving to the next PMU.

disorders are known to be a problem with that crop. Remove plants from containers or gently scrape away soil as discussed in the root and crown decay sections in the chapter "Diseases." Check to see whether the root ball is of normal size and color. Look for fungal growth or sections of dark, soft, decayed feeder roots along the face of the root ball. Examine roots on the surface of the root ball for galls typical of root-knot nematodes, and look for dark lesions, discoloration, or dry decay that might be induced by lesion or burrowing nematodes.

Follow the same pattern of inspecting each plant every time you monitor. Be sure to wash your hands thoroughly or wear disposable gloves and discard them after handling any plant suspected of being diseased; poor sanitation during scouting can spread pathogens.

Once you are familiar with the pests and problems you are likely to encounter on that crop, you can limit your targeted inspections to plant parts most likely to be infested. However, unless some plants are randomly selected and all of their parts are thoroughly examined, unanticipated problems may go undiscovered.

Indicator plants. Indicator or sentinel plants are plants that are known to be infested. By inspecting indicator plants before and after treatment, you can evaluate the efficacy of control actions. Because many controls are effective only against certain pest life stages, inspecting indicator plants at regular intervals can help you time treatment applications. The plants used to time and evaluate treatments are different from indicator plants used to detect viruses (see the chapter "Diseases").

Identify indicator plants by flagging one infested plant in several different areas of the crop. For the particular pest species of interest, use a form such as Figure 5 to record the number of each life stage present on the indicator plant. At regular intervals, inspect the same parts of the same plants, such as 2 tagged leaves or terminals on each of 2 or more indicator plants. Time treatments based on your estimate of the percentage of the pest population that is in stages susceptible to the planned control. Reinspect these indicator plants after treatment to compare numbers, assess control effectiveness, and time any reapplications.

Key plants. Key plants are species or cultivars that are most likely to be infested with specific pests or diseases at certain times of the year. Key plants may have specialized species of pests or be problem-prone cultivars, or they may not be well adapted to local growing conditions and are more susceptible to problems because they are stressed. Target key plants for more scouting. Because they are more likely to become infested, key plants can be good indicator plants.

Presence-absence sampling. Instead of counting each individual pest, presence-absence sampling (also called

Begin scouting by standing at the end of each pest management unit and giving the area an overview. Identify any portions of the crop that look off-color, stunted, or otherwise unhealthy. Target some of your scouting to include any obviously unhealthy plants, as seen here in the foreground.

binomial sampling) can save time in certain situations. To use presence-absence sampling, inspect each sample for the presence or absence of live pests or damage. Once live pests of that species or damage are found, record that sample unit (plants or plant parts) as infested and move on to another sample. Record the total number of samples inspected and the total number of samples infested. Calculate the percentage of samples that are infested:

$$\text{Percentage of samples infested} = \frac{\text{Number of samples infested}}{\text{Number of samples inspected}} \times 100$$

Compare this infestation rate among various sample dates and before and after treatment. Many of the sample record forms in this chapter can be modified to record presence-absence sampling information instead of actual pest counts. Presence-absence sampling is most useful in the few situations where researchers have determined the correlation between presence-absence sampling data and the average pest density for that crop.

Monitor control efficacy. Assessing the effectiveness of control actions is critical when developing a reliable IPM program. Before-and-after treatment comparisons of scouting records and indicator plants, combined with the use of tools such as pesticide spray droplet monitoring cards, can provide

Whitefly indicator plant monitoring record

Date 1999	Number of pest individuals per sample unit					
	Date	Eggs	First and second instars	Third instars and prepupae	Pupae	Adults
PMU no. 3	10/1	30	3			2
	10/4	35	10			1
	10/7	21	24			0
Plant no. 1	10/10	6	39			0
Cultivar Lilo						

Whitefly indicator plant monitoring record

Date 1999	Number of pest individuals per sample unit					
	Date	Eggs	First and second instars	Third instars and prepupae	Pupae	Adults
PMU no. 3	10/1	20	6			2
	10/4	74	23			1
	10/7	33	64			0
Plant no. 2	10/10	5	90	2		
Cultivar Lilo						

Comments	10/1 New infestation, mostly eggs and some adults.
	10/10 Sprayed mid AM after sampling, most whiteflies were susceptible early instars.

Figure 5. Sample form for recording numbers of whitefly life stages over several dates on two indicator plants. Depending on the pest species and the goals of your monitoring, you can combine or separate life stages into different categories, or ignore dead insects.

timely feedback on control effectiveness. Monitoring control effectiveness is especially important when using new or experimental methods. Scouting and evaluation over the long term allows you to compare quality at the end of the production cycle among crops that were managed differently.

Inspect growing areas. Scout in and around growing areas every week. In addition to examining crop plants, look for nearby problems such as torn screens, puddling water, water runoff, greenhouse doors habitually left open, and inadequate removal and disposal of crop debris. Scout for weeds in aisles, beneath benches, and between and inside beds, pots, and planting rows. Determine whether good pest exclusion and sanitation measures are being employed throughout the crop production cycle. Make sure that proper environmental conditions and appropriate growing practices are being provided. Bring any problems to the grower's attention.

Keep written records. Written records are essential for effective IPM. Critical records include PMU maps, scouting data and summaries, and pest control history. If additional records are not already being kept for production purposes, consider regularly recording crop development stages, cultural activities (such as irrigation and fertilization), and environmental conditions (such as temperature and humidity). Organize these records together in a notebook that is kept on site and is accessible to the scout, grower, and pesticide applicator.

Maps and flags. Make a map of the entire growing complex, showing physical features such as greenhouses and other buildings, and mark it with the location of each PMU. Draw a separate map for each PMU, showing the location of sticky traps and key features such as doorways and vents (Fig. 4). When infestations are isolated, use colored flagging or a copy of your original map or both to record the location of infestations. A visual survey of maps or flagged sites may reveal patterns of infestations. Marking infestations allows you to reinspect them to monitor pest development and evaluate control effectiveness. Maps and flags help the pest control operator make spot applications only where needed. Use different colors or numbers to denote different information, such as the locations of pest species and where to target control actions.

Scouting records. Develop a form for recording visual plant inspection results (Fig. 3). Sample record-keeping forms in Spanish are available in *Un Programma de Exploración para*

Use colored flags and a map to record infestations, indicator plants, and growing areas needing spot treatment.

In addition to examining crop plants, during scouting look for nearby problems. Crop debris that is not promptly removed from growing areas as shown here can be a source of pests that can move to infest nearby crops.

Young plants in propagation may need to be scouted at least every 3 to 4 days. Also inspect plants before they are transplanted or moved into production areas.

IPM scouting summary: Report of plant inspections						
Date scouted		Scout's name		Total scouting time		
Average number of pests per sample						
PMU no.	Aphids	Mites	Thrips	Powdery mildew	*Botrytis*	Other
1						
2						
3						
4						
5						
6						
7						
8						
9						
10						
Average						
Previous week's average						
Trend						
Comments (e.g., controls since last scouting or recommendations)						

Figure 6. Sample table for summarizing plant inspection records from all PMUs. This summary form, not individual records from each PMU, is presented by the scout to the grower and applicator and discussed during weekly meetings.

Cultivos Ornamentales (Guerena et al. 1997, Newman et al. unpublished). Forms should include spaces for the date, crop, scout's name, and pest management unit. Record the number of plants inspected, the number of plants infested or damaged, and a measure of damage severity or pest abundance. Record information separately for each type of pest. Some PMUs (such as field sites) may need more than one form, such as one for insects and pathogens and another for weeds (see the chapter "Weeds").

Record information so that it can be easily evaluated and compared, for example, by entering results into a computer spreadsheet program or database for analysis. Use a "comments" section to record important, nonnumerical information, such as the presence of nonproduction plants ("pet plants") that may be a source of infestations. Keep a written description of your sampling and inspection methods and follow those directions every time you monitor.

Scouting summaries. Prepare a weekly report that summarizes scouting data. A table similar to Figure 6 can be used to summarize on one page crop inspection scouting from all PMUs. The ideal summary includes a season-long graphical display for each PMU or a combination of several similar PMUs. Display the average density or percentage of crop infested by

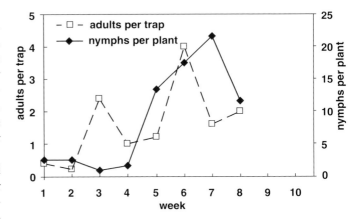

Figure 7. Average number of whitefly adults per trap or nymphs per plant found while sampling once per week during the first 8 weeks of crop growth. Graphical summaries such as this are an ideal way for the scout to present monitoring information to the grower.

each major pest versus the date counted. To make preparing the report easier, use lined graph paper or a computer graphing program. Add the most recent results each time you sample (Fig. 7).

Compare the summary results from the most recent monitoring dates to determine whether the pest population or

Pest Control Record								
				Pesticide				
Year 1999 Date	Cultivar/site/ (PMU)	Treated area size or number of containers	Target pests	Name and registration number	Type	Class	Amount of a.i. used	Equipment or method
7/21	5	¼ A spots	aphids	Soap/M–Pede 53219–6	I	CON	8 oz	WS
7/29	5	½ A	aphids mealybugs	Kinoprene Enstar II 55947–82	I	IGR	5 oz	WS
8/10	4	½ A	powdery mildew	AQ–10 55638–16	F	M	0.2 oz	WS
8/16	4	½ A	powdery mildew	AQ–10 55638–16	F	M	0.3 oz	WS
Comments								

Figure 8. A sample management record form. Determine what information is needed in state-required pesticide use reports and design your form to facilitate that record keeping. When developing your IPM program, you might want to add columns to your form for recording your material and labor costs.

damage is increasing or decreasing. Use the scouting summary to help decide if action is needed, when and where to implement controls, and whether previous management actions have been effective. Periodically evaluate the costs of monitoring, pesticide use, and other management actions and use these records to modify your programs.

Management records. Record when, where, and what control actions were taken. Management records should include the specific cultivar, location and size of the area treated, the time, and material costs. If pesticides are applied, record the name, rate, amount, chemical class, and application method (Fig. 8). Regularly review reports to ensure that pesticide types are being rotated to avoid promoting resistance. Compare summary scouting reports with the pest control reports and regularly evaluate this information to ensure that the recommended actions are being taken and that they are effective.

Determine what information is needed in any state-required pesticide use reports and design your form to facilitate that record keeping. Prepackaged, computerized record-keeping software can be purchased from some companies. Some software packages can integrate records kept from pest scouting, pesticide use, and other sources such as environmental monitoring.

Use a computer. Computers are extremely useful in planning and implementing your IPM program. A database spreadsheet program on a desktop computer allows you to readily summarize scouting data (for example, the program can calculate averages from among many samples) and graphically display pest management information. Scouting data can be sorted and presented by categories, such as cultivar, monitoring date, PMU, or pest species. Computers are also useful for pesticide record keeping, plant growth modeling, and monitoring and controlling the growing environment (see the chapter "Diseases"). Getting an online connection to the World Wide Web provides access to crop management resources at university and industry Web sites.

A handheld or palmtop computer can be programmed with a spreadsheet designed to match your scouting record-keeping form. Sampling data can be entered into the palmtop computer in the field, eliminating the need to transfer information from a paper record sheet to a desktop computer. Palmtops allow more timely and efficient summary of results. They are also versatile, often providing features such as a calculator, calendar, and phone book. Additional software available for field use may include weed identification, plant growth modeling, and degree-days calculation. Although palmtops are relatively durable, like all electronic equipment they must be protected from excess moisture and heat.

Tools such as maximum-minimum thermometers and yellow sticky traps are essential to monitor environmental conditions and pest populations and important for correct problem diagnosis. The trap shown here has been left in the greenhouse too long and is clogged with insects and debris. Traps are of no value unless they are regularly maintained and insect counts are made at least once each week.

Computerized environmental monitoring systems help growers efficiently manage the growing environment and cultural practices. An automated irrigation monitoring and management system in this greenhouse includes electronic equipment mounted on the post that relays information from tensiometers in pots to a computer in an office outside the growing area.

Diagnosing Problems

Teach employees how to recognize whether plants are healthy or stressed. Explain or illustrate the special color, growth habits, and development rates of each plant species or cultivar. When plants lack their normal characteristics, they probably are being injured. Major causes of crop damage include

- adverse environmental conditions
- improper cultural practices
- pathogens, such as fungi and viruses
- invertebrates, including insects and mites
- weeds
- nematodes

Diagnosing the cause of unhealthy crops is often difficult because the relationships between cause and effect may not be simple and direct. Similar symptoms can be produced by different stresses. Conversely, a single injury can produce multiple or variable symptoms. A combination of factors can also contribute to unhealthy plants. The conditions causing injury may not be visible to the naked eye, or damage may appear long after the cause of damage has ceased, such as previous drought stress. Correct diagnosis of the cause of damage often requires regular visual scouting of crops and growing areas, good record keeping, access to good reference material such as this manual, and experience. It may be necessary to use specialized on-site diagnostic tools and kits, such as those listed in Tables 2 and 3, or to send samples to an outside diagnostic laboratory. Refer to the chapter "Diseases" for suggestions about submitting plant samples to a diagnostic laboratory.

Generally, the first diagnostic step is to examine the crop and growing area carefully, looking for damage-causing conditions, practices, and organisms. Evaluate any pattern of symptoms. Do not base your diagnosis on a single symptom; examine as many affected plants as possible. Inspect all parts of affected plants, including roots and both sides of leaves, and inspect plants with different degrees of damage. Compare symptoms on your plants with those described in the descriptions in this manual, especially those in the chapter "Crop Tables".

When the cause of unhealthy plants is not apparent, it can be helpful to consult records from earlier in the production cycle or from previous similar crops. Key records include pest-scouting summaries and crop production records on cultural practices and environmental conditions. Compare pre-

Diagnosing and monitoring problems caused by tiny pests may require a hand lens. To identify small insects caught in this trap, hold the lens close to your eye and move the trap until the insects are in focus.

vious problems and growing conditions and practices to those known to promote specific problems, as described in this manual.

Not all possible causes of problems in flower and nursery crops are included in this manual because the scope of the manual is broad. The chapter "Crop Tables" lists mostly flower crops; consult *Pests of Landscape Trees and Shrubs* (Dreistadt 1994) for host tables for woody ornamentals. Other recommended publications include *Ball Identification Guide to Greenhouse Pests and Beneficials* (Gill and Sanderson 1998), *Integrated Pest Management For Bedding Plants* (Casey 1999), the Society of American Florists' annual conference proceedings such as *Insect and Disease Management on Ornamentals* (Heinz 1999), and *Natural Enemies Handbook: The Illustrated Guide To Biological Pest Control* (Flint and Dreistadt 1998). Refer to the literature cited and suggested reading at the back of this manual for other helpful publications, including those from the University of California and other universities, the American Phytopathological Society, the Entomological Society of America, the Weed Science Society of America, and the Western Society of Weed Science.

New pests are often introduced from other places, and these exotic pests may not be discussed in available publications. Report new or unusual pests to the local agricultural agency. If necessary, seek help from a private consultant, pest control adviser, other growers, a local Cooperative Extension advisor, or county agriculture department personnel.

Thresholds

The presence of a few pest individuals and some amount of damage usually can be tolerated. The number of pests and level of damage beyond which treatment should be taken is known as the treatment threshold, a fundamental concept in integrated pest management. Ideally, thresholds are provid-

ed to growers by University researchers or other experts who have conducted long-term research to determine the relationship between pest levels and the extent of crop damage. Few thresholds have been established for flower and nursery crops, in part because of the lack of research in comparison with the large number of crops, pests, and different growing situations. Specific thresholds or control action guidelines may be difficult to determine, but thresholds can be developed over the long term by growers who regularly monitor crops and keep and evaluate good records.

Why use thresholds. Pesticides sometimes are applied on a calendar schedule, when pest presence is only suspected or when populations are already high and difficult to control. Using thresholds can maintain or improve crop quality while reducing the frequency of pesticide applications. Less frequent applications

- help maintain pesticide efficacy by reducing the development of pesticide resistance
- reduce disruptions of cultural practices that occur during applications and reentry intervals
- may improve plant growth and quality by minimizing phytotoxicity
- increase profit by reducing costs of pesticide purchases, application labor, and regulatory compliance

When to treat. Crops are grown for profit, so thresholds are based largely on economics. Control action is warranted when the increased revenue expected from improved crop quality or yield will exceed the cost and adverse impacts (such as phytotoxicity) of control. The amount of pest presence or damage that can be tolerated is determined by many factors, including the type of pest and damage, crop species and cultivar, stage of plant development, time until harvest or sale, and market conditions. Tolerance to pests can be higher if infested plant parts are not marketed, such as older leaves on seed crops or cut terminal flowers. Thresholds can often be higher if highly effective or quick-acting methods are available for controlling the problem. Conversely, if available controls are slow-acting or only partially effective, thresholds may be relatively low for that pest. In certain situations, regulations such as quarantines may impose zero pest tolerance even when populations are low and pests do not directly damage the marketed crop.

Mother stock and new plants should have virtually no pests. If pests are present at the beginning of the crop production cycle, pests can develop through many generations before plants are shipped. Abundant pests on young plants may require repeated management actions and greatly increase the likelihood of damaged, poor-quality plants.

Treatment thresholds may be higher for mature plants of certain crops. More mature plants are often better able to tolerate some level of certain types of pests or their damage. It is unlikely that susceptible crops can be maintained pest-free

Table 4. Monitoring Methods and Preliminary Control Action Guidelines for the Key Insect Pests of Greenhouse Cut Roses.

	Aphids	Mites	Thrips	Whiteflies
monitoring method	Inspect terminal stems, buds, and leaf undersides weekly.	Inspect underside of 1 leaf (5 leaflets) above and 1 leaf below pruning break (new canes from axial bud) on 5 canes per 100-ft (30-m) row.	For each PMU or about 10,000 sq ft (900 sq m) of homogeneous beds, peel back sepals and inspect 20 buds that just underwent sepal split or tap 20 terminal buds to dislodge thrips; use 2–8 sticky traps per PMU, varying with cultivar and trap color (more if using yellow traps instead of blue).	Inspect leaf undersides weekly for all life stages; use yellow sticky traps for adults.
preliminary control action guideline	Prevent intolerable levels of honeydew or sooty mold.	>5 mites/leaflet as sampled above; avoid treating mites when using mite predators.	>25–50 thrips/trap/week if 2 traps/PMU; >10–20 thrips/trap/week if 8 traps/PMU; or ≥1–2 thrips/bud.	Prevent intolerable levels of honeydew or sooty mold, or if several whiteflies/trap.

Adjust suggested action guidelines based on the relative susceptibility of that cultivar. Adapted from Parrella and Murphy unpublished.

Appearance often determines whether customers purchase nursery ornamentals or flowers. However, the amount of pest presence or damage that can be tolerated is determined by many factors, including the type of pest and damage, crop species and cultivar, stage of plant development, time until harvest or sale, and market conditions.

Tolerate virtually no pests on mother stock and new plants.

throughout their production cycle. As crops mature, they are increasingly likely to become infested and are often more difficult to treat effectively because of the risk of phytotoxicity to colored bracts or flowers, increased difficulty in achieving good spray coverage on larger plants, and pesticide reentry intervals.

If monitoring reveals very low pest problems near the end of production, it may not be necessary to take control actions because there may be insufficient time for populations to develop to problem levels before the crop is sold. One survey of growers in the northeastern United States found that even with weekly pesticide applications, more than 80% of poinsettia growers had some whitefly-infested plants and 35% of all plants had one or more whiteflies at the time of sale. Even for highly susceptible crops like poinsettia, where the tolerance for pests is considered to be low, the presence of a few whiteflies is apparently tolerable.

How to establish thresholds. Establish thresholds by systematically monitoring plants, keeping good records, and judging the acceptability of the finished crop in comparison with pest scouting and control records. Experiment over time to develop thresholds appropriate for your situation. Be flexible in adjusting thresholds and adapt monitoring and management methods as appropriate.

Thresholds should be quantitative or numerical to be useful. For example, thresholds could be based on the average number of pests per trap each week, the percent of plants or leaves found to be damaged or infested during visual inspection, or the number of pests dislodged per shake sample. Quantitative thresholds can be developed for most pest monitoring methods, such as treating when certain conditions are conducive to disease development, or when invertebrate pests or damaged plant parts exceed specified numbers or percentages (Tables 4 to 6). For example, control action may be warranted for whiteflies when more than

Table 5. Monitoring Methods and Suggested Control Action Guidelines for the Key Pathogens of Greenhouse Cut Roses.

	Gray mold (*Botrytis*)	Downy mildew	Powdery mildew
monitoring suggestions	Each week inspect underside of leaves for downy mildew; calyx and upper side of leaves for whitish powdery mildew (new growth); flower buds for gray mold. Monitor RH and temperature.		
preliminary action guideline	Unless treated during prior week, treat at first signs on petals or leaves or when conditions are conducive for disease.		
disease-conducive conditions	60° to 77°F (16° to 25°C) and RH >90% for >6 hr continuously	RH >85% for >3 hr continuously and T <68°F (20°C)	RH ≥90% at night, RH 40–70% during day, 68° to 86°F (20° to 30°C) ≥6 hr consecutively

KEY: hr = hours
RH = relative humidity
T = temperature
Adapted from Horst 1985.

Table 6. Suggested Control Action Guidelines Used to Reduce Treatment Costs and Improve Crop Quality.

Crop	Pests	Threshold	Source
anthurium	anthracnose, mites, thrips	≥6% of flower bracts or spathes damaged	Hara et al. 1990
gypsophila	twospotted mites	>250–300 motile mites and eggs per 125–150 leaves	Price et al. 1980
gypsophila	leafminers	>25–30 live larvae per 125–150 leaves	Price et al. 1980
gypsophila	shoot- and foliage-feeding caterpillars	≥1 larva per 25 plants if plants <6 inches (15 cm) diameter; >1–5 larvae per 10 plants if plants >6 inches diameter but prior to flowering	Price et al. 1980
rose, field-grown root stock	spider mites, predominately *Tetranychus pacificus, T. turkestani*	>40% of leaves infested during weekly presence/absence sampling of 1 leaf from each of 20 of Peace scion on Dr. Huey rootstock	Karlik, Goodell, and Osteen 1995
rose, greenhouse cut	downy mildew, gray mold, powdery mildew, twospotted mite, western flower thrips	See Tables 4 and 5	

about 5 adults per trap per week are captured on 1 well-maintained 3 by 5 inch (7.5 × 12.5 cm) yellow sticky trap deployed per 1,000 square feet (90 sq m) of production. Thresholds for your situation may be very different from this.

Management

Integrated pest management employs mechanical, environmental (also called physical), cultural, biological, and chemical control methods. When action is needed, two or more methods used in combination are usually more effective than any single method used alone. Preferred techniques include using cultural practices and environmental conditions that prevent pest development. When pesticides are needed, the least toxic but effective pesticide is chosen with special consideration of the potential impact on other pests and IPM methods.

Mechanical control. Mechanical controls use labor, materials not usually considered to be pesticides, and machinery to reduce pest abundance directly. Mechanical controls include hand-pulling and applying mulch to control weeds, installing screens to exclude flying insects, and applying sticky barriers to exclude climbing pests such as ants and weevils.

Environmental or physical control. Environmental (also called physical) methods indirectly control pests and prevent damage by manipulating the environment, such as changing temperature, light, and humidity. Heat applied through solarization, steam pasteurization, or proper composting controls most soilborne pests. Altering humidity and temperature by increasing ventilation, applying heat, and changing irrigation timing and method (such as switching from sprinklers to drip irrigation) control many foliar pathogens. Improving drainage and aeration of field soils and planting mixes will prevent many abiotic and pathogenic problems.

Cultural control. Cultural controls are modifications of normal plant care activities that reduce or avoid pest problems.

Mechanical controls such as these plastic screens inside a greenhouse door help keep leaf surfaces clean and reduce windblown weed seeds and pathogens.

This card contains parasitized whitefly pupae. It can be hung on plants such as these poinsettias to introduce tiny parasitic wasps for biological control in greenhouses.

Cultural controls include choosing crop species or cultivars that are resistant to pests, rotating crops, altering planting time, and adjusting the frequency and amount of irrigation and fertilization. For example, applying too much fertilizer can induce excess succulent plant growth that favors higher populations of pests such as aphids and mites.

Biological control. Biological control uses beneficial organisms to control pests. Pathogens, parasites, and predators are the primary natural enemies used in biological pest control (see the chapters "Diseases" and "Insects, Mites, and Other Invertebrates"). Disease-suppressive composts and amendments can help prevent crop damage by certain soil-dwelling pathogens. Leaving weed seeds near the soil surface by tilling shallowly, instead of cultivating deeply, can reduce seed survival by 60% or more because seeds near the surface are more readily eaten by birds, insects, and rodents or decomposed by microorganisms. Biological control has been most successful in controlling insects and mites. For example, periodically releasing *Encarsia formosa* parasites can control greenhouse whitefly. As with other methods, biological control is most effective when integrated with other methods, such as applying selective pesticides instead of broad-spectrum pesticides that kill natural enemies.

Chemical control. Pesticides are chemicals that control or repel pests or prevent or mitigate pest problems. You can prevent crop damage or temporarily control certain pests if you choose the correct pesticide and apply it at the right time in an appropriate manner. Incorrect pesticide use, such as applying the wrong pesticide, at the wrong rate, or by the wrong method, may do more harm than good, such as by damaging crops or natural enemies. Before using a pesticide, understand its relative toxicity, mode of action, persistence, and safe and legal use. Read the information later in this chapter and consult *The Safe and Effective Use of Pesticides* (O'Connor-Marer 1999) and *Pesticide Safety: A Reference Manual for Growers* (O'Connor-Marer 1997) for more information on effective, safe, and legal pesticide use.

Sanitation and Exclusion

Sanitation and exclusion are highly effective in controlling most pathogens, invertebrates, nematodes, and weeds. While it is unrealistic for growers to strictly follow every recommendation (Fig. 9), most pest problems will dramatically decline or be avoided if exclusion and sanitation methods are adopted. Often only a few key methods are critical, as illustrated for greenhouse cut roses (Table 7). The primary strategies are to

- make the growing area as pest-free as possible before planting
- start with high-quality, pest-free stock
- keep pests out of growing areas
- regularly inspect crops and growing areas and promptly eliminate any problems

Make the growing area pest-free before planting. The most effective and least expensive time to control most pests is before planting, when virtually all control methods are available (Tables 7 to 9; Figs. 9 and 10). Control is usually more difficult after planting because many of the nonselective methods cannot be used and pests or control actions may damage crops.

Start with high-quality stock. Many pests can be transmitted in or on propagation material such as seeds, cuttings, and tubers. To reduce the possibility of contamination, use only high-quality stock from a reputable supplier and employ stringent controls if stock is produced on-site (Fig. 10). Pests

Table 7. Sanitation and Exclusion Methods for Preventing Pest Damage: An Example Using Key Pests of Greenhouse Cut Roses.

SANITATION AND EXCLUSION METHOD	PESTS CONTROLLED							
	Aphids	Mites	Thrips	Whiteflies	Botrytis gray mold	Downy mildew	Powdery mildew	Weeds
introduce only pest-free equipment, plants, and workers	●	●	●	●	●	●	●	●
screen out pests	●	●	●	●	◐	◐	◐	●
control weeds	●	●	●	●	●	○	○	●
promptly remove crop debris	◐	◐	●	●	●	◐	◐	○
rouge infected plant parts	○	○	○	○	●	●	●	○
cull unmarketable blossoms	○	○	●	○	●	○	◐	○

KEY: ● = method very important for these pests
      ◐ = somewhat important
      ○ = not important

present at the beginning of production can reproduce many generations and become high populations when plants are marketed. High populations or prolonged infestations often require more frequent and expensive control actions. Repeated controls are more likely to cause problems such as phytotoxicity or outbreaks of secondary pests such as mites. Plants received from off-site may be infested with new pest species not previously present around your growing area. Because pests can develop resistance to pesticides repeatedly applied elsewhere, such infested stock may contain resistant pest biotypes or strains that are more difficult for you to control.

The initial investment in pest-free stock can pay great dividends. Poor quality plants can cost much more in the long run due to increased management costs, lower crop quality, and lost sales revenue.

Certified and culture-indexed stock. High-quality propagators can provide plants that are not infested with any insects or weeds. Nematode-free plants for certain crops can be obtained from participants in the California Certification Nursery program. Culture-indexed or certified pathogen-free stock are available for many flower crops, including carnation, chrysanthemum, ferns, geranium, New Guinea impatiens, and orchids.

Culture-indexed plants are vegetatively propagated by specialists. Thin slices of plant tissue are cut under sanitary conditions; the tissue is grown into plants using nutrient solutions, and laboratory tests are then conducted to confirm that the new plants are free of specific bacterial, fungal, and viral pathogens. Virus-indexed plants are commonly produced from meristem culture, sometimes after treating cuttings or mother plants with heat or chemicals that inhibit virus replication. Electron microscopy, bioassays, and serological techniques such as ELISA (see the chapter "Diseases") are used to test the resulting plants for known viruses. The list of crops available as certified or indexed stock is

Poor sanitation practices in this greenhouse allow extensive growth of weeds that can be alternate hosts for insects and pathogens.

Sanitation Methods for Keeping Growing Areas and Crops Pest-Free

✓	Method	Pathogens	Insects & mites	Nematodes	Weeds
	GROWING AREA				
	Select a relatively pest-free growing site.	●	●	●	●
	Provide a smooth, well-drained planting site.	●	◖	◖	●
	Remove crop debris, old plants, and weeds.	●	●	●	◖
	Thoroughly clean the site and disinfect equipment such as irrigation systems if possible.	●	●	●	●
	Establish a vegetation-free border, ground covers, cover crops, or landscape plants that don't harbor crop pests.	●	●	◖	●
	Screen vents, entrances, and border areas.	●	●	○	◖
	Consider a plant-free period between crops to reduce pests.	●	●	◖	◖
	Rotate to crops not susceptible to the major pests of the previous crop grown on-site.	●	●	●	◖
	Introduce only pest-free growing media, equipment, plants, and workers.	●	●	●	●
	Treat and screen surface or recycled irrigation water before use.	●	◖	●	●
	Regularly inspect growing areas and eliminate remaining problems.	●	●	◖	●
	Regularly check that proper environmental conditions and cultural practices are being provided.	●	◖	◖	◖
	Minimize splashed water and airborne dust.	●	◖	◖	◖
	Take control actions before pests become abundant or damage is imminent.	●	●	●	●
	Consider disposing of infested plants and those nearby when new infestations of hard-to-control pests are limited to a small portion of the crop.	●	●	●	◖
	Promptly bag, remove, or destroy crop residue, prunings, old blossoms, and unmarketable plants.	●	●	◖	○
	Locate refuse piles and containers downwind from susceptible crops.	●	●	○	◖
	Prevent irrigation water runoff from infested plants to healthy plants.	●	◖	●	●
	GROWING MEDIA (PLANTING MIX, SOIL, AND SUBSTRATES SUCH AS ROCK WOOL)				
	Mix and store planting mix in an area not contaminated with soil, runoff water, or windblown particles.	●	●	●	●
	Keep planting mix covered until use.	●	◖	◖	●
	Pasteurize media before use or reuse.	●	●	●	●
	Do not transfer unpasteurized media from infested plants to healthy plants.	●	●	●	●

Figure 9. Sanitation checklist.

Portions of this greenhouse have been screened to prevent pest movement. If separate growing areas are not available, screening like this can isolate mother stock from production plants and can also be used to quarantine new plants.

constantly expanding. Contact your supplier or Cooperative Extension advisor for the latest information.

Quarantine new stock. Establish a special receiving and holding area for new plants. Immediately inspect new stock for pests and disease symptoms. Reject, treat, or dispose of infested material. Call any problems to the attention of your supplier. Keep plants quarantined long enough for the major potential pests of that crop to appear. For example, to detect insects, hold plants at least for the estimated egg development time using degree-days (see the chapter "Insects, Mites, and Other Invertebrates"). Until new stock has been observed long enough to know that it was received pest-free, handle plants on the assumption that they are infested.

If quarantining plants is not feasible, temporarily screen a portion of the growing area to isolate new stock from other plants. When plants are moved into production areas, group plants from the same source together. Grouping plants,

PESTS CONTROLLED

	Method	Pathogens	Insects & mites	Nematodes	Weeds
	WORKERS				
	Restrict entry into growing area to necessary personnel; supervise visitors.	●	●	◑	◑
	Begin the work day in clean areas. Then handle refuse, contaminated plants, or move to locations that may be infested.	●	●	●	●
	Avoid wearing white, yellow, or green, as these colors attract many types of insects that can hitchhike on clothing; blue attracts thrips.	●	●	○	○
	Clean shoes before entering growing areas by removing soil, then use foot baths consisting of a fiber mat or foam pads in a shallow tray containing dilute bleach or other disinfectant at entrances.	●	◑	◑	◑
	Post signs and tell employees to wash hands before work, at intervals throughout the day, and again before handling plants after eating.	●	○	○	○
	Provide convenient hand-washing facilities near entrances and at strategic locations throughout production and propagation facilities.	●	○	○	○
	Consider use of protective clothing (disposable or sterile coveralls, gloves, and shoe coverings) during potting, transplanting, pruning, or taking cuttings during propagation of highly susceptible crops and when rouging diseased plants.	●	◑	○	○
	Discard or change used protective clothing before working with pest-free plants.	●	◑	○	○
	Keep feet off benches, planting beds, and rock wool slabs.	●	◑	◑	◑
	Keep tobacco users away from crops susceptible to tobacco mosaic virus.	●	○	○	○
	EQUIPMENT				
	Remove soil, then disinfect equipment such as tools, hoses, and irrigation systems regularly throughout the production cycle.	●	◑	●	◑
	Keep containers, hose nozzles, equipment, and tools off the ground, for example, by using bench clips and racks.	●	◑	●	◑
	Thoroughly wash then disinfect containers, tools, and equipment before use and after they contact refuse, old or potentially contaminated plants, unpasteurized soil, or have fallen or been placed on the floor or ground.	●	◑	●	●

KEY: ● = very important method for that problem
◑ = somewhat important method
○ = not important method

Starting with Pest-Free Crops

✓	Method	PESTS CONTROLLED			
		Pathogens	Insects & mites	Nematodes	Weeds
	Purchase high-quality, certified, pest-free stock.	●	●	●	●
	Quarantine new stock.	●	●	◑	●
	Grow well-maintained mother stock solely for that purpose.	●	●	●	●
	Isolate mother stock from production plants.	●	●	●	●
	Use careful inspection and special pest detection tests during propagation.	●	●	●	●
	Apply effective treatments and use stringent controls during propagation.	●	●	●	●
	Do not dip or immerse cuttings unless the material contains appropriate disinfectants.	●	●	●	○

KEY: ● = very important method for that problem
◑ = somewhat important method
○ = not important method

Figure 10. Checklist for starting with a pest-free crop.

Table 8. Effectiveness of Some Media Treatments.

Treatment method	Effective against target pests			
	Fungi	Insects	Nematodes	Weeds
composting	most	yes	yes	some
dry heat	yes	yes	yes	most
solarization	most	yes	some	most
steam	yes	yes	yes	yes
chloropicrin	most	yes	some	some
dazomet	some	yes	yes	some
dichloropropene	no	some	yes	no
metam sodium	some	some	most	some
methyl bromide	most	yes	yes	most
methyl bromide (67%)/chloropicrin (33%)	yes	yes	yes	most

KEY: no   = few or no species is controlled
some = the number of species controlled
           may be less than a majority
most = the majority of species is controlled
yes   = all or almost all species are controlled

Media should be porous and moist before treatment. Temperature and other environmental conditions can affect treatment efficacy. Effective use methods and specific pest species controlled are discussed in the chapter "Diseases," except for solarization, which is discussed in the chapter "Weeds." Most fumigants are restricted pesticides; check with the County Department of Agriculture regarding use permits. Pesticide availability and registration change; check current labels and regulations before using fumigants.

instead of mixing stock from different sources together, can slow the rate of pest spread and facilitate spot treatments.

Keep pests out of growing areas. Regularly inspect crops and growing areas throughout the production cycle. Promptly eliminate any problems before pests become abundant or spread. Bacterial pathogens, eriophyid and tarsonemid mites, thrips, and certain other pests are extremely difficult to control once they become established. For difficult-to-control pests, the most effective and least expensive solution in the long run may be to immediately dispose of infested plants. Holding plants and applying ineffective controls risks spreading infestations and damage over a larger area.

Certain practices introduce pests and allow them to spread. For example, insects, nematodes, pathogens, and weeds can move into growing areas on contaminated containers, media, pallets, or plants. Dirty or contaminated shoes, hands, clothing, tools, and equipment can spread certain pests. Knowing how pests spread is critical to keeping crops pest-free.

Pathogen spread. Pathogens such as phytoplasmas and viruses that are vectored by insects can spread long distances when infective insects move. However, the main source of most pathogens is the immediate growing area, including benches, crop debris, planting beds, plants, soil, tools, and water. Many foliar-infecting pathogens soon die without live plants or suitable crop residue as a host. However, certain soil-dwelling pathogens have resting stages that persist for years.

Invertebrate spread. Mites and most tiny insects move passively by floating through air with the wind or by hitchhiking on animals, equipment, people, or plants. Larger insects are often strong fliers with well-developed senses that allow adult insects to travel far and seek out host plants. However, the major sources of most insect problems are infested crops, landscapes, and weeds within or near growing areas. Even if growing areas appear insect-free and contain no plants, certain insects can persist for weeks or longer in soil or crop residue, especially if temperatures are cool.

Weed spread. Annual weeds spread as seeds moved by water, wind, animals, equipment, and vehicles and on clothing, hair, and shoes. Although perennials can produce seed, they spread mostly as rhizomes, tubers, and other persistent propagules in containers, liners, or media. Weeds are frequently introduced through contaminated plants or media. Planting mix can become contaminated with weeds during mixing, storage, or crop production. Unpasteurized organic amendments may contain seeds or vegetative propagules.

Nematode spread. Most nematodes move only in roots, soil, or water. Foliar nematodes can spread inside infested aboveground plant parts. Equipment, shoes, and tools can spread nematode-infested soil or plant parts to uninfested growing areas. Recycled water, surface runoff, and irrigation water allowed to run from around infested plants can also spread nematodes. Any movement of unpasteurized field soils can spread nematodes.

Table 9. Some Pests Controlled by Heat Treatment of Plants.

CROPS	PESTS		
	Common name	Scientific name	Treatment suggestions
amaryllis, daffodil, gladiolus, iris, lily, tulip, and some other bulbs, corms, and rhizomes during storage	bulb flies bulb mites bulb scale mites gladiolus thrips lily bulb thrips stem and bulb nematodes tulip bulb aphid	*Eumerus, Merodon* spp. *Rhizoglyphus* spp. *Steneotarsonemus laticeps* *Thrips simplex* *Liothrips vaneeckei* *Ditylenchus* spp. *Dysaphis tulipae*	Presoak bulbs, corms, or rhizomes for 2 or 3 hr, or overnight, in 75°F (24°C) water containing a wetting agent. Immerse in 111°F (44°C) water for 1½ hr. Cool plants immediately afterwards with clean, cold water, then dry thoroughly in warm air or sunshine. Store under cool, low-humidity conditions.
caladium tubers, gladiolus corms, iris rhizomes	crown rot, southern wilt	*Sclerotium rolfsii*	Immerse tubers or rhizomes in 122°F (50°C) water for 30 min plus time necessary for plants to reach this temperature. Cool plants immediately afterward with clean, cold water. Dry thoroughly in warm air or sunshine.
calla	mosaic	Dasheen mosaic virus	Heat to 150°F (66°C) for 10 minutes, then culture tissue.
daffodil bulbs	basal rot	*Fusarium oxysporum* f. sp. *narcissi*	Store bulbs at 60° to 64°F prior to treatment to reduce heat injury. Presoak for 2–3 hr, or overnight, in 75°F (24°C) water plus a wetting agent. Maintain water at 109° to 111°F (43° to 44°C) for 3–4 hr after temperature reaches 109°F. Cool and dry bulbs immediately.
	crown rot	*Sclerotium rolfsii*	
	scorch	*Stagonospora curtisii*	
	stem and bulb nematodes	*Ditylenchus dipsaci*	
gladiolus corms	blue mold, corm rot	*Penicillium* spp.	*Cure* corms immediately after digging by storing corms in shallow trays at 95°F (35°C) and 80% RH. Use fans to provide continuous air circulation through trays and around corms. When old corms break off easily, usually after 6–8 days, break off and clean remaining new corms. Cure new corms 4 more days at 95°F, 80% RH. *Hot water treat* corms: select sound, hard, fully dormant cormels grown in warm soil and harvested before cold weather. Cure corms as above. Presoak cormels for 2 days in 60° to 80°F (16° to 27°C) water. Discard any corms that float. Immerse corms 30 min in 131°F (55°C) water. *Cool* corms immediately afterward with clean, cold water. *Dry* corms thoroughly in warm air or sunshine. *Apply* fungicide dust. *Store* corms at 40°F (4°C), 70–80% RH.
	Fusarium yellows	*Fusarium oxysporum* f. sp. *gladioli*	
	neck rot, corm disease	*Botrytis gladiolorum*, *B. cinerea*	
	dry rot	*Stromatinia gladioli*	
iris bulbs	blue mold	*Penicillium* spp.	Within 5 days of digging, cure bulbs for several days in shallow trays at 95°F (35°C) and 80% RH. Store under cool, drier conditions. Avoid injuring bulbs and do not dig them too early or too late.
iris bulbs	bulb nematodes	*Ditylenchus destructor*	Harvest bulbs 7–10 days early, immerse in 110°F (44°C) for 3 hr, cool and dry promptly. Store under cool, dry conditions.
rose	mosaic	Prunus necrotic ringspot virus	Hold mother plants at 100°F (38°C) for 4 weeks; virus will be inactive in 99% of the cuttings taken after this heat treatment.
	rose ring pattern	unknown; probably a virus	
seeds of statice, stock, zinnia and others	bacterial blight	*Xanthomonas campestris*	Soak seed in 122° to 131°F (50° to 55°C) water for 10 min to disinfect seed surface, or apply aerated steam to seed for somewhat longer. Cool seeds rapidly after heat treatment.
ranunculus seed	bacterial blight	*Xanthomonas campestris*	Soak seed in ¹⁄₁₀ dilution chlorine bleach for 30 min or ¹⁄₁₀ dilution chlorine bleach at 122°F (50°C) for 15 min. Cool seeds rapidly after heat treatment.
many hosts	cyclamen mite	*Phytonemus pallidus*	Thoroughly immerse plants in 111°F (44°C) water for 30 min or maintain 100% humidity and 111°F for 11 hours. Test some plants to determine if they will tolerate these conditions, then carefully inspect plants to ensure that treatment is effective before treating the entire crop.
	broad mite possibly other tarsonemids	*Polyphagotarsonemus latus*	

Heat can injure plant parts, causing stunting, deformation, or flower drop. Before any large-scale treatments, test crop tolerance to heat, consult an expert, or both.

Runoff among containers can spread nematodes and plant pathogens from one plant to another. Water puddling on surfaces directly contributes to problems such as foliar pathogens, fungus gnats, and weed growth.

Crop residue and used growing mix can be a source of pathogen inoculum that may spread to nearby crops. Keep refuse piles covered and away from growing areas.

Pathogen spread can be reduced by keeping equipment and tools off of floors and the ground, which may be contaminated. One method, shown here, is to clip the ends of hoses to benches or other fixtures.

This washing equipment at the end of a propagation bench encourages regular hand washing by employees, which can reduce the spread of pathogens.

Growing media treatments. Growing media, including field soil, container planting mix, and certain hydroponic substrates such as coir (coconut husk fiber) and used rock wool, should be pasteurized or otherwise treated before use or reuse whenever possible. Unpasteurized growing media and the plant debris that contaminates these media are primary reservoirs for nematodes, plant pathogens, weed seeds, and certain invertebrates. The need for media treatment is increasing as organic debris and other green waste is diverted from landfills and reused, as crop residue is managed on-site, and as media from culled plants is recycled.

Cultural controls for soilborne pests in growing media include managing drainage and runoff to avoid spreading pests in water, fallowing fields between crops so that pests die for lack of hosts, and irrigating to induce weed seed germina-

Concrete pads for ingredients of container media reduce contact with potentially contaminated soil and runoff water. Covering this growing media during storage would further prevent contamination from fungus gnats, windborne or rainborne pathogen propagules, and windblown weed seeds.

tion followed by cultivating or flaming emerged weeds. Cleaning equipment and tools before moving between fields and removing crop debris after harvest can prevent the spread of pests and pathogens. Fumigation and heating are the most widely used media treatments (Table 8). Heat treatments include solarization (see the chapter "Weeds") and steam, dry heat (such as from kilns), and heat generated by decomposer microorganisms during composting (see the chapter "Diseases"). New technologies such as microwave or gamma radiation and ohmic heating are being researched for treating media.

Biological control of soil-dwelling pathogens through disease-suppressive composts and organic amendments are discussed in the chapter "Diseases". Using reduced rates of fumigants in combination with soil amendments, biological control organisms, or heat can provide better pest control than relying on a single method alone. For example, solarization combined with certain organic soil amendments provides effective biofumigation in both open fields and container media. One experiment found that adding broccoli, cabbage, or cauliflower residue and heating media at 80° to 100°F (27° to 38°C) for 1 week reduced germination of *Pythium ultimum* and *Sclerotium rolfsii* propagules by 87 to 100%.

Heat-treating plants. Many bacteria, fungi, insects, mites, nematodes, and weeds can be controlled by exposing infested plants to dry heat, aerated steam, or hot water (Table 9). Certain viruses can be eliminated from cuttings by heat treating mother plants before propagation from meristem tissue. Heat-treating seeds is often used to eliminate *Xanthomonas* bacteria and certain other pathogens. Immersing bulbs, corms, or rhizomes into hot water before planting or storage can disinfect crops such as amaryllis, daffodil, gladiolus, lily, and tulip.

The temperature and time needed to provide control depends on the crop and pests. Too high a temperature or too long an exposure can damage plants; insufficient temperatures or too short an exposure may not kill the pests. Consult an expert before beginning any large-scale treatments. A general recommendation is to presoak bulbs, corms, or rhizomes for 2 to 3 hours, or overnight, in 75°F (24°C) water containing a wetting agent before immersing them in 111°F (44°C) water for about 1½ hours. Cool plants immediately afterward with clean, cold water; dry them thoroughly in warm air or sunshine; then store them under cool, low-humidity conditions until plants are used.

Each pest species and each crop cultivar should be tested for susceptibility on a small scale before undertaking a commercial-scale treatment program. An ice chest with an electric immersion heater may be sufficient for small volume treatments. Commercial treatment can be done in larger tanks into which stock is lowered by a hoist or forklift, treated for a period of time, and then removed. Or, stock can be placed onto a conveyer belt that moves through a hot-water tank at a calibrated speed.

Consider using a pretreatment tank to partially raise the planting stock to the required temperature, especially if stock is taken from cold storage or cold soil just before treatment. The volume of hot water in the primary tank should be large enough to prevent a significant drop in temperature when the stock is added. The shorter the treatment time, the more critical it is to quickly reach and maintain the required temperature. Depending on how quickly stock must be cooled after treatment, an additional cool-water tank or facilities for hosing down treated stock with cool water may be needed.

Accurate time and temperature controls are critical. Temperature uniformity for a treatment should be monitored by the use of several thermometers placed within the treatment tank (in California, county weights and measures offices can provide information on calibration of thermometers). Use a circulating pump or some other method to continually mix the treatment water to assure uniformity within the tank.

Environmental Management and Cultural Practices

Appropriate cultural practices and proper environmental controls are critical for effective management of many pests (see the chapter "Abiotic Disorders and Cultural Practices." Cultural practices such as planting resistant cultivars, rotating crops, and altering planting time or design are effective only if growers anticipate problems and take these steps before planting (Tables 10 and 11). Environmental controls such as modifying humidity, light, temperature, and ventilation that rely on equipment installation or physical modifications of the growing area are best done before planting, although many environmental modifications can be done anytime during the production cycle.

Resistant cultivars. The species or cultivar often determines whether certain problems are likely to develop. Pests may be able to infect or feed some on resistant cultivars without damaging plants. Before planting, determine whether species or cultivars that are less susceptible to important pests can be grown profitably (for cultivars known to be resistant or less susceptible to damage from certain insects and mites, see Table 12; for pathogens, see Table 13). Develop your own susceptibility information over time by observing multiple cultivars grown nearby at the same time. Check with the suppliers listed at the end of this book for the most recent recommendations on resistant cultivars.

Alternative crops. Consider planting alternative crop species that will perform well, can be grown profitably, and tend not to develop serious pests under conditions at your site. For example, crops that germinate quickly or start from transplants survive well and rapidly shade surrounding soil can be considered weed-resistant. Identifying the nematodes

Table 10. Environmental Control Methods for Preventing Foliar Pathogen Damage: An Example Using Key Pests of Greenhouse Cut Roses.

ENVIRONMENTAL CONTROL	PATHOGENS CONTROLLED		
	Botrytis gray mold	Downy mildew	Powdery mildew
provide good air circulation	●	●	●
prevent moisture condensation	●	●	○
control humidity	keep RH <85%	prevent RH >85% for >3 hr continuous	keep night RH <90%, keep day RH 71–84% or <40%
apply heat	heat growing area to create RH <85%	heat growing area to >80°F (27°C) daily for several hours	heat growing area to >90°F (32.5°C) for >½ hr to prevent 68° to 86°F (20° to 30°C) for 6 or more consecutive hr
use computerized environmental monitoring and control	●	●	●

KEY: ● = very important for these pests
　　　○ = not important
　　　RH = relative humidity

Table 11. Environmental Conditions and Cultural Practices That Should Be Monitored and Controlled to Help Prevent, Diagnose, and Manage Pests.

ENVIRONMENTAL CONDITION OR GROWING PRACTICE	PEST PROBLEM				
	Pathogens	Abiotic disorders	Insects & mites	Nematodes	Weeds
resistant cultivars	●	◑	●	◑	○
alternative crops	●	●	●	●	●
crop rotation	●	○	●	●	●
fallowing fields	●	○	◑	●	●
planting time, design, and grouping	●	●	●	○	●
humidity, leaf wetness	●	◑	○	○	○
nutrition and fertilization	◑	●	◑	○	◑
light	◑	●	◑	○	●
media formulation, amendment, and handling	◑	●	○	◑	◑
drainage and aeration	●	●	○	◑	◑
Irrigation Water					
frequency and amount	●	●	◑	◑	●
method and placement	●	●	◑	●	●
chemistry	●	●	○	○	○
pest contamination	●	○	◑	●	●
Temperature					
air	●	●	●	○	○
media	◑	●	○	●	●
water	◑	●	◑	○	○

KEY: ● = very important for these pests
　　　◑ = somewhat important
　　　○ = not important

that are known to attack specific crops (Table 94) will help you identify what crops to avoid when planting in soils known to be infested with those nematode species. Consult the crop tables in this manual and in *Pests of Landscape Trees and Shrubs* (Dreistadt 1994) to identify crops not known to be susceptible to serious pest problems common at your site.

If you select a more susceptible crop species or cultivar because of other priorities, be prepared for pest damage and the effort and resources required for management.

Crop rotation. Rotate crops in greenhouses and fields whenever practical. Choose crop species or cultivars that are

Table 12. Alternative Flower Crop Cultivars Less Susceptible to Some Insects and Mites.

Crop	Pest	Resistant or less susceptible alternatives
carnation	western flower thrips	Table 60
chrysanthemum	aphids, leafminer, thrips	Tables 55, 63
chrysanthemum	western flower thrips	Statesman[1]
coleus	citrus mealybug	green, nonvariegated cultivars[2]
English ivy	twospotted mite	Gold Dust, Sweet Heart, Telecurl[3]
fuchsia	fuchsia gall mite	Table 74
Geraldton wax plant	gall wasp	Lady Stephanie[4]
petunia	tobacco or petunia budworm	ivy geraniums (*Pelargonium hortorum*)
rhododendron	weevils	many rhododendron hybrids[5]
rose	western flower thrips	Table 61

Cultivars resistant to other pests are available or are being developed. Consult *Pests of Landscape Trees and Shrubs* (Dreistadt 1994) to identify woody ornamentals resistant to certain pests. Contact suppliers listed at the end of this manual for the latest information on available resistant cultivars.

Sources: 1. Van Dijken et al. 1994, de Jager et al. 1995.   4. Redak and Bethke 1995.
2. Yang and Sandof 1995.   5. Antonelli and Campbell 1986.
3. Osborne and Chase 1985.

not susceptible to the major pest species affecting the previous crop (see the crop tables). Unless soil is treated or fallowed first, do not plant susceptible crops in beds or field soils where nematodes, soil-dwelling pathogens, or insects with long-lived soil-dwelling stages such as weevil larvae have previously been a problem. In general, do avoid replanting the same crop genus into a site.

Fallowing. Consider allowing a fallow period between crops. Populations of certain pests will rapidly decline if growing areas are kept free of crops, weeds, and other pest habitats for some time after harvest. Propagules of certain pathogens will not survive long in the absence of host crops or fresh plant residue (Table 38). Adults of insects such as leafminers and thrips that drop to pupate in the soil will disperse or die if food is not present. Use degree-day models based on prevailing temperatures (see the chapter "Insects, Mites, and Other Invertebrates") to estimate how long to keep growing areas crop-free. Keep greenhouses warm during the plant-free period so that pests continue to develop; many invertebrates can survive for long periods if temperatures are cool.

Planting design. Environmental conditions in growing sites naturally vary from one area to another. Learn to recognize these variations. Locate each crop where it will best tolerate local differences in humidity, ventilation, light, and drainage. For example, if the crop is highly susceptible to foliage-infecting bacteria or fungi, avoid locating it beneath greenhouse covers or gutters that drip or leak moisture. Some portions of growing areas average higher humidity; where condensation occurs, avoid planting crops most susceptible to gray mold. Powdery mildews are more prevalent in shady areas with poor air circulation, no overhead watering, and

Table 13. Flower Crops with Alternative Cultivars Less Susceptible to Certain Pathogens.

Crop	Pathogen
many crops	Verticillium wilt
African violet	Erwinia blight, Phytophthora root decay, powdery mildew
begonia 'Rieger Elatior'	powdery mildew, Xanthomonas bacterial leaf spot and blight
calathea	Helminthosporium leaf spot (*Bipolaris setariae*)
carnation	Fusarium cutting rot, Fusarium wilt, rust, certain viruses
chrysanthemum	Fusarium wilt, Erwinia hollow stem, rust, certain viruses
croton	Xanthomonas bacterial leaf spot
daffodil	Fusarium basal rot, certain viruses
English ivy	Colletotrichum leaf spot, Xanthomonas bacterial leaf spot
geranium	gray mold, rust, certain viruses, Xanthomonas bacterial leaf spot
heather	powdery mildew, Phytophthora root and crown rot
hibiscus	Pseudomonas and Xanthomonas bacterial leaf spots
iris	Mosaic and Iris Virus 1, rust
marigold	Pseudomonas leaf spot
phlox	powdery mildew
poinsettia	powdery mildew, gray mold, Pythium and Rhizoctonia root rots, Xanthomonas bacterial leaf spot and stem rot
rose	powdery mildew
Thanksgiving cactus	*Bipolaris* or *Drechslera cactivora* stem rot, Erwinia bacterial blight, *Fusarium oxysporum* basal decay, Phytophthora and Pythium root rots
zinnia	Xanthomonas bacterial blight

Cultivars resistant to other diseases are available or are being developed. Contact suppliers listed at the end of this manual for the latest information on available resistant cultivars. Consult *Pests of Landscape Trees and Shrubs* (Dreistadt 1994) to identify woody ornamentals resistant to certain pests. Keep good monitoring records and develop your own information on pest-resistant cultivars.

Use good planting design, such as not growing potentially infested crops in hanging baskets over other hosts. For example, ivy geranium infected with *Xanthomonas campestris* pv. *pelargonii* often exhibits no symptoms or only mild symptoms. Falling infected plant parts or contaminated water dripping from baskets overhead can contribute to severely damaging infections of zonal or seed geraniums grown below.

Chrysanthemums of many different ages are being grown together in this greenhouse. This continuous cropping encourages insects and pathogen inoculum to spread to young plants from older plants that are more likely to be infested or infected.

where days are warm and nights are cool; avoid planting crops susceptible to powdery mildew in such locations unless lighting, air circulation, and temperature can be improved.

Facilitate proper management by grouping plants with compatible needs such as irrigation, light, and temperature requirements. Keep new plants from the same source together during their early growth to slow the spread of pests that may have been introduced on them and to make problems easier to detect and spot-treat. When crops susceptible to the same pests are grown, group them together throughout the production cycle so they can be more easily monitored and managed. Grouping susceptible crops together also allows more frequent spraying or other control actions to be applied only to those crops that need it while avoiding unnecessarily frequent treatment of less-susceptible crops. If possible, reduce the spread of pests by using separate growing areas, screens, or plastic sheets to isolate susceptible cultivars from other crops.

Avoid continuous cropping. Continuous cropping is the practice of growing plants of different ages together in one place or immediately replanting after harvest when pests from the previous crop may still be present. Continuous cropping encourages high populations of insects and pathogens that have developed through many generations on older plants to readily move and infest young crops at the

beginning of their production cycle. Workers moving from old crops to young crops or routine crop disturbances such as overhead irrigation or harvest can cause pests to infest a previously clean crop. If it is not possible to avoid planting young clean plants near older, infested plants, consider isolating the groups using row covers, screens, or plastic sheets.

Planting time. If hosts of serious pests are grown near a susceptible crop, evaluate whether the crop planting time can be adjusted to avoid growing it when pests can be expected to migrate from the hosts. Migration is especially devastating if it coincides with early stages of crop growth, allowing the immigrants to develop though many generations before harvest. Pests migrate from alternate hosts because numbers there have become abundant (often late in that plant's development), the crop is being harvested, or the alternate host's suitability for the pest is reduced, such as the seasonal drying of annual weeds. For example, vegetables such as celery grown in the Salinas Valley of California are alternate hosts for aphids, leafhoppers, leafminers, and thrips species that also attack flower and nursery crops.

Properly care for crops. Inappropriate irrigation is probably the most common cause of crop damage. Provide the appropriate amount, frequency, method, and quality of water to minimize or prevent problems. Overirrigation, too little water, or improper water chemistry (such as salinity, toxic elements, or alkalinity) can damage plants. Most pathogenic bacteria and fungi require moisture to infect and damage crops, and good water management is critical to effective pathogen control. Nematodes, pathogens, and weed seeds are often introduced onto crops unless irrigation drainage and runoff are handled properly. Irrigation systems that apply water at the soil surface or at the base of containers do not wash off foliar-applied pesticides, as overhead irrigation would. Pest control through cultural practices, including irrigation, is discussed in the chapter "Abiotic Disorders and Cultural Practices."

Pesticides

Many pesticides traditionally used in flower and nursery crops are broad-spectrum and relatively persistent. Broad-spectrum pesticides can cause outbreaks of secondary pests such as mites, are toxic to natural enemies, and pose hazards to workers and the environment. Longer persistence can increase pesticide resistance. Successful IPM relies heavily on biological, pest-specific, and reduced-risk pesticides. Reduced-risk pesticides have received accelerated registration approval by the Environmental Protection Agency because they have one or more desirable characteristics, including

- better worker safety
- low toxicity to nontarget organisms
- reduced potential for groundwater contamination
- low application rates
- less potential for development of pest resistance
- greater compatibility with IPM

Many IPM-compatible pesticides are relatively new, and using them effectively often requires more knowledge and skill than do older, broad-spectrum pesticides. Before choosing a pesticide, understand its relative toxicity, selectivity, persistence, and potential for causing phytotoxicity or promoting development of resistance. Consider whether the pesticide is effective in combination with nonchemical methods and IPM.

Types of pesticides. Pesticides are broadly categorized according to the type of target organism: insecticides that control insects, herbicides that control weeds, and fungicides that control pathogenic fungi. Pesticides are also categorized by the source of the material: botanicals such as neem are extracted from plants; inorganic pesticides such as sulfur and copper are refined from minerals; synthetic pesticides such as organophosphates and chlorinated hydrocarbons are manufactured from petroleum derivatives. The pest chapters in this manual concentrate on biological, organically acceptable, and reduced-risk pesticides. Consult the latest UC IPM Pest Management Guidelines: Floriculture and

Table 14. Safe Use of Pesticides.

- Read labels before purchasing or using a pesticide.
- Select the right pesticide.
- Learn and follow all applicable regulations.
- Train mixers, applicators, handlers, and other workers.
- Transport pesticides safely.
- Wear appropriate personal protective equipment.
- Mix pesticides properly.
- Use appropriate application equipment.
- Apply pesticides safely.
- Plan for accidents.
- Clean any spills immediately.
- Dispose of containers properly.
- Keep good records.

For more details, consult *The Safe and Effective Use of Pesticides* (O'Connor-Marer 1999) and *Pesticide Safety: A Reference Manual for Growers* (O'Connor-Marer 1997).

Ornamental Nurseries for more specific pesticide recommendations. Please read the following sections before choosing a pesticide, and be sure to follow label directions explicitly when using any pesticide.

Pesticides are toxic. Always use pesticides safely (Table 14) and according to the label. All pesticides are toxic (poisonous) in some way. Avoid exposing people and nontarget organisms to pesticides. Choose wisely how and when to apply pesticides. Select from among the least hazardous pesticides available for your situation.

Pesticide hazard, the ability of pesticides to produce an adverse effect, ranges from slight to extreme. Pesticides sold in the United States must have a signal word on their label indicating potential hazard of immediate or acute injury. The signal words are CAUTION (the least hazardous), WARNING, and DANGER. DANGER, the most hazardous, often includes a skull and crossbones and may also be labeled POISON. Pesticides in the DANGER category generally are available only to certified applicators and require special training and equipment for use.

In addition to acute hazard, certain pesticides are suspected of causing long-term health effects. This information is not provided on the label. A Material Safety Data Sheet (MSDS) detailing potential hazards is available for each pesticide. Request and read the MSDS for more information.

The restricted-entry interval (REI) is the required number of hours or days after application during which entry into treated areas is prohibited. REI regulations help minimize exposure to pesticides. Employers must ensure that workers who apply, handle, or mix pesticides have been properly trained. Federal Worker Protection Standards also require pesticide safety training for all employees working in fields, greenhouses, and nurseries that have been treated with pesticides, including employees who do not work directly with pesticides.

A pesticide cannot be used in greenhouses unless "greenhouse" is listed on the label. Wear proper personal protective equipment whenever using pesticides.

Selectivity. Selective pesticides are toxic only to the target organism and related species. Broad-spectrum pesticides kill many different species. Most carbamate, organophosphate, and pyrethroid insecticides are broad-spectrum, killing both pests and their natural enemies. On the other hand, many biological insecticides kill only certain pests. For example, certain strains of *Bacillus thuringiensis* (Bt) kill only certain moth and butterfly larvae. Use selective pesticides wherever possible because they are generally less damaging to nontarget organisms, are safer for use around people, and are compatible with other IPM methods.

Selectivity also refers to the manner of use. Broad-spectrum pesticides can sometimes be used selectively by modifying application timing, equipment, and method. For example, insecticides for ant control can be mixed with bait and enclosed in a container that prevents most nontarget organisms from being exposed to pesticides. Selective use includes spot treating instead of spraying the entire growing area (Fig. 11).

Persistence. The length of time a pesticide remains active after application is called persistence. Longer persistence can be desirable because it increases the length of time a pesticide controls target pests. For example, a more persistent

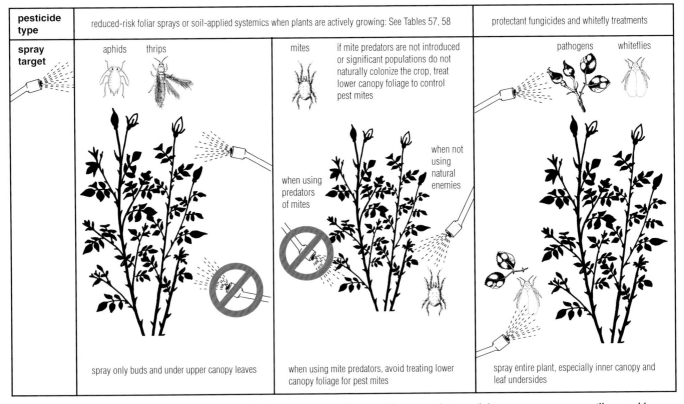

Figure 11. Selective pesticide use includes spraying only those plant parts where significant populations of the target pests occur, as illustrated here for the key pests of greenhouse cut roses. Prior to applying any pesticides, use control action guidelines to decide whether treatment is warranted (see Tables 4 and 5). Minimize pesticide use and prevent pest problems by using good exclusion and sanitation methods and appropriate environmental controls (see Table 7).

preemergent herbicide suppresses weed seedlings longer, providing crops with more time to grow without competition from weeds. However, when using broad-spectrum pesticides, the least persistent pesticide that is effective is usually the best choice for an IPM program. More-persistent herbicides can be undesirable if they prevent successful establishment of a subsequent crop. Resistance is more likely to develop among pests exposed to persistent pesticides. Persistent broad-spectrum insecticides continue to kill natural enemies that migrate in after spraying. In some cases, residues of certain pesticides in greenhouses may remain toxic to natural enemies for several months after application, preventing any naturally colonizing or introduced natural enemies from being effective. Using persistent broad-spectrum pesticides can delay safe worker reentry into crops. The restricted-entry interval (REI) is a guide to how long pesticide residue remains acutely hazardous to people. The REI does not indicate how long after application a material can affect crops or beneficial organisms. Consult Table 84 for preemergence herbicide persistence in soil; Table 57 for the relative insecticide persistence and selectivity of major classes of insecticides; and Table 66 for pesticides compatible with common insect parasites.

Phytotoxicity. Pesticides can be phytotoxic (cause damage to plants). Phytotoxicity is more likely if plants lack proper cultural care, environmental conditions are extreme, or pesticides are used carelessly. Common mistakes are applying excess amounts, allowing spray to drift onto nontarget crops, failing to obey label precautions, or using a sprayer previously used to apply herbicides to apply other pesticides. Certain active ingredients, formulations, and application methods pose a higher risk of phytotoxicity. Herbicides pose the greatest risk of crop damage if the incorrect material is chosen, if they are applied improperly, if environmental conditions favor crop damage, or if they contact nontarget plants. However, plants can be damaged by insecticides or other types of pesticides if conditions allow. Consult the chapter "Abiotic Disorders and Cultural Practices" for suggestions on diagnosing and avoiding phytotoxicity.

Resistance. Many insects and pathogens and some weeds have developed resistance to certain pesticides. Resistance occurs when a pest population is no longer controlled by pesticides that previously provided control (Fig. 12). A different type of pesticide or some other control measure must be substituted to control that pest.

Even in the absence of actual phytotoxicity, some sprays can leave visible residues such as this white powder that may be unacceptable on marketable plant parts.

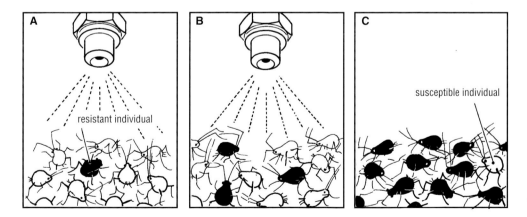

Figure 12. Resistance to pesticides develops through genetic selection in populations of pests, including insects, pathogens, and weeds. A. Certain individuals in a pest population are less susceptible to a pesticide than other individuals. B. These less-susceptible pest biotypes are more likely to survive an application and to produce progeny that are also less susceptible. C. After repeated applications over several generations, the pest population consists primarily of resistant or less-susceptible individuals. Applying the same pesticide, or other chemicals with the same mode of action, is no longer effective.

Table 15. Avoiding Pesticide Resistance.

- Scout growing areas before treatments to determine which pest species are present.
- Evaluate cost-benefit economics and use thresholds to determine whether pesticide application is justified by increased returns.
- Minimize the amount and frequency of applications and the extent of area treated, for example, by spot-spraying only locations and plant parts where target pests occur.
- Consider using biological, cultural, mechanical, and physical control alternatives.
- Rotate crops to avoid having to treat the same pests in the same location season after season.
- Rotate pesticides by making sequential applications of pesticides that have a different mode of action.
- Scout growing areas after treatment, note pests that were not controlled well, and collect and send samples to a laboratory for resistance testing.
- Take steps to avoid spreading infested plants or pests, for example by using good exclusion and sanitation.

Table 16. Common Reasons for Inadequate Control with Pesticides.

- Misidentification of pest species.
- Wrong choice of pesticide.
- Wrong choice of equipment.
- Inadequate agitation, improper calibration, or other incorrect equipment adjustments.
- Incorrect rates for the situation.
- Wrong surfactant or other adjuvants.
- Incompatibility with other materials in a tank mix.
- Poor quality spray water, such as improper pH.
- Improper timing of application, such as wrong stage of pest development.
- Inadequate coverage.
- Poor placement, such as not targeting the underside of leaves.
- Unfavorable weather or environmental conditions.
- Very high pest populations.
- Tolerant or resistant pest species or population.
- Failure to coordinate applications with other growing practices, such as overhead irrigation.
- Failure to use pesticides in combination with other methods as part of an integrated pest management program.

Avoiding resistance. Take as many steps as possible to avoid creating resistant pests (Table 15). Delay pesticide resistance by using biological, cultural, mechanical, and physical controls whenever possible. When pesticides are applied, chose selective materials, use them in combination with alternatives, and make spot applications whenever possible. If pests are frequently sprayed, avoid repeatedly applying pesticides in the same chemical class or those with the same mode of action. Unless otherwise directed on the labeling, switch to a pesticide with a different mode of action about every 2 to 3 pest generations or after about 2 to 3 applications. Consult information in the chapters "Diseases," "Insects, Mites, and Other Invertebrates," and "Weeds" to identify pesticide classes so you can select pesticides for rotation against pests.

Some growers mix two or more different types of pesticides in a single application in an attempt to overcome pesticide resistance. Pesticide mixtures are controversial; some experts believe mixtures increase resistance development over the long run. Mixtures of two or more fungicides or two or more insecticides generally are not recommended for flower and nursery crops unless synergism is known to occur among the specific pesticides used. Much of our knowledge about how to manage resistance comes from laboratory studies and theoretical models rather than from replicated field trials. Regularly consult the sources in the suggested reading at the end of this manual for new information on resistance management.

Applying pesticides effectively. Know the characteristics of your pest and pesticide in order to select the proper pesticide and determine when and how to apply it. Identify the spray target, such as terminal buds or underneath leaves; apply the proper amount of pesticide and deliver it all to the target. Spills, leaks, and drift reduce treatment effectiveness and are hazardous. Select appropriate equipment, calibrate sprayers properly, and use good application techniques.

Know whether the pesticide provides only contact efficacy (it must be thoroughly applied to cover the target) or whether the pesticide will be redistributed after application by vapor or systemic activity. Know whether the pesticide is curative or only preventive so you can time applications correctly. Many fungicides must be applied before pathogen infection takes place, especially when using inorganic or organically acceptable fungicides, and many insecticides are lethal to insect pests only during specific stages of the pests' life cycle. For example, for most caterpillar species, *Bacillus thuringiensis* (Bt) is most effective at killing young larvae, so Bt should be sprayed when actively feeding young larvae are the predominate life stage. Know whether the pesticide is broad-spectrum or pest-specific. Some herbicides must be applied before weeds emerge; others are effective only when weeds are actively growing. Making good pesticide use decisions increases the likelihood that you will obtain economically viable, environmentally sound, effective control (Table 16).

High-volume applications. High-volume sprayers thoroughly wet treated foliage until spray runs off, often applying several hundred gallons of material per acre using equipment ranging from inexpensive hand-held or backpack compressed air sprayers to hydraulic sprayers for treating large areas. High-volume sprayers usually produce a wide range of different-sized droplets, most of which are relatively large (>100 micrometers in diameter). Because large droplets settle relatively quickly, they are less prone to drift in air, reducing the likelihood of pesticide movement off-site. However, large droplets are undesirable because they

- often run off of the spray target
- tend to pool in cupped surfaces and on lower edges of plants, where the higher dose risks phytotoxicity
- often do not provide good coverage on the underside of leaves
- require a larger volume of spray than smaller droplets to thoroughly cover surfaces, resulting in a relatively high amount of active ingredient applied per unit area

When making high-volume applications, use appropriate pressures and proper nozzles to create relatively uniform-sized droplets. Place nozzles close to the targeted surfaces. Avoid moving too quickly while spraying to provide more thorough coverage. Apply spray uniformly, for example, by continually moving the nozzle in an arc when spraying with a hand wand.

Low-volume applications. Low-volume and ultra-low-volume sprayers produce very small droplets (<100 micrometers in diameter). These small droplets have a much larger surface area per volume than large droplets. Low-volume sprayers usually apply less than 30 gallons (115 l) of spray mix per acre, much less than high-volume sprayers. However, low-volume sprayers generally require a higher rate of active ingredient in the mix than high-volume sprayers. Low-volume spray use is often limited to newer pesticides, because new labels are usually the only ones that provide directions for low-volume applications.

Low-volume application equipment includes thermal-pulse foggers, mechanical generators (also called cold foggers), rotary mist applicators, and electrostatic sprayers. Low-volume sprayers have many advantages compared with high-volume sprayers when treating foliage (Table 17). The smaller diameter droplets (30–100 micrometers) from low-volume sprayers provide better coverage and are more effective than larger droplets when treating plants and foliage-dwelling pests. Because smaller droplets increase the risk of drift, take measures to prevent pesticide movement off-site, including adding appropriate adjuvants to the spray mix, using good application technique such as properly aiming sprays, employing proper nozzles, lowering spray pressure, and not spraying during adverse conditions such as high temperatures or wind.

This high-volume sprayer requires more pesticide per acre and provides poorer coverage on leaf undersides than low-volume application equipment, such as electrostatic sprayers.

Table 17. Advantages of Low-Volume Sprayers.

- Can improve spray coverage, especially underside of leaves.
- Allow reduction in the amount of active ingredient applied per acre, lowering pesticide costs.
- Use about 40 times less water or oil diluent than high-volume applications.
- Can reduce application time and labor.

Advantages of Low-Volume Electrostatic Sprayers

- Deposit about three times more active ingredient onto foliage.
- Deposit about one-third less spray onto benches and aisles.
- Apply residues that are more difficult to dislodge from foliage, reducing hazards to workers.

Electrostatic sprayers. Effective electrostatic sprayers are air-assisted devices employing an air atomizer to create tiny droplets (about 30 to 60 micrometers in diameter). This equipment operates at air pressure as low as 30 to 40 psi. Many older pesticide labels specify pesticide rates only for high-volume applications, which may involve applying 100 to 800 gallons (380–3,000 l) of diluted pesticide per acre.

Electrostatic sprayers have many advantages (Table 17) and provide equal or better pest control than conventional high-volume sprayers. With high-volume sprayers, often less than 1% of the pesticide applied reaches the target pest. Electrostatic sprayers waste less pesticide because they apply a charge (usually negative) to spray droplets, causing the droplets to be repelled from each other (so they don't clump into larger droplets) and be attracted to plants, where they stick on plant surfaces (Figs. 13 and 14). Charged particles are much less likely to drift than the noncharged particles from other spray equipment.

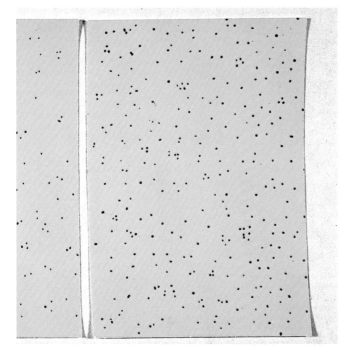

This yellow water-sensitive card produces colored spots wherever an insecticide spray droplet lands. Place cards throughout crops before treatment to assess droplet size and density and to determine how thoroughly pesticide is being delivered to the targeted plant parts.

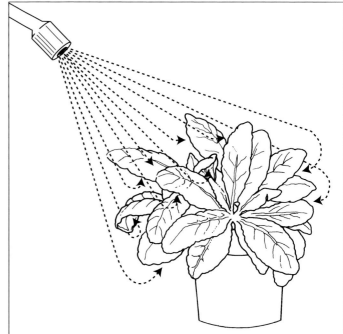

Figure 13. An air-assisted electrostatic sprayer provides good coverage on inner plant parts and leaf undersides because an electrical charge is applied to each droplet, preventing droplets from clumping together and causing spray to be attracted to plant surfaces.

Monitoring spray coverage. Use commercially available water- or oil-sensitive cards to efficiently determine how thoroughly targeted plant parts were treated. Clip or staple cards to the specific plant parts targeted for treatment, such as the underside of leaves. Also deploy cards at various canopy heights and both closer to and further from row edges to evaluate spray distribution throughout the growing area. Mark the locations where cards were deployed so the cards can be retrieved easily. Mark the locations unobtrusively and have the cards deployed by someone other than the applicator to avoid potential applicator bias when targeting sprays. The cards are moisture sensitive, so use them when rain or irrigation will not occur.

Figure 14. Spray deposition (in micrograms per cm²) on surfaces when insecticide was applied to greenhouse container plants using a conventional high-volume sprayer (runoff) versus a low-volume electrostatic sprayer. *Source:* Kabashima, Giles, and Parrella 1995.

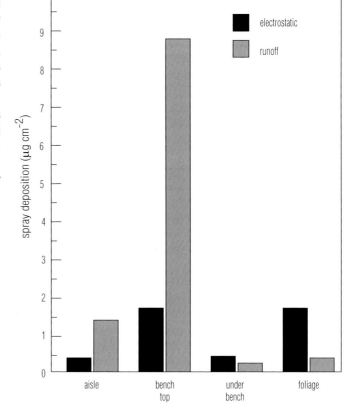

Abiotic Disorders and Cultural Practices

Abiotic (nonliving or noninfectious) disorders are diseases induced by inappropriate cultural practices or adverse environmental conditions. Common causes of abiotic disorders include too much or too little water, poor drainage of growing media, excess or deficient nutrients, salinity, improper temperature, pesticides, physical injury, and adverse weather. Abiotic disorders can directly damage plants and predispose crops to attack by certain insects and pathogens.

Some abiotic disorders can be recognized by characteristic discolored, distorted, or dying foliage. Other disorders cause symptoms easily confused with similar damage caused by insects, mites, and pathogens. Consult Table 18 to help you distinguish abiotic disorders from biotic causes of disease.

Water Excess or Deficiency

Improper irrigation is probably the most common cause of crop damage. Inadequate water amount causes foliage to wilt, discolor, and drop prematurely (Table 19). Overwatering is a more common problem than underwatering. Overwatering does not mean that too much water is applied during each irrigation, it means that water is applied too frequently, especially when drainage is poor. Excess moisture reduces gas exchange and kills roots. As roots die, foliage discolors and dies (Table 20). An inappropriate amount or frequency of irrigation predisposes crops to attack by mites and certain insects. Most pathogenic bacteria and fungi require moisture to infect plants and cause damage; good water management is critical to effective pathogen control. Table 21 summarizes good irrigation practices.

Edema
Edema (formerly called oedema) is the development of raised, scabby areas on leaves. Although affected tissue is often brown and blisterlike, it is not necrotic. The specific cause of this noninfectious disorder is not known. It often develops in the presence of light when media is cool and wet and the air is relatively warm. These conditions apparently cause excess moisture to accumulate in leaves, damaging tissue and causing formation of leaf blisters. Excess irrigation may promote edema.

Irrigation Frequency
Overwatering damage results from irrigating too frequently, especially when growing media is inadequately drained.

Necrosis developed on these hydrangea leaf tips due to insufficient irrigation frequency when plants were exposed to hot, sunny conditions.

Excess irrigation often causes abnormally small dark leaves and wilting of plants. However, because this container media is very well drained, excess irrigation with nutrient-rich water (fertigation) of the poinsettia on the left produced an oversized, unmarketable plant in comparison with the appropriately watered poinsettia on the right.

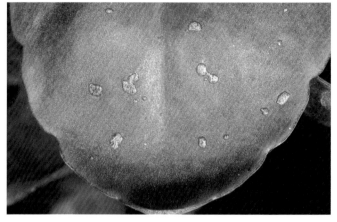

Inadequate irrigation caused this chrysanthemum to experience extreme drought for several days, resulting in permanent wilting.

Edema, scabby or blisterlike leaf spots, is visible on this kalanchoe leaf. To help reduce the risk of oedema, avoid excess irrigation and provide good drainage.

Table 18. Characteristics Useful in Distinguishing Abiotic Disorders from Biotic Causes of Disease.

	TYPE OF DISEASE	
Disease characteristics	Abiotic	Biotic
hosts	commonly affects several species and plants of various ages when grown together	commonly affects one species or cultivar or only plants of the same age
pattern of symptoms within growing area	location depends on environmental or physical factors or cultural practices; may be a regular pattern to symptom location	often initially observed on plants in apparently random locations
rate of symptom development among affected plants	relatively uniform, extent of damage appears similar among plants	relatively uneven, time of appearance and damage severity varies among affected plants
signs	no evidence of the kinds of pests known to cause the current symptoms	insects, mites, fungal mycelium, or other evidence of pests present
spread	is not infectious, commonly caused by one incident and does not spread	infectious, spreads over time if conditions are suitable
history	possibly a recurrence of causes that have previously been associated with current or prior environmental conditions or cultural practices that commonly occur in this growing area	symptoms may match those caused by pests that have affected this crop during previous growing seasons or are known to commonly affect this crop species or cultivar, such as those listed in the crop tables

Although biotic diseases involve pathogenic microorganisms discussed in the chapter "Diseases," damage results from a complex interaction among the host plant, pathogen, and the environment; damage symptoms may result from both abiotic and biotic factors combined.

Table 19. Common Symptoms of Underwatering.

- Foliage off-color.
- Leaves soft or rubbery.
- Foliage wilts.
- Leaves undersized.
- Short stem internodes.
- Hardened leaf texture.
- Marginal or interveinal leaf necrosis.
- Premature leaf senescence.
- Mites or certain leaf-sucking insects become abundant.
- Woody parts develop cankers, dieback, weeping liquid, or are attacked by wood boring insects.

Table 20. Common Symptoms of Overwatering.

- Foliage yellows or wilts.
- Leaf texture abnormally soft.
- Internodes elongated but plants stunted or tall.
- Root system undersized.
- Roots black or dark brownish.
- Nutrient deficiency symptoms appear.
- Root, stem, or foliar pathogens develop.
- Woody parts develop cankers or die back.

Table 21. Good Irrigation Management Practices.

- Use well-drained media and proper containers.
- Monitor media, plants, and environmental conditions to determine irrigation need and frequency.
- Use pulse irrigation to supply water as needed or wet all media in the entire root zone during each irrigation.
- Avoid overwatering by irrigating less frequently.
- Consider the irrigation method in relation to plant diseases.
- Monitor water quality.
- Maximize distribution or emission uniformity by using appropriate equipment and minimizing variability among emitters, nozzles, sprinklers, and other application devices.
- Maximum irrigation efficiency by applying the correct amount of water and minimizing water leaching, percolation, and runoff.
- Collect, treat, and recycle any runoff and tailwater.
- Control drainage and erosion.
- Conserve water and nutrients.

A plant's irrigation need depends in part on the frequency, amount, and method of water applied, and the type of media, plant cultivar, crop development stage, environmental conditions, and water quality.

Observing and touching media is a common method of determining irrigation need and frequency. This look-and-feel method can be highly inaccurate. Media holds moisture only at the bottom of containers, where it is not easily observed or touched. Individuals' judgments vary on what is considered to be moist. Only a portion of the water held by media is available to plants; the amount of moisture you can feel with your hand may be very different from the amount available to plants.

Tensiometer-Based Irrigation System Design

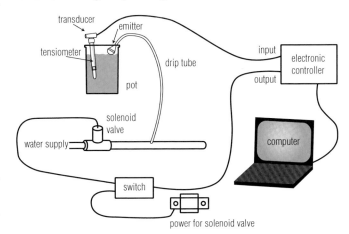

Figure 15. The basic components of one type of computer-controlled drip irrigation system. A tensiometer is used to continually monitor moisture content in the root zone of container plants. The system uses a high and a low tension point set by the grower. It provides precise, efficient, automatic irrigation that can prevent overwatering and leaching, conserving water and nutrients and avoiding wastewater disposal problems. *Source:* **By J. Henrich Leith from Leith et al. 1990.**

Timers are another common method of determining irrigation frequency. However, basic timers are not sensitive to crops' changing irrigation needs. Timers will not provide appropriate irrigation if their settings are not based on an accurate determination of the crop's varying need for water.

Consider using more sophisticated methods to determine irrigation need. Recommended methods include weighing containers periodically at intervals after irrigation to determine water loss, installing tensiometers that monitor soil moisture (Fig. 15), or irrigating based on evapotranspiration (ET). Electrical resistance blocks that imbed electrodes into a porous material are an alternative for field crops. For example, a block of gypsum buried in soil will gain or loose water depending on soil moisture. The block's resistance to electricity changes according to its moisture content. Changes in resistance are read by a special meter connected by wires to the block. Alternatively, some growers schedule irrigation based on light intensity because plants usually use more water when they receive more light. However, scheduling based solely on solar sensors can be quite inaccurate as factors such as relative humidity and temperature influence water use by crops. Computerized environmental monitoring systems can integrate information from more than one monitoring method to help growers efficiently manage irrigation.

Tensiometers. Tensiometers measure moisture tension (how difficult it is for plant roots to remove water from growing media). A tensiometer is a sealed, water-filled tube with a porous ceramic tip on the lower end that is placed at the

The change in container weight can be used to determine irrigation frequency by weighing several randomly selected containers immediately after any excess irrigation has drained and at regular intervals thereafter. Experiment to determine how dry containers can get before plants become moisture stressed, then water crops just before this water weight loss point is reached.

A tensiometer probe for measuring moisture in media is connected by wire (lower left) to a computerized environmental monitoring and control system. The white tube contains a light sensor also used to help estimate irrigation need. The light sensor is connected to an automated system for drawing shade curtains during excessively bright conditions or at night to retain heat.

root zone depth. Water is drawn out of the tip as growing media dries, creating a partial vacuum inside the tube that is measured on a gauge on the upper end of the tube. The drier the soil, the greater the vacuum inside the tube. When measuring soil moisture tension with a mechanical vacuum gauge, a standard unit of measurement is the "bar." One bar is approximately equal to 1 atmosphere or 14.5 pounds per square inch.

Electronic pressure transducers hooked up to tensiometers allow continual monitoring of soil moisture. Information from this sensor can be relayed to an electronic data logger, control timer, or computer-automated irrigation monitoring and management system. These electronic devices typically measure fluid tension in kilopascals (kPa).

Tensiometers connected to automated watering systems use a high and a low tension point set by the grower. In typical growing media, the system would be set to begin irrigating when water tension rises to about 5 kPa, a point at which plants have used much of the available water. Irrigation would be turned off when water tension drops to 1 kPa, which is just before water begins to drain out of the container bottom. Actual set points may be adjusted depending on the water-holding capacity of the media. Tensiometers should be calibrated regularly and placed in the shade beneath leaves because direct sunlight on the devices can alter sensor output.

Container weight changes. The change in average weight of containers over time can be used to determine irrigation frequency. Container weight gradually decreases after irrigation as water is lost from media through evapotranspiration. Irrigation water is applied when container weight drops to the level where much of the available water has been used. Because the amount of water available to plants depends on the planting mix and crop species, growers must experiment to determine how dry containers can become before plants become moisture stressed, then water crops just before this water weight loss point is reached. Special water scales (lysimeters) are used by researchers to monitor these container moisture changes, and similar devices containing electronic sensors for remote monitoring may be available for commercial growers. In many cases growers can adequately use this container weight method by manually weighing several randomly selected containers immediately after any excess irrigation has drained and at regular intervals thereafter using a scale sensitive enough to determine weight differences in ounces. The total weight of each container gradually increases as plants grow, but the difference in weight between dry and moist media remains relatively constant.

Evapotranspiration. Irrigation of fields and outdoor nurseries can be scheduled by monitoring evapotranspiration. This water balance method monitors outgoing and incoming water amounts to help growers maintain adequate available water for plants. Inputs include water supplied by rainfall and irrigation. Outgoing water is primarily evaporation from growing media surfaces and transpiration from plants. These water losses combined are called evapotranspiration (ET) and are expressed in inches (or cm) per day (or hour). Water is applied when evapotranspiration monitoring indicates a certain percentage of available water (perhaps 50%) has been used by plants.

Transpiration is usually estimated by consulting a published table that provides an estimated value for each plant species or for plants similar to those being grown. Evaporation outdoors can be monitored by regularly measuring water loss from a shallow pan. Automated evaporation pans use a sensor to monitor water level and send that information to a data logger or automated control system. Computer software programs are also available for predicting ET.

Many growers obtain evaporation data from universities or government agencies, such as the California Irrigation Management Information System (CIMIS). CIMIS monitors evaporation at sites throughout California and disseminates this information through many sources, including the World Wide Web site at www.ipm.ucdavis.edu maintained by the University of California Statewide IPM Project. Some computerized environmental control software will automatically access this ET information online and incorporate the data into crop management. For more information, consult the California Department of Water Resources website http://wwwdpla.water.ca.gov/cgi-bin/index or publications such as *Determining Daily Reference Evapotranspiration* (Synder et al. 1987) and *Evapotranspiration and Irrigation Water Requirements* (Jensen et al. 1990).

Irrigation frequency strategies. Two irrigation frequency strategies are commonly used to reduce water-related pathogenic diseases and abiotic disorders while efficiently applying water and nutrients to grow high-quality crops. One approach, often used with overhead sprinklers or hand-watering, is to increase the period between watering to the maximum level that is consistent with good growth, and during each irrigation, fill the entire volume of media in containers with water or thoroughly wet the plant rooting zone in field soil. Before watering again, allow growing media to drain and dry out to the point where most available water has been used.

An alternative approach, known as pulse irrigation, is to wet media with only the amount of water and nutrients that plants can use in a short amount of time. Instead of one sustained irrigation, shorter irrigation pulses are used, with several pulses spaced throughout the day when watering small containers. Pulse irrigation attempts to achieve zero runoff, saves water and fertilizer, and potentially provides more control over production costs and plant quality. Because runoff and water leaching out of containers is avoided, salinity is managed by applying good-quality water and avoiding excess

Tensiometer probes must be stored in water to keep their tips moist. This worker is inspecting probes for damage before inserting them into containers. Most test instruments, such as soluble salt and pH meters, must be inspected and calibrated at regular intervals to ensure accurate results.

application of nutrients and other salts. If leaching becomes necessary, wet the entire root zone, then apply the minimum amount of excess water needed so that salts are moved below the root zone or flushed out the bottom of containers. Efficient pulse irrigation must be automated. It is used with drip and subirrigation systems and is usually combined with collecting and recycling any excess nutrient-containing irrigation water.

Irrigation Methods

Crop quality and production costs are greatly influenced by the method used to irrigate them. The irrigation method largely determines the extent to which many pathogens and abiotic disorders develop, how efficiently water and nutrients are used, and how well you can control these problems through good irrigation management. The most common irrigation methods are overhead (either by hand or automated sprinklers), drip, and subirrigation.

Improper irrigation design and component sizing can result in a system with poor uniformity of water application and a much lower than expected application efficiency. Mainline pipes with too small a diameter are a common problem. To maintain distribution uniformity, pressure or flow regulators and pressure-compensating emitters are often

Sprinkler irrigation of newly sown flower beds in the background behind a marigold seed crop.

needed, especially if systems operate on a slope or were inadequately designed.

Irrigation system design considerations include crop species and size, type of growing medium, and environmental factors such as temperature. The system design should minimize friction loss in water mainlines and laterals and provide relatively constant pressure to each emitter, nozzle, or orifice. Factors that affect friction loss include pipe size, type, length, and number and location of outlets. Mechanical engineers have formulas for calculating these factors and compensating for potential problems during system design.

Overhead. Overhead irrigation is versatile and has relatively low initial costs. However, in comparison with drip and subirrigation, overhead watering is less precise and efficient in terms of water and nutrient use and it causes more abiotic disorders and pathogenic diseases by splashing water and media from contaminated plants to nearby plants. Disease severity is increased by systems that wet foliage frequently or for a long time because most fungi and bacteria can't infect leaves without water standing on leaves. Systems that apply water overhead or at the top of containers can also flush pathogens off foliage or out of the bottom of the container during drainage. If this water is recirculated, the pathogens are collected and can be applied to healthy plants. If poor-quality water is applied to leaves, excess salts can injure foliage. Keeping foliage dry and avoiding splashing water are the most effective strategies to prevent and control many fungal and bacterial pathogens and to avoid salt damage to foliage.

Hand-watering. Because hand-watering is often performed by employees with little training or supervision, it poses a great risk of improper irrigation amount and frequency. Train and supervise employees to hand-water appropriately. Consider installing automatic irrigation systems wherever feasible.

When hand-watering, use a water breaker or hose-end nozzle to reduce compaction and help avoid washing growing media from containers.

When hand-watering, always use a water breaker, a hose-end nozzle that decreases the force of water by increasing the cross-sectional area through which water flows. A water breaker reduces media compaction and helps avoid washing media from containers. With flats or unspaced containers, provide uniform application and minimize runoff by applying water from a distance with a relatively broad spray pattern. With spaced containers, minimize foliage wetting and water waste by narrowing the spray pattern, reducing flow rate, and placing the hose end just above the container to fill it to its rim. The flow rate for spaced containers should be fast enough to allow a quick pace but not so fast that media is compacted and water and media are extensively splashed or washed from containers. A good rate may be about 2 to 4 gallons per minute (7.6–15 l/min).

Apply water uniformly, for example, by holding the hose end over each container for the count of 5. When applying water from a distance, move the spray along benches at a steady rate; consider using a stopwatch to time or pace applications to each row or bench based on the total estimated water need for that group of plants and the flow rate. Because edge plants or those nearer heat and ventilation sources often need more water, water these drier plants first, then make a second uniform application to the entire crop.

Adjust watering frequency based on the needs of the particular species, crop age, environmental conditions, and the water-holding characteristics of media. Provide proper equipment to facilitate good watering, including shutoff valves, overhead hose guide systems, and boots and gloves so that employees can remain comfortable and water more conscientiously.

Drip. Drip irrigation, also called trickle irrigation, uses plastic tubing with point-source emitters to water individual containers. With closely spaced row crops in fields and greenhouse beds, emitters are used to apply water through perforated plastic tubes or drip tape placed on or beneath the soil surface.

Drip irrigation reduces foliar diseases by reducing humidity and keeping leaves dry; it can also help delay the onset of salinity problems in fields when water of high mineral content must be used. Many fertilizers and certain pesticides can be precisely applied through drip irrigation. Drip systems minimize application of water to bare soil where water can encourage weed growth. Although drip systems are initially expensive to install and require regular inspection and ongoing maintenance, they can provide accurate control of the amount and placement of water, thereby conserving water and improving crop growth.

Drip systems apply a relatively small volume of water at one time and must be designed and operated to meet the crop's maximum water needs. Because of the low water pressure and small diameter of tubes and outlets, drip systems are highly susceptible to clogging by sand and silt, precipitating minerals, and algal or bacterial growth. Use good-quality water, install filters, and periodically treat systems with chemicals if needed to avoid clogging. Drip systems should be inspected and serviced frequently. Monitor and adjust water distribution uniformity and periodically flush laterals. Service filters regularly, including periodic cleaning (such as backwashing, flushing, or physical cleaning) to remove contaminants.

Subirrigation. Ebb and flow (or ebb and flood) irrigation delivers water to the bottom of containers via floors and benches, capillary mats, and benches with shallow gutters or troughs. Water is carried up into the root system by the capillary and adsorptive force exerted by particles of growing media in the container. Foliage remains dry and pathogens are not spread by splashing water. Bare root systems such as aeroponics and nutrient film that constantly bathe roots with recirculated nutrient solution have similar crop production and pest management characteristics as container subirrigation systems. Although installation costs are more than for hand-watering, subirrigation requires much less labor and results in more uniform crop growth due to more even and precise watering, which reduces plant stress.

Subirrigation systems must be carefully designed to allow for adjusting the frequency and amount of irrigation to avoid oxygen stress in root systems. To the maximum extent com-

Ebb and flow irrigation reduces foliar diseases by avoiding leaf wetness that occurs during overhead irrigation. The drain gutters also facilitate good air flow among containers, helping to reduce humidity that can promote development of foliar pathogens.

patible with providing sufficient water, limit the amount applied and minimize the time that subirrigation water contacts the bottom of containers; this avoids media saturation, preventing draining out pathogens that can spread in water and contaminate other plants.

Trough or channel subirrigation provides more agitation and aeration of water than subirrigation systems that flood flat benches or floors. The increased oxygen enhances decomposition of pathogen propagules, helps reduce anaerobic conditions from media saturation, and improves root health. The spaces between troughs also allow more air movement upward between container rows, reducing humidity around plants and decreasing development of *Botrytis* and other foliar diseases. However, crops that prefer higher humidity, such as African violet and gloxinia, may benefit from the increased humidity of bench or floor flooding systems.

Subirrigation systems require especially well-drained media and containers to prevent saturating roots and depriving them of oxygen, which promotes disease development. Soilless media are commonly used to avoid clay and sand contamination of water pump systems. Group crops of similar age together and crops that require the same amounts and frequency of watering, and use the same size container for all plants on that system. Isolate young, pathogen-free plants from subirrigation water that contacts older plants, which are more likely to be infected with pathogens.

Water Quality

Irrigation water chemistry should be monitored regularly and managed carefully. Of particular concern are salinity (measured as electrical conductivity, EC), sodium adsorption level (SAR, a measure of hazard from sodium), toxic elements such as boron and chloride, nutrients such as nitrate nitrogen, and acidity and alkalinity (measured as pH and carbonate levels). For a more detailed discussion than that found in this section, consult the publications *A Grower's Guide to Water, Media, and Nutrition for Greenhouse Crops* (Reed 1996), *Fertigation* (Burt, O'Connor, and Ruehr 1995), *The Container Tree Nursery Manual* (Landis et. al 1990), and *Water Quality: Its Effects on Ornamental Plants* (Farnham, Hasek, and Paul 1985), listed in the suggested reading at the end of this book.

Recirculated and Reclaimed Water

Water quality is especially problematic when crops are irrigated with reclaimed, captured, or recirculated water. Reclaimed or recycled water includes captured surface runoff, irrigation drainage, and treated municipal wastewater. Recirculated water refers to hydroponic or subirrigation systems that recirculate water or capture and reapply irrigation drainage. These systems conserve water, avoid potentially illegal discharge of pollutants such as nitrogen, and allow reuse of leached nutrients. Rainwater runoff captured directly from greenhouse roofs before it contacts the ground can be relatively pure and ideal for high-quality uses such as irrigating cuttings and seedlings and leaching saline container media.

Recirculated and recycled water can contribute to abiotic disease induced by improper nutrients, wrong pH, and salts unless the water chemistry is carefully monitored and managed. Take steps to avoid reapplying water contaminated with soil-applied herbicides. Recirculated, recycled, and surface waters are often contaminated with pathogens such as *Phytophthora* and *Pythium*, nematodes, and weed seeds. Employ proper irrigation and good sanitation practices to avoid or reduce pest contamination of water (see the chapter "Diseases" for discussion of water treatment methods).

Salts

Salts are compounds in water or soil that break down into anions and cations. Anions are negatively charged compounds or elements, such as chloride and sulfate. Cations are positively charged particles, such as ammonium, calcium, copper, iron, magnesium, manganese, potassium, sodium, and zinc. Most nutrients become available to plants as salts. In addition to fertilizers, low-quality water and certain amendments such as manure are common sources of salts.

Water enters plant roots due to transpirational pull during water loss by leaves. Water also flows through semipermeable root membranes because the concentration of dissolved substances (solutes) inside roots is different than solute concentration in growing media, causing water to flow through root membranes due to osmotic pressure. Normally roots have higher solute concentrations than growing media, causing water to flow into roots. High levels of soluble salts in growing media or irrigation water can prevent roots from taking up enough moisture and dissolved nutrients even when the media is saturated with water. High salinity causes wilting,

Table 22. Approximate Maximum Concentration of Potential Toxicants for Water of Good to Excellent Quality.

Potential toxicant	Concentration[1]
alkalinity (carbonates + bicarbonates)	<100
boron	1.0
EC	<0.75–1.25 dS/m
chloride	<100
pH	6–7.5
sodium	<70
sulfate	<100
total dissolved solids	<480

1. Concentrations are parts per million (ppm), 1 ppm = 1 mg/l, except for EC, which is measured in decisiemens per meter (dS/m). EC can also be reported as millimhos per centimeter (mmhos/cm) or millisiemens per centimeter (mS/cm), where 1 dS/m = 1 mmhos/cm = 1 mS/cm.
Sources: Anonymous 1990; Farnham, Hasek, and Paul 1985.

necrotic leaf margins and leaf spots, root dieback, and various nutritional disorders. Roots injured by toxic salt levels are predisposed to infection by many soilborne pathogens.

Sodium chloride (table salt) can cause toxicity from sodium, chloride, increased electrical conductivity (EC), or a combination of these factors. Direct injury to foliage can occur from overhead wetting of leaves with salty water.

Table 22 lists the approximate maximum concentration of certain salts and other potential toxicants for water of good to excellent quality. Individual crops vary in their tolerance for salts. Seedlings and certain crops such as African violet, azalea, calceolaria, chlorophytum, lily, gardenia, geranium, gladiolus, and petunia are more susceptible to salt damage. Some cultivars of carnation, chrysanthemum, poinsettia, and rose are relatively salt tolerant. For more information, consult *Water Quality: Its Effects on Ornamental Plants* (Farnham, Hasek, and Paul 1985).

Monitoring salinity. Learn the salt tolerance of your crops and regularly monitor salinity. Electrical conductivity is used to estimate total dissolved salts. Salty water conducts electricity, and conductivity (EC rating) increases with increasing salt concentration. Total dissolved solids (TDS), reported in parts per million (ppm), is an older method of measuring total salt content in water and can be determined by evaporating a known weight of water to dryness and weighing the remaining salt. In general, TDS (in ppm) is approximately 640 times the EC (in dS/m, see Table 23).

Electrical conductivity is the preferred salinity measure partly because accurate, portable soluble-salt meters (EC meters) are relatively inexpensive. Instruments that send an electrical current through soil from probes on or near the soil surface are available for measuring the EC profile of field soils. These instruments avoid the need for taking soil samples and can be mounted on small vehicles for efficient sampling of field soil salinity.

Regularly sample EC on-site or send samples of media and water to an outside laboratory. Much of the benefit of knowing EC does not come from any single measurement but

Table 23. Interpretation of Electrical Conductivity (EC) for Some Soil Test Methods.

Soil 1 to 2	Soilless 1 to 2	Soil 1 to 5	Saturation extract (SME)	Interpretation	Comments
Test method[1]					
EC (dS/m)					
0.26–0.5	<1	0.1–0.25	0.75–1.5	low fertility	Often desirable for seedlings, fertigation, recirculated water, and certain salt-intolerant crops.
0.51–1.25	1.0–1.75	0.26–0.6	2–4	good for many crops	Certain established crops tolerate or benefit from higher EC.
>2	>3.5	>1	>8	commonly injurious	EC 50% or less of shown value can injure certain crops.

1. Testing laboratories add different amounts of water to extract salt from media for testing EC. One method is the saturated paste or saturation media extract (SME), where only enough water is added to completely wet soil or soilless media to simulate a typical irrigation. Other methods include diluting 1 volume of media with 2 volumes of water (1 to 2) or 1 volume of media (soil or soilless) with 5 volumes of water (1 to 5). Testing laboratories supply a chart for interpreting the EC levels according to their testing method.

Adapted from Anonymous 1990, Nelson 1991.

Table 24. Media, Plant, and Water Testing.

	Media	Media solution	Plant tissue	Plant sap	Irrigation water
	Material tested				
Timing[1]	preplant, at least once during main crop growth phase, and if deficiency symptoms occur	weekly	several times during growing season	several times during growing season	once or twice a season to continuously[2]
Information provided	pH, salinity, nutrient ratios, and fertilizer need for season	pH, salinity, and nutrients immediately available	nutrient ratios in plant tissue and whether they are sufficient for that plant growth stage	nutrient ratios in plant tissue and whether they are sufficient for that plant growth stage	alkalinity, pH, salinity, related toxicity and permeability problems, and nutrient contribution by water
Location	laboratory, partly on-site	on-site	laboratory	on-site	laboratory or on-site

1. Testing frequency depends on the source of water and nutrients. It is important to test both raw water and irrigation water at least occasionally after adding fertilizers. Consistent quality well water needs relatively infrequent testing; recirculated water fertigation systems require frequent to continuous monitoring. Specific methods vary; for example, four different methods are commonly used to prepare a media solution (see Table 23). For information on proper sampling and testing procedures, read the nutritional testing, plant sampling, and media sampling sections later in this chapter and consult publications in the literature cited and suggested reading sections at the end of this manual.
2. Automated systems are available for continuously monitoring certain water quality parameters.

Sources: Burt, O'Connor, and Ruehr 1995; Landis et. al. 1990.

derives from comparing changes in test results over time. Some experts recommend testing EC and pH in-house about once each week. Because added nutrients are often the most significant contributor to EC, monitoring EC regularly helps manage fertilization as well as avoid EC problems. Modify sampling frequency based on suspected variability. For example, irrigation water quality can be affected by season (rainy versus dry), unusual events (droughts, floods), high- versus low-usage periods, and changes in source, such as systems that draw and blend water from wells of different depths in scattered locations. Changes in fertilization or container mix ingredients can alter EC of growing media. Be aware that testing laboratories use different amounts of water to extract salt from media, so the EC values considered to be acceptable vary depending on the method used (Table 23). Be sure you know what the acceptable results should be for

your situation according to the method used, and use the same method each time. Read the suggested precautions in the section "Media Testing," below. In addition to measuring EC, on-site or laboratory tests of media, plants, and water can provide other valuable information (Table 24).

In subirrigated containers, salts tend to accumulate near the surface of media because salts move up with water. In the field, salts are often concentrated at the soil surface because they precipitate out of water that evaporates from the surface of the soil. Consider testing salts in irrigation water and at two different levels in media, just under the upper surface and at the bottoms of containers. Similarly, collect field soil from the surface and underground at the depth where most crop roots occur. Taking two separate samples allows you to test for excess salt levels in the upper level (where stems may be injured) and to test salt and nutrient levels in the root

High salinity in irrigation water applied to this chrysanthemum caused necrosis of the lower foliage. High sodium, chlorine, or EC can also cause this damage.

This marginal chlorosis and necrosis of poinsettia foliage resulted from high salinity (NaCl) in irrigation water. Symptoms of salt toxicity first appear on older leaves. Unless conditions are remedied symptoms are gradually manifested upward in the plant.

zone. Because individual elements may accumulate differently, measuring overall EC may not give sufficiently accurate results. You may need to test for each element and adjust each as needed.

The EC of container leachate can be tested as an alternative to collecting media and mixing it with water. However, unlike when testing standard mixtures of media and water (Table 23), there are no general guidelines for the acceptable EC levels of leachate. Growers can develop their own guidelines by conducting both a standard test and leachate test on the same media and comparing the EC values. By repeating both tests over time under a range of conditions, growers can learn what EC values for leachate correspond to desirable values using standard media and water mixtures.

Sodium adsorption ratio. Sodium adsorption ratio (SAR), a ratio of sodium to calcium plus magnesium, is a salinity hazard measure that can be obtained by laboratory testing of irrigation water. High SAR levels indicate water that is likely to be directly toxic to plants and high sodium concentrations in field soils reduce the soil's permeability to water. Reduced water penetration due to high SAR usually becomes a problem in the field before sodium levels become directly toxic to plants.

Although a SAR level below 3.0 is desirable, SAR levels below 6 are generally acceptable. Depending on the crop and other growing conditions, SAR of 6 to 8 may be tolerable. Severe problems can be expected at SAR above 9. The SAR level can be reduced by increasing calcium concentrations (such as by adding gypsum to media before planting) or by reducing bicarbonate (HCO_3^-) levels by acidifying water (such as by adding nitric, phosphoric, or sulfuric acid).

Salinity management. Carefully monitor water quality and fertilization to prevent excess salinity. Avoid excess fertilization. When selecting a fertilizer, consider its salt index as well as the nutritive value and specific elements present. The salt index, which is listed on well-labeled products, is a value of saltiness in comparison with sodium nitrate, a common fertilizer rated as 100. Switch to alternative forms or sources of nutrients to avoid or minimize application of the least desirable salts. Most nitrogen and potash compounds have a high salt index; phosphate compounds have a low salt index.

Employ good irrigation water management practices (Table 21). Blend water from various sources to achieve desired salinity levels. Salt can be leached away from roots by applying excess irrigation water that is low in minerals, such as high-quality well water, deionized water, captured rainwater, or water treated by reverse osmosis. However, leaching wastes nutrients and water and creates a wastewater disposal problem, so it is best to use other good practices and avoid leaching. Apply mulch around field and bedding plants to reduce evaporation; evaporation concentrates minerals near the soil surface where most roots are found.

pH

Hydrogen ion concentration (pH) affects the form and availability of nutrients. Nutrient deficiency or toxicity symptoms can develop at improper pH levels, and the effectiveness of some growth regulators and pesticides and the development of certain pathogens also depends partly on pH levels.

A scale from 0 to 14 is used to express pH. Low numbers represent acidic conditions; high numbers are basic (also called alkaline) conditions. Neutral pH is rated as 7. Because a negative logarithmic scale is used, twice as many positively charged hydrogen ions are available at a pH 6 than at pH 7. A good compromise range of pH in most floriculture and nursery crops is about 5.4 to 6.8. Each crop may prefer a more specific, narrower range of pH that depends on the type of media and water quality. Target pH levels are largely based on how they influence nutrient availability in relation to desirable or toxic levels. For example, at low pH, aluminum,

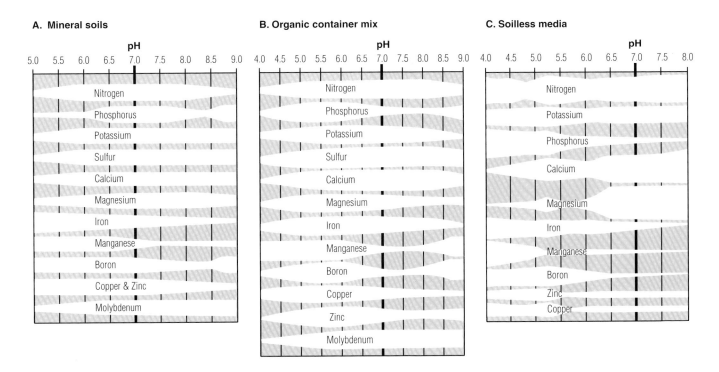

Figure 16. The approximate influence of pH on nutrient availability in A, mineral soil; B, container mix composed of sphagnum peat, composted pine bark, vermiculite, perlite, and sand; and C, soilless growing media. Wider bars indicate that the nutrient is more available at that pH. Adapted from Bailey 1996, Landis et al. 1990, Peterson 1982, and Truog 1948.

boron, iron, and manganese become more available while calcium, magnesium, molybdenum, and sulfur become less available (Fig. 16).

Learn what pH is desired and tolerated by your crop. When selecting forms and amounts of fertilizers and amendments, consider the influence on pH and specific nutrient elements. Growing media containing certain organic materials, such as sphagnum peat, often has lower than optimal pH. Adding finely ground limestone at about 3 pounds of limestone per cubic yard of media (1.75 kg/cu m) before planting will raise the pH of soil-based media by about 0.4 units (soil tests can provide more precise recommendations). Fertilizers can raise or lower pH (Table 25). For example, pH can be lowered before planting by adding sulfur, aluminum sulfate, or iron sulfate to container mix. Ammonium sulfate gradually lowers pH, acidifying growing media, while calcium nitrate fertilization gradually increases pH.

Test the pH of growing media before using it. Monitor the pH and alkalinity of irrigation water regularly throughout the crop production cycle. Make any needed adjustments before using growing media or water. Treated strips (pH paper) that change color when dipped into water can be used to estimate pH. Accurate, portable pH meters or combination pH and EC meters are relatively inexpensive. Automated, computerized pH monitoring and management systems are also available and are especially useful for recirculated water systems.

Table 25. Amendments and Fertilizers that Lower pH (Increase Acidity) or Raise pH of Media.

Lower pH	Raise pH
aluminum sulfate	calcium carbonate (limestone)
ammonium nitrate	calcium hydroxide (hydrated lime)
ammonium phosphate	calcium nitrate
ammonium sulfate	potassium nitrate
calcium sulfate (gypsum)	sodium nitrate
conifer bark and needles	
diammonium phosphate	
iron sulfate	
peat moss	
phosphoric acid	
sulfur	
urea	

Alkalinity. The term alkaline (meaning basic or high pH) is often confused with alkalinity. Alkalinity is a measure of water's ability to neutralize or buffer acids. When alkalinity is low, the pH of water and media readily change to match that of fertilizers and other chemicals that are added. If alkalinity is high, it tends to stay high (and become even higher after repeated irrigations) even when acidic chemicals are added. High alkalinity usually results in high pH, but high

This stunted, chlorotic chrysanthemum was grown under high pH. These symptoms may have developed because high pH reduces availability of phosphorus, iron, manganese, and certain other nutrients (Fig. 16).

pH does not always mean high alkalinity. A pH test by itself is not an indication of alkalinity. Regularly test both the alkalinity and pH of irrigation water.

The common practice of preventing toxicity from certain salts when pH is high by adding nitric, phosphoric, or sulfuric acids to irrigation water is not effective when alkalinity is high. Seedlings are especially sensitive to alkalinity because they are grown in a small volume of media that provides little buffering against improper water quality.

Simple on-site titration kits are available for estimating alkalinity. If alkalinity appears to be high, consider sending samples to an outside laboratory for more accurate testing. Since bicarbonates and carbonates (such as calcium carbonate) are the major contributors to alkalinity in most water, most laboratories assume that total carbonates (carbonates plus bicarbonates) equals alkalinity. Alkalinity of about 1 to 3 milliequivalents per liter of water (meq/l, where 1 meq/l = 50 ppm) is considered desirable for most irrigation water. Alkalinity of 1.5 meq/l or less is generally recommended during propagation.

Growing Media

Field soil, container mixes, and other growing media must provide roots with moisture, aeration, nutrients, and support. Support is normally not a problem unless plants are large or tall or container-grown plants are rooted in lightweight media such as peat moss. Ties, wiring, or cages for aboveground parts reduce the importance of media for support.

Aeration refers to the ability of roots to obtain adequate oxygen and to eliminate excess carbon dioxide into the atmosphere. Water-holding capacity (called field capacity in field soils and container capacity in containers) refers to the amount of water that can be held by capillary force (natural attraction between water and particles) in pore spaces among particles of growing media after excess water has drained downward. Increasing soil moisture generally reduces aeration. Increasing aeration can reduce availability of water (and water-soluble nutrients) to roots. Container media is a balanced mixture between materials that provide aeration and materials with good water- and nutrient-holding ability (Table 26).

The University of California for many years has recommended a container mix composed 50% each of fine sand and sphagnum or peat moss. This UC mix is supplemented with fertilizers. Field soil (sandy clay) is added to some UC mixes for container plants. Field soil alone is not a suitable container media because water-holding and drainage in containers differ greatly from soil in the earth. Cornell peat-lite mixes use combinations of peat moss, vermiculite (granules of the mineral mica expanded by heating), and perlite (silicacous minerals expanded with heat). Rock wool (a spun mineral resembling fiberglass), gravel, clay or pumice granules, coir (particles from coconut husk fibers), and expanded mineral products produced by heating diatomaceous earth or clay are also used as growing media.

Moisture

Inappropriate moisture is probably the most common plant production problem. Plants are about 90% water. Media must hold water and make it available (release it to roots). The water-holding capacity of field soils depends primarily on soil texture and structure (how particles are arranged or combined in aggregates). Unlike field soil, container media has no structure; its water-holding capacity is determined mostly by media texture (the size distribution of growing media particles). Texture, in combination with structure in field soils, determines the size of pore spaces, where water is held to the surface of particles by capillary action. The smaller and more numerous the pore spaces, the greater the water-holding capacity of the media (Fig. 17).

Table 26. Aeration, Water-Holding Capacity, and Nutrient Retention of Media Components.

Good aeration
fine sand[1], perlite, polystyrene

Good water-holding capacity and nutrient retention
bark[2], field soil, manure, organic compost, sphagnum peat moss, vermiculite

1. Fine sand has particles between about $\frac{1}{50}$ to $\frac{1}{100}$ inch (0.5–0.05 mm) in diameter.
2. Bark pieces in media should be $<\frac{3}{8}$ inch (9 mm) in diameter.
Adapted from Nelson 1991.

Some of the water in media adheres tightly to particles, and only a portion of it is available to plants. Both the water-holding capacity and water availability of media depend on the mixture of particle sizes (texture). Tables are available showing the size of particles of various media ingredients, the size of pore spaces between particles, and the portion of water held that is available to plants. General recommendations for container plants are that at least 60% of the sand in a potting mix should consist of particles ranging from 0.25 to 1 mm in diameter. The amount of fine sand particles equal to or less than 0.1 mm in diameter should not exceed 10% by weight. For the remaining (non-sand) materials, 60 to 100% of particles should range from 0.5 to 2 mm in diameter. None of the nonsand ingredients should be less than 0.25 mm in diameter.

Table 27 summarizes other physical characteristics considered to be desirable in container mixes. In general, water-holding capacity should be at least 40% (and preferably 50–65%) of container volume, and at least 30% of this water should be available to plants.

Aeration

In order to grow and absorb certain nutrients, roots require a continuous supply of oxygen (O_2) for respiration. Respiration generates carbon dioxide (CO_2), which must be eliminated from the root zone into the atmosphere. Adequate aeration allows diffusion of gasses through media to supply O_2 and remove CO_2. Insufficient aeration initially causes abnormally small dark leaves, slow growth, and wilting of plants even in wet soil. Leaves may turn yellow and drop and the entire plant eventually dies as roots are killed due to poor aeration.

Aeration is increased by increasing the size of pore spaces between particles. The compromise between good aeration (large pore spaces) and good water-holding capacity (small pore spaces) is achieved by appropriately mixing constituents to create media containing both large and small pore spaces. In addition to adjusting the soil mix, prevent compaction by not packing media down into containers and by not stacking containers directly onto media. Irrigate appropriately, for example, by allowing media to partially dry between irrigations to restore air to pore spaces. Aeration of field soils and ground beds is increased by planting in raised beds or on higher ground, installing drainage infrastructure, encouraging certain soil organisms (such as earthworms), incorporating amendments, and tillage.

Testing

Regularly test pH, soluble salt, and available nutrient levels in media and in irrigation water or leachate or both. Samples can be sent to an outside laboratory for testing, and relatively inexpensive and accurate pH and soluble-salt meters can be purchased for use in the field. Be consistent in the number of samples taken, the interval between sampling and fer-

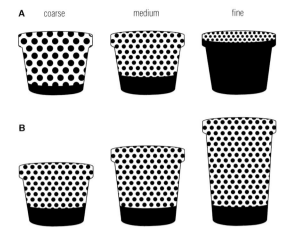

Figure 17. The water-holding capacity and aeration of container mix depends on texture (the size distribution of particles). Container mixes are composed of a range of particle sizes; the dots here represent the average particle size. The dark zone illustrates the depth of the water-saturated layer (the water-holding capacity) within containers. A. Water-holding capacity increases as average particle size decreases from coarse to fine. B. Water-holding is not affected by container height, within the normal range of container heights. *Source:* Evans 1998.

Table 27. Desirable Range of Physical Properties of Container Growing Media.

Property	Desirable range
total porosity	60–70%
air-filled capacity	10–20%
water-holding capacity	50–65%
available water	≥30%
weight per volume	70–90 lb/ft^3

Total porosity: Percentage of growing media by volume that consists of pore spaces (where air and water occur) instead of solid particles.

Air-filled capacity: Percentage of container mix by volume that is occupied by air after irrigation and drainage.

Water-holding capacity: Percentage of container mix by volume that is occupied by water after irrigation and drainage.

Available water: Portion of water held in growing media that can be extracted by plants. Because water is attracted to the surface of particles by capillary action, only a portion of water in growing media—the available water—can actually be extracted by plants. The wilting point occurs when plants have extracted all the available water.

tilization or irrigation, and what parts of the media are sampled. Avoid sampling near the edge of containers. Avoid sampling the very top of media (the upper ½ inch or 13 mm) where salts and algae can accumulate unless the test is specifically for salts as discussed earlier. Except for this topmost layer, collect soil core samples that span the entire depth of the container or the entire rooting zone in fields and beds. Collect samples from about 10 containers or 10 locations that receive the same cultural practices and that appear to have similar problems. Combine and mix these subsamples into one sample to be tested. Also consider separate sampling of media just under the soil surface and deeper in the root zone, as discussed in the salinity section. Several manufacturers supply special suction devices (soil solution access tubes) for extracting liquid from field soil for laboratory testing, but they can be difficult to use properly.

Be sure that samples being tested are representative of the media or other material being tested. Avoid basing major management decisions on a single group of samples. Inaccurate results sometimes occur due to laboratory testing errors or poor sampling practices at the growing site. Communicate with your laboratory before sampling to determine the recommended sampling method, how many samples should be collected, and how samples should be packaged and shipped. When testing on-site, be sure that meters are properly maintained and calibrated and used correctly to help make sure you get accurate results.

Heat Treatment-Induced Media Toxicity

Ammonia toxicity can occur if crops are planted into high-nitrogen organic materials such as manure, highly decomposed peat, leaf mold, and immature composts that have been heat-pasteurized. Microorganisms (mostly bacteria) must decompose organic matter to produce nitrate, which is the only form of nitrogen that most plants can use. Organic decomposition is a two-step process involving separate groups of microorganisms. First, bacteria and certain fungi convert nitrogen in organic matter into ammonium (ammonification); other bacteria convert ammonium into nitrite and then into nitrate (nitrification). Heat treatment kills these microorganisms. The ammonifying microorganisms naturally recolonize and become abundant in media within a few weeks after pasteurization, but nitrifying bacteria often require more time to recover (about 3 to 6 weeks), resulting in a temporary excess of ammonium until nitrifying bacteria become abundant. Avoid this ammonia-toxicity problem by using mostly low-nitrogen or slowly decomposing organic materials such as peat moss, by using only stable (well-decomposed) compost, or by waiting at least several weeks after pasteurization before using highly amended media.

Toxicity can also occur if certain slow-release fertilizers are mixed into media before heating. Heat can increase the breakdown of these controlled-release fertilizers, resulting in immediate availability of toxic amounts.

Steam pasteurization of media containing field soil can alter the chemical forms of manganese, making excessive (toxic) amounts of manganese readily available to plants. This high manganese availability can reduce iron availability, resulting in symptoms of iron deficiency. Manganese is abundant in many soils, but mostly in forms not readily available to plants. Manganese availability increases with increasing pasteurization time and temperature.

To minimize these problems, pasteurize media containing field soil or organic amendments at a temperature no higher than 160°F (71°C) and for no longer than recommended, commonly until the entire volume of media has reached the desired pasteurization temperature for 30 minutes. Proper pasteurization is discussed in the chapter "Diseases."

Containers

Although ornamentals are grown primarily for their foliage and flowers, the quality of aboveground parts is largely dictated by root growth and health. Proper selection, use, and maintenance of containers is vital because containers hold a discrete volume of media that supplies roots with water, air, nutrients, and physical support.

Use containers with holes as large as possible that still retain media; smaller holes increase the problem of roots plugging holes and retarding drainage. Do not add gravel, broken pieces of pottery, or similar large particles to container bottoms. Large pieces at the bottom of containers move the layer of moist media upward, away from the container bottom, reducing water-holding capacity and failing to improve aeration. Shade the sides of containers exposed to sunlight, such as containers on the ends of rows. Sunlight-induced heat injures roots and can encourage development of root pathogens. In areas with prolonged freezing conditions, protect outdoor containers from cold, such as by covering them.

Fertilization

Plants are about 90% water. The remaining portion (the dry weight) is about 90% carbon, hydrogen, and oxygen. These elements are not provided by fertilization. Carbon is obtained from carbon dioxide in the atmosphere. Hydrogen and oxygen are obtained from water. Thirteen additional nutrients, in relatively small amounts, are needed for healthy plant growth (Table 28). These thirteen essential nutrients are normally absorbed through plant roots and are provided by organic material in media and fertilization. The essential nutrients are classified as macronutrients (those constituting about 0.1 to 4% of plant dry weight) and micronutrients (equal to or less than 0.01% of plant dry weight).

Table 28. Mineral Nutrients Essential for Plant Growth.

Macronutrients	Micronutrients
nitrogen (N)	iron (Fe)
potassium (K)	chlorine (Cl)
calcium (Ca)	manganese (Mn)
phosphorus (P)	zinc (Zn)
magnesium (Mg)	boron (B)
sulfur (S)	copper (Cu)
	molybdenum (Mo)

Nutrients are listed in decreasing order of their abundance as often found in dry-weight plant tissue.

Nitrogen and potassium are required in higher amounts than other nutrients; both tend to leach out during irrigation. Nitrogen and potassium are applied through preplant incorporation of organic amendments and slow-release nutrient formulations, by periodic (such as weekly) fertilization, or through fertigation (dilute nutrients supplied during every irrigation).

Other essential nutrients can usually be provided through proper formulation and amending of media before planting. Calcium and magnesium can be provided by dolomitic limestone (calcium carbonate containing magnesium). Phosphorus and sulfur are provided by superphosphate alone or with additional gypsum (calcium sulfate). Various preplant-incorporated commercial mixtures provide iron, manganese, zinc, copper, boron, and molybdenum or any combination of these. Depending on media formulation, pH, water quality, and the particular crop, it may be unnecessary or undesirable to add certain of these micronutrients.

Consider both the specific nutrients (Table 28) and their effect on pH (Table 25) and salinity when selecting forms and amounts of fertilizers and amendments. Fertilize only when needed based on the crop's known requirements, deficiency symptom diagnosis, media testing, or foliar analysis. Although good nutrition improves growth, improper fertilization can contribute to poor water quality and promote development of plant pathogens and certain insect pests. Use the best fertilization management practices as summarized in Table 29. Also consult the World Wide Web at http://www.cals.cornell.edu/dept/flori/growon and other university and industry resources. Refer to published texts such as the *Western Fertilizer Handbook Horticulture Edition* (Ludwick et al. 1990) to obtain the formulas and adjustments for special circumstances (such as growing media composition and water quality) needed to develop a proper crop fertilization program.

Nutritional Testing

Media tests can determine current major nutrient levels, the nutrients that are available for uptake by plants, and related factors such as root-zone pH and soluble salts. However, media tests do not provide analysis of all essential nutrients. Foliar analysis determines accumulated concentrations of all nutrients and indicates past conditions and practices. Samples of media and plants can be sent to an outside laboratory for nutritional testing. Various on-site plant nutrient tests are available, including color test strips, chlorophyll meters, and portable nitrate electrodes such as the Cardy meter. However, many on-site nutrient tests only detect nitrate. A large portion of available nitrogen can go undetected by these methods if it is not in the nitrate form. The accuracy and sampling methods of on-site nutrient tests are still being evaluated. On-site tests may provide only approximate levels for a limited number of nutrients, most commonly nitrate, phosphorus, or potassium. Analyses of media, plants,

Table 29. Fertilization Best Management Practices.

- Provide most nutrients by properly amending media and adjusting pH before planting.
- Use nutrient sources that are slow-release or otherwise less likely to leach whenever practical.
- Monitor quality of media and water for potential problems, such as salinity.
- Fertilize only when needed based on crop requirements, deficiency diagnosis, media testing, or foliar analysis. Depending on media, many crops need only nitrogen and potassium application after planting.
- Use injectors or other well-measured application methods.
- Group plants according to similar fertilizer and irrigation need.
- Collect runoff water when injecting fertilizer and consider recycling fertigation runoff.
- Optimize irrigation efficiency and uniformity (see the section "Irrigation").
- Use backflow prevention devices to avoid contaminating the water supply.

and irrigation water are best used in combination as they provide different types of information (Table 24).

Plant testing. Analysis of plant tissue (usually leaves, petioles, or sap from petioles) can indicate whether adequate or potentially toxic nutrient concentrations are present before damage symptoms occur. Laboratory analysis of nutrient levels in symptomatic foliage can be compared with recommended concentrations in foliage of that crop to help diagnose the cause of problems. Recommended macronutrient levels for specific crops can vary depending on crop species, cultivar, and age and type of growing media. Recommended crop macronutrient levels for most major crops may be obtained from many university or private researchers or from suppliers or propagators of your planting stock. Recommended micronutrient levels have not been determined for many flower and nursery crops; levels in these crops are compared to a range of standard concentrations considered to be appropriate for most green plants.

Sample symptomatic plants if they are suspected of having a nutrient imbalance or select plants randomly when testing a nonsymptomatic crop. The usefulness of laboratory tests are highly influenced by sampling methods and proper testing requires that an adequate number of samples be collected from a specified portion of plants. Samples are combined for analysis to provide an overall average nutrient concentration for that crop. When sending plant tissue to a laboratory, for many crops you should sample the youngest fully expanded leaves. On chrysanthemum, these parts typically occur about one-third of the way down from the plant terminal. They should be collected about 5 to 6 weeks after pinching or after planting for a single-stem crop. Specific sampling methods depend on the crop. With roses, about thirty leaves with petioles are often combined into one sample by picking the two uppermost five-leaflet leaves from 15 stems below where color is just beginning to show on the opening flower calyx. Leaves are then thoroughly rinsed or soaked for 1 minute, preferably in distilled water, to remove any surface residue of pesticide, fertilizer, or dust, then blotted dry before packaging them appropriately (such as with ice). Consult the chapter "Diseases" for other suggestions on submitting samples to a laboratory.

With an electronic on-site testing device such as the Cardy meter, leaf petioles are crushed and the sap is placed on the end of an electrode connected to a digital display. Sap can be expressed with a garlic press or hydraulic sap press, or the petioles can be placed in a plastic bag and crushed with a rolling pin. Specific methods for collecting samples and testing plant sap on-site are provided by equipment suppliers. Consult *Fertigation* (Burt, O'Connor, and Ruehr 1995) for a review of quick-test equipment and procedures for use on-site.

Nutrient Disorders

Nutrient disorders are a common plant production problem. Deficient or excess minerals or nutrients cause foliage to discolor, fade, distort, or become spotted, sometimes in a characteristic pattern that can be recognized to identify the cause. Fewer leaves or flowers may be produced, and these may develop later than normal and remain undersized. More severe deficiency or toxicity can cause plant stunting or dieback.

Although visual diagnosis (Table 30) is a common method of diagnosing deficiencies, it can be unreliable. A single deficiency can have many different and variable symptoms. Pathogens, improper irrigation, inappropriate environmental conditions, and other nutrient disorders can cause similar damage symptoms. If visual diagnosis is possible, it means that damage has already occurred and may only be partially reversible. In addition to visual diagnosis, compare crop management records with the methods recommended for that crop and use laboratory or on-site tests of media, water, and foliar nutrient concentrations.

Management

Nutrient requirements and tolerance vary by plant cultivar, stage of growth, and environmental conditions. Excess concentrations of one nutrient can reduce the availability of other nutrients (Table 30). Therefore, plants often exhibit symptoms characteristic of a specific nutrient imbalance even though that nutrient is present at appropriate concentrations in media or water. Nutrient availability is highly influenced by type of media, pH, salinity, and over- or underwatering. Unless these other problems are identified and remedied, disorder symptoms can persist even though specific nutrients are added or withheld.

Avoid nutrient disorders by preventing root pathogen development, providing good drainage, and using good practices during fertilization (Table 29) and irrigation (Table 21). Regularly monitor nutrient, pH, and salinity conditions and correct them if needed. If appropriate cultural practices and environmental conditions are provided and a nutrient disorder has been properly diagnosed, most deficiencies can be corrected through fertilization.

Nitrogen

Nitrogen (N) availability is influenced by irrigation, temperature, pH, media, and organisms present in soil, and the form, frequency, and method of fertilization. The first symptom of nitrogen deficiency is usually the uniform yellowing of entire leaves, beginning with older foliage. However, in certain rapidly growing plants such as some poinsettias, symptoms occasionally become obvious first on younger leaves. Nitrogen-deficient plants grow slowly and leaves may drop prematurely.

Excess nitrogen kills small roots and causes leaves to turn dark green, gray, or brown along the margins. Foliage may

Chlorosis from nitrogen deficiency usually appears first on older leaves. Nitrogen deficiency symptoms can be distinguished from yellowing caused by iron or manganese deficiency or excess copper or zinc because nitrogen-deficient leaves are yellowish overall and lack the distinctly green veins characteristic of these other disorders.

Excess ammonium (NH_4^+) caused chlorosis and downward cupping of leaf margins in the poinsettia on the right.

Table 30. General Symptoms of Nutrient and Mineral Disorders.

Nutrient or mineral	Deficiency or low concentration	Toxicity or high concentration
ammonium (NH$_4^+$ nitrogen)	Symptoms resemble nitrogen deficiency (see below).	Spindly growth and pale, downward-cupping leaf margins. More common at low temperatures when nitrifying bacteria responsible for converting ammonium to nitrate are less active.
bicarbonate (calcium carbonate)	Not a problem.	Overall chlorosis and marginal necrosis of leaves. Plants stunted. Problem in arid areas with alkaline water.
boron	Chlorosis progressing to necrosis along margins of older leaves. May have slight necrosis of leaf veins or chlorotic (then necrotic) leaf spots. Leaves may become thickened and leathery. Buds die or few or no flowers develop. If severe, main terminal dies and lateral shoots develop on short internodes (witches' brooms).	Chlorotic or purplish to brown marginal necrosis or spotting of leaves. Foliage may be dry or papery. Older leaves may curl or drop. Severely affected plants can die.
calcium	Tips and margins of young leaves or bracts turn pale green, then chlorotic or necrotic and possibly distorted. Easter lilies are especially susceptible. Uncommon under proper pH and preventable by amending media with dolomitic limestone before planting.	Induces manganese and iron deficiencies. Interveinal chlorosis of young leaves.
chloride	Stunting and dieback. Deficiency is rarely a problem due to chloride's prevalence in growing media and water.	Symptoms of high EC. Chlorotic or necrotic leaf spots if applied to foliage.
copper	Upward curling of leaflets into tubes. Petioles may curl downward. Chlorotic foliage. Younger foliage most affected. Delayed flowering.	Foliar symptoms like iron deficiency; chlorosis of young leaves. Plants stunted. Roots may die.
EC	Leaves pale green throughout plant. Growth spindly. Whole plant affected. Symptoms similar to nitrogen deficiency.	Leaves dark green, stunted, leathery. Poor root growth. Foliage eventually becomes chlorotic and necrotic, especially older leaves.
fluoride	No symptoms. Not an essential nutrient.	Necrosis of leaf tips and margins. Can occur when using fluoridated domestic water. Many plants in Liliaceae and Marantaceae families are susceptible to fluoride levels in municipal water.
iron	Interveinal chlorosis. Entire leaf may turn yellow or white, except for the veins. No necrosis. Affects young leaves. Often associated with high pH.	Rarely a media problem. Foliar application can cause marginal necrosis or necrotic leaf spots.
lithium	No symptoms. Not an essential nutrient.	Marginal necrosis of older leaves.
magnesium	Interveinal chlorosis, then overall yellowing of leaves. May begin at base of the plant, often as mottling of lower leaves, then progress upwards. Some poinsettias are especially susceptible. In most crops uncommon under proper pH and preventable by amending media with dolomitic limestone before planting.	May induce potassium deficiency.
manganese	Interveinal chlorosis or whitening of young leaves. Looks like iron deficiency. As symptoms progress, may be interveinal necrotic spots, unlike iron deficiency. Flower buds may abort.	Stunted, chlorotic younger leaves. Necrotic spots between veins. Brown streaks on petioles and stems. Early senescence of older leaves.
molybdenum	Interveinal chlorosis or whitening. Discoloring begins with older leaves, similar to nitrogen deficiency. Leaf margins chlorotic, necrotic, and may curl upwards.	Uncommon. Symptoms similar to nitrogen and potassium toxicity.
nitrogen	Leaves pale green to yellowish overall. Commonly appears first on older leaves, but can be more obvious on young rapid growth of certain crops such as poinsettia. Plants stunted. Growth may be spindly. Leaves drop prematurely.	Moderate excess causes soft, overabundant, vegetative growth. Flowering is delayed in long-day plants. High excess slows growth and causes stunted, dark green foliage, especially in younger leaves. Root system commonly undersized.
pH	Induces imbalance of other nutrients. See Fig. 16.	Induces imbalance of other nutrients.
phosphorus	Foliage yellowish, reddish or purplish, especially on older leaves. Whole plant stunted. Relatively uncommon deficiency, occurring at extreme pH, low temperatures, and if phosphorus is not added to media before planting.	Apparently no primary symptoms. Induces manganese and iron deficiencies, which cause interveinal chlorosis of young leaves.
potassium	Marginal leaf scorch, interveinal chlorosis, necrotic leaf spots, leaf curling. Affects whole plant beginning with older leaves. Most common during rapid vegetative growth and in young plants. Commonly the nutrient in greatest demand after nitrogen.	Slow growth. Dark green foliage. Whole plant affected. May cause magnesium deficiency or same symptoms as high EC.
sodium	No symptoms. May not be an essential plant nutrient. Commonly present at more than adequate concentrations in media and water.	Symptoms of high EC. May affect soil structure and reduce permeability, causing poor drainage.
sulfur	Uniformly chlorotic leaves or interveinal chlorosis. Leaves small with rolled-down margins. Purple leaf veins. Purple or necrotic leaf spots. Whole plant affected, but may be visible first in younger leaves.	Stunted plants with chlorotic or necrotic leaves. Symptoms may look like high EC.
zinc	Leaves small, may grow in tufts due to reduced internode length. Symptoms commonly called little leaf disease. Chlorotic or necrotic interveinal mottling or spots on mostly younger leaves. Downward curling of petioles. Delayed opening of leaf or flower buds. Foliage may eventually turn purplish and die.	Can induce iron deficiency, causing interveinal chlorosis of young leaves. Leaves small and may curl downward. Stunted, spindly plants.

Actual symptoms vary due to disorder severity, development time, crop species and cultivar, growing conditions, and other interacting factors.

temporarily wilt or die. Excess nitrogen can delay or prevent blossoming. Plants given too much nitrogen may develop excessively succulent tissue, promoting populations of sucking insects and mites and the development of certain pathogens. Studies have found that frequently, more nitrogen is applied than crops can use. This excess fertilization wastes money. Pollution of ground and surface waters by nitrate compounds is an increasing problem.

Nitrogen is provided to plants primarily by organic matter in media and through fertilization. Common organic sources are bark, compost, manure, peat moss, and sawdust. Slow-release fertilizers that can be incorporated into media before planting include slowly soluble formulations (such as gypsum and limestone), formaldehyde urea, and sulfur- or wax-coated products. After planting, nitrogen is commonly supplied as urea (from either organic or synthetic sources), inorganic nitrate (NO_3^-), or ammonium (NH_4^+). Although crops vary in their need for nitrogen, a common rate is 100 to 200 ppm

nitrogen applied every time crops are irrigated (fertigation). Potassium (frequently supplied as K_2O) is often applied at the same time and concentration (100 to 200 ppm) as nitrogen. Higher concentrations of nitrogen (up to about 700 ppm) are often used if plants are fertilized about weekly. However, studies have found that growers often apply more nitrogen than plants can use.

Ammonium sulfate is an inexpensive and widely used form of inorganic fertilizer. Ammonium, which is adsorbed onto the surface of soil particles, may not be immediately available to plants and usually must be converted into nitrate by soil microorganisms before it can be taken up by roots. Plants generally respond to urea in the same manner as to ammonium because urea in media is converted into ammoniac nitrogen. Nitrate fertilizers are readily absorbed by plants and can quickly remedy nitrogen deficiency or promote rapid plant growth. However, quick-release fertilizers such as nitrate sometimes promote excess succulent growth,

Interveinal chlorosis on this gardenia is the classic symptom of iron deficiency. However, the cause may not necessarily be low iron concentrations. High pH or unhealthy roots caused by excess irrigation, poor drainage, or root and crown decay pathogens can prevent roots from absorbing sufficient iron.

The interveinal chlorosis in this 'Freedom Red' poinsettia (top of photo) is a symptom of iron deficiency. Manganese deficiency also causes this symptom, but manganese deficiency symptoms are usually less severe than the symptoms shown here.

Advanced manganese toxicity symptoms on the 'Bright Golden Ann' chrysanthemum on the right caused distinct chlorosis and necrotic spots between leaf veins. These older leaves will drop prematurely. This damage could be mistaken for symptoms of a virus infection.

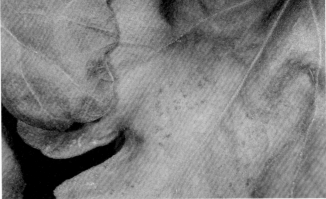

Slight chlorosis and faint purplish to brown leaf spots on the 'Bright Golden Ann' chrysanthemum on the right are early symptoms of manganese toxicity. Without careful inspection and comparison with a healthy leaf in the upper left, these symptoms can be overlooked because spots are small relative to this leaf's 2-inch (5-cm) width.

which favors pests such as aphids and mites. Quick-release fertilizers are more likely to be leached, resulting in nutrient loss and potential water pollution. A mixture of nitrate and ammonium and urea or both can provide the best growth for many crops.

Iron and Manganese

Iron (Fe) or manganese (Mn) deficiencies cause chlorosis between the veins of young leaves. The initial symptoms of these two deficiencies are indistinguishable from each other (Table 30). However, as the malady progresses, iron deficiency symptoms usually become much more severe than manganese deficiency symptoms. Adequate iron is present in most soils and organic media. However, plants are unable to absorb iron if media or water have high calcium levels or high pH, or if media is poorly drained or waterlogged. Certain plants adapted to acidic, well-drained soils high in organic matter (such as azaleas, gardenias, and rhododendrons) are especially prone to iron deficiency.

Leaf symptoms of iron deficiency can be remedied by lowering pH, increasing organic matter in media, or applying iron chelate. Iron toxicity is not a natural problem, but excess or improper use of chelates can cause foliar necrosis.

Manganese deficiency occurs in alkaline media. Leaf symptoms can be remedied by lowering soil pH, increasing organic matter in media, and by applying manganese or manganese chelates. Excess manganese can induce potassium deficiency, resulting in foliar chlorosis or necrosis (Table 30). Increasing pH reduces availability of manganese but may undesirably reduce availability of iron and possibly phosphorus (Fig. 16). Avoid fertilizing with materials containing manganese if manganese toxicity may be a problem.

Phosphorus

Phosphorus deficiency causes leaves to become purplish, reddish, or sometimes yellowish, especially on older foliage. The whole plant can become stunted. However, phosphorus deficiency is relatively uncommon. Phosphorus deficiency can be avoided in most crops by providing appropriate levels of minor elements that can influence phosphorus availability and by maintaining the proper pH. A single phosphorus application to media before planting, or one application every few years to field soil or ground beds, usually provides adequate concentrations of phosphorus. This deficiency can be remedied after planting by switching to phosphorus-containing fertilizer or by adjusting the pH. Cool temperatures can limit root growth and activity and sometimes induce this deficiency even when phosphorus levels are adequate. If induced by cool temperatures, raising media temperature several degrees will allow plants to outgrow this deficiency.

Boron

Very small amounts of boron (B) are essential for plant growth and sometimes need to be added during fertigation.

This severely phosphorus-deficient 'Freedom Red' poinsettia leaf is chlorotic and stunted. Reddening or purpling of the leaf as seen along the margins is characteristic of phosphorus deficiency.

Phosphorus deficiency in the 'Freedom Red' poinsettia at the bottom of this photograph caused purpling that is difficult to recognize. The underlying green leaf is from a properly nourished plant. When an entire crop is affected by maladies that can cause subtle symptoms, the problem can go unrecognized unless nutritional tests are conducted on plants and media.

Chlorosis confined to the margin of the lower poinsettia leaf is an early symptom of boron toxicity.

Chlorotic spots, especially around the margin of the chrysanthemum leaf on the right, were caused by excess boron in water used to irrigate the plant. As the boron excess continues the yellowish spots will eventually turn brown and die.

High boron concentrations are toxic (Table 22). Excess boron occurs in some water and soils on the western side of the Central Valley of California, parts of the Mojave Desert, and some coastal areas in southern California. Reduce boron accumulation and toxicity by applying high-quality water, improving drainage, and leaching media with good-quality water if needed. Raising pH reduces toxicity by reducing boron's availability to plants (Fig. 16). Adding calcium to media also reduces boron availability. Where boron is a problem, avoid increasing acidity because lowering pH increases boron availability.

Pesticides and Phytotoxicity

Pesticides can be phytotoxic (cause undesirable damage to plants). Herbicides must be used with great care around crops because herbicides are designed specifically to kill plants. Insecticides, fungicides, and growth regulators can also damage plants. Often it is the adjuvants or formulation characteristics that cause the crop damage, not the pesticide active ingredient.

Pesticides may cause foliage or shoots to distort or discolor and can stunt or even kill plants. Phytotoxicity is more likely to occur with certain materials, after repeated treatments or excess rates, when plants are water-stressed, or when temperatures are hot. Propagative material in a rooting stage is usually more susceptible to phytotoxicity than mature foliage. Applying nearly any material to blossoms or colored bracts risks damaging them. Mixtures of incompatible pesticides or certain formulations such as emulsifiable concentrates (EC) can be more likely to damage plants than dust or wettable powder (W or WP) formulations. Virtually any pesticide may damage crops if misapplied.

Characteristic injury symptoms can sometimes be used to determine the specific pesticide involved. However, the

Growth regulator (uniconazole) applied improperly to the Easter lily on the right caused internode compression, resulting in a bushy, stunted plant. Failing to strictly follow all label directions can result in severe crop damage.

Growth regulator (chlormequat-chloride) applied to the geranium on the right caused this temporary marginal leaf chlorosis. Because plant development functions are physiologically interrelated, using growth regulators can cause undesirable changes in plant color, shape, form, or flowering.

great variety of crops, conditions, materials, and formulations, combined with limited documentation for most ornamental crops, make phytotoxicity difficult to predict. Strictly follow all label precautions when using pesticides.

Herbicides

Herbicides can cause injury from residues in media, drift during application, vaporization after application during warm weather, and application directly onto crops. Do not allow herbicide spray, drift, or residue to contact desirable plants. Do not apply herbicides during windy or foggy conditions. Store herbicides separately from other pesticides. Use separate spray equipment for herbicides; sprayers contaminated with minute quantities of certain herbicides (such as phenoxy herbicides) can damage crops when used to apply insecticides, fertilizers, or other chemicals.

Insecticides and Other Pesticides

Acaricides, insecticides, and fungicides sometimes cause leaves, blossoms, or colored bracts to discolor and die or appear spotted or scorched. Phytotoxicity after a soil drench can also cause poor germination, seedling death, or delayed, stunted, or distorted plant growth.

Phytotoxicity is more likely from applications during or just before temperatures greater than about 90°F (32°C), cold temperatures, or if plants are stressed from drought or other factors. Some plant species are sensitive to certain insecticides, such as insecticidal soap or horticultural oil. *Managing Insects and Mites with Spray Oils* (Davidson et al. 1991) summarizes studies on the sensitivity of some ornamental crops to oil.

Consult Table 31 for suggestions on how to minimize phytotoxicity. Check the label for plant species that should not be sprayed with that pesticide. Before using a new pesticide, treating a new cultivar, or applying a material under unfamiliar conditions, test the material on that crop before using it. Spray several plants and observe them for 5 to 7 days or

Puckered, needlelike shoots and a chlorotic, incomplete blossom developed on the rose on the left after exposure to glyphosate herbicide.

Leaf yellowing developed after spraying this 'V-14 Glory' tree poinsettia during hot, humid weather. Pyrethrum and piperonyl butoxide was applied here, but many materials may cause phytotoxicity if they are applied when temperatures are high or plants are moisture-stressed.

Table 31. Minimizing Phytotoxicity.

- Minimize the number of pesticide applications.
- Test new pesticides on crops before their use is needed.
- Make a chart of crops versus pesticides and rate the potential phytotoxicity to each cultivar from each pesticide based on label information and injury observed after previous treatments and test sprays.
- Follow label rates and instructions, including avoiding excess pesticide concentrations and treating only crops listed on the label.
- Do not treat during or prior to extreme conditions, such as hot or cold temperatures.
- Be sure that crops are properly irrigated before treatment.
- Do not use tank mixes or adjuvants (spreaders, stickers, wetting agents) of unknown safety.
- Consider using dusts or wettable powder (W or WP) formulations that generally are less phytotoxic instead of emulsifiable concentrates (EC).
- Keep spray tanks well agitated.
- Prevent drift, volatile movement, and runoff of pesticides.
- Use good application technique, including applying pesticide evenly and avoiding over spraying.
- Use separate sprayers for herbicides versus other pesticides.
- Know the pesticide's persistence and avoid materials with long residual periods where they may cause problems (e.g., replanting failure due to preemergent herbicide residue).
- Avoid treating sensitive growth stages, including seedlings, fast-growing succulents, flowers, and colored bracts.
- Maximize reliance on nonchemical controls.

Adapted from Hunt 1995, Moorman 1990a, and Smitley et al. 1994.

until new growth appears to detect any signs of damage before spraying any more of the crop. Even if spraying causes no immediate damage, multiple applications can become phytotoxic, often in subtle ways, such as causing leaves to curl or lower foliage to drop. A single crop species can vary in susceptibility to phytotoxicity depending on the stage of plant growth (e.g., seedlings, blossoms) and cultivar. Although certain pesticides cause characteristic damage symptoms, symptoms can vary greatly depending on factors such as cultivar, growing conditions, and the specific pesticide used. Be aware that even in the absence of actual phytotoxicity, some sprays can leave visible residues that may be unacceptable on marketable plant parts.

Multiple sequential applications of horticultural oil for mite control caused chlorosis and necrosis where spray runoff concentrated on the margins of these rose leaves. This damage may be tolerable because it appeared mostly on older foliage that is of relatively low photosynthetic productivity, and the lower canopy foliage is not marketed when flower buds are cut. Directing sprays to the undersides of leaves will improve mite control efficacy, allowing a reduction in the number of applications.

Light

Too much or too little sunlight can damage plants. The amount of light required to cause damage varies with the species of plant, environmental conditions, and whether adequate cultural care is provided.

Sunburn

Sunburn is damage to foliage and other herbaceous plant parts caused by a combination of too much light and heat and insufficient moisture. A yellow or brown area develops on foliage, which then dies beginning in areas between the veins.

Avoid sunburn by providing shade, appropriate temperatures, and proper cultural care, especially adequate irrigation. Appropriate irrigation before discolored leaf tissue is killed can usually restore the green color to sunburned foliage.

Sunscald

Sunscald, also sometimes called sunburn, is damage to bark caused by excessive light or heat. Sunscald-damaged bark becomes cracked, sunken, and is susceptible to attack by wood-boring insects and rot fungi. Trunks and limbs can develop cankers, become girdled, and die.

Sunscald often occurs on young woody plants after bark is exposed to bright light or heat, especially after foliage is extensively pruned or harvested. Container-grown woody plants often become sunscalded during shipping or after planting because their bark is thin and not adapted to high light because their trunks were shaded by other plants grown next to them in the nursery. Even in soil that is saturated with water, sunscald may occur if plants are unable to absorb

Sunburn from excess sunlight and heat caused chlorosis and necrosis between veins of this New Guinea impatiens leaf. The cause was diagnosed using knowledge of this crop's preference for moderate temperatures and by consulting environmental monitoring records that revealed hot, bright growing conditions. A negative ELISA test ruled out impatiens necrotic spot virus and tomato spotted wilt virus, which can cause similar symptoms.

The leaf necrosis in this Oriental lily was induced by high temperatures. These symptoms could easily be confused with those caused by viruses. Diagnostic testing is needed to rule out viruses as the cause.

sufficient moisture when it is sunny or temperatures are hot or cold.

Reduce sunscald by gradually acclimating plants to bright light (providing temporary partial shade), minimizing light and heat changes to a plant's environment, and providing adequate irrigation. Mulches can reduce or increase heat and light around plants, depending on the location and type of material used (see the chapter "Weeds"). Where aesthetically acceptable, apply white interior (not exterior) latex paint, diluted 50% with water, to bark and young woody parts exposed to the sun.

Excess or Deficient Light

Each plant is adapted to certain amounts of light, depending on its species and previous growing environment. Plants typically develop larger leaves when grown at low light levels and smaller leaves when light intensity is high. Plant growth or flowering can be retarded by either too much or too little light. Deficient light causes pale, spindly, elongated growth called etiolation. Excess light can cause foliage to become chlorotic. Typical color returns when plants again receive normal light, but a prolonged light imbalance causes plants to become susceptible to other problems and possibly die.

Learn the intensity and pattern of light needed by your crop and monitor light intensity throughout the crop production. Portable light meters or foot-candle meters have traditionally been used to measure light intensity. Light meters are often weighted to measure green light, in part because light meters are often designed for use by photographers and green light is more efficiently seen by humans than blue or red light. Photosynthetically active radiation (especially blue) is most important to plants.

Handheld devices incorporating a photosynthetic photon flux (PPF) sensor are available for measuring the specific light wavelengths to which plants respond. These PPF meters may be a better choice for growers than foot-candle meters. These devices are sometimes described as PAR meters because they measure photosynthetically active radiation (PAR).

Computerized environmental monitoring and control systems with light sensors are available for predicting and managing greenhouse crop growth. These systems can calculate and adjust the light integral or sum of all light for each day, a measurement that incorporates light intensity and day length into one value.

Provide plants with appropriate levels of light by adjusting the number, intensity, and type of light available. Improve light through proper seasonal planting, keeping greenhouse covers clean, reducing dust, and spacing plants adequately. Reduce supplemental light and use greenhouse coverings, such as shade screens, to reduce damage from excess light. White shading compound sprayed onto greenhouses before hot, sunny weather is a quick and economical shading method; but once applied it cannot be adjusted, for example,

Shading from spacing pots too closely caused dieback of basal foliage on this Easter lily. Lower foliage first yellowed then progressed to this point, where labor-intensive hand trimming or decorative wrapping of the pot and basal stem may be necessary before marketing. Root rot pathogens, improper use of growth regulators, and prolonged cold storage can cause similar symptoms.

to temporarily allow in more light on cloudy days. Shade cloth inside or outside greenhouses is effective and adjustable; however, application is labor-intensive and the material becomes dirty or dusty, requiring cleaning. Mechanical curtain systems inside or outside greenhouses provide the most flexibility in controlling light and heating levels. Although installation can be relatively expensive and difficult in some greenhouses, mechanical curtains can be controlled by computerized monitoring systems to reduce labor costs, integrate shading with other environmental controls such as heating and ventilation, and greatly improve crop quality.

Container Spacing

Plants are often grown close together to maximize crop production per unit of growing space. However, growing plants too close together can increase management costs and reduce crop quality.

Plants grown more closely spaced tend to have taller stems with a more narrow diameter and lower overall biomass. Close spacing of older plants can cause yellowing and dieback of basal foliage, an aesthetic problem if plants are marketed in containers. Gray mold and other foliage diseases can more easily invade the weaker, senescing lower foliage. Closer spacing also increases disease development by raising

Spacing pots too closely caused elongation of stem internodes on this poinsettia, giving it an undesirable spindly appearance.

This African violet was subjected to refrigeration, causing the leaves to turn blackish. Within a couple days of returning to room temperature, the foliage turned brown and died. Tropical plants usually do not tolerate refrigeration.

humidity around plants and reducing the distance needed for plant-to-plant spread of pathogen propagules moving in air or in water or soil that is splashed among plants during irrigation. The distribution of sprinkler-applied irrigation and fertilization is less even and insecticide spray coverage is more difficult when plants are crowded. Pest presence can be more easily overlooked during monitoring when plants are closely spaced, and damage can become more extensive before it is recognized.

Ventilation

Ventilation is a primary method for managing growing area temperature and humidity, both of which greatly affect plant growth and foliar pathogens. Proper ventilation and use of computerized environmental monitoring and control are discussed in the chapter "Diseases" and below in the section "Greenhouse Cooling."

Temperature and Cold

The temperature of air, water, and media affects plant growth and development, including germination, stem elongation, and flowering. Temperature-related abiotic disorders include injury from cold air or cold water, sunburn, frost damage, and increased risk of pesticide phytotoxicity and possibly edema. Pathogen and insect development are also affected by temperature, as discussed in the chapters "Diseases" and "Insects, Mites, and Other Invertebrates." Heating is discussed in the chapter "Diseases."

Irrigation water temperature should be monitored and managed to stay within crop tolerances. The temperature of growing media can be managed by adjusting irrigation water temperature and applying heat beneath containers or under benches. Growing area air temperatures can be influenced by

shading, irrigation or misting, ventilation, and seasonal planting. Much of California's floriculture and nursery industry is located in coastal areas, which experience relatively moderate outdoor temperatures throughout the year. Coastal locations also minimize the need and expense for heating and cooling greenhouses.

Chilling

Plants are often chilled by holding them at 32° to 50°F (0° to 10°C) to slow growth, manage flowering, reduce ethylene production, and preserve quality during storage and shipping. However, chilling African violet and other tropical crops causes wilting of foliage and flowers and development of dark, water-soaked spots on leaves that can eventually turn light brown or bleached, and die. Chilling damage symptoms often do not become apparent until after plants are warmed to room temperature. Crop injury from cold air can occur in greenhouses if heaters are turned off too soon in the spring or turned on too late in the fall. Cold temperatures can retard or distort flower, foliage, or stem growth in certain crops. Symptoms may not appear until many days after the chilling injury, for example, when flower buds fail to develop normally.

Frost and Freezing

Cold temperatures cause shoots, buds, and flowers to curl or turn brown or black beginning at the leaf base and margins. Shoots or entire plants may be killed. Cold damage to foliage resembles some leaf anthracnose diseases—plants appear scorched because cold severely dehydrates plant tissue. This cold damage becomes most apparent after the temperature rises.

Frost and freezing occur under different conditions and have different management strategies. Freezing occurs when air temperatures are below 32°F (0°C). Frost occurs when air is above 32°F but plants drop to below 32°F because they radiate heat into the atmosphere. Protect plants from frost by covering them overnight with cloth or similar material other than plastic; remove the covers during the day. Frost protection may also be provided by moving air with high-velocity fans (commonly mounted on towers) to mix the cold surface-level air with warmer air higher above ground. Moving outdoor air and covering plants provide little or no benefit under freezing conditions unless a heat source is added, such as placing outdoor incandescent lights under plant covers.

To prevent damage from frost or freezing, do not grow species adapted to mild climates outdoors during the cold season in areas where freezing temperatures occur. Provide soil with adequate moisture to increase its ability to retain heat. At growing sites where topography varies, locate cold-sensitive crops on higher ground. Avoid placing cold-sensitive crops in low-lying spots toward which cooler air flows. During frost conditions, light smudge pots (fuel-burning devices that produce smoke) throughout the growing area if these devices are permitted in your area. Smudge pots produce a heavy smoke layer over the growing area that prevents heat loss by radiation to the night sky.

Operating sprinklers to keep foliage continuously wet can reduce damage from frost or freezing because extensive cold is required to turn water to ice. Even if the water freezes, ice-covered plants may be somewhat insulated from cooling to temperatures much below freezing. Do not operate sprinklers in combination with outdoor lights for heat because of the hazard of electrocution.

A method of applying non-ice-nucleating bacteria is also being investigated to protect plants from frost damage. Dust or bacteria on plant surfaces, including some strains of *Pseudomonas syringae*, serve as particles on which moisture from the atmosphere can condense and freeze. Some strains of bacteria that do not serve as ice nuclei have been commercially developed. Applying these non-ice-nucleating bacteria well before cold temperatures occur can allow them to develop and displace native ice-nucleating bacteria, allowing plants to tolerate somewhat colder temperatures, about 2°F (1°C) below freezing, without damage.

Greenhouse Cooling

Greenhouse cooling and heating are provided in many ways. Cooling systems are required in greenhouses because temperatures inside a greenhouse can be 20°F (11°C) or more higher than outside, even with passive ventilation (vents). High temperatures can cause sunburn, reduced flower size, delayed flowering, and bud drop.

Vents. Vents on roof ridges and sidewalls (roll-up sidewalls, roll-down sidewalls, and drop-down curtains) are used to cool many greenhouses. Because heat rises, natural ventilation can be provided by opening roof vents to allow heat to

This bleached white, yellow, necrotic agapanthus foliage was caused by freezing temperatures.

This sprinkler is one of a series linked to an environmental monitoring system. If frost is expected, the outdoor container plants are automatically blanketed by a continuous spray of water to reduce the likelihood that they will suffer frost damage.

escape, causing warm air to be replaced by cooler air drawn in by convection through sidewall vents. Some newer greenhouses are being designed with completely retractable roofs that allow greenhouses to be cooled very quickly. This allows highly effective cooling while minimizing energy costs, especially when large surface areas are provided for natural ventilation instead of using fans. Inflatable sidewalls, another option, help insulate the greenhouse when closed and provide ventilation when sidewalls are deflated. Roof and sidewall vents are best operated in combination. Vents are hand-operated on older greenhouses and mechanized on many newer or remodeled greenhouses. Mechanized vent opening and closing is often combined with motorized shade screens, all controlled by environmental monitoring sensors and computers.

Passive or natural ventilation may be inadequate, for example, if the vent surface area is too small or greenhouses are large (creating too much distance for good natural air flow), or both. Fans are often a vital component of temperature control and disease management (see the chapter "Diseases"). Also, natural ventilation alone generally will not allow greenhouses to remain cooler than outside air.

Evaporative cooling. Evaporative cooling systems, also called swamp coolers, use fans to draw in outside air and cool it by passing it through pads or thick fluted screens that are continually wetted at the top with recirculated water. This relatively economical cooling method can be used in most hot

The holes and surrounding chlorotic, pinched leaf tissue on this poinsettia are old injuries caused by rough handling. White latex is exuding from more than recent physical injury. When the exuding sticky latex dries, it prevents normal expansion of the surrounding leaf tissue. As the leaf grows, tissue surrounding the dried latex becomes injured, develops holes, and distorts.

The longitudinal discoloring on this Easter lily leaf resulted from 4-week-old injury to foliage that was sharply bent.

areas. Evaporative cooling is especially effective in growing areas with relatively low ambient humidity, such as the southwestern United States and the inland valleys of California. Although inside temperatures near the cooling pads can be about 20°F (11°C) cooler than outside, air temperatures near the exhaust end may be near ambient outside temperatures unless supplemental cooling methods such as shade are used.

Fog evaporative cooling systems suspend and disperse tiny water droplets in the air throughout the growing area. Fogging uses special nozzles with tiny openings that receive high-pressure water to produce very small droplets (<10 micrometers in diameter). Unlike traditional wetting of plants with overhead irrigation that drenches foliage, fogging or high-pressure misting minimizes condensation on leaf surfaces. Water for fogging needs to be very pure and free of particulates, minerals, and most other chemicals. Humidity created by evaporative cooling systems can contribute to pathogen infection and development, but computerized systems for monitoring and controlling temperature and ventilation can minimize this problem (see the chapter "Diseases").

Physical and Mechanical Injury

Plants can be injured by mishandling them during transport or routine cultural practices such as irrigation, pruning, and harvesting. In addition to directly damaging or killing plant parts or entire plants, wounds serve as entry sites for plant pathogens and can attract boring insects to woody stems.

Carbon Dioxide

Carbon dioxide (CO_2) deficiency occasionally occurs in greenhouses, slowing plant growth. Carbon dioxide deficiency can stunt plants, delay crop maturity, or reduce plant quality. This problem is common in greenhouses that are closed for long periods in cold areas to conserve heat, especially if the plant canopy is dense. Carbon dioxide levels in a tight greenhouse with actively growing plants can drop to 100 to 150 ppm. About 300 ppm CO_2 is generally required for good crop growth.

About 40% of plant weight is carbon. Plants take in carbon through leaf stomata as CO_2. This CO_2 is used to produce carbohydrate (sugars), the primary structural component of plants. Carbohydrate is manufactured in green plant tissue during photosynthesis:

$$CO_2 + water + sunlight \rightarrow carbohydrate + oxygen$$

Crops can usually be provided with sufficient CO_2 by venting greenhouses to bring in more outside air and by increasing air circulation within growing areas to make CO_2 more available at the leaf surface. Because most plants grow more rapidly in the presence of excess CO_2, carbon dioxide is sometimes added to greenhouse air. Potential benefits from carefully managed CO_2 injection include more rapid growth, increased plant height, greater dry weight of stems and flowers, more petals, and reduced time from planting to flowering.

Efficacy of CO_2 injection has been documented mostly in cold-winter climates. The benefit of CO_2 injection in most California growing areas is largely unknown. Vents must be kept closed and supplemental light and heat may be needed to allow plants to take full advantage of increased CO_2. These increased energy costs may outweigh any increase in crop value. Computerized systems may be necessary to optimally manage the interaction among CO_2 levels and changes in light and temperature. Accurate, reliable, and timely monitoring of CO_2 concentrations can be difficult, requiring good sampling methods and relatively expensive or high-maintenance sensors.

Excess CO_2 can stunt plant growth and cause foliar chlorosis or necrosis. About 1,200 ppm CO_2 is the maximum recommended for chrysanthemum, gerbera, and certain other crops. High CO_2 levels can be hazardous to workers. Employ proper safety measures when injecting CO_2, including ensuring that air quality is adequate for crop growth and worker heath. Improper operation of fuel-burning CO_2 generators can release carbon monoxide, ethylene, ozone, and certain other air pollutants that can injure plants or workers.

Ethylene

Excess ethylene causes premature abscission of flower buds, petals, and leaves. Wilted flowers, chlorosis, twisted growth or downward bending of stems and leaves (epinasty), and undersized or narrow leaves are other common symptoms. Ethylene is a gas produced naturally by senescing plant parts, ripening fruit, and decaying organic matter. Because incomplete combustion of fuels is a major source of ethylene, poor ventilation, faulty heating systems (especially those using lower-quality fuels), and equipment such as forklifts can be a major source of ethylene in greenhouses.

Crops vary greatly in their ethylene susceptibility. Learn the susceptibility of your crops and take steps to protect susceptible plants. After harvest, keep plants cool or treat them with commercial products that reduce ethylene production and damage. Provide adequate ventilation with fresh air during storage and shipping to dispel ethylene gas produced by plants after harvest. Avoid exposing crops or locating them near sources of ethylene. For example, ethylene is often abundant in areas where fruits and vegetables are stored, shipped, and marketed. In some produce storage, shipping, and marketing facilities, ethylene is deliberately applied to bananas and other produce to enhance ripening. Keep flower crops in a separate location.

Carbon dioxide generators can be used as an alternative to purchasing and releasing bottled CO_2 gas. This CO_2 generator is constructed mostly of aluminum, allowing it to be hung beneath a greenhouse roof. Generators can be fueled by natural gas or liquid propane and contain fans for dispersing CO_2 throughout the greenhouse.

Shattering (petal drop) occurred in the geranium on the right after the plant was exposed to low levels of ethylene.

Flower buds closed when the kalanchoe on the right was exposed to low ethylene concentrations.

Air Pollution

Air pollution damage is caused by mostly invisible gases. It is difficult to diagnose because many symptoms are similar to or aggravated by damage caused by drought, nutrient disorders, pathogens, and sucking insects and mites. Typical symptoms of air pollution damage include slow growth and discolored, dying, or prematurely dropping foliage. These symptoms may develop soon after short-term exposure to high concentrations of air pollutants or after longer exposure to relatively low pollution levels. The susceptibility of plants to air pollution damage varies greatly by species and cultivar.

Ozone, carbon monoxide, and chlorine can be damaging pollutants in greenhouse air. Chlorine used for disinfection can volatilize from treated benches and containers or move in air from on-site water treatment facilities. Crop damage from carbon monoxide, nitrous oxides, and sulfur dioxide can result from unvented or inadequately vented heaters, engine exhaust, or poorly operating equipment that burns fossil fuels. Damaging emissions are more likely to be produced when burning kerosene or fuel oil in comparison with cleaner-burning fuels such as natural or propane gas.

Ozone, sulfur oxides, nitrogen oxides, and acidic deposition ("acid rain") are common outdoor air pollutants. Outdoor air pollution damage is especially prevalent when plants are located near sources of dirty air, such as freeways or industries, or where weather and topography concentrate pollution. Some pollutants develop through complex reactions among light and chemicals such as peroxyacetyl nitrate (PAN), a photochemical smog that forms from nitric oxide and unburned hydrocarbons released into the atmosphere.

Ozone. Ozone naturally occurring in the upper atmosphere shields plants and animals from harmful solar radiation; ozone near the ground damages plants. Ozone is produced by certain electrical equipment, especially that which operates at high voltages. Outdoors, ozone is produced when the nitrogen oxides and hydrocarbons emitted during combustion are exposed to sunlight and react with oxygen.

Ozone causes pale flecks or small dark patches to appear on foliage. Discolored areas can enlarge and foliage may drop prematurely. Ozone retards growth and increases plants' susceptibility to certain diseases and insects.

Sulfur oxides. Sulfur is a common impurity in coal, oil, natural gas, and gasoline. Upon combustion, sulfur forms sulfur oxides, which are taken in through plant stomata or dissolve in moisture on leaf surfaces. This sulfur oxide converts to sulfuric acid, which burns and kills plant cells. Sulfur oxides cause small necrotic leaf spots and can bleach or kill foliage. Affected foliage may be sparse, stunted, or grow in tufts.

Management

Provide proper cultural care and control other causes of stress to keep plants vigorous and increase their tolerance to pollution. Keep equipment in good repair. Properly vent any fuel-burning activity to dispel exhaust. Develop and conduct marketing campaigns and other activities that encourage people to plant and care for plants. Growing more plants can help to purify polluted air as moderate amounts of some air pollutants, such as the sulfur in sulfur oxides, are taken in through leaf stomata and metabolized for use in plant growth. Extensive lists of plants tolerant to certain air pollutants have been developed; consider growing these tolerant crops in areas where air quality is poor.

Ozone air pollution damage can be subtle, as shown by the yellowish and brownish patches on these Japanese maple leaves.

Diseases

Disease symptoms can appear on any plant part. Symptoms of disease include roots, stems, leaves, flowers, or entire plants that discolor, wilt, distort, decay, or die. Diseases are caused by pathogens or abiotic factors such as environmental stress or inappropriate cultural practices. This chapter discusses diseases caused by pathogenic bacteria, fungi, viruses, and phytoplasmas. For diseases caused by nematodes (tiny roundworms), see the chapter "Nematodes." Abiotic or noninfectious causes of disease are discussed in the chapter "Abiotic Disorders and Cultural Practices." Table 18 lists characteristics useful in distinguishing between diseases caused by pathogens and abiotic factors. The term *pests* is used when referring to more than one cause of problems, including diseases, undesirable insects and mites, and weeds.

Plant diseases result from complex interactions among the host plant, the pathogen, and the environment (Fig. 18). Disease symptoms and damage are influenced by the disease-producing ability of the causal organism and the host plant's genetic characteristics, stage of growth, and vigor at the time of infection. In addition to the ability of cultural practices and environmental conditions to cause disease in the absence of pathogens, abiotic factors such as humidity and temperature greatly influence development of pathogenic diseases. If conditions are poor for pathogen development and plants are otherwise healthy, many pathogens have little or no effect on their hosts. The same pathogens can be devastating when conditions are favorable for the microorganism or if host plants are stressed.

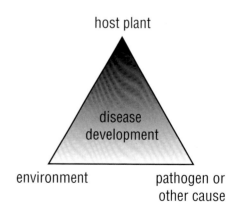

Figure 18. Diseases result from complex interactions among a susceptible host plant, an environment favorable for disease development, and virulent pathogens. Time (such as season or duration of disease-favoring conditions) is also a factor. This disease-development interaction is sometimes illustrated as a pyramid with time represented as a fourth axis.

Although pathogens are continually present in many growing areas, they are unable to damage crops unless conditions become suitable for disease development. Phytophthora root rot developed in this wilted lisianthus, probably because the plant is growing in an area where the drip irrigation system leaks, continually exposing roots to excess moisture.

Stunted growth, yellowing, and necrosis are symptoms of certain pathogenic fungi, such as Rhizoctonia root rot infecting these chrysanthemums.

Types of Pathogens

Nematodes (discussed in a separate chapter) bacteria, fungi, phytoplasmas, and viruses are the most common pathogens causing crop disease. Although pathogenic microorganisms can damage plants, many microorganisms are beneficial, such as those that control pests, degrade toxins, build soils, and decompose organic debris to produce plant nutrients.

Fungi. Pathogenic fungi cause many different symptoms, including leaf spots, wilts, root decay, dieback, and distorted or discolored blossoms. Although most pathogens are microscopic, some fungi are visible to the naked eye, such as rusts, mildews, and molds. Fungi are usually composed of fine, threadlike structures (hyphae) that form a network or mass (mycelium) on or through their host. To survive adverse conditions and facilitate dispersal, fungi produce specialized structures including rhizomorphs (rootlike or cordlike masses of hyphae that can contaminate soil and plant parts), sclerotia (compact masses of hyphae that can persist for relatively long periods), and tiny seedlike spores. The life cycles of typical fungi are illustrated for gray mold and powdery mildew in their respective sections later in this chapter.

Fungal spores can be spread by wind, water, soil movement, machinery, insects, or other things with which they come in contact, including people. Sclerotia, rhizomorphs, and some types of spores may survive for long periods in or on plants or soil. When conditions such as temperature, moisture, and the presence of a host plant are suitable for

growth, these pathogen propagules produce new fungal hyphae. If they are large enough to be seen with the naked eye or a hand lens, signs such as mycelia, masses of spores, and spore-forming structures help in identifying fungi.

Bacteria. Bacteria are microscopic one-celled organisms that feed in or on plants or other organic matter. Common symptoms of disease resulting from bacterial infection are shoot blight, leaf spots, soft rots, scabs, wilts, or cankers on stems and roots. Unlike fungi, plant-pathogenic bacteria generally do not produce spores that can survive adverse environmental conditions; bacteria must usually remain in contact with a host plant or plant debris to survive. Plant-infecting bacteria generally require warmth and moisture to multiply. They are commonly spread by water, such as overhead irrigation splashing among plants, but they can also be dispersed by insects or by moving infested plants, soil, or equipment.

Viruses. Viruses are submicroscopic infectious particles that cause stunting, discoloring, distortion, or death of leaves, stems, blossoms, or entire plants. Viruses require a living host cell in which to reproduce and generally are not viable for very long outside of living tissue. Many viruses are spread by plant-feeding insects, especially aphids and thrips. Some viruses are spread by nematodes, budding or grafting, or the movement of infected seeds, plants, plant parts, or infested equipment. Once a plant is infected by a virus, it usually remains infected during its entire life.

Damage caused by other pests can be confused with diseases, such as the pale feeding blotches and tiny specks of dark feces caused by thrips as shown here. However, some plant pathogens can be vectored by certain insects, such as aphids, leafhoppers, and thrips.

Phytoplasmas. Phytoplasmas, formerly called mycoplasmas, are minute organisms, smaller than bacteria. They are often, as with aster yellows, spread by leafhoppers.

Monitoring

Regular monitoring of environmental conditions (such as temperature, humidity, light, pH, and salinity) and cultural practices (such as irrigation, fertilization, and drainage) is critical to protecting plants from disease. Before inspecting plants, divide growing areas into pest management units (PMUs). Each PMU is a uniform crop area with similar pest management requirements, as detailed in the chapter "Managing Pests in Flower and Nursery Crops." Pest management units increase the likelihood that problems will be detected early, make scouting data easier to manage and interpret, and improve targeting of management actions.

Check plants at least weekly for symptoms of stress and disease, such as off-color or irregular growth and spotted or wilted leaves. Remove some plants from containers or gently scrape away soil and look for signs of unhealthy roots (see the section "Root and Crown Decays," below). When unhealthy plants are found, examine as many affected plants or parts of the same plant as possible. Look for plants with different stages of disease to determine how symptoms change as the disease progresses. Plant parts in the early stage of disease development often show more characteristic symptoms because secondary organisms or other factors that obscure symptoms may later become involved. Do not rely on a single symptom; the observation of several different symptoms is usually needed to identify a disease-producing agent. Look at all affected plant parts. Some aboveground symptoms such as wilt and dieback are caused by root diseases; you must expose and inspect the roots to see if they are diseased.

Compare symptoms that appear in the field with the illustrations and descriptions in this chapter, which are grouped according to the plant parts most obviously affected. Consult the chapter "Crop Tables" for lists of common flower crop damage symptoms and their causes. Consult *Pests of Landscape Trees and Shrubs* (Dreistadt 1994) for more information on pathogens affecting woody ornamental crops. See the suggested reading and literature cited at the end of this manual for other useful publications, such as those from the American Phytopathological Society.

Record keeping. Record when disease outbreaks are observed and what specific symptoms were present. Develop a standard form, which can have separate columns for insect presence and disease damage symptoms. Typically, all the monitoring information from one week for one PMU is recorded on a single form (Fig. 3). Use maps of the growing site (Fig. 4) to record the specific location and approximate extent of problems (such as the number of symptomatic plants or the size of the affected growing area). Crop maps and colored flags or stakes placed in the crop facilitate reinspection of continuing problems and targeting of control actions.

Note environmental factors that can contribute to problems, such as excess humidity or temperature, pesticide use, injuries, poor drainage, or the presence of free water. Condensation, irrigation, rain, and other water sources are especially important because most fungal and bacterial pathogens require wet plant surfaces to infect and damage crops. It can be extremely helpful to use computerized environmental monitoring systems and to record information collected manually in a form that can be entered into a computer spreadsheet or database. Computerized summaries and graphical displays of plant inspection and environmental monitoring information greatly facilitate disease diagnosis and management, as discussed in the section "Computers," below.

Tools and help. A notebook, record-keeping forms, and hand tools (such as a pocket knife and trowel) are among the essential tools for diagnosing many diseases (Table 3). A soil-sampling tube for field use and plastic bags and an ice chest for preserving samples are frequently useful.

A hand lens (about 15×) can be helpful, but a good quality 40× to 60× dissecting microscope (stereomicroscope) is even more useful. However, accurate identification of many fungi and bacteria requires culturing samples on selective media and having the results examined by an expert pathologist using a 100× to 400× binocular compound microscope. Necessary microscope accessories include glass slides with cover slips, razor blades, forceps, teasing needles, lens paper, dropper bottles, biological stains such as cotton blue, special growth media for culturing samples, and incubators for holding samples under specific light and temperature conditions while waiting for diagnostic samples to develop on petri dishes or in flasks containing growth media.

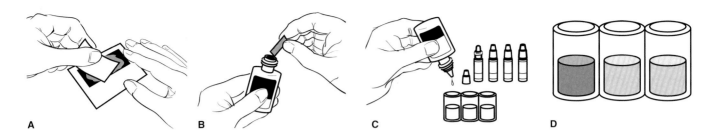

A   **B**   **C**   **D**

Figure 19. Plants can be tested by growers for *Phytophthora, Pythium,* and *Rhizoctonia* root and crown decay fungi using on-site test kits as follows. A. Collect and grind plant tissue with abrasive pads. B. Fold pads and insert them into the extraction solution. C. Apply a series of solutions to plastic wells that are coated inside with detector substances. D. Examine the plastic wells for color changes that indicate whether the target pathogen was present in the plant sample. Illustrated here is an Alert root decay test kit by Neogen Corp. Consult *Easy On-Site Tests for Fungi and Viruses in Nurseries and Greenhouses* (Kabashima et al. 1997) for more information on properly collecting samples and interpreting the results from on-site test kits. Adapted from illustration by Will Suckow.

For certain problems, consider regular use of specialized monitoring tools such as on-site pathogen detection kits (Fig. 19) and indicator plants as discussed in the section "Viruses," below. It is not always possible to identify in the field the causes of disease. Many causes of disease can be confirmed only through special laboratory tests performed on the diseased plants, nearby apparently healthy plant tissue, media, or irrigation water. Establish a relationship with a reputable diagnostic laboratory service so that when you need off-site testing, you know what services are available, how and where to ship samples, and when results can be expected. General practices for submitting a laboratory sample are summarized in Table 32.

Contact the Cooperative Extension office in your county or area for personal help from an advisor and to request a list of private laboratories that test for diseases. Correct diagnosis of the cause of problems is vital to effective management. Incorrect or ineffective actions are often taken because the cause of plant disease was misdiagnosed. Do not hesitate to consult experts.

Table 32. Suggestions for Submitting Plant Samples to a Diagnostic Laboratory.

- Write down the crop name and your name, telephone number, and any other pertinent contact information.
- Include information on the growing environment and management practices.
- Have the diagnostician visit the site if possible.
- Submit the entire plant or several whole plants.
- Don't submit completely dead plants. Provide to the laboratory plants that have earlier stages of symptoms or a range of apparent damage.
- Package and ship plants so they arrive in good condition, such as by placing each sample in a ventilated plastic vegetable bag with air holes, placing sample bags in a styrofoam chest containing ice, and shipping the container via overnight express delivery.

An IPM scout inspecting plants for disease. Regular monitoring and good record keeping are critical for effective integrated pest management.

Diagnosing Disease

Learn how to recognize whether plants are healthy or stressed and teach this information to employees who care for plants. Learn to recognize symptoms caused by the major disease categories, including damping-off, root and crown decays, vascular wilts, leaf spots, rusts, powdery mildews, gray mold, viruses, aster yellows, and galls. In some cases (such as leaf spots and vascular wilts) it's also important to learn the major divisions of these groups (such as fungal versus bacterial causes).

Learn the diseases to which your crops are prone, for example, by consulting the chapter "Crop Tables." Be sure you can recognize symptoms of those diseases and the conditions that cause them to develop.

Disease diagnosis is often difficult. Effective diagnosis requires regular scouting of crops and growing areas, good record keeping, and adequate knowledge and experience. Laboratory tests, diagnostic kits, and outside professional help may be needed to positively identify the cause of disease. Consult the chapter "Managing Pests in Flower and Nursery Crops" for specific suggestions on diagnosing and monitoring pest problems.

Many causes of disease can be confirmed only through laboratory tests performed on the diseased plants. One discolored leaf from each of several chrysanthemums is being placed into a labeled bag before submitting the leaves for virus testing.

Dying or dead plants can be a source of pathogen inoculum that may spread to nearby crops. Adjacent to the containers with dead plants are New Guinea impatiens exhibiting unhealthy growth, including stunted, chlorotic foliage and a lack of blossoms.

Disease-inducing conditions. Checking for conditions that promote disease is often more important than scouting for disease symptoms on plants. If remedial action is delayed until symptoms appear or the cause of disease has been confirmed, it is often too late to avoid permanent damage or provide effective control. Inspect growing areas regularly for improper cultural practices (such as overwatering) and environmental conditions (such as excess humidity) that promote disease. Disease monitoring should also include tools and techniques such as checking thermostat settings, recording and resetting minimum-maximum thermometers, ensuring that tensiometers are properly installed and operating, and testing for high- or low-soluble salts and proper pH levels. Computerized systems are extremely helpful in monitoring and preventing diseases such as gray mold, as discussed later in the sections on computers, disease prediction, and humidity.

Management

Use a combination of methods whenever possible to prevent and control pathogenic diseases. Management methods include sanitation and exclusion, cultural and environmental controls, pesticides, and in certain situations biological controls. Prevention is the most important disease-control strategy and the only effective option for managing some diseases. Although disease development can sometimes be stopped with systemic fungicides during early stages of infection by certain pathogens such as powdery mildews and rusts, most pathogens cannot be eliminated from their host once the plant is infected. In order to avoid damage, action often is required before infection occurs or at least at the first signs of disease.

Most pathogens require specific conditions to disperse, infect plants, and develop to the extent that plants become diseased. Whenever possible, avoid environmental conditions and cultural practices that promote diseases common to your crops. Provide proper care and minimize conditions that are stressful to plants. Stresses include insect attack, soil that is continually kept too wet or too dry, extreme temperatures, and improper fertilization. Physical damage to roots and stems, pesticide injury, poor water quality, excess salts, and growing species or cultivars that are poorly adapted for local conditions also cause stress. Disease prevention measures include planting resistant cultivars and alternative crop species, using good planting design to group plants with similar needs in locations where conditions are suitable for good crop growth, and providing appropriate cultural care and environmental conditions. Consult the chapters "Managing Pests in Flower and Nursery Crops" and "Abiotic Disorders and Cultural Practices" to learn how to care for plants, modify the environment to prevent disease, and apply key management practices that are effective against many types of pests, including pathogens.

Sanitation

Proper sanitation is often the most effective disease-prevention method. The main sources of pathogens include soil and unpasteurized planting mix, contaminated growing stock, crop debris, dirty propagation and growing areas, and anything that has contacted the ground, such as equipment, tools, and workers' hands and shoes. Mix and store growing media in an area not contaminated with natural soil. Treat growing media and used containers before reuse to prevent them from being a source of pests that can infest new crops. Keep containers and growing media covered until they are

A hose end clipped to a bench in a clean growing area. Pathogen spread can be reduced by keeping equipment and tools off of floors and the ground, which may be contaminated.

Keep dirty tools, shoes, and other soil-contaminated materials off of benches. Soil often contains pathogen propagules that can be spread to crops by splashing irrigation water or roots growing through drain holes at the bottom of containers.

Encourage employees to use good sanitation to avoid spreading pathogens on contaminated hands and tools. This worker is using disinfectant hand soap (on the post) before handling plants in a poinsettia propagation greenhouse.

used to prevent them from becoming contaminated by insects, weed seeds, runoff water, rainfall, and windborne pathogens. Clean equipment and tools before moving among fields. Remove crop debris promptly after harvest. Cull unmarketable plants. Provide and use hand-washing facilitates, shoe baths at entranceways, and sanitary coveralls to ensure that workers do not inadvertently spread pathogens as they move from one plant or growing area to another.

Key sanitation methods for preventing pathogens and other pests are summarized in Figures 9 and 10. While it is unrealistic for growers to strictly follow every method, pathogenic diseases will decline dramatically or be avoided entirely to the extent that these suggestions are adopted.

Growing Media Treatments

Whenever possible, growing media such as field soil, container mixes, and used rock wool should be pasteurized or otherwise treated before use. Unpasteurized growing media and the plant debris that contaminates these media are the primary reservoirs for nematodes, plant pathogens, weed seeds, and certain invertebrates. The need for media treatment is increasing as green waste is diverted from landfills and reused, crop residue is managed on-site, and planting mix from nonsalable plants is recycled.

Fumigation and heating are the most widely used treatments. These control most pests infesting growing media (Table 8). Heat treatments include solarization (see the chapter "Weeds") and steam and dry heat, such as from kilns. Heat generated by decomposer microorganisms during composting is a biological method of controlling pests in growing media. Biological control of soil-dwelling pathogens through disease-suppressive composts and organic amendments is increasingly being used in container mixes and some planting beds. New technologies such as microwave or gamma radiation and ohmic heating are being researched for treating growing media.

Sterilization versus pasteurization. Sterilization, killing all organisms present, is done when disinfecting benches, containers, tools, and inorganic growing media such as rock wool. Pasteurization is done when treating growing media that includes organic matter, such as soil, planting beds, and container mixes. Sterilization can cause undesirable chemical and physical changes in organic growing media, such as the nutrient disorders discussed in the chapter "Abiotic Disorders and Cultural Practices." Sterilizing growing media also creates a biological vacuum in which pathogens that reestablish can proliferate free of competition. In field soils, no treatment is likely to eliminate all organisms.

Compared with sterilization, pasteurization uses less-intensive or shorter-duration treatment, such as heating to a lower temperature. Pasteurization is a partial sterilization that kills most pests (Fig. 20), but does not greatly change the chemical composition of growing media and allows some heat-tolerant beneficial microorganisms to survive. Beneficial microorganisms are sometimes reinoculated into growing media after pasteurization to compete with pathogenic organisms.

Steam and heat. Steam, the most common method used in the past for disinfecting soil and container mixes, is coming back into more widespread use. Steam requires significant equipment, such as portable steamers or a central generator with a distribution system. However, in comparison with the fumigant methyl bromide, steam-treated beds can be replanted sooner and do not need to be cultivated or leached to avoid potential phytotoxicity from the fumigant. Steam or other heat is as effective as methyl bromide in controlling most pests in growing media (Table 8). For certain pathogens, such as crown gall, Fusarium wilt of carnations, and Verticillium wilt of chrysanthemums, heat is more effective than methyl bromide.

Steam is often applied through porous pipes on the bottom of trailers to thoroughly pasteurize container mix covered with a tarpaulin. Steam is sometimes applied through porous pipes buried under greenhouse beds that are covered with tarpaulins, a method that can pasteurize the upper 2 feet (60 cm) of soil. This technique is sometimes reversed, with steam applied on top of beds and beneath tarpaulins. The heat is drawn underground by applying suction to porous pipes buried about 2 feet (60 cm) deep and 10 feet (3 m) apart. Regardless of whether steam is applied from beneath or on top of beds, the buried pipes are also used to recover irrigation water and to provide good subsurface drainage. Placing pipes on the surface and steaming for 6 to 8 hours can sterilize approximately the upper 8 inches (20 cm) of ground beds or field soil. The actual depth of heat penetration varies depending on growing media characteristics, such as moisture. Steam heat applied from above without using buried suction pipes may not penetrate deeply enough to adequately control certain pathogens affecting some crops.

The duration of heat treatment depends on the steam or heat production and distribution system, the volume of growing media being treated, and media characteristics such as moisture. The standard pasteurization recommendation is to heat growing media so that all portions of it reach at least 140°F (60°C) for 30 minutes. Steam treatment of larger areas typically requires 4 to 8 hours to ensure media that is

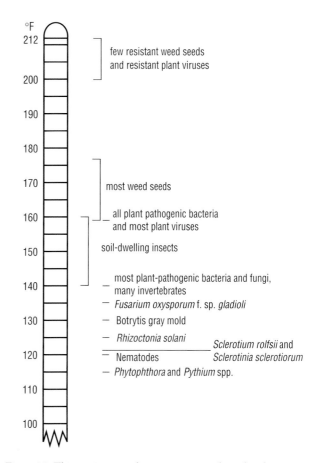

Figure 20. Thirty minutes at the temperatures indicated under moist conditions kills most pests infesting containers, equipment, or growing media while leaving some beneficial organisms behind. Temperatures of at least 140°F (60°C) for 30 minutes are usually recommended for pasteurization. Adapted from Baker and Roistacher 1957a.

more insulated or distant from the heat source reaches the recommended temperature for 30 minutes. Because steam at normal air pressure is at 212°F (100°C), steam aerator devices are used to inject cooler air into steam to lower the temperature before introducing the hot gas (aerated steam) into the growing media.

Monitor treatment time and temperature, for example, by placing at least one thermometer or thermocouple in the coolest area of the growing media being treated. The coolest spots are usually the most insulated areas or the locations far from where steam enters. Treatment time begins once all growing media (or the coolest spot) has reached the desired temperature. Before treatment, growing media should be porous (for example, beds should rototilled) and moist to about the level desired at planting time. Amendments generally should be mixed into growing media before pasteurization, especially organic materials such as peat moss, which may be contaminated with pathogens. Amendments that may not be heat-tolerant, such as certain encapsulated, slow-release fertilizers, can be added after pasteurization if they are pest-free and are added using sterile equipment and techniques that do not introduce pests.

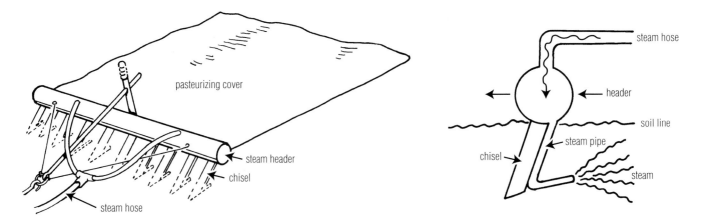

Figure 21. A plowlike steam rake can be used to treat fields with heat. Steam can be generated and piped from a central source to the rake, which is drawn across the field by a cable and winch. Alternatively, a portable steam generator can be mounted on a truck or plow, which tows the rake. Steam nozzles are located at the lower rear of chisel blades projecting down into soil (side view). A moisture-proof sheetlike cover is dragged slowly behind the plow at about 20 inches (50 cm) per minute so that treated soil stays covered and retains heat for 30 minutes after treatment (top view). Adapted from Baker and Roistacher 1957b.

Growing media is a primary source of pathogens unless media is pasteurized and properly handled. Steam is being piped into the bottom left of this trailer filled with container mix. The heat is released through porous pipes placed on the bottom inside of the cart. A metal hood over the cart traps heat to ensure that the entire volume of media is adequately heated. A metal duct at the top front of the hood directs exiting steam to a condenser where the moisture is captured.

Beneath this tarpaulin, a greenhouse planting bed is being pasteurized by applying steam through porous pipes laid on top of the bed. Steam is being introduced through the high-pressure hoses in the foreground.

Field steam. A plowlike steam rake is sometimes used to treat fields with heat (Fig. 21). Hot water or steam is applied through shanks or hollow tines to penetrate at least 1 foot (30 cm) into soil. Soil penetration of steam to an adequate depth is a major problem in field soils, and except for raised beds, methods of effectively using steam in field soils need to be improved.

Solarization. Solarization before planting kills virtually all insects, pathogens such as *Fusarium*, *Sclerotium*, and *Verticillium* species (Table 33), and many nematodes (Table 94) and weeds (Table 80). Clear plastic is used to cover bare, moist fields, greenhouse beds, or container mix. The plastic traps solar radiation and elevates growing media temperatures, killing pests near the surface. Specific recommendations on

effective use and discussion of solarization's advantages and disadvantages are provided in the chapter "Weeds."

Composting. Composting is the controlled decomposition of organic material. Many growers use composting to avoid having to dispose of green wastes and to produce their own growing media. Quality compost and other soil amendments can improve nutritional, physical, and chemical characteristics of container mix and planting beds, enhancing crop growth. Because microbial decomposition generates substantial heat, proper composting kills most pests infesting organic debris.

Composting for use in growing media requires careful monitoring and management to consistently produce material that benefits plant growth. Use controlled conditions to

Table 33. Some Plant Pathogens Controlled by Solarization.

Fungi	Bacteria
Bipolaris sorokiniana	*Agrobacterium tumefaciens*
Didymella lycopersici	*Streptomyces scabies*
Fusarium oxysporum	
f. sp. *conglutinans*	
f. sp. *fragariae*	
f. sp. *lycopersici*	
f. sp. *vasinfectum*	
Phytophthora cinnamomi	
Plasmodiophora brassicae	
Pyrenochaeta lycopersici	
Pyrenochaeta terrestris	
Pythium ultimum	
Rhizoctonia solani	
Sclerotinia minor	
Sclerotium cepivorum	
Sclerotium oryzae	
Sclerotium rolfsii	
Thielaviopsis basicola	
Verticillium albo-atrum	
Verticillium dahliae	

The fungi *Fusarium oxysporum* f. sp. *opini*, *Macrophomina phaseolina*, and *Pythium aphanidermatum* are not controlled by solarization. Other pests controlled by solarization include nematodes (Table 94) and weeds (Table 80). *Source:* Stapleton and DeVay 1995.

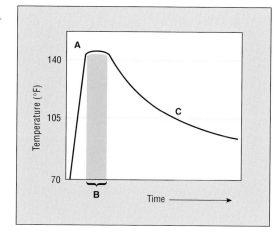

Figure 22. The three phases of composting. **A.** An initial few days during which temperatures quickly rise to above 105°F (41°C) as easily degraded substances decompose. **B.** A minimum of 3 days during which heat generated by decomposer microorganisms must reach at least 140°F (60°C) to kill most invertebrates, plant pathogens, and weed seeds. **C.** A curing phase during which temperatures decline and stabilize at just under 105°F and microorganisms naturally colonize or are inoculated into the material. Organic material cycles through these phases several times because compost temporarily cools when it is mixed. Proper composting can produce disease-suppressive growing media, but its effectiveness is influenced by many factors during the composting process and while the compost is being used.

produce uniform, well-decomposed, stable organic matter containing appropriate microorganisms (Fig. 22, Table 34). Prepare organic raw materials (feedstocks) properly before composting by grinding coarse or large materials to increase surface area for adequate water-holding ability; retain sufficient large particles to provide porosity and allow enough airflow to maintain aerobic conditions. Blend feedstocks to balance the carbon to nitrogen (C:N) ratio: at least 1 pound of nitrogen should be available for every 30 pounds of carbon (C:N of 30:1). Materials such as sawdust contain a high proportion of carbon (C:N of about 1,000:1). If high-carbon composts are used for plant production, decomposer organisms will deprive roots of sufficient nitrogen unless additional nitrogen is added to the growing media.

Mix materials well before composting. Provide adequate aeration, regular mixing, and sufficient moisture throughout the composting process. Feedstock moisture should initially be about 70% by weight, then be maintained at about 55 to 65% throughout composting. Temperatures must reach at least 140°F (60°C) for at least 3 days for heat to sufficiently destroy pathogens and weed seeds. Low pH (from organic acid production) or unpleasant odor during composting can indicate that undesirable anaerobic (oxygen deficient) metabolism is occurring.

As with other organic ingredients, compost must be blended with other materials to produce a container mix with the characteristics necessary for good plant growth (Tables 26, 27). However, composted green waste is a significantly less expensive source of organic matter for container mix than peat moss or timber by-products such as bark. In addition to compost produced on-site, commercial growing media and organic amendments produced by composting are available. Animal manure, hardwood and softwood bark, municipal green waste, municipal biosolids (sewage sludge), and wood chips are common compost constituents.

Some composts and organic amendments have disadvantages. Inadequate decomposition may be the most common problem. Immature composts can promote disease by providing food for *Rhizoctonia* species and other pathogens, which can colonize as saprophytes. Conversely, organic matter that is too mature (excessively stabilized) does not provide sufficient nutrients to support activity of biological control organisms. Compost maturity is less important in ground beds or field soils than in container mixes, as long as the compost is applied several months ahead of planting to allow for adequate decomposition.

Although proper composting eliminates most pathogens, unpasteurized soils and organic materials can be contaminated with pathogens. In contrast to the beneficial light peats from bog surfaces, dark sphagnum peat from lower bog layers (decomposition level H_4 or greater, based on an H_x rating system called the von Post scale) is commonly conducive to certain pathogens. Composted biosolids and animal manures often have high pH and high salt content, requiring amendment or mixing with other products before use. Unfavorable chemical properties in some materials can negate the beneficial effects of compost. Certain organic materials may be toxic (allelopathic) to young

Table 34. Characteristics of High-Quality Compost Used in Container Mixes.

- **Carefully monitored and managed during production** using well-defined ingredients and controlled conditions to produce a consistent and uniform product.
- **Aerobically produced** using a heat producing (thermophilic) process, which destroys pathogenic microorganisms and weed propagules.
- **Well stabilized and cured,** with adequate decomposition resulting in a high ratio of humus to total organic matter. The product should be naturally colonized with nonpathogenic microorganisms or (if desired) inoculated with biological control agents.
- **Neutral pH.** Other acceptable chemical characteristics include a high CEC (see below) and good buffering capacity (the ability to resist changes in pH despite addition of acidic or alkaline substances).
- **Low ammonium** levels and low levels or nontoxic concentrations of soluble salts.
- **No sulfide and nitrite** or other harmful compounds.
- **Nitrogen fixed stably** into humus and microbial biomass, largely as a result of having an appropriate carbon to nitrogen ratio in the feedstock and using proper composting methods.
- **Appropriate cation exchange capacity** (CEC). Clay, peat moss, and most organic composts have a high CEC; sand, perlite, and undecomposed organic materials such as rice hulls have a very low CEC. A measure of fixed negative charges in growing media, CEC indicates the ability of growing media to attract and hold positive electrical charges or cations, such as many nutrients that otherwise would readily leach during irrigation. A CEC of 6 to 15 milliequivalents per 100 cubic centimeters (meq/100 cc) of dry growing media is generally considered to be desirable.

Adapted from Grebus and Wilen 1996.

A rotating screen is removing large particles from organic material being composted in windrows in the background. Quality control measures such as this are typical of greenwaste composting operations.

plants unless materials are well composted or leached with water before use. On-site composting facilities can require much space and certain specialized equipment, such as a grinder, shredder, screens, front-end loader, and windrow turner. Composting for off-site use may be regulated.

Disease-suppressive compost. Some composts and amendments can control or suppress pathogens such as *Fusarium*, *Pythium*, and *Rhizoctonia* species that may colonize growing media after the material has been composted. The mechanisms of disease suppression are discussed below in the section "Biological Control". Composted tree bark reportedly provides some of the most effective disease suppression. Light sphagnum peats (harvested from the surface of peat bogs) have naturally undergone partial decomposition and can provide short-term disease suppression, which may be useful when crops are grown as plugs or in flats.

Disease suppressiveness develops during the final curing phase of composting (Fig. 22), when disease-suppressive microorganisms and other microflora naturally recolonize compost. Compost properly cured for 4 months or longer often is disease suppressive. However, inoculating compost with biological control agents at the beginning of curing may be needed to ensure consistent levels of disease suppression. Inoculation with beneficial microorganisms may also be needed to provide specific suppression of certain pathogens and to reduce curing time.

The disease suppressiveness of compost is influenced by many physical, chemical, and biological factors during composting and compost use. Factors affecting efficacy include the composition of starting materials; the moisture, oxygen levels, C:N ratio, salinity, pH, composting time, and temperatures maintained during composting; natural colonization or inoculation with specific beneficial organisms; the extent of pathogen contamination and the particular species of disease-causing organisms present in the soil or media; and the timing of compost use relative to crop planting and development.

Despite their increasing use and importance, the disease-suppressive characteristics of composts and amendments may be variable or undocumented. Quality control is the greatest impediment to consistent, successful use of compost for disease suppression. Unlike mycofungicides (beneficial microorganisms registered and labeled in accordance with pesticide regulations) composts and amendments are largely unregulated.

Effective disease suppression using compost requires adequate knowledge and properly prepared material. Because many commercial composts and those prepared on-site are not adequately produced and lack consistent quality, composted bark, sphagnum peat, and, increasingly, peat substitutes such as coir (dust from the fiber of coconut husks) are the principle organic materials used in commercial mixes. If compost-based potting products are purchased, establish a relationship with a reliable supplier. Purchase only adequately labeled products, such as those with an ingredients list and assay information on product nutrient content, moisture, pH, and salinity. Some outside laboratories may be able to evaluate the disease-suppressive ability of compost by conducting bioassays, which compare disease development of plants grown in standard and disease-suppressive growing media with and without pathogen inoculation. See *Compost Production and Utilization* (Van Horn 1995) and *On-farm Composting Handbook* (Rynk 1992) for more details about composting.

Fumigation. Chemical fumigation has been widely used to sterilize growing media. Fumigation before planting provides rapid broad-spectrum control of most invertebrates, microorganisms, nematodes, and weeds (Table 8). Reduced fumigant rates (sublethal fumigation) using methyl bromide or metam sodium, combined with solarization or other heat, can provide better pathogen control than using heat or fumigation alone. Sublethal fumigation and heat combined have been shown to have a synergistic effect in controlling certain fungi, including *Fusarium*, *Sclerotinia*, and *Verticillium* species.

Methyl bromide, or methyl bromide in combination with chloropicrin, are injected as a gas into soil, and the soil is immediately covered with plastic tarps. Dazomet (Basamid) and metam sodium (Vapam) are also used as broad-spectrum fumigants to control most insects and certain nematodes, pathogens, and weeds in soil. Dazomet is applied as granules that are incorporated into soil and usually followed by irrigation and the covering of growing media with tarps. Metam sodium is applied through preplant injection into growing media or by sprinkler or drip irrigation. Tarping growing media to retain the fumigant or applying clear plastic and solarizing after application increases metam efficacy and allows application of reduced rates.

Eliminate any clods and loosen and moisten growing media prior to fumigation. Fumigant escapes too quickly from soil that is too dry, but fumigants do not penetrate soil that is too wet. Pathogens are more susceptible to fumigants if soil is moist but not soggy. Keeping planting mix or field soil moist for at least 3 or 4 days prior to fumigation induces weed seed germination, increasing weed susceptibility to soil fumigants. After application, be sure that tarps are tightly sealed to retain the fumigant.

The broad-spectrum toxicity provided by fumigation can be undesirable in production systems that rely on beneficial organisms. Fumigants can temporarily raise the level of ammonia and soluble salts in soil and container mixes that include organic matter. In comparison with steam, which allows growing media to be planted within 1 day after treatment, planting may need to be delayed about 10 days to 2 weeks after removal of methyl bromide fumigation tarps to allow aeration of growing media. Posttreatment waiting periods for dazomet and metam sodium may be longer than

for methyl bromide. In addition to delayed planting, growing media may need to be leached with irrigation or aerated by cultivation prior to planting to avoid phytotoxicity to sensitive crops (Table 35) and young plants.

Fumigants can be highly toxic to people. They require stringent safety measures and their use may be restricted. A ban on methyl bromide for all uses has been proposed. Be sure the fumigant is registered for the growing situation in which you plan to use it. Follow label directions strictly; improper application is not effective and may be hazardous.

Consider alternatives before using a fumigant. Nonfumigant fungicides are available for preplant or postplant application to growing media for control of specific fungi. Also, some soil-applied fungicides control a narrow range of organisms, while others are more broad-spectrum. Narrow-range fungicides are sometimes more effective at controlling specific organisms. Consult the *UC IPM Pest Management Guidelines: Floriculture and Ornamental Nurseries* for specific chemical recommendations.

Disinfecting soilless growing media. Hydroponic systems can spread pests such as nematodes and fungal pathogens throughout the system, contaminating other plants. Steam or heat can sterilize used rock wool, clay rock pellets, coir, and other heat-tolerant growing media, but chemical disinfection of surfaces may not be sufficient to kill pathogens and other pests. Consider discarding rock wool slabs and other soilless substrates after crop harvest if heat treatment is unavailable. Rock wool is likely to harbor pests if slabs have been walked on, damaged, or exposed to unpasteurized soil; if plants grown in them were infected with root-dwelling pathogens; or if they were otherwise handled in ways likely to contaminate them.

Steam or heat sterilization of heat-tolerant soilless growing media is effective if the substrate is dry before treatment and all the material reaches 212°F (100°C) for 5 to 10 minutes. A 3-foot-high pile of rock wool slabs stacked perpendicular to each other on a pallet may need to be heated for 4 to 5 hours to ensure that all substrate reaches the desired temperature.

Sanitizing containers using heat. Most plastic can be disinfected without damaging it by using hot water up to the temperature that causes minimum softening. Remove debris

Table 35. Floriculture Crops Reported to Be Sensitive to Residue from Methyl-Bromide Fumigation.

ageratum, alyssum, antirrhinum, aster, calendula, carnation, celosia, chrysanthemum, coleus, coreopsis, datura, delphinium, dianthus, godetia, helichrysum, iberis, lobelia, matricaria, myosotis, nemesia, nierembergia, portulaca, salpiglossis, salvia, snapdragon, verbena, vinca, viola

Sensitivity to residue includes injury to transplants, reduced germination of seed planted after treatment, or both.

Source: Moorman 1990b.

such as soil, plant material, and algae and thoroughly rinse containers before disinfection. Immerse containers in hot water with a minimum temperature of 140°F (60°C) whenever possible. Containers must reach the treatment temperature for at least 1 minute; longer treatment time and higher temperatures provide more reliable control and kill more heat-resistant pests. Make sure pots, flats, and other containers are not stacked so tightly that the heat does not adequately reach all surfaces.

Disinfectants

Disinfectants are an alternative to portable steamers or hot water for decontaminating bench tops, containers, tools, and certain other equipment. Before chemical disinfection, remove debris such as soil, plant material, and algae and thoroughly rinse equipment, surfaces, and tools. Scrub plant sap from cutting blades. The effectiveness of sodium hypochlorite (commonly 0.5% bleach), quaternary ammonium compounds, alcohol, phenolic-based disinfectants (such as Lysol), and other sanitizers is reduced by soil and plant residues. If it is not necessary to rinse surfaces or equipment after disinfectant treatment, the resulting increase in disinfectant contact time generally improves pathogen control. When pruning to remove diseased plant parts, begin work on each new plant using a freshly disinfected tool while the most recently used tools are being disinfected. Tools can be soaked in disinfectant or disinfectant can be sprayed or squirted onto tools. At least 1 to 2 minutes, and possibly as much as 10 minutes, of contact time with the material between uses is required for disinfection.

Certain disinfectants such as chlorine are phytotoxic and must be rinsed away or allowed to dry before exposure to crops. Chlorine volatilizing or splashing after treatment can damage poinsettias and other crops, and it can damage clothing and break down polymers or other plastics used in containers or greenhouse coverings. Rinse, dry, and oil metal equipment and tools following treatments such as chlorine that promote rust. Protect containers and equipment from contamination during storage until they are used.

Quality Propagation Material

Many diseases can be transmitted in or on propagation material such as seeds, cuttings, and tubers. Use only high-quality stock obtained from a reputable supplier. Consider purchasing only culture-indexed or certified pathogen-free stock if available (see the chapter "Managing Pests in Flower and Nursery Crops").

Keep cuttings or other stock off the floor and ground. Do not dip or immerse cuttings unless the material contains appropriate disinfectants. Consider avoiding liquid dips entirely, as discussed in the bacterial soft rots section later in this chapter. Immersing cuttings in liquids can spread pathogens and nematodes among plants and trigger pathogen development in plants with a latent infection.

Do not interplant pathogen-free crops with plants that may be infected. Segregate new plantings by age. It is especially important to separate propagation and production plants; older plants are more likely to be infected and can serve as a source of pathogens.

Heat Treatment of Plants

Many insects, mites, nematodes, fungi, and bacteria can be killed by treating infested plants with heat. Immersing bulbs or corms in hot water has long been used to kill invertebrates and certain pathogens before planting or storage. Certain viruses can be eliminated from cuttings by heat treatment of mother plants before propagation. Treating seeds with hot water or aerated steam can eliminate bacteria and some other pathogens. See Table 9 and discussion in the chapter "Managing Pests in Flower and Nursery Crops" for a description of each treatment method, some of the pest species controlled, crops for which heat treatment is useful, and techniques for effective heat treatment of plants.

Environmental Management

A proper growing environment is critical to producing quality plants and controlling certain pathogens. This section discusses temperature, humidity, condensation, and ventilation; other environmental management considerations, including water quality, physical characteristics of growing media, air pollutants, and appropriate light are discussed in the chapter "Abiotic Disorders and Cultural Practices."

Temperature and heating. Temperature can cause abiotic injuries from freezing, frost, and inappropriate chilling (see the chapter "Abiotic Disorders and Cultural Practices"); it also influences the development of many diseases directly (Table 36) and indirectly (changes in temperature affect relative humidity). Most pathogens have specific temperature and moisture ranges within which they can infect plants and cause disease. For example, *Botrytis* species spores germinate best and cause gray mold when temperatures are between about 60° and 77°F (16° to 25°C) and free moisture is pre-

Table 36. Environmental and Cultural Factors Affecting Pathogen Infection and Development.

Factor	Effect on fungi or bacteria	
	Fungi	Bacteria
alternative crops	high	high
computerized controls	high	moderate
fertilization	variable	high
growing media	high	moderate
humidity, ventilation, condensation	high	high
irrigation	high	high
pathogen-free plants	high	high
resistant cultivars	moderate	moderate
temperature	moderate	high

sent. Some root decay and vascular wilt pathogens grow and multiply under cool conditions, but the symptoms of the diseases they cause do not become apparent until temperatures are higher, when greater demands are placed on the plant's vascular system and the plants become stressed. Effective temperature and humidity management requires good monitoring, often involving computers programmed to monitor and control the environment (Figs. 23 and 24).

Forced air, shading, and under-bench heating are common methods of controlling temperature. Central greenhouse heating systems circulate steam or hot water. Local (unit) forced-air heaters consist of a heat source (usually electricity or natural gas), a heat exchanger, and a fan. Convection heaters burn fuel and vent the resulting hot gas through long pipes that extend inside the greenhouse. Heat escapes from the surface of the pipes into the growing area before eventually being vented outside. Convection heaters can be adequate for small greenhouses if the system is designed well and maintained to prevent exhaust gas from contacting crops. Infrared radiant heaters are an energy-efficient heating method that can improve disease control. Solar, geothermal, and cogeneration (use of waste heat) are practical alternatives in certain situations.

Infrared heat. Infrared heat is an effective but little-used way to warm foliage or soil without directly heating the air. Infrared heaters emit radiant heat that is absorbed by plants, benches, and other objects. These objects give off convective heat, which warms the air. In comparison with conventional methods that warm the air in order to heat plants, radiant heat is more energy-efficient because the plants become warmer than the air, requiring about 30 to 50% less fuel in comparison with forced air or convection heaters. Air temperatures can be as much as 7°F (4°C) cooler when using infrared heat than when using conventionally heated greenhouses, and plant growth is equivalent in both systems. Infrared heating can speed crop development, prevent condensation on plants, and raise foliage temperatures above levels conducive to the development of certain pathogens. Infrared heat works best on bench or bedding crops with a uniform canopy. It does not warm the soil as well as underbench heating does.

Various types of infrared heaters are available, including equipment constructed mostly of stainless steel or aluminum and fueled by natural gas or propane. Infrared heat systems generally cost more to install than conventional systems, but this can be offset by reduced costs for energy and pathogen management.

Underbench heating. Underbench heating circulates hot water through metal, flexible rubber, or plastic heat exchangers suspended beneath benches or placed on top of benches under or among containers. This hot-water heating can also be used under rock wool. Because warmth rises,

Because warm air rises, this under-bench radiant heater through which warm water circulates can conserve energy better than heat applied overhead.

underbench heaters can provide good heat distribution throughout the greenhouse. Similar results are obtained by applying a heated solution in nutrient film hydroponics or subirrigation systems. Heating pipes can also be buried several inches below a porous concrete or gravel floor; in cold areas, a floor-heating system will require supplemental aboveground heat during winter.

Humidity. Air holds more moisture at high temperatures than at low temperatures. Because the amount of moisture air can hold is relative to temperature, the moisture content of air is measured as relative humidity (in general discussion referred to as "humidity"). If the relative humidity is high and the temperature drops sufficiently, moisture condenses from the air onto surfaces. The temperature at which this condensation occurs is called the dew point. After sunset, moisture often forms on plant parts that radiate heat and become cooler than the air. On clear nights, the period just before dawn is commonly the coolest part of the night, and dew often forms at this time.

High humidity can be caused by transpiration of plants, by evaporation from growing media and surface water, and by the weather. Managing humidity and condensation can greatly reduce disease and improve plant quality. Regularly monitor humidity, such as by using recording hydrothermographs or computerized sensors. Avoid excess irrigation, provide adequate drainage, and do not overcrowd plants. Observe how humidity varies within growing areas because of differences in ventilation, water, drainage, temperature, and other factors. Group plants in growing areas so that crops most susceptible to diseases favored by high humidity are located where humidity is lowest.

Reduce humidity and prevent condensation by increasing air movement and also by heating greenhouse air then opening vents so that the moisture-laden air escapes. A general strategy to prevent condensation, called step dehumidification, is to heat greenhouse air when humidity is high, vent the air, then close vents once the humidity drops. Repeat this process several times if necessary; lower the maximum heating temperature until both lower humidity and desired night temperatures are achieved. This process of heating and venting can be expensive, but the cost of the energy lost can be offset by reduced disease management costs and improved plant quality.

Many growers use a "purge cycle" where greenhouse air is automatically heated and vented whenever humidity reaches a set point, usually about 85 to 90% relative humidity. Computerized systems discussed later can provide better environmental control and save significant amounts of energy in comparison with simple purge cycle systems.

Condensation. Excess humidity increases the amount of condensation on the inside roof and walls of greenhouses. Condensation dripping from interior surfaces favors infection by pathogens. Excess water can excessively wet the soil below, promoting root disease. Double-layer surfaces that provide insulation, and drainage devices such as inside gutters can help control greenhouse condensation problems.

Condensation in greenhouses may be more of a problem when using DIF (the difference between day and night temperature) to regulate plant stem elongation by deliberately lowering greenhouse temperatures for several hours before and during sunrise. These lower temperatures can result in increased moisture condensation, favoring disease development. Computerized environmental monitoring and management methods are available to allow use of DIF while still effectively managing humidity.

Ventilation. Ventilation is a key method for managing growing area temperature and humidity. Gray mold, leaf spots, powdery mildew, and possibly other aerial pathogens can be controlled through ventilation or by moving air in

This propagation area is isolated from production plants to reduce pest spread from mature crops. However, water standing on the floor and algae growing on the wall where moisture condenses indicate that pathogens favored by high humidity are likely a problem in this greenhouse.

combination with temperature control to manage humidity.

Roof and sidewall vents, sidewall vents with fans, or a combination of the two, allow moist greenhouse air to be exchanged with drier, cooler outside air. Even in a closed greenhouse, horizontal air flow can lower the humidity around plant surfaces and reduce damp spots where foliar pathogens develop. Among closely spaced plants or beneath dense canopies, the relative humidity in the air can be 20% or more higher than in aisles or overhead unless plants are properly ventilated to move stagnant air. Installing relatively small circulating fans can eliminate this problem by moving the air in a circular or rotating pattern within a single greenhouse or among several connected greenhouses. Moving air causes moisture to evaporate from surfaces, drying wet leaves more quickly. The risk of spreading pathogens by moving air is relatively small compared to the benefit in reduced pathogen spore production and viability that results from air movement.

Ventilation is also needed to distribute warmed or chilled air evenly. Because warm air rises, without good ventilation the air in a greenhouse can be a much as 1°F warmer per foot (1.8°C/m) above ground level. Although heat is often applied by growers from near the roof, the heat matters most at crop level. Undesirable growth, plant stress, and economic waste occur unless temperatures are evenly distributed within growing areas.

Install efficient equipment because fans are often operated 24 hours per day. Locate each fan at least 10 to 15 feet (3–4.5 m) from walls, at least 2 feet (60 cm) above the top of the crop, about 6 to 10 feet (1.8–3 m) from the floor, and at least 1 foot (30 cm) from the roof. The overall horizontal air flow fan capacity should be about 3 to 4 cubic feet (0.09–0.12 cu m) per square foot (0.09 sq m) of growing area, with a velocity no greater than 200 feet (60 m) per minute across the plants. The optimal air movement speed is about 50 to 100 feet (15–30 m) per minute throughout the entire growing area, a gentle breeze. Use a smoke bomb to observe and measure air movement.

Increasing plant spacing improves air circulation, which immediately reduces the humidity around plants. Arrange plants in parallel rows so that fans blow air down the gap between rows. Grow plants on raised benches, where air circulation is usually better than on the ground. Use slatted or mesh bench tops to permit air to move up from beneath plants. Ridge and furrow or ebb and flow subirrigation can improve air movement through gaps commonly left among plants. Screens to exclude pests can greatly reduce ventilation unless the greenhouse is appropriately modified, such as by increasing the surface area of vents (see the chapter "Insects, Mites, and Other Invertebrates"). See the section on greenhouse cooling in the chapter "Abiotic Disorders and Cultural Practices" for more discussion of ventilation.

In fields and outdoor nurseries, the air nearest the ground is usually the warmest, although under certain frost condi-

Moving air with horizontal fans can help to control many foliar pathogens in greenhouse crops. Among closely spaced plants or beneath dense canopies, relative humidity in air can be 20% higher than in aisles or overhead unless ventilation is used to move stagnant air. Moving air also causes moisture to evaporate from surfaces, lowering the humidity on leaves.

This polyethylene tube evenly distributes warm, humidity-controlled air throughout the greenhouse. The total volume of greenhouse air must be cycled through the climate control system at intervals that vary depending on conditions. The resulting even temperatures and relatively dry air provide good growing conditions and help control many foliar diseases.

tions, the air near the ground can be the coldest. Although special tower-mounted fans are sometimes used for frost control, as discussed in the chapter "Abiotic Disorders and Cultural Practices," outdoor ventilation is managed primarily through seasonal planting and good selection of growing sites in relation to local topography and prevailing winds and other weather conditions. Windbreak plantings, screens, or structures can reduce ventilation; good weed control, increased plant spacing, and pruning or harvesting plants increase ventilation.

Positive pressure ventilation. Use positive pressure ventilation in greenhouses whenever possible to exclude pests and improve plant quality. With positive pressure, outside air is filtered and passed through a heating/cooling system before being blown into the greenhouse. The air is then evenly distributed throughout the growing area, commonly through inflatable polyethylene tubes just below the greenhouse roof. Forcing cool air downwards and allowing warm air to rise out of vents can reduce temperature differentials throughout the greenhouse. More even temperature distribution reduces plant stress and helps to avoid condensation, improving disease control. Proper air flow also provides cultural benefits, such as improved pollination and stronger stem growth resulting from mechanical air pressure. The system fan can be run even when no heating or cooling is required, providing temperature uniformity throughout the greenhouse, conserving heat, and reducing moisture condensation. Positive pressure ventilation combined with screening effectively excludes many insects that directly damage crops or vector pathogens.

Light. Sunburn, sunscald, and poor crop growth because of too much or not enough light is discussed in the chapter

"Abiotic Disorders and Cultural Practices." Although light also influences certain pathogenic diseases, there has been little research on the practicality of using light to directly control crop pathogens; light is generally managed for plant production. Using reflective mulch to reduce colonization of young field crops by pathogen-vectoring insects such as aphids and leafhoppers is one well-documented use of light manipulation. See the reflective mulches section in the chapter "Insects, Mites, and Other Invertebrates" for more information.

Ultraviolet-absorbing films. Some fungi require certain wavelengths of ultraviolet light for spore production. Special plastic coverings or vinyl films absorb or block ultraviolet (UV) light below about 360 to 380 nanometers (nm). These films may help control *Alternaria* and possibly other fungi in greenhouses by inhibiting spore formation. Because certain insects apparently use UV light to help locate their host plants, UV-absorbing plastics are also being researched for discouraging thrips, whiteflies, and other insects from entering greenhouses. There are currently few specific recommendations for manipulating UV light for pest control, but prolonging the life of plastic greenhouse coverings subject to degradation by UV may be adequate justification for using UV-absorbing films.

Computers. Special tools, equipment, and advanced technologies are increasingly important in flower and nursery crop production. Many businesses use computers to handle inventory (such as reading and tracking bar codes) and manage production, accounts receivable, and administrative functions. Plant growth models allowing "what if?" projections based on various settings for temperature, light, and other parameters are available for certain major crops.

Computers help users summarize and display scouting data, diagnose crop problems, predict development of certain diseases, time management actions, maintain plant quality, comply with regulations, and profitably produce a desired crop on schedule.

Substantial amounts of information and software programs are computer-accessible from storage devices such as diskettes, compact disks or CDs, and on-line sources. Connecting to the Internet allows prompt electronic communication (e-mail) with other connected users, and connecting to the World Wide Web (WWW or Web) portion of the Internet allows users to access university, industry, and private computers containing text, data, pictures, and software programs. Many Cooperative Extension services provide on-line information to help care for plants and diagnose, identify, and treat pest problems. Through the Internet, growers also can interact with buyers, suppliers, and other growers to conduct a great variety of business and educational activities. See the list of suggested World Wide Web sites at the back of this manual for more information.

Automated monitoring and control. Automated irrigation, fertilization, and water quality monitoring are increasingly parts of successful growers' operations. Environmental control equipment ranges from simple thermostats to highly versatile computer systems (Fig. 23, Table 37). Certain tasks cannot be done effectively without computers, such as calculating irrigation rates based on plant need and coordinating fertilization with irrigation. Automated systems can trigger frost protection systems and adjust irrigation frequency based on plants' changing water needs, such as by reducing irrigation during cool, cloudy weather. Only computers can integrate environmental sensors and controls to optimize management of multiple interrelated factors, such as temperature, relative humidity, light, and carbon dioxide levels (Fig. 24). For example, to prevent conditions conducive to gray mold infection, computers can integrate air temperature and leaf wetness to control greenhouse heating, ventilation, and irrigation systems. Computerized environmental monitoring improves scouting efficiency by indicating critical periods to inspect plants, improving control action timing, and alerting growers when to avoid cultural practices that promote disease development.

Graphical tracking or plant growth modeling and prediction are available for some major crops, including African violet, chrysanthemum, Easter lily, hydrangea, oriental lily, poinsettia, and Thanksgiving cactus. Benefits of these newer technologies include fewer production inputs such as energy, labor, water, fertilizer, and pesticides, which reduces cost; reduced water runoff, which benefits the environment and avoids violation of water quality discharge regulations; more consistent and higher quality plants; better crop timing for predictable marketing; and increased sales and profit.

Consult your Cooperative Extension advisor or competent environmental computer experts (see the list of suppli-

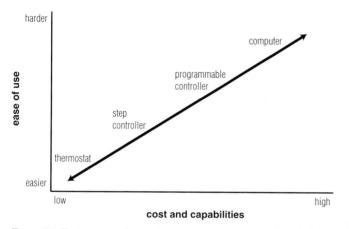

Figure 23. Environmental control systems range from simple on/off devices such as thermostats and timers to sophisticated computers. Computers can perform many tasks that simpler controllers cannot, such as integrating environmental sensors and controls to optimize management of multiple interrelated factors, including temperature, relative humidity, light, and carbon dioxide levels. However, computers can cost more to set up and operate.

Table 37. Environmental Control Equipment.

Equipment	Function	Advantages	Disadvantages
on/off controls, such as thermostats and timers	Switches equipment on and off at a specified setting.	Simple and inexpensive.	Limited abilities; cannot be integrated with other controls; cannot collect data.
controller	Integrates the operation of multiple on/off switches, allowing coordinated operation of groups of equipment; can provide successive stages of heating and cooling by turning on or off one, several, or all units to achieve specified settings.	Provides more uniform overall control than on/off switches. Step controllers are inexpensive and relatively simple to operate; programmable controllers are more versatile, can better integrate some basic functions such as temperature and time, and can collect some data.	No or limited integration with other types of control; no or limited data collection ability. Generally limited to specific predesigned tasks; settings usually must be predetermined by the grower.
computer	Provides highly integrated monitoring and control of complex and diverse equipment; collects, analyzes, and summarizes data.	Can completely integrate multiple functions (e.g., temperature, venting, lighting, irrigation, etc.); comprehensive data collection; versatile and programmable for a variety of tasks, which can be upgraded.	May or may not be less expensive or complicated to operate than programmable controllers; susceptible to moisture and other damage, so some components must be located outside the immediate growing area.

ers at the end of this manual) for help in deciding what type of computerization is appropriate for your operation.

Disease prediction. The likelihood that important diseases will occur can be predicted in certain crops based on specific information about environmental conditions, pathogen biology, and the host crop. This information has been incorporated into mathematical models in user-friendly computer software that predicts disease risk and provides control advice. Disease prediction improves scouting efficiency by

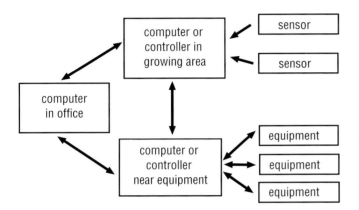

Figure 24. Many crop production activities can be monitored and managed from a central location using computers. Shown here is a generalized design of a greenhouse environmental computer monitoring and control system. Each sensor is a device specialized to monitor temperature, relative humidity, light, soil moisture, carbon dioxide levels, or another environmental condition. Equipment includes heaters, fans, irrigation valves, and motorized vents and shade screens that modify the environment. Computers use sensor information and settings selected by the grower to monitor and provide the desired growing conditions. The sensors are located in representative environments, commonly near the center of the growing area at the level of plant growing points, and not near heaters, fans, or in direct sunlight.

Good monitoring of this growing area includes yellow sticky traps for flying insects and a humidity sensor in the white cylinder. The sensor is connected to a computerized environmental monitoring and control system that includes temperature and light level sensors (not shown) that collect information used to trigger operation of heaters, ventilation fans, and motorized shade screens.

indicating critical monitoring periods; it can also reduce fungicide application frequency and improve efficacy by indicating optimal treatment timing. Disease prediction alerts growers when to avoid cultural practices that promote disease development and when to apply environmental controls that reduce infection and disease.

A generalized *Botrytis* (gray mold) prediction model is available in commercial software for use in greenhouse crops. This model is based on the fact that *Botrytis* spores can germinate only when temperatures are moderate to warm, about 60° to 77°F (16° to 25°C), and relative humidity exceeds 90% for at least several continuous hours. The risk of germination and crop infection increases the longer these conditions prevail. Combining prediction of infection risk with monitoring of spore levels or knowledge about practices that promote high airborne spore populations (spore showers) can be extremely useful in planning management activities and improving crop quality (see the section "Gray Mold," below).

Watch for development of disease prediction programs specifically for flower and nursery crops. For example, environmental monitoring can be used to help growers decide whether to treat for any of the three major foliar and flower pathogens of greenhouse cut roses (powdery mildew, downy mildew, and gray mold, Table 5). A more accurate model to predict treatment need for powdery mildew is being developed for greenhouse roses based on temperature, humidity, and leaf wetness. This rose model is adapted from models widely used by growers in California to accurately predict development of powdery mildew, downy mildew, and gray mold in grapes. Consult your Cooperative Extension advisor or environmental monitoring expert for the latest information on computerized disease prediction.

Cultural Practices

Proper cultural practices can prevent or control many pathogenic diseases. This section discusses disease management in relation to certain cultural practices; irrigation, fertilization, water quality, and related topics are discussed in this chapter, but discussion is limited to how they affect disease. The major discussion of irrigation, fertilization, water quality, and related topics is in the chapter "Abiotic Disorders and Cultural Practices." Resistant cultivars, alternative crops, crop rotation, and similar activities that help control many types of pests are among the cultural practices discussed in the chapter "Managing Pests in Flower and Nursery Crops."

Irrigation. Many diseases can be avoided by properly managing the amount, frequency, timing, and method of irrigation and also by monitoring water quality. Appropriate irrigation amounts and frequency are critical to avoiding and managing root and crown decays. Too much or too frequent irrigation promotes development of these soilborne pathogens. One irrigation strategy to reduce disease is to increase the period between watering to the maximum consistent with good growth. An alternative method is to wet soil or each container with just the amount of water and nutrients that the plant can immediately use, providing several irrigation pulses spaced throughout the day if necessary.

Overhead irrigation splashes soilborne and foliar pathogens among plants. Wet foliage promotes infection and development of many pathogens, such as anthracnose, bacterial blights, and gray mold. Disease severity is increased by systems that wet foliage frequently or for a long time because most fungi and bacteria need a minimum time of free water continuously on leaves. Keeping foliage dry and avoiding splashing water are the most effective and vital strategies to prevent and control many fungal and bacterial pathogens. Direct overhead water at the base of plants and not from above foliage and use drip or subirrigation systems whenever possible. Systems such as ebb and flow (or flood) for floors and benches, capillary mats, and shallow gutters or troughs deliver water to the bottom of containers. Because water is carried up into the root system by capillary action, foliage remains dry and pathogens are not spread by splashing water.

Systems that apply water overhead or at the top of containers flush pathogens off foliage or through growing media and out of the container bottom. If this water is recirculated, these pathogens are collected, contaminating the water that is reapplied. Bare root systems (such as aeroponics and nutrient film techniques that constantly bathe roots with recirculated nutrient solution) or improperly managed subirrigation

Rainfall and fog drip runoff from these coastal greenhouses is being collected for storage elsewhere before the water is reused on-site. This conservation method provides high-quality irrigation water.

systems can spread pathogens from one root system to another. Systems using recirculated or surface runoff water can contribute to abiotic disease induced by improper nutrients, incorrect pH, or excessive salts unless water chemistry is carefully monitored and managed.

Recirculated and reclaimed water. Flower and nursery crops are increasingly irrigated with recirculated, reclaimed, recycled, or captured water, partly to conserve water and partly to avoid problems in discharge water, such as nitrogen contamination. When using recirculated or recycled water, carefully monitor and manage water chemistry to avoid disorders induced by improper nutrients, pH, and salts (see the chapter "Abiotic Disorders and Cultural Practices"). Avoid reapplying water contaminated with soil-applied herbicides (see the chapter "Weeds").

Water that is recirculated (such as in hydroponic systems), reclaimed (such as from municipal wastewater), or drawn from surface sources (such as rivers or irrigation canals) is often contaminated with pathogens that can be applied to crops during irrigation. Some bacteria (such as *Erwinia* and *Pseudomonas* species), fungi (*Fusarium*, *Phytophthora*, *Pythium*), nematodes, and possibly certain viruses (tobacco mosaic) can be introduced to crops in recirculated water. The importance of low-level pathogen contamination of water in relation to crop disease development is not well-known. However, irrigating pathogen-free plants with *Phytophthora*- or *Pythium*-contaminated water over several weeks has been shown to cause infections on plant roots. A small number of infected plants in a nursery can release large numbers of pathogen propagules into recirculated irrigation water.

To help avoid disease problems when reusing water, purchase and grow pathogen-free stock, manage irrigation properly, and use good sanitation practices. Keep plants unstressed to avoid or reduce disease development and minimize pathogen contamination of water. Consider having water tested at regular intervals to detect pathogens, estimate their population levels and determine their seasonal fluctuations, and identify disinfection methods effective against any pathogens detected. If water is contaminated, treat it if possible. Relatively rapid treatment methods may be required while recirculating water during crop production. Slower treatment methods can be used on water held between crops.

Water treatment. Irrigation water can be treated by bromination, chlorination, heating, filtration, ozonation, and ultraviolet light. Although water treatment can be important in eliminating waterborne pathogens, there is little information regarding the practical effectiveness of economical methods to control plant pathogens in water. Water commonly contains suspended and dissolved impurities that degrade treatment efficacy, requiring treatments that are more intense, longer in duration, and more expensive. Many growers have avoided installing water treatment facilities because of the capital cost and the uncertainty regarding their efficacy, and many have increased fungicide applications instead. However, such prophylactic chemical treatments may not be a sustainable approach.

Bromine, chlorine, and ozone. Chlorine and ozone are widely used to treat large volumes of drinking water and are used by some growers to disinfect irrigation water. Some growers use bromide treatment, and hydrogen peroxide and iodine are also being studied for similar uses. These materials are strong oxidizing agents that degrade cell walls and membranes, killing microbes. Although bromine, chlorine, or ozone treatment is relatively rapid, a holding tank or reservoir may be needed to allow adequate contact time and still meet peak irrigation demands. Water may need to be exposed to these chemicals for about $1/2$ to 1 hour to achieve adequate control; the actual treatment time depends on factors such as the organic matter content, temperature, and the concentration of treatment chemical. Bromination, chlorination, and ozonation can cause air pollution hazards to workers and crops, corrode equipment, and require careful and safe use.

Chlorine gas is the cheapest method of chlorination, but it is extremely hazardous. Growers in California who store and use large amounts of chlorine are subject to stringent federal, state, and local regulations. Chlorine gas is not widely used by growers because it is highly toxic and its use is heavily regulated. Tablet and liquid bromine or chlorine are safer to use but more expensive. Because organic contaminants interfere with bromine and chlorine efficacy, water may need to be pretreated or extra bromine or chlorine may need to be added. Accumulation of bromine or chlorine salts from treated water can damage plants.

Ozone (O_3) is produced by irradiating water with a lamp emitting electromagnetic radiation at a wavelength of 185 nanometers or by passing air through a corona discharge generator, then bubbling the ozonated air through water. In comparison with bromine and chlorine, ozone may require longer contact time to be effective. Ozone gas is less hazardous than chlorine gas, and ozonation does not add salts to irrigation water. Because ozone may be more effective when applied to acidic water, some growers lower the pH before treating water. Ozonation is highly effective in low-volume irrigation systems and avoids the potential salt accumulation of bromine or chlorine.

Filtration. Activated-charcoal, sand, membranes, and certain other filters are an effective but slow water treatment method. Activated charcoal or carbon primarily removes organic compounds; used activated charcoal is classified as a hazardous waste and is expensive to dispose of. For this reason, it is rarely used on a large scale. Reverse osmosis filtration through a membrane removes pathogens and salts but

This chlorination unit is used to kill plant pathogens in surface water pumped from a stream. Chlorine is stored in the white tank in the background behind the gray water storage tank and is injected into water by the orange and gray equipment in the foreground.

also filters out returned fertilizers. Filters that allow fertilizer but not pathogens to pass through are being developed.

Low-flow filtration such as sand filtration, one of the most widely used water treatment methods, can provide relatively inexpensive treatment. Very large containers of sand (with particle sizes ranging from about 0.2 to 2 mm) act as an impact filter; particles, including fungal spores, are removed as water drains slowly down through the sand. Sand filters also serve as a substrate for colonization by beneficial microorganisms that may consume and decompose pathogens. The upper few inches of sand are periodically disposed of to remove debris, so new sand must be added when the filtration layer becomes too thin. The major disadvantage is that a large surface area of sand is required to filter a relatively small volume of water. Sand filtration is used primarily by smaller growers because of its relatively limited water capacity.

Heat. Heat kills pathogens by disrupting their membranes and proteins. About 10 seconds at 194°F (90°C) eliminates most plant-disease-causing organisms. Lower temperatures for longer times are also effective (Fig. 20). For example, *Fusarium* spores are killed by heating water for 10 minutes at 140°F (60°C) or for 40 to 60 minutes at 122°F (50°C). Heating irrigation water has been employed in the Netherlands, but it can be an expensive process. Solar energy, geothermal, waste heat, or combination systems able to treat both water and growing media can make it more cost-effective. As with most other systems, partial purification or filtration may be necessary before heating since soluble impurities can precipitate or coagulate at high temperatures, fouling heating systems.

In a typical system, recirculated water is drained into a recatching tank, which screens out organic particles. Water is then pumped to another tank and preheated through a heat exchanger. The preheated water is pumped to a second heat exchanger, where it is heated to about 200°F (94°C) for about 30 seconds. This method requires about 1 cubic foot (0.03 cu m) of natural gas to treat each 1 cubic foot of water. Alternatively, some growers pass filtered water through a single set of coils that are flame heated. This method requires only about 0.6 cubic foot (0.02 cu m) of natural gas to treat each 1 cubic foot of water, but achieves lower water temperatures, which kill most but not all pathogens.

Ultraviolet light. Ultraviolet (UV) light kills microorganisms by damaging nucleic acids (DNA and RNA). Mercury-vapor lamps emitting radiation at about 200 to 280 nanometers are a common source of UV radiation. Long lamps are encased in quartz sleeves in pipelike chambers, where water is pumped through and irradiated. The treatment dose is determined by the number and power of lamps (radiation intensity) and the rate of water flow (exposure time).

Suspended solids and dissolved organic compounds greatly reduce UV efficacy, so effective mechanical (e.g., sand filtration) or activated-charcoal pretreatment of water usually is necessary. Radiation intensity decreases sharply with increasing distance from the lamp. Because only a thin film of water can be treated at once using current technology, rapid treatment of large volumes of water is both difficult and expensive. New technologies such as UV-emitting lasers, pulsed-power, and narrow-wavelength excimer lamps are expected to improve the commercial feasibility of large-scale UV water treatment. Special care must be taken in hydroponic systems where iron chelates are used as a nutrient source; UV light can break down iron chelates, leading to iron deficiency unless iron nutrition is monitored and properly managed.

Fungicides. Many conventional pesticides available for application to foliage or growing media are not labeled for use in treating irrigation water. Pesticide rates and activity can be different in water than when used on foliage or growing media. Correct calibration and application can be difficult, and the pesticides may accumulate or interact in recirculated water, causing phytotoxicity. Because of regulatory and environmental concerns regarding surface water and groundwater contamination, few products are likely to be labeled for application to water. Because it is generally illegal to discharge pesticide- or nutrient-contaminated water, disposal of wastewater is an expensive problem. Furthermore, prophylactic chemical treatment of soil, plants, or water can be expensive and can also promote resistance to fungicides.

Drainage. Poor drainage weakens plants and favors root-infecting fungi, abiotic disorders, and increased populations of fungus gnats and shore flies. Blend appropriate ingredients and handle them properly to provide adequate aeration and drainage in container mixes. Improve field soil drainage before planting by gently grading soil surfaces, installing sub-surface drains or sumps, breaking up compacted soil layers, or sloping the base of compacted subsoils. Provide good drainage by planting in raised beds and reducing compaction by staying out of fields when soils are excessively wet. Further avoid soil compaction by minimizing traffic around plants and mulching walkways between rows. Grow container plants on benches using proper containers and well-drained growing media. For more information, see the discussion of aeration and moisture in growing media in the chapter "Abiotic Disorders and Cultural Practices."

Fertilization. Crop nutrition can affect disease development. For example, *Xanthomonas campestris* pathovars affecting English ivy, ficus, schefflera, and other crops may be less severe when crops are fertilized in excess of recommended rates. Excess fertilization also can reduce development of *Pseudomonas cichorii* affecting ficus and schefflera and *Erwinia chrysanthemi* affecting chrysanthemum and dieffenbachia. However, *Pseudomonas syringae* is more severe on impatiens and possibly other hosts when plants receive higher-than-recommended fertilizer rates. Lower fertilization may reduce development of black root rot (*Thielaviopsis basicola*) in many bedding plants. Using nitrate nitrogen instead of ammonium sources reduces *Fusarium* development in aster, chrysanthemum, gladiolus, hebe, and possibly other crops. Research has shown that silicon used as a soil drench or foliar spray can control certain pathogens even though silicon generally is not considered to be an essential plant nutrient.

In addition to pathogenic diseases, certain invertebrate pests and many abiotic disorders can be affected by fertilization rates, frequency, and timing, and by the form, source, and type of nutrients. Despite the relationships between crop nutrition and pests, the practical use of fertility management for disease control is limited because nutrition generally is optimized for good plant growth. Crop nutrition is influenced by various environmental conditions (such as temperature and light), cultural practices (such as irrigation methods, rates, and frequency), and especially by fertilization. For more information, see the sections on fertilization and nutrient disorders in the chapter "Abiotic Disorders and Cultural Practices."

Crop rotation. Rotation can reduce the potential for disease in field crops for a period of time. Rotation prevents pest population buildup and can reduce densities of soil organisms that cannot persist without hosts. Learn the persistence of disease propagules before replanting (Table 38). Rotating the site out of crops susceptible to certain diseases for that period of time may avoid disease development. For example, the resting stages of some bacterial and fungal pathogens last about 1 to 3 years. *Fusarium oxysporum* f. sp. *gladioli* affecting gladiolus, ixia, tigridia, and tritonia can be controlled by growing other crops in infested soils for 4 or more years. *Armillaria* in woody roots, *Verticillium*, and certain other

Table 38. Approximate Time Required for Rotation to Nonhost Crops or Fallowing of Fields to Control Disease Propagules in Soil or Soil Infested with Crop Residue.

Pathogen			
Common name	Scientific name	Crop	Rotation or fallow time (years)
Alternaria leaf spot	*Alternaria* spp.	many hosts	2–3
bacterial wilts[1]	*Pseudomonas, Xanthomonas* spp.	many hosts	2–3
basal rot[2]	*Fusarium oxysporum* f. sp. *narcissi*	daffodil	4
black leaf spot	*Pseudomonas syringae*	bird of paradise, larkspur, safflower, snapdragon	1–2
cottony rot	*Sclerotinia sclerotiorum*	many hosts	3
crown gall	*Agrobacterium tumefaciens*	many hosts	3
Fusarium yellows[2]	*Fusarium oxysporum* f. sp. *gladioli*	gladiolus, ixia, tigridia	4
Ramularia leaf spot	*Ramularia deusta*	sweat pea	2
scab	*Pseudomonas gladioli*	gladiolus	3
Septoria leaf spot	*Septoria* spp.	many hosts	2–3
smoulder	*Botrytis narcissicola*	daffodil	1–2
smut	*Entyloma, Urocystis* spp.	many hosts	1
Stemphylium leaf spot	*Stemphylium* sp.	gladiolus	2

1. Each *Xanthomonas* pathovar is specific to related plants and cannot infect crops in another plant family.

2. Fusarium wilt fungi are host-specific; crops from other genera will not be affected by replanting soil infested with special forms of *Fusarium* (f. sp.) infecting other genera. Some *Fusarium* f. sp. persist longer than those listed here, and short rotations against *Fusarium* affecting certain other crops may not be effective.

fungi persist in soils for many years, so short rotations do not control them.

Fallowing. Fallowing takes fields out of production temporarily. Populations of nonpersistent pathogens (Table 38), nematodes, and invertebrates that feed on roots or pupate in soil will decline or be eliminated if their host plants are not present. Fallowed fields are not planted for a period of time, and the soil usually is kept bare of vegetation through tillage, herbicides, or a combination of methods. Alternatively, cover crops (see the chapter "Weeds") or natural vegetation can be grown if the species used are known to be nonhosts of the pathogens or other pests for which fields are fallowed.

Deep plowing. Deep plowing uses modified mold board plows (such as Kverneland and Wilcox plows) to cut and then invert furrow slices. By taking soil and surface residue from the upper profile and burying it deeper underground, pathogen inoculum and infected crop residue can be buried where it is not reached by shallow roots and can be gradually decomposed by microorganisms. Deep plowing can prevent spread of *Sclerotinia* species that lack a spore stage in California and persist only in soil. Deep plowing to incorporate debris can reduce the spread of leaf-infecting pathogens such as *Alternaria* and *Septoria* that persist in crop residue on the soil surface.

The effectiveness of deep plowing varies with the soil profile: it is effective only in deep soils. Some portion of the pathogen population will remain near the surface after plowing. Deep plowing may not be desirable if pathogens are limited to small clumps in the field; plowing infested soil will distribute pathogens more widely throughout the field. Clean equipment thoroughly before leaving the infested field.

Flooding. Flooding, preceded by incorporation of organic matter into the soil to promote anaerobic microorganism activity, has been shown to reduce *Fusarium* and *Verticillium* prior to planting cotton in the San Joaquin Valley. Before resistant cultivars were developed, flooding was widely used to control Verticillium wilt and Fusarium wilt of cotton in China and to control Fusarium wilts of banana in Central America; it may have some value in controlling these pathogens infecting field-grown flowers.

Planting time. It may be feasible to adjust the planting time of certain crops to coincide with low pathogen levels or a reduced likelihood of infection due to less-suitable weather or other conditions. The specific causes and seasonal pattern of pathogen infection and development in relation to the crop must be well-known for planting time adjustments to provide any control. There are no specific pest-management-based planting date recommendations in floriculture. However, vegetable crops susceptible to damage from silverleaf whitefly and viruses vectored by thrips are more heavily damaged if planted during the fall because populations of insect vectors outdoors are much higher during the fall than in the spring. Many flower and nursery crops are susceptible to these same pests.

Weed and Insect Control

Pasteurize, compost, or otherwise treat growing media before planting to eliminate viable weed propagules such as seeds, stolons, and rhizomes. Be aware that seeds of many weed species are killed by heat only at extreme temperatures (Fig. 20). Control weeds around growing areas because many weeds may be reservoirs of viruses or fungi such as *Botrytis* and fungi may spread from weeds to crops by wind or splashing water. Some species of aphids and thrips can spread certain viruses when they move from virus-infected weeds to crops. Leafhoppers vector aster yellows; fungus gnats may spread certain root-infecting pathogens. Even insects that do not vector pathogens can weaken or injure plants, increasing crop susceptibility to disease-producing organisms.

Biological Control

Many naturally occurring organisms and organic compounds kill or retard pathogen growth, and fungi and bacteria also are commercially available for disease control. Currently, the most practical methods for growers to control pathogens biologically are applying registered mycofungicides, composting to destroy pathogens, and producing growing media that may be disease-suppressive. Some growers who formerly relied on soil fumigation using methyl bromide have replaced most of this fumigant with using disease-suppressive compost in container mixes and ground beds. Certain commercial beneficial organisms are also available for direct application to growing media. However, effective use of soil-applied beneficial microorganisms often requires a good understanding of the ecology of the specific microbes in that soil, and this information is often lacking.

Biological control of plant pathogens can be divided into two general categories: general suppression and specific suppression. General suppression tends to be effective against pathogens that produce small propagules, such as *Pythium* and *Phytophthora* species. The infective propagules of these

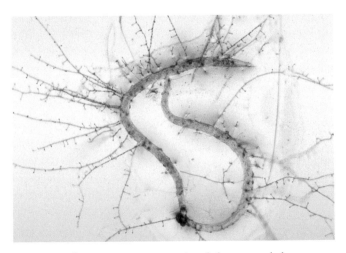

Many naturally occurring microorganisms help to control plant pathogens. The fungus *Hirsutella rhossiliensis* has killed this cyst nematode (*Heterodera* sp.). The fungal hyphae strands radiating from this dead soil-dwelling nematode develop protruding structures that produce sticky spores that attach to and infect passing nematodes.

pathogens generally require an external nutrient source (such as organic material in growing media) to germinate and cause infection. The presence of large numbers of diverse, nonpathogenic microorganisms can result in general disease suppression of these pathogens due to competition, antibiosis, or induced resistance as discussed later.

Large propagules (such as sclerotia) are produced by pathogens such as *Rhizoctonia*, *Sclerotinia*, and *Sclerotium* species. Because these infective propagules contain their own nutrient reserve, competition is relatively ineffective against them. These pathogens must instead be controlled through specific biological control mechanisms including hyperparasitism, antibiosis, and induced resistance.

Biological control agents are living organisms that must be treated differently than chemical fungicides. The products must be stored under proper conditions because viability and effectiveness can be affected by changes in the environment, such as moisture, temperature, and the presence of pesticides. The majority of chemical pesticides are most effective soon after application, then residual effectiveness gradually declines. Some biocontrol agents may also be applied in large numbers, then gradually decline. Alternatively, initial populations of some biological control agents may not provide maximum protection until some lag time after application when the beneficial organisms have reproduced and spread throughout the growing media; protection may then last for many months.

Parasitism and predation. Predation and parasitism are primarily used in the biological control of pest insects (see the chapter "Insects, Mites, and Other Invertebrates"). Predation and parasitism of microorganisms are less well-known, but it is known that certain nematodes consume root rot fungi and some microorganisms (hyperparasites or mycoparasites) consume other microbes. *Ampelomyces quisqualis* (AQ-10) applied as a foliar spray to roses and other crops infects powdery mildew fungi, reducing powdery mildew growth and eventually killing some colonies of the pathogen. *Trichoderma harzianum* (Bio-Trek), available as a seed treatment, parasitizes certain pathogenic fungi and may control *Fusarium*, *Pythium*, *Rhizoctonia*, and *Sclerotinia*. Some mycoparasites also produce antibiotics that weaken hosts before they parasitize them.

Antibiosis and antagonism. Some microorganisms can produce compounds that kill or suppress populations of other microscopic species. Streptomycin (Agrimycin-17) is a by-product of soil-dwelling *Streptomyces griseus* bacteria. Streptomycin is produced commercially as a seed dip to prevent damping-off and for use as a cutting dip or foliar spray to control bacterial leaf, stem, or wilt diseases infecting crops such as chrysanthemums, dieffenbachia, philodendrons, and roses.

Certain *Bacillus*, *Pseudomonas*, and *Streptomyces* species used as seed inoculants produce antibiotics that prevent infection by *Pythium* and *Rhizoctonia* damping-off fungi. An advantage of live biocontrol agents, in comparison with sprays or dips such as streptomycin, is that live microorganisms produce high amounts of pathogen-antagonistic compounds at the plant surface, but the overall amount released into the environment is low. This natural production reduces worker exposure and reduces the opportunities for development of chemically resistant pathogen populations.

The K-84 strain of *Agrobacterium tumefaciens* (formerly called *A. radiobacter*) is a commercially available microorganism (marketed as Galltrol) that produces an antibiotic specific against other *Agrobacterium* bacteria. Crown gall, *Agrobacterium tumefaciens*, can be prevented on most hosts by dipping roots or cuttings for 30 seconds before planting or immediately after wounding in a protective suspension of *Agrobacterium tumefaciens* K-84.

Many other promising beneficial fungi are also being evaluated. Tests on various ornamental and vegetable crops have found that *Pythium ultimum* and *Rhizoctonia solani* damping-off fungi do not cause disease if *Gliocladium* (=*Trichoderma*) *virens* and certain *Trichoderma* species fungi are added to soilless potting mixes before planting.

Competition and exclusion. Competition for moisture, nutrients, and favorable growing sites may be the most important biological control strategy for diseases. If competitor species that do not attack living plants are applied or are naturally present before the pathogen population can become high, these competitors serve as biological control agents by excluding or limiting development of the disease-causing organisms. Competition or exclusion by nonpathogenic microorganisms is effective when growing media contains a complex of active microorganisms.

For example, when organisms that cause root disease readily colonize pasteurized growing media, pathogens can quickly build up to large populations in the biological near-vacuum by acting as saprophytes feeding on the available organic matter. Applying certain nonpathogenic microorganisms to seeds or transplants or to growing media after pasteurization allows these beneficials to get a head start in colonization; through competition and exclusion these nonpathogens may prevent later-arriving pathogens from becoming abundant. These beneficial microorganisms can prevent diseases such as damping-off resulting from infection by *Pythium* and *Rhizoctonia* species. Commercial products available for use in competition and exclusion include a seed inoculant, *Bacillus subtilis* (Kodiak).

Induced resistance. Resistance to certain bacteria, fungi, and viruses can be systemically induced in plants, similar to the way humans are vaccinated against certain diseases. Some plants develop physical or chemical barriers to damage from insects or pathogens. For example, infection of gladiolus corms by the pathogen *Fusarium oxysporum* f. sp. *gladioli* can be prevented if corms have first been exposed to nonpathogenic *Fusarium moniliforme* f. sp. *subglutinans*. How resistance is induced in plants is poorly understood, and protection is often temporary or only partially effective.

Suppressive Soils

Some naturally occurring soils and peats improve plant growth despite the presence of certain plant pathogens. For example, Fusarium wilt of carnation is greatly reduced or avoided when carnations are planted in certain soils from the Salinas Valley of California. Although it is not well understood why some natural soils suppress disease, it is thought that they are effective in part because the soils contain *Pseudomonas* species or other microorganisms that induce resistance or produce natural antibiotics. Suppressive soils are sometimes ineffective when moved to a different location; on-site production of naturally suppressive growing media is a more practical approach to disease suppression in many situations, as discussed earlier in the section on disease-suppressive compost.

Mycorrhizae

Many soil-dwelling microorganisms improve plant growth in ways other than their ability to control pathogens. Mycorrhizal fungi, which occur in most flowering plants, form beneficial associations with plant roots. Mycorrhizae improve plants' ability to absorb nutrients, may aid in water uptake, and make roots more resistant to infection by certain fungi such as *Fusarium*, *Phytophthora*, and *Pythium*. Endomycorrhizae commonly form a loose mycelial growth on roots, sometimes containing visible pearl-like reproductive structures. Ectomycorrhizae commonly cause roots to appear swollen or galled.

Commercial inoculants are available for inoculating seeds or roots with spores of mycorrhizal fungi such as *Gigaspora* and *Glomus* species. Mycorrhizal fungi can be isolated from soil containing fungi known to be beneficial. Much of the study of mycorrhizal interactions has been with forest trees, and mycorrhizae are widely applied in nursery production of conifer seedlings. There are no specific recommendations for mycorrhizal use in flower and ornamental nursery crops.

Pesticides

Many flower and nursery crops can be produced at high quality with little or no fungicide use if environmental control, cultural management, good sanitation, and resistant cultivars are used. Proper management to prevent disease usually is the most effective control strategy. Although populations of gray mold and other pathogens have developed resistance to many fungicides, pesticides are available to control certain plant pathogens, primarily fungi. Consult the latest *UC IPM Pest Management Guidelines: Floriculture and Ornamental Nurseries* for recommended fungicide uses.

Fungicides require careful selection and timing to be effective. Fungicides are commonly used where disease-promoting conditions are difficult to avoid, as with the young field-grown floral crop being treated in the background behind a marigold seed crop.

Fungicides are commonly used where disease-promoting conditions cannot be avoided and crop species or cultivars highly susceptible to disease-producing agents are grown. Many fungicides only prevent infection of healthy plants, while some materials have eradicative action against certain pathogens. Fungicides require careful selection and timing to be effective. Fungicides sometimes cause phytotoxicity, discoloring plants or stunting growth.

Fungicides. Inorganics (sulfur, copper, bicarbonates), certain botanicals (neem and cinnamaldehyde), various synthetic (petroleum-derived) materials, and beneficial microorganisms (mycofungicides) are available as fungicides. Pathogen control is a relatively new use for soap, horticultural oil, neem oil, and bicarbonates. Horticultural oil, neem oil, or oil in combination with bicarbonates such as potassium bicarbonate or sodium bicarbonate (baking soda) have been shown to control powdery mildew on lilac, hydrangea, phlox, poinsettia, rose, and some other ornamental plants. Although certain antitranspirants control powdery mildew, they may not be registered (legally permitted) for pathogen control and can be phytotoxic under certain growing conditions. Check labels for registrations and contact Cooperative Extension advisors or suppliers for the latest information on new materials.

Inorganics, oil, and soap may prevent the infection of only healthy, spray-covered tissue and do not act systemically to kill existing pathogens, so repeated applications may be necessary during critical growing stages. Bordeaux mixture, fixed copper, oil, soap, and sulfur also can be damaging to some plants, particularly during warmer temperatures. Be aware that oil and sulfur in combination can be highly phytotoxic.

Sulfur. Sulfur is commonly applied to prevent (not cure or eradicate) powdery mildew, rusts, and certain leaf spot diseases (such as black spot of roses). Sulfur is applied as a dust or formulated as a flowable or wettable powder and sprayed onto foliage. Micronized (flowable) sulfur commonly provides better coverage and easier handling than other sulfur sprays or dusts to control pathogens and mites. Pure sulfur is generally suspended in air using heaters or vaporizing devices called sulfur pots. However, it is questionable whether these uses of vaporized sulfur are legal.

Lime sulfur can eradicate powdery mildew, and the residual sulfur acts as a protectant. However, lime sulfur can be quite phytotoxic to green plant tissue. Sulfur—especially lime sulfur—can damage foliage if temperatures exceed about 85°F (30°C).

Copper. Fixed coppers include cupric oxide and tribasic copper sulfate. Bordeaux mixture is a combination of bluestone (copper sulfate) and lime (calcium hydroxide). Copper fungicides prevent infection by aerial fungi and bacteria, which cause leaf spots and foliar blights. Most copper fungicides resist weathering because they are only slightly soluble in water and have an ionic attraction to plant surfaces. Copper salts of fatty and rosin acids ("organic copper") control fungal leaf spots while avoiding the visible residue that commonly results from fixed coppers. In comparison with ready-made products, Bordeaux mixture is more effective when prepared fresh and applied soon.

Synthetics. Synthetic fungicides are available for disease control as directed on the product labels. Common chemical groups for pathogen control include acylalanines, benzimidazoles (including thiophanates), sterol or demethylation inhibitors, dithiocarbamates, dicarboximides, and substituted aromatics (Fig. 25). Some synthetic fungicides have systemic activity and are often easier than inorganics to apply, are more effective, provide control at lower rates, and are less likely to damage some plants. Because legal and appropriate uses can change frequently, specific fungicides are generally not mentioned in this manual. Consult the most recent *UC IPM Pest Management Guidelines: Floriculture and Ornamental Nurseries*, other publications, professional pest control advisers, and Cooperative Extension advisors for currently registered and recommended fungicides.

Mycopesticides. Mycopesticides are commercially available beneficial microorganisms or their by-products that control pathogens. They sometimes are called mycofungicides because most products control fungi (for a discussion of how they work, see the biological control section earlier in this chapter). Because mycopesticides must be registered and labeled according to pesticide regulations, the testing requirements and available information on them may be more extensive in comparison with the microbes available in amendments or inoculants because amendments and inoculants are largely unregulated.

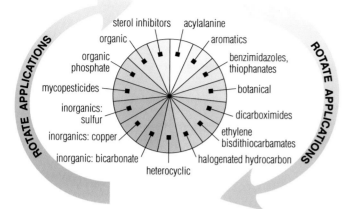

Class of Fungicides	Common Names of Some Fungicides
acylalanine	mefenoxam
aromatics	chlorothalonil, pentachloronitrobenzene, piperalin
benzimidazoles, thiophanates	thiabendazole, thiophanate-methyl
botanical	neem oil
dicarboximides	iprodione, vinclozolin
ethylene bisdithiocarbamates	mancozeb, maneb, thiram
halogenated hydrocarbon	methyl bromide
heterocyclic	captan
inorganic, bicarbonate	potassium bicarbonate
inorganics, copper	Bordeaux, copper oxides, copper sulfate
inorganics, sulfur	sulfur, lime sulfur
mycopesticides[1]	*Agrobacterium, Ampelomyces, Gliocladium, Streptomyces, Trichoderma*
organic	stylet oil
organic phosphate	fosetyl-al
sterol inhibitors	fenarimol, myclobutanil, triadimefon, triflumizole, triforine

1. These beneficial microorganisms are classified into separate genera and can prevent different pathogen problems (see Table 39).

Figure 25. The class (chart wedges) and corresponding common names (shown in table) of selected fungicides. Fungicides in the same class have a similar mode of action, and a fungus resistant to one chemical usually is cross-resistant to all other chemicals in the same class. Some pathogens, such as *Botrytis* (gray mold), have developed multiple resistance; they are resistant to chemicals from different classes. If crops are frequently sprayed, rotate applications among chemicals from three or more different classes to slow development of resistance.

Various mycopesticides are available as seed treatments, cuttings dips, or amendments to soilless mixes or organic growing media prior to or during planting (Table 39). Most only prevent disease, but some (Streptomycin) have curative action. Much work has focused on improving mycopesticide formulations. Watch for the availability of new products.

ROOT, CROWN, AND STEM DISEASES

Many fungi and some bacteria cause decay of roots, basal stems, and the crown area where roots and stems meet. The most important of these pathogens include *Phytophthora*, *Pythium*, and *Rhizoctonia* fungi, which can affect almost every flower and nursery crop species.

Damping-Off

Damping-off disease of seedlings usually results from infection by *Pythium* species and *Rhizoctonia solani*. *Alternaria*, *Botrytis*, *Fusarium*, and *Sclerotinia* species are also occasionally responsible for damping-off. Damping-off may result in decay of seeds or seedlings before emergence or, more commonly, postemergence rot at the soil line, which causes seedlings to collapse. Older seedlings infected at the soil line may remain upright but are hard, stunted, and may die.

Rhizoctonia and *Pythium* are common soil fungi discussed later in the sections on these pathogens. *Pythium* thrives under wet conditions, while *Rhizoctonia* can cause disease when conditions are somewhat drier. These fungi spread mechanically as mycelia (not common for *Pythium*), sclerotia, or resting spores in infested runoff water, growing media, and containers; they also spread in soil particles contaminating flats, tools, or baskets or in soil under benches, which may contaminate the end of a watering hose. The fungi are carried in infected plant tissue, and seeds occasionally carry damping-off pathogens. Vigorous seedlings growing under good conditions may survive in the presence of these fungi, while weaker seedlings succumb when conditions are good for disease development.

Control damping-off primarily through good sanitation, quality planting material, and proper cultural and environmental controls as summarized in Table 40. Certain composts, amendments, or mycofungicides may provide natural suppression of some damping-off fungi as discussed in the biological control and mycopesticides sections and Table 39. Sowing seed in a layer of screened light sphagnum peat, vermiculite, perlite, or sterilized and well-drained growing media also helps avoid damping-off. However, some peat moss can carry these pathogens.

Fungicide drenches are often used, but they may be phytotoxic to seedlings; it may be better to use good sanitation and proper cultural and environmental controls. Incorporation of granular fungicide in growing media before planting can also cause phytotoxicity problems with seedlings of some species, particularly if the ingredients are not well distributed through the growing media. If experience has shown

Table 39. Some Botanicals, Inorganics, and Mycopesticides for Pathogen Control.

Pesticide (trade name)	Pathogens controlled	Application methods	Crops
Agrobacterium tumefaciens (=*A. radiobacter*) strain K-84 (Galltrol-A, Norbac)	crown gall, *Agrobacterium tumefaciens*	preventive as container drench or cutting, root, or seed dip	*Prunus* and *Rosa* spp. bare-root and transplant nursery stock, woody ornamentals
Ampelomyces quisqualis (AQ-10)	powdery mildew	foliar spray at the first signs of powdery mildew	rose, field, and greenhouse flowering herbaceous and woody ornamentals
Bacillus subtilis (Kodiak)	damping-off fungi, including *Pythium*	seed inoculant	all agricultural seeds
copper, complex (Phyton 27) or hydroxide (Kocide, Nu-Cop)	Botrytis blight, downy mildew, powdery mildew	preventive foliar spray	herbaceous, foliage, and woody ornamentals
cinnamaldehyde (Cinnacure, Cinnamite, No Mas)	powdery mildew	foliar application	roses, bedding plants, container stock, flowers, nursery trees
Gliocladium virens GL-21 (SoilGard)	*Pythium* and *Rhizoctonia*	preventive as granule incorporation in soil or soilless growing media with incubation for about 1 day before planting	bulbs, potted plants, rooted cuttings, seeds, tissue culture transplants
lime sulfur	powdery mildew	mostly eradicant foliar spray with some protectant properties	not for use in greenhouses
neem oil (Triact)	black spot, downy mildew, powdery mildew, rust	mostly eradicant foliar spray with some protectant properties	field and nursery foliage, flowering ornamentals
oil (JMS Stylet Oil, Sunspray)	powdery mildew	foliar spray	chrysanthemum, dieffenbachia, philodendron, poinsettia, and roses
potassium bicarbonate (Kaligreen)	powdery mildew	eradicant foliar spray	roses
soap (M-Pede, Safecide)	powdery mildew	mostly eradicant foliar spray with some protectant properties	herbaceous, foliage, and woody ornamentals
Streptomycin (Agri-Mycin 17)	bacterial blights, cankers, leaf spots and wilts; crown gall	curative as cutting dip, foliar spray	herbaceous ornamentals and foliage plants, including chrysanthemum, dieffenbachia, philodendron, and rose
sulfur	powdery mildew, rusts	dust, wettable foliar spray	roses
Trichoderma harzianum, T. polysporum, T. viride (Bio-Trek, Planter Box, RootShield)	*Pythium, Phytophthora, Rhizoctonia,* damping-off and certain other soil-borne fungi	seed and bulb dip, soil drench, granule incorporation	greenhouse and nursery herbaceous and woody ornamentals

Consult a current label for approved uses of these pesticides. For example, greenhouse must be listed on the label or the pesticide cannot be used in greenhouses.

Table 40. Cultural Practices and Environmental Conditions Affecting Damping-Off.

Cultural practice or environmental condition	Promotes damping-off	Discourages damping-off
quality of stock	dirty or pathogen-infested; weak or slow germinating seed	clean or certified pathogen-free; vigorous seed germination
planting depth	deep	appropriate depth or shallow
plant spacing	crowded, over-sowing	well-spaced; one seedling per container or cavity
growing media	pathogen-infested, fine-textured, compacted	pasteurized, mixed particle sizes, good porosity
drainage	poor; low-lying soil or poorly drained media	good; raised beds, well-drained media, level fields
containers and growing area	dirty, infested	clean, disinfected
nutrition	high nitrogen	well-balanced fertilization
irrigation	frequent, heavy application; contaminated or uncertain water quality	appropriate, some drying between applications; pathogen-free water used
environment	high humidity, low light, extreme temperatures, slow-growth conditions	moderate or low humidity, adequate light, ideal temperatures, conducive to rapid emergence
direct control	no beneficial microorganisms or fungicides used	beneficial microorganisms or pesticides used on seeds, young stock, or media

that particular plant species or cultivars are highly susceptible to damping-off, consider spot applications on just those
plants. Pay careful attention to the appropriate dosage delivery for the size of the container or bed. Make any fungicide
applications before extensive damage has occurred.

Root and Crown Decays

Pythium, *Phytophthora*, *Rhizoctonia*, and *Thielaviopsis* species
are common fungi that infect roots and crowns of plants.
Virtually all flower and nursery crops are susceptible to
attack by one or more of these pathogens. Several noninfectious or abiotic disorders also damage roots and basal stems.
Other causes of similar symptoms that may be confused with
root and crown diseases include too much or too little water,
mineral toxicity, and herbicides as discussed in the chapter
"Abiotic Disorders and Cultural Practices."

Damage
Dull-colored foliage or wilting followed by yellowing of
plants are often the first aboveground symptoms of root and
crown disease. Plants may be stunted, with noticeably smaller plants occurring only in certain spots. This is commonly
followed by the death of many of the plants. Pathogens can
be difficult to distinguish from other causes of unhealthy
plants, but in comparison with cultural or environmental
problems (Table 18), pathogens commonly do not affect all
plants to the same degree.

Aboveground symptoms are the result of dying roots and
basal stems. If root decay is not severe and conditions favor
new root growth, plants may recover and sometimes never
show aboveground symptoms. If conditions remain conducive to disease development and poor for plant growth,
aboveground symptoms become severe and plants die.

Identification and Biology
Healthy roots are firm and whitish. Infected roots and
stems often are dark, soft, decayed, break off easily, or have
brownish tips. If the outer part of the root easily pulls or
slips away from the central portion, it is likely that root
decay is present.

In woody plants, infection by *Phytophthora* (and sometimes *Pythium*) can cause distinct margins between healthy
and infected wood. Healthy wood is whitish or yellowish;
infected wood is commonly discolored brown or reddish and
looks like it is soaked with water. Woody roots decaying from
Phytophthora (and sometimes from *Pythium*) are firm and
brittle, although roots eventually soften as a result of secondary decay organisms.

It is important to know the specific genus or group of
pathogens present because most fungicides control only certain pathogens. No fungicide will be effective if root damage
is being caused by excess irrigation or other nonpathogenic
factors that also can kill roots.

A seedling decayed at the soil line from infection by a *Pythium* species
damping-off fungus. Good sanitation and proper cultural and environmental controls are the primary methods for avoiding damping-off.

Pythium and *Phytophthora* species (now considered to be
parasitic algae, not true fungi) can be difficult to identify.
They produce no fruiting bodies visible to the naked eye,
and fruiting bodies are used to identify many pathogens.
Thielaviopsis species produce a large number of dark spores,
which blacken basal stem lesions; these spores can be identified through microscopic examination by a plant pathologist. *Dematophora*, *Rhizoctonia*, *Sclerotium*, and *Sclerotinia*
species sometimes produce whitish mycelia or cottony fungal
growth around rotted basal stems.

Root and crown rot fungi are common in cultivated soils.
They spread in contaminated water, infected plant tissue,
and by movement of mycelia, sclerotia, or resting spores in
soil or other growing media. They can also spread on contaminated flats, tools, pots, baskets, benches, and the ends of
watering hoses. Propagules of some species of these fungi can
survive in soil for years.

Monitoring
Regularly (at least weekly) monitor growing areas for poor
sanitation, inadequate drainage, and inappropriate cultural
practices (especially excess irrigation), as discussed in the
sanitation and exclusion section in the chapter "Managing
Pests in Flower and Nursery Crops." Also inspect plants for
discoloring, wilting, or possible fungal growths that may
indicate advanced stages of disease development. Regularly
inspect roots of a few plants from each crop. Remove plants
from containers or gently pull away soil and examine roots
for signs of root disease. Be sure to wash your hands thoroughly or wear and discard disposable gloves after handling
diseased plants to avoid spreading pathogens.

Have damaged roots tested to determine which pathogens,
if any, are present and to help select among fungicides if
chemical treatment is planned. As with many pathogens,
confirmation of the specific pathogen present can require taking a sample of suspect tissue, culturing it on laboratory
media, then examining it under a microscope. Instead of
sending samples to a laboratory, test kits are available to identify certain pathogens.

Disease test kits. Kits for on-site pathogen testing employ a serological technique called ELISA (enzyme-linked immunosorbent assay). Separate kits are available for *Phytophthora*, *Pythium*, *Rhizoctonia*, *Xanthomonas*, and possibly other genera of pathogens. These tests can confirm pathogen presence within a few hours with no need for specialized equipment or facilities. However, caution must be exercised when using test kits. For example, because they are closely related, several species of *Pythium* also react with *Phytophthora* test kits and vice versa.

These kits are relatively simple to use (Fig. 19). Samples are collected from tissue with a viable infection. Infected tissue is ground and suspended in liquid. A few drops of this liquid are added to plastic wells, which are then incubated and rinsed with a series of solutions. If the pathogen for which the test is sensitive is present in the sample, a visible color change will occur with coatings on the inside of the plastic wells. Read *Easy On-Site Tests for Fungi and Viruses in Nurseries and Greenhouses* (Kabashima et al. 1997) for more information on properly collecting samples and interpreting the results from on-site test kits.

Management

Because pathogenic fungi are almost always present on floriculture and nursery plants, good cultural practices and sanitation are critical control measures. Avoiding excess moisture in the root zone and minimizing other plant stresses are also key management practices for most root and crown rots.

The lisianthus on the right is pale and wilted because of a *Pythium* infection that caused sparse, brown, decaying roots. Excess irrigation and poor drainage are primary causes of root and crown decays.

Pasteurize growing media before planting. Consider using disease-suppressive compost, amendments, or microorganisms as discussed in the biological control, composting, and mycopesticides sections above. Use only pathogen-free plants. Disinfect containers, tools, benches, and other materials that may contact plants. Provide good drainage, for example by using light, well-drained growing media and raised beds. Avoid overwatering. Use pathogen-free irrigation water. Rogue infected plants and prevent contaminated runoff. Control fungus gnats and shore flies and the conditions that promote their populations (see the chapter "Insects, Mites, and Other Invertebrates"); fungus gnats may spread spores or hyphae of *Pythium*, *Thielaviopsis*, and other fungi.

Chemical control may be warranted when other procedures have not been followed or if plants are especially susceptible to root and crown decays. Unlike cultural practices and sanitation, which are effective against all root and crown rots, most fungicides control only certain pathogens; proper identification of the disease-causing organisms is often necessary for effective chemical control.

Pythium Root Rots
Pythium spp.

Yellow, stunted, or wilted plants are often the first symptoms of a *Pythium* infection. *Pythium* infects young tissue, often root tips. It causes a dark brown to black wet rot that softens and disintegrates tissue. *Pythium* commonly attacks below the soil surface, spreading from root tips into primary roots and sometimes extending infection into the base of the stems. *Pythium* development is favored by wet, poorly drained conditions. Besides damaging or killing older plants, *Pythium* causes seed and seedling damping-off.

There are many species of *Pythium*; a few are beneficial parasites of pathogenic species. Among pathogenic species, some have a limited host range, while others, such as *Pythium ultimum*, have many hosts. *Pythium aphanidermatum* and some other species are active only at relatively warm temperatures, above 77°F (25°C). Many other species are active only when soil is cool. Pathogenic *Pythium* species are present in practically all cultivated soils, and a field may contain several different pathogenic *Pythium* species.

Use pathogen-free growing media, plants, water, and equipment to avoid *Pythium* contamination. Provide good drainage. Avoid anything that may weaken plants, making them more susceptible to infection, including too much or too little water or nutrients and extreme temperatures (Table 40). Fungicides, where necessary, including some mycofungicides (Table 39) can help prevent infection by *Pythium*. See the water treatment section for suggestions on managing *Pythium* species, which are common in surface and recirculated water.

Phytophthora Root and Crown Rots
Phytophthora spp.

Phytophthora infection may cause leaves to discolor, wilt, and drop prematurely. Infected plants are stunted, stems die back, and the entire plant may be killed. *Pythium* and *Phytophthora* are related; they thrive under wet conditions, often have the same hosts, produce the same symptoms, and can occur together. *Phytophthora* can directly infect stems and larger roots and very commonly infects the crown area, especially in woody plants. Depending on the species, *Phytophthora* may infect only small feeder roots or rootlets, major roots, or all roots and the crown. Under wet conditions, aerial parts including branches and roots also can be infected. All *Phytophthora* species require high soil moisture, but temperature requirements vary. *Phytophthora cinnamomi* develops rapidly during warm, moist conditions. *Phytophthora cactorum* requires cool, moist conditions.

Symptoms of *Phytophthora* infection depend on the environment and the pathogen and host plant species. On woody plants, a vertical discoloring, stain, or canker is commonly visible on infected trunks. Depending on the host plant, black or reddish sap may ooze from darkened areas of infected bark. To confirm infection in woody plants, cut away the outer bark around the stain streaks or canker. Look for discolored wood and the distinct margin that may occur between infected (discolored) and healthy wood.

On herbaceous plants, *Phytophthora* can be difficult to distinguish from other pathogens that cause decayed roots. *Phytophthora* produce no fruiting bodies visible to the naked eye. Consult the chapter "Crop Tables" for plants susceptible to *Phytophthora*, primarily to *P. cinnamomi*. Use an outside laboratory or the relatively quick and simple on-site test kits to confirm pathogen identity.

Avoid Phytophthora root and crown rots by using pathogen-free growing media, plants, water, and equipment. Provide good drainage and do not overwater. The same fungicides used against *Pythium* generally have activity against *Phytophthora*. See the water treatment section for suggestions on managing *Phytophthora* species in surface and recirculated water.

Rhizoctonia Root Rot
Rhizoctonia solani

Several *Rhizoctonia* species fungi cause root rot, but the most common is *Rhizoctonia solani*. It causes wilting and death in several hundred genera of plants. *Rhizoctonia solani* is especially severe among seedlings and is one of several fungi that cause damping-off. Moist, brown lesions or cankers commonly form at the base of infected petioles or on lower stems, usually at the soil line. Crown areas decay, and roots are also sometimes infected and become dark and decayed, especially in peat-containing mixes. Decayed tissue may become

This undersized and chlorotic gerbera shows the foliage dieback characteristic of Phytophthora root rot. **Pythium** and **Phytophthora** thrive under wet conditions, often have the same hosts, produce the same symptoms, and can occur together.

Yellowing and dieback of basal periwinkle stems caused by Rhizoctonia root rot. The pathogen persists in soil, so pasteurize growing media before planting and use good sanitation practices to avoid introducing the fungus.

covered with white, cottony fungal growth, but this cottony growth is uncommon with Rhizoctonia root rot.

Rhizoctonia root rot is favored by relatively high temperatures and intermediate moisture, neither too wet nor too dry. The fungus persists in growing media and is common in many soils. In addition to outside laboratory testing, quick

Basal stem canker on a periwinkle typical of that caused by **Rhizoctonia solani**. Pasteurizing growing media and using good sanitation can often prevent development of this pathogen.

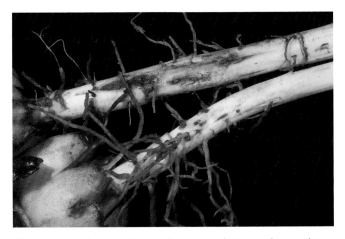

Rhizoctonia species typically cause brown stem lesions such as on this Oriental lily. The fungus causes wilting and death of plants in several hundred genera.

and relatively simple on-site test kits are available for confirming the presence of *Rhizoctonia*. Consider limiting use of the *Rhizoctonia* test to bench-grown crops, including most greenhouse and shadehouse plants, that are less than 1 year old and have not contacted unsterilized soil. Because many *Rhizoctonia* species are not pathogenic and the test kits currently do not distinguish between *Rhizoctonia solani* and other *Rhizoctonia* species, younger, bench-grown plants are less likely to be contaminated by nonpathogenic *Rhizoctonia* species.

Pasteurize growing media before planting and use good sanitation. To prevent damping-off, do not overirrigate; provide good drainage and avoid improper practices as summarized in Table 40. Certain fungicides are registered for control when used as soil drenches, preplant fumigants, or seed treatments. Certain beneficial microorganisms applied as soil amendments may provide natural suppression of *Rhizoctonia*, as discussed in the biological control and mycofungicides sections (Table 39). Adding composted pine or hardwood bark to container mixes has been reported elsewhere to prevent or reduce Rhizoctonia root rot, but this has not been demonstrated to be effective in California.

Thielaviopsis Root Rot
Thielaviopsis basicola (=Chalara elegans)

Stunted growth and chlorotic foliage are the aboveground symptoms of black root rot or Thielaviopsis root rot. Infected plant roots become decayed and frequently thickened. Decayed roots may be very black, but this very dark soft decay commonly occurs only in mixes containing soil. Stems below ground may develop black, longitudinal cracks. *Thielaviopsis* produces basal stem and root lesions that are drier than the stem lesions of *Rhizoctonia*. The basal lesions soon turn black because a large number of dark brown to black, barrel-shaped clamydospores are produced in the infected tissues. These spores help distinguish *Thielaviopsis basicola*, but laboratory culturing is required to positively identify this pathogen. *Thielaviopsis basicola* is more difficult to isolate than other common fungi and it may be overlooked during diagnostic laboratory culturing.

Black root rot is especially troublesome in field-grown flowers and some plugs. At least 120 species of plants in 15 families are susceptible to this pathogen. Important flower hosts include begonia, cyclamen, geranium, kalanchoe, pansy, peony, petunia, poinsettia, primula, snapdragon, sweet pea, verbena, and vinca.

Thielaviopsis spreads in infected plants, soil, water, and windblown particles. Disease development is favored by wet, cool soil and any conditions that weaken plants. Poor drainage, high pH, and possibly excess fertilization promote pathogen development. The pathogen is most active at 55° to 61°F (13° to 16°C) or cooler. It is suppressed by temperatures above 72°F (22°C). *Thielaviopsis* is virtually inactive above 86°F (30°C). Disease development is greatly reduced at pH 5.5 or below, and the pathogen is not a problem at pH 4.5 to 5.0. Many plants do not grow well under such acidic conditions, but the specific pH that inhibits black root rot can differ among plant species and cultivars; low pH that is higher than 5 may still provide control in certain crops.

Control black root rot by starting with pathogen-free plants, sterile containers, clean growing areas, and pasteurized growing media. Peat moss and other unpasteurized organic amendments may be contaminated with *Thielaviop-*

sis. Flooding fields for 3 to 6 weeks greatly reduces *Thielaviopsis basicola* in soil if temperatures are above 68°F (20°C); pathogen inoculum in soil increases during prolonged flooding if temperatures are cooler than 68°F. Use good sanitation and cull severely infected plants. Provide crops with good drainage and proper irrigation. Allow growing media to dry between irrigations. Use the lowest rate of fertilizer consistent with good plant growth. Minimize plant stress to help control this disease, especially in plug production. Benzimidazole fungicides, such as thiophanate compounds, can provide control when used as a soil drench or possibly as a heavy spray to run off.

Armillaria Root Rot
Armillaria mellea

Oak root fungus disease, also called shoestring fungus disease or Armillaria root rot, affects mostly woody plants but also affects certain herbaceous perennials. The fungus is prevalent in soils where natural forests, oaks, or other native trees once grew, such as riverbanks, former river beds, and areas subject to flooding. Flower crop hosts include amaryllis, aucuba, azalea, begonia, bird of paradise, calla, camellia, carnation, daffodil, dahlia, eucalyptus, ficus, fuchsia, gardenia, geranium, heather, hibiscus, hydrangea, jade plant, leptospermum, peony, poinsettia, prickly pear cactus, rhamnus, rose, and watsonia. Consult *Pests of Landscape Trees and Shrubs* (Dreistadt 1994) or *Resistance or Susceptibility of Certain Plants to Armillaria Root Rot* (Raabe 1979) for an extensive list of woody plant hosts.

Damage
Armillaria infects and kills cambium tissue, causing major roots and the main stem near the ground to die. The first aboveground symptoms are often undersized, discolored, and prematurely dropping leaves. Branches die, often beginning near the top of plants; on herbaceous hosts, stems become discolored and cankered. Eventually the entire plant can be killed. Young woody plants and herbaceous hosts often die quickly; mature woody plants may die quickly or slowly, depending on whether conditions are more favorable to disease development or good plant growth.

Identification and Biology
Armillaria forms characteristic white mycelial plaques that have a mushroomlike odor when fresh. Mycelia grow between the bark and wood on woody hosts and can grow through soft plant tissue and appear on the surface, especially with herbaceous hosts. These distinctive white fans are visible when the bark is removed from infected roots and the lower trunk or when fleshy tissue such as corms and tubers are opened. Dematophora root rot also causes white growths that may be confused with *Armillaria*. *Dematophora* tends to occur in smaller patches and grows throughout the wood

Armillaria root and crown rot infects many species of woody plants. White mycelial plaques of this fungus have been revealed here by cutting beneath the bark on the lower trunk just above the soil line. Because *Armillaria* persists in soil for years and is difficult to eliminate, growing resistant species is often the only effective control.

rather than just under the bark, and Dematophora root rot is less common than Armillaria root rot.

During cool, wet conditions outdoors in the fall or early winter, clusters of mushrooms may form at the base of *Armillaria*-infected woody plants. *Armillaria* mushrooms are honey yellow to brown and 1 to 10 inches (2.5–25 cm) in diameter. They have a ring on the stalk just under the cap, and white spores are shed from this cap.

Armillaria frequently produces rootlike structures (rhizomorphs) that attach to the surface of roots or the root crown. Rhizomorphs have a black to dark reddish brown surface. When pulled from their host or pulled apart, their cottony interior becomes visible. When similar-sized roots are pulled apart for comparison, the roots have a more solid, woody interior than do rhizomorphs.

Armillaria thrives under moist conditions. Plants become infected through root contact with infected roots or when healthy roots contact rhizomorphs attached to infected roots. *Armillaria* rhizomorphs do not grow through the soil. The fungus can survive for many years in dead or living roots of woody plants. Armillaria root rot can develop slowly, and symptoms may not appear until the fungus is well established.

Management
Preventing infection of new plants and planting resistant species are the only effective controls for *Armillaria*. Where Armillaria root rot has been a problem, consider avoiding field plantings of susceptible crops. Consult *Resistance or Susceptibility of Certain Plants to Armillaria Root Rot* (Raabe 1979) or the chapter "Crop Tables" to identify crops not reported as susceptible to *Armillaria* and consider planting

these alternative crops. Because general plant health and care greatly influence disease susceptibility, lists of crops reported as susceptible or resistant provide only a general guideline to the likelihood of disease. Reduce disease susceptibility by providing plants with appropriate cultural care, especially proper irrigation and adequate drainage.

Use pathogen-free stock and pasteurize growing media before planting to avoid infection in container-grown ornamentals. Fumigants and other methods of pasteurization before planting provide some control in the field, but fumigation of field soil usually does not kill the fungus in all roots, especially those deeper in soil. Prepare the site well if infested soils must be replanted with susceptible crops. Remove as many roots as possible that are $\frac{1}{2}$ inch (13 mm) in diameter or larger from the soil before planting because these can harbor *Armillaria*. Before replanting or using chemical or heat pasteurization, aerate and air-dry the soil by deep tilling once or more during dry weather. Before any heat or chemical treatment, soil should be moist and warm.

No chemicals are available to cure *Armillaria*-infected plants. In established vineyards and orchards, sublethal heating of infested roots via solarization has helped to control *Armillaria mellea*. Sublethal heating weakens the *Armillaria* pathogen enough to allow biological control by *Trichoderma viride* and other heat-resistant beneficial microorganisms. There are no reports of this method's effectiveness in flower or nursery crops.

Dematophora causes whitish growth beneath bark and on bark and growing media around the base of a trunk. Minimize Dematophora root rot by pasteurizing growing media, using pathogen-free stock and good sanitation, providing good drainage, and avoiding excess irrigation.

Dematophora Root Rot
Dematophora (=Rosellinia) necatrix

Dematophora root rot, also called white root rot, is less common than other soilborne pathogens, but it rapidly kills plants when it occurs. Ornamental nursery hosts of Dematophora root rot include ceanothus, cotoneaster, holly, and viburnum. Notable flower hosts are iris and peony.

After infection by Dematophora root rot, just a portion of the plant canopy or the entire plant will yellow, wilt, and turn brown. Stems killed by *Dematophora* fungi often retain dry foliage. A white mycelial mat may be visible around lower stems or in soil growing over infected roots. Minute white growths may be visible beneath the bark and in the wood of infected woody plants. These whitish patches are much smaller than *Armillaria* mycelia and lack the characteristic mushroomlike odor produced by *Armillaria*. If soil is excavated, white strands can be observed growing from *Dematophora*-infected roots into the adjoining soil. A dark crust may also form over dead roots or around the crown.

Dematophora root rot is most active during mild, wet conditions. It infects primarily through healthy roots growing near infested plants or in infested growing media. When *Dematophora*-infected tissue is sealed in a moist chamber, such as plastic bag or jar, it produces a distinctive white fluff within a few days. However, if *Dematophora* is suspected, it is best to seek expert confirmation promptly.

Minimize Dematophora root rot by pasteurizing growing media, using pathogen-free stock, providing good drainage, and avoiding excess irrigation. Use good sanitation and immediately rogue infected plants. If soil will be replanted, remove soil around the infected plants that were rogued and replace it with pathogen-free soil because *Dematophora* can grow through the soil. No chemicals have been found to be effective against this pathogen.

Bacterial Soft Rots
Erwinia spp.

Erwinia species including *Erwinia carotovora* and *E. chrysanthemi* are common soft rot bacteria that infect flower and vegetable crops. Flower hosts include African violet, agapanthus, aglaonema, amaryllis, begonia, calla, Christmas cactus, chrysanthemum, cyclamen, daffodil, dahlia, dieffenbachia, dracaena, freesia, hyacinth, impatiens, iris, larkspur, Marguerite daisy, orchids, philodendron, poinsettia, statice, stock, and tulip.

Soft rot bacteria cause infected tissue to turn brown, become mushy, and develop a very disagreeable odor. Succulent stems such as cuttings, and corms and tubers in storage or in the field, are commonly affected. Stem tissue turns brown and deteriorates near the soil. Plants grow slowly and seedlings collapse. The bacteria spread in water and can persist in undecomposed organic debris and in symptomless host plants. High temperatures and high humidity favor disease development.

Use disease-free cuttings, corms, and other stock. Avoid planting too deeply. Provide good drainage. Do not overwater. Bacteria commonly infect through wounds, so avoid injuring plants. Reduce infections in corms and tubers by keeping humidity and temperatures low during storage. Regularly inspect crops for disease and immediately rogue infected plants when you find them. Avoid using liquid cutting dips, such as growth regulators or rooting hormones, even if they contain a compatible antibiotic. Read the bacterial wilts section below for more details on managing bacterial pathogens.

Some cultivars are more susceptible to bacterial rots than others. For example, 'Red Torch,' 'Tempo,' and 'Tempter' chrysanthemums are more susceptible to soft rot than many other cultivars. Seek information on resistant cultivars (Table 13) and consider planting them.

Cottony Rot
Sclerotinia spp.

Cottony rot, also called Sclerotinia rot or white mold, forms mostly on herbaceous plants in several dozen genera of flower crops. The most common causal fungus, *Sclerotinia sclerotiorum*, is also a primary pathogen of many vegetables including carrot, celery, and lettuce. Several other less common *Sclerotium* species have a more narrow host range, such as *S. bulborum* that causes black slime disease of hyacinth, iris, and narcissus bulbs.

Cottony rot produces a prominent white flocculent growth that covers infected root crowns and stems, and less commonly grows on flowers, leaves, and terminals. Plant tissue beneath the white mycelium turns soft and watery. Infected stems become bleached pale, girdled, and die. Hard black sclerotia (fungal resting bodies) form on the cottony growth or in diseased tissue, particularly in plants with hollow stems. The disease is most commonly found on the lower parts of the plant because the fungus is soilborne. Moisture or high humidity help the pathogen develop.

In the absence of a suitable host, sclerotia can survive in soil for 2 to 3 years. Sclerotia undergo a dormant period, which is broken by low temperatures. When conditions are cool and moist, plants can be directly infected from sclerotia in the soil. In spring as temperatures warm and conditions are wet, sclerotia also produce $\frac{1}{8}$- to $\frac{1}{4}$-inch (3–6-mm) diameter saucer-shaped spore-forming structures (apothecia) on stalks that forcibly discharge spores into the air. These airborne spores germinate and cause infections if they land on wet, dead, or inactive tissue, such as flower petals or injured or senescent plant parts. Once these spore-initiated infections have colonized dead or inactive tissue, the pathogen can spread and invade nearby healthy plant parts.

To kill *Sclerotinia* sclerotia, pasteurize soil before planting

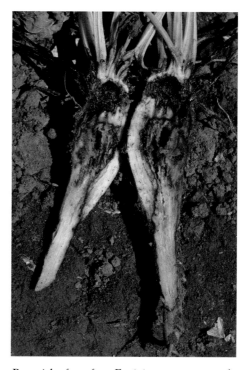

Bacterial soft rot from *Erwinia carotovora* caused this severely infected taproot to turn brown and mushy. Succulent stems such as cuttings, and corms and tubers in storage or in the field, are commonly infected.

whenever possible. Deep incorporation of plant residue, removing and disposing of debris, or rotating to nonhost crops for three years greatly reduces *Sclerotinia* levels and subsequent disease. Where feasible, avoid overhead irrigation to reduce spore production, spread, and germination; spores of the cottony rot fungus cannot infect dry or healthy plant tissue. Irrigate early in the day so plants dry quickly. Eliminating nearby weeds and avoiding planting near major vegetable crop hosts reduces incidence of the disease.

Where conditions are conducive for disease development, protective fungicides can be applied to foliage of susceptible hosts. Thorough plant coverage is essential; adding a spreader-sticker can increase fungicide effectiveness. Incorporation of appropriate fungicides into soil will inhibit germination of sclerotia.

Southern Blight
Sclerotium rolfsii

Southern blight, also called southern wilt, southern stem rot, and southern root rot, has a wide host range. Hosts include field-grown vegetables and ornamentals listed in the chapter "Crop Tables."

Initial symptoms of southern blight are similar to those of other basal stem rots, such as cottony rot and Rhizoctonia stem rot. Lower leaves yellow or wilt and basal stems decay,

White cottony hyphae and black, brown, and white mustard-seed-like sclerotia produced by tissue infected with Sclerotium root rot. Sclerotia range from about ⅟₅₀ to ⅕ inch (0.5–5 mm) in diameter, depending on the pathogen species and situation. These sclerotia are about ⅟₂₅ inch (1 mm) in diameter.

followed by collapse and death of the plant. The main diagnostic feature for southern blight is mustard-seed-like sclerotia developing in a white fungal mat. Sclerotia are ⅟₅₀ to ⅕ inch (0.5–5 mm) in diameter, round, tan to brown, and they form within abundant white hyphae or mycelia growing on decaying tissue and in and on nearby soil.

Southern blight fungus is soilborne, attacking plants at or below the soil line. In addition to persisting as sclerotia in soil, it can be carried on bulbs and other planting stock. The disease occurs mostly during summer months, being favored by warm, moist soil.

To help control southern blight, solarize or otherwise pasteurize soil before planting. Use only pathogen-free stock. Avoid overwatering and provide good soil drainage, for example, by planting in raised beds. Certain fungicides applied around plant bases before infection can prevent disease development. The fungus is killed by exposure to a temperature of 122°F (50°C) or higher for 30 minutes. Caladium tubers, iris rhizomes, gladiolus corms, and some other plants can be treated with hot water to eliminate the fungus (Table 9). Soil fumigation between crops can also provide control.

Botryosphaeria Canker and Dieback
Botryosphaeria spp.

Botryosphaeria canker and dieback develops from infection by Botryosphaeria species fungi, most often Botryosphaeria dothidea or B. ribis. Botryosphaeria affects only woody plants, including croton, eucalyptus, protea, and rose.

Botryosphaeria causes stems to discolor and die. Often only scattered branches are killed on the plant. Infected branches first turn reddish brown, then become mostly grayish brown and eventually drop their leaves. Infected stems may have cankers or exude drops of yellowish sap.

Botryosphaeria spreads in splashing water. It infects only weakened plants, often those stressed from poor environmental conditions or inadequate care. Infection commonly occurs during spring and may develop slowly for months before symptoms become visible.

To help control Botryosphaeria, keep plants vigorous. Provide good cultural care, especially proper irrigation; use drip irrigation where feasible. Rogue affected plants and dispose of crop debris away from the growing area.

Crown Gall
Agrobacterium tumefaciens

The crown gall bacterium causes distorted and gnarly growths or galls, principally on the basal stem and root crown at the soil line or just below the soil surface. Galls sometimes also form on roots, limbs, and trunks of many species of woody plants. Under moist conditions, galls may appear on upper stems or even leaves of chrysanthemum and some berry crops. Crown gall hosts include carnation, chrysanthemum, croton, dahlia, euonymus, geranium, gypsophila, Marguerite daisy, marigold, peony, rose, snapdragon, and yarrow, as well as most fruit trees and ornamental Prunus species.

Damage

Plants infected with crown gall exhibit distorted callus growth or galls on the lower stem. Roots may be gnarled, stunted, or "hairy" with mostly small rootlets. Infected plants may become distorted, grow slowly, and become stressed and susceptible to drought or other problems. Galls can crack and become colonized by secondary pathogens. Foliage of infected plants may be chlorotic and leaves may be small.

Woody plants are usually not killed by crown gall unless galls occur in the root crown area when plants are young. Crown gall appears to have a relatively minor affect in many situations once plants have become well established. If galls are large or plants are young or herbaceous, plants may be more seriously affected and possibly killed.

Identification and Biology

The surface of crown-galled tissue is usually rough. Crown galls on young plants can be tiny and smooth; galls on mature woody hosts can become massive. Secondary galls sometimes form above the sites of the primary gall on stems of certain hosts. The secondary galls are usually smaller and occur as separate or unbroken elongated masses of tissue breaking through the bark surfaces.

Galls caused by A. tumefaciens appear similar to damage caused by certain other organisms. Normal callus growth around grafts or wounds and root nodules due to nitrogen-fixing bacteria or ectomycorrhizae can resemble crown galls. Before taking any control action, determine the actual cause of galls. Consult Table 41 for a list of other causes of gall-like

Table 41. Characteristics Useful in Distinguishing among Common Causes of Galls.

Cause	Plant parts affected	Distinguishing characteristics
crown gall	basal stem, root crown; uncommon on more aerial parts	Surface same color as healthy plant tissue; swellings cannot be rubbed off of plant; surface as firm as and same color as surrounding ungalled tissue. On woody hosts, when cut with a knife, crown galls are softer than normal wood and lack the typical pattern of annual growth rings.
bacterial fasciation	crown, stems, foliage, buds	Plant often becomes extensively distorted, and secondary decay may be present; develops under wet conditions.
boring insects	roots, stems, foliage	Tunnels, frass, cast skins, or the insects themselves may be observed in and around galls; insects may be secondary, attracted to galls originally formed due to other causes.
woolly aphids	roots, bark, foliage	Whitish flocculent material around galls during certain times of the year; aphids or cast skins commonly visible.
beneficial nitrogen-fixing bacteria	roots	Galls easily rub off roots; a thumbnail can easily be pressed into galls. They occur only on plants in certain groups, especially legumes.
clubroot	roots	Plasmodium microorganisms, affects mostly *Brassica* spp. and a few flower crops such as alyssum.
ectomycorrhizae	roots	Roots appear more forked than nonmycorrhizal roots; forms a thin (1 to 40 hyphal diameters thick) white, brown, yellow, or black fungal sheath or threadlike mold growth around the outside of feeder roots and adjacent soil, which may be too small to be visible to the naked eye; when sectioned and examined under a microscope, intercellular fungus growth can be observed between epidermal and cortical cells of roots.
root knot nematodes	roots	Surface of galls is as firm as surrounding ungalled tissue; swellings cannot be rubbed off; cutting into gall may reveal pinhead-sized, shiny, white female nematodes inside, which look like tiny, pear-shaped pearls that are visible if galls are inspected through a hand lens.
gall midges, gall wasps	stems, foliage	Maggotlike insects or emergence holes present in distorted tissue. Relatively few flower hosts, common in chrysanthemum and verbena. Many woody plants host gall midges or cynipid gall wasps.
fungal leaf galls	foliage, stems	Fungi, including *Exobasidium* and *Taphrina* spp., have relatively few flower hosts; commonly found in azalea and leatherleaf fern.
eriophyid or tarsonemid mites	buds, stems, foliage	Tiny mites, cast skins, or excrement occur in and around distorted tissue. A microscope may be needed to discern mites.
sucking insects	buds, stems, terminals	Thrips, aphids, bugs, or other insects or their cast skins or excrement are present. Sucking insects commonly feed on new growth, which later distorts.

Consult the chapter "Crop Tables" to identify known hosts and help distinguish among causes of galls affecting flower crops. Consult *Pests of Landscape Trees and Shrubs* (Dreistadt 1994) for woody ornamental plants susceptible to *Agrobacterium* and other causes of galls.

plant growths. Also consult the chapter "Crop Tables" to help identify whether that crop has been reported as a host of crown gall. Send galled tissue and nearby soil samples to a laboratory for confirmation if the cause of galls is in doubt.

The crown gall bacterium is common in many agricultural soils and can persist in soils for long periods. The bacteria enter plants through wounds commonly inflicted by handling in the nursery or during transplanting. Bacteria also enter established plants when soil enters growth cracks or wounds, such as injuries caused by cultivation or pinching.

Crown gall bacteria transfer a portion of their genetic material into host plant cells, stimulating plant cambium to produce actively growing, disorganized, tumorlike tissue. Gall development is favored by rapid plant growth. Infected tissue often sloughs off plants. This causes some bacteria to contaminate soil, and this infested soil can become the source of new infections.

Crown gall often kills woody plants if they are infected while young, as with this euonymus. Sanitation is the most important management strategy. An excellent biological control agent, the K-84 strain of *Agrobacterium tumefaciens* (Galltrol, Norbac), is available for preventing crown gall before planting by dipping or spraying seeds, cuttings, or roots.

Management

Sanitation is the most important management strategy for crown gall, especially where cuttings are produced or handled. Clean tools, containers, and work surfaces frequently and treat them with a commercial disinfectant. Purchase only high-quality stock. Propagate from and grow only disease-free plants. Infected plants growing in hydroponic substrates can be a source of bacteria that can spread throughout the crop. Avoid injuring plants, especially around the soil level and when plants are wet. Rogue infected plants.

Crown gall bacteria are especially abundant where previously infected plants have grown. Where crown gall has been a problem, pasteurize soil or plant only nonhost species for at least 3 years after removing all hosts. In hot areas, solarization before planting can reduce crown gall bacteria in soil. Heat is the only effective method of soil pasteurization; common fumigants are only partially effective against crown gall.

Infection may be prevented by dipping cuttings in an antibiotic, but, dips are undesirable if plants are susceptible to other bacterial infections. An excellent biological control agent, the K-84 strain of *Agrobacterium tumefaciens*, formerly called *Agrobacterium radiobacter* (Galltrol, Norbac), is available for preventing crown gall. This biological control agent produces an antibiotic that reduces or eliminates infection by most strains of pathogenic crown gall bacteria if applied within 24 hours of wounding plants. After wounding plants and before planting, dip or spray seeds, cuttings, or roots with a solution containing K-84. *Agrobacterium tumefaciens* K-84 also can be used as a dip for ungerminated seeds or as a preventative (but not curative) soil drench.

Galls on woody plants such as roses can be eliminated by painting galls with a mixture of chemicals (marketed as Gallex) toxic to gall tissue but nontoxic to healthy woody tissue. Apply this bactericide as directed on the product label.

VASCULAR WILT DISEASES

Various fungi and bacteria cause vascular wilt disease of flower and nursery crops. *Fusarium* and *Verticillium* are the most common causes, although certain other fungi and bacteria can also cause vascular wilt. Wilt pathogens disrupt the plant's vascular system, the network of phloem and xylem tissue that transports nutrients and water among plant parts. Infected vascular tissues sometimes turn brown and xylem vessels of stems and roots may become clogged with fungal hyphae and spores, bacteria, or other substances. By interfering with the plant's distribution of nutrients and water, diseases of vascular systems cause foliage to fade green, yellow, or brown and then wilt. Wilt symptoms commonly start in scattered portions of the canopy or begin on one side of the plant. Shoots and branches eventually die and plants can be killed quickly, especially if they are young. Mature woody plants can take many years to die and may suddenly recover if conditions become favorable for plant growth and poor for disease development.

Fusarium Wilt
Fusarium oxysporum

Fusarium wilt is caused by the fungus *Fusarium oxysporum*. Although other *Fusarium* species can also cause plant disease, these other *Fusarium* species are not wilt pathogens. *Fusarium* species are divided into various special forms (f. sp.), subspecies or populations that are physiologically distinct but morphologically indistinguishable. Each f. sp. of *Fusarium* is specific to certain hosts and does not infect plants in other genera. Although Fusarium wilt infects a few woody hosts (such as conifer seedlings, hebe, and palms), Fusarium wilt affects mostly herbaceous plants. Most flower and herbaceous nursery crops are subject to infection by one or more *Fusarium* f. spp.

Damage

Fusarium wilt causes foliage to yellow, curve, wilt, then turn brown and die. Lower foliage is usually affected first. On many hosts, symptoms may appear on only one side of the plant. Plants infected when they are young often die.

Identification and Biology

Symptoms occur primarily on aboveground parts. Roots do not rot in early stages of the disease; roots rot later, when secondary pathogens become active as a result of the severe weakening of plants. Cross-sections of basal stems may reveal brown rings, vascular tissue (xylem) that has turned brown, often all the way from the shoot to the soil line. Masses of spore-bearing stalks (sporodochia) are sometimes visible on dead tissue and may look like small pink cushions.

Like *Verticillium*, *Fusarium* infects through roots by hyphae that germinate from long-lasting chlamydospores (survival

Freesia corms cut open to reveal brown vascular discoloration from *Fusarium* infection (top) compared with a healthy corm. Control Fusarium wilt through pasteurization of growing media and use of good sanitation and cultural practices.

structures) in the soil. Spores are spread on contaminated tools and workers and by splashing water. The fungus is frequently spread in infected cuttings taken from infected mother plants that appear to be healthy. Spores or microscopic bits of infected tissue often cling to seeds, infecting new plants as they germinate. Spores also can become airborne in moisture or in dust composed of infected plant debris.

Fusarium wilts are favored by warm air and soil temperatures, about 75° to 86°F (24° to 30°C). The disease may not develop at soil temperatures below about 68°F (20°C), and infected plants may remain symptomless when temperatures are low.

Management

Control Fusarium wilt through sanitation, cultural practices, and pasteurization of growing media. Choose resistant cultivars (labeled "F" or "F resistant") if available, especially for field-grown crops and perennials. Because Fusarium wilt fungi are host-specific, replant infested fields using a crop from a different genus. Rotate to other crops for 4 or more years before replanting with hosts susceptible to the *Fusarium* f. sp. infesting that soil. Provide proper cultural care to reduce crop susceptibility to infection and damage. Avoid applying excessive fertilizer, especially urea, which may promote Fusarium wilt. Soil pH higher than 6.5 may reduce incidence of Fusarium wilt in carnation and some other crops.

Pasteurize growing media before planting. Steam heat is effective in raised beds, but in ground beds steam applied at the surface does not penetrate deeply enough to provide control throughout the rooting zone. Solarization, as discussed in the chapter "Weeds," can temporarily reduce *Verticillium* and *Fusarium* fungi in the upper few inches of soil in areas with warm weather. Whether this control will be adequate depends on factors such as location and the species, rooting depth, and pathogen susceptibility of the crop.

Fumigants such as methyl bromide and basamid can provide some control, but the control may not persist long enough to prevent damage to crops that grow in field soils or ground beds for longer than about 6 to 12 months. A study of carnations that are highly susceptible to *Fusarium oxysporum* f. sp. *dianthi* found that no method (including heat or fumigation) provided 12-month control in heavily infested ground beds. Effective control was achieved only by converting ground bed production to raised beds, applying steam through pipes buried underneath beds, sanitizing irrigation systems, then tarping the surface around plants to exclude recontamination of growing media.

Verticillium Wilt
Verticillium spp.

Verticillium wilt is caused by several species and varieties of *Verticillium* fungi, most commonly *Verticillium dahliae* and *V. albo-atrum*. Verticillium wilt affects mainly herbaceous

Vascular discoloring of xylem in a woody stem infected with Verticillium wilt. Sanitation and resistant plants are the primary strategies for avoiding infection by *Verticillium*.

plants, but the fungus also occurs in many woody plants listed in *Plants Resistant or Susceptible to Verticillium Wilt* (McCain et al. 1981) and *Pests of Landscape Trees and Shrubs* (Dreistadt 1994).

Damage

Although symptoms of *Verticillium* infection depend on the host plant and environment, certain symptoms usually occur. Infected leaves wilt and turn yellow, first at the margins and between veins; foliage then turns tan or brown and dies, progressing upwards from the base to the tip of the plant or branch. Browning of older leaves while younger leaves remain green also is characteristic. Woody plants are often affected first on one side of the plant or only in scattered portions of the canopy. Water-conducting tissue in branches and stems may darken in some hosts (such as snapdragons) but not others (such as roses). *Verticillium* causes no leaf or stem lesions, and roots appear normal, although secondary decay pathogens can later become active after the plant is weakened. Infection usually occurs during cool conditions but damage may not become apparent until warm weather when plants are more stressed.

Identification and Biology

The survival structures of Verticillium wilt (microsclerotia) reside in the soil for about 4 years or longer. When it is cool and roots are present, microsclerotia germinate and hyphae grow from them. Hyphae infect plants through roots, then spread upward in the current year's growth, blocking the plant's ability to transport nutrients and water. In some (but not all) woody plants, peeling back the bark on newly infected branches may reveal dark stains following the grain on infected wood. Depending on the plant species, these stains are dark gray, black, brownish, or greenish. A laboratory culture from newly infected wood is often required to confirm the Verticillium wilt fungus.

During early stages of disease development, woody plants infected with Verticillium wilt often develop yellow or brown foliage in scattered portions of the canopy, as with this young Japanese maple.

Management

Sanitation and resistant plants (Table 42) are the primary strategies for managing Verticillium wilt. Plant only culture-indexed or pathogen-free stock. Infected plants of some types (such as chrysanthemums) often are not killed by the fungus and, during periods of rapid vegetative growth, can appear symptomless. Cuttings taken from symptomless infected plants can introduce the pathogen to new areas.

Plant in sterile soilless growing media or pasteurize media before planting. Solarization (see the chapter "Weeds") can reduce *Verticillium* and *Fusarium* fungi in the upper few inches of soil, but *Verticillium* propagules can occur down to about 16 inches (40 cm) below the soil surface. With certain crops affected by *Fusarium*, rotating fields into nonsusceptible crops can allow replanting with a susceptible crop after about 4 years (Table 38). Because fungal resting structures can persist in soil for many years, long rotations with nonsusceptible crops do not eliminate the pathogen, and susceptible crops should not be replanted there. Cover crops of cereal rye or ryegrass have helped to reduce soil levels of *Verticillium* in some vegetable crops, but the practicality and effectiveness of *Verticillium* control using cover crops has not been evaluated in flower and nursery crops.

Many crops are naturally resistant to *Verticillium* (Table 42); plant these in *Verticillium*-infested fields. Resistant strains (labeled as "V" or "V resistant") have been selected or bred for some otherwise susceptible crops, and these resistant cultivars are also a good choice. Keep plants vigorous by providing proper cultural care. Good cultural practices can allow some infected plants to perform well.

Table 42. Some Flower Crops Resistant to Verticillium Wilt.

Common name	Scientific name
African violet	*Saintpaulia ionantha*
ageratum	*Ageratum* spp.
alyssum	*Alyssum* spp.
anemone	*Anemone* spp.
baby's breath	*Gypsophila paniculata*
baby-blue-eyes	*Nemophila menziesii*
balloon flower	*Platycodon grandiflorum*
begonia, fibrous	*Begonia semperflorens*
begonia, tuberous	*Begonia tuberhybrida*
browallia	*Browallia* spp.
buttercup, Persian	*Ranunculus asiaticus*
calendula or pot marigold	*Calendula officinalis*
candytuft	*Iberis* spp.
carnation	*Dianthus caryophyllus*
Christmas rose	*Helleborus niger*
cleome	*Cleome* spp.
columbine	*Aquilegia* spp.
coral bells	*Heuchera sanguinea*
cup flower	*Nierembergia frutescens*
English daisy	*Bellis perennis*
evening primrose	*Oenothera* spp.
gaillardia	*Gaillardia* spp.
geum	*Geum* spp.
hollyhock	*Althaea rosea*
honesty or silver dollar	*Lunaria annua*
lantana	*Lantana* spp.
monkey flower	*Mimulus* spp.
moss rose	*Portulaca grandiflora*
nasturtium	*Tropaeolum majus*
nemesia	*Nemesia strumosa*
pansy or violet	*Viola* spp.
periwinkle	*Vinca minor*
potentilla	*Potentilla* spp.
primrose	*Primula* spp.
scabiosa	*Scabiosa atropurpurea*
sun rose	*Helianthemum nummularium*
sunflower	*Helianthus* spp.
sweet William	*Dianthus barbatus*
wallflower	*Erysimum* (=*Cheiranthus*) *cheiri*
wishbone plant	*Torenia fournieri*
zinnia	*Zinnia* spp.

These hosts resist infection caused by *Verticillium albo-atrum* and *V. dahliae*. Consult *Pests of Landscape Trees and Shrubs* (Dreistadt 1994) or the source of this table, *Plants Resistant or Susceptible to Verticillium Wilt* (McCain et al. 1981), for resistant woody container plants.

Bacterial Wilts

Vascular wilt disease can be caused by many pathogenic bacteria, including certain *Clavibacter* (=*Corynebacterium*), *Erwinia*, *Pseudomonas*, and *Xanthomonas* species. Pathogens that cause bacterial spots, blight, and soft rots can also cause vascular wilt if the infecting bacteria become systemic. Many wilt bacteria affecting flower crops are primarily pathogens of vegetable crops. A few species of wilt-causing bacteria affect mostly flower crops, such as *Pseudomonas caryophylii*, which causes bacterial wilt of carnation. Fireblight, caused by *Erwinia amylovora* infecting rosaceous hosts, and lilac blight, caused by *Pseudomonas syringae*, are important bacterial wilt pathogens infecting woody ornamental plants.

Damage
Wilt bacteria enter the plant's vascular system, multiply there, and interfere with the plant's translocation of water and nutrients. Symptoms include yellowing, drooping, wilting, and death of aboveground parts.

Identification and Biology
Sending samples to a diagnostic laboratory for culturing or indexing, or (in some circumstances) use of on-site test kits, are the only reliable methods for confirming the presence of bacterial pathogens. Outside laboratories can test for many of the common *Clavibacter*, *Erwinia*, *Pseudomonas*, and *Xanthomonas* species that infect flower and nursery crops, including *E. amylovora*, *E. carotova*, *E. chrysanthemi*, and the *Xanthomonas campestris* pathovars *begoniae*, *campestris*, *dieffenbachiae*, and *pelargonii*. Consider prompt use of specialized testing whenever pathogens are detected, as discussed in the root and crown decays section earlier in this chapter.

The presence of oozing liquids sometimes can be used in the field to help distinguish bacterial wilt from fungal wilt. Fungal infections usually remain confined within the vascular system until the plant dies; bacteria often dissolve cell walls early during disease development, causing plant tissue to rupture. Dark liquid may ooze from stomata, cracks, cavities, or lesions in bacteria-damaged tissue.

Cutting an infected stem with a sharp razor blade can sometimes help in diagnosis. When bacterial vascular wilts are present, a thin bridge of sticky substance often can be observed between the cut surfaces as the two pieces of stem are slowly pulled apart. If a small piece of infected stem or leaf is placed in a drop of water and viewed under a microscope, masses of bacteria may be seen flowing from the cut ends of the vascular bundles. Liquid masses of bacteria naturally exuding from plant lesions (bacterial streaming) can sometimes be observed by examining a thin slice of infected tissue using a compound microscope.

Wilt bacteria persist in infected plants, in crop debris in soil, and in or on seeds or vegetative propagation material.

They commonly enter plants through wounds or natural openings such as stomata. Most bacteria are easily spread by direct plant-to-plant contact, splashing or dripping water, infested growing media, infected plant material, during handling or on tools, and possibly by some insects or nematodes.

Management
Once plants become infected with bacteria, it's probably best to immediately rogue symptomatic plants and the plants near them before the pathogen spreads throughout the crop. Bactericides are generally of limited effectiveness; infected plants usually cannot be cured. Figure 26 outlines a general strategy for managing bacterial diseases.

Good sanitation to prevent infection is the most important management strategy for new and uninfected crops. Pasteurize growing media and containers before planting or rotate fields into nonhost crops for 2 or 3 years. Immediately dispose of crop debris away from growing areas. Reduce new infections by protecting plants from wind and rain, which often spread bacteria. Avoid spreading bacteria mechanically. Reduce infection by minimizing the length of time that foliage is wet and by reducing humidity. Minimize wounding of plants. Controlling insect or nematode vectors may help to reduce pathogen spread.

Avoid bacterial wilts by starting with pathogen-free plants. Culture-indexed stock is available for carnation, geranium, and certain other crops. Disinfect seed surfaces using heat (Table 9) or chemicals to prevent introduction of *Xanthomonas* and certain other pathogens. Copper compounds can reduce infections if they are incorporated into the container mix or soil before planting. Antibiotics can be used in dips or incorporated into container mixes. However, antibiotics are broken down rapidly when mixed into growing media, and liquid dips should be avoided as discussed

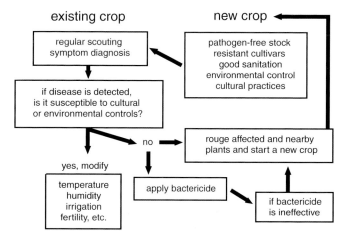

Figure 26. A general strategy for managing bacterial pathogens in flower and nursery crops.

below. Some bacteria have developed resistance to certain antibiotics and application of these materials will not prevent infection by resistant bacteria. Even if bacteria are not resistant, plants infected with bacteria usually cannot be cured with chemicals. Preventative bactericide applications may mask symptoms and still not control the disease.

Cultivars vary greatly in susceptibility to vascular wilts; consider using resistant cultivars when available (Table 13). Changing light, temperature, and fertilization can help to control certain bacterial diseases, but the specific response varies depending on the pathogen and plant species. Seek information on whether managing these factors can be helpful in your specific situation; light, temperature, and fertilization generally must be optimized for crop growth, not pathogen control.

Dips. Dipping cuttings or corms in a registered antibiotic is commonly used to help prevent disease development. *Strep-*

Dark, wilted lilac leaves and blossoms caused by Pseudomonas bacterial blight. Sending samples to a diagnostic laboratory or (in some circumstances) using on-site test kits is the only reliable method for confirming the presence of bacterial pathogens.

The presence of oozing liquids sometimes can be used in the field to help distinguish bacterial wilt from fungal wilt. Bark removed at the base of this bud reveals discolored phloem in this rosaceous plant infected by *Pseudomonas syringae*.

tomyces species mycofungicides also are available for control of *Erwinia*. Avoid using liquid cutting dips, such as growth regulators or rooting hormones, even if they contain a compatible antibiotic. Bacteria can contaminate dips and readily spread among plants during dipping, even when the initial incidence of contamination is very low. Bactericides generally are not 100% effective, and immersing cuttings with latent infection may trigger disease development. These problems are compounded because dips are often misused, for example, by not changing the solution as often as recommended because of the desire to save time or money. Dry dips are sometimes available and can avoid some of the problems associated with liquid dips.

FOLIAR AND FLOWER DISEASES

Many pathogens cause leaves or flowers to discolor, distort, wilt, or die. This section discusses gray mold, powdery mildews, leaf spots, rusts, blights, and other fungi and bacteria that infect foliage and flowers. Root, crown, and stem rots and vascular wilts discussed above also cause symptoms in aboveground parts; abiotic or noninfectious disorders, foliar- or root-feeding nematodes, invertebrates such as insects and mites, phytoplasmas, and viruses also damage foliage and flowers. It is important to identify correctly the cause of unhealthy plants in order to take effective management actions.

Gray Mold
Botrytis cinerea

Gray mold, also called Botrytis blight, attacks most flower and nursery crops. It is probably the most important pathogen affecting aboveground parts of flower crops. Gray mold usually results from infection by *Botrytis cinerea*, but several other *Botrytis* and *Botryotinia* species fungi cause similar damage to crops such as Easter lily and tulips. These pathogens are managed the same ways as *B. cinerea*.

Damage
Gray mold causes brown, water-soaked spots or decay on leaves or petals. Symptoms often start as tiny, almost translucent spots. Infected terminals and stems may be girdled and rot. Diseased tissue wilts and infected seedlings can die.

Identification and Biology
Gray mold is named for the fuzzy gray, brown, or tan spores of *Botrytis cinerea* that develop on rotted tissue when conditions are humid. Spores are produced on dark, hairlike stalks (conidiophores). Spores are readily dislodged and once airborne are the primary method of spreading the fungus (Figs. 27 and 28).

Botrytis cinerea cannot directly colonize healthy green tissue. Active, healthy tissue other than petals are seldom infected directly. Only tender plant parts (such as seedlings

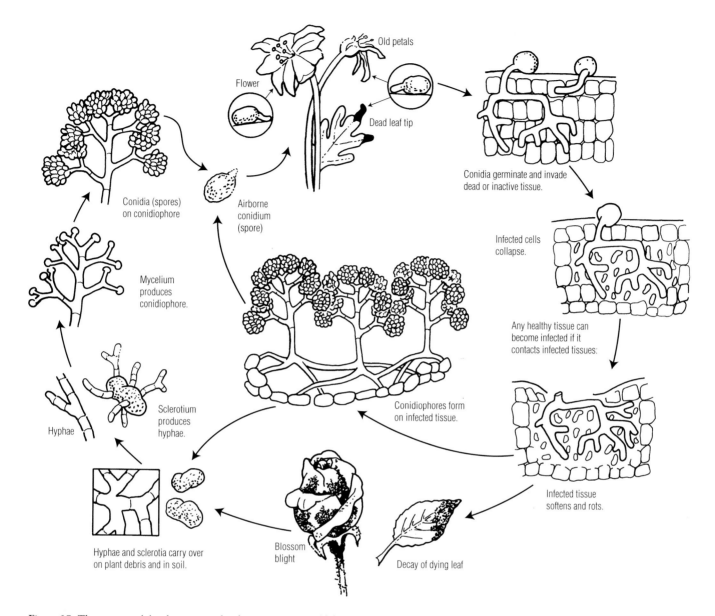

Figure 27. The stages and development cycle of common gray mold disease. Spores (conidia) can initiate infections only when they contact plant tissue that is already declining or injured (top). However, any healthy tissue can become infected if it contacts tissue that is already infected. Adapted from Agrios 1997.

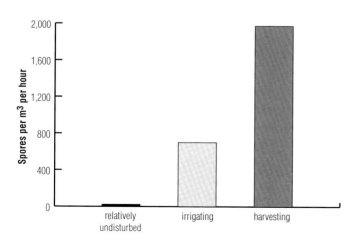

Figure 28. The approximate number of airborne gray mold spores collected during 1 hour from 1 cubic meter (35 cu ft) of greenhouse air during the production of geranium stock. Unless stringent sanitation measures are used to cull plant tissue infected with gray mold, normal cultural practices that disturb the crop can produce large numbers of airborne spores. These spore showers spread the pathogen among plants throughout the growing area. Adapted from Hausbeck and Pennypacker 1991.

and petals), weakened tissue (such as cutting stubs and tissue damaged by other pathogens), or injured, old, or dead parts are attacked on most crops. Once established, the fungus can move from an infected leaf or fallen petal and invade healthy tissue it contacts. For example, petals shed from hanging baskets can promote infection of otherwise healthy leaves on the crops below.

Moisture is the primary factor limiting this disease. Gray mold spores germinate and produce new infections only after about 6 or more consecutive hours in contact with water, including free moisture from splashing, condensation, and exudation or when relative humidity is higher than about 90%. High humidity and wet plants are common throughout the year in greenhouses. In the field in California, humidity can be high any time of year in coastal areas and high inland during the rainy season (late fall through early spring). Gray mold can grow on almost any moist, decaying, herbaceous vegetation. Other crops, landscapes, weeds, and plant debris can be pathogen reservoirs, producing gray mold spores that spread in air to crops.

The optimal temperatures for gray mold development are 60° to 77°F (16° to 25°C). Gray mold is particularly troublesome under moderate temperatures and high humidity. However, *Botrytis* is active over a broad temperature range. Refrigeration near 32°F (0°C) retards development but does not stop fungal growth. Cold-stored plants can be infected with symptomless latent infections that can develop rapidly and quickly damage plants when tissue is warmed, as often occurs during and after shipping infected plants.

Management

Good cultural practices, sanitation, and proper environmental controls are the most effective management strategies. These methods, discussed earlier in this chapter and in the chapter "Managing Pests in Flower and Nursery Crops," can virtually eliminate gray mold problems.

Sanitation. Strict sanitation is vital; abundant airborne spores develop on old or dead plants. Rogue affected plants; cull unmarketable or old blossoms, disbuds, prunings, fallen leaves, and other susceptible plant material on a frequent or daily basis during periods favorable to the disease. Dispose of plant residue in covered containers away from production areas. Refuse piles near growing areas, such as outside greenhouse vents, are a major source of *Botrytis* spores. Spores can also be carried by wind from off-site where there is no sanitation. It is difficult to eliminate all herbaceous debris that might be a source of spores, so sanitation must be ongoing and used in combination with other methods.

Botrytis spore populations can increase dramatically in growing areas during and after activities that physically disturb the crop. Hand-watering, culling, harvesting, and similar activities produce airborne spore showers; spores are knocked from infected surfaces, become airborne, and settle elsewhere throughout the crop. One study found that in comparison with an undisturbed crop, airborne gray mold spores increased over tenfold when plants were watered with drip tubes; airborne spore density increased almost a thousandfold during harvesting of plants (Fig. 28).

Because large spore showers can occur during harvest, consider holding freshly cut plants at less than 60% relative humidity for at least 1 day before shipping flowers or placing cuttings into propagation. This low-humidity holding period greatly reduces viability of *Botrytis* spores, which can germinate in fresh cutting wounds and develop rapidly under humid conditions during shipping or while rooting cuttings in dew chambers or mist benches. Make every effort throughout the production cycle to promptly remove senescing, dead, or infected plant material before abundant spores are produced.

Cultural control. Avoid overhead irrigation, especially during bloom. If plants are sprinkled or misted, do so early in the day so that plants dry as rapidly as possible and are not wet overnight. Increase the interval between irrigations to the maximum extent consistent with good growth. Group plant material by maturity and susceptibility so that older or more susceptible plants are isolated and less likely to contaminate other crops, especially young plants where disease has a long time to develop before harvest. Do not hold well-rooted cuttings in propagation areas. Once rooted, cuttings no longer require such a humid environment and commonly have senescing older leaves that are highly susceptible to infection. Remove propagative material and finished plants from shipping containers immediately.

Environmental control. Avoid temperature and moisture conditions that favor disease; moisture management is generally more practical than temperature controls. Keep relative humidity below 85% whenever possible. Do not allow plants to remain wet or humidity to remain high for more than about 5 to 6 consecutive hours. Provide good air circulation; moving air horizontally at about 30 feet per second can arrest *Botrytis* development. Reduce crowding, which improves ventilation and increases light access to plants, thereby reducing senescence of lower leaves and reducing the likelihood that shaded lower foliage will become an infected source of sporulation.

Heat greenhouses and open vents to expel moisture-laden air and reduce humidity. The energy costs of heat can be expensive, especially if not carefully managed, such as by using computerized controls. Computerized environmental monitoring and control systems are especially useful in managing gray mold while minimizing energy costs. Only computers can efficiently integrate temperature and wetness monitoring 24 hours a day to control greenhouse heating, ventilation, and irrigation systems to prevent conditions conducive to gray mold infection.

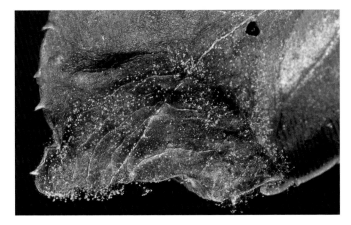

Gray mold has infected the tip of this New Guinea impatiens leaf. The fuzzy growth on the lower edge near the leaf tip is composed of minute spores developing on the end of tiny stalks. Good cultural practices, sanitation, and proper environmental controls are the most effective management strategies to prevent gray mold.

Brown, decayed snapdragon blossoms infected with gray mold. Much of this crop damage could have been prevented by heating and ventilating this greenhouse to prevent prolonged humid conditions.

Gray mold fungal spores are visible on the leaves and stem on the left. Certain crops are highly susceptible to gray mold, such as this field-grown peony.

Gray mold sporulates best under ultraviolet light (355 nm wavelength). Ultraviolet light-absorbing greenhouse coverings may help reduce pathogen infection.

Avoid shipping or storing plants in plastic or other moisture-impermeable materials. Adding packets of calcium chloride or other water absorbents to packaging may retard *Botrytis* infection of cut roses and other flowers during shipping.

Chemical control. Fungicides are commonly used in greenhouses when practices and conditions favoring disease cannot be avoided. Gray mold fungicides are only preventative and must be applied prior to infection. Improve spray coverage by not crowding plants. Treat early in the production cycle to reduce foliar infections that serve as sources that later infect petals. Target sprays later in production to protect healthy plant tissue from anticipated *Botrytis* spore showers. For example, consider applying a protective fungicide 1 to 3 days before harvesting cuttings and performing other major activities that disturb and wound plants.

Consult the latest *UC IPM Pest Management Guidelines: Floriculture and Ornamental Nurseries* for recommended fungicides. Relatively few fungicides are effective against gray mold. Many populations of *Botrytis* are resistant or insensitive to benzimidazoles (such as thiophanates) and dicarboximides. A material may not necessarily be effective against *Botrytis* just because it is registered for this pathogen. Minimize the development of resistance by relying on nonchemical methods. Apply fungicides only when necessary. If plants are sprayed frequently, retard resistance development by rotating applications among effective materials from different chemical groups (Fig. 25). Growers relying primarily on fungicides risk serious crop losses due to gray mold.

Biological control. *Trichoderma harzianum*, a black yeast (*Exophiala jeanselmei*), or a black yeast combined with a naturally occurring coryneform bacterium, reduced gray mold in experiments when sprayed onto greenhouse rose petals. These nonpathogenic microbes colonize plant surfaces and

Overcrowding plants contributes to the development and spread of gray mold. Close inspection of these potted New Guinea impatiens being grown on a gravel floor in a greenhouse would reveal that the wilted plants (center right) have become heavily infected with gray mold.

Plant debris near production areas is a major source of gray mold spores and other pests. Promptly remove crop residue and compost or dispose of it away from crops.

through competition prevent gray mold from developing on dead or dying tissue. There are many reports from Europe of beneficial *Trichoderma* species sprayed in the field onto grapes and vegetables during flowering to reduce gray mold infection. However, gray mold control has been inconsistent using biological control, and there may be no mycofungicides registered for gray mold control in California.

Powdery Mildews

Powdery mildews are a group of fungi that produce gray or white powdery growth on leaves and sometimes on other green plant parts. Many nursery and flower crops are suscep-

tible to one or more genera and species of powdery mildew. For example, species of *Erysiphe*, *Leveillula* and *Sphaerotheca* are found principally on herbaceous plants. *Microsphaera*, *Podosphaera*, *Phyllactinia*, and *Uncinula* species infect primarily woody plants.

Damage

Powdery mildew may have little affect on the plant, or the damage may be significant and cause infected leaves to distort, discolor, dry, and drop prematurely. Powdery mildews exist only in living tissue and many have evolved to avoid seriously damaging their hosts. Many powdery mildews cause only whitish discoloring, which may not be a problem unless present on marketed plant parts. Other powdery mildews grow extensively into tissue and slowly debilitate their hosts. The type and severity of symptoms depend on the species or cultivar of the host plant, the age of tissue when infected, environmental conditions, and the specific powdery mildew species involved.

Identification and Biology

Powdery mildew is usually recognized by whitish powder or light-colored mats of spores that are produced on vegetative strands growing on plant surfaces. New, developing infections are often bright white while older infections are often grayish. Some powdery mildews form fungal threads with spores on short, erect branches that resemble tiny chains when viewed through a hand lens. However, under some conditions, threads are so sparse that the mildew can be detected only by examination under strong light with a dissecting microscope.

The microscopic structure of sexual spore cases (cleistothecia) is used by plant pathologists to discriminate one genus of powdery mildew from another. If only asexual spores (conidia) are present, some powdery mildews are identified as *Oidium* species because asexual spore characteristics can rarely be used to distinguish one genera of powdery mildew from another. The specific powdery mildew present is usually identified in the field by using a list of known hosts such as that provided in the chapter "Crop Tables." Each powdery mildew is specialized to infect only hosts in one genus or family; infection cannot spread to plant species in other families. For example, *Sphaerotheca pannosa* infects only certain plants in the rose family (roses and stone fruits) and *Sphaerotheca pannosa* var. *rosae* infects only roses. Most Asteraceae can be infected by *Erysiphe cichoracearum*. Because the family Asteraceae (formerly called Compositae) includes many crop genera and species, this powdery mildew has a relatively large number of hosts.

All powdery mildews are managed in the same way, so it is generally not necessary to identify the species present. Do learn whether the crop species is highly susceptible to powdery mildew, because some plants are severely damaged by these fungi (requiring immediate action), while other crop

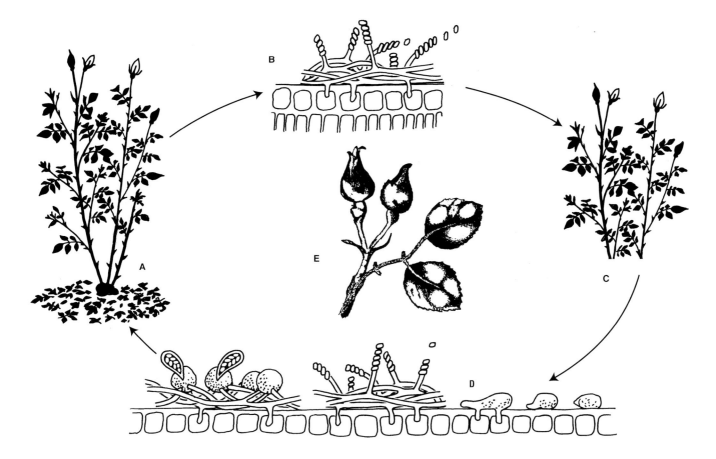

Figure 29. Life cycle and stages (magnified) of a typical powdery mildew, illustrated with *Sphaerotheca pannosa* infecting rose. A. The fungus persists in infected buds, canes, and fallen leaves. B. Hyphae develop from infected plant tissue and produce terminal conidia (asexual spores). C. New growth becomes infected. D. Sources of infection are airborne conidia that land and germinate (right) and growth from adjoining tissue by hyphae (center), which also develop more conidia. Cleistothecia (ascospore-forming structures) may also be produced (left). However, in California sexual reproduction is uncommon with many powdery mildews so cleistothecia are rarely seen. E. Powdery fungal growth is often visible on the surface of infected leaves and sepals and occasionally on petals (not shown).

species or cultivars are more tolerant. It also is critical to determine correctly whether the problem is actually powdery mildew and not other fungi (such as downy mildew) or materials (such as spray residue, irrigation salts, or insect excrement) that resemble powdery mildew.

Powdery mildews are favored by shade or low light. Greenhouses are often ideal for their development. Outdoors, powdery mildews are particularly severe in semiarid areas, such as most of California, and are less troublesome in high-rainfall areas. Powdery mildews are favored by warm days and cool nights; at leaf temperatures above 90°F (32°C) some powdery mildew spores and mycelia are killed.

Powdery mildews are obligate parasites and do not require plant stress or injury to infect hosts. Powdery mildews spread by windborne spores. Unlike most other fungi, no external moisture is required for spore germination; the presence of free water can actually reduce germination and kill some spores. Powdery mildews survive in the absence of susceptible hosts by forming a sexual stage (cleistothecium) that is resistant to drying. On roses and many perennial plants,

mycelia can survive in dormant buds and on woody stems until foliage develops and environmental conditions become suitable for disease development (Fig. 29).

Management

Monitor crops regularly for the presence of powdery mildew and for conditions that promote its development. Widespread, serious infections that appear to develop explosively almost overnight in crops such as poinsettia are the result of undetected low-level infections that spread spores throughout the crop. Manage powdery mildew in established plantings primarily through early detection, sanitation, cultural control, environmental control, and fungicides.

Cultural control. Rogue infected plants or prune out diseased tissue where feasible to reduce spore production and spread. It is probably best to prune or rogue powdery mildew-infected plants when plants are wet, unless other foliar diseases that spread and infect plants when tissue is wet or wounded are a concern in that crop. In some crops such as poinsettia, diligently removing and immediately bagging infected leaves is an important control measure.

Overhead sprinkling or syringing plants with water can reduce infection; powdery mildew spores cannot germinate when plants are wet, and some spores are killed by moisture. However, sprinkling foliage can promote other diseases, so consider the other problems to which the crop is susceptible when deciding if overhead watering is appropriate. Powdery mildew conidia spores are produced in a diurnal cycle and released early in the morning. If plants are sprinkled, do so only from morning through midafternoon; overhead water will be most effective during this period, and this timing allows plants to dry before nightfall, reducing the likelihood that sprinkling will promote other diseases.

The best control is through the use of resistant species or cultivars. Resistant cultivars have been identified for a few flower and nursery crops (Table 13); however, despite its effectiveness and great potential, relatively little attention has been paid to developing flower cultivars resistant to powdery mildew. Seek the latest information on resistance from suppliers or Cooperative Extension advisors. Develop your own information through regular monitoring and good record keeping, comparing the relative extent of disease development when different cultivars are grown together.

Environmental control. To reduce the incidence of powdery mildew, plant in a sunny or well-lit location. Although spores can germinate and infect under relatively low humid-ity, some powdery mildews develop more rapidly and prolifically at higher humidities. Avoid overcrowding plants; provide good air movement. Horizontal fans provide good control of powdery mildew infecting certain greenhouse-grown crops such as roses. Read the ventilation and humidity sections earlier in this chapter for information on effective environmental controls.

Chemical control. Fungicide application to highly susceptible crops may be warranted at the earliest signs of disease. Once powdery mildew growth is extensive, it is usually too late for fungicides to prevent damage. Most fungicides act primarily as either an eradicant or protectant. Protectants prevent powdery mildew from damaging healthy, treated foliage. Protectants such as sulfur have no eradicant ability and cannot stop tissue from being damaged if it is already infected when treated. Eradicants can stop pathogen development and prevent further damage when applied to infected tissue. Materials such as piperalin that are only eradicants do not prevent healthy tissue from becoming infected in the future. Certain synthetic materials (such as thiophanate-methyls) have some activity as both protectants and eradicants if they are thoroughly applied, often in combination with a surfactant to achieve good wetting. Few if any materials perform very well both as eradicants and protectants. Some materials are phytotoxic to blossoms or bracts in color. Some powdery mildews have developed resistance to certain fungicides.

Pale whitish growth on the upper leaf surface of poinsettia resulting from the growth of powdery mildew *(Erysiphe euphorbiae)*. Early detection and prompt action before the disease becomes widespread are critical to avoiding extensive powdery mildew damage. Yellow spots on the leaf on the right are an early symptom of infection.

Powdery mildew usually does not damage flowers. These pink aster blossoms are not infected even though fungal growth heavily covers the stems and leaves.

At least one mycofungicide is registered for powdery mildew control in greenhouses, nurseries, and field-grown ornamentals and is used by some rose growers and others. *Ampelomyces quisqualis* (AQ-10) is a nonpathogenic, beneficial fungus that acts as a hyperparasite or mycoparasite of powdery mildew fungi, reducing powdery mildew growth and eventually killing some colonies of the pathogen. Apply this mycofungicide at the earliest signs of disease, before powdery mildew becomes extensive. Because it is a fungus, *Ampelomyces* is not compatible with certain fungicides, such as dithiocarbamates and sulfur. Consult a current label and product representatives for more information.

Cinnamaldehyde (Cinnacure, Cinnamite, No Mas), a botanical, is registered for powdery mildew control on roses and other ornamental crops. Cinnamaldehyde also controls certain invertebrates, including aphids and mites.

Sulfur may be the most commonly used protectant fungicide. Regular sulfur use often can prevent powdery mildew from becoming a serious problem. Sulfur's effectiveness increases with increasing temperature, but plant damage may result if temperatures exceed about 85°F (29°C). As with other protectants, repeated applications are generally necessary to protect new growth and to renew deposits removed by rain or irrigation. Sulfur is applied as a dust or wet spray (flowable or wettable powder formulation). Some greenhouse growers heat pure sulfur in vaporizers (sulfur pots) or, in cold areas, paint a slurry of sulfur in water onto steam heating pipes, from which sulfur vaporizes. It is questionable whether these vaporized sulfur uses are legal.

Lime-sulfur has eradicant action, and the residual sulfur provides some protection. However, the residue can be unsightly. Lime-sulfur can damage plants if temperatures exceed about 85°F (29°C), and certain crops are affected even below that temperature.

Certain oils (e.g., JMS Stylet Oil) can provide good powdery mildew control. Potassium bicarbonate or sodium bicarbonate (baking soda) in combination with horticultural oil have controlled powdery mildew on lilac, hydrangea, phlox, poinsettia, rose, and certain other crops. Potassium salts of fatty acids, also called soaps (M-Pede, Safecide), can reduce powdery mildew development. Neem oil and soap have primarily eradicant properties, but also provide some protection. Be aware that oil and sulfur in combination can be highly phytotoxic.

Antitranspirants have provided some protectant control of powdery mildews in certain crops. However, antitranspirants may not be registered for this use and can be phytotoxic under certain growing conditions. Check labels for permitted uses. Consult the latest *UC IPM Pest Management Guidelines: Floriculture and Ornamental Nurseries* for fungicide recommendations and watch for new fungicide registrations and information.

Downy Mildews

Downy mildews are primarily foliage blights that affect many ornamentals, grains, and vegetables. *Peronospora* and *Plasmopara* species commonly infect flower crops, most often when they are grown in the field.

Downy mildew is named for its soft and fluffy gray, purplish, or light brown sporulation on the underside of leaves and sometimes on stems or buds. Pale yellow areas or irregular purplish red to dark brown necrotic lesions are sometimes visible on the upper surface of infected leaves. In certain plant species, the fungus can become systemic when young shoots are infected, resulting in stunted, malformed, yellowish growth. Infected plants usually do not die, but sometimes they defoliate.

Downy mildew can be confused with powdery mildew. However, grayish downy mildew patches are almost always limited to the underside of leaves, while powdery mildew growth is common on both sides of the leaf, and in general, the whitish to gray growth is more extensive and prominent with powdery mildew than with downy mildew. The conditions conducive to development of these diseases are very different. Downy mildews are favored by low temperatures. High relative humidity (≥90%) or free moisture is required for downy mildew spores to germinate and infect plants. Powdery mildew development is retarded when foliage is wet.

Downy mildew spores are produced only on living plants. Spores usually are short-lived; under ideal cool, moist conditions, spores may persist for several days. Spores become airborne and after landing on a susceptible host they germinate and infect within 8 to 12 hours if free water is present. In the absence of a live host, downy mildew fungi can produce persistent spores that resist drying. Infection is sometimes carried in seeds or bulbs.

A magnified view of downy mildew on the underside of a leaf. Unlike powdery mildew, which commonly produces pale, powdery growth on extensive areas on both sides of leaves, the grayish patches caused by downy mildew are almost always limited to the underside of leaves, and the grayish growth is less extensive.

Downy mildew sometimes causes pale yellow blotches or irregular brown to purplish red necrotic lesions on the upper surface of infected leaves. To avoid downy mildew, keep foliage dry, provide good air circulation, and maintain low humidity.

This blackish sooty mold on ceanothus grows on honeydew secreted by plant-juice-sucking insects such as aphids, mealybugs, scales, and whiteflies. Sooty mold can be controlled by managing the insect pests.

Pale brown spots with purplish margins on sweet William leaves caused by the fungus *Mycosphaerella dianthi*. To avoid fungal leaf spots, pasteurize growing media, use pathogen-free stock and good sanitation, maintain low humidity, and keep foliage dry.

To control downy mildew, provide good air circulation and maintain low humidity, as discussed in the humidity and ventilation sections above. Avoid wetting foliage; use drip instead of overhead irrigation where feasible. Immediately rogue affected plants to reduce disease inoculum. Several fungicides can prevent infection of healthy tissue, and fungicide use may be necessary to prevent damage to susceptible crops if conditions are good for disease development. Downy mildew eradicant fungicides are available, but registrations may be limited and resistance is becoming a problem.

Sooty Molds

Sooty molds are dark fungi that grow on plant surfaces that have become covered with honeydew excreted by insects such as aphids, mealybugs, scales, and whiteflies. Sugary material secreted by certain plants is also a substrate for sooty mold growth. Sooty mold is generally harmless to plants, except when it is extremely abundant and prevents enough light from reaching leaf surfaces, causing plants to become stressed. Sooty mold itself normally is not a problem unless it occurs on marketable portions of the plant. The presence of sooty mold indicates that insects were abundant or may need to be controlled.

If sooty mold is extensive, do not apply fungicides; control the insects that produce the honeydew on which sooty mold grows. Insecticidal soap, horticultural oil, and many other insecticides control most exposed-feeding, plant-juice-sucking insects, as discussed in the chapter "Insects, Mites, and Other Invertebrates." A forceful stream of water can dislodge and help control many Homoptera, and water helps wash away honeydew and sooty mold.

Leaf Spots

Many pathogens, environmental conditions, cultural practices, and certain invertebrates cause leaf spots. Table 43 lists some common causes of leaf spots, which are discussed in those sections in this manual. This section discusses fungi and bacteria that cause leaf spots, blotches, blight, and some other symptoms. Key management practices include good sanitation, keeping foliage dry, and managing humidity, for example, by adequately spacing plants, and heating and venting moist greenhouse air around sunset.

Fungal Leaf Spots

Most flower and nursery crops are susceptible to one or more species of fungi that cause leaf spots or blight. This section discusses *Alternaria*, *Septoria*, *Heterosporium* species, and a group of fungi that produce anthracnose diseases. Other common fungi that cause leaf spots include *Ascochyta*, *Colletotrichum*, *Cercospora*, *Curvularia*, *Drechslera*, *Entomosporium*, *Gloeosporium*, *Mycosphaerella*, *Phomopsis*, *Phyllosticta*,

Table 43. Some Causes of Leaf Spots and Irregular Discoloring or Necrosis of Foliage.

Cause	Comments
air pollution	Problem where air quality is poor in the field or in greenhouses, e.g., from heater emissions or volatile chemicals.
anthracnose	Commonly conspicuous tan to brown spots or irregular dead areas, promoted by moisture during new growth.
bacterial spots	Spots commonly have vein-limited, different-colored margins; dark, liquid exudate common if conditions are wet.
chewing insects	Insect presence or insect by-products usually help to identify.
edema	Blisters or pimplelike lesions. A noninfectious disorder of uncertain cause that may develop under moist conditions when growing media is warm and air is cool.
eriophyid mites	Tiny elongated mites barely visible with a hand lens.
foliar nematodes	Damage commonly progresses upward from base of plants; restricted by veins so damage appears angular; microscopic roundworms occur in foliage. Relatively uncommon in California.
fungal leaf spots	Spots usually circular and commonly have distinct margins and different-colored borders; older plant parts are commonly affected first.
mites	Minute pale speckling of foliage; fine webbing or tiny mites may be present.
pesticide injury	Commonly caused by insecticides, but fungicides and herbicides also can damage plants.
rusts	Orange, yellow, brown, or purple spore masses usually present on leaf undersides.
scale insects	Do not resemble most other insects; usually legless, immobile, roundish, and convex or flattened. Unlike causal agents of disease, tiny sucking insects can usually be scraped off plant surface.
sucking insects	Feeding damage, excrement, or cast skins; presence of aphids, lace bugs, plant bugs, shore flies, thrips or other insects usually helps to identify.
sunburn	Yellow or brown areas beginning between leaf veins; plants drought-stressed.
viruses	Foliage or flowers may be discolored, distorted, mottled, streaked, or stunted.
water deficiency	Often begins as yellow or brown area between leaf veins; foliage may be wilted or off-color and dull green.

Biotic causes often are host-specific. See the chapter "Crop Tables" for help in diagnosis.

Septoria, and *Stagonospora* species; they have similar biology and management as the fungi discussed here.

Leaf spot fungi primarily cause circular to irregular brown, yellow, reddish, or black spots or blotches on leaves and sometimes on stems. Spots often have a distinct margin and may be bordered by lighter or darker discoloring. Centers of spots are frequently dead. Infected leaves may show spots or may wilt, dry, and die. Blossoms and young stems are also sometimes affected and may become spotted or wilted and die. Only portions of the plant, such as lower leaves or new leaves, may show symptoms, or the entire plant may be affected and die, especially when plants are young.

Alternaria

Alternaria species infect the leaves, stems, and flowers of many annual plants. Infection commonly causes numerous dark brown to black spots on each infected leaf. Spots may develop in concentric rings or appear targetlike, although viruses and bacteria can also cause targetlike leaf spots. As the disease progresses, the plant may appear yellowish and leaves may dry or drop prematurely. Stem lesions or cankers may develop, sometimes girdling and killing stems and sometimes causing damping-off of seedlings, which collapse near the soil line.

Entomosporium leaf spot appears as dark brown lesions with light brown centers. Older infections cause leaves to redden and senesce. This damage to *Rhaphiolepis* in a container nursery could be avoided if foliage were kept dry, for example, by irrigating with drip emitters instead of overhead sprinklers.

Alternaria species persist in infected crops, seeds, and plant debris. Spores are carried mainly in wind currents but can also be spread among nearby plants by splashing water.

To help control *Alternaria* species, use pathogen-free stock, keep foliage dry, and use good sanitation. Consider applying protectant fungicides if disease-conducive conditions are expected to prevail, as discussed in the section on management of fungal leaf spots. Certain *Alternaria* species in the greenhouse have been drastically reduced by covering the greenhouse with special film that absorbs UV light, inhibiting *Alternaria* spore formation.

Septoria

Septoria species cause round, angular, flecked, sunken, or irregular spots mostly on older leaves. The spots usually begin as small yellowish specks that later enlarge and turn grayish, tan, or white and may eventually become dark brown or purplish. The spots are sometimes surrounded by a narrow yellow zone. The circular or irregular spots range in size from barely visible to over 1 inch (2.5 cm) in diameter. Small black spore-producing structures (pycnidia) form within the spots, appearing as dark dots. Infected leaves usually turn yellow and may wilt and die, often starting with lower foliage and progressing upward. Leaves sometimes drop because an abscission layer may form on petioles of infected leaves.

Septoria species fungi persist mainly as spores on crop debris, mycelia in plant tissue, and in or on infected seeds. Fungi spread by splashing water. Disease is most severe when wet conditions coincide with new plant growth. See the fungal leaf spot management section for suggested control methods.

Anthracnoses

Anthracnoses, often called leaf, shoot, or bud blight, are a group of diseases resulting from infection by various fungi, including *Colletotrichum*, *Discula*, *Gloeosporium*, *Glomerella*, and *Mycosphaerella* species. Anthracnoses infect many nursery and flower crops, causing conspicuous tan to brown spots or irregular dead areas on leaves or stems. Depending on the species of fungus and host plant, foliage may also distort, turn yellow, wilt, drop prematurely, or die; lesions or cankers may form on stems and crown tissue can decay. Small tan, brown,

Several genera of fungi cause leaf and shoot blights called anthracnose. This shoot dieback and midvein leaf necrosis was caused by *Discula platani* (=*Apiognomonia veneta*) infecting sycamore.

black, or tarlike spots or lesions appear on infected leaves of some hosts. If leaves are very young when infected, they may become curled and distorted, with only a portion of each leaf dying; affected leaves may look like they have been damaged by frost.

Anthracnose fungi persist primarily in infected plant parts and crop debris. On woody hosts, fungi can persist in lesions on young stems. Spores produced in infected tissues are spread readily by splashing water to nearby succulent growth. See the fungal leaf spot management section below for suggested control methods.

Heterosporium

Infection by *Heterosporium* species fungi causes disease that is sometimes called fairy-ring leaf spot or fire because infected parts may appear scorched or have distinct spots with different-colored margins. Infected foliage develops lesions and discolors, wilts, and dies back. Dark spores may be apparent within spots. On hosts such as lily, the flower buds, stems, and bulbs also may be infected. Additional hosts include carnation (where the fungus is also named *Cladosporium echinulatum*), iris (*Heterosporium gracile*, also named *Mycosphaerella macrospora*), and sweet William.

In most flower crops, each host plant genus is infected by a different species of *Heterosporium*. Fungal spores survive on living and dead leaves and on crop debris in soil, and are also spread by air. Because disease development is favored by wet, humid conditions and cool to moderate temperatures, heating greenhouses adequately to avoid overly cool temperatures provides some control.

Fungal Leaf Spot Management

Pasteurize growing media before planting. To avoid infection in young plants, use seed or other stock that is pathogen free, if available, or use treated seed. Avoid overhead watering. Keep foliage dry, as discussed in the humidity and condensation sections. Use good sanitation. Promptly remove and dispose of crop debris and diseased tissue from which fungi spread. For woody crops grown outdoors, prune and dispose of infected tissue in the fall. Rotate crops for 2 or 3 years into nonhost species to greatly reduce inoculum in fields where infected crops have grown (Table 38).

Where prolonged wet conditions favor disease development, protectant fungicide applications may help to prevent infection on many hosts if thoroughly sprayed on uninfected new growth. If fungicides are relied on for control and moist conditions prevail, additional applications may be needed at intervals to protect new growth.

Bacterial Spots and Blights

Bacterial spots and blights are often caused by various strains or pathovars (pv.) of *Pseudomonas* and *Xanthomonas*. Flower and nursery crops infected by bacterial spots and blight include anthurium, begonia, bird of paradise, cassia, cosmos, chrysanthemum, cordyline, daffodil, delphinium, dieffenbachia, geranium, gerbera, gladiolus, hibiscus, impatiens, ivy, larkspur, oleander, orchids, primrose, ranunculus, safflower, schefflera, and snapdragon.

Damage

Bacterial spots often start as tiny water-soaked areas on leaves, stems, or blossoms. Spots or blotches turn dark gray or blackish as they enlarge and sometimes have yellow borders. The initial spots are commonly circular, but because their growth is often limited by major veins, larger blotches often become angular in dicotyledonous plants, while infections in monocotyledonous plants appear as streaks or stripes. As the disease develops, spots coalesce and cause plant tissue death or necrosis (blight); growing points may turn black and die back, and cankers may form on stems, girdling and killing plants.

Under wet or humid conditions, infected tissue may exude brownish masses of bacteria, which spread and start new infections. Wet, dead tissue may tear or fall out, leaving holes and giving foliage a shredded or ragged appearance.

Identification and Biology

The specific bacteria that cause spots or blight cannot usually be positively identified in the field. Symptoms can easily be confused with those from other causes, such as foliar nematodes. Diagnosis in the field is based primarily on characteristic symptoms of bacterial infection, known-host lists such as the crop tables, and knowledge of whether previous environmental conditions or cultural practices were conducive to bacterial disease development.

In the early stages of infection before secondary organisms become common, if microscopic examination of tissue by an expert detects pathogenic bacteria and does not detect any pathogenic fungi, this indicates that bacteria are a likely cause of disease. Positive identification can be made in a laboratory using selective growth media or ELISA tests. On-site ELISA test kits may be available for certain pathovars of *Xanthomonas* or other bacteria. Care must be taken in using and interpreting the results of on-site test kits, as discussed in the virus and the root and crown decays sections of this chapter.

Bacteria persist in or on infected plants, crop debris, seeds, contaminated soil, and infested containers and equipment. Splashing water and mechanical means such as contaminated tools or workers spread bacteria to healthy tissue, where the microorganisms infect through wounds or natural openings when plant surfaces are wet.

Management

Key management practices include planting pathogen-free, resistant cultivars; using good sanitation practices; and keeping foliage dry. Use bacteria-free seed, culture-indexed cuttings, or other pathogen-free stock, if available, especially for

Foliar leaf spots caused by the bacterium *Xanthomonas campestris* pv. *pelargonii*. Geranium, like certain other crops, is highly susceptible to bacterial leaf spot when temperatures are warm and plants are irrigated overhead because splashing water readily spreads bacteria and promotes infection.

highly susceptible crops such as geranium. Heat treatment can eliminate bacteria from seed (Table 9), and certain cultivars are resistant to bacterial infection (Table 13). Do not carry over highly susceptible crops from year to year. Employ good sanitation. Thoroughly clean and disinfect growing areas between crops. Rogue infected plants immediately and promptly remove crop debris. Avoid handling plants when they are wet. Do not grow susceptible crops in hanging baskets over other hosts. For example, do not grow ivy geranium (*Pelargonium peltatum*) over zonal geranium (*P. hortorum*). Ivy geranium infected with *Xanthomonas campestris* pv. *pelargonii* often exhibits no symptoms or only mild symptoms but infected plant parts dropping from above or contaminated water draining from overhead containers can contribute to severely damaging infections of zonal or seed geraniums grown beneath hanging containers.

Avoid overhead irrigation; the bacteria are spread easily by splashing water. Consider using drip systems with individual watering tubes. Manage subirrigation systems to avoid drainage out of containers that may be contaminated. Keep foliage dry. Maintaining appropriate fertilization (not too much or too little) may help to reduce disease development.

Registered antibiotics, copper compounds including Bordeaux mixture, and certain other metal-containing fungicides can help prevent infection if thoroughly applied to cover plants and if reapplied when new growth appears. However, good sanitation and cultural practices are generally more effective, and pesticides should be employed only in combination with these other measures.

Rusts

Rusts are among the most easily recognized plant pathogens. These parasitic fungi are named for the dry, brown, orange, purple, reddish, or yellowish spore masses or pustules that many species form, commonly on lower leaf surfaces. Each species of rust is specific to a certain host genus or species and cannot spread to unrelated plants. Rust-causing fungi include *Coleosporium*, *Melampsora*, *Phragmidium*, *Puccinia*, *Pucciniastrum*, *Tranzschelia*, and *Uromyces* species.

Rusts infect many different crops, attacking mostly leaves and stems and occasionally infecting flowers. Moderate populations of rust pustules on foliage generally do not harm the plants but are aesthetically objectionable if infected parts are marketed. The upper surface of heavily infected leaves can become spotted or turn yellow or brown, and infected leaves may curl, wither, and drop prematurely. Severely infected plants may be stunted. Some rust species cause tissue swellings, galls, or cankers, especially on woody plant parts. These rusts can cause stem dieback and, rarely, can kill the entire plant.

Rusts are spread primarily by windblown spores. Spores spread only from living tissue, and plants must be wet to become infected. In addition to orangish pustules, many rusts also form black overwintering spores on leaves in the autumn that start the disease cycle in the spring. Some rusts have a complex life cycle, alternating generations between two host species. Others, such as the rose rust (*Phragmidium mucronatum*) are apparently restricted to one host species.

Rust fungi infect under mild, moist conditions. Reduce infections by minimizing the length of time that foliage is wet. Avoid overhead watering, which favors rust spore germination and spread. Alternatively, water early in the day so that plants dry more quickly. Use good sanitation; rogue affected plants or plant parts as soon as they appear and remove and dispose of infected crop debris. Prevent excess humidity, provide good air circulation, and don't crowd plants.

Some crops are resistant to rust (Table 13), including certain cultivars of larkspur and rose and a few cultivars of snapdragon. Consult suppliers or Cooperative Extension advisors for the latest information on resistant cultivars and consider using these to avoid rust problems. Certain rusts, such as geranium rust (*Puccinia pelargonii-zonalis*), may be controlled by treating cuttings with hot water; however, it can be difficult to eliminate the pathogen without causing some plant damage. Fungicides applied at the first signs of infection can also prevent serious damage from most rust fungi. Certain horticultural oils (JMS Stylet Oil), neem oil, and possibly potassium salts of fatty acids, also called soaps (M-Pede), may provide some control of rusts.

Chrysanthemum White Rust
Puccinia horiana

Chrysanthemums (*Dendranthema* spp.) are infected by two rusts. Common rust (*Puccinia chrysanthemi*) has been present throughout the United States for many years. Common rust causes powdery brown pustules on stems and both surfaces of the leaf. Infected foliage may turn yellow overall and develop yellow or brown spots, and leaves may drop. Common rust mostly causes minor damage in the field and is uncommon in greenhouses. As with most rust species, *P. chrysanthemi* is managed by resistant cultivars, sanitation, irrigation, humidity control, and fungicide applications where appropriate.

Chrysanthemum white rust (*Puccinia horiana*) is established in Asia, Europe, and South America. It is a recent introduction to the United States, where it is being subjected to an eradication program. White rust has been found infecting commercial and residential plantings of florist's chrysanthemum (*Dendranthema grandiflora*) and hardy chrysanthemum (*Chrysanthemum morifolium*) and the perennial garden plant *C. pacificum*. White rust is named for the white (sometimes pinkish or brownish) pustules it causes on leaf undersides. Chrysanthemum white rust distorts, discolors, defoliates, and kills chrysanthemums. Before pustules form and foliar damage becomes extensive, careful inspection can reveal pale green, yellow, or white spots or lesions on the upper surfaces of infected leaves. Common rust and white rust can be reliably distinguished through microscopic examination by an expert; diagnostic uredospores are found in the pustules of common rust but are absent in white rust pustules.

Where white rust occurs, it causes damage primarily in greenhouses; it usually is not damaging outdoors because direct sunlight and low humidity destroy white rust spores. However, white rust can survive outdoors where temperatures are mild and humidity is high. Residential and outdoor chrysanthemum plantings in coastal areas of California, Oregon, and Washington can serve as a reservoir of infection that is difficult to eliminate. When infection spreads from outdoors to chrysanthemums in greenhouses, crops can be devastated.

White rust in commercial plantings has spread primarily on infected plant material, so use only pathogen-free certified chrysanthemum stock. The fungus survives for extended

Rose leaves infected with rust. Orangish fungus pustules develop on the underside of infected leaves, and discolored tissue becomes apparent on the upper leaf surfaces. Good sanitation, keeping foliage dry, and maintaining low humidity can largely eliminate rose rust in greenhouses.

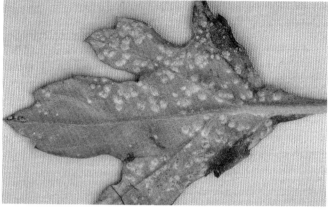

STEVEN T. KOIKE

White and pinkish pustules cover the underside of this leaf infected with chrysanthemum white rust. Immediately report suspected white rust infections to local agricultural officials.

Fasciation results in thick, flattened, and sometimes twisted stems, as with this snapdragon. Manage fasciation as if it were a bacterial infection and take additional measures because the cause also may be viral or genetic.

periods only when in contact with host plant tissue, so use good sanitation practices. Although the rust spreads locally as windborne basidiospores, in the absence of a host, spores survive only about 5 minutes at 80% relatively humidity and only 1 hour at 90% relative humidity. Infected hosts produce and release spores only during high relative humidity (96–100%). A film of free water must cover plant tissue in order for spores to penetrate tissue and initiate an infection. Infection is avoided by keeping humidity low and foliage dry, such as by avoiding overhead irrigation and using a combination of heat and ventilation. Dipping chrysanthemum cuttings in an effective fungicide and making at least two subsequent applications may help to prevent white rust from developing, but repeated applications of certain materials may be damaging to the crop.

White rust is a quarantined pathogen. Report any suspected white rust infections to your county department of agriculture. In the United States, regulations require that infected plants be destroyed to prevent disease establishment. Growing, selling, or shipping any chrysanthemums from designated eradication zones may be prohibited during certain parts of the year. In order to break the disease cycle, all chrysanthemums must be removed, bagged, and disposed of in the trash (not composted) during this period. In designated eradication zones, these regulations apply to everyone: commercial growers, distributors, and retailers as well as homeowners.

Fasciation

Fasciation is an abnormal flattening of stems, often appearing as if several adjoining stems have fused. Many plants can be affected, including alyssum, aster, carnation, chrysanthemum, delphinium, geranium, gypsophila, impatiens, liatris, Marguerite daisy, nasturtium, petunia, primula, Shasta daisy, snapdragon, and sweet pea. In ornamental cut willow, fasciation is considered desirable.

Fasciated plants have short, swollen clumps of distorted shoots. Leaves growing from distorted stems are abnormally abundant and undersized. Distortion often develops at the plant base, and crowns may appear galled. Sometimes only new terminal growth is affected.

Distorted shoots caused by fasciation may be confused with symptoms caused by aster yellow phytoplasmas. However, on fasciated plants, petals develop normal color and shape, even though distorted stems may affect overall plant appearance, such as causing abnormal spacing among clusters. Aster yellows distinctly affects flowers, commonly causing flowering parts to become green leafy structures.

The cause of most fasciations is not understood; some may be genetic or caused by bacterial or viral infections. Because the bacterium *Rhodococcus fascians* is often involved, manage fasciation as if it were a bacterial infection and take additional measures as the cause may be viral or genetic.

Fasciation bacteria survive on infected plants and debris. They spread in water and may infect through wounds. Control bacterial fasciation primarily through good sanitation and use of pathogen-free plants. Avoid injuring the base of plants, especially when plants are wet. Keep the base of plants dry. To control fasciation due to all potential causes (bacterial, genetic, viral), do not propagate or graft symptomatic plants. Label cuttings by the mother plant; rogue plants that later appear affected and dispose of the mother plant from which they were cut. If affected plants are not rogued, at least prune and dispose of distorted tissue and do not propagate from those plants.

Viruses

Viruses are submicroscopic particles that infect cells and alter their host's development. Most crops are susceptible to infection by one or more plant viruses.

Damage

Viruses can retard plant growth and change the appearance of foliage, flowers, and fruits. Virus-infected leaves can become discolored (spotted, streaked, or mottled), distorted, or stunted. Veins may lose their color (clearing) or develop outgrowths (enations). Flowers can be dwarfed, deformed, streaked, or faded, or they can remain green or develop into leaflike structures. In comparison with herbaceous plants, most woody ornamentals are less seriously affected by viruses, although plant growth rate may be slowed.

Although viruses rarely kill plants, they sometimes dramatically alter plant appearance, which can greatly reduce the value of ornamental crops. Conversely, certain virus-infected plants are propagated for the aesthetically desirable ornamental effects of the virus. These include the pink and white petal blotching and streaking resulting from infection by tulip breaking virus and the variegated foliage caused by abutilon mosaic virus.

Identification and Biology

Most viruses are named for the first reported host or the major host in which they are found and the most conspicuous symptom they produce: for example, the hibiscus chlorotic ringspot virus causes discolored yellow blotches or rings on hibiscus leaves. Certain viruses are host-specific and cause characteristic damage (see the chapter "Crop Tables"). Other viruses cause varied symptoms and infect many different crops (Table 44). Some hosts can be infected and show no symptoms.

Viruses consist of nucleic acids surrounded by a protein coating and are too small to be seen with a light microscope. Viruses have been placed into taxonomic groups (such as families and genera) according to their similarity in appearance when viewed with an electron microscope. These groups are usually named for their appearance or for the most important or first-discovered virus with that appearance. Cucumoviruses are named after cucumber mosaic virus, potyviruses are named after potato virus, and tospoviruses are named after tomato spotted wilt virus. Ilarviruses, such as prunus necrotic ringspot, are named by combining the first one or two letters of words used to describe their appearance; ilarvirus is the shortened name for "isometric labile ringspot viruses."

Viruses usually infect through a wound; once a plant becomes infected, the virus often spreads systemically within the plant. Viruses require assistance to spread from one plant to another; many are transmitted by invertebrates that feed on plant juices, especially aphids and thrips. Mites, nematodes, and fungi also transmit viruses affecting certain plants. Viruses can be spread in vegetative plant parts used for propagation, such as cuttings from infected stock plants and in bulbs, corms, and rhizomes. Very few viruses can be spread mechanically in sap that contaminates hands or tools. A few viruses spread in infected seed or pollen.

Field identification of viruses has traditionally relied on recognition of damage symptoms and host lists, and knowledge of local disease history and how specific viruses develop and spread. Although visual diagnosis is common, it often is inaccurate. Virus symptoms can easily be confused with those from other causes, such as nutritional disorders, herbicide or other chemical damage, and nonviral pathogens. Symptoms may vary in different cultivars. Some plants host many different viruses, and multiple viruses can occur in a plant at the same time.

Many control strategies are specific to a given virus; effective management requires timely and accurate virus identification. Proper identification allows you to determine how the virus is spread and what plants are susceptible. Identification is increasingly important as crop species and cultivars resistant to specific viruses are identified and developed, and virus complexes are better understood.

Microscopic identification. Electron microscope analysis has traditionally been used for expert diagnosis of most viruses. However, electron microscopes are expensive, and the results take at least several days and require highly trained operators. Interpreting results is tricky, and similar viruses often cannot be distinguished microscopically. There are only a few experts who can perform this work.

Bioassays. Indicator inoculations or bioassays are performed by outside laboratories and can sometimes be used on-site by growers. Indicator bioassays typically involve grinding tissue from symptomatic plants and rubbing the extracted juice onto several different plants (such as certain well-studied *Nicotiana* species) that are known to develop symptoms when infected with specific viruses. Bioassays can be used to diagnose many viruses. However, indicator inoculations are relatively slow, require pest-proof greenhouses for rearing indicator plants, and demand labor to grow the specific cultivars of plants (and sometimes the insect vectors) that are needed in the transmission studies.

Roses are susceptible to several common viruses that cause a wide variety of discoloring on foliage, such as this vein clearing. Stunted growth or spring dwarfing is another symptom of viruses in roses.

Table 44. Some Hosts and Transmission Methods of Viruses with a Wide Host Range.

Virus common name (family or genus)	Vector or method of transmission	Hosts		
		Ornamentals	Other crops	Weeds and natives
bean yellow mosaic (potyvirus)	aphids	freesia, fuchsia, gladiolus, sweet pea, violet	legumes, including beans, clovers, fava bean, pea, soybean	*Chenopodium* spp., clovers, sweet clover
beet curly top (rhabdovirus)	leafhoppers	celosia, coreopsis, cosmos, geranium, Marguerite daisy, nasturtium, pansy, petunia, strawflower, stock, sweet William, zinnia	beans, beets, borage, buckwheat, celery, clovers, cress, cucurbits, fava bean, fennel, flax, horseradish, pepper, potato, radish, rhubarb, tobacco, tomato, vetch	*Atriplex* spp., *Chenopodium* spp., clovers, fennel, *Polygonum* spp., *Rumex* spp., Russian thistle, shepherd's-purse
cauliflower mosaic (caulimovirus)	aphids	honesty, lunaria, stock	crucifers, including broccoli, cabbage, cauliflower, Chinese cabbage	mustard, *Raphanus* spp., shepherd's-purse
cucumber mosaic (cucumovirus)	aphids	aster, begonia, buddleia, calendula, columbine, dahlia, daphne, delphinium, freesia, fuchsia, geranium, gladiolus, iris, larkspur, ligustrum, lily, lobelia, nasturtium, passion vine, penstemon, periwinkle, primula, snapdragon, vinca, zinnia	buckwheat, carrot, celery, cucurbits, cowpea, pepper, potato, spinach, tobacco, tomato	*Commelina*, lambsquarter, lupine, milkweed, nightshade, pigweed, pokeweed
impatiens necrotic spot (tospovirus)	thrips	African violet, begonia, browallia, calla, chrysanthemum, cineraria, cyclamen, dahlia, exacum, gloxinia, impatiens, kalanchoe, lisianthus, lycium, odontoglossum orchids, phalaenopsis orchids, pouch flower, primrose, snapdragon, stephanotis, streptocarpus	see tomato spotted wilt	see tomato spotted wilt
prunus necrotic ringspot (ilarvirus)	grafting, pollen	*Prunus* spp., rose	apple, hops, *Prunus* spp.	*Prunus* spp.
tobacco mosaic (tobamovirus)	mechanical, carried in seed, soilborne	delphinium, flowering tobacco, petunia, phlox, wisteria	beans, tobacco, tomato	*Emilia* spp.
tomato spotted wilt (tospovirus)	thrips	African violet, ageratum, alstroemeria, amaryllis, anemone, aralia, aster, begonia, calendula, calla, carnation, Christmas cactus, chrysanthemum, cineraria, columbine, coreopsis, cosmos, dahlia, dieffenbachia, everlasting, exacum, forget-me-not, fuchsia, geranium, gerbera, gladiolus, gloxinia, godetia, gypsophila, hydrangea, impatiens, larkspur, lily, lisianthus, marigold, nasturtium, peony, periwinkle, petunia, phlox, poppy, pouch flower, primrose, ranunculus, sage, saponaria, scabiosa, schefflera, snapdragon, statice, stephanotis, stock, sweet pea, verbena, zinnia	artichoke, beans, cauliflower, celery, clover, cowpea, endive, fava bean, lettuce, papaya, pea, peanut, pepper, pineapple, spinach, tobacco, tomato	bindweed, bittercress, chickweed, *Emilia* spp., jimsonweed, knotweed, lupine, malva, *Mesembryanthemum* spp., miner's lettuce, nightshade, oxalis, physalis, pigweed, shepherd's-purse
turnip mosaic (potyvirus)	aphids	anemone, begonia, nasturtium, petunia, safflower, statice, stock, sweet William, wallflower, zinnia	Brussels sprouts, cabbage, cauliflower, cress, horseradish, mustard, radish, rhubarb, Swede turnip	cruciferous weeds

This is only a partial listing of host plants; for example, over 400 plant species are hosts for cucumber mosaic and over 600 plant species are hosts for tomato spotted wilt. More than one type of virus within that group may be involved with some diseases; for example, hosts of impatiens necrotic spot virus (INSV) are poorly known. Many plants reported as infected by tomato spotted wilt virus (TSWV) may actually be infected by INSV or both TSWV and INSV. Tomato spotted wilt is not thoroughly understood and may be more than one virus.

Serological and molecular identification. Rapid, sensitive, and accurate virus identification uses molecular techniques. Molecular methods recognize nucleic acid structures unique to each virus or specific antigens (substances such as pathogen proteins that induce an immune response in their hosts). Antigens are commonly identified using ELISA (enzyme-linked immunosorbent assay), which is discussed in the root and crown decays section earlier in this chapter.

DNA or RNA hybridization or amplification (such as polymerase chain reaction or PCR) and gel electrophoresis are used to identify nucleic acid structure, the specific sequence of nucleotides in genetic material.

Molecular tests require research on each specific virus and are commercially available from certain laboratories for many viruses (Table 45), but not for all viruses affecting flower and nursery crops. Simple ELISA test kits also are available for growers to monitor and identify certain viruses on-site.

Monitoring

Locating the sources of virus infection and identifying infected plants are critical for effective virus management. Strive for early virus detection, which is especially important when producing or using vegetatively propagated plants. Thoroughly inspect all incoming plants and examine crops at least weekly for symptoms of virus and the presence of insect vectors. Use yellow sticky traps (and possibly blue traps for thrips) throughout growing areas for early detection of insects, as detailed in the chapter "Insects, Mites, and Other Invertebrates." Check regularly to see that good sanitation and virus and insect exclusion are being practiced. Routinely look around growing areas for alternate hosts and reservoirs of insects and virus diseases, including weeds, crop residue, old plants, and "pet" plants (those that will not be marketed but are kept for pleasure around growing areas).

Although routine visual inspections are important, growers who rely only on inspection may not become aware of a problem until a virus is widespread in a crop. Once symptoms become obvious, losses can be high. Some plants do not exhibit symptoms at all or not until long after infection, for example, until flowering. Symptomless plants can be a source of virus that can spread, even when populations of insect vectors are low. In addition to visual inspection, consider routine use of indicator bioassays, on-site test kits, and outside laboratory testing for viruses in both symptomatic

and symptomless plants of susceptible crops. Especially monitor mother blocks and areas where cuttings or other new plants are received or shipped out for propagation.

If tospoviruses vectored by thrips are the primary concern, consider using indicator plants as discussed in the tospoviruses monitoring section later in this chapter. This indicator plant method could be modified to monitor other insect-vectored viruses if suitable indicator cultivars are identified and the blue surfaces used to attract thrips are changed to yellow to attract other adult insects that vector viruses, such as winged aphids.

Virus tests. Viruses affecting many major flower and nursery crops can be detected by sending samples to an outside laboratory (Table 45). Additionally, on-site kits are available to detect impatiens necrotic spot virus, tomato spotted wilt virus (Fig. 30), certain fungi as discussed in the root and crown decays section above, and possibly other pathogens.

In comparison with indicator bioassays, laboratory tests or on-site kits may be better able to identify the specific virus that is present. In addition to plant parts, certain tests

Table 45. Outside Laboratories Can Test for Many Viruses Commonly Affecting these Flower Crops.

African violet, aster, begonia, carnation, chrysanthemum, dahlia, geranium, gladiolus, hibiscus, impatiens, kalanchoe, lily, marigold, orchids, petunia, poinsettia, rose

Tests for additional crops are constantly being developed. Contact a Cooperative Extension advisor or private laboratory for the latest information on available tests.

The necrotic, chlorotic terminal leaves on these chrysanthemums are advanced symptoms of impatiens necrotic spot virus. Without good monitoring, this problem can go undetected and unmanaged until near harvest, resulting in devastating crop losses.

This chlorotic leaf blotch moving along veins in chrysanthemum is an early symptom of impatiens necrotic spot virus. A virus infection was confirmed by an ELISA test of liquid extracted from this leaf.

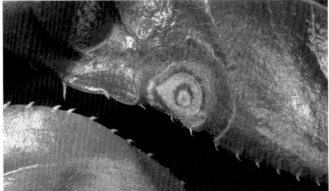

Ringspot symptoms of tospovirus in New Guinea impatiens. The only control for tospoviruses is prevention, such as excluding thrips and promptly roguing infected plants.

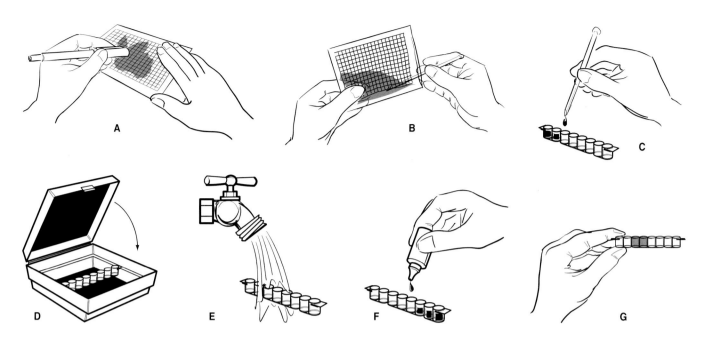

Figure 30. On-site test kits can be used to detect certain plant pathogens. Tests contain all needed materials, require only a few minutes, and provide results within several hours. Illustrated here is a QTA-Tospo kit test from Agdia for impatiens necrotic spot virus and tomato spotted wilt virus. Use the kits as follows (more detailed information can be had from kit suppliers). A. Place symptomatic plant tissue into the mesh-lined pouch provided with the kit and crush the sample by placing the pouch on a hard surface and rubbing it with the blunt end of a pen. B. Squeeze the sealed end of a straw and insert the open end into the pouch, then release pressure on the straw so that the liquefied plant sample is drawn up into the straw. C. Place drops of sample into a sample well, which is on a plastic strip containing wells for additional samples and control wells without sample liquid to help ensure accurate results. D. Place the plastic well strip into a moist container to allow the samples to react with the coating on the inside of the wells. E. After 1 hour, rinse the wells with water. F. Add the special solution, and place the wells in a moist container for another hour. Repeat this rinse and wait procedure. G. After 30 to 60 minutes, if the target virus is present a visible color change occurs in the test wells. See *Easy On-Site Tests for Fungi and Viruses in Nurseries and Greenhouses* (Kabashima et al. 1997) for more information. Source: Illustration by Will Suckow from Kabashima et al. 1997.

can be conducted on insects. Insects for testing can be picked off sticky traps or collected from plants or growing area surfaces using a hand-held insect suction device called an aspirator, as illustrated in the chapter "Insects, Mites, and Other Invertebrates."

On-site test kits allow growers to detect and confirm virus presence quicker than off-site laboratories. For propagators and growers of sensitive crops who will benefit from frequent and numerous tests, on-site test systems can be more economical than using an outside laboratory. Impatiens necrotic spot virus and tomato spotted wilt virus tests require only a few minutes, and the results are provided within several hours. Contact suppliers and read *Easy On-Site Tests for Fungi and Viruses in Nurseries and Greenhouses* (Kabashima et al. 1997) for more information on collecting samples for testing and interpreting results.

Negative results in a specific ELISA test do not rule out the possibility that another virus is causing disease. Bioassays discussed above can be used to diagnose most viruses. Although bioassays can be used on-site by knowledgeable growers with proper facilities, they are commonly done by outside laboratories. When sending samples off-site, make arrangements in advance with a reputable laboratory. To ensure that samples arrive in good condition, consider sending the entire plant or plants and use express delivery (Table 32).

Chlorotic line patterns indicate that this leaf is infected with impatiens necrotic spot virus, a diagnosis confirmed by an ELISA test. Although some customers desire this appearance because of its ornamental effect, infected plants are a source of virus that can be spread by thrips to nearby susceptible crops that are more severely damaged by tospoviruses. The appearance of many virus-infected crops makes them unmarketable.

These lesions and discoloring in leaves and stems are among the symptoms of tomato spotted wilt virus infecting field-grown ranunculus. Locating and eliminating nearby weed hosts of thrips and viruses dramatically reduced tospovirus infection in subsequent crops at this site.

Management

Most plants infected with a virus cannot be cured. Roguing infected plants is often the only way to eliminate virus from a crop. Virus-free plants can sometimes be obtained from infected mother plants by growing mother plants at 100°F (38°C) for 3 to 4 weeks and then culturing shoot tip meristems. For example, in plants infected with prunus necrotic ringspot, the virus can be inactive in 99% of the meristem cultures after this heat treatment. In some cases, virus multiplication inhibitor chemicals can also be used alone or in combination with heating. Plants propagated from infected mother plants will usually be infected. Once a plant becomes infected with a virus, it usually remains infected throughout its life. There is often no treatment or effective chemical that allows virus-free material to be obtained from infected mother plants. Starting with virus-free stock, using good sanitation and exclusion, and controlling insect vectors or other methods of spread are the primary control methods for viruses.

Sanitation. Prevention is often the only effective method of virus control. To avoid spreading viruses, use good sanitation (Figs. 9 and 10) and cultural practices, for example, install screens to exclude thrips and other insect vectors (see the chapter "Insects, Mites, and Other Invertebrates"). Control nearby weeds that serve as reservoirs for viruses and insects. Break the virus cycle by employing a plant-free period (no crops or weeds) between crops; if possible, keep greenhouses plant-free and warm for at least two weeks so that adults can emerge from any pupae and starve before feeding on plants and spreading viruses. Pasteurize beds between crops to eliminate pupating thrips. Use only virus-free propagation material if available and avoid carrying over stock plants that may be infected. If a virus is present, consider growing less-susceptible crop species or virus-resistant cultivars if available. Regularly inspect the crop and rogue infected plants. If plants are infected with viruses vectored by insects, immediately rogue the plants into a covered container to prevent any insects from escaping or spreading.

Minimize the number of greenhouse entrances; limit access only to essential workers. Train workers to use good sanitation and cultural practices and to recognize virus symptoms and insect vectors. Keep tobacco smoke and tobacco smokers away from crops susceptible to tobacco mosaic virus. Tobacco mosaic virus can be carried on hands of people who have been handling any tobacco product.

Virus-free plants. Purchase and plant only high-quality, certified virus-free stock or seeds and use indexed stock whenever available. Virus indexing eliminates viral pathogens from the propagative material of many flower crops, including chrysanthemums, carnations, foliage plants, geraniums, hydrangeas, lilies, and orchids. Culture- or virus-indexed plants are initially free of the internal pathogens for which they are indexed. Indexed plants are not necessarily disease resistant and can become infected later if good prevention and production practices are not employed.

Propagators should establish mother blocks only from material that has been thoroughly and repeatedly tested and found to be virus-free. Isolate mother blocks from production plants to reduce the likelihood of reinfection. Use especially stringent sanitation and exclusion procedures in propagation areas. Do not allow workers and equipment to move from production areas into propagation areas. Monitor for the presence of viruses at each cycle of plant multiplication. Mark new propagules to indicate the mother plants so that the stock and the mother plants can be rogued if infection is discovered later.

Impatiens Necrotic Spot Virus and Tomato Spotted Wilt Virus

Impatiens necrotic spot virus (INSV) and tomato spotted wilt virus (TSWV) often infect flower crops. The disease once thought to be caused by TSWV is now known to be caused by at least several similar yet distinct viruses, including INSV and TSWV. What was once known as TSWV is now known to be a complex of many viruses in the tospovirus group. TSWV is not thoroughly understood, and it may not be known which viruses are most common in your growing area.

Damage. Many flower crops are susceptible to one or more of the tospoviruses (Table 44). However, there are extreme

Table 46. Known Thrips Vectors of INSV, TSWV, and Certain Other Tospoviruses.

Common name	Scientific name	Tospoviruses
blossom or cotton bud thrips	*Frankliniella schultzei*	GRSV, TCSV, TSWV
flower thrips	*Frankliniella intonsa*	GRSV, TCSV, TSWV
melon thrips	*Thrips palmi*	GBNV, TSWV, WSMV
onion thrips[1]	*Thrips tabaci*	TSWV
tobacco thrips	*Frankliniella fusca*	TSWV
western flower thrips	*Frankliniella occidentalis*	INSV, GRSV, TCSV, TSWV
no common name	*Thrips setosus*	TSWV

KEY: GBNV = groundnut bud necrosis virus   INSV = impatiens necrotic spot virus   TSWV = tomato spotted wilt virus
GRSV = groundnut ringspot virus   TCSV = tomato chlorotic spot virus   WSMV = watermelon silver mottle virus

1. The ability of onion thrips to vector TSWV is uncertain. Onion thrips apparently does not spread the currently known isolates of TSWV but reportedly were an important vector in the past.

differences in the extent to which infected cultivars develop symptoms. Poinsettia and rose are among the few major flower crops that are not susceptible to tospoviruses.

Tospoviruses produce a broad range of symptoms, including stunting, yellow or white spotting, black or brown stem or leaf necrosis, ringspots, defoliation, vein necrosis, and dark or yellow linear patterns, mottling, or mosaic. Some viral symptoms are easily confused with improper nutrition, other abiotic disorders such as air pollution or pesticide phytotoxicity, or fungal or bacterial leaf spots, root decays, and vascular wilts. Lesions or necrotic tissue caused by INSV may be susceptible to secondary infection by *Botrytis*. Plants are often more severely damaged by the viruses if infected when young. However, some plants (such as cyclamen) can be infected for extended periods and remain symptomless.

Identification and biology. It is not possible to reliably distinguish TSWV from INSV based on symptoms; these viruses have wide, overlapping host ranges. ELISA techniques can, however, confirm virus presence and distinguish between INSV and TSWV.

INSV and TSWV are transmitted in propagative material and by thrips (Table 46). Although at least seven species of thrips can transmit TSWV, western flower thrips is the most important vector of TSWV in floriculture and nurseries and is at the time this is written the only confirmed vector of INSV.

The first larval stage (first instar) is the only stage at which thrips can acquire the virus. A thrips that did not feed on an infected plant in the first instar cannot acquire or transmit the virus, even if it feeds on infected plants as an adult. Only plants that are infected with virus and suitable for development of thrips from egg through adult are important in virus transmission. Thrips that acquire virus during their first instar remain infective to plants as they mature into adults. Infective adults then transmit the virus when they move and feed on susceptible plants. Primary infection occurs when infective adults move into a susceptible crop and feed. Secondary infection occurs when immature thrips acquire the

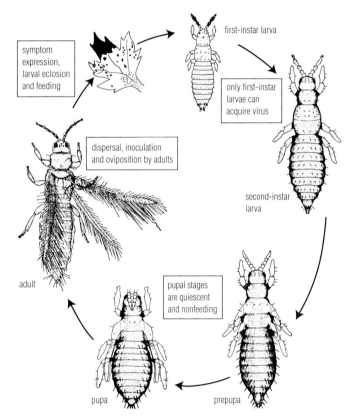

Figure 31. Life cycle of a tospovirus-vectoring thrips. Thrips can acquire virus only during their first larval stage. Larvae remain infected as they mature and transmit virus as adults when they move and feed on uninfected plants. Adapted from Ullman et al. 1997; adult thrips from Anonymous 1952; immature thrips from McKenzie 1935.

virus by feeding on infected crop plants, then as adults move and feed on other crop plants within the growing area (Fig. 31). The relative importance of primary infection (infective thrips arriving from outside the crop) versus secondary infection (thrips movement within crops) is poorly known; both causes are managed by reducing thrips numbers and preventing thrips movement among plants.

Monitoring. Detect virus presence early by using a combination of visual inspection, bioassays, on-site test kits (Fig. 30, Table 47), and outside laboratory testing as discussed above in the virus monitoring section. Especially monitor mother blocks, areas where cuttings or other new plants are received or shipped, and crops highly susceptible to damage. Consider using indicator plants to determine if tospovirus is being spread in growing areas and to identify the source of infective thrips. Virus indicator plants are different from the insect-infested sentinel plants (also called indicator plants) discussed in the chapter "Insects, Mites, and Other Invertebrates." Use yellow or blue sticky traps to monitor for the presence of thrips (see the chapter "Insects, Mites, and Other Invertebrates"). Consider using directional trapping, pairs of traps oriented at right angles to each other to identify the direction from which thrips are arriving. Routine spraying when thrips are found is not recommended because the number of thrips present does not necessarily reflect the prevalence of infective thrips, nor do thrips numbers reveal their source. Routine spraying often causes pesticide resistance and seldom eliminates problems with tospoviruses. Use of petunia indicator plants and directional traps in combination alerts growers to the presence of infective thrips and helps locate their source.

Indicator plants. Certain cultivars develop distinct symptoms soon after infection by a specific virus. Place individual plants of these susceptible cultivars throughout the growing area and along crop borders. Inspect these indicator plants about twice each week to detect the presence of virus vectors using the methods summarized in Table 48. These indicator plants provide an early warning to help you locate infective thrips and their host plants, directing you where to remove host plants and control thrips to protect crops.

Table 47. Viruses that Can Be Detected Using Commercially Available On-Site Test Kits.

Tospovirus	Serogroup	Hosts
Tomato spotted wilt (TSWV)	I	over 600 dicot and monocot plant species, most notably many vegetables, but some ornamentals as partially listed in Table 44
Impatiens necrotic spot (INSV)	III[1]	primarily herbaceous ornamentals, as partially listed Table 44, but also vegetables

Also available is a single kit providing a broad-spectrum test for multiple tospoviruses, including INSV and TSWV. On-site tests may be available for other viruses; contact product suppliers for the latest information.

1. Serogroup III includes isolates formerly named TSWV Impatiens (TSWV "I" strain). Other currently recognized tospoviruses include serogroup II, tomato chlorotic spot (TCSV) and groundnut ringspot (GRSV); and serogroup IV, groundnut bud necrosis (GBNV) and watermelon silver mottle (WSMV).

Table 48. Methods for Using Thrips Virus Indicator Plants.

- Grow indicator plants in 3-inch (7.5-cm) pots in a pestproof greenhouse. Use excellent sanitation and exclusion methods to ensure that plants are pathogen free prior to being placed in the general growing area.
- Start using the indicator plants when they are young and contain about 10 to 15 leaves per pot.
- Distribute plants in self-watering containers throughout the propagation area or growing area beginning several weeks before susceptible crops are grown there.
- Consider variables such as crop susceptibility and value and available monitoring resources in deciding how many indicator plants to use. Deploying about 2 to 3 indicator plants per acre (5 to 7 per ha) of field crop or for every 10,000 square feet (900 sq m) of greenhouse growing space may be adequate in many situations.
- Concentrate indicator plants near vents, entranceways, or along field borders where especially susceptible crops will be grown.
- Place plants so they are at or slightly above the crop canopy.
- To attract thrips, place each indicator plant on or near a blue surface. Attach a *non-sticky* blue card to each indicator plant, paint or cover pots with blue, place the self-watering pot on a blue sheet of plastic or in an aluminum pan or tray painted blue, or use a combination of these methods.
- Force thrips to feed on foliage of indicator plants by promptly removing flowers as soon as they appear. If flowers are present, thrips will likely feed on flowers instead of foliage, delaying or preventing development of conspicuous foliar symptoms.
- Locate yellow sticky traps for insect monitoring throughout the growing area to detect insect vectors. Place a pair of traps near each indicator plant, orienting traps at right angles to each other, one trap facing north-south and the other east-west, so the direction from which thrips are coming can be identified by observing which trap side catches the most thrips.
- Provide indicator plants with good cultural care throughout the cropping cycle, especially adequate water and fertilizer, so that plants remain attractive to insects.
- Periodically replace indicator plants with younger plants that may be more attractive to pests.
- Check indicator plants carefully for virus symptoms (small, new leaf spots) at least once a week; twice weekly or even daily inspections are better. Early morning is the best time to examine petunias.
- Consider confirming that symptomatic foliage is infected by using on-site rapid tests kits or commercial laboratory testing.
- Replace and isolate infected indicator plants and dispose of them once the virus is confirmed.
- Combine information from directional sticky traps and indicator plants to locate sources of infective plants needing removal, and identify where exclusion, targeted sprays, and other methods should be directed to control thrips.

The pale scars on the leaf on the right resulted from feeding by thrips that were not infected with virus. Dark lesions on the petunia leaf on the left developed 4 days after feeding by thrips carrying the virus. This 'Celebrity Blue' petunia is a good cultivar to use as a virus indicator plant because it develops distinct local lesions within days of feeding by virus-vectoring thrips.

This virus indicator plant in a self-watering container was placed on a blue plate because blue is highly attractive to western flower thrips. The directional sticky traps (2 traps oriented at right angles) will indicate the direction from which infective thrips are migrating if virus symptoms appear on the petunia indicator plant.

Table 49. Some Hosts of Aster Yellows and Phytoplasma Organisms Spread by Leafhoppers.

Ornamentals	Other crops	Weeds and natives
alyssum, anemone, aster, calceolaria, calendula, candytuft, celosia, centaurea, chrysanthemum, cineraria, cosmos, delphinium, gladiolus, gloxinia, godetia, gypsophila, hydrangea, larkspur, Marguerite daisy, marigold, nasturtium, peony, petunia, primrose, Queen Anne's lace, ranunculus, sage, scabiosa, snapdragon, statice, stock, strawflower, sunflower, sweet William, veronica, zinnia, and others	buckwheat, carrot, celery, lettuce, onion, parsley, parsnip, potato, safflower, spinach, tomato, and many others	California poppy, dandelion, plantain, and many others

Petunia cultivars 'Burgundy Madness,' 'Carpet Blue,' and 'Summer Madness' are good indicator plants for INSV and TSWV. These petunias are suitable because they attract the insect vector (thrips), are unsuitable for complete life cycle development of the vector, and seldom become infected systemically, so they are unlikely to act as a reservoir from which virus can spread. Conspicuous symptoms (local lesions) become apparent on petunia foliage within 3 to 7 days after feeding by infective thrips. Lesions are small brown to black spots, which look very different from the whitish feeding scars left by noninfective thrips. Certain fava beans (*Faba vulgaris*) have also proven useful as indicator plants, but the most reliable cultivar, 'Little Toto,' may be unavailable; fava bean should be avoided because it is a good thrips host. Contact your Cooperative Extension advisor or plant supplier for other suggestions.

Management. No cure for tospoviruses is available. Manage tospoviruses by roguing infective plants and controlling thrips. Stringent sanitation and exclusion are the most effective management strategies. Propagate and grow only certified or culture-indexed, virus-free plants if available. Start crops using thrips-free plants and growing areas. Eliminate nearby alternate host plants. Although tospoviruses do not persist long on tools, mechanical transmission may be possible when moving rapidly from one plant to another, such as when taking cuttings; consider sterilizing tools before contacting each new plant during propagation as discussed in the disinfectants section earlier in this chapter.

Monitor regularly for thrips using traps and visual inspection. Regularly inspect crops for virus symptoms. Consider routine use of sensitive indicator plants, laboratory tests, and on-site ELISA test kits to help detect and confirm virus presence. Immediately rogue affected plants. Consider rotating susceptible crops with a crop that is not susceptible to tospoviruses and is a poor host of western flower thrips. In addition to poinsettia and rose, crops reportedly not susceptible to tospoviruses include *Boltonia*, croton, *Euryops*, *Helenium*, iris, *Lobelia*, *Melampodium*, *Phlox*, *Salvia*, and *Tiarella* species. Geraniums (*Pelargonium* spp.) can become infected but little loss of this crop has been reported. Watch for the availability of new virus management tools, such as better monitoring and genetic engineering of plants to resist pathogens.

Phytoplasmas

Phytoplasmas, formerly called mycoplasmas, are minute organisms that are smaller than bacteria and cannot be seen with a light microscope. They infect many weeds, vegetables, and flower crops (Table 49).

Phytoplasmas cause yellowing, dwarfing, abnormal shoots, and greening of flower parts, which develop into leaflike structures. Clusters or tufts of spindly, yellow, upright shoots commonly develop around the base of infected plants, often on one side of the plant. Corms or tubers can mature early, be undersized, or have stunted roots if they are infected early during the current season. When corms or tubers infected during the previous season are grown, they develop many thin, weak, yellowish leaves, distorted flower spikes, and green blossoms. No chemicals are effective against phytoplasmas; they are best controlled by proper sanitation, excluding insect vectors, and using pathogen-free stock.

Aster Yellows

Aster yellows is the most important phytoplasma infecting flower and nursery crops. Aster yellows is poorly understood and may be a complex of related phytoplasmas and phytoplasmalike organisms. It is vectored by several species of leafhoppers but is not spread by seed, handling, or other insects.

Control aster yellows in the same manner as discussed above for insect-vectored viruses. Start production using pathogen-free plants and good sanitation. Do not plant susceptible crops downwind from other hosts or near weeds that may host leafhoppers and phytoplasmas. Regularly inspect crops and rogue infected plants. Monitor growing areas and eliminate nearby weeds, especially biennial and perennial weeds that host leafhoppers. Control or exclude leafhoppers, as discussed in the chapter "Insects, Mites, and Other Invertebrates." Reflective mulch has been shown to repel leafhoppers vectoring corn stunt spiroplasm (a bacterialike organism) and use of reflective mulch may be beneficial in reducing insect-vectored pathogens affecting young field-grown flower crops as discussed in the chapter "Insects, Mites, and Other Invertebrates."

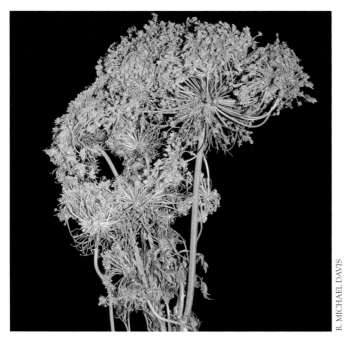

R. MICHAEL DAVIS

Flower parts develop into green, stunted growth, such as this on Queen Anne's lace and other hosts, when infected with aster yellows. This pathogenic phytoplasma, formerly called a mycoplasma, is spread by leafhoppers.

Insects, Mites, and Other Invertebrates

Invertebrates are animals that do not have an internal skeleton or backbone. In addition to insects and mites, the most common invertebrates attacking flower and nursery crops, this chapter also discusses snails, slugs, sowbugs, millipedes, and related invertebrates. Nematodes, which are also invertebrates, are discussed in a separate chapter.

Life Cycles

Most invertebrates begin life as an egg that hatches into an immature form called a nymph or a larva. Invertebrates grow by periodically forming a new outer skin or exoskeleton (molting) and shedding their old skin. In addition to the change in size, many invertebrates change shape with each successive molt, a process known as metamorphosis.

Insects, the most common terrestrial invertebrates, can be divided into two major groups based on their metamorphosis (Table 50): complete and gradual. Insects with complete metamorphosis undergo major changes in form between the immature (larval) stages and adult. Complete metamorphosis is illustrated here for caterpillars (Fig. 32) and later in the sections on bulb flies, fungus gnats, and parasitic wasps. Insects with gradual metamorphosis, also called simple or incomplete metamorphosis, undergo less drastic changes in form as they mature; immatures (nymphs) become more like adults each time they molt, as illustrated for aphids (Fig. 33). Each progressively larger nymphal or larval stage is called an instar and is numbered beginning with the stage that emerges from an egg, called the "first instar." The development of many other invertebrates, including centipedes, millipedes, symphylans, and mites, is similar to the gradual metamorphosis of insects.

Certain invertebrates have metamorphosis that is intermediate between complete and gradual. For example, the immature stages of thrips are often called larvae instead of nymphs. Because last-instar nymphs in thrips and whiteflies change greatly in appearance, they are often called pupae even though these groups do not have a true pupal stage.

Table 50. Comparison between Gradual and Complete Metamorphosis in Insects.

	Gradual metamorphosis	Complete metamorphosis
Life stages	Three major life stages: egg, nymph, and adult.	Four major life stages: egg, larva, pupa, and adult.
Change in form	Immatures become more like adults each time they molt; no pupal stage. Immatures differ from adults primarily in their smaller size, lack of wings, and often different color. Immatures are called nymphs.	Major changes in form between immatures and adults; transformation occurs in the nonfeeding pupal stage. The immature feeding stage is called a larva.
Mouthparts	Many have sucking mouthparts, including aphids, thrips, scales, and whiteflies.	Mostly chewing insects, including borers, caterpillars, leafminers, weevils, and white grubs.
Feeding habit	Adults and nymphs feed; both stages commonly occur on the same plant parts, often together in groups.	Adults and larvae commonly have different feeding habits; for example, adult weevils feed on foliage while larvae chew roots. In groups such as moths and flies, only the larval stage chews plants; the adults take in only nectar and water.

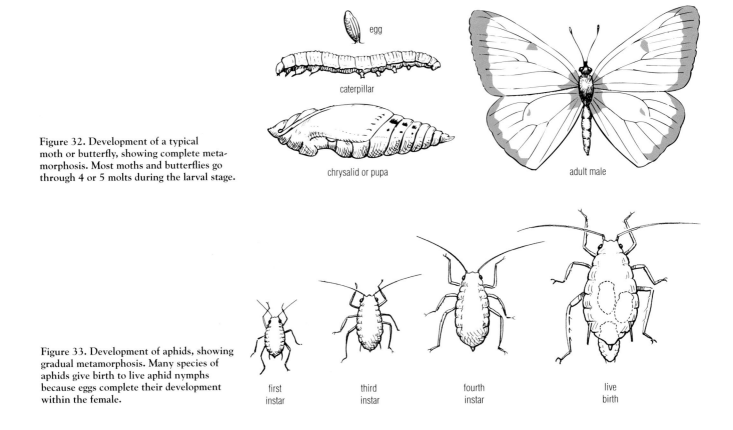

Figure 32. Development of a typical moth or butterfly, showing complete metamorphosis. Most moths and butterflies go through 4 or 5 molts during the larval stage.

egg

caterpillar

chrysalid or pupa

adult male

Figure 33. Development of aphids, showing gradual metamorphosis. Many species of aphids give birth to live aphid nymphs because eggs complete their development within the female.

first instar

third instar

fourth instar

live birth

Damage

Invertebrates cause four major types of damage to floral crops. First, pests injure plants directly, usually while feeding. Second, some invertebrates spread plant pathogens. Third, pest by-products or the presence of invertebrates can be aesthetically objectionable. Finally, due to quarantines, infestation by certain pests may limit or prevent marketing of a crop.

The importance of pest presence or damage is determined by many factors, including the type of damage, the market for which the crop is destined, crop species or cultivar, the size and stage of the pest, plant age, and the plant part affected. For example, little or no apparent damage or obvious pest presence is typically tolerable on marketable portions of the plant; leaf mining on older chrysanthemum foliage may not reduce marketability because lower foliage is removed prior to shipping and by retail florists during arrangement. Armyworm chewing can devastate gypsophila flowers and foliage; however, feeding by moderate armyworm populations early in the season on nonmarketed (older) leaves may stimulate new terminal growth and increase yields.

Feeding damage. Invertebrates have either chewing or sucking mouthparts. Mites and insects such as thrips, whiteflies, aphids, and mealybugs have tubular sucking mouthparts. These pests suck plant fluids, causing buds, leaves, or

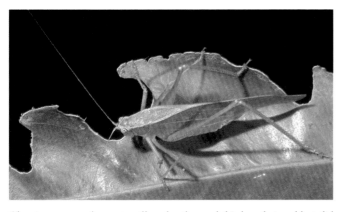

Chewing pests such as caterpillars, beetles, and this broadwinged katydid cause identifiable holes or cuts in foliage.

Damage caused by certain invertebrates can be confused with damage caused by pathogens or other pests. Larvae of an introduced *Liriomyza* species leafminer caused these necrotic spots on lantana by tunneling between the leaf surfaces.

Sucking pests, such as this adult stink bug, feed through tubular mouthparts. Feeding injury causes plant parts to discolor, distort, or drop.

Certain pests, such as these female green shield scales and their flocculent egg masses, are damaging because plants infested with them cannot be shipped out of the county or out of California due to quarantines. Other examples include the brown garden snail (not shown).

flowers to discolor, distort, wilt, or drop. Invertebrates such as caterpillars, weevils, and snails have chewing mouthparts. Chewing pests usually cause identifiable holes or cuts in foliage or flowers; they can also clip away plant parts, sometimes consuming entire plants. Because some chewing pests attack roots or tunnel inside plant tissue, their feeding can cause wilting or discoloring of foliage that may be confused with damage symptoms caused by sucking pests, pathogens, or poor cultural practices.

Disease vectors. Aphids, whiteflies, thrips, and some other insects that suck plant juices may ingest viral particles when they feed on infected plants. These insects can spread the virus when they move and feed on healthy plants. A given insect can generally spread only certain diseases, and each disease affects only certain plants. Tomato spotted wilt virus and impatiens necrotic spot virus are the most notorious viral pathogens of floral crops (see the chapter "Diseases").

These diseases affect many different species of crops and weeds and are vectored primarily by western flower thrips.

Some nonviral diseases may also be vectored by insects. For example, leafhoppers spread aster yellow phytoplasma pathogens. Other diseases not specifically spread by invertebrates may enter plants at sites where tissue is injured by invertebrate feeding, especially when feeding injury occurs on roots or stems near the soil.

Pests and pest by-products. Although easily overlooked at low densities, the visible presence of pests or their by-products is usually unacceptable on marketed plant parts. Caterpillars and other chewing pests produce dark excrement or droppings (frass), which can contaminate plants. Greenhouse thrips and plant bugs produce dark, watery, or varnishlike frass on foliage. Aphids, whiteflies, soft scales, and some other Homoptera (sap-sucking) insects excrete excess plant fluids as honeydew, which makes a sticky mess on plants and provides a medium for the growth of sooty mold. Some caterpillars and mites cover plants with silken webbing. As invertebrates shed their skins as they grow, cast skins may stick to or lodge in plants, reducing the crop's market value.

Quarantines. Many of the worst pests of flower and nursery crops are not native to the United States—they were introduced from other regions. Just as the United States attempts to protect crops by prohibiting import of foreign pests, other nations impose quarantines against pests that occur in our country but not theirs. Quarantines may require special inspections or treatment before crops can be exported. At foreign ports, infested crops may be refused entry, impounded, or disinfected in ways that damage the crop, resulting in loss of the commodity. Some quarantines are imposed between states, like that prohibiting shipment of plants infested with brown garden snail.

Diagnosing Problems

Successful pest management requires proper identification of pest and natural enemy species and accurate diagnoses of the problems affecting the plants. One approach to diagnosis and identification is to use the chapter "Crop Tables"; match the symptoms on your plants with those described in the table for that species, then refer to the more detailed information to confirm the cause and rule out other causes that produce similar symptoms. Alternatively, if you know what kind of pest you have (e.g., whiteflies or scale insects), you can refer to that section of the manual and use the photographs and descriptions to help identify common species. Because of the broad scope of this manual and because new species are frequently introduced from other places, not all possible flower and nursery crop pests are included in this manual. Nursery growers of woody ornamentals should use this manual in combination with *Pests of Landscape Trees and Shrubs* (Dreistadt 1994). Take pests or damaged plant parts that you can't identify to a local Cooperative Extension or county agriculture department expert.

After identifying the invertebrates that attack your plants, learn about their biology and potential damage. You may find that some species, while present near the damage or symptoms, are innocuous or beneficial. Damaging species may be susceptible to control only during certain life stages that you must be able to recognize. The most effective or appropriate control action(s) may vary with pest density and life stage, plant development, and other factors, such as history of control methods employed at that site.

Monitoring

Monitoring, also called scouting, is the gathering, recording, and evaluation of information about your crop and its pests or disorders collected on a regular basis. Because insect and mite populations can increase rapidly, inadequate monitoring increases the likelihood that problems will not be detected until pest populations are high, damage becomes extensive, and management options become more limited.

Visually inspecting plants at least once a week in combination with proper use of yellow sticky traps is the minimum monitoring that should be used in each crop. For certain problems, special techniques, like shaking foliage or installing special traps (Table 51) should be used in addition to visual inspection and yellow sticky traps. Select appropriate scouting methods based on knowledge about pest biology, the goals of your monitoring, and available resources.

Yellow sticky traps, shaking plants, degree-day (heat accumulation) monitoring, and other specialized techniques used

Visual inspection is the most common monitoring method. Regularly scout the entire growing area in a consistent, uniform manner.

Diagnosing and monitoring problems caused by tiny pests may require a hand lens. A hands-free magnifier, such as this one mounted on an adjustable headband, can also be helpful.

Table 51. Invertebrate Monitoring Methods.

Method	Invertebrates detected
	ESSENTIAL METHODS
visual inspection of plants and growing areas	Most exposed-feeding species and their damage and evidence of parasitism and predation. Monitoring may require a hand lens or other magnifier.
sticky traps	Adults of many types of insects, including fungus gnats, leafminers, shore flies, thrips, whiteflies, winged aphids, and beneficial aphid midges and parasitic wasps.
	SPECIAL METHODS
indicator or sentinel plants	Most exposed-feeding species and their damage. Inspect the same infested plants before and after treatment to determine whether pests are in the stage(s) susceptible to planned control actions and to evaluate treatment efficacy.
shaking plants	Adults and larvae or nymphs of most exposed, readily dislodged species, including bugs, lacewings, lady beetles, leaf beetles, leafhoppers, mites, nonwebbing caterpillars, psyllids, thrips, and adult parasites and whiteflies.
carbon dioxide exhalation and shaking	Thrips hidden in buds, which are stimulated to move by a long, gentle breath into terminals, then dislodged and revealed by shaking plant tips over white paper on a clipboard.
degree-day monitoring	Many pests and some beneficials for which researchers have determined development thresholds and rates (see Tables 52, 53, 65).
potato traps	Root-feeding fungus gnat larvae, which migrate to feed on the underside of raw potato pieces imbedded about ½ inch (13 mm) deep into container media. Pick potato piece up and look for larvae on the underside of each disk and the soil surface immediately beneath the disk once or twice a week.
pheromone-baited traps	Moths listed in Table 71. Used in greenhouses only if screened. Also traps males of certain scale insects (e.g., California red, San Jose), but of uncertain value in flower and nursery crops; certain parasite adults attracted to their host's pheromone.
black light or visible light traps	Night-flying adults of moths, certain other pests (such as scarab beetles), and certain beneficials (such as green lacewings).
double-sided sticky tape	Scale and mealybug crawlers.
pitfall traps with or without a bait attractant	Adult weevils, centipedes, millipedes, predaceous ground beetles, and ground-dwelling spiders.
trap boards	Certain ground-dwelling invertebrates, including snails, slugs, and adult weevils.
flushes using pyrethrum or soap; or flooding with plain water in field soil	Relatively mobile species in hidden places, including fungus gnat and shore fly larvae, millipedes, and symphylans in soil. Thrips and possibly other species in buds may also be flushed with pyrethrum.
timed counts	Exposed pests (e.g., caterpillars), some beneficials (e.g., lady beetles), and certain types of damage (rolled leaves) that are relatively large and obvious but occur at relatively low density so that individuals are not observed faster than they can be counted.
host collection and rearing	Immature stages of species that feed inside their hosts; only the adult stage of many insects can be positively identified to species.

primarily for invertebrates are discussed in this chapter. Visual inspection, indicator plants, and other methods used for a variety of types of pests are discussed in the chapter "Managing Pests in Flower and Nursery Crops." Forms for recording monitoring data and tips for interpreting monitoring information are also presented there. Also see the pest management units discussion in the chapter "Managing Pests in Flower and Nursery Crops." A pest management unit (PMU) is a contiguous area for which monitoring results are summarized each time that you scout. Each PMU is typically a crop area with similar pest management requirements, such as the same or similar cultivar and age of plants grown with the similar cultural practices. By dividing the overall growing area into smaller units (PMUs), scouting data is easier to manage and control actions can be better targeted according to need.

Different species can resemble each other, as with these lygus bug nymph (photo left) and two cotton aphids. Correct species identification is critical to selecting effective management methods. Bugs lack the pair of tube-like projections (cornicles) near the rear of aphids.

Sticky traps. Adults of whiteflies, thrips, and some other pests and beneficials (Table 51) can be monitored with yellow sticky traps. Traps warn of pest presence, hot spots, and migration. Traps provide a relative measure of insect density; comparisons of the number of adults caught among sample dates may indicate whether pest density is changing or remaining relatively constant over the long term. Traps are often a very efficient and important monitoring tool, alerting growers to pests early, before damage is observed in crops.

Traps may not be a good tool for deciding treatment need or timing. Immature stages in crops commonly cause the most damage, and traps typically capture only airborne adults. Adult trapping sometimes is not a reliable indicator of pest presence or abundance on the crop, and traps must be used in combination with visual inspection of plants. For example, plant inspection and traps provided similar measures of whether whitefly abundance was changing during much of a 9-week sampling period, as illustrated in Figure 7. However, during weeks 3, 5, and 7, relatively large differences in population trends were observed in traps in comparison with on plants. Relying on just one of these measures would have given a very different impression of pest density changes in comparison with using trapping and plant inspection in combination.

Unless other guidelines are recommended, use at least one sticky trap per 10,000 square feet (900 sq m) of growing area. When monitoring whiteflies, use about 1 trap per 1,000 square feet (90 sq m) of growing area. Although actual trap density will be dictated by the growing area and the time and effort devoted to trapping, each pest management unit should have at least one trap. Use bright yellow traps, each 3 by 5 inches or larger. If western flower thrips is the primary species of concern, consider using blue sticky traps as discussed in the thrips section later in this chapter.

Orienting traps horizontally (facing the soil) is sometimes recommended when monitoring pests such as fungus gnats emerging from media. However, in most programs, to catch the most insects, orient the longest part of the trap vertically (up and down). Place each trap so that the bottom of the trap is even with the top of the plant canopy. For rapidly growing crops, locate the trap's bottom a few inches above the canopy so that the plants don't overgrow the traps. As plants grow, move each trap up so that its bottom remains about even with the top of the canopy. Use one or two clothespins to attach each trap to a bamboo post or wood dowel embedded in the growing media or stand. Alternatively, hang traps from rafters or wires strung between posts.

Number each trap and map its location in your growing area. Inspect each trap at least once or twice weekly. It is easiest to replace traps each time you inspect them. Traps can be wrapped in clear plastic and taken to a more comfortable location for counting later that day. Alternatively, replace traps when they become too fouled to count insects quickly. If traps are reused, note this because catches become cumulative and you must subtract the number of insects present last time traps were checked.

Since many insects in traps may be harmless or beneficial, carefully identify insects before taking action. Use the illustrations and photographs here and in the individual pest sections to help you in identification. Additional high-quality color photographs and distinguishing line drawings of commonly trapped insects are available in *Sticky Trap Monitoring of Insect Pests* (Dreistadt, Newman, and Robb 1998). You can also wrap used traps in clear plastic (such as Saran wrap) to preserve them and take traps containing unknown pests to a Cooperative Extension or county agricultural department expert for help in identification.

Count the number of each type of pest caught. Record these data in a form like Figure 34. It is not necessary to count all insects on the entire trap; counting the insects in a vertical, 1-inch-wide (2.5-cm-wide) column on both sides of the trap gives results that are representative of the entire trap. Do not reduce traps to 1-inch vertical strips, as smaller traps may be less attractive to insects.

Interpreting trap information. Regularly summarize trap data to facilitate comparison, for example, by graphing the average of all traps from each sample date (Fig. 7). Interpreting trap information requires knowledge, skill, and practice and may be more art than science. Traps catch both migrating insects as well as adults that emerged from the crop. Canopy density, plant foliage quality, and temperature influence adults' tendency to fly. Wind and ventilation fans can discourage flight, reducing trap catches. The number of adults trapped may temporarily drop after a pesticide application, even if there has been relatively little change in immature populations on foliage. Conversely, adult numbers of some species may temporarily increase in traps after applying an adulticide, so the numbers caught for several days after an application should not be used when comparing adult densities among sample dates. Foliage disturbances, such as sprinkling with water or shaking plants to promote pollination or

Yellow sticky traps are used to monitor adults of many insect pests. Orient each trap vertically and place the bottom of the trap even with the top of the plant canopy. As plants grow, move the traps up so that the bottom remains about even with the top of the canopy.

Yellow Sticky Trap Record Form

Trap location _____   Scout's name _____

Date traps out _____   Date traps collected or checked _____

Trap no.	Days trap was up	Number of insects*						Others/ Comments
		Leafminers	Thrips	Whiteflies	Fungus gnats	Shore flies	Aphids	
Total								
Average								
Previous avg.								
Trend								

Comments

*Insects per trap or per 1-inch-wide column (note which).

Be sure to record when traps are changed. Unless traps are collected each time they are checked, numbers in traps are cumulative. If traps are reused, note this because catches become cumulative; in order to determine the number of insects caught during the most recent period in reused traps, you must subtract all previous catches.

Figure 34. Sample sticky trap record form. Be sure the location of each trap is recorded, such as on a map of the growing area as in Figure 4. You can copy (or enlarge) this sample to create your own original form.

monitor adults, increase trap catches. Even large numbers of pest species in traps do not necessarily indicate that control action is needed.

Consistent use of well-maintained traps is an important tool for experienced users in determining whether treatments are warranted, as discussed in the thresholds section later in this chapter. However, because many variables influence trap catches, always use traps in combination with foliage inspection.

Shaking plants. Certain mites and insects, including those listed in Table 51, can be monitored by shaking or tapping plants, also called branch beating. Determine whether pests that are readily dislodged are present by holding a collecting surface such as a clipboard with a white sheet of paper beneath the plant. Shake the plant or sharply tap it or its container

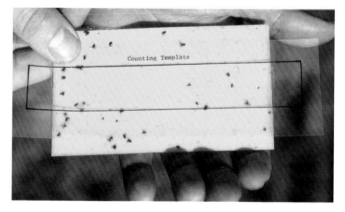

An accurate estimate of pest populations can be obtained by counting only a vertical column 1 inch (25 mm) wide, as illustrated here by the counting template placed over a trap. However, do not reduce traps to 1-inch vertical strips, as smaller traps may be less attractive to insects.

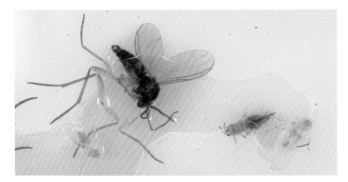

A fungus gnat (left) is much larger than a thrips (center right) or a whitefly (far right) in this sticky trap. A second whitefly lays across one of the fungus gnat's legs (lower left). Traps must be inspected every few days because, for example, the whitish wings and entire body of the whitefly will become almost invisible in the trap adhesive.

Liriomyza species leafminers are robust flies and mostly black and bright yellow. Adults have short bristles on their body and a yellow patch on their thorax.

Instead of counting insects on traps in the field, traps can be wrapped in clear plastic and taken to a more comfortable location for counting later that day.

Monitor pests that are readily dislodged by shaking the plant or sharply tapping it or its container two or three times. Hold a collecting surface such as a clipboard with a white sheet of paper beneath the plant. Examine the paper and record whether live individuals of species of concern to you are present.

two or three times. Examine the paper and note whether live individuals of species of concern to you are present.

In certain situations, such as when sampling flower heads for thrips, it may be easier and worth the destruction to clip the flower heads before shaking or beating them over paper. Adult thrips hidden in buds are stimulated to move by carbon dioxide; exhale a long, gentle breath into terminals, then shake terminals over a collecting surface. If plants are large or hardy, you can place a sweep net over foliage and shake it; empty the contents onto a clean surface and look for dislodged pests. Another method is to insert branches or bend the top of the plant into a white 5-gallon (19-l) bucket and beat the plant parts against the side for several seconds. If you're uncertain of the species' identification, use an aspirator (Fig. 35) to collect tiny or fast-moving insects so that you can freeze or kill them and examine them more closely.

If more precise data are needed and you have more time, beat sampling can be used as a quantitative measure. Use the same size collecting surface and the same method and number

of beats or shakes per plant each time you sample so that results are comparable between locations or over time. Monitor at about the same time of day on each date. Shake a set number of plants or a known amount of foliage each time you sample. For each shake sample, count and record the total number of each insect or use presence-absence sampling by recording only whether each type of pest was found in that shake sample. Compare numbers from one sample date to the next to determine whether pest populations are increasing or decreasing.

Degree-day monitoring. The growth rates of plants and invertebrates are closely related to temperature. Generally, the higher the temperature, the more rapid the development. Because of variation in temperatures, calendar dates are not a good guide for timing management actions. Measuring the amount of heat accumulated over time provides a physiological time scale that is biologically more useful than calendar days for timing control actions and deciding when to rotate pesticides to delay resistance development.

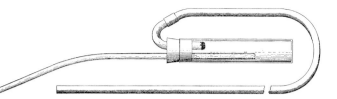

Figure 35. Use an aspirator to collect tiny or delicate insects from plants, growing areas, or sample collecting surfaces. Bend two copper tubes that fit snugly into a two-holed cork or cap. Place a screen over the inside of one tube (to prevent insects from being sucked out of the container into your lungs) and attach a flexible hose to the outside of that tube. Draw insects into the container by placing the outside end of the unscreened tube near the insect and sucking through the hose. Consult the list of suppliers at the end of this manual for sources of monitoring equipment such as aspirators. *Source: Anonymous 1952.*

ommended rotation time is every 2 to 3 pest generations. Monitoring degree-days instead of the calendar is a better method for determining when to rotate chemicals because the time for one generation can vary from days to months, depending on the pest species and temperature.

The unit used to measure physiological time is the "degree-day." Although overlapping pest generations limit degree-day (DD) use in flower and nursery crops in comparison with its extensive use in many nonfloral field crops, degree-days are still useful (see the individual pest sections later in this chapter). For example, when beet armyworm adults or other moths are caught in traps (an indication of pest egg-laying), degree-days can be used to determine when to begin spraying. Degree-day monitoring helps growers determine when specific life stages of pests are likely to be present so that pesticides that are effective only against certain life stages can be applied at the correct time.

Degree-days are also useful in managing pesticide resistance. When pests are frequently sprayed, growers should rotate applications among three or more materials with different modes of action to avoid exposing the same pest individuals to more than one type of insecticide. The rec-

One degree-day is defined as 1 degree above the lower threshold temperature maintained for a full day. The lower threshold temperature is the temperature below which no development or activity occurs. Pests do not feed, grow, or reproduce unless temperatures are above this threshold. Because development also slows and eventually stops if temperatures are too warm, an upper threshold is sometimes used when calculating degree-days in hot areas for certain pests. Each invertebrate species has a specific lower and sometimes an upper development threshold. The lower development threshold and the number of degree-days required to complete each life stage must be known in order to use degree-days for pest management.

Most computerized environmental monitoring and control equipment can automatically calculate degree-days. Dedicated devices installed in growing areas can also record temperatures and calculate degree-days. A programmable calculator, desktop computer, or printed chart for certain pests can be used to calculate degree-days if temperature records are available. Degree-day calculations and temperature data from a statewide weather monitoring system can also be accessed via Internet at the UC Statewide IPM Project's website at www.ipm.ucdavis.edu.

Degree-days for each day are estimated by subtracting the threshold temperature from the average daily temperature for that date. This manual calculation method is illustrated in Table 52, using a monitoring example detailed in the

Table 52. Approximating Degree-Days (DD) Manually.

Add the daily minimum and maximum temperature and divide by 2 to get the average daily temperature.	$\dfrac{78°F + 54°F}{2} = 66°F$			
Subtract the lower threshold temperature (for example, 50°F for cabbage looper, as listed in Table 53) from the average daily temperature. The result is the approximate number of degree-days accumulated that day.	$66°F - 50°F = 16\ DD$			

		Temperature, °F		
	Day	Minimum	Maximum	Average	DDs

Add up the degree-days accumulated for each day until you reach the sum when specific actions are recommended. For example, cabbage looper eggs hatch about 98 DD after being laid. Assuming that the beginning of egg laying (Day 1) coincides with when the first moths are caught in traps (as explained in the caterpillars section) and using the temperatures shown here, the soonest time to spray for caterpillars would be 6 days after catching the first moth, because this is when the number of degree-days required for egg hatch has been exceeded. Because moths may be caught and lay eggs over a prolonged period, you might wait longer than 6 days after catching the first moth before you begin spraying; the youngest larvae cause relatively little damage and delaying the first spray allows a single application to kill more of the larvae hatching from eggs laid later.

Day	Minimum	Maximum	Average	DDs
1	54	78	66	16
2	56	76	66	16
3	56	78	67	17
4	54	74	64	14
5	55	79	67	17
6	56	82	69	19
Accumulated Total Average				99

This "manual" method of degree-day estimating becomes significantly inaccurate when temperatures are near the threshold; for example, when the high temperature is above the lower threshold, but the mean is below the threshold, no degree-days accumulate using this manual method even though degree-day accumulation and insect development actually does occur. Computerized estimates available via the Internet at www.ipm.ucdavis.edu and elsewhere are more accurate. Growers can also purchase environmental computer monitoring systems or portable, compact, electronic temperature recorders that calculate and display degree-days.

Table 53. Lower Threshold Temperature and Generation Time of Some Flower and Nursery Crop Pests and Beneficials for Which Degree-Day Development Can Be Used to Facilitate Monitoring and Management.

Common name	Scientific name	Lower threshold (°F)[1]	Generation time[2] Degree-days	Days[3]
armyworm	*Pseudaletia unipuncta*	50	909	36
beet armyworm	*Spodoptera exigua*	54	930	44
black cutworm	*Agrotis ipsilon*	51	1,157	48
bollworm, corn earworm, or tomato fruitworm	*Helicoverpa zea*	55	760	38
cabbage aphid	*Brevicoryne brassicae*	44	283	9
cabbage looper	*Trichoplusia ni*	50	792	32
California red scale	*Aonidiella aurantii*	53	1,173	53
California red scale parasite	*Aphytis melinus*	50	408	16
convergent lady beetle	*Hippodamia convergens*	55	518	26
cotton aphid or melon aphid	*Aphis gossypii*	42	203	6
diamondback moth	*Plutella xylostella*	45	518	17
greenhouse whitefly	*Trialeurodes vaporariorum*	46	673	23
greenhouse whitefly parasite	*Encarsia formosa*	51	434	18
green peach aphid	*Myzus persicae*	39	254	7
lygus bug	*Lygus hesperus*	54	623	30
mite predator	*Metaseiulus occidentalis*	48	430	16
Pacific spider mite	*Tetranychus pacificus*	52	218	10
pea aphid	*Acyrthosiphon pisum*	42	197	6
San Jose scale	*Quadraspidiotus perniciosus*	51	1,050	44
serpentine leafminer	*Liriomyza trifolii*	50	565	25
silverleaf whitefly	*Bemisia argentifolii*	57	455	25
tobacco budworm	*Helicoverpa virescens*	55	760	38
twospotted spider mite	*Tetranychus urticae*	53	196	9
variegated cutworm	*Peridroma saucia*	45	1,216	41
western flower thrips	*Frankliniella occidentalis*	50	317	13
whitefly predaceous lady beetle	*Delphastus pusillus*	52	675	29

1. Upper threshold temperatures are also available for certain pests. Using upper thresholds in addition to lower thresholds can improve accuracy in growing areas with hot temperatures.

2. Generation times are for development from egg to adult. Some species have significant pre-egg laying (preovipositional) times; this time from adult emergence until egg laying is not included here. Some values are the average from more than one reported study. It may be helpful to obtain more precise values from the UC Statewide IPM Project website or by consulting your Cooperative Extension advisor.

3. Approximate generation time in days is when temperatures average 75°F (24°C). Because the number of days for one generation varies greatly depending on temperature, degree-days are a better estimate than calendar days.

caterpillars section later in this chapter. However, instead of this manual method, computerized "sine wave" calculation methods are recommended because they provide more accurate estimates.

Degree-day monitoring does not tell you whether control action is warranted; you must still monitor plants to decide whether thresholds are exceeded. Degree-day monitoring tells you when pests will reach susceptible life stages. If pests are abundant, monitoring degree-days helps eliminate the guesswork otherwise required to determine when to time a control action. Researchers have determined the threshold temperature and developmental times for many important flower and nursery crop pests, including those listed in Table 53.

Tolerate virtually no pests on mother stock and young plants in propagation. Pests can develop though many generations and increase to large numbers if crops are infested when plants are young.

Weeds in or near growing areas, such as outside entryways and other openings to greenhouses and nurseries, can host insect pests. Silverleaf whiteflies are infesting the underside of this thistle growing in a nursery container. Adult whiteflies can disperse to infest nearby crops.

Thresholds

A certain number of pest individuals and some amount of damage usually can be tolerated; this concept is fundamental to integrated pest management. Crops are grown for profit, so control action thresholds are based largely on economic criteria; action is warranted when it will improve crop quality or yield and result in increased revenue that exceeds the cost and adverse economic impacts of management. The importance of pest presence or damage is determined by many factors, including the type of pest and damage, crop species and cultivar, stage of plant development, time until harvest or sale, market conditions, and whether or not marketable plant parts are affected. In some situations, quarantines or other regulations may impose zero pest tolerance even when populations are low and pest species are not directly damaging to the crop.

Control action guidelines are available for certain insects (Tables 4, 6) and other pests affecting some flower crops. Although specific action thresholds and guidelines can be difficult to determine, thresholds can be developed over the long term by growers who regularly monitor crops and keep good records. See the thresholds discussion in the chapter "Managing Pests in Flower and Nursery Crops."

Management

Many growers have relied primarily on pesticide applications to control invertebrates. However, it is increasingly difficult, and in some instances impossible, to obtain satisfactory control by relying only on pesticides. Pesticide resistance and increasing regulation are among the reasons why alternatives such as exclusion, sanitation, resistant cultivars, and biological control must be used instead of or in combination with pesticides. In addition to effective controls, satisfactory management of invertebrates requires adequate knowledge, trained personnel, regular monitoring, and a comprehensive, integrated program that begins well before problems occur.

Integrated pest management is a strategy for preventing and minimizing pest damage that relies on a combination of techniques, including biological, cultural, environmental, and chemical controls. Decisions to employ methods are based on knowledge of pest biology and information from scouting or monitoring. Effective pest management begins when you prepare the growing area before planting, select plants adapted to that location, modify the environment, and properly plant and care for the crop. By providing proper cultural care and suitably modifying environmental conditions (such as temperature, humidity, light) you keep plants vigorous so they are less likely to be attacked by certain pests and are better able to tolerate any damage. An overview of the major control techniques is provided below. Consult the individual pest sections for information specific to certain pests.

Sanitation

Make the growing area as pest-free as possible before planting. Start with pest-free, high-quality planting stock. Do not introduce potentially infested plants or equipment into clean areas. Quarantine new plants by receiving them in a separate area, carefully inspecting them, and holding plants long enough to determine that they are pest-free. Before planting and regularly throughout the production cycle, thoroughly inspect in and around greenhouses for potential sources of pests.

Bag or destroy any crop residue immediately to prevent pest population buildup that can infest other crops. Avoid continuous cropping, which lets pests that have developed into high populations on older plants infest young crops. Consider immediately disposing of infested plants and those nearby when new infestations are limited to a small portion of the crop. Consult the sanitation methods summaries (Fig. 9, Table 7) and read the more detailed sanitation discussion in the chapter "Managing Pests in Flower and Nursery Crops."

Exclusion

Keeping pests out of growing areas (exclusion) is often the most effective control method. Exclude insects from field crops by using row covers or field cages. Isolate infested plants in greenhouses by using plastic sheeting or screening. Keep doors closed, except when entering or leaving the greenhouse. Construct double doors at greenhouse entrances. With double doors, workers and equipment must pass through a plant-free space between the two sets of doors

These culled plants and used growing media awaiting recycling can be a major source of insect pests and pathogens. Cover greenwaste, store debris well away from crops, or promptly compost crop residue to avoid this problem.

before entering the growing area. Create a positive pressure entrance by installing fans on the greenhouse wall so that they blow into the space between the two doors. This causes air to flow out the outside door, repelling windborne insects. To more effectively exclude insects, provide positive pressure ventilation throughout the greenhouse (see the chapter "Diseases"). Consult the exclusion methods checklist (Fig. 10) and read the more detailed exclusion discussion in the chapter "Managing Pests in Flower and Nursery Crops."

Insect screening. Microscreening can be an integral component of an integrated pest management program. Screen vents and doorways to greatly limit the movement of insect pests into the greenhouse. Some growers have reduced their pesticide use by 90% by using proper screening in combination with insect-free stock and good sanitation. Screens also keep predators and parasites from migrating out of the greenhouse where they are being released for biological control. Because some screens are small enough to exclude certain pests but large enough to allow smaller parasites to pass through them, screens may sometimes be used to create small biological control production areas within greenhouses. For example, growers could raise *Encarsia formosa* parasites on whiteflies in an enclosure screened with, for example, Lumite 2:1 twill weave polyethylene fiber (0.116 sq mm hole size). Parasites could pass through the screen and attack whiteflies throughout the greenhouse, but the whiteflies in the enclosure could not pass through the screen.

Screen material generally must have openings as small or smaller than the insects it excludes (Table 54). However, virtually any size screen will reduce the number of insects migrating into crops. Shade cloth or relatively large-mesh screen effectively excludes larger moth species, which are often drawn by lights at night. In the case of thrips, where the holes in most screens are larger than the pest's smallest dimension, screens still discourage many or even most thrips from passing through.

Screening reduces airflow. Choose the proper screen size mesh and surface area to assure adequate greenhouse ventilation. If you install screening over fans or vents, increase the surface area over the fan or vent to compensate for the reduction in airflow to prevent excess humidity and temperature in the greenhouse. For example, if 20 percent of the screen material is open (a proportion equal to 0.2), the screened area must be at least five times larger ($1/0.2 = 5$) than the surface area of unscreened vents in order to provide the same air flow after screening. The actual calculation of screen area and material should be considered carefully before installing screens. Growers must know their ventilation fans' static pressure limits (the fans' ability to move air against resistance). They should estimate the total volume and rate of air exchange desired in the greenhouse (such as 1 air change per minute). It may be necessary to use specific formulae or a device (a manometer) to estimate or measure

Table 54. Approximate Screen Hole Size Suggested for Excluding Insects.

Common name	Scientific name	Suggested maximum hole size[1]		
		Largest width		
		Inches	Micrometers	Area (sq mm)
greenhouse whitefly	Trialeurodes vaporariorum	0.011	288	0.08
green peach aphid	Myzus persicae	0.013–0.037	340–930	0.12–0.87
melon aphid	Aphis gossypii	0.017	435	0.19
serpentine leafminer	Liriomyza trifolii	0.025–0.037	640–930	0.41–0.87
silverleaf whitefly	Bemisia argentifolii	0.017	435	0.19
western flower thrips	Frankliniella occidentalis	0.008	192	0.04

1. Because the hole size of commercial screens is reported as hole width or area (length × width) using various units, several measures are provided here.

1 inch = 25.4 millimeters (mm) = 25,400 micrometers.
Sources: Bethke and Paine 1991, Bethke et al. 1994.

Double doors at greenhouse entrances and positive pressure ventilation prevent insect-contaminated air from flowing into greenhouses.

Screens retrofitted onto the vents, fans, and walls of this greenhouse, in combination with good sanitation, reduced insecticide use by 90% and resulted in better-quality plants.

air pressure differences in the greenhouse ventilation system. Manometers can also be used to measure air flow after screen installation and periodically afterwards, for example, to assess whether screens have become excessively clogged with debris. For help during the screen design process, consult *Insect Screening for Greenhouses* (Ross and Gill 1994) or a Cooperative Extension advisor, environmental engineer, or greenhouse or screening manufacturer.

Screen must be installed and maintained in a manner that provides good pest exclusion. Screens must be periodically cleaned, such as with a forceful stream of water directed outward from inside the greenhouse. Employees must understand that doors cannot be left open. Tears in screen material must be quickly repaired. Screening must be employed in combination with the control of weeds and other hosts around the greenhouse. Plants must be inspected and be pest-free before entering the growing area.

Ultraviolet-absorbing films and screens. Certain plastic coverings, vinyl films, and screens absorb or block ultraviolet (UV) light (light below about 360 to 380 nm). Applying these UV-absorbent materials to greenhouse covers may

Insect microscreening reduces airflow. To compensate for this problem, this grower increased the ventilation surface area by adding a relatively simple screened enclosure to the greenhouse wall containing air intake vents.

Cloth mesh row covers such as these can exclude insects from field-grown seedlings. This can be useful during the first few weeks of plant growth, especially when excluding insects that vector plant viruses. Carefully shake off soil and plant debris before reusing or storing covers to minimize potential movement of weed seeds or pathogen propagules on contaminated covers.

Reflective mulch covering planting rows prior to transplanting a crop into this field. Reflective mulch can dramatically reduce insect populations and infection by certain viruses in young field-grown crops.

discourage aphids, thrips, whiteflies, and certain other insects from entering greenhouses. Films that absorb UV also may reduce sporulation by certain pathogens, such as *Alternaria* species. There currently are few specific recommendations for manipulating UV light for pest management. Prolonging the life of plastic greenhouse coverings subject to degradation by UV light may be adequate justification for using UV-absorbing films or screens.

Row covers. Row covers, hot caps, and other types of cages were developed primarily to speed growth of young field-grown plants during early spring by raising temperatures beneath the cover. Row covers can also be used to screen beds and benches in greenhouses and nurseries as well as excluding pests from young field-grown crops. They can exclude migrating aphids, cucumber beetles, flea beetles, leafhoppers, leafminers, thrips, whiteflies, and other pests that feed on crops or vector viruses or other pathogens.

Any type of covering that excludes insects but allows light and air penetration can be used. Wood, wire, or plastic frames covered with muslin, nylon, or other mesh can be used for several years. Floating row covers can be placed on top of beds with no frames or hoops. The crop itself lifts the fabric as it grows. Vented polyethylene, spunbonded polyester, point-bonded polypropylene, and woven plastics are available for this use. Floating row covers are useful on sturdy crops that do not grow too tall. Use hoops, plastic tunnels, or wire strung between posts to hold up covers on plants that grow upright or have sensitive tips that might be damaged when pushing against covers.

Apply row covers during planting or before crops emerge. Field plants are normally covered or caged only temporarily, while plants are young and most susceptible to damage by many pests. Once plants get larger or temperatures get warmer, remove covers to provide enough growing space and

to prevent overheating. A drip or furrow irrigation system is necessary when using row covers.

Reflective mulch. Reflective mulch confuses and repels certain flying insects searching for plants, apparently because reflected ultraviolet light interferes with the insects' ability to locate hosts. Most uses of reflective mulch have been against winged aphids, but infestation of young plants by leafhoppers, thrips, and whiteflies has also been prevented or delayed. Although few floral crops have been studied, reflective mulches have been shown to be effective in many vegetable row crops attacked by melon aphid, silverleaf whitefly, and western flower thrips. In field-grown crops especially sensitive to viruses, the added cost of reflective mulch may be justified because the mulch can be significantly more effective than insecticides in preventing insect-vectored pathogen infection: insects that migrate in often have time to feed long enough to transmit viruses before being killed by pesticide residue on treated crops.

Reflective mulch may be useful in flower and nursery crops grown in the field from seed or small transplants. It is most effective during early growth when plants are small; as plants grow larger, it is less effective, and other methods may be needed. Reflective mulches cease to repel insects when the plant canopy covers more than about 60% of the soil surface.

Transplant through holes in the mulch or apply the mulch before plants emerge from the soil by leaving a thin mulch-free strip of soil along the planting row or by spraying a liquid mulch through which plants can emerge. Reflective mesh is also available for application over top a crop that can lift this light-weight material as plants grow. Various materials, such as plastic (polyethylene or nylon) film, can be used. Silver or gray are the most effective colors for reflective mulch or mesh, but white also works. Commercially available products include aluminum-metalized polyethylenes (such as those manufactured by Adcock and Sonoco, listed in the suppliers at the end of this manual) and silver embossed polyethylene (from AEP Industries, Polyon). White synthetic latex with silver pigment added is effective and easy to spray on soil before plants emerge, but it may not be reflective enough to use as reflective mulch. Aluminum foil is also effective, but it is expensive, delicate to handle, and probably is not commercially feasible on a large scale.

Reflective mulch may improve crop growth beyond that provided by pest control, possibly due to warmer night soil temperatures, more even soil moisture, and increased light levels. Consult the chapter "Weeds" before using mulch; certain mulches have other beneficial or negative effects, such as weed control, water conservation, or increasing crop susceptibility to root diseases.

Barriers. Barriers can exclude certain types of flightless invertebrates, including ants, larvae of armyworms and cutworms, snails and slugs, and many species of weevils. Control these pests by using unclimbable barriers to prevent ground-dwelling pests from climbing bench legs, to isolate pest-susceptible plants from surrounding areas that may be infested, and to segregate older plants likely to be infested from young plants more likely to be uninfested. Barriers include copper bands that repel mollusks, as discussed in the snails and slugs section later in this chapter; strips of heavy aluminum or other metal to exclude armyworms, as discussed in the caterpillars section later in this chapter; and various commercial or homemade slippery or sticky materials. One method is to sink the lower edge of aluminum strip flashing into the ground and coat the upper 1 inch (25 mm) of the barrier with grease on both sides or coat at least the side toward plants most likely to be infested. A band of commercially available sticky material (such as Tangle-foot or Stickem) also excludes flightless invertebrates. Grease or sticky material can be applied to encircle bench legs. Alternatively, coat the inside of containers that are inverted over the top of legs or blocks on which bench tops rest (Fig. 36). Using inverted containers at the top of legs instead of using containers on the floor eliminates worker

Figure 36. Exclude weevils and certain other flightless pests by applying grease or commercially available sticky material on bench legs. Or, (where indicated by arrows) coat the inside of containers inverted over the top of legs or blocks on which bench tops rest. Putting the inverted containers at the tops of legs gets them out of the way and keeps them from collecting debris or becoming fouled.

and equipment contact with sticky material or grease and reduces barrier fouling with debris or water.

Cultural Controls

Cultural controls are modifications of normal planting or plant care activities to reduce or avoid pest problems. Planting resistant cultivars (Table 12), altering planting times, or changing irrigation or fertilization practices are common cultural controls (see the chapter "Managing Pests in Flower and Nursery Crops"). Because practices such as selecting cultivars resistant to certain pests may favor other pest species (Table 55), growers need to learn the common local problems and possible pests for their crops by scouting regularly in order to make the best choices for their growing situation.

Mass Trapping

Pheromone-baited sticky traps effectively monitor certain pests, as discussed in the caterpillars section later in this chapter, and have been used experimentally for pest control.

Table 55. Comparative Susceptibility of Some Chrysanthemum Cultivars to Insect Damage.

Susceptibility[1]	Leafminers	Aphids	Thrips
Most susceptible	White Diamond	White Diamond	Pink Lady
	Pink Lady	Splendor	Fontana
	White View Time	White View Time	White Diamond
	Iridon	Fontana	Splendor
	Fontana	Iridon	White View Time
Least susceptible	Splendor	Pink Lady	Iridon

1. Cultivars are listed in order of decreasing susceptibility.
Source: Schuch et al. 1996.

Although yellow sticky ribbons can be used for pest monitoring, they are primarily used in experimental mass trapping insect control programs.

These aphids have turned orangish and fuzzy because they were killed by a naturally occurring fungal disease. Some insect-specific diseases are commercially available for controlling certain pests.

Standard-size or extra-large yellow sticky traps or yellow sticky tape strung along rows are used by some growers for trapping adult pests. There is little information on the effectiveness of control using traps; mass trapping may be unreliable and commercially infeasible on a large scale.

When traps are used for control, the apparent number necessary is substantial, reportedly 1 or more yellow sticky traps for every 40 square feet (3.7 sq m) of growing area. Sticky tapes may be a better choice for mass trapping. Conduct any mass trapping in combination with good sanitation and exclusion. Begin any mass trapping early in the season when populations are still low. Experiment first on a small, relatively isolated crop. Apply other measures if monitoring reveals that pest populations are continuing to increase.

Biological Controls

Biological control—the use of natural enemies to control pests and reduce damage—is increasingly being used in floral nursery crop pest management. Although biological control can be highly effective against certain pests, its use must generally be integrated with other methods, such as good exclusion and using only pesticides that are compatible with natural enemies. Because at least some low-level pest population must be present for biological control to be effective, one approach is to use biological control early in the production of a crop then rely more heavily on pesticides if needed prior to harvesting and marketing. Three primary groups of natural enemies are used in biological pest control: pathogens, parasites, and predators. Consult the *Natural Enemies Handbook* (Flint and Dreistadt 1998) and other publications listed in suggested reading for more detailed information on natural enemy identification, biology, and use.

Pathogens. Pathogens are microorganisms, including bacteria, fungi, nematodes, protozoa, and viruses, that infect and kill the host. Naturally occurring pathogens often help control pests. Certain of these pathogens are commercially available as microbial or biological pesticides. *Bacillus thuringiensis* (Bt), a naturally occurring bacterial pathogen of caterpillars, is the most widely used pathogen for pest control. Various Bt subspecies are commercially available for controlling foliage-feeding caterpillars (ssp. *aizawai* and *kurstaki*), leaf beetle larvae (ssp. *tenebrionis*), and larvae of mosquitoes, black flies, and fungus gnats (ssp. *israelensis*). As with most bacteria, Bt must be eaten by the insect before it can infect and kill its host. Other commercially available pathogens or their by-products for invertebrate control include the fungus *Beauveria bassiana*, the entomopathogenic nematodes *Heterorhabditis* and *Steinernema* species, and spinosyns.

Parasites. Parasites (more precisely called parasitoids because they kill their host) are smaller than their host and develop inside, or are attached to the outside, of the host's body. Typically the immature stage of the parasite feeds on the host, and the adult is free living. Each immature parasite usually kills only one host individual during its development (Fig. 37). Adults of certain parasites feed on the same pest species within which the immature parasites develop. In many species, this easily overlooked host feeding by adults is often a more important source of pest mortality that parasitization by immature stages.

Predators. Predators feed on more than one individual prey during their lifetime and are commonly about the same size or larger than the animals they eat. Many predators feed on a variety of insects, mites, and other invertebrates. These "general predators" feed on prey that is abundant and can be important in suppressing pests. Some also feed on pollen, nectar, and honeydew in addition to prey. Use the methods detailed in the conservation section later in this chapter, to increase numbers of predators. By conserving general preda-

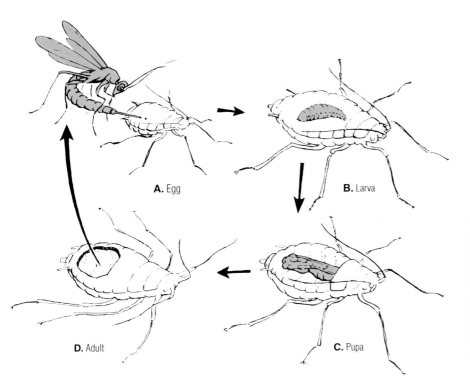

A. Egg

B. Larva

D. Adult

C. Pupa

Figure 37. The life cycle of a typical parasite is illustrated here with a species that attacks aphids. *A.* An adult parasite lays an egg inside a live aphid. *B.* The egg hatches into a parasite larva that grows as it feeds on the aphid's insides. *C.* After killing the aphid, the parasite pupates and develops into an adult wasp. *D.* The wasp chews a hole and emerges from the dead aphid, then flies off to find and parasitize other aphids. Typically, each parasite during its immature development kills only one host individual.

tors, some predators may already be present to help provide control if pest outbreaks do occur.

Kinds of biological control. Classical biological control, conservation, and augmentation are three tactics for using natural enemies. Classical biological control is the importation, release, and establishment of natural enemies of pests. Conservation is the use of management practices that conserve beneficial organisms that are already present or that may naturally colonize the site. Augmentation is the release of collected or insectary-reared natural enemies.

Classical biological control. Classical biological control is used primarily against pests that have been introduced from elsewhere. Many organisms that are not pests in their native habitat become unusually abundant when they arrive in a new area that lacks their natural controls. Researchers go to the pest's native habitat and collect the natural enemies that kill the pest. Natural enemies found to be beneficial are introduced into the new environment. If they become established, these introduced natural enemies may reduce their host to a level at which it no longer causes damage. By law, exotic natural enemies from foreign countries must be introduced only by qualified scientists with approved quarantine facilities. Be aware of these natural enemies and conserve them if you encounter them.

Classical biological control has primarily been used in field-grown perennial crops. Eucalyptus psyllid, several species of whitefly (ash, bayberry, and woolly), and certain species of scale insects are among the pests of flower or nursery crops

that have been controlled by introduced natural enemies. These insects in many situations are no longer pests, except where natural enemies are disrupted, such as by honeydew-seeking ants or pesticide applications.

Conservation. Predators and parasites that occur naturally in the field or that migrate into greenhouses sometimes control pests. Conserve resident natural enemies whenever you can by choosing cultural, physical, or chemical controls that do not interfere with or kill them. Avoid applying broad-spectrum persistent pesticides, or apply them in a selective manner. Natural enemies tend to be more susceptible to pesticides than are pests. In addition to immediately killing natural enemies that are present at the time of spraying (contact toxicity), the pesticides that are most disruptive to biological control leave residues on foliage that kill predators or parasites that migrate in many days or weeks after spraying (residual toxicity). Even if beneficial organisms survive an application, low levels of pesticide residues can alter the behavior of a natural enemy, reducing its ability to reproduce and to locate and kill pests.

Some ants are important predators of pests, but the common Argentine ant (also predaceous) and certain other ant species are often pests because they attack predators and parasites of honeydew-producing insects and disrupt biological control. See the ants section later in this chapter, for details on controlling ants that feed on honeydew produced by aphids, soft scales, whiteflies, mealybugs, and other sucking insects.

Dust can interfere with natural enemies and cause outbreaks of pests such as spider mites. Reduce dust by growing

Blue gum psyllids infesting *Eucalyptus pulverulenta* leaves. This pest in California has been biologically controlled by an introduced parasitic wasp that feeds inside psyllids, causing the psyllid bodies to become puffy mummies.

Learn to recognize predators and parasites. Obtain a colorful *Natural Enemies Are Your Allies!* poster (Flint and Clark 1990) and display it so that you and others can become familiar with common beneficial species.

windbreaks, installing plastic dust barriers, planting bare soil, sprinkling dirt surfaces with water before they experience heavy traffic, posting speed limits and driving slowly on dirt roads around fields, and minimizing cultivation and other disturbance of dry soil near crops.

Beneficials may require vegetation for hiding from their own natural enemies, for overwintering, and to protect them from adverse weather or environmental conditions. A diverse environment also generally harbors low populations of many different plant-feeding arthropods, which may serve as alternate hosts for the more general natural enemies. Environmental diversity helps maintain beneficials so that they remain in the local habitat and are present to help prevent and control pest outbreaks.

Most adult parasites and many adult predators feed only on pollen and nectar. Even if pests are abundant for the predaceous and parasitic stages, all life stages of the natural enemy may be uncommon or absent and biological control may be ineffective if food is unavailable for egg-laying adults. Growing certain insectary plants or a variety of plant species can provide natural enemies with food and shelter and increase populations of beneficials. Artificial foods containing sugars, yeasts, and proteins are commercially available to attract and feed green lacewings and certain other beneficials. However, there is relatively little research-based information on the effectiveness of insectary plants or how to practically employ artificial foods for pest management; field use is largely experimental.

Augmentation. When natural enemies are not present or their numbers are too low, populations can be augmented (see the releasing natural enemies effectively and nurse plants sections later in this chapter). Many natural enemies are commercially available (Table 56) through mail order (see the list of suppliers at the back of this manual). A good place to start with augmentation is in situations similar to those where researchers or other pest managers have previously demonstrated success. Desperate situations where pests are already abundant or damage is common are not a good opportunity for augmentation. Much of the information on releases in this manual has been extrapolated from field crops or greenhouse vegetables. Damage thresholds in those systems are commonly higher than in greenhouse flower crops.

Begin small by testing the effectiveness of a release on an isolated portion of the crop. Because pest presence is necessary to sustain natural enemies, choose crops where some levels of the target pests and their damage can be tolerated. Begin making releases early in the production cycle. Consider what other pests may occur in the crop and how they can be managed in ways that are compatible with biological control. Make other necessary changes in production practices, for example, by avoiding use of pesticides that harm natural enemies.

Inoculation and inundation are two tactics for augmenting natural enemies. In inoculation, relatively few natural enemies are released when pest populations are low. The introduced predators or parasites reproduce, and it is their progeny, not the released individuals, that are expected to provide biological control. Releasing the mealybug destroyer lady beetle (*Cryptolaemus montrouzieri*) in the spring to

Table 56. Some Commercial Natural Enemies Available for Release Against Pests.

Target pest	Natural enemy Common name	Scientific name	For more information
aphids	aphid midge	*Aphidoletes aphidimyza*	Table 67
	convergent lady beetle	*Hippodamia convergens*	
	lacewings	*Chrysoperla* spp.	
	microbial insecticide	*Beauveria bassiana*	
	minute pirate bugs	*Orius insidiosus, O. tristicolor*	
	parasitic wasps	*Aphelinus, Aphidius* spp., *Diaeretiella rapae*, others	
broad mites	predaceous mites	*Neoseiulus* spp.	Table 73
caterpillars	egg parasites	*Trichogramma* spp.	pages 157–159, 206–208
	entomopathogenic nematodes	*Steinernema carpocapsae, Heterorhabditis bacteriophora*	
	larval parasites	several host-specific ssp.	
	microbial insecticides	*Bacillus thuringiensis* ssp. *kurstaki*, Bt ssp. *aizawai*, *Beauveria bassiana*	
fungus gnats	entomopathogenic nematodes	*Steinernema carpocapsae, S. feltiae*	Table 70, pages 157–159
	microbial insecticide	*Bacillus thuringiensis* ssp. *israelensis*	
	predaceous mite	*Hypoaspis miles*	
mealybugs	citrus mealybug parasite	*Leptomastix dactylopii*	pages 151–152, 157, 184–186
	lacewings	*Chrysoperla* spp.	
	mealybug destroyer	*Cryptolaemus montrouzieri*	
	microbial insecticides	*Beauveria bassiana*	
scale insects	predaceous lady beetle	*Rhyzobius* (=*Lindorus*) *lophanthae*	page 189
	red scale parasite	*Aphytis melinus*	
	soft scale parasites	*Metaphycus helvolus, Microterys flavus*	
serpentine leafminer	parasitic wasps	*Dacnusa, Diglyphus* spp.	pages 169–170
	parasitic nematode	*Steinernema carpocapsae*	
snail, brown garden	predatory snail	*Ruminia decollata*[1]	pages 222–223
spider mites	lacewings	*Chrysoperla* spp.	Table 73, pages 151–152
	predatory cecidomyiid	*Feltiella* sp.	
	predatory mites	*Amblyseius, Metaseiulus, Neoseiulus, Phytoseiulus* spp.	
thrips	greenhouse thrips parasite	*Thripobius semiluteus*	Table 62
	lacewings	*Chrysoperla* spp.	
	microbial insecticide	*Beauveria bassiana*	
	minute pirate bugs	*Orius insidiosus, O. tristicolor*	
	predatory mites	*Amblyseius, Euseius, Iphiseius, Neoseiulus* spp., *Hypoaspis miles*	
weevils	entomopathogenic nematodes	*Steinernema carpocapsae, Heterorhabditis bacteriophora*	pages 157–159, 210
white grubs	parasitic nematodes	*Steinernema carpocapsae, Heterorhabditis bacteriophora*	pages 157–159, 211
whiteflies	lacewings	*Chrysoperla* spp.	pages 151–152, 176-179
	microbial insecticide	*Beauveria bassiana*	
	parasitic wasps	*Encarsia, Eretmocerus* spp. and others	
	predaceous lady beetle	*Delphastus pusillus*	

See the list of suppliers at the end of this manual for sources of natural enemies. Other newly registered insect pathogens not listed here may also be available.

1. Releases are legal in California only in certain southern parts of the state. See the snails and slugs section later in this chapter, or contact your County Agricultural Commissioner for more details.

control mealybugs is an example of inoculative release. The mealybug destroyer is effective in killing mealybug species that feed openly on foliage or stems, but it overwinters poorly outdoors in California and needs to be reintroduced to target areas in the spring.

Inundative releases involve large numbers of natural enemies, often released several times over a growing season. The natural enemies released, and possibly their progeny, are expected to provide biological control. Periodically releasing

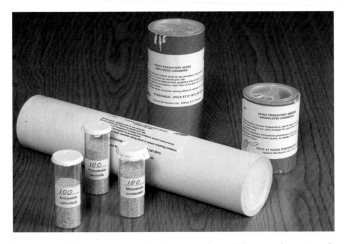

Many natural enemies are available for purchase. When resident natural enemies are insufficient, releases can augment biological control in certain situations.

Trichogramma species (parasitic wasps) to destroy moth eggs is an example of inundative biological control.

Releasing natural enemies effectively. Effectively releasing natural enemies requires knowledge, practice, and imagination. Good monitoring and effective pest exclusion can be critical. Anticipate pest problems and plan releases ahead of time. Begin making releases early in the season, before pests are too abundant or intolerable damage is imminent. Since pests must be present to provide food for natural enemies, be prepared to tolerate some pests and possible damage; the low damage thresholds in many ornamental crops are an impediment to biological control.

Natural enemies may not always be able to keep pest populations below acceptable damage thresholds. Some of the natural enemy species that are available may be the easiest and most economical to produce and sell, but not the most effective species for control.

Releases often fail because information or experience was inadequate, the wrong species was released, natural enemies were of poor quality, the timing was incorrect, pesticides were applied, or the beneficials were overwhelmed by a migration of pests.

The releases. Increase the likelihood that natural enemy releases will be effective by accurately identifying the pest and its life stages. Parasites and many predators attack only certain pest stages; release the beneficial species when the pest is in its vulnerable life stage or stages. The pest life stage that can be effectively controlled with natural enemies may be different from the pest stage that damages plants. For example, *Trichogramma* species kill only eggs of moths and butterflies; they are not effective against caterpillars. *Trichogramma* must be released when moths are laying eggs, before the caterpillars become abundant.

Remember that natural enemies are living organisms that require water, food, shelter, and suitable growing conditions. Natural enemies may be adversely affected by extreme conditions such as hot temperatures. Residues of certain pesticides can persist for weeks or months, harming natural enemies long after losing their effectiveness against pest species. Overhead irrigation may drown natural enemies. Many beneficial species stop reproducing under short day length or prolonged cool conditions. Supplemental light may be necessary for some predators and parasites to be effective year-round. Environmental conditions required by natural enemies (such as long days) may not be compatible with production needs of certain crops.

Natural enemy quality. The quality of commercially available natural enemies is not regulated and may sometimes be poor due to production practices, inadequate packaging, or unsuitable conditions during shipment. Obtain beneficials from a quality supplier, as suggested by supplier membership in the Association of Natural Bio-Control Producers. Find out when and how they will be shipped and what day they are expected to arrive. Release the beneficials as soon as conditions are suitable and learn how to store them until they can be released.

Evaluate the quantity and quality of each shipment of natural enemies. Take samples to estimate numbers or emergence. For example, when beneficials arrive in parasitized hosts, count parasite exit holes immediately after parasites arrive. Recount and compare the number of emergence holes about 10 days after deploying parasites. Another method is to isolate a few infested unsprayed plants or deliberately infest clean plants, introduce the natural enemies, then reinspect plants after a few days to determine whether natural enemies have established and are reproducing.

When natural enemies (typically predators) arrive in a shaker-type container, estimate their numbers and calibrate your application rate by making one shake over a sheet of white paper and counting the number of apparently alive or active natural enemies. Repeat this several times to estimate the average number of predators per shake. If predators or parasitized hosts arrive on leaves, use a hand lens or dissecting binocular microscope to examine the underside of a leaf from each of several plants and estimate the natural enemies per leaf. Contact the supplier immediately if natural enemy quality is unsatisfactory.

Besides emergence or immediate viability upon arrival, sex ratio, longevity, and size of individual insects can influence the effectiveness of any particular batch of beneficials. It is often impractical for most growers to assess these and certain other attributes contributing to natural enemy quality.

Releases in an IPM program. The best control may be obtained when a combination of more than one species is released. Releases are likely to fail unless growers also use good monitoring, exclusion, sanitation, and other compatible control methods. Controls for other pests in the crop and production practices must not be damaging to natural enemies. In many cases, the value of the plants and availability of alternatives may not justify the cost and effort of releasing natural enemies.

Avoid applying broad-spectrum or persistent pesticides; if they must be used, apply them as spot sprays. Many pyrethroids and organophosphates are especially toxic to natural enemies (Table 57). Plants received from propagators often have insecticide residue that may persist for several weeks or more than a month, killing natural enemies. Before exposing parasites or predators to new plants or foliage sprayed with materials of unknown toxicity, confine several beneficials in each of several clear, ventilated containers, each with a leaf from a different plant. If most parasites or predators are dead within a few hours, delay releases until residues have degraded. Use low-persistence materials or alternative methods to provide any necessary pest control until it is safe to introduce beneficials. Some suppliers recommend specific waiting periods before release based on the particular natural enemy species and the specific pesticide applied. Consult the *Natural Enemies Handbook* (Flint and Dreistadt 1998) and other publications listed in suggested reading for more detailed information on incorporating natural enemy use into IPM programs.

Nurse plants. Nurse (or banker) plants may be an economical way for sophisticated users to produce natural enemies for their own use in certain situations. Natural enemies produced on-site are more readily available when needed. Users can rear species or strains that may not be commercially available or are better adapted for local conditions because the initial beneficial population can be collected in that area. By doing their own rearing, users become more familiar with natural enemy identification and biology. The major disadvantage is that on-site production requires time and space to grow susceptible plants, rear the target pest or suitable alternative host, and produce sufficient numbers of good-quality beneficials. Problems in producing any one of these three (plant, pest, beneficial) can frustrate the entire project.

When heavily infested plants are found, instead of treating or disposing of the plants, consider caging or covering them and (if in containers) move them from the general growing area to an isolated or enclosed location. Observe the plants to determine whether they have been naturally colonized by locally occurring beneficial species or strains that can be reared. Alternatively, purchase or collect the appropriate natural enemies and introduce and confine them on the infested plants. Once the natural enemies reproduce and become abundant, release the beneficials into the crop.

Nurse plants are most feasible where relatively simple procedures have been demonstrated, such as rearing certain

Table 57. Relative Toxicity to Natural Enemies of Insecticides.

Insecticide	Toxicity[1]	
	Direct contact	Residual contact
microbials	no	no
botanicals	yes/no[2]	no
oil, soap	yes	no
IGRs	yes/no[2]	yes/no[2]
carbamates, organophosphates	yes	yes
pyrethroids	yes	yes

For more detailed information, consult the latest UC IPM *Pest Management Guidelines: Floriculture and Ornamental Nurseries.*

1. Direct contact toxicity is killing within several hours from spraying the beneficial or its habitat. Residual contact toxicity is killing or sublethal effects (such as reduced reproduction) due to residues that persist.
2. Toxicity depends on the specific material and natural enemy.

predatory mites on mite-infested bean plants or on bean pollen without host mites. In some situations, natural enemies can be introduced from nurse plants without introducing pests. Mealybug destroyer lady beetles or *Leptomastix* parasites discussed in the mealybugs section later in this chapter, can be reared in wide-mouth jars or buckets containing sprouted potatoes or *Coleus* infested with mealybugs. Mealybug parasites and predators can fly but mealybugs cannot, so a band of Vaseline, sticky material, or other barrier applied inside near the top of the container prevents mealybugs from walking out while allowing the parasitic wasps and adult lady beetles to fly away to nearby crops.

Certain screens are small enough to prevent whiteflies from escaping but large enough for whitefly parasites to pass through. Parasitic wasps and predaceous *Aphidoletes* have been introduced for aphid control by rearing them on plants heavily infested with an aphid species that does not attack broadleaved plants, such as the greenbug (*Schizaphis graminum*), which is easily cultured on cereals and grasses.

Important Natural Enemies

Common pests for which natural enemies can be purchased and released are listed in Table 56; conserving resident natural enemy populations can often be more effective and economical than purchasing and releasing them. Introduction methods vary depending on the pest, crop, and growing conditions and on the species, life stage, and packaging of the natural enemies. This section discusses several groups of common natural enemies; specific natural enemies for particular pests are discussed in the pest sections later in this chapter.

Green and brown lacewings. Green lacewings (family Chrysopidae) and brown lacewings (Hemerobiidae) are named for the many-branched veins in their wings. Adult green lacewings have golden eyes, green slender bodies, and green wings with netlike veins. Adult brown lacewings look like green lacewings, except that brown lacewings are typically about one-half as large and are brown instead of green.

Green lacewings lay their tiny oblong green to gray eggs on slender stalks. Depending on the species, eggs are laid singly, in rows, or in clusters. The oblong eggs of brown lacewings are laid singly on plants and look similar to the syrphid egg pictured in the aphids section later in this chapter.

Lacewing larvae have flattened bodies that are tapered at the tail and are usually pale with darker markings. They develop through three instars. Larvae have tubular sucking mouthparts, distinct legs, and look like tiny alligators. In comparison with green lacewings, brown lacewing larvae are more slender and smaller. Unlike green lacewings, brown lacewing larvae often move their head rapidly from side to side when seeking prey.

Green lacewings pupate in round, whitish cocoons attached to plants or substrates near where larvae fed. Brown lacewings pupate in a flat, white, silken cocoon. Brown and green lacewing biology is similar, except that brown lacewings prefer cooler temperatures and appear to be less common.

Green lacewings are sometimes called aphidlions because they often feed on aphids; however, lacewings also prey on mites and a wide variety of small insects, including caterpillars, leafhoppers, mealybugs, whiteflies, and insect eggs. All lacewing larvae are predaceous; depending on the species, adult green lacewings may feed on insects (*Chrysopa* spp.) or only on honeydew, nectar, and pollen (*Chrysoperla* spp.). Brown lacewings are predaceous as both larvae and adults. They feed on mites and soft-bodied insects, especially aphids, mealybugs, scales, and whiteflies.

Green lacewings (*Chrysoperla* spp.) can be purchased as eggs or larvae. Releasing larvae may be more effective than dispersing eggs. Eggs can be held at room temperature until larvae begin hatching, then distributed. However, larvae will cannibalize each other if held together.

Lacewing adults tend to disperse before laying eggs. Although lacewings released as immatures may provide control, they may disperse after pupating and not reproduce where released. Application of Wheast (a proteinaceous by-product of cheese making) combined with sucrose has been found to attract adult green lacewings and stimulate them to lay more eggs in some field crops. The benefit of lacewing attractants has not been tested in floral crops.

Predaceous bugs. Although many bugs are plant-feeding pests, other species are predaceous. Beneficial groups include assassin bugs (family Reduviidae), bigeyed bugs (subfamily Geocorine, family Lygaeidae), damsel bugs (Nabidae), and minute pirate bugs (Anthocoridae).

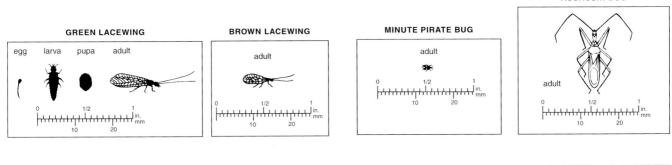

Green lacewing larvae are flattened, tapered at the tail, have distinct legs, and look like tiny alligators. This third-instar *Chrysoperla rufilabris* is eating a rose aphid by using its long, curved, tubular mandibles to puncture and suck the fluids out of its prey. Lacewings' varied prey include caterpillars, leafhoppers, mealybugs, psyllids, whiteflies, and insect eggs.

This adult minute pirate bug (*Orius tristicolor*) is feeding on an aphid. *Orius* also eats mites, psyllids, thrips, and insect eggs.

In addition to naturally occurring populations that may be important in the field, some minute pirate bugs (*Orius* spp.) are commercially available. *Orius* prey mostly on aphids, mites, psyllids, thrips, and insect eggs. Adults are ¹⁄₁₂ to ¹⁄₅ inch (2–5 mm) long, oval, black or purplish with white markings, and have a triangular head. As with most true bugs, adults have a triangular or X-shaped pattern on the back caused by the folding of their half-dark and half-clear wings. Nymphs emerge from obscure, oval eggs laid in plant tissue; they are pear shaped, yellowish or reddish brown, and so small that they may be overlooked in monitoring.

Predaceous beetles. Beetles (order Coleoptera) are the most diverse of all insects, with over a quarter of a million known species in about 150 families. About 40 beetle families contain predaceous species. Important groups include lady beetles, ground beetles, soldier beetles or leather-winged beetles, and rove beetles.

Lady beetles. Adult lady beetles (family Coccinellidae) are easily recognized by their shiny, convex, half-dome shape. They have short, clubbed antennae. Some species are brightly colored while others are plain and dark. Most adults and larvae feed on mites or soft-bodied insects such as mealybugs, scales, and whiteflies. Many species eat only certain types of insects; for example, most of the larger, reddish orange lady beetles eat primarily aphids. Most adult lady beetles can feed on nectar, honeydew, and pollen, which are important food sources when prey are scarce. Eggs are oblong or spindle shaped; depending on species, eggs are laid singly or in clus-

ters near prey. Larvae are active, elongate, and alligatorlike, usually with long legs. The roundish pupae are usually attached to plants and are often colorful, elaborately sculptured, or have spines. Larvae and pupae of the common convergent lady beetle are pictured in the aphids section.

Ground beetles. Most ground beetles (family Carabidae) are predaceous as adults and larvae, feeding on snails, slugs, root-feeding insects, and insect larvae and pupae. Adults are commonly black or dark reddish, although some species are brilliantly colored or iridescent. Most species have a prominent thorax that is wider than their head. Their long antennae are eleven-segmented and not clubbed at the end. They dwell on the ground, have long legs, and are fast runners. Adults usually hide during the day and feed at night.

PREDACEOUS GROUND BEETLES

Predaceous ground beetles have long legs and a prominent thorax that is wider than their head, and they are fast runners. Adults usually hide during the day and stalk prey on soil or in litter at night. They feed on soil-dwelling larvae and pupae of insects such as cutworms and wireworms and other invertebrates such as snails and slugs.

CONVERGENT LADY BEETLE

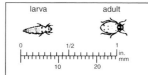
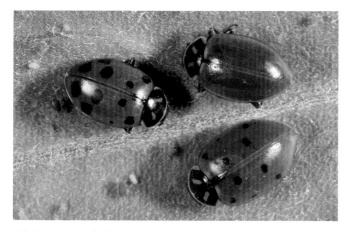

Adult convergent lady beetles are mostly orange and typically have 12 black spots; however, many individuals have fewer spots and some have none. Naturally occurring populations are important predators of aphids.

SOLDIER BEETLE

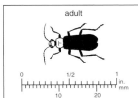

Adult soldier beetles are long and narrow, usually with an orangish head and thorax and dark wing covers. Soldier beetle adults are often observed feeding on aphids or pollen.

SYRPHID

PREDACEOUS MIDGE

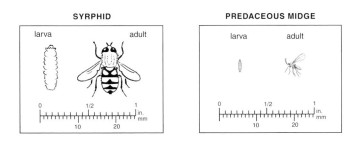

Eggs are laid in moist soil, sometimes in specially molded mud cells attached to plants or stones. Larvae dwell in litter or soil. They are elongate, have a large head with distinct mandibles, are sharply tapered toward the rear end, and usually have ten well-defined segments. Carabids pupate in a cell in soil or litter. Most species take about a year to complete the cycle from egg to adult, and adults live about 2 or 3 years.

Soldier beetles. Adult soldier beetles or leather-winged beetles (family Cantharidae) are elongate, often with a red, orange or yellow head and abdomen and black, gray, or brown, soft wing covers. Adults of some species feed on pollen and nectar and are often found on flowers. Others are predaceous on aphids and insect eggs and larvae or feed on both flowers and insects. Larvae are dark, elongate, and flattened. Larvae feed under bark or in soil or litter, primarily on eggs and larvae of beetles, moths, butterflies, and other insects.

Predaceous flies. Predaceous flies (order Diptera) are mostly small and soft-bodied. Flies differ from most other insects because they have only one (instead of two) pairs of wings. At least 20 families of flies have species that are predaceous as larvae or adults. The most frequently observed predaceous flies are flower flies (family Syrphidae), aphid flies (Chamaemyiidae), and predaceous midges (Cecidomyiidae). Adults in these groups are not predaceous; they eat pollen and nectar. Adult syrphids look like honey bees but do not sting, as seen in the picture of an adult syrphid in the aphids section. Adult syrphids are often seen feeding on flower nectar. Adults of the other predaceous flies are tiny, delicate insects. Adults lay their oblong eggs singly or in scattered groups on plants near prey, as illustrated in the aphids section.

Larvae of these flies prey on soft-bodied pests such as aphids, mealybugs, mites, and some scales. Larvae are maggotlike and can be green, yellow, brown, orangish, or whitish.

The large hover fly larva *(Scaeva pyrastri)* is light green with a white line down its back. At first glance this beneficial might be mistaken for a pest caterpillar. However, syrphid larvae are legless while caterpillars have 3 pairs of short legs on their thorax. Larvae of some syrphids and all aphid flies and predaceous midges are much smaller than caterpillars and can easily be overlooked among a colony of aphids.

Adults of many beneficial tachinid species are robust and dark. They look like house flies, except that tachinids have stout bristles at the tip of the abdomen. Tachinids are important parasites of beetles, bugs, and larvae of armyworms, cutworms, leafrollers, and loopers.

Larvae molt through three stages before forming oblong to teardrop-shaped pupae.

Parasitic flies. At least twelve families of flies contain parasitic species. Flies are second only to the Hymenoptera in their importance as parasites. Tachinidae is the most important family of flies providing biological control. Most are internal parasites of immature beetles, moths, and butterflies; other hosts include true bugs, grasshoppers, and earwigs. Adults are often dark, robust, hairy flies that look like a house fly.

Some adult tachinids can lay eggs or larvae in or on their host. However, most parasitic flies do not have a well-developed egg laying organ. Many flies oviposit or larviposit on plants. Some species enter their host by being eaten. After killing their host, fly larvae may leave the dead skin and pupate elsewhere. Tachinid pupae are commonly oblong and dark reddish and often occur in litter beneath plants.

Parasitic wasps. Wasps (order Hymenoptera) are the most important parasites or parasitoids. Parasitic Hymenoptera commonly are small to minute wasps that do not sting humans. Thousands of species occur in over 40 families, and most species of insects are attacked by one or more species of parasitic Hymenoptera.

The family Aphelinidae attacks aphids, caterpillars, mealybugs, psyllids, true bugs, and whiteflies. Most Aphidiidae are internal parasites of aphids. Encyrtidae attack spiders and all kinds of insects, most commonly scales and mealybugs. Other important parasite families include Braconidae, Chalcididae, Eulophidae, Ichneumonidae, and Trichogrammatidae.

Pesticides

Pesticides are substances applied to kill or repel pests and to prevent or reduce pest damage. Many pesticides are available that have low toxicity to workers and natural enemies, including microbials (also called biologicals), soaps, oils (narrow-range or superior), botanicals, and insect growth regulators (IGRs). These reduced-risk pesticides (Table 58) are usually more compatible with other integrated pest management methods than broad-spectrum carbamate, organophosphate, and pyrethroid pesticides. However, in part because of their more specialized and selective modes of action, these alternative pesticides often require more knowledge, skill, and careful application to be effective. Use these alternative pesticides whenever possible to provide good control of target pests, to reduce or avoid secondary outbreaks of other potential pests (Figure 38), and to minimize hazards to workers and natural enemies that help control pests.

Understand the relative toxicity, mode of action, persistence, and safe and legal use of pesticides. You then can use reduced-risk pesticides effectively, more favorably manage natural enemies, and avoid potential problems. For example,

An adult *Trichogramma pretiosum* wasp laying its egg inside a *Heliothis* moth egg. This parasite is about the size of the period at the end of this sentence.

Many pests have developed resistance to certain pesticides. Consider sending samples to a diagnostic laboratory if resistance is suspected. In this picture, spider mites are being brushed from a leaf into an acaricide-treated petri dish. Mites will be brushed into several other dishes containing a range of pesticide concentrations and checked for mortality after several hours to determine whether they are resistant to the pesticides.

Table 58. Some IPM-Compatible, Biological, and Reduced-Risk Insecticides and Miticides for Flower and Nursery Crops.

Insecticide common name	Aphids	Caterpillars	Fungus gnats	Leafminers	Mealybugs	Mites	Scales	Thrips	Weevils	Whiteflies
abamectin	○	○	○	●	○	●	○	◑	○	○
azadirachtin, neem	◑	●	●	◑	○	○	○	◑	○	◑
Bacillus thuringiensis ssp. *israelensis*	○	○	●	○	○	○	○	○	○	○
Bacillus thuringiensis ssp. *kurstaki*, ssp. *aizawai*	○	●	○	○	○	○	○	○	○	○
Beauveria bassiana[1]	◑	◑	○	○	◑	○	○	●	◑	●
buprofezin	●						●			●
cinnamaldehyde	◑	○	○	○	○	●	○	●	○	●
cyromazine	○	○	●	●	○	○	○	○	○	○
diflubenzuron	○	●	●	○	○	○	○	○	○	○
fenoxycarb	●	○	○	○	○	○	○	◑	○	●
Heterorhabditis bacteriophora	○	○	○	◑	○	○	○	○	●	○
imidacloprid	●	○	○	○	●	○	●	●	●	●
kinoprene	●	○	●	○	●	○	●	○	○	●
oil	●	◑	○	○	●	●	●	◑	○	●
pyrethrum	●	◑	●	◑	○	◑	○	○	○	●
pyridaben	●	○	○	○	○	●	●	○	○	◑
rotenone		◑								
soap	●	◑	○	○	●	●	●	◑	○	●
spinosad	○	●	○	●	○	○	○	●	○	○
Steinernema carpocapsae	○	○	◑	◑	○	○	○	○	●	○
Steinernema feltiae	○	○	●	○	○	○	○	○	○	○

KEY: ○ = not effective   ◑ = efficacy uncertain or variable in part depending on pest species and life stage   ● = effective

Consult Table 59 for trade names and chemical classification of these pesticides. Check current labels for permitted uses. For example, a pesticide cannot be used in greenhouses unless greenhouse is listed on the label. For detailed recommendations, consult the latest *UC IPM Pest Management Guidelines: Floriculture and Ornamental Nurseries*.

1. Allow at least 48 hr between application of *Beauveria bassiana* and fungicides.

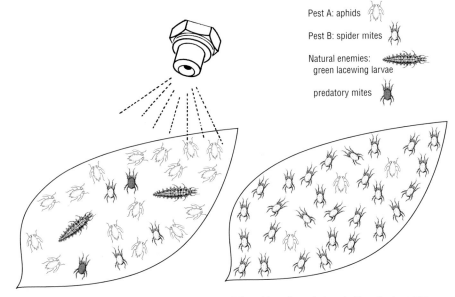

Pest A: aphids

Pest B: spider mites

Natural enemies: green lacewing larvae

predatory mites

A pesticide applied to control pest A also kills natural enemies that are controlling pest B.

Released from the control exerted by natural enemies, pest B builds up to economically damaging levels.

Figure 38. Destruction of natural enemies often results in secondary outbreaks of insects and mites. For example, spider mites are often present on plants at low densities but become excessively abundant and cause damage when pesticides applied against other species kill the natural enemies of the spider mites. Here a pesticide applied to kill aphids (Pest A) not only killed aphids but also killed predaceous green lacewing larvae and predatory mites, leading to a secondary outbreak of spider mites (Pest B).

many broad-spectrum pesticides can be hazardous to workers, prompting longer worker reentry intervals after application that can interfere with other crop production practices. For more discussion on pesticides, see the chapter "Managing Pests in Flower and Nursery Crops" and consult *The Safe and Effective Use of Pesticides* (O'Connor-Marer 1999) and other publications listed in the suggested reading.

Pesticides can damage plants (cause phytotoxicity), especially if plants lack proper cultural care, environmental conditions are extreme, or pesticides are used carelessly. See the phytotoxicity section in the chapter "Abiotic Disorders and Cultural Practices" for help in diagnosing and avoiding pesticide phytotoxicity.

Pesticide resistance. Populations of many flower and nursery pests have developed resistance to certain pesticides (Fig. 12), primarily carbamates, organophosphates, and pyrethroids. Resistant pests can no longer be controlled by the pesticides that previously were effective against them. See the pesticide resistance section in the chapter "Managing Pests in Flower and Nursery Crops" for recommendations on avoiding pesticide resistance (Table 15). Always use pesticides in combination with other IPM methods. Unless otherwise directed on the labeling, delay resistance development by switching to a pesticide with a different mode of action (Table 59) about every 2 to 3 pest generations. Monitoring temperatures using degree-days is an accurate method of determining pest generation time (Table 53) and when to rotate to pesticides with a different mode of action. Pesticides in different classes usually have a different mode of action. However, because carbamates and organophosphates have the same mode of action, rotating between pesticides in these two groups will not help avoid resistance.

Types of Insecticides

Pesticides for controlling insects, mites, and other invertebrates are briefly described in this section and later in the sections on each type of pest. These discussions emphasize lower-toxicity and reduced-risk pesticides that are most compatible with other IPM methods. Although many of these pesticides selectively control only certain types of invertebrates, they can often be mixed and applied together to control a broader range of pests. For example, entomopathogenic nematodes combined with Bt or insecticidal soap can be applied to plants infested with a complex of soil- and foliage-feeding pests, including aphids, armyworms, cucumber beetles, loopers, weevils, and white grubs. For detailed recommendations, consult the latest *UC IPM Pest Management Guidelines: Floriculture and Ornamental Nurseries*.

Microbial or biological insecticides. Microbial pesticides, sometimes called biologicals, are naturally occurring pathogens or their by-products that are commercially pro-

duced for pest control. Most microbials affect only a certain group or several related groups of pests. These commercial products present little or no toxicity to humans. Most have low toxicity to beneficial insects or significantly lower toxicity to natural enemies than persistent, broad-spectrum pesticides. *Bacillus thuringiensis* (Bt), the most widely used pathogen for pest control, is discussed and illustrated in the sections on caterpillars and fungus gnats. Microbials that control plant pathogens, also called mycofungicides, are discussed in the chapter "Diseases." Abamectin, *Beauveria bassiana*, entomopathogenic nematodes, and spinosyns are discussed below.

Abamectin. Abamectin (Avid) is a mixture of similar avermectins, compounds derived from the soil bacterium *Streptomyces avermitilis*. Commercial abamectin is a fermentation product of this bacterium. It acts as an insecticide and miticide that affects the nervous system of invertebrates and paralyzes them. It controls several pests, including leafminers and mites. Abamectin has some systemic activity and a short residual toxicity of several days or less.

Beauveria. *Beauveria bassiana* (BotaniGard) is a fungus that can control aphids, thrips, whiteflies, and certain other insects. *Beauveria* is highly compatible with other biological and integrated control methods. Its use is recommended mostly in greenhouses, in part because ultraviolet radiation that is partly filtered by greenhouse coverings causes the material to decompose outdoors. *Beauveria* does not appear to have special humidity requirements, and its residue on leaf undersides can persist more than a week. Excellent spray coverage is required. Two or more applications may be required at a frequency of about 3 to 7 days, depending on the pest species and population density, host crop, and growing environment. Its efficacy does not become apparent until several days after the first application because the pathogen requires some time to infect and develop in its host. The haemocyls (body fluid) of infected insects often develop a pinkish appearance. This color helps confirm that insects have been killed by the application. This beneficial fungus is incompatible with certain fungicides, which must not be applied within 48 hours of applying *Beauveria*. Certain spray adjuvants may also have fungicidal properties that make them incompatible as a mix with *Beauveria*. Store the product in a dry, cool location, less than 68°F (20°C), until used.

Entomopathogenic nematodes. Nematodes are tiny (usually microscopic) roundworms. Pest species feed on plants as discussed in the chapter "Nematodes." Nematodes that kill insects are discussed here; these beneficials are called entomopathogenic nematodes because hosts are killed by the nematode in combination with associated bacteria, usually within several days of infection.

Table 59. Chemical Classification of Some Pesticides Used to Control Insects, Mites, and Other Invertebrate Pests of Flower and Nursery Crops.

Pesticide classification	Common name (Trade names)
acetaldehyde	metaldehyde (Clean Crop, Cooke, Corry's, Deadline, Durham)
botanical: alkaloid, pyridine	nicotine (Nicotine smoke generator)
botanical: dicarboxylic acid; IGR: ecdysone hormone mimic	azadirachtin (Azatin, Neemazad), neem (Triact)
botanical: pyrethrins	pyrethrum (PT 1600 X-Clude), pyrethrum + piperonyl butoxide (Pyrenone)
botanical: rotenoid; metabolic inhibitor: electron transport chain site I	rotenone + pyrethrins (Pyrellin E.C.)
botanical: unsaturated carbonyl	cinnamaldehyde (Cinnacure, Cinnamite)
carbamate	aldicarb (Temik), carbaryl (Sevin), methiocarb (Mesurol)
chlorinated hydrocarbon	dicofol (Kelthane), endosulfan (Thiodan), oxythioquinox (Joust, Morestan)
chloronicotinyl, pyridine	imidacloprid (Marathon, Merit)
IGR: chitin synthesis inhibitor	cyromazine (Citation), diflubenzuron (Adept, Dimilin)
IGR: juvenile hormone analogue	fenoxycarb (Award), kinoprene (Enstar II)
inorganic: iron phosphate	iron phosphate (Sluggo)
inorganic: silica gel	silica gel + pyrethrins (Drione, Eliminator, Micro-cide, Tri-die)
inorganic: sodium aluminofluride	cryolite (Kryocide, Prokil)
metabolic inhibitor: electron transport chain site I	pyridaben (Sanmite)
metabolic inhibitor: electron transport chain site II	hydramethylnon (Amdro, Combat, Maxforce)
microbial: avermectin, macrocyclic lactone	abamectin (Avid)
microbial: entomopathogenic fungus	*Beauveria bassiana* (BotaniGard)
microbial: entomopathogenic nematode	*Heterorhabditis bacteriophora* (Cruiser)
microbial: entomopathogenic nematode	*Steinernema carpocapsae* (Savior, Scanmask, Vector)
microbial: entomopathogenic nematode	*Steinernema feltiae* (Nemasys M, X-Gnat)
microbial: spinosyns	spinosad (Conserve)
microbial: thuringiensin	*Bacillus thuringiensis* ssp. *aizawai* (Xentari)
microbial: thuringiensin	*Bacillus thuringiensis* ssp. *israelensis* (Gnatrol)
microbial: thuringiensin	*Bacillus thuringiensis* ssp. *kurstaki* (Biobit, Bio-worm Killer, BT Worm Killer, Caterpillar Clobber, Condor, Crymax, Cutlass, Dipel, Mattch, MVP, Worm-Ender)
organophosphate	acephate (Orthene), chlorpyrifos (Dursban, Lorsban), diazinon (Knox-out), dimethoate (Cygon), disulfoton (Disyston), malathion, oxydemeton-methyl (Metasystox-R), naled (Dibrom)
organosulfur	propargite (omite)
organotin	fenbutatin-oxide (Isotox, Rosepride Orthenex)
potassium salt of fatty acids	soap (M-Pede)
pyrethroid ester	bifenthrin (Talstar), cyfluthrin (Decathlon), fenpropathrin (Tame), fluvalinate (Mavrik), lambda cyhalothrin (Demand, Scimitar), permethrin (Ambush, Astro, Pounce), resmethrin (PT 1200)
sulfur, inorganic	sulfur (Cooke, Drexel, Wilbur-Ellis)
superior-type petroleum oils	oil (Saf-T-Side, SunSpray)

Check current labels for permitted uses. For example, greenhouse must be listed on the label or the pesticide cannot be used in greenhouses. Classifications followed by a colon (botanical, IGR, microbial) are subdivided into groups of pesticides that have a different mode of action, are effective against different types of pests, or both. A pest resistant to one class of chemicals (e.g., microbial: avermectins) may still be susceptible to pesticides in a different subgroup of that class (e.g., microbial: spinosyns). Because carbamates and organophosphates have the same mode of action (inhibiting nerve system cholinesterase) rotating between pesticides in these two groups generally will not help to avoid pesticide resistance.

IGR = insect growth regulator

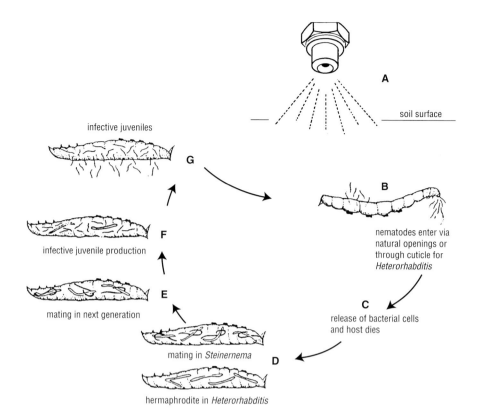

Figure 39. Life cycle of beneficial nematodes. *A.* Infective-stage nematodes are applied to soil. *B.* The nematodes seek a host and enter it. *C.* Once inside, the host is killed by nematodes and mutualistic bacteria carried by the nematodes. *D.* Nematodes feed, grow, mature, and reproduce. The initial development of nematodes in the host differs because there are no separate male and female nematodes in the first generation of *Heterorhabditis*, which are hermaphrodites. *E.* All generations of *Steinernema* and subsequent generations of *Heterorhabditis* in the host produce both males and females. *F.* Females produce infective-stage juvenile nematodes inside the dead host. *G.* Infective nematodes exit and seek hosts. Nematodes persist in media and in dead hosts and, under suitable conditions, can provide residual control. The entire life cycle from infection of the host to release of the new infective generation takes 7 to 14 days. Adapted from Kaya 1993.

Many insects are susceptible to entomopathogenic nematodes (Fig. 39). *Heterorhabditis* and *Steinernema* species (families Heterorhabditidae and Steinernematidae, respectively) entomopathogenic nematodes are commercially available for application primarily against soil-dwelling insects, including larvae and pupae of fungus gnats, white grubs, and weevils. They are also available to control other insects living in moist or humid environments, such as larvae of armyworms, cutworms, and wireworms. To help entomopathogenic nematodes infect and kill immature insects, drench the soil or container media when pest larvae or pupae are present and keep the growing media warm, at least 60°F (16°C), and moist (well-irrigated), but not soggy, before application and for 2 weeks afterward.

Certain pests that bore into plant tissue, such as leafminers, can be controlled by nematodes if the nematodes can be applied to reach their hosts (see the leafminers section). At high relative humidity, certain nematode species, such as *Steinernema carpocapsae*, are more tolerant of desiccation and may be able to control foliage-feeding insects like the diamondback moth (*Plutella xylostella*).

Heterorhabditis bacteriophora (formerly *H. heliothidis*) and *Steinernema carpocapsae* are the nematode species most commonly available commercially. As with all natural enemies, these species differ in the conditions under which they are most effective (Fig. 40).

Obtaining a relatively fresh product, such as by ordering directly from nematode producers, is critical. Nematodes are perishable, so store them under cool, dark conditions. In addition to applying nematodes in conventional sprayers, nematodes can also be applied through irrigation systems as long as they are not mixed with fungicides or other potentially toxic materials. Irrigation water should be well-aerated to provide nematodes with adequate oxygen. Each batch of nematodes should not be immersed for longer than about 24 hours before application.

Spinosyns. The spinosyns (Spinosad) are produced by fermentation of by-products from the bacterium *Saccharopolyspora spinosa* (Actinomycetes). Spinosyns are toxic to most caterpillars, fly larvae, thrips, and certain species of beetles and wasps. One of the most effective microbials, they also have relatively low toxicity to people.

Soap. Potassium salts of fatty acids, usually called soaps, are effective against mites and exposed insects, including aphids, immature scales, psyllids, and whiteflies. Soaps also have some fungicidal activity (see the chapter "Diseases"). Insecticidal soap has low toxicity to humans and wildlife. Although it can damage certain plants, especially species with dull leaf surfaces or many hairs, it can be applied to most crops without risk of phytotoxicity unless several successive applications are made. Before treating a new cultivar for the first time, make a test application on a few plants and observe them for damage over several days before treating the entire crop. Do not treat water-stressed plants or spray when it is expected to be hot or windy.

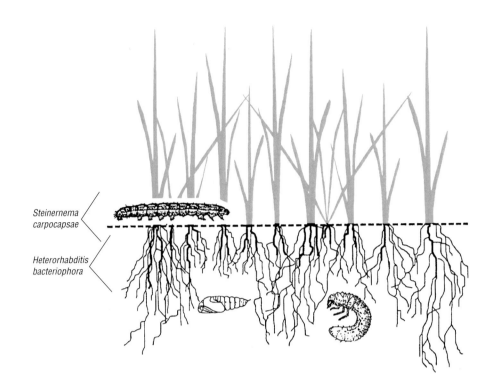

Figure 40. All natural enemies differ in the conditions under which they are effective. Understanding their biology greatly increases the effectiveness of control actions. As shown here, a combination of two commercially available entomopathogenic nematode species can be applied to control different life stages of the same insect pest or more than one species occupying different habitats. For example, *Steinernema carpocapsae* is a sit-and-wait forager that infects hosts that move near the soil surface, such as cutworms and armyworms. *Heterorhabditis bacteriophora* actively searches for prey below the soil surface and attacks hosts such as root-feeding grubs and underground pupae of moths. As with virtually all natural enemies, besides differences in behavior and habitat, the effectiveness of nematode species depends on the host species. *Source:* Kaya 1993.

Steinernema carpocapsae

Heterorhabditis bacteriophora

Oil. Narrow-range or horticultural oil, also called supreme or superior oil, is a highly refined petroleum product manufactured specifically to control pests on plants. Plant-derived oils, such as those made from neem (*Azadirachta indica*), are also available. In comparison with motor oils or many other petroleum products, narrow-range oils have low toxicity to humans and most wildlife. Some products may irritate skin and, as with all pesticides, should be kept away from the eyes.

Oil smothers insects by clogging spiracles, the tiny openings in their bodies through which they breathe. Narrow-range oil apparently also disrupts cell membranes, interfering with normal metabolic activities. Oils kill exposed soft-bodied immature and adult pests, including scales, aphids, mealybugs, mites, and whiteflies. Oil also kills pest eggs, which are unaffected by most other pesticides. Adults of some insects (such as whiteflies) may be temporarily repelled from oil-treated plants. Applying oil may also reduce transmission of viruses by aphids, thrips, and other sucking insects. Oils also controls certain plant pathogens (see the chapter "Diseases").

Oil can damage certain plants. Leaf, stem, or petal burn (marginal necrosis) can occur, or the color of foliage that is glaucous (waxy whitish or bluish) can change. Before treating a new cultivar for the first time, consider making a test application on a few plants and observe them over several days for damage before treating the entire crop. Do not apply oil when plants are drought stressed, when it is windy, or when temperatures are over 90°F (32°C) or below freezing. Do not apply oil in combination with sulfur or fungicides.

Avoid spraying oil when the relative humidity is expected to be above 90% for 48 hours. High humidity reduces the evaporation of oil, increasing its effectiveness against pests but also increasing the likelihood of phytotoxicity.

Use oils that say "supreme," "superior," or "narrow-range" on the label. These have a minimum unsulfonated residue (UR) of 92 percent and a minimum percent paraffin (%Cp) of 60, characteristics that make an oil relatively safe for plants. Some "dormant oils" and other oils are not safe for use on green plant tissue. For more details on effectively using oils see *Managing Insects & Mites With Spray Oils* (Davidson et al. 1991).

Botanicals. Botanical pesticides, including azadirachtin, cinnamaldehyde, pyrethrum, and rotenone, are derived from plants. They are effective against many exposed-feeding insects. Most botanicals are of low toxicity to humans; nicotine sulfate is a highly toxic exception. Botanicals break down rapidly after application, which makes them relatively safe for the environment. Most have only contact toxicity, so they must be applied when and where pests are present to be effective, although azadirachtin has some systemic activity.

Azadirachtin is extracted from the seeds of the neem tree. Neem extracts are very toxic to a wide range of invertebrate pests, deter certain pests from feeding or laying eggs on treated plants, and have systemic activity allowing the material to move within plants.

Natural cinnamaldehyde is derived from the bark of several *Cinnamomum* species trees, which are the source of the food spice cinnamon. The cinnamaldehyde used in pesticides

(Cinnacure, Cinnamite, No Mas) is synthesized. It can control algae and certain fungi, insects, and mites, including exposed eggs of mites and certain insects. For good control, treated surfaces should remain wet for about $\frac{1}{2}$ hour after application. Cinnamaldehyde provides contact toxicity only. Most residue is gone from plants within a few hours and application may be most effective early in the morning or later in the afternoon when the material may volatilize less quickly.

Pyrethrum (PT 1600 X-Clude) is derived from chrysanthemum flowers grown in Africa and South America. Many pyrethrum products (such as Pyrenone) include the synergist piperonyl butoxide. Insects may only be temporarily paralyzed (knocked down) and pests may recover from temporary effects of exposure to pyrethrum unless piperonyl butoxide is added. Rotenone is obtained from the roots of certain tropical plants. For ornamental use, rotenone may be available in commercial products only in combination with pyrethrum (Pyrellin).

Insect growth regulators. An increasingly important pest control material, insect growth regulators (IGRs) are often not immediately toxic to insects, but over the long term they can be among the most effective pesticides available if properly used. They act by interfering with a specific insect growth function, such as preventing the insect from molting. Because it can be several days to a week or more between each molt of a caterpillar, the pest will not be affected until the normal molting time arrives, so the effect of some IGRs is not immediately apparent. Insect growth regulators often have less adverse impact on beneficials than broad-spectrum insecticides, yet they can be very effective against certain pests. They have several modes of action (Table 59); most are synthesized from petroleum, but the botanical azadirachtin is also a growth regulator.

Pyrethroids. Pyrethroids, which are more persistent and more toxic to pests than natural botanicals, are synthesized from petroleum to produce chemical structures similar to naturally occurring pyrethrum insecticides. They have a relatively low toxicity to humans and other mammals. However, some pests rapidly develop resistance to pyrethroids (Fig. 12) and pyrethroids can be very toxic to natural enemies (Table 57), leading to resurgence or secondary pest outbreaks where natural enemies are important. Because most available pyrethroids (Table 59) are in the same class (pyrethroid esters), pests that develop resistance to one pyrethroid become resistant to other pyrethroids.

Inorganics. Inorganic insecticides are elements or salts usually refined from minerals. Sulfur, probably the first effective pesticide discovered, is commonly used to control mites and plant fungal diseases, such as powdery mildew. It is available in various dust, wettable powder, and vapor formulations. Do not treat plants labeled as sus-

ceptible to damage by sulfur and do not apply it during very hot or humid weather. Sulfur generally is not compatible with oil, fungal microbial pesticides, and predatory mites. Sulfur can irritate the skin and is harmful if inhaled, so wear appropriate protective personal equipment during application.

Synthetics. Organophosphates and carbamates are commonly used insecticides that are synthesized from petroleum. Most kill a wide variety of pests that are sprayed or that contact or eat treated foliage. Because they also kill many natural enemies and promote the development of resistance, consider using effective alternatives if they are available. Organophosphates and carbamates inhibit cholinesterase, an important enzyme in the nervous system of insects and vertebrates. Pests that develop resistance to organophosphates usually are resistant to carbamates and vice versa. Because all insects and mammals use cholinesterase to regulate nerve activity, these pesticides can adversely affect nontarget organisms. Workers may be injured if they are exposed to a large enough dose. Carefully follow all precautions on the pesticide label when using these materials.

Thrips

Over a dozen species of thrips (order Thysanoptera) attack flower and nursery crops in California. Western flower thrips (*Frankliniella occidentalis*) is the most serious problem; it can infest almost every species of flower crop. Banded greenhouse thrips (*Hercinothrips femoralis*), flower thrips (*Frankliniella tritici*), gladiolus thrips (*Taeniothrips simplex*), greenhouse thrips (*Heliothrips haemorrhoidalis*), and onion thrips (*Thrips tabaci*) are other relatively common species (see the chapter "Crop Tables"). *Thrips palmi* has become a pest in Florida and Hawaii and it may be introduced and become established in California.

Damage

Thrips feed on flowers, buds, terminals, bulbs, and corms. Damage does not become visible until some time after feeding. Once surrounding tissue grows, damaged leaves, buds, or petals become silvery, stippled, blotched, streaked, papery, or deformed. Infested buds or flowers may drop or fail to open. High populations of some species leave black, varnishlike specks of excrement.

Western flower thrips spreads impatiens necrotic spot virus and several strains of tomato spotted wilt virus. This ability to vector viruses is often the most serious damage from thrips. Thrips acquire viruses only as larvae when they feed on infected plants (Fig. 31). Adult thrips spread viruses as they feed among healthy plants. These viruses are incurable once plants are infected; virus prevention relies on eliminating infected plants and controlling western flower thrips.

Identification and Biology

Adult thrips are narrow, less than 1/20 inch (1.3 mm) long, and most often yellow, brownish, or shiny blackish. Adults have long fringes on the margins of their wings and move readily with the wind. Females insert tiny eggs into plants, commonly into leaves or buds. The elongate larvae are translucent white to yellowish. The pale prepupae and pupae occur mostly in the soil.

Adults and larvae puncture and kill individual plant cells. Western flower thrips and some other species also feed on pollen and mites. Thrips have several generations per year; the development time depends on the temperature (Table 52).

Most thrips can be positively identified to species only by an expert. Fortunately, most species of thrips are controlled by the same management methods. Learning whether a crop species or cultivar is highly susceptible to damage from thrips or thrips-vectored viruses and taking stringent preventive measures in those susceptible crops are probably more important than identifying the species.

Yet there are important differences among thrips. Onion thrips (*Thrips tabaci*) is frequently confused with western flower thrips and its close relatives, *Frankliniella* spp. Because western flower thrips and onion thrips behave differently, it can be very helpful to distinguish between them (Fig. 41). Western flower thrips is much less susceptible to most pesticides, and onion thrips is of relatively little importance in transmitting major viruses in flower crops. Accurately identifying thrips species is also important when using certain biological controls. For example, the parasite *Thripobius semiluteus* controls only greenhouse thrips, a relatively sluggish species that feeds openly in groups on the underside of leaves. This behavior helps to distinguish greenhouse thrips from most other pest species of thrips, which move relatively quickly and feed hidden within terminal plant parts such as buds (Fig. 42).

Western flower thrips feeding on the buds caused this color streaking in chrysanthemum petals once blossoms opened. This thrips can infest most species of floral crops.

Frankliniella spp.

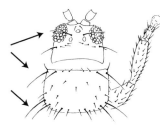

One pair of long setae (hairs) and some short hairs on head between compound eyes and ocelli; four long hairs on the both front and rear of pronotum (top of first thoracic segment, the segment containing first pair of legs).

Continuous row of short hairs behind forewing main vein.

Thrips tabaci

Only short hairs on head between compound eyes and ocelli; four long setae along rear of pronotum.

Row of hairs behind forewing main vein has 6 or 7 hairs near the base and 3 to 5 hairs near the tip, but row is not continuous.

Figure 41. Characteristics for distinguishing *Frankliniella* species (such as western flower thrips) from onion thrips (*Thrips tabaci*). Adapted from Malais and Ravensberg 1992. Illustrations from Papp and Kono 1977, reprinted with permission of California Department of Food and Agriculture.

These scabby brown western flower thrips feeding scars on rose sepals are unlikely to affect crop marketability. However, this injury indicates that thrips may be feeding in unopened buds. Unacceptable injury to blossoms occurs in many rose varieties when pest populations exceed 1 to 2 thrips per bud.

Monitoring

Early detection is critical. Thrips damage or virus infection does not become visible until some time after plants have been fed upon. Damage is not reversible and control becomes increasingly difficult as the population density of the thrips increases. In addition to monitoring thrips, monitor for thrips-vectored viruses, as discussed in the chapter "Diseases."

Traps. Sticky traps are a very important detection tool because traps capture adults before the insects or their damage are observed on plants. Yellow traps are effective for most insects, but blue sticky traps are more attractive to western flower thrips and certain other thrips species. In crops such as chrysanthemums, which are affected by many pests, yellow traps can be more efficient than blue because yellow attracts other insects; the same yellow traps can be used to monitor many different potential pests. Blue traps may be warranted for crops especially susceptible to thrips or where thrips are the major insect of concern, such as in African violets or roses. However, blue traps are harder to read than yellow traps because the insects are more difficult to discern against the darker background. Deploy at least one trap per 10,000 square feet (900 sq m) of growing area and check them at regular intervals. Place additional traps near doors and vents and in crops that are especially susceptible to thrips or virus damage.

Although trapping can be very efficient in detecting thrips, traps also catch migrating adults; the number of thrips in traps is not always a good measure of thrips density in the crop. Where different species or cultivars are grown together, it may be uncertain which plants were the source of the adults in the traps. The number of thrips also may not be a good indicator of potential virus spread because not all thrips are infectious (see the sticky traps section earlier in this chapter for discussion of interpreting catch information). Use traps in combination with plant inspection. Where viruses are a problem, use traps in combination with indicator plant monitoring, as discussed for viruses in the chapter "Diseases."

Visual inspection. Examine plants at least once a week for damage, thrips, and natural enemies of thrips. Check for thrips by tapping or shaking flowers or terminals over white paper or your hand. To uncover more thrips, take a deep breath, gently blow on the terminal or flower head for several seconds, then tap the terminal in combination with exhalation; the carbon dioxide in breath brings more thrips out of their protected habitats. Because thrips can move rapidly, an alternative method is to place randomly collected blossoms or partly open buds into a container with several drops of ethyl acetate. Wait at least ½ hour, then remove plant samples and shake them onto black or white paper, where the dead thrips will be dislodged and more readily

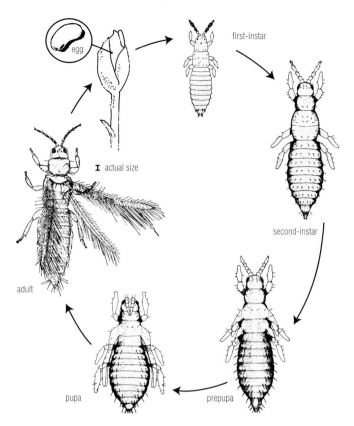

Figure 42. Most thrips develop through six life stages: adult, egg, first- and second-instar nymphs (sometimes called larvae), prepupa (or early pseudopupa), and pupa (or late pseudopupa). Prepupae and pupae of many species occur mostly in growing media or litter, but some are found in protected places in foliage or flowers. Only adults and nymphs are motile and feed. Western flower thrips develop from egg to adult in about 12 days at 86°F (30°C) and 40 days at 59°F (15°C). *Sources:* Adult from Anonymous 1952; immatures from McKenzie 1935.

Western flower thrips feeding damage includes black frass (feces) specks (on left leaf) and feeding scars that range from pale (on both leaves) to brownish (right leaf). Thrips also can introduce viruses, causing distinctly different symptoms.

observed and counted. Certain cultivars or colors tend to be more infested than others, so spend more time inspecting these once you identify them. Use plant inspection in combination with traps.

Tolerance levels. For most crops there are no treatment guidelines based on thrips density. Plants highly susceptible to viruses should be kept virtually free of thrips. Greenhouse cut roses are an exception (Table 4). Roses, however, are apparently not affected by tospoviruses, and research indicates that, except for the more susceptible cultivars, rose buds can tolerate up to about 2 thrips per bud without significant damage. Deciding when to treat most other crops is difficult and subjective; often there is no simple relationship between thrips density and plant damage, and thrips density in traps does not always correlate with thrips density in crops. However, growers who regularly inspect plants and consistently employ well-maintained traps can establish thresholds over the long term by judging the acceptability of the finished crop in comparison with historic monitoring records. Consult the thresholds section earlier in this chap-

Western flower thrips adults usually are mostly yellowish, often with a brown or blackish abdomen. In addition to direct feeding damage, this thrips is the primary vector of impatiens necrotic spot virus and tomato spotted wilt virus.

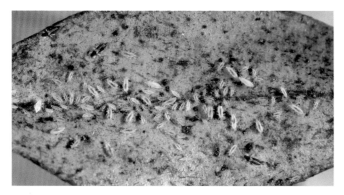

High populations of greenhouse thrips cover the lower leaf surface with black, varnishlike specks of excrement. This species can be controlled with contact sprays of oil or insecticidal soap because, unlike western flower thrips and other species that feed hidden in plant parts, greenhouse thrips feed openly on leaves in dense colonies of adults and immatures.

ter, keep good records, and adjust thresholds or monitoring methods as appropriate. Make treatments based on the visual presence of thrips in the crop, attainment of specified threshold levels of adults in traps based on past experience, and the presence of viruses in indicator plants. A combination of these methods will probably work best.

Management

Thrips can be difficult to manage, and even a few can cause serious damage if they vector viruses to sensitive crops. Most of the life stages of thrips are protected in plant parts or media, and populations can develop rapidly. Some thrips have become resistant to pesticides.

Prevent or minimize infestations by starting with clean plants, eliminating sources of thrips, and keeping pests out of growing areas. Consult the sanitation and exclusion sections in the chapter "Managing Pests in Flower and Nursery Crops," especially Figures 9 and 10, for more information on these critical control methods. Use less-susceptible cultivars, which also enhance the effectiveness of other control measures. Greatly reduce thrips damage by limiting pollen availability, culling unmarketable blossoms, growing blossoming crops separately from crops harvested before extensive flowering, and avoiding continuous cropping. Apply insecticides judiciously, such as by careful selection of active ingredients, rotation to minimize development of resistance, and targeting of plant parts most likely to be infested. Natural enemy introductions may be useful in certain situations.

Susceptible cultivars. Crop species and cultivars vary significantly in their susceptibility to thrips and viruses. For example, chrysanthemum cultivars vary one-hundred-fold in the extent to which western flower thrips feeding discolors foliage, and some cultivars of carnation (Table 60) and rose (Table 61) host more thrips than others. In the case of roses, cultivars with sepals that remain tightly wrapped around the bud until near harvest host fewer thrips than roses with sepals that open early. Where thrips feeding or virus infection has been a serious problem, seek information on less-susceptible crops and determine whether these can profitably be grown.

Pesticides. Chemical control of thrips is difficult. Most stages are protected from sprays: eggs are imbedded in tissue, larvae live in developing terminal leaves or buds, and pupae are found in media. Reinfestation occurs when thrips are carried into crops by wind or fly from nearby host plants. Western flower thrips is resistant to many pesticides. Use pesticides only in combination with good sanitation and exclusion; spraying alone is unlikely to provide good control over the long run.

Most insecticides primarily affect newly hatched larvae and recently emerged adults. To reduce high populations, make about three applications about 5 days apart. If temperatures are cool, increase the interval between applications.

Sequential applications catch thrips that were not in susceptible stages when the earlier applications were made. Provide good coverage of flowers, buds, and shoot terminals where most thrips occur. Ultra-low-volume or fog applications can reach more protected plant parts and spread the same amount of pesticide over a larger foliage area than high-volume (wet) sprays. Soil drenches may provide some control, but this has not been documented and actions targeting pupae do not kill thrips until after they finish feeding as nymphs on the plant.

Abamectin, azadirachtin, *Beauveria bassiana*, cinnamaldehyde, fenoxycarb, imidacloprid, and spinosad are IPM-compatible, biological, and reduced-risk insecticides that can control thrips. Except for greenhouse thrips that feed openly, oil and soap provide only moderate control of most species. However, horticultural or stylet oil can help reduce virus transmission by thrips and certain other infective insects. Materials that have been applied frequently or over long periods in an area are unlikely to be effective against thrips. Reduce the development of resistance by not exposing the same individual thrips to more than one type of pesticide; rotate insecticides by class (Table 59) every 2 to 3 thrips generations (about 4 to 6 weeks at 80°F). See the degree-days section earlier in this chapter for information on estimating thrips generation time. For specific pesticide recommendations consult *UC IPM Pest Management Guidelines: Floriculture and Ornamental Nurseries*.

Biological control. Resident populations of predaceous thrips, minute pirate bugs, and predaceous mites help control plant-feeding thrips in natural situations, but without augmentation they cannot be relied upon for adequate control in greenhouses and nurseries. Release of insectary-reared predaceous mites and minute pirate bugs have provided good control of thrips in some greenhouse vegetable crops, but results have been variable in flower crops, where thresholds are lower. For crops that are not highly susceptible to viruses transmitted by thrips and where some thrips feeding can be tolerated, natural enemy releases may control thrips on aboveground plant parts if the releases are begun early during production and combined with good sanitation and

Chrysanthemum buds recently discarded on the greenhouse floor can be a source of thrips. Place prunings and other crop debris into covered containers and dispose of waste away from crops to reduce the spread of pests.

Table 60. Comparison of Abundance of Western Flower Thrips in Some Carnation Cultivars.

Cultivar	Thrips per flower
Red Mini	39
Deep Pink	63
Blaze	69
Lavender Lace	70
Pike's Peak	70
Orchid Beauty	72
Hot Pink	73
Tangerine	73
White Sim	81
Chianti	84
May Brit	86
Red Sim	87
Parade	90
Pink Nora	90
Yellow Corona	115
Pink Mini	121

All cultivars were grown together in a commercial greenhouse. The number of thrips per flower is the average of all stages combined (except eggs) per harvested flower over 4 months. *Source:* Robb 1989.

Table 61. Comparison of Abundance of Western Flower Thrips in Some Rose Cultivars.

Cultivar	Thrips per flower
Cara Mia	2
Coquette	3
Prive	3
Samantha	3
Lavonde	4
Volare	4
Jack Frost	5
Mercedes	5
Royalty	5
Sonia	5
Golden Fantasie	9
Junior Bride	10
Golden Times	11
Gabriella	12
Sassy	16
Candea	17

All cultivars were grown together in a commercial greenhouse. The number of thrips per flower is the average of all stages combined (except eggs) per harvested flower over 4 months. *Source:* Robb 1989.

exclusion, such as screens (Table 54). Use only pesticides that are relatively compatible with natural enemies (see Table 66). Follow guidelines presented early in this chapter on releasing natural enemies effectively. Table 62 lists some commercially available thrips natural enemies and their attributes.

Bulb and Corm Thrips

Lily bulb thrips (*Liothrips vaneeckei*), gladiolus thrips (*Thrips simplex*), western flower thrips, and a few other species feed on bulbs or corms, either in storage or in the field. Thrips are best controlled during storage and by planting only clean stock in thrips-free media. Controls during storage include hot water (Table 9), insecticide dips, and fumigants. New methods, such as controlled atmosphere treatments during storage, are also being developed. The best control methods depend on the pest and crop species, risk of phytotoxicity, local storage conditions, and other pests, such as diseases, that may need to be controlled in storage.

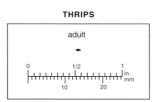

THRIPS

adult

A black and yellow adult *Thripobius* parasite (center left) among parasitized (black) and unparasitized (yellow) greenhouse thrips nymphs. Parasitized thrips blacken and swell at the head as the wasp larva matures inside. Adult greenhouse thrips are also black, but adult thrips are mobile and larger than the parasitized nymphs, which do not move.

Weeds and flowering plants such as this ice plant can be a source of thrips that can move into growing areas.

Table 62. Commercially Available Thrips Natural Enemies.

Natural enemy	Comments
Neoseiulus (=*Amblyseius*) *cucumeris*; *Neoseiulus barkeri* (=*Amblyseius mckenziei*); *Iphiseius* (=*Amblyseius*) *degenerans*	Predaceous mites that attack thrips nymphs and some eggs on foliage and flowers; mites also feed on spider mites, pollen, and fungi. Predators prefer 70° to 85°F (21° to 29°C) and relatively high humidity. If temperatures are less than about 80°F (27°C) and day length is less than about 13 hours, mites may stop reproducing and become ineffective. High numbers are needed, but these mites are relatively inexpensive. Suggested release rates are 10–50 mites/plant/week. If pollen is present as an alternate food, releases can begin early, before thrips are apparent.
Hypoaspis (=*Geolaelaps* or *Stratiolaelaps*) *miles*	Predaceous mite that can feed on thrips pupae in media near surface. Released primarily for fungus gnat control. High mite populations have reportedly reduced thrips pupal emergence by 30–60%. However, actions targeting pupae do not kill thrips until after thrips nymphs finish feeding on the plant. Suggested release rates are about 30–200 mites per square yard (40–250 per sq m) every 1–2 weeks for at least several releases.
Orius insidiosus; *Orius tristicolor*	Predaceous minute pirate bugs that eat all thrips stages and feed on aphids, mites, and small caterpillars. *Orius* reproduction is increased if relative humidity is ≥50%; reproduction stops under short day length. Often disperses from plants unless pollen is present. Suggested release rates range from 1–2 *Orius* per plant to 2,000–4,000 per acre (5,000–10,000 per ha). *Orius* can be shaken from plants before plants are sold and rereleased onto the remaining crop.
Thripobius semiluteus	Parasitic wasp that attacks only greenhouse thrips nymphs. Parasitized nymphs become swollen around the head and, about 2 weeks before the wasp's emergence, turn black, in contrast to the yellow color of unparasitized nymphs. The black parasitized nymphs are smaller than mature thrips and do not move. *Thripobius* develops from egg to adult in about 3 weeks when temperatures average 70°F (21°C). Suggested release rates are several thousand *Thripobius* per acre per week, beginning when greenhouse thrips nymphs first appear. Continue releases until at least 60% of nymphs are parasitized.

See the releasing natural enemies effectively section earlier in this chapter for details and qualifications on using biological control.

Field management strategies to control thrips include thorough incorporation or removal and disposal of crop residue after harvest, leaving fields fallow between cropping, rotating sites into nonhost crops for a season, and pasteurizing growing media before planting.

Leafminers

Larvae from several families of flies and moths mine leaves of flower and nursery crops. These pests are referred to collectively as *leafminers*. The most common and damaging species are small flies (family Agromyzidae), especially *Liriomyza* species that attack many different hosts. The most important species are the serpentine leafminer (*Liriomyza trifolii*) and the pea leafminer (*L. huidobrensis*). The chrysanthemum leafminer (*Phytomyza [=Chromatomyia] syngenesiae*), often seriously damages greenhouse-grown chrysanthemums in Europe, but this species is relatively uncommon in the United States.

Damage

Adult female leafminers puncture leaves and sometimes petals to feed on exuding sap. These punctures eventually turn white, giving foliage a stippled or speckled appearance. Females lay eggs in a portion of the leaf punctures. Eggs hatch into larvae, which are the most damaging leafminer stage. Each larva makes a winding tunnel (mine) or sometimes a blotch between the lower and upper leaf surface. The mine becomes longer and wider as the larva grows, making mined leaves unattractive and unmarketable. Relatively high damage can be tolerated in certain crops where foliage is not marketed, such as gerbera and seed crops. Mining usually has little impact on plant growth and rarely kills plants. Unusually heavy damage can slow plant growth and may cause infested leaves to drop.

Identification and Biology

Adult *Liriomyza* are small, active, black and yellow flies. Each female lays several dozen to several hundred tiny eggs in leaves. Larvae are yellow cylindrical maggots. Pupae are oblong and brown to gold.

It is difficult to distinguish among *Liriomyza* species. *Liriomyza trifolii* is smaller and has noticeably more yellow in comparison with the more creamy or whitish colored *L. huidobrensis*, which mostly mines the lower leaf surface, so its damage is most obvious when viewing leaves from their underside. *Liriomyza trifolii* mostly mines the upper leaf mesophyll, so its damage is most visible from above. Because of its smaller size, *Liriomyza trifolii* produces narrower mines that are often near the leaf margin and wind in a somewhat circular manner. *Liriomyza huidobrensis* frequently mines leaves near their base, often along middle veins. The adult *Phytomyza syngenesiae* is covered with short, stout bristles,

giving it an overall grayish appearance. It pupates in leaf mines, distinguishing it from *Liriomyza* spp., which drop to the soil to pupate. In California, *P. syngenesiae* is most often found infesting cineraria and Marguerite daisy. Whether species identification is important depends largely on what control methods are used.

Most leafminers, including all *Liriomyza*, are controlled using some of the same methods, such as exclusion screens (Table 54) and foliar contact sprays against adults. Species identification is important in certain situations as discussed below, such as when control actions target prepupae or pupae, or when biological controls are applied.

Leafminers have many generations per year. The generation time varies with temperature (Table 53) and host plant; egg to adult development ranges from about 2 weeks at 95°F (35°C) to 8 weeks at 60°F (16°C). One generation commonly requires 25 to 30 days at average greenhouse temperatures. Eggs hatch in about 2 to 5 days. Larvae develop through three instars and feed in the leaf for about 1 week. Mature third-instar *Liriomyza huidobrensis* and *L. trifolii* cut a slit in the leaf and drop to pupate on lower leaves or in the upper surface of media. *Chromatomyia syngenesiae* pupates inside leaves, so leafminer prepupae and pupae are not susceptible to soil drenches or *Hypoaspis* predator mites that feed on the surface of growing media. Pupal development time ranges from about 1 month at 60°F (16°C) to 9 days at 80°F (27°C).

Monitoring

Yellow sticky traps are the best method for early detection of leafminers. Use traps in combination with foliage inspection for larval mines because larvae are the most damaging life stage. Examine leaves for mines at least once each week. Take action promptly if mines are developing in marketable plant parts; uncontrolled leafminer populations can increase rapidly (see the thresholds section earlier in this chapter for help in deciding when to treat).

In chrysanthemums, a presence-absence sampling method has been developed for estimating leafminer density. Quantitatively estimating leafminer density can be especially helpful to growers who are developing treatment thresholds or estimating the number of leafminer parasites to release in an augmentative biological control program. For more information, consult *The Development of Sampling Strategies for Larvae of Liriomyza trifolii in Chrysanthemum* (Jones and Parrella 1986) and *Toward Predictable Biological Control of Liriomyza trifolii (Diptera: Agromyzidae) Infesting Greenhouse Cut Chrysanthemum* (Heinz, Nunney, Parrella 1993).

Traps. Deploy traps in greenhouses throughout the production cycle at a density of at least 1 trap per 10,000 square feet (900 sq m) unless other guidelines are recommended. Traps usually catch adults before leaf mining by larvae becomes obvious. Besides early pest detection, traps can indicate leafminer migration, hot spots in the growing area, or changes in pest density in the crop. Although no thresholds have been established based on the number of adults trapped, increased adults in traps can help experienced users decide whether treatment is warranted. Spray timing generally cannot be based directly on adult catches; few available materials are effective against leafminer adults.

Management

A combination of sanitation, exclusion, cultural practices, and pesticides are the most frequently used methods to control leafminers. Regular monitoring is also a vital component of leafminer management. Biological control can be effective under certain circumstances if good exclusion and sanitation are also employed. Some growers are experimenting with mass trapping of leafminers in greenhouses by deploying long strips of sticky yellow tape to attract and capture adult insects.

Consult the sanitation and exclusion sections earlier in this chapter for vital information on keeping leafminers out of crops (Figs. 9, 10). Do not bring stippled or mined plants into the growing area. Quarantine stippled plants for several days before using them to see if mines develop. Examine the crop and nearby plants for stippling and leaf mines at least once each week throughout production. Dispose of infested plants and plant debris. Control weeds that can host leafminers. Avoid continuous cropping. Provide a host-free period between crops; leafminers can emerge from pupae in soil for two weeks or more after all host plants have been removed. Isolate young plants from older crops likely to be infested. Avoid excess fertilization.

Resistant cultivars. When growing more-susceptible cultivars, group them together so they can be more intensively monitored and managed. Consider growing less-susceptible cultivars, especially if plants are grown near other hosts or leafminer populations are high. For example, chrysanthemum cultivars can vary ten- to twentyfold in their susceptibility to *Liriomyza trifolii* (Table 63). The susceptibility to aphids, leafminers, and thrips has been compared for several popular chrysanthemum cultivars (Table 55). The resistance of commercial cultivars is not sufficient to provide adequate leafminer control; however, using the resistance in available cultivars can improve the effectiveness of other control measures. Contact cultivar suppliers for current information on susceptibility to leafminers of various cultivars or develop you own information by comparing damage when growing multiple cultivars.

Pesticides. Spraying alone is unlikely to provide effective long-term control. Pesticides are more effective when used in combination with good sanitation and exclusion. When insecticides are relied on, begin applications as soon as mines are found in marketable plant parts or when past experience with sticky traps indicates that adult populations are likely reaching intolerable levels. If pesticides are necessary, use reduced-risk insecticides (Table 58).

If effective larvicides are available, use them, these generally provide better control than adulticides. Nematodes (see below) and a few insecticides are effective against larvae. Larvae are protected in leaf tissue where they can be killed only by nematodes that actively seek out and penetrate leaf openings or by larvicides that have systemic activity allowing them to penetrate the leaf tissue (such as abamectin, azadirachtin, and cyromazine). For example, the botanical larvicide azadirachtin can be quite effective in killing larvae, but mortality is often delayed until leafminers pupate, and this mortality is not easily observed. Larvicides can be used alone or at the same time as adulticides.

It is very difficult to control leafminers with adulticides. If effective materials are available, several applications generally will be needed to kill adults that are present and those that emerge from pupae after the initial spray. Apply contact sprays or fogs during daylight from early morning to mid-morning, when adult leafminers are more active. Spray perimeter plants most thoroughly, as they tend to be more heavily attacked than interior plants. Fog applications kill more adults than wet foliar sprays.

Table 63. Relative Susceptibility of Some Chrysanthemum Cultivars to the Leafminer *Liriomyza trifolii*.

Least susceptible

Accent, Albatross, Arctic, Baby Tears, Buckeye, Dark Yellow Fuji Mefo, Detroit News, Fred Shoesmith, Freedom, Fuji Mefo, Goldburst Mefo, Golden Crystal, Golden Knob Hill, Improved Mefo, Jackstraw, Mandarin, Nob Hill, Orange Bowl, Puritan, Red Stingray, Red Torch, Snow Crystal, Spirit, Splash, Splatter, Statesman, Stingray, Sunny Mandalay, Super White, Super Yellow, Surf, Tempo, Tinker Bell, Torch, Winter Carnival, Yellow Jacket, Yellow Mandalay, Yellow Knob Hill, Yellow Torch

Susceptible

Amber, Beauregard, Bright Golden Anne, Bright Yellow May Shoesmith, Charisma, Cloud-9, Cream Yellow Princess Anne, Dark Red Beauregard, Dignity, Golden Polaris, Golden Yellow Princess Anne, Jade, Jasmine, May Shoesmith, Paragon, Peacock, Polaris, Promenade, Ruby Mound, Solarama, Tip, Wildfire, Wild Honey, Yellow Cloud-9

More susceptible

Blue Marble, Florida Marble, White Marble

Highly susceptible

Iceflo, Icecap, Manatee Iceberg

For each cultivar, damage from adult stings and larval mines combined was compared with Manatee Iceberg, a cultivar classified as highly susceptible. In comparison with the amount of damage to Manatee Iceberg, the approximate percentage of damage sustained by each cultivar was: least susceptible, ≤25%; susceptible, 26–50%; more susceptible, 51–75%; and highly susceptible, >75%. Actual leafminer damage depends on many factors. Susceptibility to leafminers is one consideration among many when selecting a crop cultivar. *Source:* Yoder Brothers 1988.

Winding tunnels caused by leafminer larvae feeding in gerbera. White spots on the lower leaf were caused by adult feeding punctures. Heavily stippled leaves or petals may appear bleached or turn brown.

A greenish larva of the parasite *Diglyphus begini* (center) feeding on an orangish leafminer larva covered with dark excrement, viewed here through the leaf surface.

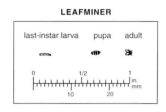

LEAFMINER

last-instar larva	pupa	adult

Adult *Liriomyza* species flies are small and mostly black with bright yellow. Yellow sticky traps are an effective method of detecting this pest and adults of many other insects.

Insecticides do not generally control leafminer eggs and pupae. Soil drenches (including entomopathogenic nematodes, organophosphates, and pyrethroids) may be available for use against pupae, but there is little information on their effectiveness.

Insecticide resistance is a serious problem with leafminers. Carbamate, organophosphate, and especially pyrethroid insecticides have been used for many years and are often ineffective against leafminers due to resistance. Leafminers also appear to be developing tolerance or resistance to newer insecticides, including abamectin and cyromazine. See the pesticide resistance section earlier in this chapter and also the chapter "Managing Pests in Flower and Nursery Crops" for information on how to minimize resistance problems. Regardless of the chemical used, unless otherwise directed on the labeling, rotate to a material with another mode of action after about 2 to 3 leafminer generations, which is usually about 4 weeks at 75°F (24°C). See the degree-days section earlier in this chapter for the best method of determining generation times for chemical rotation. Chemicals belonging to different classifications (Table 59) generally have different modes of action. For specific pesticide recommendations consult the latest *UC IPM Pest Management Guidelines: Floriculture and Ornamental Nurseries*.

Entomopathogenic nematodes. Foliar applications of *Steinernema carpocapsae* nematodes can control leafminers in greenhouses and possibly outdoors in humid locations. For nematodes to be effective, conditions must be dark and moist for a few hours after application, such as around sunset in greenhouses with plants rooting on mist tables. These beneficial nematodes enter mines through leaf punctures made by adult leafminers and feed only on insects. In comparison with more conventional insecticides, which generally kill late-instar leafminers, nematodes kill early-instar leafminers before mines become large.

Mix and apply nematodes as labeled. Because exposed nematodes are killed by UV light and dry conditions, consider adding thickeners, antidesiccants, or UV protectants to the mix or make applications in the evening or both. Relative humidity must be high (≥70%), or a film of water should be allowed to remain on foliage for several hours so that nematodes stay moist while seeking prey. Temperatures should be about 68° to 78°F (20° to 26°C) for optimal nematode activity. Repeat these treatments about every 4 to 7 days for about two weeks to allow killing of leafminers that were in nonsusceptible stages (eggs, pupae, and adults) when treatments are begun. Continue monitoring for leafminers and repeat treatments if necessary.

Because conditions are constantly moist, nematodes can be especially effective for leafminer control in cuttings during rooting on mist tables. To reduce wash-off of nematodes, apply nematodes to foliage at the end of rooting cycles or immediately after watering during less-frequent misting cycles. If overhead irrigation systems are adapted to keep the water well aerated and mixed, nematodes may be efficiently applied in the irrigation water. Each batch of nematodes should not be immersed for longer than about 24 hours before application. Nematode application avoids the phytotoxicity problems associated with some other materials, especially on young, stressed plants. For more information, see the entomopathogenic nematodes discussion in the pesticides section earlier in this chapter.

Biological control. Parasitic wasps, including species in the genera *Dacnusa*, *Diglyphus*, and *Opius*, often control leafminers in natural habitats. For example, adult female *Diglyphus* species host-feed on second-instar *Liriomyza* leafminers and lay eggs near third instars, in both cases killing these hosts. Leafminer parasites often migrate into crops and can be abundant later in the production cycle. Augmentative biological control is highly feasible in certain crops where some level of damage can be tolerated, especially early in the production cycle. One approach in greenhouse-grown cut flowers is to use biological control early in the production cycle, when leafminers are attacking older foliage that will not be marketed, and then apply pesticides later in the production cycle, if needed to protect younger, harvested foliage.

Commercially available parasites (including *Diglyphus begini*, *Diglyphus isaea*, and *Dacnusa sibirica*) generally must be carefully introduced and managed to provide adequate control in flower crops. *Diglyphus begini* releases have been effective in greenhouse-grown cut chrysanthemums (resulting in less than 1 leafminer larva per 1,000 leaves 40 days after planting) and in greenhouse-grown gerbera and nonpot marigolds where some damage to leaves is tolerable because older foliage is not harvested.

Begin any parasite releases during the first 2 weeks after planting, even if few leaves are obviously mined then. In this type of preventive program (where natural enemies are released in anticipation of leafminer problems) general recommendations for *Dacnusa* or *Diglyphus* are about 500 parasites per acre twice each week for 2 to 3 weeks. About twice that number per week for 4 to 6 weeks may be needed to control moderate leafminer populations if preventive releases are not initiated early or early releases provide inadequate control.

Successful parasite introductions require careful monitoring to ensure that leafminers are becoming parasitized and pest populations are not becoming excessive. Good pest exclusion is needed to prevent released natural enemies from being overwhelmed by leafminers migrating into the crop. Parasite releases can be expensive, and commercial parasite availability may be limited. Parasite releases may be economically feasible only at low pest densities, such as about 1 live leaf miner per 100 leaves. Avoid using broad-spectrum pesticides for leafminers or other pests; carbamate, organophosphate, and pyrethroid adulticides may kill parasites for weeks after their effectiveness against pests has worn off.

Whiteflies

Whiteflies (family Aleyrodidae) are not true flies (order Diptera); they are in the order Homoptera and are related to aphids and scales. Over 50 whitefly species occur in California, and most are uncommon. Introduced species, especially silverleaf whitefly (*Bemisia argentifolii*) and greenhouse whitefly (*Trialeurodes vaporariorum*) are the most common whiteflies infesting flower and nursery crops (Table 64).

Damage

Whitefly nymphs and adults have piercing-sucking mouthparts and primarily feed in phloem tissue. Feeding by high densities of whiteflies causes loss of plant fluids, resulting in leaves that discolor, shrivel, and drop prematurely. Whitefly feeding can stunt plant growth and may sometimes kill young plants. Adult whiteflies can be a nuisance when they fly from infested foliage. Honeydew excreted by adults and nymphs creates unsightly, sticky foliage and promotes growth of sooty mold. Some species of whiteflies can induce plant growth disorders, such as leaf and stem chlorosis and distortion, or transmit viruses. Thus far, whitefly transmitted viruses (such as geminiviruses) have not been reported in flower and ornamental nursery crops in California.

Identification and Biology

The name *whitefly* refers to the adults, which are shaped like tiny moths or flies with mealy white wax covering their wings and yellowish bodies. Some species have dark wing markings that are helpful for identification. However, adults of most species look very similar to each other and can be distinguished only by an expert. Late fourth-instar nymphs, usually called pupae, are used for accurate whitefly identification (Fig. 43).

Whiteflies eggs are usually laid on the underside of leaves. Eggs are oblong, tiny, and have a short stalk inserted into leaf tissue. Eggs are white to yellowish when laid and commonly darken before hatching. The tiny crawlers (mobile first-instar nymphs) emerge from eggs and wander for up to several hours before settling on a leaf to feed. Most whiteflies remain virtually immobile during development through the fourth instar. After the first molt, the semitransparent nymphs become flattened and oval, resembling tiny scale insects. Nymphs of some species secrete a waxy covering. The species commonly infesting flower and nursery crops have several generations per year. All stages are present year-round in greenhouses and outdoors under mild conditions.

The time required to complete a single generation varies from one to several months, depending on host plants and especially on temperature (Tables 53, 65), as discussed earlier in the degree-days section.

Metamorphosis of fourth instars differs from that of most Homoptera. Early fourth instars are flattened. As they develop, they become plump and in most species filaments develop or become more prominent (the "prepupal" stage). The final stage is called a "pupa," even though whiteflies have incomplete metamorphosis and do not have a true pupal stage. In many species during this pupal stage the red eyes of the developing adult can often be seen through the pupal case at one end of the body. Although pupae of many species of whiteflies are covered with curly wax, the most common whiteflies attacking flower and nursery crops have a mostly transparent pupal cover.

Pupal appearance is used to identify whitefly species. Adult wing posture and markings, the species of host plant, pattern of egg laying, and extent of waxiness can also help distinguish among whitefly species (Fig. 43).

Monitoring

To monitor whiteflies, visually inspect foliage for immature stages and use yellow sticky traps for adults. Consider using indicator or sentinel plants to time and evaluate control actions (Fig. 5). A good monitoring program also includes regular inspection in and around the growing area to eliminate other sources of whiteflies and careful examination of new plant material before it is brought into the growing area.

Monitoring temperature to determine whitefly generation time helps determine when to rotate pesticides for resistance management. Use degree-days (Table 65) to determine the application frequency of materials that control only certain life stages as described below. Degree-day monitoring also helps time natural enemy introductions.

Gently shaking foliage can flush out adults. Shaking can help locate whitefly infestations as discussed in the shaking plants section earlier in this chapter, but shaking plants may not be necessary when sticky traps are used.

Traps. Yellow sticky traps are the most efficient tool for detecting whitefly infestations. Besides alerting you to the presence of whiteflies with less effort than inspecting foliage, traps help you to locate whitefly hot spots and indicate infestation sources, such as vents, doorways, nearby plantings, or new stock. Use traps in combination with foliage inspection.

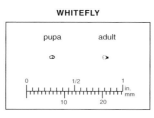

WHITEFLY

pupa   adult

Silverleaf whitefly adults on the underside of a gerbera leaf. Insecticides for whiteflies and certain other pests may be ineffective unless the spray thoroughly covers the underside of leaves where the pests occur.

Whitefly species are identified by the appearance of their pupae. The silverleaf whitefly pupa (center) does not have long filaments projecting from its outer margin. However, the smaller early-instar whitefly nymphs (upper right and lower left) are the stages most susceptible to pesticides.

The adult iris whitefly (*Aleyrodes spiraeoides*) has one or two dark blotches on each forewing. Pupae of this species can be confused with silverleaf whitefly because both lack filaments around their margins. Iris whitefly is much less common than silverleaf whitefly and, as shown here, leaves much more wax on the plant where eggs were laid.

Table 64. Some Flower Crops Susceptible to Whiteflies.

	Whitefly species						
Crop	**Greenhouse**	**Silverleaf**	**Giant**	**Iris**	**Bandedwinged**	**Citrus**	**Other**
African boxwood							bayberry
anthurium		●					
aquilegia					●		
aster	●	●		●			
azalea	●	●					azalea
begonia	●	●	●				
bird of paradise			●	●			
bouvardia	●	●	●	●			
calendula		●					
camellia	●						
celosia		●					
chrysanthemum	●	●					
cineraria	●						
cornflower		●					
cyclamen		●					
dahlia	●						
English daisy	●						
eucalyptus			●		●		woolly
fig	●	●					
fuchsia	●		●	●	●		
gardenia	●	●				●	
geranium	●	●	●		●		
gerbera	●	●					
gladiolus	●		●	●			
gloxinia	●						
hibiscus	●	●	●		●		

Table 65. Approximate Development Times for Some Whiteflies and Their Natural Enemies.

	Time in days when temperatures average 82°F or 28°C (time in Fahrenheit degree-days)							
Species, lower threshold	**Egg**	**First instar**	**Second instar**	**Third instar**	**Early fourth or fourth instar**	**Prepupa and pupa**	**Egg to adult**	**Female longevity**
greenhouse whitefly, 46°F (7.8°C)	5 (191)	3 (90)	2 (65)	2 (79)	2 (61)	6 (202)	18 (655)	12 (432)
silverleaf whitefly, 57°F (14°C)	5 (136)	3 (80)	3 (59)	3 (68)	—	5 (118)[1]	18 (455)	18 (441)
Encarsia formosa, 51°F (10.6°C)	—	—	—	7 (202)[2]	—	8 (258)[3]	14 (434)	12 (372)
Delphastus pusillus, 52°F (11.2°C)	4 (123)	2 (54)	1.5 (42)	2 (54)	3 (87)	6 (192)	20 (594)	60 (1,800)

Because development time varies dramatically with temperature, degree-day values are a better estimate of development time than calendar days. The sum of immature development may not equal egg to adult development time, in part because different groups of insects and separate threshold temperatures were sometimes used in estimating development for different life stages of the same species. Reported values vary; seek the latest information if precise estimates are important. Thresholds and *Delphastus* degree-days are estimates.

1. All fourth instar or pupal stages combined.

2. From oviposition through third instar combined (the white scale stage).

3. For black scale stage on greenhouse whitefly (when pupa darkens).

Sources: van Roermund and van Lenteren 1992; Enkegaard 1993, Hoelmer, Osborne, and Yokomi 1993; Heinz et al. 1994; Drost et al. 1998.

Crop	Whitefly species						
	Greenhouse	Silverleaf	Giant	Iris	Bandedwinged	Citrus	Other
hydrangea	●	●	●				nesting
impatiens	●						
iris				●			
ivy						●	
lily	●						
marigold	●	●					
nasturtium	●		●				
orchids			●				
pansy	●			●			
petunia		●					
philodendron			●				
poinsettia	●	●	●		●		
portulaca					●		
pouch flower		●					
primula	●						
rhododendron	●						azalea
rose	●						
sage	●	●					
schefflera			●			●	
Shasta daisy		●					
smilax	●					●	
verbena	●						
vinca		●					
violet	●			●			
zinnia	●	●					

For whiteflies infesting woody ornamental crops, consult *Pests of Landscape Trees and Shrubs* (Dreistadt 1994).

Deploy traps in greenhouses throughout the production cycle. Good whitefly detection requires a higher density of traps than with most other insects; the recommended density is about 1 trap per 1,000 square feet (90 sq m) of growing area. See the sticky traps section earlier in this chapter for more information.

Visual monitoring. Regularly inspect the underside of leaves, especially if foliage is shriveled or discolored. Look for whitish adults, waxiness, and immature insects. Once located, examine them through a hand lens to confirm that they are whiteflies. Because honeydew, sooty mold, and discolored or shriveled leaves are characteristic of heavier infestations, it is important to inspect regularly under healthy-looking leaves and use traps to detect infestations early before damage becomes obvious.

Monitor beneath both new and old leaves on a portion of the crop throughout the growing area at least once each week. Concentrate on plants near areas where adults were trapped. When an infested plant is found, dispose of it if possible. Examine neighboring plants at an increasing distance from infested plants to determine the extent of the infestation. Flag or record the location and extent of infestations so you know where to return to apply spot treatments or monitor again later. Record your results using a form similar to Figure 3.

Whitefly life stages are not evenly distributed throughout the plant. Because whitefly immatures do not move after the crawler stage, monitoring results are influenced by what parts of the plant are examined. The predominant stage present on a leaf depends on the age of the leaf; older (usually lower) foliage has older life stages, which are larger and more easily seen. To get an overall indication of the relative abundance

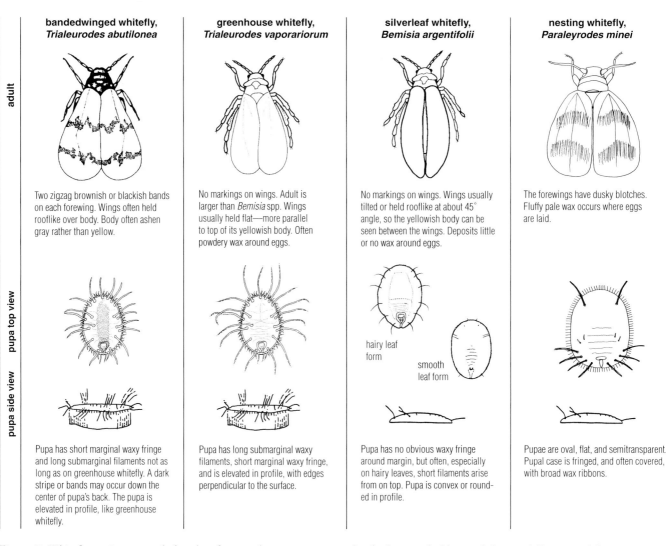

Figure 43. Whitefly species commonly found on flower and nursery crops can often be distinguished by pupal shape and filaments, adult wing posture and markings, and the waxiness associated with colonies. The silverleaf whitefly and sweetpotato whitefly are difficult to distinguish and are discussed together here. *Sources:* Flint 1995, giant and nesting whitefly adults and pupae by David H. Headrick.

of each whitefly life stage, inspect at least one new and one old leaf on each sample plant. To estimate parasite activity, inspect older leaves where whiteflies have developed to the fourth instar and immature parasites have been present long enough for parasitism to become visible.

Be aware that because empty pupal cases and egg shells persist on leaves, counts of these stages are cumulative among sample dates and counting them may lead to overestimation of whitefly densities. Distinguish live insects from empty pupal cases and base management decisions on the numbers of live insects.

Indicator plants. Use infested plants as indicator or sentinel plants by monitoring them at regular intervals to select and time control actions (see the chapter "Managing Pests in Flower and Nursery Crops," especially Figure 5). Most pesticides and parasite releases are effective only against certain whitefly life stages. Learn to distinguish the different life

stages and determine which stages are present at each inspection. Inspect indicator plants to decide what method or material to use by determining whether whiteflies are in the stage(s) susceptible to planned control actions. Reinspect indicator plants several days after treatment to evaluate the effectiveness of control.

Tolerance levels. Tolerance for whiteflies varies with many factors, including crop species and cultivar, time until harvest, market conditions, and whether whiteflies infest salable plant parts. See the thresholds section earlier in this chapter for information on deciding when to treat.

Tolerate virtually no whiteflies on mother stock, other propagative material, and new introductions into the growing area. Plants can be treated more effectively when they are young, and potential phytotoxicity limits chemical options once crops like poinsettia show color. Whiteflies present at the beginning of production can develop through

	iris whitefly, ***Aleyrodes spiraeoides***	**citrus whitefly,** ***Dialeurodes citri***	**giant whitefly,** ***Aleurodicus dugesii***
adult	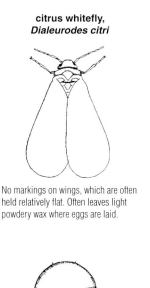 One or two grayish blotches visible on forewings. Much wax on foliage where eggs are laid, often in circles.	No markings on wings, which are often held relatively flat. Often leaves light powdery wax where eggs are laid.	Grayish blotches or mottling on wings. Larger that other species, about ³⁄₁₆ inch (4 mm) long. Often feed in groups. Make spiraling wax patterns during egg-laying on leaves.
pupa top view	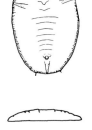		
pupa side view	Pupa has no waxy fringe or filaments. Unlike the *Bemisia* spp., there usually is much wax on leaf around groups of whiteflies.	Yellow to transparent case, rounded or relatively flat in profile. No waxy fringe or filaments. Distinct Y-shaped pattern from three spiracular (breathing tube) furrows, one on each side and at the rear.	Distinctly elevated in profile with edges perpendicular to the leaf surface. Covered with frostlike or powdery wax. Long wax strands hang from infested leaves, giving foliage white bearded appearance.

many generations before plants are shipped, requiring repeated management actions and greatly increasing the likelihood of damaged, poor-quality plants.

It may not be possible or necessary to keep susceptible plant species and cultivars whitefly-free throughout the production cycle (see the example on whitefly-infested poinsettia in the thresholds section in the chapter "Managing Pests in Flower and Nursery Crops").

Management

Good sanitation, exclusion, and cultural practices are the most effective methods for avoiding whitefly problems. Control is difficult, and damage may be unavoidable, once whiteflies become abundant. Prevent or minimize infestations by starting with clean plants, eliminating sources of whiteflies, and keeping pests out of growing areas. Use less-susceptible cultivars. Alter planting time if possible to prevent the early growth of susceptible field-grown crops from coinciding with large numbers of whiteflies migrating from outside growing areas. Avoid excess irrigation and fertilization, which increase susceptibility of certain crops to whiteflies. For more information on management options, see the sanitation, exclusion, and cultural controls sections earlier in this chapter; see also the chapter "Managing Pests in Flower and Nursery Crops," especially Figures 9 and 10.

Monitor plants carefully throughout production. If whiteflies are detected, determine the source and severity of the infestation; take action early when spot treatments can be effective before infestations spread. Natural enemy releases can control whiteflies on some greenhouse crops. Insecticides are the primary control strategy once flower and nursery crops are infested.

Pesticides. Whiteflies are difficult to control with pesticides. Immatures develop on the lower surface of leaves where thorough spray coverage is difficult. Pesticide resistance readily develops, and adults migrate into crops from many other hosts. Whiteflies have multiple, overlapping generations, allowing rapid population increase.

Some insecticides temporarily reduce whitefly populations if applied at the proper time in an effective manner. Monitor carefully and make spot applications while infestations are localized, before whiteflies become widespread and abundant. Concentrate control actions early in the production cycle, before a dense plant canopy shields lower foliage from spraying. Thorough coverage on the underside of leaves is essential. Applications made to the upper leaf surface do more harm than good because spraying kills the actively searching beneficials.

Eggs and pupae are not susceptible to most insecticides. Early-stage nymphs or adults are more susceptible to pesticides than later nymphs. Insecticides are effective only if they are applied when susceptible life stages predominate. If nonsusceptible life stages predominate, use an alternative material or method, or delay treatment until susceptible stages are present. If all stages are present on the plants, several applications may be necessary to expose most individual whiteflies to insecticide at times when they are susceptible.

The frequency and number of applications necessary to control a population when all stages are present depends primarily on the pest species, temperature, and the material used. For example, at an average temperature of 82°F (28°C), silverleaf whitefly is in the first and second instars (combined) for about 6 days. Therefore, sequential applications must be made about every 6 days to ensure that each individual is sprayed during a susceptible stage of its life cycle.

Whiteflies have developed resistance to many broadspectrum insecticides, including chlorinated hydrocarbons, organophosphates, and pyrethroids. Resistance to oil has not been observed. Delay resistance by rotating applications among insecticides with a different mode of action; chemicals belonging to different classes (Table 59) generally have different modes of action. Rotate insecticides every two to three pest generations, about every 2 to 3 months at average greenhouse temperatures. See the degree-days section earlier in this chapter for information on determining generation time. An ideal way to delay resistance development is to use biological, cultural, and physical controls.

The need for frequent applications may indicate that other recommended methods (clean stock, sanitation, exclusion, etc.) are being neglected. Spraying alone is unlikely to provide adequate long-term whitefly control. Repeated applications can increase phytotoxicity and worker reentry problems, as well as promote resistance.

When spraying, spot applications will be more effective than widespread treatments. Rely on short-persistence insecticides (oil or soap) or selective materials whenever possible. Oil or soap can be combined with other insecticides to increase the effectiveness of the other materials. Unlike most other materials, oil kills whitefly eggs. Thorough oil

coverage also has been found to repel adult whiteflies from landing for about 1 week after application to certain crops, including chrysanthemums.

Many reduced-risk pesticides are available for whitefly control (Table 58). Use only pesticides compatible with biological control (Table 66) if natural enemies will be released or may become naturally abundant. For specific pesticide recommendations consult the latest *UC IPM Pest Management Guidelines: Floriculture and Ornamental Nurseries*.

Biological control. Many whitefly species in their native habitats are well controlled by natural enemies. Parasitic wasps, such as *Amitus*, *Encarsia*, and *Eretmocerus* species, are among the most important natural enemies of whiteflies. Minute pirate bugs (*Orius* spp.), green lacewings, lady beetles, and bigeyed bugs (*Geocoris* spp.) are common predators. Insect-specific fungi include *Beauveria bassiana* and *Paecilomyces fumosoroseus*.

Where beneficials are naturally occurring or are being introduced, encourage their activity by minimizing pesticide applications and using only selective or short-persistence materials. If releases are planned, follow the advice in the releasing natural enemies effectively section earlier in this chapter. Impediments to effectively releasing natural enemies to control whiteflies include clumped whitefly distribution, reduced suitability of some crops, and displacement of greenhouse whitefly in some crops by silverleaf whitefly. Releases are more likely to be effective if success has previ-

Table 66. Some Insecticides, Miticides, and Fungicides Compatible with *Encarsia* and *Eretmocerus* spp. Parasites.

Pesticide	Type
abamectin	A, I
azadirachtin	I
Bacillus thuringiensis	I
Beauveria bassiana	I
chlorothalonil	F
cinnamaldehyde	A, I
fenoxycarb	I
iprodione	F
kinoprene	I
metalaxyl	F
oil	A, F, I
Steinernema, *Heterorhabditis* spp. nematodes	I
soap	A, F, I

KEY: A = acaricide F = fungicide I = insecticide

Consult Tables 58 and 59 for the types of invertebrate pests controlled and the class of these materials.

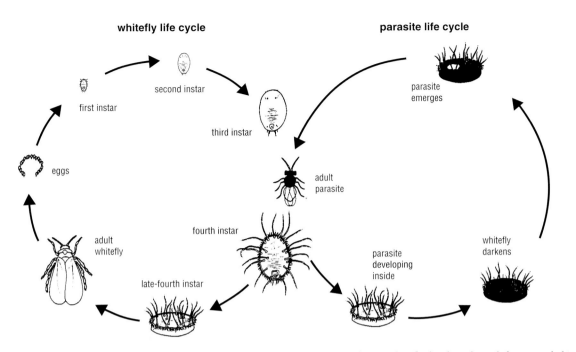

whitefly life cycle

parasite life cycle

first instar

second instar

third instar

eggs

adult
whitefly

fourth instar

adult
parasite

late-fourth instar

parasite
developing
inside

parasite
emerges

whitefly
darkens

Figure 44. Life cycles of the greenhouse whitefly and *Encarsia formosa*. Greenhouse whitefly develops through four nymphal instars. The female *Encarsia* lays one egg per host in a late-second-instar through early-fourth-instar whitefly. The immature parasitoid develops through three instars as it feeds inside and eventually kills the whitefly nymph, which blackens as the parasitoid matures.

ously been reported on that crop, such as with gerbera, marigold, and poinsettia.

Greenhouse parasite releases. The wasp *Encarsia formosa*, probably the most commonly used greenhouse parasite, kills whiteflies through host feeding and parasitism. Commercial *E. formosa* is used in certain greenhouses to control greenhouse whitefly (*Trialeurodes vaporariorum*). The Beltsville strain of *E. formosa* attacks silverleaf whitefly.

During host feeding, the female *E. formosa* punctures whitefly nymphs with her ovipositor and consumes the exuding body fluids, resulting in dead, flattened nymphs. Females lay about 50 to 200 eggs during their life. The eggs hatch into parasite larvae that develop through three instars and kill the whitefly (Fig. 44). *Encarsia formosa* develops from egg to adult in about 14 days if temperatures average about 82°F (28°C) (Table 65).

After the parasite larva finishes feeding and pupates, the mature wasp chews a circular hole in the pupal case and escapes. This circular hole contrasts with the longitudinal or T-shaped slit or ragged tear left in empty pupal cases by emerging whiteflies. Parasites also leave black to orangish deposits (excrement or meconium) in the empty pupal case. The case is mostly clear if a whitefly emerged.

Start any parasite introductions early when whitefly numbers are low. Introduce sufficient numbers of parasites low in the plant canopy at the correct time(s). Release parasites when the susceptible late-second through early-fourth instars are the most abundant life stages. Concentrate releases where infested plants are most abundant or begin releases

before whiteflies are observed infesting the crop. Most users make multiple releases of commercial parasites at intervals of 1 to 2 weeks, at least until many (50% or more) whitefly pupae are parasitized. Parasites also can be introduced by placing banker or nurse plants containing parasitized whiteflies throughout the crop, as discussed earlier in this chapter.

Temperatures of about 65° to 85°F (18.5° to 30°C) and relative humidities averaging 50 to 80% are optimal for *E. formosa*. The growing area should be well lit (650 footcandles or more) to promote parasite egg laying. Parasite development within the whiteflies is inconspicuous until about 7

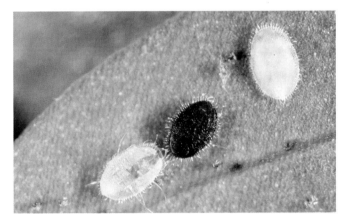

Greenhouse whitefly pupae have a distinct fringe of filaments that protrude around the perimeter of the upper edge of the pupa. These fringes are visible here in the clear, empty pupal skin (left) of an emerging adult whitefly. A parasitized greenhouse whitefly pupa (center) looks like a dark black scale insect. An unparasitized whitefly pupa (right) is whitish or yellowish green.

The adult *Encarsia formosa* is a tiny wasp with a dark head and yellowish abdomen. This commercially available wasp is an important parasite of greenhouse whitefly.

An adult *Delphastus pusillus* lady beetle feeding on a silverleaf whitefly nymph. *Delphastus pusillus* is dark brown to black; the heads of males are light brown as seen here, and the heads of females are black.

to 10 days after parasitism. Whitefly nymphs containing young parasites (the white scale stage) look like unparasitized whiteflies; both are whitish or yellowish green. As parasites mature, the host's appearance changes. The change varies with the species of parasite and whitefly.

Greenhouse whitefly nymphs turn dark brown or black (the black scale stage) about 7 to 10 days after being parasitized by *E. formosa*. Silverleaf whiteflies parasitized by *E. formosa* do not blacken and are more difficult to recognize; the ridges on the clear pupal case turn brown, and the browning becomes more pronounced as the parasite develops. Prior to emergence from silverleaf whitefly, the wasp's dark head and thorax and yellowish abdomen become visible through the pupal case when it is examined with a hand lens.

Silverleaf Whitefly
Bemisia argentifolii
Silverleaf whitefly is the most serious whitefly pest of flower and nursery crops in the United States, especially in greenhouses and outdoors in areas with a relatively mild winter

climate. Silverleaf whitefly was formerly called sweetpotato whitefly (*B. tabaci*) strain B; the two species are difficult to distinguish morphologically. It is probable that many past reports of sweetpotato whitefly infestations, including those in the chapter "Crop Tables," actually refer to the silverleaf whitefly. The same guidelines are used to manage both species.

Although researchers are developing new control methods, silverleaf whitefly can be difficult to manage. Prevention, exclusion, sanitation, and spot applications of insecticides as discussed above are the primary management methods. Although natural enemy releases for silverleaf whitefly control have given variable results, they are being used by some growers. Releases of the Beltsville strain of *Encarsia formosa* reportedly have provided some control; this is not the same *Encarsia formosa* strain that has long been used for greenhouse whitefly. *Encarsia luteola*, *Encarsia pergandiella*, and *Encarsia transvena*, along with *Eretmocerus californicus* and *Eretmocerus eremicus*, are silverleaf whitefly parasites occurring naturally in the field. These parasites apparently are better adapted to *Bemisia* species than the greenhouse whitefly parasite *E. formosa*.

Eretmocerus eremicus and possibly other *Eretmocerus* species may be commercially available. In poinsettias, releasing 1 to 3 parasites per plant per week has been effective if releases are begun early during production. Pest density must be less than about 1 silverleaf whitefly (nymph, pupa, and adult stages combined) per 10 cuttings or young plants. These suggested thresholds are based on inspecting the bottom three leaves from each of 50 randomly selected poinsettias per pest management unit or homogenous planting. For more information on releasing parasites, consult *A Grower's Guide to Using Biological Control for Silverleaf Whitefly on Poinsettia in the Northeastern United States* (Hoddle n.d.). Other good practices, such as exclusion and applying only pesticides that are compatible with biological control, must also be used.

Giant Whitefly
Aleurodicus dugesii
The introduced giant whitefly is a pest in southern California and the southern United States. It is named for its relatively large size (Fig. 43). After emerging from pupal cases, most adults remain on the leaf where they emerged, laying eggs until they die. Many adults will remain on a dying or fallen leaf and perish as the leaf dries.

This clustering tendency allows a relatively large number of whiteflies to be destroyed by removing relatively few leaves. Monitoring to detect infestations early is extremely critical. Early detection allows new infestations to be largely eliminated by hand-picking and bagging foliage for disposal before whiteflies disperse.

Directing a strong stream of water to the underside of infested leaves (syringing) also is highly effective. Syringing performed as well or better than chemical treatments in a University of California study. Contact insecticides have difficulty reaching whiteflies in part because of the abundant wax they produce. Syringing improves plant appearance by removing honeydew and has much less negative effect on biological control than applying pesticides does.

At least three species of introduced parasitic wasps have become established on giant whitefly in southern California: *Encarsia noyessi* (family Aphelinidae), *Entedononecremnus krauteri* (Eulophidae), and *Idioporus affinis* (Pteromalidae). It is hoped that natural enemies will eventually provide effective biological control, as they have against certain other introduced whiteflies that attack ornamentals, including ash whitefly (*Siphoninus phillyreae*), bayberry whitefly (*Parabemisia myricae*), citrus whitefly (*Dialeurodes citri*), and woolly whitefly (*Aleurothrixus floccosus*). Conserve these natural enemies whenever possible, such as by avoiding application of broad-spectrum insecticides. Because giant whitefly may be a quarantined pest, plants may be required to be pest-free, which may require that some pesticides be applied prior to marketing.

Aphids

Aphids (family Aphididae) are small, soft-bodied insects that suck plant juices. Several hundred species are occasional or frequent pests.

Damage

Feeding by high aphid populations can slow plant growth or cause leaves to yellow, curl, or drop. Infested leaves or stems may distort. Aphid cast skins may persist as unsightly white flecks on foliage long after aphids have left the plant. Aphids secrete honeydew, which attracts ants and results in growth of blackish sooty mold. Some aphids transmit certain viruses that cause diseases in some flower crops.

Identification and Biology

Aphids feed in groups on leaves or stems and do not rapidly disperse when disturbed. A few species feed on roots. Adult aphids usually are less than 1/12 inch (2 mm) long and are pear shaped with long legs and antennae. Aphids vary in color even within a species; they are often green, yellow, white, brown, red, or black. Some species, such as woolly aphids, are covered with a waxy white to grayish coating. Adults may be winged or wingless. A pair of tubelike projections (cornicles) near the rear end of the body distinguishes most aphids from other insects.

Under warm conditions, aphids may go through a complete generation in 6 to 7 days. There are many generations per year, and populations can increase rapidly, especially when temperatures are moderate. Extreme temperatures may retard aphid growth and reproduction. Most aphids are females that reproduce without mating. Throughout most of

Beardlike wax strands beneath leaves and blackish sooty mold caused by giant whitefly nymphs infesting hibiscus. Because this pest spreads slowly, infestations can be controlled by carefully monitoring the crop and promptly disposing of infested leaves where giant whiteflies are first found.

Giant whitefly adult females make pale wax spirals on the underside of leaves, where they lay eggs.

the year, adult aphids (winged or wingless) give birth to live young. Aphids may produce overwintering eggs outdoors in locations with cold winters.

Although many aphids look similar, most species feed only on closely related plant species and cannot spread to unrelated plants. The most important species infesting flower and nursery crops are melon (or cotton) aphid (*Aphis gossypii*) and green peach aphid (*Myzus persicae*), which can feed on many different plants. It can be helpful to distinguish between these species (Fig. 45) to improve control efficacy. For example, in chrysanthemums, green peach aphids are commonly most abundant on growing tips, while melon aphids are more distributed throughout the plant canopy, mostly on the underside of leaves. Concentrating scouting efforts and pesticide applications where the particular aphid is more abundant will improve control. Aphid species can also vary in their susceptibility to pesticides, in part due to differences in pesticide resistance.

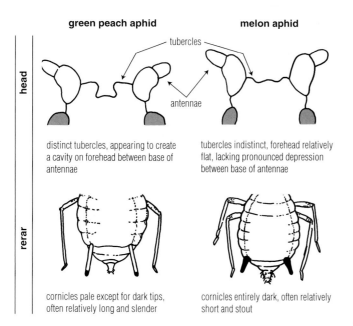

green peach aphid   **melon aphid**

head

tubercles

antennae

distinct tubercles, appearing to create a cavity on forehead between base of antennae

tubercles indistinct, forehead relatively flat, lacking pronounced depression between base of antennae

rear

cornicles pale except for dark tips, often relatively long and slender

cornicles entirely dark, often relatively short and stout

Figure 45. Distinguish green peach aphid from melon aphid by examining their antennal tubercles (projections on the forehead between the base of antennae) and cornicles (pair of tubes projecting near the rear).

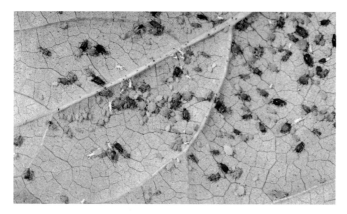

Melon or cotton aphids are commonly blackish or dark green, but they can also be yellow to whitish. They feed on many plants and can spread certain plant viruses.

The blackish sooty mold (right leaf) and pale cast skins (left) on lower-canopy cineraria leaves are evidence of aphids infesting terminal buds (not shown).

Monitoring

Visually inspect plants for aphids at least once a week when aphids are expected to be present. Examine new growth and the underside of leaves for aphids. Inspect the upper surface of foliage for whitish cast skins, shiny honeydew, and blackish sooty mold. To estimate infestation levels or to compare aphid densities before and after treatment, it may be helpful to use presence-absence sampling or indicator plants, as discussed in the monitoring section earlier in this chapter and in the chapter "Managing Pests in Flower and Nursery Crops."

Yellow sticky traps capture winged adult aphids, but traps are not the best monitoring tool because most aphids are wingless, including reproductive adults. However, traps can indicate aphid hot spots and migration and can detect many other insects. Place traps throughout the growing area, especially near vents and doors, to detect aphid migration. Learn to distinguish aphids from other insects (see the sticky traps section earlier in this chapter).

Management

Physical, cultural, chemical, and biological controls are all important aphid management methods. Use these methods in combination to provide good control. Prevent or minimize infestations as discussed in the sanitation and exclusion sections earlier in this chapter and in the chapter "Managing Pests in Flower and Nursery Crops," especially Figures 9 and 10. Bring only aphid-free plants into the growing area. Eliminate weeds and other sources of aphids. Keep pests out of growing areas by using screening, positive pressure ventilation, row covers, or reflective mulches. Aphids are attracted to yellow; avoid yellow clothing and equipment when moving from outdoors into aphid-free greenhouses, especially during times of the year when aphids are abundant outdoors or may be migrating.

Cultural controls. Aphids prefer succulent new tissue; avoid practices that stimulate excess new growth, such as applying more nitrogen or water than necessary. Use slow-release fertilizers where feasible. Unless otherwise necessary, avoid pinching or shearing plants, which stimulates new growth.

Aphids often prefer certain plant cultivars over others. Suppliers may have information on cultivars that are less susceptible to aphids. Careful aphid monitoring and record keeping allows growers to develop their own information on less-susceptible cultivars.

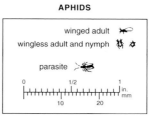

APHIDS

winged adult

wingless adult and nymph

parasite

0   1/2   1
in.
mm
10   20

Reflective mulch. Reflective mulch confuses and repels aphids and certain other winged insects searching for new plants. Spray-on or plastic film reflective mulch prevents or delays aphid infestation of young plants and greatly reduces aphid-borne virus infections in some field crops. Although few flower crops have been studied, this method may be useful during early growth of many flower and nursery crops grown in the field from seed or small transplants, as discussed in the reflective mulch section earlier in this chapter.

Insecticides. Reduced-risk insecticides that control aphids include azadirachtin, *Beauveria bassiana*, cinnamaldehyde, fenoxycarb, imidacloprid, kinoprene, and pyridaben (Table 58). A forceful stream of water where practical can also reduce populations. Narrow-range oil and insecticidal soap provide temporary control if applied to thoroughly cover infested plant parts. Oil and soap provide no residual control, so application may need to be repeated. However, unlike some conventional materials, aphids have not been found to be resistant to soap or oil. Because aphid predators and parasites often become abundant only after aphids are numerous, applying nonpersistent or selective insecticides may provide more effective long-term control on outdoor plants because these materials do not kill natural enemies that migrate in after the spray.

Many other foliar-applied insecticides are registered for aphid control. However, some commonly used carbamate, organophosphate, and pyrethroid insecticides are ineffective against certain populations of green peach aphid, melon aphid, and some other species because aphids have developed resistance to them. To reduce resistance development, employ other methods instead of or in addition to spraying.

Where plants are frequently sprayed, rotate among at least three insecticides with different modes of action (see Table 59) every two to three generations, about every 2 to 3 weeks for green peach aphid when temperatures average 75°F (24°C). See the degree-days section earlier in this chapter for more information on aphid generation time.

Because infestations often begin as locally dense colonies, insecticides can be confined to spot treatments if plants are carefully monitored to detect aphids early. With many insecticides, the recommendation is for two applications made about 7 to 10 days apart. Where natural enemies are important, make only spot applications if possible and use only biological, selective, or short-residual pesticides. For specific pesticide recommendations, consult *UC IPM Pest Management Guidelines: Floriculture and Ornamental Nurseries*.

Biological controls. Aphids are susceptible to naturally occurring fungal diseases when conditions are humid. Look for dead aphids that have turned reddish or brown and have a fuzzy, shriveled texture unlike the smooth, bloated mummies formed when aphids are parasitized. Fungus-killed aphids sometimes have fine, whitish mycelia (threadlike strands) growing over their surfaces.

Resident predators and parasites frequently control aphids outdoors. Natural enemies also move into greenhouses, although densities may be low. Aphid predators include lady beetle larvae and adults; larvae of lacewings, syrphid flies, and aphid midge flies (Fig. 46); and minute pirate bugs. Many small wasps, including *Aphelinus*, *Aphidius*, *Ephedrus*, *Lysiphlebus*, *Praon*, and *Trioxys* species, are also important aphid natural enemies. These parasites reproduce by laying their eggs in aphids (Fig. 37). The immature wasp feeds in

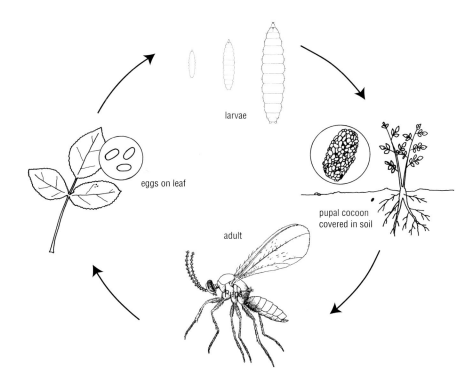

larvae

eggs on leaf

pupal cocoon
covered in soil

adult

Figure 46. Life cycle of a predaceous aphid midge. Adults are delicate flies with long slender legs. Adults consume only honeydew and liquids and are active only during dark or dusk. Each female lays about 70 tiny eggs. The larvae are yellowish maggots that develop through three instars; they impale aphids and suck out their body contents. Each larva eats about 10 to 100 aphids, depending on the size of the aphids and environmental conditions. Pupae occur in the top 1 inch (2.5 cm) of media. Egg to adult development time is about 3 weeks at 72°F (22°C). Aphid midges may stop reproducing and become ineffective if exposed to day length less than about 16 hours; outdoors they overwinter as mature larvae in cocoons. *Sources*: Larvae from Peterson 1960, adult from Quayle 1932.

Table 67. Some Commercially Available Natural Enemies of Aphids.

Natural enemy	Comments
aphid midge (*Aphidoletes aphidimyza*)	Tiny flies (family Cecidomyiidae) with predaceous larvae (Fig. 46). Does best in greenhouses or outdoors where humidity is high. Supplied commercially as pupae in containers from which adults emerge. Adult *Aphidoletes* lack the distinct Y-shaped vein found on the wings of similar-looking adult fungus gnats. Suggested release rates are at least two introductions about 2–4 weeks apart, each release with 2–5 or more pupae per 11 square feet (1 sq m) of growing area. Drop pupae on soil directly beneath infested foliage.
aphid parasites, including *Aphidius colmani, A. matricariae, Diaeretiella rapae*	Tiny wasps that lay eggs in many species of aphids (Fig. 37), including *Aphis, Brachycaudus,* and *Myzus* species. Parasitized aphids become tan mummies. Other parasite species may be available. Releasing parasites approximately every 11 feet (3.3 m) has been suggested for greenhouse containers.
convergent lady beetle (*Hippodamia convergens*)	Common orange-and-black-spotted species.
green lacewings (*Chrysoperla* spp.)	Each alligatorlike larva can consume several hundred or more aphids over its life. Shipped as eggs or young larvae. Because most aphids are eaten by older larvae, there is about a 2-week lag in any control until lacewings grow older. Suggested release rates are at least 2 larvae per square foot (0.09 sq m) of growing area released each week for several weeks. Cannibalistic larvae should be well-dispersed; a distance of about 2.3 feet (0.76 m) between release points has been suggested in greenhouse containers.
minute pirate bugs (*Orius insidiosus, O. tristicolor*)	*Orius* spp. are released primarily against thrips. Natural populations outdoors feed on aphids, but there is little information on release for aphid control.

Sources: Flint et al. 1995, Dreistadt and Flint 1996, Ehler and Kimsey 1995, Stary 1993.

and kills its host, causing the aphid to mummify (become slightly puffy and turn tan or black). A round hole can be observed where the adult parasite has chewed its way out of the aphid mummy. See the biological control conservation section earlier in this chapter for information on pesticide management, ant control, and other methods of enhancing native predators and parasites.

Several commercially available aphid predators and parasites (Table 67) can be introduced in greenhouses and interiorscapes. There is little commercial-scale experience on the effectiveness of introducing predators or parasites for aphid control in flower and nursery crops in the United States, but some promising research and problems with pesticide-resistant aphids make natural enemy introductions an increasingly attractive alternative.

Predators are most likely to be effective when released on dense colonies of aphids (localized hot spots in the crop). Parasitoids search for hosts throughout the crop and may be a better choice if aphids are relatively few and scattered. Predators and parasitoids can be released in combination. Biological control is more likely to be successful on crops where some low density of aphids can be tolerated, such as aphids that feed primarily on foliage in a crop sold as cut flowers. If natural enemy introductions are planned, consult the nurse plants and releasing natural enemies effectively sections earlier in this chapter.

Convergent lady beetle. The convergent lady beetle (*Hippodamia convergens*) is available from many commercial sources and is relatively inexpensive when purchased in bulk through the mail. Commercial convergent lady beetles are collected in the Sierra Nevada, where they overwinter in large aggregations. Although resident convergent lady beetles are important predators, beetles collected from aggrega-

tions have a strong tendency to disperse; most commercial beetles will soon fly away when released outdoors.

Because each adult lady beetle can eat about 100 aphids a day, releasing relatively large numbers of convergent lady beetles can temporarily reduce aphid densities. Release on potted plants has temporarily controlled melon aphids on chrysanthemums in the field and greenhouse and has controlled rose aphids (*Macrosiphum rosae*) on roses. Releases were effective against relatively high aphid populations (dozens of aphids or more per leaf or terminal); the effectiveness of lady beetles released on low-density aphid infestations on flower crops has apparently not been studied.

Beetles store well in the refrigerator (don't freeze them) and can be periodically released as needed. If cold-stored, warm them to room temperature for a few hours about once each week and mist beetles with water or sugar water. Commercial lady beetles are often thirsty when they are received; spraying them with sugar water before release increases their survival. Wetting plants before release and releasing lady beetles in the evening when it is cooler may reduce beetle dispersal. Screening vents and fans to prevent beetles from escaping may allow releases to be effective in greenhouses.

Root Aphids

Several aphids attack basal stems and underground plant parts. The aster or erigeron root aphid (*Aphis middletonii*) attacks aster and cornflower as well as many weeds in the family Asteraceae. Aster root aphids are pear shaped, light gray to dark green, and they are found in the field on basal stems and roots near the surface. Infested plants may become stunted and have yellow foliage.

The tulip bulb aphid or iris root aphid (*Dysaphis tulipae*) attacks freesia, gladiolus, iris, lily, and tulip. It is pear shaped

Although this older (lower) lily foliage is heavily covered with sooty mold (left leaf), the aphids are dead and mummified (right leaf), and the new growth that will be marketed is aphid-free and undamaged by sooty mold due to releases of the parasite *Aphidius matricariae* in this greenhouse.

An orange convergent lady beetle pupa and several dark orange-spotted lady beetle larvae are shown here among whitish aphid cast skins.

Adult flower flies, also called syrphid or hover flies, often have black and yellowish abdominal bands. They resemble honey bees, but syrphids have only two wings and cannot sting. Flower fly larvae (pictured earlier in this chapter) are common aphid predators.

Syrphid eggs are laid singly on their sides near aphids or other prey. The eggs are oblong, usually whitish to gray, and when viewed through a hand lens have a surface covered with crossing strands or lines. Brown lacewing eggs look similar, but they have a smoother surface and a tiny knob that projects from one end of the egg.

and waxy, and is yellow, pink, gray, or green. This tiny aphid is easily overlooked, as it occurs under leaf sheaths and on basal stems in the field and on roots, corms, and rhizomes in storage. Heavy infestations during storage cause direct feeding damage; once in the field, plants grow poorly, are stunted, and produce fewer blossoms. Infestations in the field are a concern primarily because this aphid vectors viruses in lily and tulip.

Inspect bulbs regularly during storage. Control aphids in storage using the methods discussed in the bulb flies section later in this chapter. Immersing bulbs in hot water, at about 111°F (44°C), for 1½ hours kills root aphids (Table 9). Plant only aphid-free stock. Use row covers or reflective mulch to prevent or reduce infestations in the field. Dipping bulbs in insecticide before planting, drenching soil, or spraying basal stems may help control infestations in the field. Control nearby alternate hosts.

Mealybugs

Mealybugs are slow-moving insects that suck plant juices. Citrus mealybug (*Planococcus citri*), longtailed mealybug (*Pseudococcus longispinus*), Mexican mealybug (*Phenacoccus gossypii*), and obscure mealybug (*Pseudococcus viburni* =*Pseudococcus affinis*) are common pest species.

Damage

Mealybugs are usually a problem only on perennial crops. They tend to congregate in large numbers, forming unsightly, white cottony masses on plants. Feeding can distort new growth, and infested foliage may turn yellow or drop prematurely. Mealybugs produce sticky honeydew, which attracts ants and promotes growth of blackish sooty mold. High mealybug populations can cause plants to decline; young plants may be killed.

Identification and Biology

Adult female mealybugs are wingless, soft-bodied, grayish insects about 1/20 to 1/5 inch (1–5 mm) long. They are elongate, segmented, and covered with whitish or cottony wax. Many species have wax filaments radiating from the body, especially at the tail.

Woolly aphids and cottony cushion scale may sometimes be confused with mealybugs because they also produce a whitish waxy material. The white, fluted egg sacs of cottony cushion scale are attached to a bright orange, red, yellow, green, or brownish body part. Underneath most aphids' loose, cottony, waxy covering, their bodies appear pear-shaped, and some aphids in a colony may have wings; only male mealybugs have wings and males are rarely seen. Male mealybugs are tiny and delicate; their bodies are commonly yellow or red with two long whitish tail filaments.

Most female mealybugs lay tiny yellow eggs in an ovisac, a mass intermixed with white wax. Mealybug nymphs are oblong, whitish, yellowish, or reddish and may or may not be covered with wax. Both nymphs and adults can crawl slowly. Depending on the species, host, and climate, mealybugs outdoors overwinter only as eggs or females, or as all stages. Most mealybugs have several generations each year, requiring several weeks to several months to develop from egg to adult, depending on the temperature.

If sanitation and chemical control strategies are relied upon, it is generally not necessary to distinguish one mealybug species from another; management guidelines for most above-ground feeding species are the same. If biological control is planned, determine what species is present; each natural enemy species controls only certain mealybug species. To identify mealybugs to species, take them to a Cooperative Extension or agriculture department expert.

Management

Inspect plants regularly for waxy whitish material, honeydew, and sooty mold. Look for columns of ants, which can indicate that mealybugs or other Homoptera are present. Although mealybugs can infest all parts of the plant, branch crotches, the underside of foliage, and stems near the soil are favored, so concentrate inspections in these protected locations.

Tag several infested sentinel or indicator plants and compare mealybug densities on these plants before and several days after treatment. If contact insecticides are planned, monitor sentinel plants by examining colonies with a hand lens to determine that crawlers are present before treating. Dissect some egg sacs and look for crawlers beneath the whitish material. Sticky tape traps wrapped around infested stems, as discussed for scale crawler monitoring later in this chapter, can also be used to monitor mealybug crawlers.

As with most pests, mealybug management is easier and more effective if infestations are detected early. Sanitation, insecticides, and natural enemies can provide control.

Sanitation. Carefully inspect new stock to be sure that it is free of mealybugs. Bring only clean plants into the growing area. Isolate infested plants, where practical, to prevent mealybugs from spreading to nearby crops. If plants are heavily infested, it may best to discard them instead of expending control efforts and risking further spread. Depending on the species of mealybug, an alternative to disposing of heavily infested plants is to use them to culture natural enemies, as discussed in the nurse plants section earlier in this chapter.

Insecticides. Chemical control of mealybugs is difficult; mealybugs' flocculent wax makes good spray coverage difficult. Available reduced-risk insecticides include *Beauveria bassiana*, imidacloprid, kinoprene, oil, and soap. Carbamates, organophosphates, pyrethroids, and some botanicals also control mealybugs if the insects come in contact with the materials. Contact sprays are most effective against the crawler stage (the recently emerged first-instar nymphs). Monitor crawlers as discussed in the sticky tape traps section earlier in this chapter and the indicator plants section in the chapter "Managing Pests in Flower and Nursery Crops." Apply contact sprays when crawlers are active. Because eggs are unaffected by most materials (except possibly oil), a second application may be needed after about 2 weeks to kill mealybugs that were in the egg stage during the first application. When contact materials are used, thorough coverage is critical, especially on inner and under parts of plants where mealybugs are more protected from sprays. Adding a spreader-sticker can improve coverage but may increase risk of phytotoxicity. Systemic insecticides and aerosols or fumigants that provide good penetration can help overcome the difficulty of controlling these pests infesting protected plant parts. A forceful stream of water, where practical, can be applied to reduce populations. For specific pesticide recommendations, consult *UC IPM Pest Management Guidelines: Floriculture and Ornamental Nurseries*.

Biological control. Naturally occurring lady beetles, green lacewings, and parasitic wasps provide good control of many mealybug species outdoors unless these beneficials are disrupted. Where natural enemies are present, conserve them by avoiding persistent, broad-spectrum pesticides and by controlling ants and dust. Where some mealybugs can be tolerated, natural enemy releases may be effective against above-ground-feeding species. Properly identify the species of mealybug before introducing parasites or the mealybug destroyer lady beetles. Lacewing larvae, the mealybug destroyer lady beetle, and certain other predators feed on most mealybug species (Table 56). Parasitic wasps are specific to certain mealybug species.

After purchasing a few of the *Cryptolaemus* mealybug destroyers or *Leptomastix* parasitic wasps as discussed below, growers can rear their own natural enemies in wide-mouth jars or buckets containing sprouted potatoes or other plants infested with mealybugs. A band of Vaseline or commercial sticky material applied inside near the top of the container prevents mealybugs from crawling out while allowing wasps and adult beetles to fly away. These homemade insectaries can be scattered throughout the crop, as discussed in the nurse plants section earlier in this chapter, as long as insecticides are not applied for other pests and ants are controlled.

Citrus Mealybug
Planococcus citri

Citrus mealybug is probably the most common mealybug species attacking flower and nursery crops. Unlike the long filaments at the rear of many other species, including long-tailed mealybug and obscure mealybug, the filaments around the margins of citrus mealybug are not appreciably longer at the posterior end than on the sides. In addition to methods discussed above for other species, biological control can be effective against citrus mealybug.

Citrus mealybug parasite. *Leptomastix dactylopii* is an important commercially available parasite that attacks only the citrus mealybug. This yellowish brown wasp lays its eggs in late-instar nymphs and adult mealybugs, preferring hosts in warm, sunny, humid environments. *Leptomastix* can complete one generation in 2 weeks at 85° (30°C) and 1 month at 70°F (21°C). Suggested release rates are two or more releases at 1 to 2 week intervals, each release consisting of about 6 parasites per square yard (0.8 sq m) of infested growing area.

Leptomastix is effective at lower host densities than the mealybug destroyer, so these beneficials complement each other. Release of *Leptomastix* in combination with *Cryptolaemus* has reportedly given good control of citrus mealybug infesting a wide range of ornamentals in European greenhouses, including African violet, bromeliads, cattleya, croton, geranium, and *Pilea*.

Mealybug destroyer. The mealybug destroyer lady beetle (*Cryptolaemus montrouzieri*) is an important predator of the citrus mealybug, most other exposed mealybug species, and some other ovisac-producing insects such as the green shield scale. Mealybug destroyer adults are dark brown or blackish lady beetles with an orangish head and tail. The larvae are covered with waxy white curls and resemble mealybugs, except that the lady beetle larvae are more active, grow larger, and can be recognized as alligator-shaped predators if the wax is gently scraped off to expose the pale body. This waxiness may help to disguise mealybug destroyer larvae from predators, which may explain why it is not often attacked by mealybug-tending ants. Both adult and larval lady beetles feed on all mealybug stages, but adults and young larvae prefer mealybug eggs and young nymphs. One lady beetle generation from egg to adult requires about 1 month at 70°F (21°C) and 2 months at 80°F (27°C). The predator prefers this temperature range and 60 to 80% relative humidity.

The mealybug destroyer survives poorly over the winter outdoors in California. In cold areas in the spring or at previously sprayed sites, it may need to be reintroduced locally to provide control. Besides its proven usefulness in citrus orchards, releases have reportedly controlled mealybugs infesting some interior landscapes and greenhouse gardenias.

Adult mealybug destroyers require mealybug eggs as food to stimulate production of their own eggs, which are laid into mealybug egg masses. Unlike introductions of most other natural enemies, it is best not to reduce mealybug populations with an insecticide before releasing these lady beetles. If mealybug eggs are not abundant, adults tend to fly away. Mealybug destroyer releases are likely to prove satisfactory only if released on hot spots where mealybugs (and

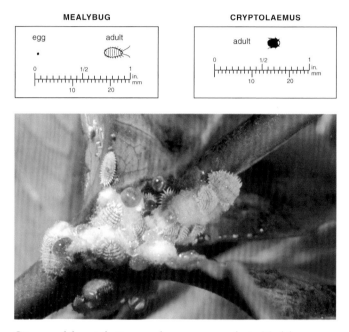

Citrus mealybugs infesting greenhouse-grown gardenia. Mealybugs cover themselves with flocculent white wax. Several of the mealybugs seen here are excreting honeydew droplets.

These oblong brown to orangish pupae belong to the citrus mealybug parasite (*Leptomastix dactylopii*). After emerging, the adult parasite leaves a round hole or hinged cap on the end of each pupal case.

especially their egg sacs) are relatively abundant. Growers must be able to tolerate some mealybugs. It will be 2 weeks or more before mealybug destroyer larvae become evident, and beetles must reproduce and develop into a second generation of lady beetles before mealybug destroyers become abundant enough to provide control; typically this requires waiting 2 months or more after the initial inoculative release. Suggested release rates are about 2 beetles per small plant or 2 square feet (0.2 sq m) of infested growing area.

Longtailed Mealybug
Pseudococcus longispinus

Longtailed mealybug can infest many ornamentals. The mealybug destroyer is relatively ineffective against it because longtailed mealybug gives live birth to nymphs and produces

GROUND MEALYBUG

The adult mealybug destroyer is a mostly dark lady beetle with an orange head and tail. The mealybug destroyer larva also shown here is covered with pale wax strands and resembles its mealybug prey.

A cluster of citrus mealybug eggs revealed by pulling away their waxy covering. The most effective time to spray mealybugs is when crawler-stage nymphs are hatching from eggs.

no egg masses. If adult mealybug destroyers do not eat mealybug eggs, they lay few eggs of their own.

Parasitic wasps including *Anagyrus fusciventris*, *Anarhopus sydneyensis*, and *Arhopoideus peregrinus* help keep longtailed mealybug populations at low levels outdoors, but these species may not be commercially available. If longtailed mealybug is a problem in greenhouses, rely on sanitation and chemical controls.

Ground Mealybugs
Rhizoecus spp.

Ground or root mealybugs commonly live in the soil and feed on the roots of many different plants. Several native and introduced ground mealybug species occur throughout the United States; *Rhizoecus falcifer* is apparently the most common in California. High populations on a plant can cause general decline (yellow foliage and slow growth) and can kill young plants. Ground mealybugs may be covered with white wax and their short antennae and legs may be visible, but they do not have obvious filaments along their sides and tail.

Use good sanitation and physical and cultural controls to avoid ground mealybug problems. Pasteurize media before planting. Place containers over a surface of several inches of gravel or grow plants on benches to reduce ground mealybug movement into containers. Provide good drainage; standing water and contaminated runoff may spread ground mealybugs. Dispose of plant refuse and old, unmarketable plants, which can harbor mealybugs. Provide appropriate irrigation and other plant care to prevent stress that can increase damage from root mealybug feeding.

A soil-applied insecticide may control root mealybugs in containers. Some insect growth regulators can also be applied to control ground mealybugs; check pesticide labels for permitted uses. Insecticidal soap in water poured onto media in containers as labeled may reduce ground mealybug populations. Natural enemy releases are not effective against root mealybugs.

Scales

Scale insects, order Homoptera, are easily overlooked because they are small and immobile most of their lives and do not resemble most other insects. Scales usually are a problem only on perennial plants.

Damage

Scales feed by sucking plant juices. Their feeding can distort new growth, turn foliage yellow, cause premature leaf drop, and stunt plants. Some scales inject toxins while feeding that may spot or streak foliage. Certain scale species produce sticky honeydew that attracts ants and causes growth of blackish sooty mold. The scale bodies themselves may give plants a crusty appearance. Severely infested young plants may be killed.

Identification and Biology

Adult female scales are wingless and lack a separate head or other easily recognizable body parts. Most common scales belong to one of two groups: armored scales or soft scales. Soft scale pests of flower and nursery crops include black scale (*Saissetia oleae*), brown soft scale (*Coccus hesperidum*), and hemispherical scale (*Saissetia coffeae*). Armored scale pests include California red scale (*Aonidiella aurantii*), greedy scale (*Hemiberlesia rapax*), oleander scale (*Aspidiotus nerii*), oystershell scale (*Lepidosaphes ulmi*), and San Jose scale (*Quadraspidiotus perniciosus*).

Armored scales (family Diaspididae) are less than ⅛ inch (3 mm) long, circular to irregular, and flattened; they often appear as grayish, brownish, or yellowish encrustations on plants. Each scale has a platelike shell or cover that usually can be removed to reveal the soft insect body underneath. Unlike soft scales, armored scales do not excrete honeydew. The life cycle of a typical armored scale is illustrated in Figure 47.

Female soft scales (family Coccidae) are usually smooth and brown, black, or grayish. In comparison with armored scales, mature soft scales are larger, about ¼ inch (6 mm) long or less, and more bulbous. The scale's surface is the actual body wall of the insect and cannot be removed. Soft scales, including black and brown soft scale, are prolific honeydew execrators. Outdoors, most species of soft scales, except for brown soft scale, have only one generation per year. In greenhouses with relatively constant conditions, scales that normally have one generation per year outdoors may have multiple overlapping generations.

Adult male scales are tiny pale-colored insects with one pair of wings and a long tail filament. Males are rarely seen in many species and do not feed as adults. In many species, males apparently do not exist; females reproduce without mating.

Scale eggs develop beneath the cover of the female. The newly hatched crawlers (mobile first instars) emerge and crawl on stems and foliage or are spread by the wind or on people or equipment. Crawlers are usually pale yellow to orange and about the size of a period. After crawlers settle and start feeding, armored scales remain at the same spot for the rest of their lives. Soft scale and cottony cushion scale nymphs can move slowly throughout much of their life; on deciduous perennials, they often move from foliage to bark before leaf drop in the fall (Fig. 48).

It is important to recognize the different life stages of scales, especially crawlers, in order to control them. If biological control is planned, correct identification of the scale species is also necessary. Excellent information sources on

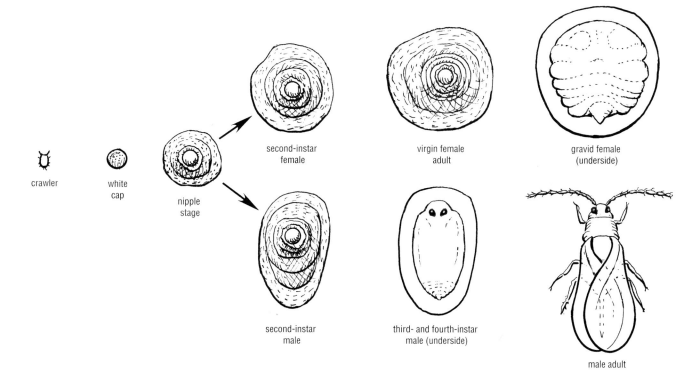

Figure 47. Life cycle of the California red scale, a typical armored scale. Eggs hatch into tiny crawlers which soon settle and secrete a cottony (white cap) cover and later a more solid cover (nipple stage). After the first molt, males begin to develop an elongated scale cover, and female covers remain round. Females molt three times; the final stage is the mated female, which has a rounded scale cover with a legless, wingless, immobile female beneath. Males molt four times. They develop eyespots, which can be seen when scale covers are turned over in the third and fourth instar. The adult male has legs and two wings. Armored scales typically have several generations each year. Depending on the temperature, egg to adult development time for armored scales typically ranges from about 2 to 4 months.

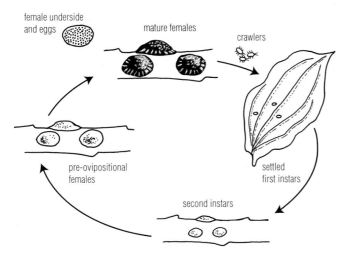

Figure 48. Life cycle of a typical soft scale. This species moves between bark and foliage; some scale species occur only on bark. Most species of soft scale have only one generation each year.

scale biology and identification listed in the suggested reading at the end of this manual include *The Scale Insects of California Part 1: The Soft Scales* (Gill 1988), *The Scale Insects of California Part 2: The Minor Families* (Gill 1993), and *The Scale Insects of California Part 3: The Armored Scales* (Gill 1997).

Monitoring

Monitor scales regularly on plants selected at random from throughout the crop. Inspect plants for scales, scale-associated ants, honeydew, sooty mold, and damage. Where natural enemies are important, learn to recognize them. Parasitized scales often darken, and one or more holes may be chewed in the scale cover by emerging adult parasites. Consult the presence-absence sampling and indicator plants sections in the chapter "Managing Pests in Flower and Nursery Crops" for suggestions on how to determine whether scales are increasing and to evaluate whether treatment was effective.

The most effective time to apply a contact insecticide is when crawlers are active. If female scales are present and spraying is planned, use sticky tape traps to monitor for crawlers. Or, instead of using traps, it may be sufficient to time sprays by using a hand lens to inspect under and around female scales on a regular basis to determine whether crawlers are present. However, a few crawlers may be present throughout much of the year, especially in greenhouses or if scales have several generations each year. Traps provide a quantitative comparison of crawler density among sample dates, which greatly improves decision making.

When managing many high-value plants infested with California red scale or San Jose scale, pheromone traps and degree-day monitoring can be used to time controls, as detailed in *IPM for Citrus* (UCIPM 1991) and *IPM for Almonds* (UCIPM 1985), respectively.

Sticky tape traps. Traps made of sticky tape are an efficient method of monitoring scale crawlers. On each of several plants infested with female scales, snugly wrap a stem with transparent tape that is sticky on both sides (this tape is available at stationery stores). Double over the loose end of the tape several times so you can pull the end to easily unwind it. Place a tag or flag near each tape so you can readily find it. Change the tapes at regular intervals, about weekly. After removing the old tape, wrap the stem at the same location with fresh tape. Preserve the old sticky tapes by sandwiching each tape unrolled between a sheet of white paper and a sheet of clear plastic. Label the tapes with the collection date, location, and host plant.

Scale crawlers get stuck on the tapes and appear as yellow or orange specks. Examine the tapes with a hand lens to distinguish the crawlers (which are round or oblong, orangish, and have very short appendages) from pollen and dust. Apply a contact insecticide when crawlers are abundant. If a single application is planned, visually compare the tapes collected on each sample date. The best time for a single spray is after a sharp increase in crawlers in traps or soon after crawler numbers have peaked and begun to decline.

Management

Diligent sanitation and exclusion, careful pesticide use, and in some instances natural enemies, can control scales.

Sanitation. Inspect new plants carefully for scales; reject or thoroughly treat them if infested. When more-mature plants are infested, isolate, discard, or treat them. Screen greenhouse openings to exclude windborne crawlers. Begin the work day in clean areas; crawlers can be carried on workers or equipment that contact infestations. Remove potentially infested plant debris or prunings from growing areas. For more information, see the sanitation and exclusion sections earlier in this chapter.

Insecticides. Many insecticides are registered for control of scales on flower and nursery crops, including the reduced-risk pesticides buprofezin, imidacloprid, kinoprene, and pyridaben (Tables 58, 59). For example, imidacloprid is a systemic materials that can be applied to growing media to control soft scales. Insecticidal soap and narrow-range oils (labeled "supreme" or "superior" oil) kill scales on contact; oil or soap are also preferred insecticides when natural enemies are present or are being introduced. Various carbamates, organophosphates, and pyrethroids are available, but these are less compatible with IPM programs.

Because crawlers are the stage most susceptible to insecticides, monitor crawlers as discussed above before spraying. When applying contact insecticides, thorough coverage on the underside of foliage is needed to kill scales.

Dormant-season application of narrow-range oil to roses and other woody ornamentals kills scales overwintering on bark. Dormant-season oil also kills eggs of overwintering aphids and mites.

Biological controls. Black scale, brown soft scale, California red scale, and many other species are controlled by natural enemies under certain circumstances. Lady beetles, green lacewings, and certain bugs, mites, and thrips are common predators of scales. Parasitic wasps are often the most important natural enemies, including *Aphytis*, *Coccophagus*, *Encarsia*, *Metaphycus*, and *Microterys* species. If scales are a problem, learn whether that species has effective natural enemies (Table 68), and if so, what can be done to promote these beneficials. When natural enemies are present or are being introduced, avoid using broad-spectrum, persistent pesticides, and control ants and dust. Read the ants and biological control conservation sections in this chapter for more information.

Natural enemies are commercially available for release against certain scale species. There is little information on the effectiveness of releases for scale control in flower and nursery crops. If releases are planned, consult the releasing natural enemies effectively section earlier in this chapter.

Soft scale parasites. Metaphycus helvolus (family Encyrtidae) is a tiny wasp, $\frac{1}{25}$ inch (1 mm) long, that kills black scale, brown soft scale, and soft scales of several other species. The yellowish orange females attack first and second instars, killing them by laying eggs in them or by feeding on their body fluids. Parasite activity can be recognized with a hand lens by inspecting scale covers for the round exit hole chewed by the emerging adult parasite.

Commercially available *Metaphycus helvolus* can be released when first- and second-instar scales are common; in black scale, this is the young, flattened, brownish stage when an H-shaped ridge is apparent on the scale's back. Another commercially available parasitoid species, *Microterys nietneri* (=M. *flavus*), attacks only brown soft scale.

Soft scale predators. The lady beetle *Rhyzobius* (=*Lindorus*) *lophanthae* feeds on many armored and soft scales. About $\frac{1}{12}$ inch (2 mm) long, it is blackish with tiny dense hairs on top and reddish or yellowish underneath. Although naturally occurring populations are important outdoors, there is little information on the effectiveness of releasing commercially available beetles. Because they tend to be associated with high scale populations, releasing beetles on hot spots might be effective in combination with parasites, which can seek lower density scales throughout the crop.

Cottony cushion scale natural enemies. Cottony cushion scale is usually well controlled in landscapes and orchards by two introduced natural enemies, but sometimes it infests perennial container plants. The vedalia beetle (*Rodolia cardinalis*) is a red and black lady beetle introduced from Australia. Adult beetles feed on cottony cushion scales and females lay their eggs underneath the scale or attached to scale egg sacs. The reddish larvae move into the egg masses and feed; more-mature larvae feed on all scale stages.

The parasitic fly *Cryptochaetum iceryae* (family Cryptochaetidae) deposits its eggs inside the bodies of cottony cushion scale. The larvae feed within the scale; later their dark, oblong pupal cases may be seen there. This parasitic fly produces up to eight generations per year.

Neither species is commercially available. If not present naturally, it may be possible to collect them from a cottony cushion scale infestation on common hosts such as *Coccculus laurifolius*, *Nandina domesticum*, or *Pittosporum tobira*. If scales cannot be tolerated until natural enemies become abundant, narrow-range oil or other insecticides provide control if applied when the tiny reddish scale crawlers are active.

California red scale parasite. The wasp *Aphytis melinus* (family Aphelinidae) is the most important parasite of California red scale. Properly timed releases of commercially available *A. melinus* can reduce California red scale populations in citrus orchards, and the wasp is widely released there. *Aphytis* kills

Table 68. Some Common Scales and Important Natural Enemies that Can Control Them.

Common name	Pest Scientific name	Type	Natural enemies
black scale	*Saissetia oleae*	S	parasitic wasps *Metaphycus bartletti*, *M. helvolus*
brown soft scale	*Coccus hesperidum*	S	parasitic wasps *Coccophagus scutellaris*, *Metaphycus luteolus*, *Metaphycus* spp.
California red scale	*Aonidiella aurantii*	A	parasitic wasps *Aphytis melinus*, *Aphytis lingnanensis*, *Comperiella bifasciata*, *Encarsia perniciosi*
cottony cushion scale	*Icerya purchasi*	M	predatory lady beetle *Rodolia cardinalis*; parasitic fly *Cryptochaetum iceryae*
green shield scale[1]	*Pulvinaria psidii*	S	mealybug destroyer lady beetle *Cryptolaemus montrouzieri*
hemispherical scale	*Saissetia coffeae*	S	parasitic wasps *Metaphycus helvolus*, *Metaphycus* spp.

KEY: A = armored, family Diaspididae
    M = family Margarodidae
    S = soft, family Coccidae

1. Green shield scale has been rated a "B" pest by the California Department of Food and Agriculture. Biological control can be important in limiting scale populations during production, but plants may be required to be entirely free of this pest to be marketed, which will necessitate thorough spraying and careful inspection before shipping.

scales by puncturing them and feeding on the exuding fluid or by laying an egg under the scale cover, where the immature parasite feeds. *Aphytis* leaves a flat and dehydrated scale body beneath the scale cover where the parasite's cast skin and fecal pellets may be observed. The adult wasp may emerge through a small, round exit hole in the scale cover or push out from beneath the scale cover, so that parasitized scales often slough off. *Aphytis melinus* prefers to parasitize the adult virgin female scales (Fig. 47), so release *Aphytis* when this scale stage is common. Virgin female California red scales have a wide, gray margin extending beyond the insect body, and the scale cover and body can be readily separated. The short life cycle of *Aphytis* (10–20 days) allows two to three parasite generations for each scale generation. Consult *Life Stages of California Red Scale and Its Parasitoids* (Forster, Luck, and Grafton-Cardwell 1995) and *Integrated Pest Management for Citrus* (UCIPM 1991) for more details on using A. *melinus* and other red scale biological control agents.

Green Shield Scale
Pulvinaria psidii

Green shield scale is a relatively new species in California. Its hosts include anthurium, aralia, begonia, camellia, croton, *Ficus*, hibiscus, gardenia, pittosporum, plumeria, *Schefflera*, *Schinus*, and *Syzygium*. Heavy infestations produce copious honeydew and extensive sooty mold growth, and mature females cover plants with flocculent white egg sacs.

The green, yellowish, or brownish female scale is about ⅛ to ⅙ inch (3–4 mm) long, and several times longer than this when a cottony egg sac is produced. Unlike most other species of scales, which settle and feed in one spot soon after emerging from eggs, immature green shield scales are relatively mobile. They can feed in one spot for days, then slowly crawl to infest adjoining plants. The mealybug destroyer appears to be an important predator of this pest. Some species of native parasites are attacking green shield scale.

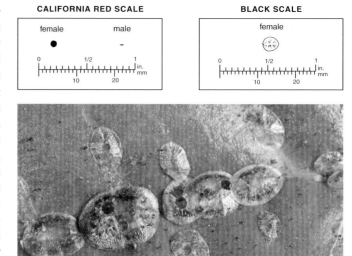

| CALIFORNIA RED SCALE | | BLACK SCALE |
| female | male | female |

Dead brown soft scale nymphs with emergence holes of the parasite *Microterys flavipes*. Brown soft scale and certain other scale species can be biologically controlled. Take steps to conserve natural enemies whenever possible.

An enlargement of scale crawlers caught in a sticky tape trap. Crawlers are the stage most susceptible to pesticides. Monitoring with sticky tape traps is an efficient method for timing applications.

Brown soft scale, unlike most soft scale species, has multiple overlapping generations, so life stages of different size commonly occur together. Shown here are tiny yellow crawlers, yellow second instars, and orangish to dark brown females.

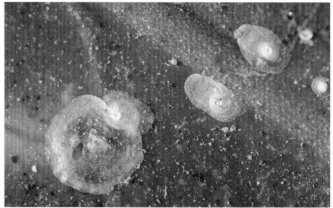

Several oblong males and a roundish female California red scale. The female was killed by a parasite that left a hole in the platelike scale cover, which can usually be removed to reveal the soft insect body underneath.

Green shield scale infestations are often tended by Argentine ants, which carry scales from one plant to another, attack parasites, and can prevent biological controls agents from becoming abundant. Green shield scale may be quarantined, prohibiting nurseries from shipping plants unless they are pest-free, which can require repeated insecticide applications.

Ants

Ants (family Formicidae) are in the order Hymenoptera, along with bees and wasps. Many species of ants are beneficial in their roles as predators of pests or important nutrient recyclers. Ants are pests if they annoy workers handling infested plants and when their activities increase pest populations, for example by interfering with biological controls.

Damage

Certain ants (e.g., *Solenopsis* spp.) occasionally chew tender twigs and bark of young woody plants, but ants are primarily an indirect pest because they can promote populations of other pests. Ants feed on honeydew excreted by Homopteran insects, including aphids, mealybugs, soft scales, and whiteflies. Ants move these honeydew-producing insects from plant to plant and protect them from predators and parasites that might otherwise control them. Ants can also disrupt the biological control of some non-honeydew-producing pests, such as mites and armored scales, if these pests occur on the same plants as honeydew-producing species. Where natural enemies are present, if ants are controlled, populations of many pests will gradually be reduced as natural enemies become more abundant.

Identification and Biology

Adult ants are divided into three social classes: winged males that occur only during the mating season, queens that spend most of their life in the nest laying eggs, and workers. Most ants are wingless workers that forage for food outside the nest or care for the tiny, pale, grublike immatures in the nest. Most ants nest underground or beneath rocks, buildings, or other objects, where the tiny, elliptical, pale eggs are laid.

Ants are sometimes confused with termites, but these groups are readily distinguished by differences in their antennae, body shape, and wings, if present (Fig. 49). Argentine ants and certain fire ants are important pests in flower and nursery crops. Consult *Ants of California with Color Pictures* (Haney, Phillips, and Wagner 1987) for identification of common ant species.

Management

Inspect plants and growing areas regularly for ants, which often occur in trails. Look for sticky honeydew, blackish sooty mold, and the honeydew-producing insects associated with ants. Depending on the situation, ants may be controlled through barriers or by insecticide baits or sprays. Controlling honeydew-producing insects that attract ants often results in ant control. Promising research indicates that Argentine ants in orchards can be controlled with farnesol, a behavior-modifying chemical or pheromone; watch for new information and commercial availability of this product.

Deny ants and other flightless pests access to plants by applying sticky material (such as Tanglefoot or Stickem) to encircle bench legs. To avoid getting sticky material on workers and equipment, coat the inside of inverted cups or trays placed over the top of legs or blocks on which bench tops rest (Fig. 36). Moats of water or oil also exclude ants; set bench legs in pans and fill pans with water when watering plants. Look for the availability of special benches that divert irrigation runoff from bench tops into containers around bench legs, automatically filling the ant-excluding moats whenever plants are watered.

Silica gel combined with pyrethrins is available for application to ant mounds. Silica gel apparently injures ant cuticles (outer skin) causing them to dehydrate and die. Place enclosed pesticide baits, such as ant stakes containing an insect growth regulator, near nests or plants or along ant

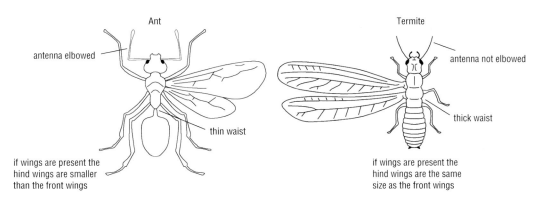

Figure 49. Ants are distinguished from termites by ants' narrow waist, elbowed antennae, and hind wings (if present) that are much shorter than the forewings.

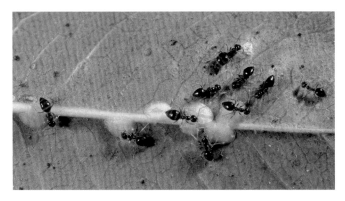

Ants can disrupt biological control by protecting pests from attack by parasites and predators. These honey ants *(Prenolepis imparis)* are tending European fruit lecanium scale nymphs.

A southern fire ant nest exposed to reveal pale pupae and larvae, winged reproductives, and worker ants. Their yellowish red head and thorax and dark brown abdomen distinguish southern fire ant workers from workers of harvester ants and other fire ant species found in California.

A container of poison bait for ant control. Applying insecticide mixed with bait minimizes nontarget impacts. Although baits take several days to provide control, they can be highly effective because the poison is carried underground, killing queen ants and causing the colony to die.

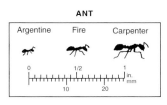

trails. Pesticide baits act slowly but can be more effective than sprays because worker ants carry the poisoned bait back to their underground nests, killing the reproductive queens and causing the entire colony to die. For the most effective and economical ant control, treat in the late winter or early spring when ant populations are low. Periodic moistening and stirring of certain baits may improve their attractiveness to ants. Surface sprays or drenching soil around nests with certain insecticides (such as diazinon) can temporarily reduce ant populations.

Argentine Ant
Linepithema humile (=Iridomyrmex humilis)

The introduced Argentine ant is probably the most common ant pest species in California. This species does not usually chew plants. In nursery and flower crops it primarily is an indirect pest because it aggressively tends honeydew-producing insects. Abundant ants can annoy workers. Colonies sometimes nest in container soil, requiring treatment before plants can be marketed.

The wingless Argentine ant workers are relatively small, about $^1/_{10}$ inch (2.5 mm) long. They are uniformly dark brown and travel in characteristic trails on bark or on the ground. Argentine ants can quickly relocate their ground nests in response to changes in temperature, soil moisture, and available food. Relocating colonies can be recognized by workers carrying pale ant larvae and pupae. Populations of Argentine ants increase greatly during summer and early fall. Late winter and early spring usually are the best times to apply controls, before ants and the pests they tend become abundant.

Red Imported Fire Ant
Solenopsis wagneri (=S. invicta)

The red imported fire ant is a widespread severe pest throughout the southern United States. It has recently been introduced into California, where it is a more aggressive and prolific pest than native fire ants. Red imported fire ant has a painful sting that can severely injure people or animals attacked by swarming ants. Even a single sting can be life-threatening to the small percentage of people who are allergic. Although primarily predators of insects and other invertebrates and therefore beneficial in certain situations, fire ants also feed on crop seeds, tend honeydew-producing insects, and sometimes feed on crops, such as by stripping bark from young plants. The large nesting mounds of fire ants can damage farm equipment and interfere with cropping of fields. Fire ant quarantines may restrict shipment of container plants and certain other products from infested areas, adding significant treatment and inspection costs to container crop production.

A red imported fire ant queen can lay hundreds of eggs each day in an underground nest. Eggs hatch in about 7 to 10 days, then develop through larval and a pupal stage in about 2 to 4 weeks. Fire ants can be distinguished from other ants

Table 69. Characteristics Helpful in Distinguishing Three Species of Fire Ants Found in California.

Characteristic	Common name, *Solenopsis* spp.		
	Desert fire ant, *S. aurea*	Red imported fire ant, *S. wagneri*	Southern fire ant, *S. xyloni*
worker length	≤⅛ inch (3 mm)	1/12–¼ inch (2–6 mm)	1/12 to ⅕ inch (2–5 mm)
worker color	golden yellow	uniformly dark reddish brown	yellowish red head, dark brown abdomen
location	deserts	irrigated or moist locations	coastal, inland
mound	variable; often use other ants' nest	usually domed mounds	irregular craters

Positive ant species identification requires expert knowledge or reference to appropriate technical publications and an examination under magnification of certain physical characteristics, including the number of antennal segments and projections (nodes) on the abdomen.

in California by the great variability in size of worker ants. These highly variable workers can be observed together in the same trail. Size, color, and location help to distinguish the red imported fire ant from native California fire ants (Table 69). The red imported fire ants may also be confused with harvester ants, which are also called red ants. However, harvester ants are not aggressive unless disturbed. Workers of the California harvester ant (*Pogonomyrmex californicus*) are uniformly red, more robust (stout) than fire ants, and uniformly sized, about ¼ inch (6 mm) long.

Fire ants are spread long distances primarily by people moving ant-infested soil. To prevent infestations from spreading, container nurseries in quarantined areas may be subject to a nursery certification program. Quarantines may require drenching all containers with insecticide and inspecting them before shipping plants, regardless of whether fire ants have been found in the immediate vicinity of that growing site.

Inspect incoming soil and container plants to avoid introducing fire ant colonies into growing areas, especially if material is arriving from areas known to be infested. Red imported fire ants are controlled by baiting infested areas, drenching individual mounds, or both. Granules of an insect growth regulator such as fenoxycarb (Award) or hydramethylnon (Amdro, Combat, Maxforce) are typically broadcast throughout the infested area. Although they can be highly effective, it typically takes several weeks after first applying these IGRs before a reduction in ants is observed. When baiting, use only a fresh product. Make bait applications when red imported fire ants are active and soil temperatures are about 65° to 90°F (19° to 33°C). Make broadcast applications of registered materials only onto dry surfaces when no rain or overhead irrigation is expected for at least 2 days after application. If individual mounds are to be treated, wait at least 2 or 3 days after any baiting before drenching each mound. Insecticide drenches usually consist of a dust, granule, or liquid insecticide containing a registered carbamate, organophosphate, or pyrethroid insecticide.

LEAFHOPPER

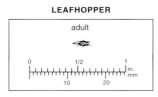

Leafhoppers and Sharpshooters

Leafhoppers (family Cicadellidae), including species called sharpshooters, suck plant juices. Leafhopper feeding causes leaves to appear stippled, pale, or brown, and shoots may curl and die. Certain species secrete honeydew on which foliage-blackening sooty mold grows. Potato leafhopper (*Empoasca fabae*) and certain other species inject toxins while feeding. Feeding, toxins, and egg laying by most leafhopper species can cause foliage to distort, discolor, and sometimes die. Leafhoppers are usually not abundant enough for their feeding or egg-laying damage to be a problem, although high populations can be a major nuisance because of the copious amount of liquid excreted by certain species.

Leafhoppers are pests primarily because some species vector pathogens. The aster leafhopper and several other species vector the aster yellows phytoplasma, which infects many flower crops (see the chapter "Diseases"). Glassy-winged sharpshooter (*Homalodisca coagulata*), blue-green sharpshooter (*Graphocephala atropunctata*), smoke tree sharpshooter (*Homalodisca lacerta*), and possibly other leafhopper species vector a strain of *Xylella fastidiosa* bacteria that causes oleander leaf scorch. Related strains of *Xylella fastidiosa* cause Pierce's disease in grapes and certain other crops. The relationships among leafhopper species, host plants, and pathogenic *Xylella* are not fully understood.

The adult aster leafhopper is grayish to yellowish green with black markings. Adults of this species have six dark lines on the face (not shown) that are visible with a 10× hand lens. This insect spreads the aster yellows phytoplasma pathogen.

Most adult leafhoppers are slender and less than or about equal to ¼ inch (6 mm) long. Some species are brightly colored, while others blend with their host plant. Leafhoppers are active insects; they crawl rapidly sideways or readily jump when disturbed. Adults and nymphs and their pale cast skins are usually found on the underside of leaves.

Females insert tiny eggs in tender plant tissue, causing pimplelike injuries. Wingless nymphs emerge and molt four or five times before maturing in about 2 to 7 weeks. Leafhoppers overwinter as eggs on twigs or as adults in protected places such as bark crevices. In cold-winter climates, leafhoppers may die during winter and in spring migrate back in from warmer regions. Most species have two or more generations each year.

Leafhoppers can be detected by visually inspecting plants for insects or their damage. Shaking or tapping plants, commonly called branch beating, to cause leafhoppers to jump or fly, or placing yellow sticky traps along crop borders or within plantings, can also be used to detect leafhoppers.

Rely on cultural and physical methods to control leafhoppers and aster yellows. Control methods for oleander leaf scorch are still being investigated. One method being studied is to lower populations of pathogen-vectoring glassy-winged sharpshooters using parasites, such as the leafhopper egg parasite *Gonatocerus ashmeadi* (Mymaridae).

Exclude leafhoppers from growing areas whenever possible. Inspect plants thoroughly and bring them into enclosed growing areas only if they are pest-free. Use screening, positive pressure ventilation, and row covers to exclude leafhoppers from crops as discussed in the exclusion sections earlier in this chapter. Reflective mulch has been shown to repel leafhoppers vectoring corn stunt spiroplasm (a bacterialike organism) and use of reflective mulch as discussed earlier in this chapter may be beneficial in reducing insect-vectored pathogens affecting young field-grown flower crops.

Aster yellows infect many weeds, pasture plants, and crops such as alfalfa, celery, and oats. When possible, avoid planting susceptible flower and nursery crops near these alternate hosts, especially if weeds will dry up or crops will soon be harvested. Eliminate weeds, which can host leafhopper-vectored pathogens and leafhoppers that can migrate to crops. If nearby alternate hosts cannot be eliminated, consider maintaining (such as by irrigating or strip harvesting) border plants to reduce outward migration of leafhoppers.

If insecticides are applied, rather than treating the flower and nursery crop, it can be more effective to treat nearby alternate hosts to reduce leafhopper migration. Treating crops is relatively ineffective against migrating leafhoppers because leafhopper feeding can transmit the phytoplasma before the insects are killed by the insecticide. Insecticide sprays or dips can eliminate leafhopper nymphs from infested stock, but eggs are laid in plant tissue where they are protected from most insecticides. Consider rejecting infested stock, which may already be infected with disease that is not

An adult (right) and nymphal glassy-winged sharpshooter. Adults are about ½ inch (13 mm) long, distinctly larger than most other leafhoppers, and can feed on a wide variety of woody ornamental species. Glassy-winged sharpshooter is one of several leafhopper species that vectors *Xylella* bacteria that cause oleander scorch and Pierce's disease.

yet exhibiting symptoms. Insecticidal soap or oil kills immature leafhoppers on contact. Some other insecticides (such as dimethoate, carbaryl, chlorpyrifos, malathion, and permethrin) may be more effective, but it is extremely difficult to adequately control populations with insecticides. Adults move readily and brief feeding by just one leafhopper can infect a plant with phytoplasma.

Aster Leafhopper
Macrosteles quadrilineatus (=M. fascifrons)
Aster leafhopper occurs throughout the United States. It is one of several dozen leafhopper species that transmit aster yellows, which are one or more phytoplasma pathogens that infect many crops. The aster leafhopper is also called the six-spotted leafhopper because of three pairs of black dots on its head. Adults are mostly light green to yellow, with some black on their thorax and abdomen. Their wings are transparent to somewhat smoky. Nymphs are mostly dark green. Hosts of aster leafhopper include most of the flower crops susceptible to aster yellows as listed in the chapter "Crop Tables"; alfalfa and cereal grains; vegetable crops, including carrot, celery, lettuce, and potato; grasses, including crabgrass, Kentucky bluegrass, and quackgrass; and many species of weeds. Consult *Pests of Landscape Trees and Shrubs* (Dreistadt 1994) for leafhopper pests of woody ornamentals.

True Bugs

Many different kinds of true bugs (order Hemiptera) occasionally damage flower and nursery crops. Lygus bug (*Lygus hesperus*) and other plant bugs (family Miridae) are the most common pests. Lace bugs (family Tingidae) and stink bugs (Pentatomidae) are occasional pests. Some bugs are beneficial predators, including assassin bugs, bigeyed bugs, and minute pirate bugs (see the predaceous bugs section earlier in this chapter). Spittlebugs are not true bugs; they are in the order Homoptera and are more closely related to leafhoppers and aphids.

Spittlebug nymph foam on a sweet William stem. Spittlebug feeding is usually harmless to plants; the insects can be controlled with a forceful stream of water. Despite the name, spittlebugs are homopteran insects, not true bugs.

The adult lygus bug has a distinct yellow or pale green triangle behind its head. Nymphs are pale yellowish green. The most effective control for many pest bugs is to manage their populations on nearby noncrop plants before bugs migrate into crops.

Pest bugs suck plant juices, sometimes causing tissue to become distorted or drop. Some bugs leave black specks of excrement on the underside of foliage where they feed. Pale white or yellow stippling forms around feeding sites of certain bugs, giving foliage a bleached appearance. Leafhoppers, mites, thrips, and certain other invertebrates can cause similar leaf stippling. Carefully inspect foliage (usually the underside of leaves) to observe the pests and determine what type of invertebrate is causing damage.

Nearly all true bug adults have thickened forewings with membranous tips. When bugs rest, they can be recognized by the characteristic triangular or X-shaped pattern on the back formed by the overlap of dissimilar parts of their folded wings. Most species have several generations per year. Depending on the species, eggs are laid exposed on plants, inserted into plant tissue, or deposited in litter. The flightless nymphs usually develop through five instars, gradually changing each time they molt and becoming winged adults without any pupal stage.

Lygus bugs and stink bugs are most likely to damage crops when nearby herbaceous plants on which they feed dry up or are cut, prompting the bugs to move. Screen growing areas, if possible, to excluding migrating bugs. Reduce lygus bug and stink bug movement by controlling weeds and reducing nearby herbaceous noncrop hosts where bugs feed and overwinter. Alternatively, maintain (such as by irrigation and strip harvesting) nearby alternate hosts so that bugs are not

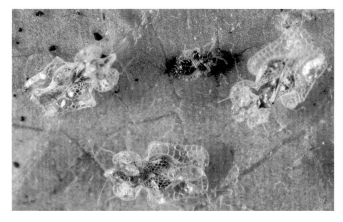

Lace bug adults and nymphs usually occur on the underside of leaves, often among dark excrement left by adults.

Bleached foliage caused by *Corythucha* species lace bugs feeding on photinia. Leafhoppers, mites, thrips, and certain other true bugs cause similar leaf stippling. Correctly identify the cause of this damage before taking control action.

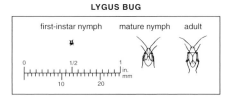

LYGUS BUG

first-instar nymph   mature nymph   adult

0   1/2   1   in. mm
10   20

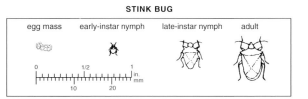

STINK BUG

egg mass   early-instar nymph   late-instar nymph   adult

0   1/2   1   in. mm
10   20

induced to move. Reduce organic debris and rubbish near crops, which may shelter bugs, especially during overwintering. Populations of bugs infesting crops may be reduced by applying a registered insecticide to foliage when nymphs are abundant; systemic insecticides are the most effective. No treatment will restore damaged foliage; discard plants or prune out damaged parts and provide good cultural care to promote healthy new growth.

Most species of lace bugs attack only woody perennial plants in a closely related group; they will not move to or feed on unrelated plants. Lace bugs attacking flower and nursery crops are managed primarily by spraying nymphs and adults on infested plants. Azalea lace bug (*Stephanitis pyrioides*) is one of the few well-studied species in this group. Besides using insecticides, azalea lace bug populations in landscape plantings are reduced by adequate irrigation, providing plants with partial shade, and encouraging various lace bug predators and parasites.

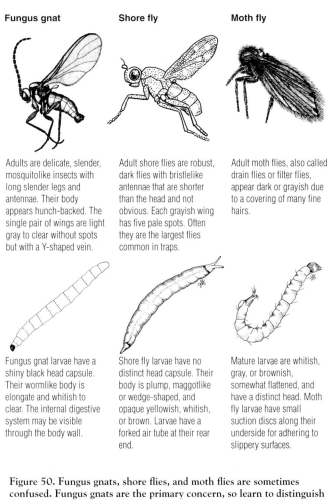

Fungus gnat

Adults are delicate, slender, mosquitolike insects with long slender legs and antennae. Their body appears hunch-backed. The single pair of wings are light gray to clear without spots but with a Y-shaped vein.

Fungus gnat larvae have a shiny black head capsule. Their wormlike body is elongate and whitish to clear. The internal digestive system may be visible through the body wall.

Shore fly

Adult shore flies are robust, dark flies with bristlelike antennae that are shorter than the head and not obvious. Each grayish wing has five pale spots. Often they are the largest flies common in traps.

Shore fly larvae have no distinct head capsule. Their body is plump, maggotlike or wedge-shaped, and opaque yellowish, whitish, or brown. Larvae have a forked air tube at their rear end.

Moth fly

Adult moth flies, also called drain flies or filter flies, appear dark or grayish due to a covering of many fine hairs.

Mature larvae are whitish, gray, or brownish, somewhat flattened, and have a distinct head. Moth fly larvae have small suction discs along their underside for adhering to slippery surfaces.

Figure 50. Fungus gnats, shore flies, and moth flies are sometimes confused. Fungus gnats are the primary concern, so learn to distinguish these groups. *Sources:* Fungus gnat adult and larva and moth fly adult by C. Feller from Gorham 1991, other larvae by J. L. Lockwood from Dreistadt 1997.

Fungus Gnats, Moth Flies, and Shore Flies

Fungus gnats, moth flies, and shore flies are sometimes confused. They have similar biology and appearance, prefer overwatered conditions, and often occur together. Fungus gnats are the primary concern, so learn to distinguish them from moth flies and shore flies.

Distinguish among these flies by their appearance (Fig. 50), behavior, and location when resting. Fungus gnats at rest hold their wings slightly spread when viewed from above. They are weak flyers and are often observed running or resting on growing media, foliage, or litter. Fungus gnats also resemble adult aphid midges (*Aphidoletes* spp.), a commercially available and naturally occurring predator with larvae that feed on aphids and other soft-bodied pests. Adult *Aphidoletes* can be caught in yellow sticky traps along with the pest species discussed here, but *Aphidoletes* lack the distinct Y-shaped vein found on the wings of similar-looking fungus gnats.

Moth flies (family Psychodidae) are usually observed resting with their wings held rooflike over their body. Often they rest around drains, urinals, and on bathroom walls. Shore flies (Ephydridae), such as the common species *Scatella stagnalis*, are stronger, faster fliers than fungus gnats. Shore flies have less of a tendency to take flight in comparison with the more easily disturbed fungus gnats.

Fungus Gnats
Bradysia spp.

Fungus gnats (families Mycetophilidae and Sciaridae) are tiny, delicate flies. *Bradysia coprophila* and *B. impatiens* (family Sciaridae) are the most common greenhouse pest species. They occur in wet greenhouses or outdoors among organic debris where conditions are mild and damp.

Damage. Fungus gnat larvae are primarily a pest of seedlings and cuttings. Larvae feed on or inside roots near the surface of media and sometimes chew lower stems or leaves touching media. Feeding by larvae can reduce germination, stunt growth, and cause foliage to wilt and yellow. Besides affecting young plants in propagation areas, larvae sometimes damage older, container-grown plants of certain susceptible species, including begonias, carnations, geraniums, and poinsettias.

Feeding by fungus gnat larvae wounds roots, which can allow entry of pathogenic fungi. Larvae themselves can be contaminated with pathogens in their gut and may introduce these pathogens to plants while feeding. Adult fungus gnats have been found to be contaminated with fungi including *Botrytis*, *Fusarium*, *Phoma*, *Pythium*, and *Verticillium* species. Adults may spread these pathogens when they fly from infected plants to healthy crops. However, the importance of fungus gnats in plant disease development is uncertain.

Possibly the greatest problem is when plants are shipped with fungus gnat-contaminated media; retailers and consumers do not appreciate tiny flies emerging from their plants. Although adults do not bite, flying adults can annoy workers during production.

Identification and biology. Adult fungus gnats are dark brown or black, delicate, mosquitolike flies. Adult females lay tiny eggs in clusters of 2 to 30 or more in moist media (Fig. 51). Larvae develop through four instars, feeding mostly on root hairs, algae, and decaying organic matter. If conditions are especially moist and fungus gnats are abundant, larvae traveling in groups on media surface can leave slime trails that look like those of slugs. The oblong, somewhat silken fungus gnat pupal case occurs in damp media where larvae feed.

Fungus gnats have several generations each year. If uncontrolled, heavy populations of fungus gnats and shore flies can build up in growing areas. Infested media, growing beds, and wet areas under and around plants are the primary sources of fungus gnats and shore flies. Where outdoor temperatures are mild, adults may also migrate into crops from consistently wet, organic-rich areas nearby, but the growing area itself is the source of most infestations.

Monitoring. Regularly survey growing areas for excessively moist conditions and organic debris that can be reduced to limit reproduction of these flies. Yellow sticky traps are an efficient way to monitor adults. Adults can also be observed resting on plants, media, or walls or flying around growing areas. Overhead sprinkling or tapping containers disturbs adults and causes them to fly up from media. Fungus gnats are most common outdoors in interior areas of California during winter and spring. They occur any time of year in moist coastal regions and in greenhouses.

Because adults may be migrants and most control is directed at larvae, it is best to confirm that larvae are present before treating growing media. Larvae and pupae can be detected by digging in the topmost surface of infested media or by inspecting the underside of fallen leaves and the surface of media covered by organic debris.

If the precise source of infestations is unknown, consider using adult emergence traps or apply a pyrethrum flush to growing media to locate larval feeding sites. Potato disks placed on media are useful for confirming larval presence and monitoring fungus gnat larval densities, such as before and after treatment to evaluate control efficacy.

Sticky traps. Place yellow sticky cards throughout the greenhouse to capture adults. Learn to distinguish fungus gnats from other pests in traps. Concentrate traps in propagation areas and in especially susceptible crops. Sticky cards placed flat just above media can catch about 50% more fungus gnats than vertical traps. However, because this horizontal orien-

tation is not useful for catching most other insects, conventional vertical orientation is most efficient for an overall IPM program (see the sticky traps section earlier in this chapter).

Potato disks. Fungus gnat larvae migrate to feed on the underside of potato pieces placed in media. Use raw potato pieces of relatively uniform size, about 1 inch (25 mm) thick and 1 inch diameter or square. Cut raw potatoes into cubes, slice small potatoes into disks, or use a vegetable corer to extract a 1-inch-diameter column from a potato and slice the column into disks 1 inch thick. Partly bury several cubes or disks in the topsoil of containers so that the potato piece is imbedded about ½ inch (13 mm) deep into media. Suggested trap densities range from about 10 potato disks or cubes per 10,000 square feet (900 sq m) of production area to about 10 traps per 1,000 square feet (90 sq m) of propagation area when growing susceptible crops. Once or twice a week, pick up and examine the underside of each disk and the soil surface

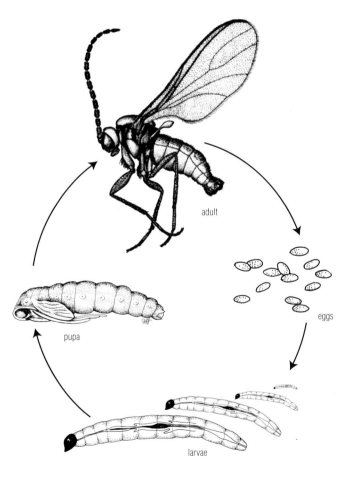

Figure 51. Life cycle and stages of a fungus gnat. Larvae develop through four instars or sizes. Fungus gnats have many annual generations; egg to adult development time varies with temperature and is about 3 weeks at 75°F (24°C), as shown here. *Sources:* Adult by C. Feller from Gorham 1991, larvae and pupa by J. L. Lockwood from Dreistadt 1997.

immediately beneath the disk. Count and record the number of larvae present to estimate pest density and compare numbers before and after treatment to determine whether larvae are being controlled. Replace raw potato pieces with fresh potato cubes or disks about every 2 weeks.

Emergence traps. If the precise source of fungus gnat larvae in a growing area is not known, consider using small emergence traps to determine where adults are coming from. Invert several clear plastic cups or halves of petri dishes over each batch of suspect media, soil, compost, or other moist, organic-rich material. Examine traps over the next several days for adults that have emerged from pupae in the media. If traps contain adult fungus gnats, the media is infested with larvae.

Pyrethrum flush. Pyrethrum, a naturally occurring botanical insecticide, is highly irritating to insects. Mobile stages of many insects can be induced to leave hidden places if they are exposed to pyrethrum. Apply pyrethrum to the surface of media suspected of harboring fungus gnat or shore fly larvae. If media is contaminated, within a few minutes larvae will emerge onto the surface and can be readily observed wriggling vigorously. Other hiding invertebrates, such as centipedes, millipedes, and springtails may also be induced to reveal their presence when pyrethrum is applied.

Management. Cultural control, sanitation, and exclusion can adequately control fungus gnats, shore flies, and moth flies in many situations. Good water management is the most important control strategy. Shore flies are relatively difficult to control with most pesticides but are largely eliminated by cultural methods that control algae. Good cultural methods and sanitation should be applied continuously because they also greatly reduce disease problems.

If cultural control, sanitation, and exclusion are insufficient, consider applying biological or chemical controls if monitoring indicates these flies are abundant or increasing, especially in propagation areas. Because more than one-half of their life span is spent as larvae and pupae confined in media, most direct control targets these stages rather than the mobile and short-lived adults. If growing areas are infested, consider treating container plants before marketing to prevent objectionable adult populations from emerging after crops are shipped.

Cultural control, sanitation, and exclusion. These fly larvae thrive under moist conditions. Avoid overwatering, keep surfaces dry, and eliminate water puddling. Repair irrigation system leaks and provide good drainage. Use ventilation and temperature control to reduce condensation. Keep greenhouses free of weeds, dead plants, crop residue, algal scum, and organic debris where these flies breed. Cleaning floors, benches, and walls between crops using a portable steam machine can be very effective at controlling algae and these flies.

Do not introduce infested plants or media into growing areas. Compost and other moist organic amendments are often contaminated with fungus gnats unless organic material is pasteurized immediately before use. Periodically turn and aerate compost piles, keep them covered, and locate compost and organic debris away from growing areas. Keep sterile organic media well covered until use.

Insecticides. The most effective insecticides for fungus gnat control apparently are soil drenches of insect growth regulators to control larvae. Available insecticides include diflubenzuron, cyromazine, fenoxycarb, kinoprene, and certain other reduced-risked insecticides, including azadirachtin and imidacloprid. Some carbamates and organophosphates can also be applied as soil drenches. To improve pesticide coverage, avoid crowding plants. Leave head space at the top of containers so enough drench can be applied to drain down through the top several inches of media. Some pyrethroids and possibly other materials applied by fogging can reduce adults; however, actions targeting larvae provide more effective control.

Bti. Bacillus thuringiensis subspecies *israelensis* (Bti), or Bt H-14 (Gnatrol), is a biological insecticide that is toxic only to fly larvae (Table 70). Because Bti does not reproduce or persist, severe infestations in media and under benches will

Table 70. Commercially Available Biological Pesticides and Natural Enemies for Fungus Gnat Control.

Biological	Comments
Steinernema feltiae	Nematode effective under moist conditions at 60° to 90°F (16° to 32°C). Can be applied as a soil drench in conventional spray equipment. May be applied during irrigation if system is adapted to keep water well aerated and mixed, and each batch of nematodes is not immersed for longer than 24 hours before application. Nematodes reproduce and actively search for hosts, so they may provide season-long control after several initial applications to establish populations.
Hypoaspis (=*Geolaelaps* or *Stratiolaelaps*) *miles*	Predaceous mite (family Laelapidae) $\frac{1}{25}$ inch (1 mm) long. The light brown adults and whitish nymphs feed in the upper $\frac{1}{2}$ inch (1.2 cm) of moist soil. Preys on fungus gnat eggs and young larvae, thrips pupae, springtails, and other tiny invertebrates. Develops from egg to adult in about 10 days at 80°F (27°C) and 30 days at 60°F (16°C). Recommended release rates are about one-half dozen to several dozen mites per container or 1 square foot (0.09 sq m) of growing area applied before or within about 2 weeks after planting and while pest populations are still low. Mixing mites into media before planting is not recommended; *Hypoaspis* does not survive well deep below the surface and mites can be killed by physical injury during media mixing.
Bacillus thuringiensis ssp. *israelensis* (Bti)	A naturally occurring, spore-forming bacterium produced commercially by fermentation. Bti applied at labeled rates provides temporary control and is toxic only to fly larvae.

These materials are essentially nontoxic to people and are compatible for application in combination.

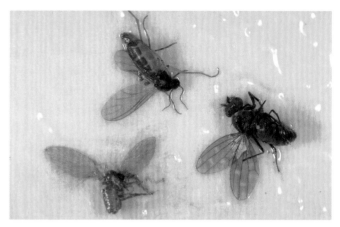

The adult fungus gnat (left) is a delicate, mosquitolike fly with slender legs and long, segmented antennae. The shore fly adult (right) is a dark, robust fly with short, bristlelike antennae. Shore flies have dark wings with clear or light spots.

The fungus gnat (top) has long, slender legs and antennae; its wings are light gray to clear with a Y-shaped vein. The shore fly (right) has short, bristlelike antennae and 5 pale spots on each wing. The moth fly (lower left) has wings that appear to be covered with fine hairs or fur. Of the three, fungus gnats are the primary concern, so learn to distinguish them in sticky traps.

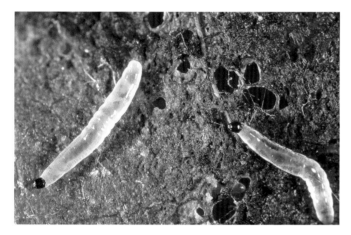

Fungus gnat larvae are elongate, whitish to clear, and have a shiny black head capsule. Because most of this pest's life cycle is spent as larvae and pupae, target most control actions against these immature stages.

Fungus gnat larvae left these shiny trails on the media of a container-grown greenhouse rose. Excess irrigation and poor drainage promote fungus gnat damage.

require several treatments at about 3- to 5-day intervals. Weekly treatment may be needed to provide season-long control where larval populations are a problem.

Bti is applied with conventional spray equipment as a soil drench. It can also be injected in irrigation water, but it should not be mixed with fertilizers, fungicides, or other materials with high levels of copper or chlorine; these materials can kill Bti. Chlorine levels in potable water are not a problem.

Biological control. Naturally occurring predators such as rove beetles (family Staphylinidae) provide some control in areas not sprayed with insecticides. If broad-spectrum materials are not applied as drenches, about two applications of commercially available nematodes or *Hypoaspis* predaceous mites at about 1 week intervals can provide relatively long-term suppression of fungus gnat populations because these

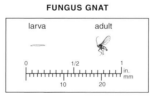

FUNGUS GNAT

larva   adult

0   1/2   1
|----------|----------| in.
       10   20   mm

beneficial populations are self-reproducing. Like Bti, nematodes are applied with conventional sprayers or with irrigation water if strong nutrient solutions are not used (Table 70). The nematode *Steinernema feltiae* is apparently more effective against fungus gnats in comparison with other available nematode species. Fungus gnat larvae turn milky white once they become infected with nematodes. Mites can be applied to beds and under benches using the commercial shipping container as a shaker. Because these predators are relatively mobile, it may not be necessary to distribute them into every individual container. Evaluate predator quality and calibrate shaker application rates as described in the releasing natural enemies effectively section earlier in this chapter.

Moth Flies

Moth flies (family Psychodidae) are also called drain flies, filter flies, or sewer flies. They thrive under moist conditions where decaying organic material is prevalent. Moth fly larvae have been reported to feed on plant roots and may be an occasional pest in wet production areas. Moth flies can occur together with shore flies and fungus gnats; fungus gnats are the more important pest.

Adults are usually about ⅛ inch (3 mm) long. They appear grayish or dark because of the many fine hairs covering their wings and body (Fig. 50). Indoors, moth flies are commonly observed resting on bathroom walls and around drain surfaces with their wings held rooflike over their body.

Mature larvae are less than ¼ inch (6 mm) long. They are whitish, gray, or brownish, somewhat flattened, and have a distinct head (Fig. 50). Moth fly larvae have small suction discs along their underside for adhering to slippery surfaces. Larvae feed in decaying organic matter, commonly in drains on the gelatinous film on drain plugs, screens, and pipes.

Control moth flies using good cultural practices, sanitation, and exclusion as described in the fungus gnats section above. Avoid overwatering, eliminate stagnant water, and provide good drainage. Keep growing areas free of crop residue, excess organic matter, and algal scum. Clean growing areas between crops using a portable steam machine or other methods. Regularly brush or wash away muck that collects around drain screens and inside the top of drain pipes. Biological and chemical control of moth flies has not been investigated.

Shore fly larvae have no distinct head capsule, and the body is opaque yellowish, whitish, or brown. Both the dark brown pupa (at the top of this photo) and larva have a forked air tube at the rear end.

Shore Flies

Shore flies (family Ephydridae), including the common species *Scatella stagnalis*, feed primarily on algae. They are considered relatively harmless because adults and larvae do not feed on crops. However, adult shore flies, like fungus gnats, are a nuisance when present in large numbers. Abundant adults can leave unsightly frass spots on foliage. Shore flies may spread soil-dwelling pathogens, but this is uncertain and may be of little importance. Shore flies are often confused with fungus gnats; both prefer overwatered conditions and often occur together. Adult shore flies are robust with short legs. Adults can be distinguished by their short antennae, light wing spots, and lack of a forked wing vein (Fig. 50).

Shore fly larvae occur in or on algal scum or very wet, decomposing organic matter. The larva's plump body takes on the color of their food, often green, yellowish, or brown. Larvae have no distinct head capsule, but their dark mouthparts and internal organs may be visible through their relatively clear integument. Larvae also have a suctionlike organ near their tail, which is retractable into their body and therefore may not be apparent. Shore fly larvae and pupae have a distinctive forked, dark-tipped breathing tube at the end of their tail. The dark oblong pupae, and the tiny oblong white eggs laid by adults, occur in damp media or algal scum where larvae feed. Shore flies have several generations each year.

The same cultural, sanitation, and physical control methods detailed in the fungus gnats section are effective against shore flies. It is especially important to avoid overwatering, repair irrigation system leaks, eliminate stagnant water, and provide good drainage. If cultural and physical controls are inadequate or impractical, chemical control of algae can largely eliminate shore flies.

Hydrated lime, potassium salts of fatty acids, and certain other materials are available to control algae under and around benches. Copper sulfate can be applied about once per month as labeled. A slurry of 1 to 1½ pound of lime per gallon of water (0.37–0.56 kg per 3.8 liters) applied about every 3 to 4 months controls algae. Prevent contact with plants as these materials are phytotoxic. Some counties may restrict growers' use of hydrated lime. Avoid contaminating water.

Bulb Flies

Maggots of several species of flies infest bulbs of all types, including amaryllis, daffodil, hyacinth, iris, lily, and tulip. The narcissus bulb fly (*Merodon equestris*) may be the most important species. Lesser bulb flies (*Eumerus* spp.) are sometimes a problem.

Damage

Larvae feed in bulbs, causing yellow foliage and stunted plants. If infested, large bulbs produce fewer leaves and distorted growth. Instead of a single large shoot, small leaves may emerge in a ring around the central growing point that has been killed by a larva. Blooms and small bulbs often die. Narcissus bulb fly attacks healthy plants; lesser bulb flies apparently are secondary pests, preferring bulbs and root-stocks that are already diseased or decayed. Bulb flies are primarily a problem in the field and in stored bulbs. However, bulb fly populations can develop in greenhouses if infested bulbs are brought in from outside.

Identification and Biology

Bulb flies are in the family Syrphidae, a group of mostly beneficial species that eat aphids (see the biological control and aphids sections earlier in this chapter). Adults are stocky, hairy flies, blackish to dark green with pale yellow, orange, or gray markings. Adult bulb flies look like small bumble bees and may also resemble other beneficial species, including leafcutting bees (family Megachilidae), predatory flower flies (Syrphidae), and bee flies (Bombyliidae). On warm, sunny days, adults often hover around blooming plants, where they feed on pollen and nectar. Narcissus bulb fly adults are about ½ to ⅝ inch (12–14 mm) long. Adult lesser bulb flies are less than or about equal to ¼ inch (6 mm) long.

Bulb fly eggs are chalky white and about 1/16 inch (1.5 mm) long. Eggs are laid on or near bulbs where larvae feed (Fig. 52). Bulb fly larvae are plump, wrinkled, dirty yellow, gray, white, or brownish maggots with a short brown or blackish breathing tube at their rear. Narcissus bulb fly larvae grow to about ¾ inch (19 mm) long. Lesser bulb fly larvae are about one-half this size. Larvae pupate in a brownish case inside the bulb or in nearby soil. Usually only one narcissus bulb fly maggot infests each bulb, hollowing the center and filling the bulb with brown excrement. Many lesser bulb fly maggots can occur in a single bulb.

Bulb flies usually have one generation per year, overwintering in the field as mature larvae within bulbs. They pupate in spring, then emerge as adults. Because not all flies develop at the same rate, adults can be present in the field and lay eggs from early spring through midsummer. Multiple generations may occur in greenhouses and possibly outdoors in mild-winter areas where hosts are grown year round.

Monitoring

Damage may not be obvious until after bulbs are harvested. In the field, damage becomes apparent when bulbs are unproductive the season after being infested; by this time, insects often have pupated and left the damaged bulbs. Because the current-season infestation is in bulbs that may appear normal in the field, crops must be carefully monitored to effectively manage bulb flies.

If bulb flies have been a problem, regularly inspect bulb crops on sunny days and look for robust, hairy flies that may be laying eggs near the base of plants. Females may be observed repeatedly extruding and withdrawing their ovipositor as they

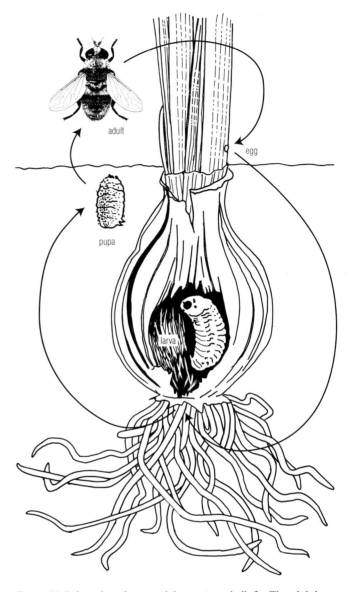

Figure 52. Life cycle and stages of the narcissus bulb fly. The adult lays an egg in spring or summer on exposed bulbs or stems at or near the base of plants. After 5 to 14 days, the egg hatches and a larva wriggles down into the soil or moves down along the outside of the bulb. It feeds on the basal plate (the bottom of the bulb where roots emerge), then enters and feeds inside the bulb. The larva develops through three instars over a period of 9 to 10 months. In spring the lava pupates in a brownish case inside the bulb, or it emerges and pupates nearby in topsoil. Pupation takes 4 to 8 weeks, after which the adult emerges, mates, and females lay eggs. Adults live about 2 to 3 weeks. *Source:* Adult from Doucette 1959.

use the tip of their abdomen to seek soil crevices or spaces between bulb scales in which to lay their eggs. Capture adults observed around crops by using a sweep net. Alternatively, place yellow sticky traps just above the crop canopy to monitor adults. Traps will catch many different species of insects, including similar-looking species that are beneficial pollinators or predators. Have the insects you capture properly identified before taking action based on the presence of adults.

Unproductive bulbs or those with few shoots or blooms may indicate a bulb fly infestation; however, bulbs may be unproductive for other reasons. If bulb flies are suspected, dig up some bulbs and examine them out of the ground. Brush or scrape away soil from the base and look for a small hole or sunken, brown area on the bottom of the bulb in the normally white root ring at the edge of the basal plate. A tunnel entrance or discoloration can indicate infestation by a bulb fly maggot. Cut the brown spot with a knife and look for the discoloring to extend into the bulb. Brownish bulb fly frass and a maggot may also be found.

Examine bulbs for damage at the end of the field season when mature bulbs are harvested and also after storage before planting. Bulbs that have been infested commonly feel soft and spongy, particularly at their smaller (neck) end. When cut into, damaged bulbs are hollow and are filled with brown excrement from maggots.

Management

Prevention is the most effective bulb fly control strategy. Purchase and plant only pest-free bulbs. Handle bulbs carefully during digging and in storage to avoid injuring bulbs. Plant only in sterile media or treat infested soil before planting. Consider rotating infested sites into nonbulb crops because bulb fly pupae can persist in the soil. Avoid continuous cropping of bulbs in the same soil. If the soil is not infested, use row covers or screens to keep adults away (see the exclusion section earlier in this chapter). Soil-dwelling predators (including rove beetles and ground beetles) and at least one parasite (an ichneumonid wasp) are natural enemies of bulb flies.

Inspect bulbs before selling or planting them. Look for bulbs damaged by maggots, other insects, mites, and disease. Treat soft or spongy (damaged) bulbs or bag and dispose of them away from crops.

Immersing bulbs in hot water at about 111°F (44°C) for about 1½ hours kills bulb fly larvae and most other invertebrates (Table 9). If infested bulbs are large, they may again become productive, although blooming may be delayed for a season. Large bulbs can be replanted after treatment, although it is probably best to grow them separately from undamaged bulbs. If damaged bulbs are small, they are unlikely to be productive; it is probably best to discard them.

Dipping bulbs in insecticide before planting or drenching soil after planting may prevent maggots from entering bulbs. Although insecticide dips or soil drenches can reduce damage the following season by preventing larvae from infesting undamaged bulbs, dips or drenches will not control maggots already inside bulbs.

Periodic surface cultivation when adults are ovipositing can provide some control by disturbing egg-laying sites—most larvae will die unless they contact a bulb soon after hatching from the egg. Thoroughly harvest bulb crops and promptly dispose of any plant debris. Deep cultivation to bury infested crop residue and pupae after harvest may help to reduce infestations.

Gall Makers

Galls are distorted and sometimes colorful swellings in plant tissue, abnormal plant growth caused by the secretions of certain plant-feeding pests. Invertebrates that cause galling include certain species of aphids, adelgids (aphidlike insects), cynipid wasps, eriophyid mites, gall midges, moths, and sawflies. Consult Table 41 for a list of microorganisms, nematodes, and other common causes of plant galls and how to distinguish among them.

Most gall-making pests that attack flower and ornamental nursery crops usually do not infest these hosts until after they are planted in gardens and landscapes, such as larvae of cynipid wasps that attack oaks. Major exceptions include gall mites (discussed in the mites section later in this chapter) and certain nematodes and pathogens discussed in the chapters on those topics. This section discusses gall midges. Other types of gall-making insects are most often a problem in perennial flower and nursery crops when these plants are grown in the nursery for more than one year before they are marketed.

Gall Midges

Hundreds of species of gall midges (family Cecidomyiidae), also called gall gnats or gall flies, occur in the United States. Not all of these flies feed on plants or are pests. Certain species, such as the aphid midge (*Aphidoletes aphidimyza*) are beneficial predators. Each gall-forming species is specialized to feed on only one or a few closely related hosts, such as the honeylocust pod gall midge (*Dasineura gleditchiae*) which infests only honey locust (*Gleditsia* spp.).

Adult gall midges are tiny, delicate flies, often with long slender antennae. They resemble fungus gnats and flies in certain other families. Adult gall midges lay minute eggs on foliage, usually on new growth. The eggs hatch into tiny white, yellowish, reddish, or orange maggots. In gall-making species, these larvae bore into tissue or cause tissue to form into galls that surround the larvae, which feed inside. Larvae usually pupate inside galled plant parts or drop to growing media as mature larvae to pupate, or both, depending mostly on the crop and pest species and the time of year. Most species have several annual generations.

Pasteurizing growing media and starting with pest-free stock often prevents gall midge infestations during the relatively short period that most flower and nursery crops are produced. Screening or row covers can exclude egg-laying adults. Hand-picking galled tissue or culling infested plants may provide control if employed when new infestations are first detected.

Horticultural oil applied to new shoots where adults lay eggs can control honeylocust pod gall midge and possibly

An orangish adult female violet gall midge *(Prodiplosis violicola)* and several whitish midge pupal cast skins on a curled violet leaf. The curling was caused by midge larvae feeding inside the leaf. Pasteurizing growing media and excluding insects prevents this problem in nurseries.

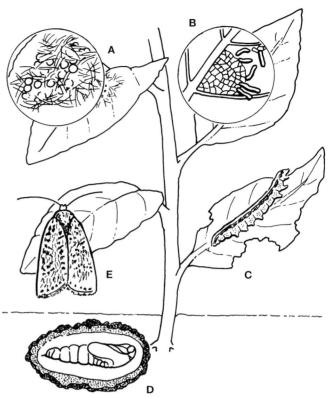

Figure 53. Life cycle of the beet armyworm, a pest of many flower crops. A. Eggs are laid in a cluster on foliage and covered with hairs from the female. B. Young larvae feed inside buds or in groups that skeletonize the leaf surface as they develop through 5 instars. C. Older larvae feed singly, chewing through leaves or stems. D. Mature larvae pupate in a cell or within loose silken webbing on or near the soil surface. E. The adult emerges and mates, and females seek a host plant and lay eggs. Because many species are potential pests and biology and behavior depend on the species, monitoring and control are more effective if you identify the species present and learn about their biology before taking action.

BEET ARMYWORM

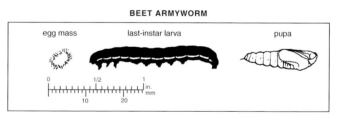

other species. Carefully time applications by monitoring for adults. Direct sprays to susceptible plant parts, usually the youngest, most succulent new terminal growth. Reduced-risk insecticides, including abamectin, azadirachtin, and cyromazine, may be effective if these pesticides are labeled for flies, gnats, or midges. Predatory mites or entomopathogenic nematodes may help to control soil-dwelling pupae, but their efficacy against pupating gall midges is largely unknown.

Persistent, broad-spectrum insecticides applied to foliage or drenched onto container media can be effective. Most foliar pesticides must be applied when egg-laying adults are present, before damage has become significant. Although certain pesticides, such as azadirachtin and orthene, have systemic effects, few if any pesticides will kill larvae feeding in galls. No treatment will restore already galled plant parts.

Caterpillars

Caterpillars are the immature or larval stage of moths and butterflies (order Lepidoptera). Only the larval stage chews plants. Although adults consume only liquids, such as nectar and water, they are important because they spread throughout the crop, choosing which plants to lay eggs on.

Damage

Caterpillars chew irregular holes in foliage or blossoms or entirely consume seedlings, young shoots, buds, leaves, or flowers. Some caterpillars fold or roll leaves together with silk to form shelters. Caterpillar feeding can kill or retard the growth of young plants. Any amount of chewing damage on marketable parts may make plants unmarketable. Most flower and nursery crops are susceptible to damage from

caterpillars of one or more species, as listed in the chapter "Crop Tables." Consult *Pests of Landscape Trees and Shrubs* (Dreistadt 1994) for caterpillar pests of woody ornamentals.

Identification and Biology

Moths and butterflies have complete metamorphosis and develop through four life stages (Fig. 32). Adults have prominent, delicate wings covered with tiny scales that rub off and appear powdery when touched. After mating, the female moth or butterfly lays her eggs singly or in a mass on or near the host plant or nearby soil. Eggs usually hatch in several

A rose bud mined by a caterpillar next to a chewed blossom with black frass (feces). Various noctuid caterpillars can cause this damage, including green fruitworms (*Amphipyra, Grapholitha,* and *Orthosia* spp.) and tobacco budworm (*Heliothis virescens*).

Beet armyworm feeding damage on kalanchoe. This pest has a broad host range. It can often be excluded from greenhouses by installing and maintaining screens.

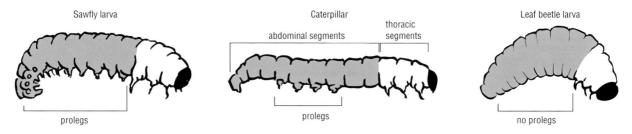

Figure 54. Distinguish caterpillars from larvae of beetles and sawflies by examining the number and arrangement of their appendages. These insect larvae have three pairs of true legs, one pair on each thoracic segment. Sawfly larvae also have a pair of appendages (prolegs) on most or all of their abdominal segments, a total of more than five pairs of prolegs. Caterpillars have prolegs on five or fewer abdominal segments, but never on their first two abdominal segments. Beetle larvae have no prolegs.

days, except for species that spend the winter in the egg stage outdoors.

The emerging larvae move singly or in groups to feeding sites on the plant (Fig. 53). In addition to three pairs of legs on the thorax (the area immediately behind the head), caterpillars have leglike appendages (prolegs) on some, but not all, segments of the abdomen. These prolegs distinguish caterpillar larvae from similar larvae of leaf beetles and sawflies (Fig. 54).

Most caterpillars eat voraciously and grow rapidly. Some species feed almost continuously. Others, such as cutworm larvae, hide in soil during the day, emerging to feed at night. Caterpillars shed their old skins about five times before entering a nonactive pupal stage. Some species pupate in silken cocoons, and most species pupate in a characteristic location, such as on the host plant or in litter beneath the plant.

The adult moth or butterfly emerges from the pupal case after several days to several months, depending on the species and season. Some common caterpillars have only one generation per year outdoors; other species have several generations each year and can cause damage throughout the growing season.

Because pest caterpillars comprise many species with different biologies and behaviors, control is more effective if you identify the species present and learn about the biology before taking action.

Monitoring

Learn how to recognize infestations early. Plants with a history of damage or plants prone to certain pests may need to be monitored at least once a week during critical parts of the year. Monitor to determine whether populations warrant control and to time management actions. Monitor plants at least once after taking action to assess the effectiveness of your actions. Keep thorough monitoring records. Record the location, date, environmental conditions, and host plants where caterpillars are a problem. Consult these records during subsequent years to help anticipate problems and plan control actions.

Several methods are available for monitoring caterpillars or their damage, including timed counts and shaking plants (Table 51). Visual inspection and pheromone-baited traps, generally the most useful techniques, are discussed below. Choose a sampling method appropriate to your plant and pest situation. Be consistent in your methods so you can compare results among sample dates.

Visual inspection. Randomly select leaves, growth terminals, or entire plants and visually inspect them for caterpillars, silken webbing, or chewing damage. Also look for dark fecal pellets (frass) on chewed plants or on media beneath the plant. Each type of caterpillar excretes characteristic frass. These fecal pellets increase in size as the larvae grow. Pellets

Table 71. Moth Species with Commercially Available Pheromone-Baited Traps.

Common name	Scientific name
beet armyworm	*Spodoptera exigua*
black cutworm	*Agrotis ipsilon*
bollworms and budworms	*Heliothis* or *Helicoverpa* spp.
cabbage looper	*Trichoplusia ni*
diamondback moth	*Plutella xylostella*
fall armyworm	*Spodoptera frugiperda*
obliquebanded leafroller	*Choristoneura rosaceana*
omnivorous leafroller	*Platynota stultana*
omnivorous looper	*Sabulodes aegrotata*
orange tortrix	*Argyrotaenia citrana*
sunflower moth	*Homoeosoma electellum*
variegated cutworm	*Peridroma saucia*
western yellowstriped armyworm	*Spodoptera praefica*

See the suppliers at the end of this book for sources. Suppliers will have an up-to-date list of commercially available pheromone-baited traps.

A tobacco budworm *(Heliothis virescens)* larva feeding on cosmos. Sticky traps baited with pheromone (sex-attractant) are available for detecting adults of this species and certain other important pests.

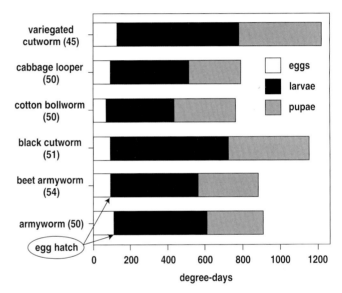

Figure 55. Degree-days required for development of eggs, larvae, and pupae of some common caterpillars (the species' lower development threshold in °F is given in parentheses). Assuming that the first moths or the peak density of moths caught in traps coincides with the beginning and peak of egg-laying, respectively (when degree-days = 0), control actions can be timed by monitoring degree-days starting when moths are trapped. The most effective time to apply *Bacillus thuringiensis*, for example, would be when the degree-days accumulated after moth catch are within the left half of the black bar segment (when most caterpillars are in the younger instars). See the beginning of this chapter for information on calculating degree-days.

are generally produced in greater amounts with an increase in the number of larvae or an increase in temperature, which causes caterpillars to feed faster. Chewing damage, webbing, or frass indicate past insect activity. Because insect populations can change rapidly due to factors such as weather or natural enemies, make sure that caterpillars susceptible to treatment are still present before taking control actions.

Pheromone-baited traps. Traps are commercially available that capture adults of many caterpillars attacking flower and nursery crops (Table 71). These traps typically consist of a sticky surface and a dispenser containing a pheromone (sex attractant) to lure adults of one sex (usually the male). Traps also indicate when adults are active and when more intensive inspection of plants may be warranted. Because both sexes are active around the same time, traps can be used to determine when females are laying eggs and to time control actions. If you know how long it takes for larvae to hatch from eggs after adults are caught (usually several days), you can use traps to time applications. Because the rate of development is related to temperature and heat accumulation, calculating degree-days is the most reliable method for timing treatments (Table 53, Fig. 55). For species that overwinter as eggs, traps are useful for altering you to the presence of these pests, but traps may not be helpful in timing applications.

Although traps can help detect pests and time monitoring and controls actions, they do not reliably indicate numbers and are probably not useful for determining treatment thresholds. Moths in traps are not definite proof that nearby crops are infested with caterpillars. Inspect crops to confirm that they contain eggs or larvae before basing treatments on trap catches.

To determine when specific moths are active in an area, hang at least two traps at chest height in the crop. Deploy traps during the season when adults are expected. Separate each trap from other traps by at least several hundred feet. Reapply sticky material or replace the traps when they are no longer sticky. Pheromone dispensers may need to be replaced about once a month, especially if the weather has been hot. Check with trap distributors for specific recommendations.

Check traps at least once a week. On each date, record the number and species of moths trapped. Because some pheromones may attract more than one moth species and not all species are pests, correct identification is important. Identify species by comparison to photographs in the University of California IPM manuals listed in the suggested reading at the end of this manual or take traps containing moths to a Cooperative Extension or agriculture department expert to be identified.

Management

A combination of physical, cultural, and chemical methods can provide good control of caterpillars, and biological control may be useful in certain situations. The use of pheromone dispensers to confuse moths and reduce mating, or deploying many traps (mass trapping) to capture moths has controlled some species in other situations. Although pheromone-baited traps are useful for monitoring, little is known about using pheromones for moth control in flower and nursery crops.

Physical and cultural controls. Screen greenhouse openings, doors, or individual growing areas to exclude moths, especially if greenhouses are lit at night. Moths of most species fly at night, and many are attracted to lights. Apply row covers to exclude egg-laying moths from seedling flats or field rows as detailed in the exclusion section earlier in this chapter.

Armyworms and saltmarsh caterpillars that migrate in from nearby vegetation may be stopped by surrounding growing areas with a strip of heavy aluminum or copper foil 6 inches (15 cm) tall with the top part bent away from the crop (as described for snail control later in this chapter. Bury the bottom edge about 1½ to 2 inches (3.7–5 cm) into soil so caterpillars cannot crawl under it.

Most noncrop plants host caterpillars; if possible, avoid growing crops near other major hosts or when moths may be expected to migrate. Eliminate nearby weeds, which may host caterpillars. Provide proper cultural care to allow older plants to outgrow and replace any damaged tissue after infestations are controlled.

Seek information from suppliers on resistant cultivars. Develop your own information by comparing and recording damage from different cultivars grown together. For example, petunia cultivars vary in susceptibility to the tobacco or petunia budworm (*Heliothis virescens*); ivy geraniums (*Pelargonium peltatum*) are rarely damaged by this budworm, in contrast with susceptible standard geraniums (*Pelargonium hortorum*).

Figure 56. Several subspecies of *Bacillus thuringiensis* (Bt) are widely used to control certain insects. *Bacillus thuringiensis* ssp. *aizawai* and ssp. *kurstaki* control moth and butterfly caterpillars. A. Bt must be sprayed during warm, dry conditions to thoroughly cover foliage where young caterpillars are actively feeding. B. Within several hours of consuming treated foliage, caterpillars are infected, become relatively inactive, and stop feeding. C. An enlarged view of Bt in the gut of a caterpillar. The rod-shaped bacteria contain reproductive spores and protein toxin crystals (endotoxins). These spores and protein crystals are separate components in some commercial Bt formulations. The separate components and one whole bacterium (greatly enlarged) are shown here. D. Within several days of ingesting Bt, caterpillars darken and die, and their carcasses eventually decompose into a dark, liquid, putrid mass.

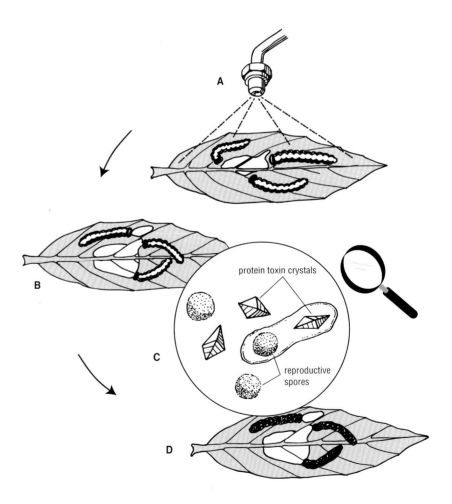

protein toxin crystals

reproductive spores

Mating confusion. Infusing the air with insect pheromone can prevent moths from finding mates, preventing or reducing moth reproduction. This method uses the same species-specific sex attractants (pheromones) discussed earlier in the monitoring and mass trapping sections. Instead of attracting moths to be captured in pheromone-baited sticky traps, however, hollow plastic wicks, aerially dispersed flakes, mechanical puffers, or other devices are used to disperse pheromone into the air. To be effective, adequate pheromone concentrations must be maintained throughout the pest's mating season around crops in locations where pest moths occur.

Mating confusion has been highly effective against certain pests such as pink bollworm attacking cotton. However, mating confusion for flower and nursery crops may be relatively expensive and is largely experimental. Specific recommendations are generally unavailable for important details, such as the appropriate distance between pheromone dispenser locations, the treatment area size, the frequency at which dispensers need to be replaced, and the minimum concentration of pheromone that must be maintained around the growing environment.

Insecticides. *Bacillus thuringiensis* ssp. *aizawai* and *Bacillus thuringiensis* ssp. *kurstaki* are commercially available pathogens of caterpillars. *Bacillus thuringiensis* (Bt) is effective against young larvae that feed openly on foliage; Bt subspecies that are commercially available for other pests, such as fungus gnats or shore flies, are not effective against caterpillars. Bt is an almost ideal insecticide from an environmental and safety point of view because it affects only caterpillars. When moth or butterfly larvae are infected by Bt, they stop feeding within a day and usually die within a few days (Fig. 56).

Unlike broad-spectrum insecticides that kill on contact, caterpillars must eat Bt-sprayed foliage in order to be killed. Proper timing and thorough spray coverage are very important when using Bt and other microbial insecticides. Bt is most effective on early instars. Apply Bt during warm, dry weather when caterpillars are feeding actively. Sunlight soon inactivates Bt on foliage, so caterpillars hatching a few days after the application may not be affected. Directing sprays to the more shaded underside of leaves can improve Bt's persistence. A second application about 7 to 10 days after the first may be required. Be aware that Bt products differ in their effectiveness against caterpillars.

Other reduced-risk insecticides effective for caterpillar control include azadirachtin, diflubenzuron, and spinosad. For best control, time foliar sprays to coincide with newly hatched larvae. Broad-spectrum carbamates, organophosphates, and pyrethroids can be used when environmental conditions are not suitable for reduced-risk insecticides. For example, if infestations are not discovered until older caterpillars predominate, these will be less susceptible to Bt, and insect growth regulators may not provide control fast enough. However, broad-spectrum insecticides adversely

A pheromone-baited sticky trap opened to reveal captured moths. Because moth flight coincides with female egg laying, traps are useful for timing control actions.

Caterpillars stop feeding soon after eating foliage treated with *Bacillus thuringiensis* (Bt). Within several days, Bt-killed larvae, such as this looper, turn dark and soft.

CABBAGE LOOPER

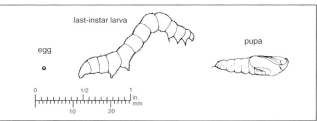

affect natural enemies. Confine these treatments to plants that are infested.

Leafrolling and webmaking caterpillars may be more effectively controlled if pyrethrum or pyrethrins are used alone or mixed with other pesticides to irritate larvae, inducing larvae to leave protected places and increase their contact with insecticide. Spot application to soil using certain insecticide baits, such as carbaryl baits, can be effective against cutworms. Products containing apple pomace as the bait may be more effective than those containing only bran baits. Users generally must contact the manufacturer or its representatives to determine what baits are used in formulated pesticide products because the bait and other "inert" ingredients usually are not listed on product labels.

Biological controls. If you avoid the use of broad-spectrum insecticides that destroy them, predators and parasites sometimes kill enough caterpillars to control populations outdoors. Predators include assassin bugs, bigeyed bugs, damsel bugs, ground beetles, spiders, wasps, and birds. Naturally occurring and commercially available minute pirate bugs and lacewing larvae eat moth and butterfly eggs or caterpillars, but there is little information on the cost or effectiveness of releasing caterpillar predators.

Most caterpillars are attacked by one or more species of parasitic wasps. Many moth eggs are destroyed by tiny *Trichogramma* species wasps. Evidence of *Trichogramma* includes eggs with tiny holes from which parasites emerged and unhatched eggs that are darker than normal, indicating they may contain parasites.

Trichogramma often occur naturally on plants infested with moth eggs; several species are available by mail from commercial insectaries. Researchers have successfully released *Trichogramma* to control caterpillars including bollworm, (*Helicoverpa zea*), omnivorous leafroller (*Platynota stultana*), and omnivorous looper (*Sabulodes aegrotata*). There is little information on *Trichogramma* use in flower and nursery crops. For more information on *Trichogramma* releases, consult *The Trichogramma Manual* (Knutson 1998), *Natural Enemies Handbook* (Flint and Dreistadt 1998), and *Pests of Landscape Trees and Shrubs* (Dreistadt 1994).

If natural enemies are present or are being released for caterpillars or other pests, the biological insecticide *Bacillus thuringiensis* or certain other reduced-risk insecticides can be applied to kill caterpillars while leaving most natural enemies unharmed.

Caterpillars are often killed by diseases caused by naturally occurring bacteria, fungi, or viruses. Caterpillars killed by disease may turn dark and soft; their carcasses may hang limply from foliage or stems and eventually degenerate into a sac of liquefied contents. Although disease outbreaks can rapidly reduce caterpillar populations, they often do not occur until caterpillar populations have become high. Viral and fungal diseases of some caterpillars are being commercially developed; watch for the availability of these new products.

Weevils

Over 1,000 species of weevils or snout beetles (family Curculionidae) occur in California. Several species are pests in container nurseries, certain field-grown crops, and sometimes in greenhouses. Black vine weevil (*Otiorhynchus sulcatus*), which occurs throughout the United States, is believed to be the most common pest weevil species in California. Other important species include obscure root weevil (*Sciopithes obscurus*), strawberry root weevil (*Otiorhynchus ovatus*), and Woods weevil (*Nemocestes incomptus*). Whitefringed beetles (*Graphognathus* spp.), are serious pests in the southeastern United States. Whitefringed beetles are regularly found in soil and container plants shipped from infested areas, but quarantines have so far excluded them from becoming established in the western United States.

Damage
Adult weevils chew foliage, causing characteristic notching on leaf edges. Although leaf notching may be unsightly, the serious damage is caused by larvae. Young larvae chew the outer surface of young roots. More mature larvae chew older roots and basal stems, girdling plants near the soil surface and causing decline in mature plants and death in young plants. The larvae are a major pest of young plants in containers, preferring well-drained organic container mixes. Most feeding and damage outdoors occurs in the spring. Black vine weevil attacks plants in at least 29 families, including most plant species in the families Ericaceae, Rosaceae, Saxifragaceae, Taxaceae, and Vitaceae (see the chapter "Crop Tables").

Identification and Biology
Weevils are inconspicuous. The larvae live in soil and adults feed at night, hiding in litter during the day. The head of adult weevils is elongated into a snout and their antennae are elbowed and clubbed. Black vine weevil, whitefringed beetles, and many other weevil species are flightless because their wing covers are fused. Only females are known for many species. Females can produce eggs without mating, commonly laying them on or into soil near host plants. The female adults must feed for about a month before laying eggs.

The larvae develop in soil through 6 instars over a period of 2 to 8 months. They are whitish grubs with a brown head and commonly have a C-shaped posture.

Black vine weevil overwinters outdoors primarily as a late-instar larva. A few individuals of this and other species can overwinter as adults. Weevils overwintering as late instars form pupae in spring. Adults emerge from the soil about 2 weeks after pupation and begin feeding during the night. Adults are present outdoors in California from March through September, and each adult lives for several months. Outdoors, weevils usually have one generation per year. In greenhouses, weevils may have more than one generation per year, with all stages present throughout the year, except that adults suspend egg laying under short day length.

Monitoring
Inspect soil and roots of incoming container plants to be sure that they are not infested with weevils. Use one or more methods to regularly monitor crops susceptible to weevil damage. Inspect foliage for adult weevils, chewing, and symptoms of root damage (such as yellowing or wilting foliage). Examine roots for larvae and damage, and trap adults. If plants are young, even a few weevils or slight chewing of foliage warrants action to prevent serious damage to roots from larvae.

Regularly inspect susceptible foliage for weevil feeding, concentrating inspections in spring. Identifying the seasonal pattern and time of adult emergence allows control actions to be targeted against recently emerged adults during their first few weeks of feeding, before egg laying begins. Weevils overwintering as adults feed sooner in spring than those overwintering as mature larvae. Because most of the pest damage is caused by weevils overwintering as mature larvae, early feeding damage by a few overwintering adults can make it difficult to identify when to initiate control actions against most of the weevil population, which emerges later.

Monitor plants for signs of damage. If notched or jagged edges of leaves are observed, but there are no slime trails from snails or slugs and no leaf-feeding caterpillars, katydids, or other insects, the damage was likely caused by weevils. Also observe nearby *Epilobium* species weeds, such as fireweed or willow herb, (see the chapter "Weeds"), which are preferred hosts of black vine weevil. Chewed *Epilobium* leaves can indicate that weevils are present. If weevils are suspected, determine whether adults are present or remove plants from containers and inspect roots and soil for larvae or pupae.

Adult weevils are most likely to be found on plants during warm, calm, dry nights, especially during the several weeks after adults emerge from pupae. To determine if adult weevils are present, starting 2 hours or more after dark, use a narrow-beam, high-intensity flashlight to look for adults on the foliage of plants that have suspected weevil damage. Or, if plants are relatively large or sturdy, sample them as detailed in the shaking plants section earlier in this chapter; sweep foliage with a net or hold a tray, clipboard, or framed cloth beneath plants and beat or shake foliage at night to dislodge weevils onto the collecting surface.

As an alternative to sampling foliage at night, trap adults by taking advantage of their need to seek shelter during the day. Use one of three trapping methods discussed below and dispose of any trapped beetles by dropping them into alcohol or a bucket of soapy water. Trapping helps confirm weevil presence, monitor changes in density, and time control actions. Persistent adult trapping year-round may also reduce local weevil populations.

Traps. Pitfall traps may be the most effective method of trapping adult weevils in nurseries. Construct each trap from a wide-mouth plastic cup or dish that is several inches deep and a funnel or a smaller tapered cup. Cut off most of the funnel's spout or the bottom of the smaller cup and snugly insert it, smaller hole down, into the larger cup. A single cup may be used if the sides are regularly lubricated with oil or silicone spray to prevent the beetles from climbing out. Bury each trap so that its top is flush with, or slightly below, the soil surface (Fig. 57). Drill small holes in the bottom of the cup to allow water to drain. Or, keep water out by covering each trap, such as by using an inverted gallon pot after first

The notched viburnum leaf edges shown here are characteristic weevil chewing damage.

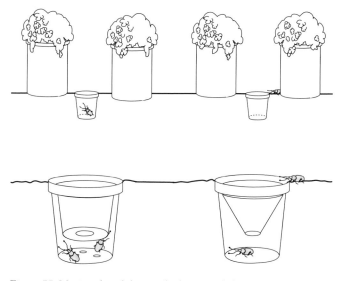

Figure 57. Monitor for adult weevils, for example by using pitfall traps. Each trap can be a single container if the inside walls are kept lubricated. It can be more effective to construct traps from one funnel or cup fit inside another larger cup, making it more difficult for weevils to climb out. Bury traps in the soil near plants so that beetles walking on the soil surface fall into them. Drill several small drainage holes in the bottom of each trap or keep sprinkler water out by covering each trap with an inverted gallon pot after first cutting legs in the pot's rim.

cutting legs in the pot's rim so weevils walking along the ground have access to the trap.

Bury pitfall traps throughout the nursery, especially among susceptible crops and just within the inside corners of any exclusion barriers (see below). Check each trap about weekly. Record when weevils first appear (for treatment timing) and note the total number of weevils caught in all traps (to estimate population density and for comparison before and after control actions). Don't be surprised to find a variety of ground-dwelling creatures in traps, including beneficial predaceous ground beetles and spiders.

An alternative to pitfall traps is to place small boards, about 10 by 10 inches (25 cm by 25 cm), on the ground or bench tops. The underside of boards is an attractive hiding place to adult weevils. Cutting shallow trenches about ⅖ inch (1 cm) deep running the entire length of the underside of boards may increase their attractiveness to weevils. Place several trap boards among each group of host plants. Inspect the underside of the boards and the ground or bench beneath them during the day when beetles are resting. During rainy weather, boards may be more effective than pitfall traps.

Another monitoring method is to wrap trunks, containers, or stakes driven into the ground among plants with several layers of folded burlap, corrugated plastic tree wrap, or corrugated cardboard with the smooth paper removed on one side and the corrugated side placed against the bark, container, or stake. Climbing weevils are attracted to these resting places. Gently remove the wrapping during the day, carefully inspect it, and count and dispose of any weevils.

Management

Avoid replanting susceptible crops at infested sites. Grow species or cultivars that are less susceptible to weevil damage. For example, many rhododendron hybrids resist weevil damage (Table 12, also see *Pests of Landscape Trees and Shrubs* [Dreistadt 1994]). Grow older plants that are more likely to be infested away from younger stock susceptible to weevils. Provide proper cultural care to keep plants vigorous and better able to tolerate damage. Because most weevils are flightless, barriers can effectively exclude them and other flightless pests from plants (Fig. 36). Disking border areas and infested fields between crops can provide some control, especially if cultivation is timed to coincide with the period when weevils are pupating.

Insecticides. Different treatment methods targeting weevil adults and larvae may be needed on highly susceptible crops and growing areas with persistent problems. Soil-dwelling larvae and pupae are susceptible to insect-parasitic nematodes. Drenching growing media with commercially available *Heterorhabditis bacteriophora* (formerly *H. heliothidis*) will kill immature stages in soil (Figs. 39, 40) and possibly adults hiding in litter. Apply nematodes during late spring through fall outdoors, when weevil larvae or pupae are expected to be present. In hot areas, apply nematodes in the early morning or evening. The soil must be warm, at least 60°F (16°C), and moist but not soggy before application. If persistent, broad-spectrum pesticides are not applied to media, nematodes can reproduce and persist, providing long-term control. See the entomopathogenic nematodes discussion earlier in this chapter for more information.

A drench of persistent, broad-spectrum insecticides (such as diazinon) or soil incorporation of pyrethroid granules (bifenthrin) can also be effective against weevils. Foliar applications of persistent carbamates, organophosphates, and pyrethroids can control adults. Foliar application may be preferable to soil treatment if no foliar damage can be tolerated or conditions are not suitable for nematodes, such as when it is cool or dry. The inorganic insecticide cryolite (sodium aluminofluoride) is effective when consumed by foliage-feeding adults. Available foliar insecticides include carbamates (bendiocarb), a chlorinated hydrocarbon (endosulfan), organophosphates (acephate, chlorpyrifos), and pyrethroids (fluvalinate, permethrin).

Monitor traps and, unless no foliar damage is tolerable, wait 2 or 3 weeks after adults first appear before spraying foliage. Delaying application while more weevils emerge will maximize control from a single application; few if any weevils will have laid eggs by then because they must feed for about a month before they lay eggs. If weevil emergence is prolonged, a second foliar spray may be warranted about 3 to 4 weeks after the first application. Foliar application is most effective if applied late in the afternoon and especially 2 or 3 hours after dark. Instead of monitoring adults, some growers spray foliage when damage is observed; however, it is difficult to distinguish new damage from old, and timing based only on foliar damage is less effective than that based on adult monitoring.

Weevils, such this Fuller rose beetle, have a long, snoutlike head. Weevils are easily overlooked because adults feed on foliage at night and larvae live in soil.

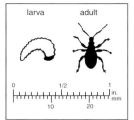

BLACK VINE WEEVIL

larva   adult

Entomopathogenic nematodes can be applied to kill many soil-dwelling insects. Shown here are a healthy black vine weevil pupa and larva (left) and two yellowish pupae and a brownish larva infected with *Steinernema feltiae* nematodes (right).

White Grubs

White grubs are larvae of scarab beetles (family Scarabaei-dae), including chafers such as *Cyclocephala* spp., Hoplia beetles (*Hoplia* spp.), and May and June beetles such as *Cotinus* spp. Japanese beetle (*Popillia japonica*) is an important white grub species in the eastern United States; it is occasionally introduced and eradicated in the West.

Many scarabs feed only in vertebrate feces; these dung beetles are beneficial, helping to recycle nutrients and reduce breeding by filth flies. Adults of pest species chew foliage and blossoms, sometimes aggregating in masses to mate and feed. The most serious damage is caused by larvae of species that live in the soil. These white grubs chew roots and basal stems of turf, landscapes, and certain flower and nursery crops. Infested plants become stunted. Foliage discolors and wilts from root damage and stem girdling. Small plants can be killed, especially those grown in containers.

Most white grubs are C-shaped, dirty whitish, and about ½ to ¾ inches (13–19 mm) long at maturity. These larvae commonly have a swollen abdomen and prominent legs near their dark head. Larvae of most species can be distinguished only by an expert. *Hoplia* species are some of the most common white grub pests of flower crops such as roses in California. The adults are about ¼ to ⅜ inches (6–9 mm) long, shiny, and mostly reddish brown with a silvery abdomen. However, larvae of *Hoplia* species apparently do not feed on rose roots even though migratory adults are often attracted to field-grown roses during a few week period in late spring.

White grub eggs are laid in soil near host plants and hatch in several weeks. White grubs feed mostly during mild or warm weather, burrowing deeper underground outdoors to hibernate over winter. Larvae of many species feed for 2 or 3 years before pupating in an earthen cell, from which adults emerge during warm weather.

Because they have a prolonged larvae stage and most damage is caused by older larvae, white grubs are less of a problem in annual crops if the soil is well cultivated, fumigated, or solarized between plantings. Entomophagous nematodes of the *Steinernema* and *Heterorhabditis* species are effective against larvae and pupae when applied to the soil (see the weevils section earlier in this chapter). Some conventional insecticides such as diazinon also are effective. Milky spore disease (*Bacillus popilliae*), which may be commercially available, kills immature Japanese beetles and persists in soil for many years after application. Registered carbamate, organophosphate, or pyrethroid insecticides can be applied to foliage when adults are active.

Hand-picking or knocking Hoplia beetles from plants into a containers may provide control. Adult *Hoplia* species prefer light colored rose blossoms including yellow and white. Concentrate monitoring (look for adults and damage) and any foliar spraying there.

An adult hoplia beetle and its feeding damage on rose petals. Because adult *Hoplia* species apparently prefer light-colored blossoms, concentrate monitoring on apricot, white, and yellow flowers if blossoms are present.

White grubs, such as these of the northern masked chafer (*Cyclocephala borealis*) are usually C-shaped and whitish with prominent legs near the brown head. The grub on the right has been killed by commercially available *Heterorhabditis bacteriophora* entomopathogenic nematodes.

Adult Japanese beetles are mostly a shiny metallic green with coppery brown wing covers and tufts of short white hairs along their sides. This beetle has two white eggs of the tachinid parasite *Hyperecteina aldrichi* on its thorax. In the western United States, report suspected Japanese beetles to the local agricultural department.

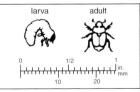

WHITE GRUB

larva   adult

0   1/2   1   in.
                    mm
       10   20

Predaceous and parasitic flies, including those in the families Asilidae, Pyrgotidae, and Tachinidae, are important natural enemies of white grubs outdoors in areas not frequently sprayed with broad-spectrum insecticides.

Cucumber Beetles, Flea Beetles, and Leaf Beetles

Cucumber beetles, flea beetles, and leaf beetles (family Chrysomelidae) are pests of many flower and nursery crops. Cucumber beetles common in California include the western spotted cucumber beetle (*Diabrotica undecimpunctata undecimpunctata*) and the western striped cucumber beetle (*Acalymma trivittata*). Common flea beetles include several *Epitrix* and *Phyllotreta* species. Most chrysomelids are relatively specialized, feeding on only one or several closely related hosts. Cucumber beetles and most species of flea beetles attack primarily herbaceous plants. Flower crops attacked by these chrysomelids include centaurea, lily, pansy, Queen Anne's lace, sage, solidago, stock, and sunflower. Larvae of the western spotted cucumber beetle feed

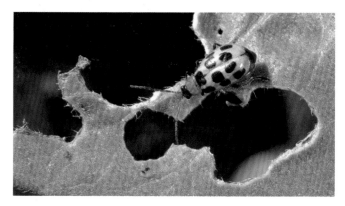

An adult western spotted cucumber beetle and its feeding damage on sunflower. Larvae of cucumber beetles and flea beetles are hidden in the soil, where they feed on roots. However, adults often chew foliage of plant species on which larvae are unable to feed.

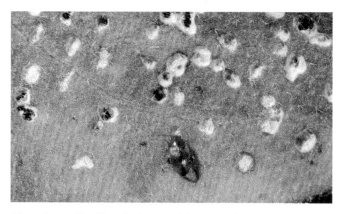

Chewed, pitted leaf from feeding by adult tobacco flea beetles *(Epitrix hirtipennis)*. A brownish adult is visible here. The immature stages of this pest occur in soil where larvae feed on roots.

on roots of cucurbits, grains, legumes, and many weeds. The western striped cucumber beetle infests only Brassicaceae. Most leaf beetles are pests of one genus or a few closely related species of woody plants. Consult *Pests of Landscape Trees and Shrubs* (Dreistadt 1994) for important pest and woody ornamental host species.

Adult chrysomelids chew holes in leaves; some species also consume shoots and blossoms. Larvae of cucumber beetles and flea beetles chew roots, which can stunt crops. Seedlings can be destroyed within a few days. Older plants often tolerate relatively large numbers unless feeding causes aesthetic damage to marketable plant parts. Leaf beetles feed on foliage of the same host plants as both larvae and adults. Adults and larvae of cucumber beetles and flea beetles may feed on the same or different species of plants. Pupae of all groups occur primarily on or in soil or organic debris beneath larval host plants. Most species have several annual generations and overwinter as adults in protected or weedy places near their hosts.

Exclude chrysomelids when possible by using row covers and screens as discussed in the exclusion section earlier in this chapter. For species such as cucumber beetles that also feed on grasses and certain weeds, eliminating these nearby alternate hosts can help reduce crop damage. Western striped cucumber beetle larvae feed exclusively on Cucurbitaceae family plants. Avoid planting flower and nursery crops susceptible to feeding by adults of this species near cucurbit vegetable crops.

Certain reduced-risk insect growth regulators (such as imidacloprid) can provide control. *Bacillus thuringiensis* ssp. *tenebrionis* (formerly called ssp. *san diego*) may be available for foliar application to control adults and larvae of certain leaf beetles. Entomopathogenic nematodes may provide some control of root-feeding larvae. Carbamate, organophosphate, and pyrethroid insecticides are also available for foliar or soil drench applications.

Earwigs

Earwigs (order Dermaptera) feed on dead and living plants and animals. They are beneficial decomposers and predators of aphids and other soft-bodied pests. They also can be serious pests, especially when plants are young. Earwigs chew seedlings and succulent stems, usually feeding at night. They leave numerous irregular holes or ragged edges in foliage. Earwig damage may resemble damage caused by caterpillars or snails and slugs. To distinguish these pests, look for webbing, frass, and life stages characteristic of caterpillars and slime trails left by snails and slugs.

Earwigs are elongate, flattened, and dark and shiny. At maturity they range from about $\frac{1}{4}$ to 1 inch (6–25 mm) long. They have prominent pincers or cerci at their rear. Wings, when present, are folded into a compact mass so that abdominal segments are visible from the top. The European earwig (*Forficula auricularia*) is probably the most common species in California. It was introduced from Europe and occurs throughout North America.

Earwigs lay their eggs in a chamber in the ground, where the female guards the eggs and feeds the young until the nymphs have molted into the second instar. Gradual metamorphosis occurs through 4 or 5 instars. Females lay about two batches of eggs per year, which hatch in about 2 to 10 weeks, depending on temperature. Nymphs reach maturity in about 2 months. They have one, and possibly two or more generations per year. Adults can be active throughout the year, but they hibernate in soil outdoors in cold areas.

Use traps or inspect dark places during the day to determine whether earwigs are present and to get an idea of their abundance. Look for earwigs under containers and by disturbing organic litter. Earwigs are attracted to rolled newspaper, short segments of bamboo tube, or old garden hose cut into short tubes and left out overnight among plants. In the morning, shake the earwigs from these traps into a pail of soapy water. A low-sided cat food or tuna fish can makes an excellent trap; just add ½ inch (12 mm) of oil and place cans among plants. Fish oil is especially attractive to earwigs, but vegetable oil with a small amount of bacon grease added also attracts earwigs and is less expensive. Dump out the cans and refill them with oil as they fill up with earwigs killed by the oil. If cats or other animals are present in growing areas, cover traps with a large mesh screen (such as chicken wire) to prevent animals from feeding on the odorous oil. Persistent trapping can reduce local earwig populations and may provide some control.

Reduce earwig populations by eliminating their refuges, including plant debris, litter, boards, old containers, and material stored on the ground near growing areas. If populations are severe, a registered carbamate (carbaryl), organophosphate (chlorpyrifos, diazinon, malathion), or pyrethroid (resmethrin) insecticide applied to surfaces can reduce earwig numbers. Silica gel can kill earwigs that contact it if treated areas are kept dry. Commercial baits containing insecticide also kill earwigs.

An introduced parasitic tachinid fly (*Bigonicheta spinipennis*) and some small vertebrates kill many earwigs in areas not frequently sprayed with broad-spectrum insecticides.

Mites

Mites are not insects; they are arachnids, belonging to the same class as spiders and ticks. Unlike insects, mites do not have antennae, segmented bodies, or wings; they have a main body with appendages. Table 72 lists common mites infesting flower and nursery crops.

Mites puncture plant cells with their mouthparts and suck the exuding fluid. Some mites also inject plant toxins when they feed. Mite feeding causes plant tissue to discolor, distort, or drop. Plants rarely die from mites, but crops may be unmarketable due to aesthetic damage.

Mites begin as eggs that hatch into six-legged immatures (larvae). Later-stage immature spider mites are called nymphs. Spider mite nymphs and adults have eight legs, but otherwise look similar to mite larvae (Fig. 58). Mites in certain other groups, like the family Eriophyidae, have only four legs as larvae, nymphs, and adults.

Because of their tiny size and diversity, the species of most mites can be positively identified only by an expert. Identification of families is usually sufficient (Table 72) because mites within these groups have a similar life cycle and management.

Spider Mites, False Spider Mites, and Red Mites

These mites in the families Tetranychidae and Tenuipalpidae can infest almost every species of flower, foliage, and nursery crop. *Tetranychus* species, especially twospotted spider mite (*Tetranychus urticae*), and privet mite (*Brevipalpus obovatus*) are common pests.

Damage. Tetranychids and tenuipalpids cause leaves to become stippled or flecked with pale dots where mite feeding has killed tiny areas of plant tissue. As areas of feeding damage coalesce, foliage appears bleached or bronzed. Severe mite populations stunt plant growth and can cause leaves to drop. When abundant, *Tetranychus* species cover leaves, shoots, or flowers with large amounts of fine webbing, which is why they are called spider mites. Mite damage is more likely in hot, dry environments and when plants are drought stressed because these conditions favor reproduction of pest mites and suppress predatory mite populations.

EARWIG

adult

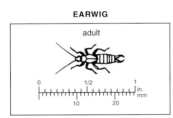

0   1/2   1 in.
├┼┼┼┼┼┼┼┼┼┼┼┼┼┼┼┼┼┤ mm
        10   20

Earwigs can be a serious pest by feeding on young plants. However, earwigs are mostly predaceous and in established crops can be beneficial predators of various other pests.

Table 72. Common Mites and Host Crops.

| Mites | | |
Common name (Family name)	Species	Hosts
blister mites, bud mites, gall mites, rust mites (Eriophyidae)	carnation bud mite (*Aceria paradianthi*)	carnation
	fuchsia gall mite (*Aculops fuchsiae*)	fuchsia; see Table 74
bulb mites, mold mites, pollen mites (Acaridae)	bulb mites (*Rhizoglyphus* spp.)	bulbs, including amaryllis, freesia, gladiolus, hyacinth, lily, narcissus, onion, and tulip in storage and in the field
	mold or pollen mite (*Tyrophagus putrescentiae*)	gerbera, gladiolus, orchids
predaceous or phytoseiid mites (Phytoseiidae)	see Table 73	commonly on foliage where spider mites, red mites, and false spider mites occur
spider mites and red mites (Tetranychidae), false spider mites (Tenuipalpidae)	carmine mite (*Tetranychus cinnabarinus*), privet mite (*Brevipalpus obovatus*), twospotted mite (*Tetranychus urticae*)	primarily foliage of many species of flower, foliage, and nursery crops
tarsonemids (Tarsonemidae)	broad mite (*Polyphagotarsonemus latus*), cyclamen mite (*Phytonemus pallidus*)	African violet, azalea, begonia, bouvardia, carnation, chrysanthemum, cyclamen, dahlia, exacum, fuchsia, geranium, gerbera, gloxinia, impatiens, ivy, kalanchoe, larkspur, Marguerite daisy, petunia, pouch flower, schefflera, snapdragon, verbena, zinnia
	bulb scale mite (*Steneotarsonemus laticeps*)	amaryllis, daffodil, gladiolus

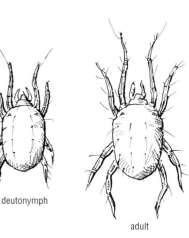

Figure 58. Spider mites, false spider mites, red mites, and phytoseiid species predatory mites develop through five stages. Adults and the two nymphal stages have eight legs. The stage emerging from eggs, called a larva, has six legs. The time required for spider mites to complete one generation ranges from about 1 week at 80°F (27°C) to 3 weeks at 63°F (18°C). All stages occur together on leaves, except outdoors during overwintering when females are found in crevices, under bark, or in litter; eggs are laid in bark crevices.

egg   larva   protonymph   deutonymph   adult

Identification and biology. Spider mites and red mites have tiny globular or spherical bodies that are translucent to colored and often are covered with long bristles. Immature and adult twospotted spider mites are commonly yellowish or greenish with two dark spots or irregular dark blotches on the midbody. Females often turn orange and stop reproducing under cool temperatures and short day length. The eggs are spherical and clear to pale yellow; they look like tiny drops on a leaf. Females can lay up to about 1 dozen eggs per day; eggs are usually laid in fine webbing. Spider mite colonies are most abundant in groups on the underside of leaves, but they can occur on both sides of leaves, especially when populations are high.

Red mites (*Oligonychus* and *Panonychus* spp.) and their eggs are commonly red or brown; although in the same fam-ily as spider mites, these tetranychids produce little or no silken webbing.

False spider mites produce little or no silk and are more flattened than spider mites or red mites. Their eggs are oval, and all stages are commonly red to brown.

Adults and nymphs in all of these groups have eight legs, except for the stage hatching from eggs, which has six legs (Fig. 58). Because all mites are tiny, unless plants are routinely inspected with care, mite damage to plants can usually be observed before you notice mites themselves.

Monitoring and thresholds. About once a week inspect growing areas for weeds that host mites and examine the crop for mites and damage. Concentrate inspections on plant species or cultivars especially susceptible to mite damage and focus on areas with a history of mite problems, such as near entranceways in greenhouses. Randomly select plants in these areas and inspect middle to lower leaves for damage. If stippled or distorted leaves are observed, remove and turn leaves over and inspect them with a hand lens to determine if live mites or fine webbing are present. Also examine the underside of nearby healthy plant parts to determine the extent of developing infestations. Stippled and distorted foliage can be caused by other pests, including lace bugs, plant bugs, and thrips, but these insects often leave specks of dark excrement on lower leaf surfaces and they do not make webbing.

You can also sample tetranychids, tenuipalpids, and predaceous mites by holding a sheet of white paper on a clipboard beneath the plant and tapping the foliage sharply. Inspect the paper for any dislodged mites; to the naked eye they look like moving specks. Some of these mites may be beneficial predators helping to control pest mites. See the shaking plants section earlier in this chapter for more details. Special mite brushing machines and disks for counting dislodged mites under a microscope are used in some nonfloral crops where quantitative sampling programs and thresholds have been developed.

Low populations of mites can be tolerated in certain crops, such as greenhouse cut roses (Table 4). Presence-absence sampling as discussed in the chapter "Managing Pests in Flower and Nursery Crops" is useful for monitoring mites and determining treatment need in field-grown roses. For example, in field-grown production of bareroot roses ('Peace' with 'Dr. Huey' rootstock) in the San Joaquin Valley, no yield or crop quality loss occurred and no treatment was needed even though at least 40% of leaves were infested with *Tetranychus* species during weekly inspection of one leaf from each of 20 plants.

Management. Carefully inspect new plant material with a 10× to 15× hand lens before bringing it into the greenhouse; disinfest plants if they harbor mites. Tetranychids and tenuipalpids feed on many different plants, so control potential host weeds around growing areas.

Mites are easily spread by wind or on infested plants, equipment, and workers. Start with clean plants and use good sanitation to avoid spreading mites. Routinely employ cultural practices and physical controls that limit mite populations. Careful pesticide application can control outbreaks. Release of commercially available predaceous mites may be helpful in some situations, for example, after a soap or oil application. Some crop cultivars are less susceptible to mites than others (see Table 74 example). Ask suppliers for information on resistant cultivars. Careful monitoring and record keeping may allow growers to develop their own information on less-susceptible cultivars; consider growing these where mites have been a problem.

Cultural and physical controls. High foliar nitrogen levels can favor outbreaks of some mites. Do not apply more nitrogen

than necessary, and when possible use less soluble forms. Urea-based "timed released" formulations and most organic fertilizers generally release nitrogen more slowly.

Spider mites develop best under hot, dry conditions. Predatory mite egg hatch and reproduction is retarded by low humidity. Plants that are stressed, especially due to drought, are more likely to experience mite outbreaks and less able to tolerate feeding damage. Provide plants with appropriate cultural care, especially adequate irrigation. Regular overhead sprinkling helps control some mites; sprinkling alleviates drought stress, dislodges some mites, slows mite dispersal, and reduces dust and low humidity that interfere with some predators. Take additional measures to reduce dust around crops; for example, use plastic dust barriers, impose speed limits on dirt roads, and cover bare soil. Where practical, tetranychid and tenuipalpid mite populations can be reduced with a forceful stream of water directed at the underside of leaves.

Chemical control. Abamectin, cinnamaldehyde, and pyridaben are botanicals or IGRs that can be effective in controlling mites. Narrow-range oil and insecticidal soap are low-residual-toxicity pesticides that provide control if applied to thoroughly cover plant parts where mites are feeding. Oil reportedly has little impact on predatory mites and can be a good choice if spraying is needed when natural enemies are present. For crops and growing situations where phytotoxicity is a concern, reduced rates (1% soap or 0.25–0.5% oil) can provide control. More-persistent acaricides are available, including some carbamates, organophosphates, and pyrethroids. However, these materials can induce physiological changes in mites or host plants and kill mite predators, sometimes increasing spider mite populations even though the labels may say they control mites. Insecticides applied for other pests during hot, dry conditions often cause dramatic outbreaks of mites within a few days.

Stippled, bleached rose foliage caused by a twospotted spider mite infestation. Spider mite outbreaks are often induced by drought stress or pesticides sprayed against other pests.

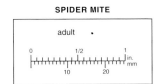

SPIDER MITE

adult   •

Twospotted spider mites are yellowish or greenish and have an irregular dark blotch on each side of the midbody when viewed under magnification.

Dense spider mite populations produce extensive webbing. The underside of heavily infested leaves may appear to be covered with sand or have a salt-and-pepper appearance. Each tiny particle is a spider mite body or cast skin, which can be distinguished by examining the leaf under magnification.

This *Phytoseiulus persimilis*, an important predator mite, is eating a twospotted spider mite egg. To promote populations of this predator, avoid broad-spectrum, persistent pesticides and provide adequate humidity.

Because mites typically remain beneath foliage or protected in tissue, regardless of the material used, thorough spray coverage is essential when treating. Mite eggs tolerate most pesticides; exceptions include cinnamaldehyde and oil, which kill all exposed stages. With most materials, make two applications about 5 days apart to kill mites that were eggs during the first application.

Resistance to acaricides such as abamectin, chlorinated hydrocarbons (dicofol), and organosulfurs (propargite) occurs in some mite populations. To preserve the effectiveness of pesticides, rely to the maximum extent possible on cultural, physical, and biological methods. Materials that have been frequently applied or used over long periods in that area (or at the location where introduced mites came from) are unlikely to be effective, although resistance to oil or soap has not been reported. If plants are frequently sprayed, reduce resistance development by rotating among acaricides from at least three different classes (Tables 58, 59). Switch to another class of materials about every two to three generations, about every 3 to 4 weeks for twospotted mite when temperatures average 75°F (24°C). See the degree-days section earlier in this chapter for more information on determining generation time. For specific pesticide recommendations, consult *UC IPM Pest Management Guidelines: Floriculture and Ornamental Nurseries*.

Biological control. Native natural enemies often control mites outdoors; outbreaks often occur because natural enemies have been disrupted. Where natural enemies are present, avoid using broad-spectrum pesticides. Control dust and provide adequate humidity for predatory mite reproduction.

The most important natural enemies of plant-feeding mites are predaceous mites, commonly found on the underside of leaves in the interior portions of outdoor plants. Other important predators include the spider mite destroyer lady beetle (*Stethorus picipes*), the sixspotted thrips (*Scolothrips sexmaculatus*), minute pirate bugs, brown and green lacewings, and predaceous Cecidomyiidae midges (*Feltiella* spp.).

Naturally occurring viruses that are harmless to plants and people also sometimes control mites. Virus-infected mites crawl stiffly, curl up, then die. In dry weather, the dead mites dry up and blow away; under humid conditions, dead mites become tiny reddish to black watery spots on leaves.

Introducing predaceous mites or other predatory species in some situations can control spider mites in greenhouses. Predators are widely used to control mites infesting greenhouse vegetable crops in Europe and Canada. Trials in chrysanthemum, gerbera, and rose indicate that predaceous mite releases can work in certain flower crops.

Predaceous mites. Most predaceous mites are long-legged, pear-shaped, and shiny. Many are translucent, although after feeding they often take on the color of their host and may be bright red, yellow, or green. Predaceous mite eggs commonly are pale or colorless and oblong in comparison with spider mite eggs, which are commonly spherical and colored to opaque. One way to distinguish plant-feeding mites from the predaceous species is to observe mites closely with a good hand lens. Predaceous species appear more active and move faster than plant-feeding species; they stop only to feed. Many predaceous mites feed not only on all stages of plant-feeding mites but also on thrips (Tables 56, 73), scale crawlers, pollen, and fungi.

If resident predators are insufficient, several species of predaceous mites are commercially available (Table 73). If predator introductions are planned, read the releasing natural enemies effectively section early in this chapter. Predators require proper environmental conditions, such as adequate humidity and compatible management practices to be effective. For example, bending rose canes to increase flower production increases humidity within the lower canopy, providing a more favorable environment for predatory mites than in traditional trellis production.

When using predatory mites, regularly monitor pest and mite populations to evaluate control efficacy and to determine whether predatory mite releases or other control methods are warranted. Monitor the quality and quantity of any commercial predators; predators sometimes arrive dead or in poor condition (lethargic and discolored from starvation or other causes). Release recommendations vary from crop to crop. The number of predators needed depends on many factors, including the severity of the spider mite infestation, temperatures, and whether humidity is sufficient to favor increased reproduction and survival of predators. Suggested predaceous mite releases rates are about 2 to 20 per square foot (20–220 per sq m) of growing area. Make several releases at one- or two-week intervals, beginning before pest mites become abundant. If plant-feeding mites are common, apply oil, soap, or another insecticide with relatively low impact on predators to reduce pest populations, then introduce predators after leaves dry. Control dust and avoid using persistent pesticides (Tables 57, 58) for at least several weeks before beginning releases.

Cyclamen Mite and Broad Mite

Cyclamen mite (*Phytonemus pallidus*) and broad mite (*Polyphagotarsonemus latus*) are the most important flower and nursery crop pests in the family Tarsonemidae.

Damage. Feeding by tarsonemids causes leaves to become cupped, dwarfed, and thickened. Leaves or flowers may become discolored, bronzed, or stiff. Infested buds discolor, deform, or drop. Internodes may be short, giving plants a stunted or tufted appearance. Tarsonemids infest many plants, as listed in the chapter "Crop Tables."

Identification and biology. A 20× hand lens, or preferably a binocular dissecting microscope, is needed to see cyclamen mites and broad mites because they are about one-fourth the size of tetranychid spider mites. Adult cyclamen mites can be translucent white, pinkish orange, or pale yellow; broad mites are often translucent, yellowish, or greenish, and female broad mites have a white stripe down the center of their back. Broad mites have a tapered body that is widest between their second pair of legs and more narrow toward

Stunted, curled, brown-edged cyclamen leaves caused by cyclamen mite feeding. This mite damage can easily be confused with damage from abiotic disorders, thrips, or viruses. To avoid ineffective control actions, carefully examine plants with a hand lens, and preferably with a dissecting microscope, to confirm mite presence before taking control action.

Table 73. Some Commercially Available Predaceous Mites.

Predator	Comments
Galendromus (=*Metaseiulus*) *occidentalis*, western predatory mite	Light-colored mite that tolerates hot climates if relative humidity is ≥50%. Some pesticide-tolerant strains are available. Often released against *Tetranychus* species. Eggs are commonly colored pale salmon.
Iphiseius (=*Amblyseius*) *degenerans*	Continues to reproduce under short day length, and its eggs tolerate relatively low humidity. Also used to control western flower thrips.
Neoseiulus (=*Amblyseius*) *californicus*	Commonly used in greenhouses. It tolerates temperatures up to 85° to 90°F (30° to 33°C) but needs relative humidity ≥65%. It persists well when pest populations are low.
Phytoseiulus longipes	Looks like *P. persimilis*, but will tolerate lower (40%) relative humidity at 70°F (21°C). At higher temperatures, it requires more humidity than *P. persimilis*.
Phytoseiulus persimilis	Orangish general predator active at 60–90% relative humidity and 70° to 100°F (21° to 38°C). A strain that tolerates temperatures over 100°F is available. Often released against *Tetranychus* species.

Sources: Easterbrook 1992; Fan and Petitt 1994; Osborne, Ehler, and Nechols 1985.

the rear; cyclamen mites have sides that are more nearly parallel, not sharply tapered. Cyclamen mite eggs are smooth pale ovals, about one-half the length of adults; broad mite eggs are equally tiny, but are studded with rows of tiny pegs protruding from the egg's upper surface.

The hind legs of tarsonemid females are threadlike; adult males have relatively stout legs, which they use to grasp an immature female and carry it on their back. Tarsonemids develop through four life stages: egg, nymph, pseudopupa, and adult. One generation is completed in about 5 to 21 days, depending on temperature. In contrast with tetranychids and tenuipalpids that prefer warm temperatures, tarsonemids do best under cool, moist conditions.

Monitoring and management. Because tarsonemid mites are too small to be seen with the naked eye, knowledge of what plants are most susceptible (Table 72) and regular, careful visual inspection of these plants for damage are the key monitoring methods. Damage is easily confused with that from abiotic disorders, phytotoxicity, thrips, or viruses. To avoid ineffective actions when tarsonemids are suspected, plants must be carefully examined with a hand lens, or preferably a dissecting microscope, to confirm mite presence as the cause of damage. Cyclamen mites usually feed on new growth in buds and young apical leaflets or in distorted flowers or terminal leaves. Broad mites frequently feed on both older and newer growth, usually on the lower surface of leaves and often all over the plant.

Regularly inspect crops throughout production and disinfest or dispose of infested plants. Carefully inspect all incoming stock to detect any infestations. Reject infested plants or disinfest them. Thoroughly immersing plants in 111°F (44°C) water for 30 minutes or maintaining 100% humidity and 111°F for 11 hours may control tarsonemids. Test some plants to determine if they will tolerate these conditions, then carefully inspect plants to ensure that treatment is effective before treating the entire crop. Disinfect containers and tools, such as by dipping them in hot water, to minimize mite spread on contaminated surfaces. Mites can hitchhike on plants, workers, equipment, or even whiteflies and other insects that contact infested plants, so start the work day in uninfested areas. Because tarsonemids feed on many different plants, keep growing areas free of weeds that may host mites. Use other good practices detailed in the sanitation and exclusion sections.

Tarsonemids require a relative humidity of greater than about 70% to reproduce; inducing rapid growth of infested plants under low humidity can cause mite populations to crash and allow new growth to develop free of damage, if the crop will tolerate this treatment.

Control with acaricides can be difficult because tarsonemid mites rapidly develop resistance and live within buds or beneath distorted foliage, protected from sprays. Many of the acaricides effective against spider mites do not control tarsonemids. When spraying, thorough coverage is critical. Use pesticides that are at least somewhat selective for pest mites whenever possible and avoid acaricides that may be more toxic to predators than pests. Naturally occurring predators such as sixspotted thrips and predatory mites, including several *Typhlodromus* species, can help provide control in field situations. Release of *Neoseiulus* (=*Amblyseius*) *barkeri* or *N. cucumeris* predaceous mites have controlled broad mites infesting vegetables, tropical foliage plants, and ivy in small greenhouse areas. It is uncertain whether releases are effective on a large scale in commercial floriculture.

Bulb Mites

Bulb mites (*Rhizoglyphus* spp., family Acaridae) infest flower crop bulbs (Table 72) in storage and in the field. The specific effects of bulb mites are not well known; the mites appear to be secondary pests, attacking weakened tissue. These mites thrive in association with bulb and root diseases; damage from *Fusarium*, *Pseudomonas*, *Stromatinia*, and some other pathogens may be more severe and more difficult to control when bulb mites are present. Infested fleshy bulb scales commonly turn reddish brown. Bulb mite-infested roots, rhizomes, or basal stems can become soft and decayed during storage or in the field.

Bulb mites are pearly white to brownish with stubby legs. Adults are about 1/32 inch (0.8 mm) long, relatively large in comparison with most other pest mite species. Each female can produce about 100 eggs, which are laid on or near injured bulb tissue as well as between bulb scales. Egg to adult development time is about 10 days at 80°F (27°C).

Avoid injuring bulbs during digging, handling, or storage; injuries promote attack by diseases and mites. To help discourage mites, prevent disease development in the field by using resistant cultivars, sterile planting media, appropriate irrigation, adequate drainage, and fungicides. Remove or deeply bury crop debris and employ other good sanitation measures because bulb mites can persist for long periods solely on decayed crop residue. Fallowing fields, rotating to non-host crops, and flood irrigation also reduce populations.

Bulb mites are pearly white with stubby legs. This adult was one of many found under scales of tulip bulbs in cold storage.

Use appropriately cool temperatures, about 35° to 40°F (2° to 5°C), when storing bulbs. Use low humidity, controlled atmosphere (such as high carbon dioxide), and appropriate fungicides to prevent diseases. Promptly remove and dispose of bulbs that become decayed or are soft when squeezed.

Store and plant only disease- and mite-free bulbs. Immersing bulbs in hot water, about 111°F (44°C), for about 1½ hours (see Table 9) can kill all stages of bulb mites, bulb scale mites (*Steneotarsonemus laticeps*), and bulb flies; however, hot water treatment weakens bulbs and preventive measures are preferred. Soaking bulbs in certain acaricides as directed prior to planting also kills mites. Dusting bulbs with sulfur kills bulb mites; because of potential pathogen problems, dust pesticides may be preferred over liquid treatments before storage.

Gall Mites, Bud Mites, and Rust Mites

Mites in the family Eriophyidae commonly feed in buds or distorted plant tissue. Some species are free-living on foliage. Eriophyids distort, stunt, and discolor leaves, terminals, or buds, which may drop prematurely. Each species attacks only one plant species or a group of closely related plants; unrelated weeds or crops are not a source of these pests. Floricultural pests include camellia bud and rust mites and the fuchsia gall mite.

Eriophyids are wormlike or wedge shaped, and often are yellow, pinkish, or white. Adults and immatures have four legs, which appear to be coming out of the head. Eriophyids are minute; they can barely be seen with a 10× hand lens. A microscope is required to clearly distinguish them. If you have difficulty establishing or propagating known host plants, dissect new terminal growth and inspect plant tissue under magnification to determine whether eriophyids are present and possibly causing the poor plant growth.

Eriophyids are difficult to control because they feed protected within plant tissue. Employ good sanitation; quarantine and inspect plants for mites or damage before bringing them into the growing area. Use only clean stock. Consider immediately disposing of infested plants and those nearby when limited infestations are discovered. Once damage occurs, it is not reversible and it may be more cost-effective to discard infested plants than to risk the further spread of the pest and the need for more extensive, repeated control efforts. Some acaricides provide control if plants are treated when mites or damage are first detected on young growth. Acaricides that penetrate plant tissue or have systemic action are more effective. Treat obviously infested plants and nearby hosts.

Fuchsia gall mite. Fuchsia gall mite (*Aculops fuchsiae*) occurs on growing tips year-round and in flowers during blooming. Growing resistant fuchsia (Table 74) is the most effective management method. Although many of the more resistant fuchsia have smaller flowers, growers and retailers

Fuchsia gall mite feeding caused these *Fuchsia magellanica* leaves and shoots to thicken and distort. Many fuchsia cultivars and species are resistant to this pest.

Table 74. Susceptibility of Some Fuchsia Species and Cultivars to Fuchsia Gall Mite.

Low susceptibility or resistant[1]

Baby Chang, Chance Encounter, Cinnabarina, *F. boliviana*, *F. microphylla* ssp. *hindalgensis*, *F. minutiflora*, *F. radicans*, *F. thymifolia*, *F. tincta*, *F. venusta*, Isis, Mendocino Mini, Miniature Jewels, Ocean Mist, Space Shuttle

Moderate susceptibility[2]

Dollar Princess, Englander, *F. aborescens*, *F. denticulata*, *F. gehrigeri*, *F. macrophylla*, *F. procumbens*, *F. triphylla*, Golden West, Lena, Macchu Picchu, Pink Marshmallow, Postijon, Psychedelic

High susceptibility[3]

Angel's Flight, Bicentennial, Capri, China Doll, Christy, Dark Eyes, Display, Firebird, First Love, *F. magellanica*, Golden Anne, Jingle Bells, Kaleidoscope, Kathy Louise, Lisa, Louise Emershaw, Manrinka, Novella, Papoose, Raspberry, South Gate, Stardust, Swingtime, Tinker Bell, Troubadour, Vienna Waltz, Voodoo, Westergeist

1. No control needed.
2. Pinching or pruning galled tissue whenever it occurs provides adequate control.
3. Pruning galled tissue followed by spraying may be necessary every several weeks to provide high aesthetic quality.

Sources: Koehler, Allen, and Costello 1985; Costello, Koehler, and Allen 1987.

can promote these less-problem-prone cultivars to consumers by using resistance information as a marketing tool. If high susceptibility fuchsias are grown, pruning or pinching off and destroying infested terminals, or pinching followed by a systemic material such as acephate, may be necessary every several weeks to provide high aesthetic quality.

Snails and Slugs

Snails and slugs are pests in wet or humid areas such as in greenhouses and in outdoor locations with mild winters.

Damage

Snails and slugs feed on many species of plants, primarily seedlings and low-growing or herbaceous crops. They clip stems and chew irregular holes with smooth edges in leaves. They also leave slime that dries into silvery trails on foliage, media, and containers. Some states have quarantines against the brown garden snail (*Helix aspersa*), an introduced species common in California. Quarantines prevent infested plants from being marketed in other states. Even if the plants are infested only with nonquarantined species of snails, plants can be rejected because these other species sometimes are mistaken for brown garden snails.

Identification and Biology

Snails and slugs have a similar biology and structure, except that snails have a conspicuous spiral shell. Snails and slugs are mollusks that glide along on a muscular "foot" that constantly secretes mucus. Besides the muscular body and the snail's shell, the most readily identifiable body parts are tentacles (antennalike sensory stalks) on the head that retract when disturbed.

The most common species of snail pest in California is the brown garden snail. At maturity its shell is about 1¼ inches (30 mm) in diameter. The shell is yellowish brown and usually has light to dark brown spiral bands streaked with white. *Succinea ovalis*, another common species, has a shell that is up to about ½ inch (12 mm) long. *Succinea* has a delicate, almost translucent, yellowish green shell with inconspicuous lines. The brown garden snail's muscular body is brown, while *S. ovalis* has a translucent, greenish yellow body. *Succinea ovalis* occurs throughout the United States and feeds only on decaying organic matter; it does not damage plants. Learn to distinguish these species (Fig. 59). Because *S. ovalis* is sometimes mistaken for the quarantined brown garden snail, presence of *S. ovalis* can prevent interstate plant shipments. *Deroceras*, *Limax*, and *Milax* species are also common

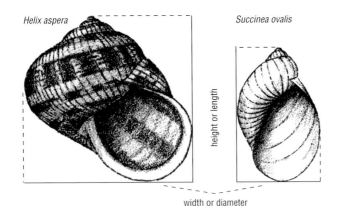

Figure 59. The brown garden snail (*Helix aspersa*) and *Succinea ovalis* can be distinguished by comparing their relative width and height. When viewed with their opening (aperture) toward you and their tip pointed upward, the shell of *S. ovalis* is conspicuously higher than wide. The width of a brown garden snail shell is equal to or greater than its height. These similar species are sometimes confused, but it is important to be able to distinguish them. Brown garden snail is quarantined by some states, and shipment of infested plants is prohibited. *Succinea ovalis* occurs throughout the United States and is not quarantined. Adapted from Kono and Papp 1977; illustrations reprinted with permission from California Department of Food and Agriculture.

slugs, including the gray garden slug (*Deroceras=Peroceras reticulatum*), the banded slug (*Limax poirieri*), and the greenhouse slug (*Milax gagates*).

Snails and slugs are most active under mild temperatures and damp, dark conditions. They feed and reproduce year-round in greenhouses. Outdoors during cold weather, snails and slugs hibernate in the topsoil. During hot, dry periods, slugs remain in the soil, while snails seal themselves off with a parchmentlike membrane, often attached to containers or benches. Slugs feed at or near the soil surface, such as on the underside of leaves touching the ground. Snails are more arboreal, feeding both near the ground and well above ground. On taller plants, such as trees and shrubs, snails either move back to the soil during the day or remain inactive above ground attached to plant parts or surfaces near where they feed during night.

Snails and slugs are bisexual (hermaphroditic). Brown garden snail eggs are about ⅛ inch (3 mm) long, spherical to somewhat teardrop-shaped, and brown, orange, translucent, or white. Eggs are deposited in a cluster on topsoil or media, often in a shallow depression or hole. Each adult brown garden snail lays up to about 80 eggs a month (the total from several clusters) if conditions are suitable. Slug eggs usually are laid in a mass on or near the soil surface; they have a gelatinous shell and somewhat milky appearance.

Monitoring

Regularly inspect growing areas if snails or slugs have been a problem or if shipments will be subject to quarantines. Chewed plants and dried silvery trails on and around foliage indicate snail and slug activity. However, high populations of fungus gnat larvae also leave silvery trails resembling snail and slug trails on growing media. Check for snails and slugs around bait stations. Look on foliage during cloudy days and soon after sunrise or use a flashlight and examine plants at night. During the day, search for snails under dense foliage, beneath pots and benches, and in other protected places. Because they lack a moisture retaining shell, slugs mostly remain in topsoil during the day.

To estimate snail and slug density, regularly inspect under a set number of pots or flats or use special traps. Moist burlap bags or wood traps are attractive hiding places and can be placed at intervals around plants. Wood traps consist of wood squares about 12 inches on a side, raised off the ground by 1-inch runners. Record the approximate number of snails and slugs each time containers or traps are inspected; place bait at these traps or crush any pests present or scrape them into a container for disposal. Compare pest numbers before and after treatment.

Containers of beer also attract slugs, and to a much lesser extent snails. Use relatively flat containers, about the dimensions of an 8-ounce can of tuna. Fill the cans with beer and bury them with their tops about level with the soil surface or place traps on benches or in beds. Beer becomes less attractive to snails after several days so it should be replaced at least twice a week. If the plants are sprinkler irrigated, keep water out by covering each trap with an inverted gallon pot after first cutting legs in the pot's rim so the snails and slugs have access to the trap. Because snails and slugs caught in beer traps are killed, other monitoring methods may be better where decollate snails (see below) are common predators or are being introduced.

Management

Control snails and slugs with a combination of physical, cultural, and chemical methods. Biological control may also be useful in certain situations.

Physical and cultural controls. Inspect inside and underneath containers and flats any time they are moved and before bringing them into the growing area. Crush any pest snails and slugs or scrape them into a container for disposal. Because snail and slug populations are promoted by wet, humid conditions, avoid overwatering. Switch from sprinkler to drip irrigation where practical. Irrigate early in the day so surfaces dry by evening. One study found five times greater damage from slug feeding when plants were irrigated during evening in comparison with plants irrigated 2 hours after sunrise. If it is feasible to apply a waterproof covering over plants, covering plants during nights when rain is expected and then irrigating during mornings if needed may greatly reduce mollusk feeding damage.

Reduce snail and slug survival by reducing their hiding places around plants, including boards, stones, debris, empty containers, unmarketable plants, and weeds. Where practical, grow plants on benches, because they are less frequently damaged there in comparison with plants on the ground. Shallow cultivation may provide some control by mechanically injuring and burying mollusks, exposing subsurface soil to drying, and smoothing surfaces to eliminate soil clods and depressions that provide damp refuges.

Barriers. Snails and slugs avoid crossing copper. Wrap copper flashing or screen around beds, bench legs, containers, or growing areas to exclude snails and slugs. A 6-inch (15-cm) vertical copper screen partially buried about 2 inches (5 cm) deep in the ground stops snails and slugs from crawling through the topsoil or over the barrier. Thin copper is marketed in rolls (Snail-Barr) specifically for snail exclusion; it is commonly wrapped around tree trunks and attached with staples to exclude snails from citrus. One edge of the material is designed to be bent out, improving its exclusion efficacy. The bands may need to be cleaned occasionally, but they will exclude snails and slugs for several years after installation. If growing areas are already infested, use molluscicide or other methods to kill snails and slugs that are present in combination with copper barriers to reduce recolonization.

Copper sulfate or Bordeaux mixture (copper sulfate and hydrated lime) can be sprayed under and around benches or on bench legs and the outside of containers to repel snails

An adult brown garden snail and a young snail. The brown garden snail's muscular body is brown; it has a mottled brown shell up to about 1¼ inch (30 mm) in diameter.

Slugs and their chewing damage on chrysanthemum. To help control snails and slugs, avoid excess irrigation, irrigate in mornings instead of evenings, and provide good drainage.

Snail eggs are laid in clusters, often in slight depressions in the soil surface. Brown garden snail eggs are about ¼ inch (6 mm) long and clear, whitish, orangish, or dark brown. Eggs are spherical or may appear teardrop-shaped due to a protuberance at one end. Snail eggs resemble Osmocote fertilizer pellets, but fertilizer pellets vary in size while all snail eggs in a cluster are about the same size.

and slugs. This also reduces the inoculum of certain diseases. These materials are phytotoxic; prevent contact with plants. Sticky material containing copper sulfate to repel snails and slugs may also be available for use (see Fig. 36).

Pesticide baits. Molluscicides are usually combined with bait to attract and kill snails and slugs that feed on them. Poison baits can provide effective, temporary control of snails and slugs, but baiting may not be necessary where the recommended integrated program of reducing moisture and hiding places, installing barriers, and possibly biological control is employed. Baits are toxic to the predatory decollate snail, and certain products may be hazardous to pets.

Molluscicide susceptibility varies depending on the species (and possibly the age) of the pest and environmental conditions. Metaldehyde and methiocarb are two commonly used molluscicides, which usually are formulated with a bran bait. When choosing between metaldehyde and methiocarb, in general, methiocarb is more effective under prolonged cool, wet, or foggy conditions while metaldehyde is more effective if conditions during the day are warm and sunny. Metaldehyde does not kill snails and slugs directly; rather, it makes them lethargic (unable to seek shelter during the day) and causes excess mucous production, so they die from desiccation and exposure to light. If it is cool and wet during the day, mollusks poisoned by metaldehyde may recover. The time of baiting greatly affects control. For example, when metaldehyde is used outdoors it should be

Drip irrigation emitters have been left on the ground instead of in pots, as is visible at the middle left and lower right of this picture. Damp conditions and poor weed management contribute to pest problems, such as snails and slugs.

applied during a cool, damp period—when snails are most active—just before dry, warm day time weather is expected. If cool damp conditions persist throughout the days after baiting, methiocarb would have been a better choice. Metaldehyde is effective against brown garden snail and most other snails and slugs, but it is not very effective against *Succinea ovalis*; this species lives in damp media and litter, so it is not prone to desiccation after ingesting metaldehyde. Methiocarb is effective against *S. ovalis*.

An iron phosphate and bait combination (Sluggo) has become registered for snail and slug control. Poisoned mollusks reportedly stop feeding within a few hours but can take several days to a week to die. Iron phosphate bait granules may be active on the soil surface longer that other baits, especially if conditions are wet.

Irrigate before applying bait to promote snail and slug activity. Make spot applications instead of widespread applications. Apply bait in the evening and in a narrow strip around sprinklers or in other moist and protected locations to which plant-eating snails and slugs are drawn. Apply bait in relatively protected, damp locations, such as near drip irrigation emitters. Do not make molluscicide applications if heavy rain is expected soon and avoid irrigating overhead for several days after application, as baits decompose upon exposure to excessive moisture. Metaldehyde and possibly certain other molluscicides are decomposed by sunlight.

Beer-baited traps have been used to trap and drown mollusks, primarily slugs. However, they attract slugs and some snails within an area of only a few feet, must be refilled every few days to keep the level deep enough to drown the mollusks, and are more effective if the beer is relatively fresh (less than several days old) rather than flat. Traps should have vertical or steeply slanted sides to minimize crawling out of snails and slugs. Traps should protrude no more than about ¾ inch (19 mm) above the ground surface.

Biological controls. Snails and slugs have many natural enemies, including pathogens, snakes, birds, ground beetles, and flies in the family Sciomyzidae. *Scaphinotus* spp. ground beetles (Carabidae) are important snail predators outdoors in some areas, such as in coastal northern California. Toads were formerly kept in greenhouses to consume slugs and reportedly still are in certain operations. These agents alone may not provide effective control. Minimizing the use of broad-spectrum pesticides outdoors helps improve natural enemies' contribution to pest control.

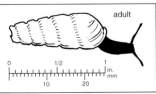

DECOLLATE SNAIL

adult

Snails and slugs are repelled by copper strips. This copper foil can be wrapped around bench legs, planting beds, or groups of containers to prevent mollusks from colonizing uninfested growing media.

Adult garden symphylans have 15 to 22 body segments (usually 15) and 10 to 12 pairs of legs. They have prominent antennae with 25 to 50 tiny, beadlike segments.

GARDEN SYMPHYLAN

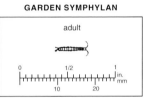

The predatory decollate snail (*Rumina decollata*) consumes young to half-grown brown garden snails and has been effective in controlling snails within several years after introduction into citrus orchards. Because it also feeds to some extent on seedlings and succulent young plants, decollate snail introductions are not recommended for nurseries. Decollate snail introductions in California are permitted only in southern California and certain counties in central California. Releases in most other areas are illegal because they might decimate native snail and slug populations of ecological importance in natural areas. Check with your local agricultural or wildlife protection agency to determine if decollate snail introductions are permitted in your area. For more information on releasing decollate snails, see *Integrated Pest Management for Citrus* (UCIPM 1991).

Garden Symphylan

Symphylans (class Symphyla) are slender, soft-bodied, wingless, soil-dwelling animals related to insects and centipedes. They are sometimes called garden centipedes, but centipedes are beneficial predators. Most symphylan species have been poorly studied. Some species are believed to feed primarily on fungi and decaying plant material in soil. Some feed primarily on tiny soil-dwelling animals, including mites, nematodes, and springtails. At least one common species of garden symphylan, *Scutigerella immaculata*, sometimes feeds on flower and nursery crops and container plants in fields, greenhouses, and nurseries.

Damage

Symphylans are pests when they feed on seeds, fine roots, and root hairs. Under moist conditions, they can chew basal stems and foliage touching soil. Tiny dark spots, actually small pits or depressions, may appear on damaged tissue. Feeding by high-density symphylan populations can stunt plant growth, cause foliage to wilt or discolor due to root damage, and may kill young plants. Symphylan damage to roots may facilitate infection by soil-dwelling fungal diseases such as *Fusarium*. Symphylans attack aster, chrysanthemum, gladiolus, lilies, rose, smilax, snapdragon, and numerous other flower and vegetable crops.

Identification and Biology

Symphylans are tiny, white, fast-moving arthropods. Larvae have six pairs of legs when they hatch from eggs and may be confused with springtails. However, springtails are much smaller and are true insects, which have only three pairs of legs. Adult symphylans can reach $3/8$ inches (9 mm) long and have prominent antennae with 25 to 50 beadlike segments. Adults have 15 to 22 body segments (usually 15) and 10 to 12 pairs of legs (Fig. 60). Immature stages have fewer legs (as few as 6 pairs) and fewer segments. Symphylans may be confused with centipedes or millipedes, but adult millipedes and centipedes have more legs and segments. Symphylans are translucent white, except that gut contents are visible through the integument running the length of the body, so that they may appear dark or colored, depending on their diet.

Adults lay tiny white eggs in groups of about 6 to 24 tied together with silk. Growth from egg to adult requires about 6 to 9 weeks, allowing for several generations each year. Garden symphylans commonly live 6 to 12 months and sometimes longer. Outdoors in California, symphylans occur near the soil surface during fall through spring, but migrate to 1 foot or more below the surface during summer if conditions are hot or dry.

Management

To determine whether symphylans are present, gently lift plants and surrounding soil. Quickly place them into a

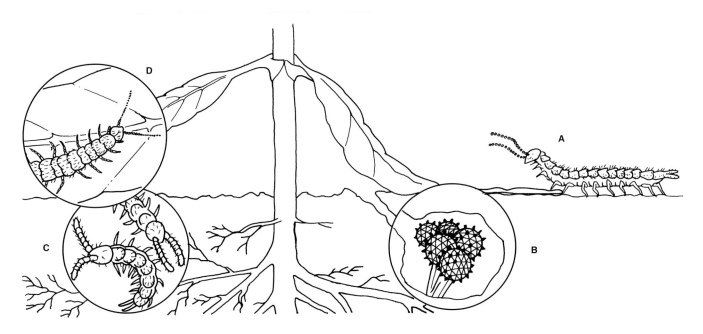

Figure 60. Life cycle of the garden symphylan. **A.** Adults feed at or below the soil surface. **B.** Eggs are laid in a crevice in soil or in decaying vegetation and are webbed together into a cluster attached to substrate with a silken stalk. **C.** Newly emerged nymphs have six pairs of legs. They develop through six instars, adding a pair of legs, another body segment, and more antennal segments each time they molt. **D.** Adults and nymphs feed on plant parts touching the soil surface, but under dark, damp conditions they will climb and feed on low-growing plant parts.

container of water and gently agitate them. Examine the water surface for any dislodged symphylans, which will float. Soaking entire containers in a bucket with water covering the media surface may also induce symphylans to float to the top. Be sure to distinguish symphylans from other tiny soil-dwelling animals that may be present.

Manage symphylans by altering their habitat, reducing moisture, and using good sanitation. Remove damp litter and other organic debris near plants where symphylans reproduce and hide. Reduce humidity, provide good drainage, avoid overwatering, and switch to drip irrigation where feasible. Irrigate early in the day, so that areas can dry before dark.

Greatly reduce or avoid damage in greenhouses by not planting directly in the ground; plant susceptible crops in raised beds, in containers (on benches where feasible), or in inorganic media. Pasteurize growing media before planting. Avoid moving contaminated media, which spreads symphylans.

If fields are relatively flat and surrounded by a dike, flooding for 3 weeks greatly reduces symphylan populations. Deep cultivation to promote soil drying or allowing bare soil to remain fallow, especially during hot weather, provides some control. Vigorously disturbing soil before planting may kill many symphylans, which have a delicate body.

There is little information on biological or chemical control of symphylans. True centipedes, small beetles (families Staphylinidae and Carabidae), and certain soil-dwelling mites prey on symphylans. Entomopathogenic nematodes (such as *Steinernema feltiae*) applied to media and litter may reduce symphylan populations, but their effectiveness against this pest is not documented. Some broad-spectrum insecticides may be available for use as a soil drench to control garden symphylans. Fumigating field soils before planting if warranted can reduce severe populations. However, control may be incomplete because garden centipedes can live deeply in soil.

Centipedes and Millipedes

Centipedes (class Chilopoda) and millipedes (class Diplopoda) occur in damp and loose soil, in organic debris or litter, and in manure. Living plants are not a primary food of either group. Centipedes are mostly predaceous, but some species of millipedes can be occasional pests, chewing tender shoots, small roots, and seedlings. Millipedes and centipedes are often confused because both have an elongate, dark body with many legs (Table 75).

The greenhouse millipede (*Orthomorpha gracilis*) is brown with pale sides; it attacks roots of flower and nursery crops outdoors and in the greenhouse. The small brown common millipede (*Diploiulus luscus*) is widely distributed outdoors and occasionally occurs in greenhouses. The bulb millipede (*Nopoiulus minutus*) occasionally chews bulbs; it is brownish with a row of black dots on each side. *Scutigera* and *Scolopendra* species are common centipedes.

Because they feed mostly in damp, protected locations near the soil surface or during the night, millipedes are easily overlooked. Lift and examine beneath containers, organic litter, or other materials covering the soil surface to observe

Table 75. Differences among Centipedes, Millipedes, and Symphylans.

	Centipedes	Millipedes	Symphylans
Feeding Habits	Largely predaceous, feeding on soil-dwelling insects, snails, and earthworms. Algae and plant material are occasional foods.	Primarily eat dead and decaying plant material, but some species feed on living plants.	Varied diet, including soil-dwelling mites, nematodes, springtails, fungi, and decaying plant material. Pest species chew roots and may feed on seeds and wet foliage touching soil.
Legs	One pair of legs per body segment; 15 to 181 total pairs of legs at maturity.	Two pairs of legs per body segment, except on first few segments.	One pair of legs per body segment, 6 to 12 total pairs of legs.
Body shape	Body relatively flat on top.	Body usually rounded on top.	Up to 22 body segments, usually 15 at maturity.
Biting or stinging	Usually have venom-bearing claws that can cause painful wounds.	Have no venom, but when disturbed they often produce odorous, irritating secretions.	Do not bite or sting.
Evasive action	Commonly run to cover when disturbed.	Often coil their body around their head when disturbed.	Actively run to cover when exposed to light.

whether millipedes are present. Placing pitfall traps or funnel traps in the soil as discussed in the weevils section earlier in this chapter is another monitoring method.

Habitat modification, as detailed for the garden symphylan, provides the most effective control. Remove decaying vegetation and other moist organic debris that harbor centipedes and millipedes around growing areas. Reduce humidity and excess water. Grow plants on benches where feasible. Pasteurize media before planting.

Natural enemies of millipedes include centipedes, predaceous beetles (families Carabidae and Staphylinidae), parasitic flies, parasitic nematodes, and various microorganisms. Except for nematodes, there has been little study on millipede biological control. Entomopathogenic *Steinernema feltiae* nematodes reportedly provide some millipede control in greenhouses (see the weevils section earlier in this chapter). An insecticide recommended for that purpose can be applied to surfaces to reduce severe millipede populations.

Pillbugs and Sowbugs

Pillbugs and sowbugs (class Isopoda) are soil-dwelling crustaceans related to crayfish. Isopods are common outdoors and in greenhouses where moisture and organic matter are abundant. Although they feed primarily on decaying vegetation, they can also chew young roots, seedlings, and tender shoots, and stems near the ground. At least some species of pillbugs can also be beneficial predators of insect eggs. The greenhouse pillbug (*Armadillidium vulgare*) and dooryard sowbugs (*Porcellio* spp.) occur throughout the world.

Pillbugs and sowbugs are covered with gray, brown, or purplish segmented plates; they resemble tiny armadillos. They have seven pairs of legs and at maturity are about ½ inch (13 mm) long. Pillbugs and sowbugs are most readily distinguished by their behavior: when disturbed, pillbugs roll their body into a ball, while sowbugs run and hide. Young of both

The millipede (bottom) has two pairs of legs per segment, is rounded on top, and can feed on crops growing under very damp conditions. The centipede (top) is elongate, flattened on top, and has one pair of legs on each segment. Centipedes are beneficial predators.

The outer body of sowbugs consists of gray, brown, or purplish segmented plates. Sowbugs can become pests only if conditions are frequently humid or damp.

groups emerge from eggs held in a pouch in the female. The young look like adults, but are smaller. They have 1 to 3 generations per year.

Confirm whether sowbugs or pillbugs are present by inspecting damp, dark hiding places during the day; look under containers and flats and disturb the surface of media or organic debris near plants.

Control sowbugs and pillbugs through cultural and physical means and by spot application of insecticide if necessary. Remove litter and other organic debris where sowbugs and pillbugs feed and hide near plants. Store materials off the ground wherever possible to reduce hiding places. Provide good drainage, avoid overwatering, and switch to drip irrigation where feasible; sowbugs and pillbugs soon die in dry conditions. Irrigate early in the day, so areas can dry before dark. Entomopathogenic *Steinernema feltiae* nematodes reportedly provide some control of sowbugs in greenhouses (see the weevils section earlier in this chapter). Severe populations may be reduced by spraying soil surfaces and benches with an insecticide recommended for that purpose.

Springtails

Springtails (class Collembola) occasionally occur in great numbers among seedlings in greenhouses and in damp media rich in organic matter. They are most common in rotting wood and decaying leaf litter. Springtails are primarily decomposers, consuming decaying vegetation, fungi, and algae. Some species attack living plants, chewing roots and succulent plant parts near soil, thereby stunting plant growth or killing seedlings.

Immature springtails are usually opaque or white and are often confused with immature symphylans. Upon maturity, springtails may become grayish or have bright colors, including blue, red, or yellow. Springtails are one of the most primitive groups of insects; they are entirely wingless. They have segmented bodies, three pairs of legs, and are usually $\frac{1}{16}$ inch (2 mm) long or smaller. Springtails are named for the tiny forked appendage many species have folded underneath the rear of their body; when quickly extended, the appendage propels these tiny animals into the air.

Control springtails primarily through cultural and physical means as detailed for the garden symphylan. Reduce moisture, eliminate organic debris, and pasteurize media before planting. Spraying media surfaces or benches with an insecticide recommended for that purpose can temporarily reduce high populations.

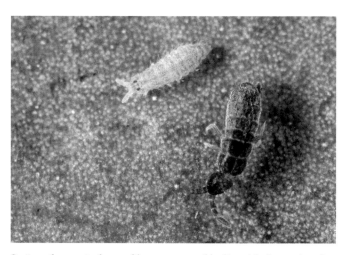

Springtails are wingless and have segmented bodies with three pairs of legs. Most are about $\leq\frac{1}{8}$ inch (3 mm) long.

SPRINGTAIL

adult

Weeds

Weeds are plants that have detrimental economic, ecological, or health effects, such as reducing crop quality and yield. Weeds compete with crops for growing space, nutrients, sunlight, and water. Some weeds can host whiteflies, thrips, nematodes, and mites, or they can harbor other pests such as snails and slugs that attack crops. Weeds can also host pathogens that can spread to nearby crops, such as plant viruses vectored by aphids and thrips (Table 44) and rusts spread by wind. Weeds can increase harvesting costs. If shipped with plants for market, weeds may reduce sales revenue due to poorer crop quality. Certain weeds, such as nutsedge in containers, may cause the crop to be rejected or discarded.

Noncrop plants can be beneficial when grown as windbreaks or cover crops. Cover crops bordering fields can reduce erosion, provide a filter strip to minimize chemical movement off-site, and serve as alternate hosts for beneficial insects. Effective use of noncrop plants requires careful management. Consider the potential advantages and disadvantages of using cover crops and hedgerows in order to maximize their advantages and minimize their potential to become weeds.

Thresholds

Consider the potential for crop damage when deciding whether, when, and how to control weeds. Determine treatment need by assessing whether the weeds are likely to

- significantly reduce yields by competing with crops for space, nutrients, sunlight, or water
- produce seeds or other propagules that will increase management costs and interfere with crops
- host pests that can spread to crops
- interfere with harvest
- reduce crop quality and sales revenue
- result in regulatory action such as quarantines

Crop yield. In general, crop yield reduction from weed competition is proportional to weed density. However, whether control action is justified to minimize weed competition is affected by many factors besides weed density, including weed species biology, dates of crop and weed emergence, crop value, and the timing and method of previous and planned control actions.

Assess what period of weed-free growth is needed to optimize yields. At some low weed density, the value of increased yield from weed control will be less than the cost of weed control. This control action threshold is difficult to determine. Many crops will be relatively unaffected by competition if the crops are provided with weed-free growth during the first several weeks after seedling emergence or if weeds are controlled until the crop canopy develops sufficiently to shade out later-emerging weeds.

Weeds and insects can damage crops. This annual sowthistle is infested with silverleaf whiteflies, which have a broad host range and can disperse from this weed to crops. Weeds can host other pests, such as rust pathogens, or aphids and thrips that vector viruses.

Weeds compete with crops for light, nutrients, and water. To avoid yield reductions, the crop in the foreground requires weed-free growth during at least the first several weeks after seedling emergence. Once the crop has matured, as shown in the background, later-emerging weeds may not significantly reduce crop yield, but they can contribute to problems such as increasing the soil seed bank.

Seed production. Even if weeds are not abundant enough to affect crop yield, quality, and harvest, control action may be justified to prevent weeds from producing seed. The hardest weeds to evaluate are those that you cannot see—the weeds in the soil seed bank. The seed bank is all viable seeds in the soil and on the soil surface, seeds that can germinate and grow if conditions become suitable. Ongoing weed control over the long term will reduce the number of viable seeds in the soil, thereby reducing weed control costs in future crops. Control action is warranted against even a few weeds if the level of weed seeds in the soil is relatively low.

Whenever possible, weeds should be controlled while they are young, certainly before they produce seeds or other propagules. However, deciding specifically when to act to prevent seed production can be complicated. For example, when mowing grains grown as cover crops or annual grasses growing as filter strips bordering crop areas, regrowth allows potential seed production during more than just one time of year. Mowing too soon or too frequently before seedhead development can increase the number and cost of mowings during a season without significantly reducing seed production. Repeated mowing without other control methods can induce weed shifts to low-growing broadleaf species and grasses that produce seed on plant parts below mowing levels.

Monitoring

Before planting, evaluate whether container mixes or field soils are heavily infested with weed seeds. Do not assume that media such as peat moss or compost is weed-free. One method is to moisten samples of the field soil or the container mix and observe them for weed germination.

Scout in and around growing areas to determine when, where, and how to manage weeds. Monitor for weeds during at least two seasons: in fall or winter to detect winter annual weed species and again during spring or summer to detect summer annuals and perennials. Identify and record weed location, growth stage, species (Table 76), and density. In a greenhouse or nursery, look for and identify weeds growing in aisles and liners (small containers that will be transplanted), beneath benches, and between, near, or in beds and pots. In the field look for weeds between and in planting rows. Also inspect areas bordering fields, greenhouses, and nurseries.

Divide growing areas into pest management units (PMUs) to facilitate monitoring and recordkeeping. Map the location of PMUs and weed infestations as described in the chapter "Managing Pests in Flower and Nursery Crops." For each PMU, use a separate weed recordkeeping form, such as the example in Figure 61. Estimate and compare weed density before and after control actions, especially when using experimental methods. Rate infestations as light, medium, or heavy (Fig. 61) or use a more quantitative method for assessing weed density. One method is to select a representative

Table 76. Some Flower and Nursery Crop Weeds.

Weed				Problem site		
Common name	Scientific name	Plant type	Life cycle	Container nursery	Field	Greenhouse
algae, green	many species	Aq	P	●	○	●
bermudagrass	Cynodon dactylon	G	P	●	●	○
bindweed, field	Convolvulus arvensis	B	P	○	●	○
bittercress, lesser seeded	Cardamine oligosperma	B	A	●	●	●
bluegrass, annual	Poa annua	G	A	●	●	●
chickweed, common	Stellaria media	B	A	●	●	●
clover, white	Trifolium repens	B	P	○	●	○
crabgrass, large	Digitaria sanguinalis	G	A	●	●	○
cudweeds	Gnaphalium spp.	B	A or Bi	●	●	○
dock, curly	Rumex crispus	B	P	○	●	○
duckweed	Lemna spp.	Aq	P	●	○	●
fieldcress, creeping	Rorippa sylvestris	B	P	●	●	●
filarees	Erodium spp.	B	A	○	●	○
fleabane, hairy	Conyza bonariensis	B	A	●	●	○
goosefoot, nettleleaf	Chenopodium murale	B	A	●	●	○
groundsel, common	Senecio vulgaris	B	A	●	●	●
henbit	Lamium amplexicaule	B	A	○	●	○
horseweed or marestail	Conyza canadensis	B	A	●	●	○
knotweed, common	Polygonum arenastrum	B	A	○	●	○
lambsquarters, common	Chenopodium album	B	A	○	●	○
lettuce, prickly	Lactuca serriola	B	A	●	●	○
liverworts	Marchantia spp.	L	P	●	○	●
malva or little mallow or cheeseweed	Malva parviflora	B	A or Bi	○	●	○
mosses	many species	L	P	●	○	●
mustards	Brassica spp.	B	A	○	●	○
nettles	Urtica spp.	B	A	○	●	○
nightshades	Solanum spp.	B	A	○	●	○
nutsedges	Cyperus spp.	S	P	●	●	○
oat, wild	Avena fatua	G	A	○	●	○
oxalis or creeping woodsorrel	Oxalis corniculata	B	P	●	●	●
pearlwort, birdseye	Sagina procumbens	B	A or P	●	●	●
pigweeds	Amaranthus spp.	B	A	○	●	○
purslane, common	Portulaca oleracea	B	A	●	●	○
ryegrasses	Lolium spp.	G	A	○	●	○
sowthistle, annual	Sonchus oleraceus	B	A	●	●	○
spurges	Chamaesyce (=Euphorbia) spp.	B	A	●	●	●
willow herbs or fireweeds	Epilobium spp.	B	A	●	●	●

KEY: ● weed can be a problem at that growing site
      ○ generally not a problem at that growing site
      A   annual
      Aq aquatic
      B   broadleaf

      Bi biennial
      G   grass
      L   lower plant, bryophyte
      P   perennial
      S   sedge

| Crop _____ | Year _____ | Location _____ |
| PMU# _____ | Scout _____ | |

Common Name	Season	Infestation Density[1]					
		Sample Dates					
ANNUAL GRASSES							
bluegrass, annual	W						
crabgrass, large	S						
oat, wild	W						
ryegrasses	W						
ANNUAL BROADLEAF WEEDS							
bittercress, lesser seeded	W						
chickweed, common	W						
cudweeds (Bi)	S						
filarees	W						
fleabane, hairy	S						
goosefoot, nettleleaf	W						
groundsel, common	W						
henbit	W						
horseweed or marestail	S						
knotweed, common	S						
lambsquarters, common	S						
lettuce, prickly	W						
malva or mallow or cheeseweed (Bi)	S-W						
mustards	W						
nettles	W						
nightshades	S						
pearlwort, birdseye (P)	W						
pigweeds	S						
purslane, common	S						
sowthistle, annual	W						
spurges	S						
willow herbs or fireweeds	W						
PERENNIALS							
algae, green	S-W						
bermudagrass	S						
bindweed, field	S						
clover, white	W						
dock, curly	S						
duckweeds	S-W						
fieldcress, creeping	W						
liverworts	S						
nutsedges	S						
oxalis or creeping woodsorrel	W						

KEY: Bi   biennial or annual life cycle   S-W   summer and winter germination
        P   perennial or annual life cycle   W   winter (fall and winter) germination
        S   summer (spring and summer) germination

1. Infestations can be rated as L = light   M = medium   H = heavy.

Figure 61. Record form for weeds sampled on six dates. Scout for weeds during at least two seasons to detect species that germinate during fall and winter (winter) and spring and summer (summer). Adapted from Kempen 1993.

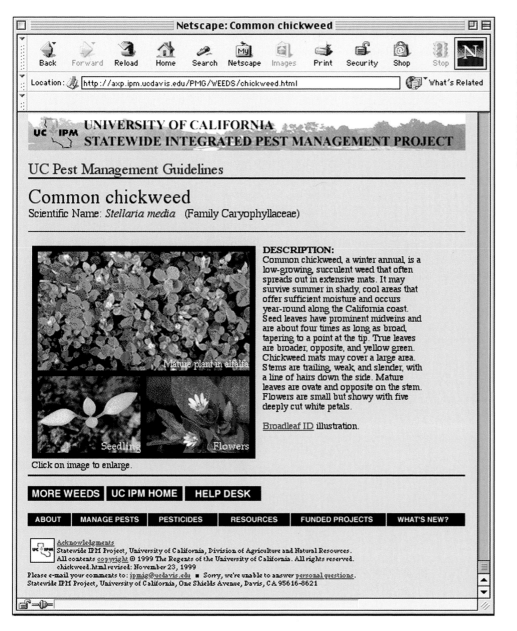

An example of pest identification information accessible through the Internet. The UC IPM Project's World Wide Web site at http://www.ipm.ucdavis.edu and other online sources provide a wealth of information on pest identification and management. Online information includes herbicide recommendations in the *UC IPM Pest Management Guidelines: Floriculture and Ornamental Nurseries.*

area of the crop (such as one-half of a field row or a specific number of square feet of growing area), count all the weeds in that area, then multiply the number of weeds by the total number of similar areas to estimate the total weed population.

Many different species of weeds can infest field-grown crops; which species are present depends mostly on the weed and cropping history in and around the field. Relatively few species of weeds occur in most greenhouses and nurseries. Consult Table 76 and the end of this chapter to identify some common floriculture and nursery weeds and learn their growing habits. More-detailed, well-illustrated sources include publications listed in suggested reading at the back of this book, such as *Weeds of the West* (Whitson et al. 1991)

and the UC IPM Project's World Wide Web Site at www.ipm.ucdavis.edu. Cooperative Extension advisors, county agricultural commissioners, knowledgeable pest control advisers, certified nurserymen, and botanical garden and arboretum personnel can also help you identify weeds.

Learn the type (broadleaf, grass, or sedge) and life cycle (annual, biennial, or perennial) of problem weeds in order to effectively manage them. For example, most selective postemergence herbicides control certain grasses or broadleaf weeds but not both types of plant. Selective herbicides for grasses do not control sedges. Many weeds germinate only during certain times of the year or in response to specific environmental conditions that growers can recognize. Use this knowledge to effectively time control actions.

Management

Control weeds using a combination of chemical, cultural, mechanical, and physical methods. Physical controls include applying mulch or steam or solar heat pasteurization of growing media. Mechanical controls include cultivation, flaming, hand-weeding, mowing, and screens to exclude waterborne or windblown seeds. Irrigation management is a primary cultural control strategy, but cover crops, crop rotation, and adjusting planting density and time are other cultural controls for certain situations. Chemical controls include preemergence and postemergence herbicides and sometimes soil fumigation.

The method of weed control depends on the growing site (field, greenhouse, or nursery), the target weed species, the grower's needs and management style, whether control actions are taken within or outside growing areas (Fig. 62, Table 77), and the time. Controls can be done before planting (preplant), after planting but before weeds emerge (preemergence), or after weeds emerge (postemergence).

To minimize or avoid weed competition, always

- control weeds before planting, when possible
- start with weed-free seeds, plants, and media
- use good sanitation and exclusion throughout the crop production cycle

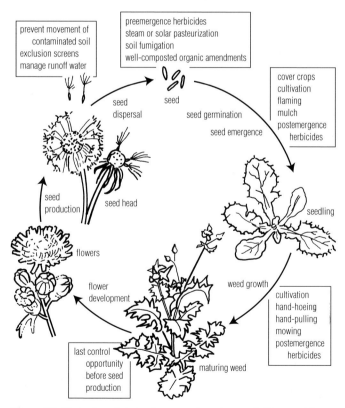

Figure 62. Methods and timing for annual weed control, illustrated here with annual sowthistle.

- prevent weed emergence in crops
- scout regularly in and around growing areas for weeds
- control any emerged weeds while they are young and before they produce propagules

In greenhouses and container-grown nursery plants, you can avoid most problems by using weed-free container mix and stock and by preventing establishment of weed seeds that are carried in by wind, water, equipment, tools, or other contamination sources. Also make sure that liners (small container plants) are weed-free before purchase and transplanting. Once weeds grow among container-grown and greenhouse crops, hand-weeding is often the only option. There are few selective postemergence herbicides for floral crops and few herbicides are registered for greenhouse use.

For field crops, good site selection and preplanting weed control are critical, especially when perennial weeds are present. In established field crops, manage weeds primarily by close cultivation, cover crops, exclusion, hand-weeding, mowing, mulching, and selective herbicides. Promptly remove the crop and all weeds after harvest to eliminate them as hosts of other pests and to prevent weeds from contributing to the soil seed bank.

Weed Control Before Planting

The most critical time for weed management is before planting, when virtually all control options are available. Once crops are planted, many control methods become unavailable (Table 77). Weed management after planting is usually more difficult and expensive; either a selective herbicide must be available for that crop or other methods that may injure the crop must be used (such as hand-weeding or cultivation). When weeds are present, control them before they mature, flower, and produce seed or other propagules.

Choose a Weed-Free Growing Site

When selecting a new growing site, choose an area that is relatively free of weeds, especially perennial species. Perennial weeds are often more competitive than the crop. Weeds from bordering areas and underground propagules will continually invade fields, nurseries, and greenhouses. Select a location away from areas such as unmanaged fields where windblown seeds can be a significant problem. Annual sowthistle, common groundsel, cudweed, hairy fleabane, horseweed, prickly lettuce, and willow herbs are among the weeds that produce seeds that are easily dispersed by wind.

Prepare the Site

Control perennial weeds before grading, cultivating, or installing irrigation equipment. Inspect the site. If perennial weeds are found, control them at the proper stage of growth for maximum effectiveness. For example, postemergence herbicides are often applied before grading or cultivation in areas infested with perennial weeds such as bermudagrass.

Table 77. Weed Control Methods and When and Where to Use Them.

Method	Where to use			When to use		
	Greenhouse	Field	Nursery	Before planting	After planting	Anytime outside growing areas
monitoring or scouting	●	●	●	●	●	●
weed-free site selection	●	●	●	●	○	◐
site preparation	●	●	●	●	○	○
solarization	●	●	●	●	○	○
pasteurization	●	●	●	●	○	○
composting container mix	●	●	●	●	○	○
weed-free stock	●	●	●	●	○	○
modified planting time, spacing, or depth	◐	●	◐	●	○	○
crop rotation	◐	●	◐	●	○	○
cover crop or living mulch	○	●	○	●	●	●
cultivation	○	●	○	●	●	●
sanitation and exclusion	●	●	●	●	●	●
flaming	◐	●	◐	●	○	●
hand-weeding	●	●	●	●	●	●
herbicides	◐	●	●	●	●	●
irrigation and runoff water management	●	●	●	●	●	●
mowing	○	●	○	●	○	●
mulch	◐	●	●	●	●	●
screens or hedgerows	◐	●	●	●	●	●
biological control[1]	○	◐	○	○	◐	●

KEY: ●   method can be used
         ◐   method may or may not be feasible depending on the growing situation
         ○   method usually not useful in that situation
1. Current uses are very limited, as discussed later in the biological control section.

Bermudagrass should have 4 to 6 inches (10–15 cm) of vigorous growth and not be moisture-stressed when the herbicide is applied. This perennial weed control can add 1 to 2 months to the time required for site preparation.

Fields. Cultivate or grade soil to provide a smooth, weed-free planting site for field-grown ornamentals. Irrigate to induce weed seed germination and then kill the weeds with cultivation, flaming, or herbicides. Soil solarization, steam rakes, or fumigation can also be used in combination with cultivation before planting. A combination of methods may be needed, especially if the soil contains an abundance of weed seeds or is heavily infested with underground propagules such as tubers or rhizomes of perennials.

Containers. Create a weed-free, well-drained growing area for container plants by installing a drainage system and applying gravel, concrete, a geotextile (weed-barrier fabric) or other mulch, preemergence herbicide, or a combination of these to the ground and greenhouse floors. Maintain a vegetation-free strip of at least 6 feet (2 m) around greenhouse foundations. One method is to close greenhouse vents and windows and apply herbicide outside greenhouses. Alternatively, establish turf or another ground cover as a border around growing areas as discussed in the cover crops section later in this chapter. In addition to weed control, a ground cover border such as turf will filter runoff water and silt that contain substances that might otherwise move off-site, such as nitrates and preemergence herbicides.

Greenhouses. Before planting, control established weeds in greenhouses by manual removal, emptying the growing area and solarizing, fumigating, applying postemergence herbicides, or a combination of these methods.

Sanitation and Exclusion
Keep weeds out of growing areas by using good sanitation and exclusion practices before planting and during the growing season. Most annual weeds spread as seeds moved in soil; seeds are also moved by wind, irrigation water, surface water

Few herbicides are registered for greenhouse use. This weed-free growing area was created by using a concrete walkway and water-permeable geotextile beneath gravel, and controlling all weeds around the outside of the greenhouse.

Allowing extensive weed growth around potted plants is a poor production practice. These weeds are a source of seeds that repopulate the seed bank and contaminate pots. Weeds can also harbor insects, nematodes, and pathogens that can spread to crops.

These weedy pots in a greenhouse are the result of poor sanitation practices and will require handweeding before sale.

runoff, animals, people, vehicles, and tools. Perennial weeds are spread from one site to another primarily as nutlets, rhizomes, and tubers. These propagules infest soil, contaminated materials such as containers and liners, and organic amendments and growing media that are unpasteurized or become contaminated during mixing and storage.

The best way to prevent greenhouse and container weed problems is by using pasteurized media and weed-free crop seeds or transplants, and by controlling weeds around growing areas. Hand-weed containers with established plants before moving them into clean growing areas. Screen irrigation intake systems, greenhouse vents, and other openings to exclude waterborne and windblown seeds. Cooperate with neighbors to control invasive weeds on nearby properties. Consider installing fences or planting hedgerows around nurseries and fields (see the screens and hedgerows section later in this chapter).

Growing Media

Before planting, eliminate weeds from growing media, including container mixes, field soil, and planting beds. Container mixes and greenhouse beds are usually weed-free if they have been pasteurized and kept covered to prevent contamination. Effective heat or chemical pasteurization requires adequate pretreatment preparations. Moisten media several days before treatment so it is damp but not soggy; this initiates weed seed germination, making weeds easier to control. Also mix or cultivate to loosen the media and eliminate clods.

Monitor for weed seeds in container mixes and organic amendments such as compost and peat if they will not be pasteurized before use. Place several samples of the media in one or two flats and keep them moist. Check them periodically for about two weeks. If weeds grow, pasteurize the media before use. Improve storage and handling practices to prevent recontamination.

Steam and Heat Pasteurization

Use steam, dry heat (such as from kilns), or solarization to pasteurize growing media before planting. In the past, steam was the most common method for treating container mixes and planting beds. Although its use has declined, steam is coming back into widespread use. Steam heat is as effective as methyl bromide in controlling most pests (Table 8). However, methods of effectively using steam in field soil need to be improved. Heat generated by microorganisms during proper composting also controls most weeds as discussed in the chapter "Diseases." New technologies, such as microwave or gamma radiation and ohmic heating, are being researched for treating media.

Solarization

Solarization kills pests before planting by using solar radiation to heat growing media. Clear (not black) plastic, 1.5 to 2 mils (0.0015–0.002 inch [0.038–0.05 mm]) thick, is used

Table 78. Advantages and Disadvantages of Solarization.

Disadvantages

- Doesn't work well in cloudy, cool, windy areas.
- In the field, it requires a crop-free period of 4 to 6 weeks during a sunny time of year that is warm or calm or both.
- Effective use requires careful preparation (such as moist, smooth, debris-free soil) and adequate execution (such as tear-free plastic with sealed edges).
- Certain pests are resistant to solarization.
- Soil-contaminated plastic is often too dirty and damaged to reuse and many recyclers will not accept it.

Advantages

- Safe, relatively simple, and scaleable for use in any size field or greenhouse.
- Costs less than methyl bromide if it is used for both pathogen and weed control, and is typically cheaper than hand-weeding or metam sodium treatment.
- Often stimulates plant growth beyond that resulting solely from pest control, possibly because solarization increases nutrient availability and gives a competitive advantage to certain heat-tolerant beneficial soil microorganisms.
- Can improve soil texture and quality, facilitating planting and seedling emergence.

Table 79. Key Requirements for Effective Solarization.

- Moist but not soggy soil.
- Smooth, clod- and debris-free soil that is ready to plant.
- Adequate solar radiation (about 450 lumens per day) for 4 to 6 weeks.
- Intact, clean, clear plastic tarps (preferably UV-inhibiting treated plastics) with sealed edges and seams.

to cover bare, moist fields, greenhouse beds, or container mix. The plastic traps solar radiation and elevates media temperatures. In addition to using it in hot climates, field solarization can be effective in many cool coastal areas if it is applied during periods of high radiation and low wind. Solarization of container mixes, greenhouses, and raised beds is more effective in these cooler climates than solarizing field soils. The effectiveness of solarization can be improved by applying reduced rates of fumigants before or after solarization or by incorporating crop residues, green and animal manures, or inorganic fertilizers into the soil before applying the plastic. For example, one experiment found that adding broccoli, cabbage, or cauliflower residue and heating media at 80° to 100°F (27° to 38°C) for 1 week reduced germination of *Pythium ultimum* and *Sclerotium rolfsii* by 87 to 100%. Consult *Soil Solarization* (Elmore et al. 1997) for a detailed discussion of solarization.

Solarization controls many pests if users recognize its shortcomings (Table 78) and use effective techniques (Table 79). Solarization can control nematodes, soilborne pathogens (Table 33), and seeds and seedlings of most annual and certain perennial weeds (Table 80). Solarization easily controls most winter annuals, including malva, a weed not controlled by methyl bromide fumigation; but solarization does not control white sweetclover (*Melilotus alba*). Although summer

Table 80. Susceptibility of Weed Species to Solarization.

Common name	Susceptibility
bermudagrass	S
bindweed, field	R
bittercress, lesser seeded	S
bluegrass, annual	S
chickweed, common	S
crabgrass, large	S
fleabane, hairy	S
goosefoot, nettleleaf	S
groundsel, common	S
henbit	S
horseweed	S
johnsongrass	U[1]
knotweed, common	S
lambsquarters, common	S
lettuce, prickly	S
liverworts	S
mallow, little (cheeseweed)	S
mustard, black	S
nettles	S
nightshade, black	S
nightshade, hairy	S
nutsedge, purple	R
nutsedge, yellow	U
oat, wild	S
oxalis or creeping woodsorrel	S
pearlwort, birdseye	S
pigweeds	S
purslane, common	S
ryegrasses	S
shepherd's-purse	S
sowthistle, annual	S
spurges	S
sweetclover, white	R
willow herbs or fireweeds	S

KEY: R = resistant
S = susceptible
U = unpredictable, weeds may or may not be controlled

1. Seed is susceptible but control of emerged plants is unpredictable.

Adapted from Elmore et al. 1997.

This field is being prepared for solarization by covering moist, smooth, debris-free soil with clear plastic.

Solarization controls most annuals and the parts of certain perennials that are within a few inches of the soil surface. These propagules of yellow nutsedge can be too deep underground to be controlled by solarization.

annuals are less temperature sensitive, they are usually controlled well. Purslane is less susceptible to solarization than other summer annuals. If purslane is controlled, this is a good indication that soil has been adequately heated.

Established perennials generally are not controlled well by solarization because their roots or propagules are growing below the depth of good solar heat penetration. Solarization does control seeds of bermudagrass, field bindweed, and johnsongrass, and will control rhizomes of bermudagrass and johnsongrass if they are within a few inches of the soil surface. Yellow nutsedge is only partially controlled and purple nutsedge is usually not controlled by solarization.

Field solarization. In California's Central Valley, soil can be solarized anytime from late May through September. In south coastal California, mid-July through August is usually the sunniest, calmest time of year. Along coastal areas of central and northern California, August to October and May through June are usually best; these are transitional periods when fog or wind can be at a minimum.

Soil must be bare and moist for maximum solar heating. Before applying plastic, scrape vegetation off, mow weeds closely to $\frac{1}{2}$ inch (12 mm) tall, rake soil free of any residue, then cultivate no deeper than about 4 inches (10 cm). Smooth the soil and otherwise prepare fields so that the soil is ready for planting and soil disturbance after solarization is minimized.

Irrigate soil thoroughly just before covering it. Soil moisture should be at least 70% of field capacity to a depth of 2 feet (60 cm) to ensure adequate heat conduction and to make soil organisms more vulnerable to the heat. After watering, lightly work the soil surface to even it, then lightly irrigate again if the surface has dried. Alternatively, apply plastic before irrigation then water using preinstalled drip lines under the plastic or water running down furrows or tracks made by tractor wheels. Do not irrigate during solarization as applying water will lower soil temperatures.

If plastic may become heavily contaminated with windblown dirt or debris, consider using plastic screens or other contamination barriers along field edges. Plant soon after removing the solarization plastic. After solarization, avoid deep cultivation. Working the soil deeper than about 3 inches (7.5 cm) can bring to the surface weed seeds that were buried too deeply to have been killed.

Field and greenhouse solarization. Solarization is most effective when plastic is laid closely on a smooth surface. Be sure ground beds and soil are free of clods, protruding rocks, excess plant debris, and trash. Air gaps created by clods or air pores in dry soil are poor conductors of heat. The plastic can be applied by machine or hand to cover the entire field, selected strips, or only the planting beds. Seal the tarp edges with soil to retain heat and prevent the plastic from being blown away. Use care during application and keep workers and equipment off of the plastic surface; the tarp surface must be protected from punctures during solarization to achieve the highest soil temperatures. If holes form in the plastic while on the soil, seal them with clear patching tape.

Greenhouse solarization. Solarization in greenhouses can reach much higher temperatures than outdoors, a desirable benefit during cooler weather and in coastal areas. Clean the greenhouse covering to remove any whitewash or dirt. Level the soil of planting beds, irrigate, and then cover the beds with clear plastic. After applying plastic, close the greenhouse and solarize it for up to 4 to 6 weeks. Depending on the situation, it may or may not be necessary or desirable to close the greenhouse tightly during solarization. Closing the greenhouse tightly will significantly increase temperatures inside and shorten the time needed for solarization. Higher temperatures may be needed when solarizing during cold, overcast, or windy weather. However, tightly closed greenhouses can get very hot, possibly damaging plastics such as irrigation pipes.

Container media solarization. Solarize planting mix in containers, flats, or plastic bags outdoors by placing them inside a tightly closed polyethylene tunnel or tent (Fig. 63). Covering media with a double layer of clear plastic can increase temperatures up to 50°F (28°C) above the temperatures achieved by a single layer, allowing media to be solarized in about 1 week. When using double plastic layers, leave a gap of at least ½ inch (12 mm) between each layer of plastic, such as by placing a plastic hoop frame between the two layers.

Alternatively, spread a sheet of plastic out flat on the ground. Place flats, trays with small pots, or polyethylene planting bags of media on one-half of the sheet (Fig. 64). Fold the other half of the plastic over on top and seal the edges so that the media is sandwiched between the plastic. Bulk media can be spread on the plastic to a depth of no more than 12 inches (30 cm). Instead of folding over a single sheet of plastic, media can be placed on disinfected blacktop, concrete, greenhouse benches, black plastic, or other materials that will not allow reinfestation from soil or other potentially contaminated sources. An additional layer of clear plastic is then placed on top, providing a solarization cover that creates a still-air chamber. Although clear plastic is usually used for solarization, in warmer areas of California growing media inside black plastic sleeves left outside in the sun can also reach 158°F (70°C) during solarization.

Be sure that the moisture content of media is near field capacity. When solarizing container mix, monitor and record soil temperature using a minimum-maximum thermometer that is tolerant to high temperatures or use thermocouples with a digital temperature logger. Monitor temperatures in the coolest part of the media, which usually is at the bottom center of the pile or bag. Ensure that all media reaches a minimum temperature of 158°F (70°C) for 30 minutes.

Plastic disposal. Avoiding environmental contamination and disposing of plastic after solarization can often be a problem. UV-treated plastics thicker than 4 mils (0.1 mm) may be useable for more than one season if they are handled carefully. It can be difficult in California to find recyclers that accept soil-contaminated plastic. Most plastic in California is disposed of in landfills. Some grower organizations periodically sponsor plastic drop-off days at certain locations where relatively clean plastic, such as about 5% or less soil contamination by weight, is accepted for recycling.

Certain plastics are designed to biodegrade after 6 to 12 weeks. Although these can be effective for solarization, they are not currently recommended. Their biodegradation has been inconsistent, and buried plastic remains in soil until it is brought to the surface and exposed to sunlight.

Repeated Irrigation and Cultivation

The soil seed bank can be depleted before planting by irrigating soil and then killing emerged seedlings by cultivating, flame weeding, or applying postemergence herbicides. This

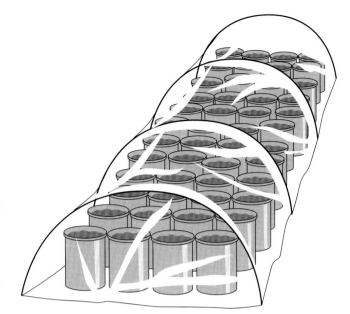

Figure 63. A clear polyethylene tunnel or tent for outdoor solarization of container mix. Wires or plastic hoops are arched over container mix in flats, pots, or plastic bags. The hoop frame is covered with clear plastic and the tunnel edges are tightly sealed, for example, by burying them in soil.

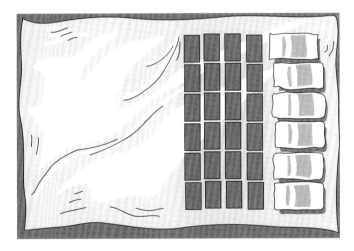

Figure 64. These flats and plastic bags of container mix are awaiting solarization. Media is placed on top of a sheet of clear plastic that is spread flat on the ground. The left half of the plastic sheet will be folded over on top of the growing media and will then be sealed around the edges. Flats or trays of small containers can be stacked before covering them, as long as sufficient space is provided to allow good air movement between layers. The plastic bags containing growing media can be any color.

method is especially effective against annual weeds.

Cultivate, prepare, and irrigate beds about 10 days before planting. About 7 to 10 days later, remove the newly emerged weeds, for example, by scraping bed surfaces. Minimize soil disturbance or more seeds will be brought to the surface for germination. If several weeks are available before planting, this "water-wait-then-cultivate" (or flame or spray) process can be repeated one or more times at intervals of 7 to 10 days. Make each subsequent cultivation shallower than the last so that deeply buried seeds are not brought to the surface. Plant as soon as possible after the last control action.

Repeated Dry Cultivation

Certain perennial weeds, such as bermudagrass, Johnsongrass, and purple nutsedge, can be killed by cultivating the soil and allowing it to dry. This brings propagules (rhizomes or nutlets) to the surface, where they are dried by the sun and killed or use up their stored reserves by sprouting. Cultivate 3 or 4 times during dry summer weather and keep the soil dry at all times. Allow sufficient time between each cultivation so that the exposed propagules die and the sprouts have too few leaves to begin producing more propagules. Although the cultivation interval depends on prevail-

Broadleaf weeds growing where wood chip mulch has become too thin are being killed with a propane weed flamer. In comparison with untreated weeds in the foreground, treated weeds near the nozzle have wilted from brief heating of their basal stems. These treated weeds will turn brown and die within a few days.

ing conditions, it can be judged in part by feeling the soil to determine if the top few inches have dried, by cutting or breaking open rhizomes or nutlets to assess whether their centers have dried completely, and by learning the maximum number of leaves on sprouts before they begin producing propagules.

Keep soil dry at all times or propagules will not die. Do not use dry cultivation unless it will be repeated as necessary; otherwise, tillage can increase weed problems by breaking up and spreading propagules. Confine dry cultivation to areas known to be infested with weeds susceptible to dry cultivation. Repeated dry cultivation may not be appropriate in locations where wind erosion is a significant problem.

Flame Weeding

Flame weeding or flaming uses special hand-held or tractor-mounted controlled flamers fueled with propane or kerosene to briefly expose weeds to high temperatures without exposing them for so long that they catch fire and burn. Flaming can kill weeds during bed preparation, in certain mulches, and outside growing areas. Shielded flamers can be used for weed control between established crop rows. Since no soil disturbance occurs, flame weeding is a good alternative to cultivation, which can bring new seeds to the surface. Seedlings and broadleaf annuals are most susceptible to flaming; although grasses and perennials are partially controlled, they often regrow, requiring retreatment.

Flaming in combination with irrigation can deplete the weed seed bank prior to planting. Irrigate, wait for seedling emergence, flame the seedlings, then plant. Alternatively, prepare the beds, plant, and irrigate the crop seeds. At approximately one-half to two-thirds of the time needed for crop emergence, flame beds to kill any emerged weeds. This gives the crop a competitive advantage by allowing it to emerge before the weeds.

Move the flame across beds carefully so that seedlings are touched by flame only briefly. Keeping the flame in one spot too long can heat soil below the surface, risking crop damage. Be sure that soil is moist before flaming to minimize heat transfer to germinating crop seeds.

How to flame. Only brief contact with high temperatures is needed to disrupt plant cells. *Do not flame weeds to the point where they char or burn.* Kill seedlings by moving a high-temperature flame over them once lightly. Kill larger weeds by briefly touching the basal stem area of each plant with the tip of a flame. It is not necessary to flame foliage, as aboveground parts die if the basal stem is killed. Flame during early morning or late evening when winds are low and the flame is more easily visible. Plants may wilt, change color, or appear unaffected soon after flaming. Even if no immediate change in the weeds is apparent, flaming will eventually cause them to yellow and die.

Move at a slower pace when flaming grasses because their growing points can be somewhat protected below the soil surface. When flaming grasses or perennials, it can be more effective to flame them again about a week after the initial treatment. For best effectiveness, flame weeds when they are less than 2 to 3 inches (5–7.5 cm) tall, especially grasses and perennials.

Proper flaming produces little smoke or other emissions, so air quality impacts should not be a problem. Consider avoiding the practice during "spare the air days" because of the hydrocarbon emissions of the fuel and the small amount of smoke that occurs if weeds are inadvertently overheated. Take care to avoid starting a fire. Use good judgment to identify hazardous situations where flaming should be avoided, such as immediately adjacent to structures or piles of dry debris. Keep fire suppression equipment handy, such as a fire extinguisher, shovel, and water, in case of accidents.

Herbicides

Use herbicides in combination with other methods as part of an integrated weed management program. Depending on the chemical and the situation, herbicides can provide convenient, cost-effective weed control before planting, within crops, and outside of growing areas.

Control weeds before planting whenever possible. Few selective herbicides are available for application to flower and nursery crops. Also, crops from a different genus or family are often grown near each other in small blocks or adjoining rows; once crops are present, it can be difficult to use selective herbicides that are not phytotoxic to some of the crops in the area. Consult Tables 81 and 82 before choosing a herbicide.

Table 81. Herbicide Selection Criteria.

- What are the weed species to be controlled?
- What is the life cycle of targeted weeds (annual, biennial, or perennial)? When do they germinate?
- Will a herbicide that is registered for that use control the weeds that are present?
- What crops are being grown and what is their sensitivity to herbicides?
- How might environmental conditions, soil characteristics, and water quality affect herbicide performance?
- What application procedures are required (for example, mechanical incorporation for certain preemergence herbicides)?
- What equipment is available?
- How will herbicide use and irrigation be coordinated? For example, can the herbicide be applied through drip irrigation, does the chemical require postapplication irrigation, and does it perform best with or without overhead irrigation?
- Will the timing of control be prior to or after emergence of the crop or weeds or both, and how does this timing affect herbicide selection?
- What duration of weed control is desirable?
- What is the level of residual activity of the herbicide, and will it persist too long and adversely affect subsequent crops?
- Will the herbicide pose a risk of environmental contamination, such as groundwater contamination or other contamination off-site?

Herbicides are classified according to when they are applied relative to plant growth, how they control weeds (their mode of action, Fig. 65), and how they are formulated. They can be applied prior to planting (preplant), after the crop is planted but before crop seedlings or weeds have emerged (preemergence), or after weeds are present (postemergence). Different herbicide formulations may be appropriate for different situations, and the application equipment needed depends on the formulation. Common formulations are granules (which are applied dry and then watered in) and

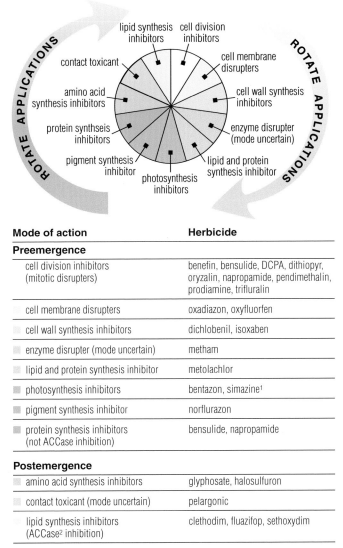

Mode of action	Herbicide
Preemergence	
cell division inhibitors (mitotic disrupters)	benefin, bensulide, DCPA, dithiopyr, oryzalin, napropamide, pendimethalin, prodiamine, trifluralin
cell membrane disrupters	oxadiazon, oxyfluorfen
cell wall synthesis inhibitors	dichlobenil, isoxaben
enzyme disrupter (mode uncertain)	metham
lipid and protein synthesis inhibitor	metolachlor
photosynthesis inhibitors	bentazon, simazine[1]
pigment synthesis inhibitor	norflurazon
protein synthesis inhibitors (not ACCase inhibition)	bensulide, napropamide
Postemergence	
amino acid synthesis inhibitors	glyphosate, halosulfuron
contact toxicant (mode uncertain)	pelargonic
lipid synthesis inhibitors (ACCase[2] inhibition)	clethodim, fluazifop, sethoxydim

1. Simazine is a postemergence herbicide.

2. ACCase or acetyl-CoA carboxylase is an enzyme necessary in lipid biosynthesis. Lipids, including fats and waxes, are principal structural components of living cells.

Figure 65. One method of avoiding weed resistance to herbicides is to rotate applications among 3 or more chemicals with different modes of action. Above are the modes of action of selected herbicides used in flower and nursery crops. Sources: Anonymous 1998, Weller 1997.

Table 82. Weed Species Susceptibility to Herbicides.

PREEMERGENCE HERBICIDES

BROADLEAF WEEDS	Life cycle	Benefin	Bensulide	DCPA	Dichlobenil	Dithiopyr	Isoxaben	Metam sodium	Metolachlor	Napropamide	Norflurazon	Oryzalin
bindweed (Pr)	Pe											
bindweed (Se)	Pe					—						
chickweed	A											
cudweed	A											
dock (Pr)	Pe											
dock (Se)	Pe					—						
fieldcress, creeping	A										—	
fiaree	A					—						
fleabane, hairy	A											
goosefoot, nettleleaf	A											
groundsel, common	A											
henbit	A								—			
horseweed	A					—						
knotweed	A											
lambsquarter	A											
lettuce, prickly	A					—						
liverwort	Pe					—	—				—	
mallow, malva, or cheeseweed	A					—						
mustard	A											
nettle, burning	A											
nightshade, black	A					—						
nightshade, hairy	A					—						
nutsedge, purple	Pe											
nutsedge, yellow	Pe											
oxalis or creeping woodsorrel	Pe										—	
pearlwort, birdseye	Pe	—		—	—	—		—	—		—	
pigweed	A											
purslane, common	A											
sowthistle, annual	A					—						
spurge, prostrate	A								—			
willow herb or fireweed	A	—	—	—	—	—			—		—	

GRASSES

GRASSES	Life cycle	Benefin	Bensulide	DCPA	Dichlobenil	Dithiopyr	Isoxaben	Metam sodium	Metolachlor	Napropamide	Norflurazon	Oryzalin
barnyardgrass	A											
bermudagrass (Pr)	Pe											
bermudagrass (Se)	Pe											
bluegrass, annual	A											
crabgrass	A											
johnsongrass (Pr)	Pe											
johnsongrass (Se)	Pe				—							
oat, wild	A											
ryegrass, Italian	A											

KEY:
- Pe perennial weeds
- A annual weeds
- Pr established perennial
- Se seedling
- ▪ controlled
- ▨ partially controlled
- ▢ not controlled
- — not rated

PREEMERGENCE HERBICIDES

Oxadiazon	Oxyfluorfen	Pendimethalin	Prodiamine	Simazine	Trifluralin

POSTEMERGENCE HERBICIDES

Bentazon	Bromoxynil	Clethodim	Fluazifop	Glyphosate	Halosulfuron	Pelargonic	Sethoxydim

GRASSES

GRASSES

Certain herbicides are not recommended for use in greenhouses, including atrazine, dichlobenil, oxyfluorfen, prometone, phenoxy acids (e.g., 2,4-D), and benzoic acids (e.g., dicamba and triclopyr). Check current labels for registrations and directions before using a herbicide. Susceptibility to herbicides depends on factors such as the weed species biotype and soil and environmental conditions. The ratings provided here are approximate. See Table 84 for the product or trade name of preemergence herbicides listed here. Adapted from Cudney n.d.

Table 83. Common Reasons for Inadequate Weed Control with Herbicides.

- Misidentification of weed species.
- Wrong choice of herbicide or adjuvant.
- Improper timing of application, such as targeting the wrong weed life stage or applying when weeds are not in a susceptible condition.
- Ineffective application techniques, such as inadequate coverage, poor placement or targeting, and improper equipment calibration.
- Incorrect application rates for the situation.
- Very high weed populations.
- Unfavorable environmental conditions, soil characteristics, or water quality.
- Off-season weed emergence.
- Tolerant or resistant weed species.
- Failure to use herbicides in combination with other methods as part of an integrated weed management program.

Table 84. Approximate Residual Persistence of Preemergence Herbicides.

Chemical name	Trade name	Persistence (months)[1]
benefin	Balan	1–4
bensulide	Betasan	8–10
DCPA	Dacthal	2–4
dichlobenil	Casoron	3–12
dithiopyr	Dimension	1–6
EPTC	Eptam	1–8
isoxaben	Gallery	1–4
metam sodium	Vapam	0.4–1
metolachlor	Pennant	0.2–1
napropamide	Devrinol	2–12
norflurazon	Predict	3–12
oryzalin	Surflan	6–10
oxadiazon	RegalStar, Ronstar	4–6
oxyfluorfen	Goal	1–4
pendimethalin	Pendulum, Pre-M	2–8
prodiamine	Barricade, Endurance, Factor	3–12
simazine	Princep	6–20
trifluralin	Treflan	3–12

1. Persistence is the length of time after application that herbicide residue may continue to provide preemergence weed control or remain phytotoxic to susceptible crops. Actual herbicide persistence varies according to factors such as application rate, chemical formulation, moisture, organic matter content, soil type, species of plant, and temperature.

emulsifiable concentrates, flowables, solutions, and wettable powders (which are mixed with water and sprayed). Most weed species are susceptible to several different herbicides (Table 82). However, as with other methods, even under optimum conditions herbicides rarely give 100% weed control (Table 83). For specific herbicide recommendations, consult the latest *UC IPM Pest Management Guidelines: Floriculture and Ornamental Nurseries*.

Preemergence herbicides. Preemergence herbicides are usually quite effective and relatively inexpensive. Although they must be applied before weed seeds germinate, they kill germinating seedlings for several weeks or months after application (Table 84). Preemergence herbicides are usually absorbed by roots and either kill the root growing point or are translocated to other plant parts where they disrupt growth processes.

Most preemergence herbicides are placed on the surface and watered in by sprinkler irrigation or rainfall. Certain herbicides must be mechanically worked into the soil to place them at the proper location to control weeds. Preemergence herbicides are applied to noncropped areas such as under or on top of mulch and to bare soil around growing areas. Certain preemergence herbicides can be applied on the surface of containers and planting beds after establishment of a tolerant crop species. Because preemergence herbicides generally do not kill established plants, they are relatively safe for application around established woody plants.

Each crop species may vary in its tolerance to herbicides. Potential phytotoxicity and many other factors must be considered when selecting a preemergence herbicide. Some preemergence herbicides can retard the root growth of established plants, especially nonrooted cuttings, young plants, and herbaceous species. The soil residue of certain herbicides can affect germination or transplants of certain crop species for several months to a year or more after application. Avoid these long-residual herbicides in herbaceous plantings with a short rotation. Because annual flower crops are frequently rotated, hand-weeding, mechanical cultivation, selective postemergence herbicides, or a combination of these methods is often used instead of preemergence herbicides.

Postemergence herbicides. Postemergence herbicides are applied to weeds that have emerged. Depending on the herbicide, postemergents either control weeds systemically or on contact. Contact postemergence herbicides usually kill only those green plant parts contacted by the herbicide. Thorough coverage is important for good control. Postemergence contact herbicides are most effective against small annual weeds.

Systemic or translocated herbicides can enter plants through the leaves or roots, or both. Most foliar-applied translocated herbicides are transported primarily to roots and shoot growing tips, so it may not be necessary to spray the entire plant to kill it. Translocated herbicides can control either annual or perennial weeds. Established perennial weeds generally require a systemic herbicide, often with repeated treatments, to ensure that their underground propagules are killed. For best control with systemic herbicides, perennial weeds should be growing vigorously and have an abundance of mature leaves when they are sprayed. Adequate soil moisture is critical to maximum translation. Depending on the season and stage of plant growth, the effect of some translocated herbicides may not be apparent until long after they are applied. For example, the effects of glyphosate may not be apparent until 2 or 3 weeks after application, especially during cool weather and against certain species of weeds.

Selectivity. Selective postemergence herbicides kill only certain types of plants and can be used around tolerant crop species, such as by applying them over the top of the crop or by some other method as directed on the product label. For example, clethodim (Envoy), fluazifop (Fusilade), or sethoxydim (Poast) can selectively control most annual grasses and bermudagrass without injury to most broadleaf crops.

Some herbicides are nonselective; they kill both weeds and desirable plants that are sprayed. For example, pelargonic acid and related fatty acids (Scythe) kill most young plants on contact. Nonselective postemergence herbicides are used primarily before planting or outside growing areas. Some of these nonselective herbicides can be applied under benches and along walkways in greenhouse. Avoid applying nonselective herbicides around crops unless contact with crop plants can positively be avoided. Certain formulations of some nonselective herbicides can be applied very carefully around crops by using special equipment such as a wick or wiper applicator or a properly directed low-pressure hooded or shielded sprayer.

Phytotoxicity. Herbicide injury to floral crops can result from misapplication of a herbicide or by using a herbicide that is not selective on a crop. Crops may be damaged by direct spraying, by herbicides that reach plants through drift, by roots picking up herbicide, or by herbicides volatilizing after application and moving in the air. Phenoxy herbicides such as 2,4-D can drift or volatilize after application and move relatively long distances, causing subtle to severe damage to broadleaf crops. If glyphosate drifts or is sprayed onto thin-barked roses during the dormant season, herbicide damage may not be visible until several months later when distorted new shoots and foliage are produced. Surface water or recycled water can contain herbicide residues that can damage a crop.

Certain preemergence herbicides and some selective postemergence herbicides can be applied around tolerant established crops. However, herbicide selectivity is affected by many factors, such as stage of growth and the plant's growing environment. Young plants and crops protected in greenhouses are often less tolerant to herbicides than more mature crops and plants grown outdoors. Carefully evaluate the potential for phytotoxicity before using herbicides around crops, especially when multiple crops of differing sensitivity are grown in close proximity. To avoid potential crop injury, know the weed spectrum, crop sensitivity, and herbicide selectivity for the various crops. Pay special attention to good application techniques and proper equipment calibration, nozzle selection, and operating pressure. Read

Control weeds before planting whenever possible. It can be difficult to use selective herbicides that are not phytotoxic to at least a few of the crops being grown when plants from different genera or families are grown together in small blocks or adjoining rows.

These puckered shoots and chlorotic leaves (right) were caused by glyphosate drift onto the rose's basal trunk. The effects of glyphosate may not be apparent until weeks after application. The cause of damage can be difficult to diagnose because the symptoms can be confused with those from other causes, such as viruses.

labels carefully before any application. Consult the phytotoxicity section in the chapter "Abiotic Disorders and Cultural Practices" for more information.

Herbicide-resistant weeds. Tolerance and resistance prevent some herbicides from controlling certain weeds. Tolerant plant species have a natural lack of susceptibility to certain herbicides (Table 82). Tolerance can be desirable because it allows development of selective herbicides, such as those that control either grasses or broadleaf weeds but not both types of plants. However, because of a lack of competition from susceptible species, repeated application of selective herbicides can allow tolerant weeds to increase unless other methods are used to control tolerant weeds.

Resistance occurs when a pest population is no longer controlled by pesticides that previously provided control (Fig. 12). It develops because individuals in a species vary in their susceptibility to pesticides. For example, repeated exposure of a weed population to the same herbicide or other herbicides with the same mode of action causes an increase in the number or proportion of plants with the biotypes resistant to that class of herbicides. With repeated selection pressure from herbicide reapplications, resistant biotypes will dominate the population. A different type of herbicide or other measures must be substituted to control that weed species. Take steps to avoid development of herbicide resistance, for example, by making sequential applications of herbicides that have a different mode of action (Fig. 65) and using other methods recommended by the Weed Science Society of America (Table 85).

Fumigation. Chemical fumigation, typically using methyl bromide, has been widely used to sterilize container mix and field soil because it provides rapid, broad-spectrum control of most soil-dwelling pests (Table 8). Fumigation is generally not warranted for weed control unless it is also needed to control pathogens. Fumigants can be highly toxic to people and require stringent safety measures. Fumigant use is increasingly restricted. Consider alternatives to fumigation whenever possible.

In addition to methyl bromide, dazomet (Basamid) and metam sodium (Vapam) are also used as broad-spectrum soil fumigants. In comparison with methyl bromide, these fumigants generally have a longer waiting period before planting the crop and are less effective in controlling certain weeds, in part because they are relatively ineffective against dormant seeds or seeds with impermeable seed coats. However, dormant seeds of certain weeds are not controlled by any soil fumigants. For example, methyl bromide generally does not kill seeds of field bindweed, malva, and many clovers.

Prior to chemically fumigating for weed control, keep container mix or field soil moist for 3 or 4 days. Preapplication moisture induces weed seeds to absorb water and begin to germinate, increasing weed susceptibility to soil fumigants. Recommendations on fumigation of growing media are discussed in the chapter "Diseases."

Weed Control Around Crop Plants

Cultivating, hand-weeding, mulching, and applying preemergence and selective postemergence herbicides are methods regularly used to control weeds where crop plants are growing. Cover crops and flaming can be employed in certain situations. Always use good exclusion, irrigation, and sanitation practices throughout the cropping cycle to minimize weed problems. If crops become severely infested with weeds and require intensive, ongoing control actions, the most efficient strategy over the long term may be to remove crops from the growing area and control weeds with steam, fumigation, solarization, herbicides, or a combination of methods.

Planting Adjustments

Establish a crop canopy that quickly shades soil and outcompetes weeds. Use transplants instead of direct seeding to give the crop a head start over weeds. To reduce the amount of empty growing space and prevent light from reaching the soil (where it can be used by weeds), plant crops uniformly, use rows on beds, space plants closely, and increase planting density. Plant in straight rows to allow closer cultivation. Plant at a uniform depth to induce even crop emergence; this allows well-timed weed control actions such as flaming or contact herbicides after planting but before crop emergence.

Table 85. Steps for Avoiding Herbicide Resistance.

- Scout growing areas before applying any herbicide to determine what weed species are present.
- Evaluate economics to determine whether herbicide application is justified by increased returns.
- Consider the use of alternatives, such as cultivation, mulches, or solarization.
- Rotate crops to avoid growing the same crop in the same location season after season.
- Limit herbicide application and minimize use of a single herbicide, or herbicides with the same site of action, during a growing season.
- Vary herbicides by using mixtures or make sequential applications of herbicides that have different modes of action.
- Scout growing areas after applying herbicides and note weed escapees or species shifts.
- Avoid spreading weed seeds from infested areas, for example, by controlling runoff water and cleaning equipment before moving to another site.

Adapted from Retzinger and Mallory-Smith 1997.

Once established, a well-maintained, densely planted crop excludes most annual weeds by outcompeting them for light, as shown with this gypsophila.

Planting time adjustments can minimize certain weed problems. Planting during good growing conditions, such as at the correct air and soil temperature and soil moisture, facilitates rapid crop germination and growth. Delayed planting may allow use of methods such as solarization or irrigation followed by shallow cultivation. Planting after the seasonal emergence of key annual weeds allows use of non-selective controls to reduce weeds.

Irrigation Management

Proper irrigation management can help control weeds. Prevent weed seed contamination by installing and maintaining filters or treating recycled and surface irrigation water. Eliminate seed-producing weeds near irrigation ditches and other surface water sources if this is feasible. Certain weeds such as algae, annual bluegrass, dallisgrass, liverworts, moss, and nutsedges thrive under excessively damp conditions. Avoid excess irrigation by reducing irrigation amount, frequency, or both to the extent compatible with good crop growth. Keeping the soil surface moist favors germination and establishment of annual bluegrass, common groundsel, lesser seeded bittercress, and oxalis, and frequent, shallow irrigation is usually not necessary after crop establishment. Prevent standing water, provide good drainage, and maintain irrigation systems to eliminate leaks. Group crops by water need to improve irrigation efficiency, facilitate weed control, and improve crop growth.

Instead of irrigating overhead, use subsurface irrigation where feasible. Subsurface irrigation keeps the top of media dry, reducing germination of windblown seeds. Subsurface irrigation combined with mulching container surfaces can be especially effective in preventing weed growth. Subsurface irrigation reduces or eliminates irrigation water runoff and herbicide leaching.

Herbicide and irrigation coordination. Irrigation practices influence herbicide efficacy, leaching, and runoff. For example, frequent light irrigation when temperatures are warm increases the herbicide degradation rate, reducing the persistence of preemergence herbicides. Chose chemicals carefully, adjust herbicide application frequency and rates, and use good water management practices to minimize irrigation-related herbicide problems.

Poor water quality (such as high pH or dissolved organic compounds) can reduce herbicide performance. Before using water to apply herbicides, modify water quality if needed, or use suitable water from an alternative source.

Herbicide leaching and runoff. Leaching is herbicide movement in water through soil or other growing media, including downward movement into the soil profile that can cause herbicides to contaminate groundwater. Runoff is movement of water over the soil surface away from the application location. Excess irrigation increases the likelihood that her-

Light is reflecting from standing water on the weed control plastic under this bench. Algae cover the aisles, indicating walkways are frequently damp. Better irrigation management, improving drainage under benches, and applying a water-permeable geotextile or gravel barrier will eliminate standing water, reducing humidity and eliminating habitat for certain pests such as fungus gnats.

bicide will move off-site in eroded soil, runoff water, or leachate. During the first irrigation after herbicide application, apply only enough water, about ½ inch (12 mm), to move herbicide into growing media, thereby minimizing herbicide erosion, leaching, and runoff. Consider planting turfgrass borders, filter strips, or buffer strips around production areas, especially on slopes, to help reduce off-site movement of soil and herbicide. Space containers more closely together to reduce the amount of overhead water that misses containers. Minimize the amount of water applied and use pulsed irrigations (several short waterings versus one long irrigation) to reduce herbicide leaching and runoff. Check and maintain the irrigation system output rate and uniformity and use subirrigation, drip irrigation, or microsprinklers instead of overhead irrigation whenever possible to help reduce herbicide movement in water or on soil.

Recycled water can pose a risk of damaging crops by reapplying herbicide that leached into irrigation water. In container-grown plants, consider avoiding the use of herbicides that have a low adsorption onto soil, a K_{OC} of less than 500 (see Fig. 66), and a moderate to high water solubility, greater than about 5 to 7 mg/l. These herbicides with relatively low adsorption and high solubility pose the highest risk of leaching.

Mulch

Mulch is any material applied to cover the soil. Mulches can be living or dead cover crops, inorganics such as gravel, organic materials such as bark or compost, or synthetics such as plastics. Mulch prevents the establishment of most annual and certain perennial weeds by limiting the light available for seed germination and growth. A synthetic mulch also forms a physical barrier that blocks seeds on the surface from

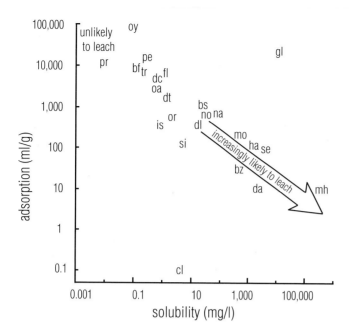

KEY:

bf	benefin	mh	metam sodium
bs	bensulide	mo	metolachlor
bz	bentazon	na	napropamide
cl	clethodim	no	norflurazon
da	dazomet	or	oryzalin
dc	DCPA	oa	oxadiazon
dl	dichlobenil	oy	oxyfluorfen
dt	dithiopyr	pe	pendimethalin
fl	fluazifop	pr	prodiamine
gl	glyphosate	se	sethoxydim
ha	halosulfuron	si	simazine
is	isoxaben	tr	trifluralin

Figure 66. Approximate likelihood of herbicide leaching, as measured by plotting herbicide water solubility against soil adsorption potential on a logarithmic scale. The actual risk of leaching is also influenced by other factors, including irrigation or rainfall, soil type, and herbicide persistence. Solubility is at 68° to 77°F (20° to 25°C) and pH 7 measured in milligrams of herbicide active ingredient per liter of water (mg/l), units that are equivalent to parts per million (ppm). Adsorption is given as the soil organic carbon distribution or partition coefficient (K_{oc}) in ml/g. K_{oc} is a standard measure of adsorption, calculated as the ratio of sorbed pesticide to dissolved pesticide divided by the weight fraction of organic carbon present in soil. Adapted from Ahrens 1994.

Table 86. Effectiveness of Some Synthetic Mulches in Preventing Weed Emergence.

Weed barrier fabric		Number of shoots emerging through weed barrier after 30 days			
Product name	Polypropylene type	Yellow nutsedge	Pigweed	Johnsongrass	Bermudagrass
DuPont Typar 307	nonwoven, spun-bound	0.0	0.0	0.0	2.5
DuPont Typar 312	nonwoven, spun-bound	0.0	0.3	0.0	0.8
Weed Barrier Mat	woven	0.3	0.0	0.3	0.0
DeWitt Pro 5	woven	1.0	0.5	2.3	1.5
Geoscape Landscape Fabric	nonwoven, meshed	0.8	0.0	0.3	9.3
Amoco Rit-a-Weed	nonwoven, meshed	2.5	8.3	7.0	17.5
Phillips Duon Fiber	nonwoven, meshed	3.3	7.8	6.5	12.0
Weedblock Fabric	nonwoven, perforated	1.8	20.3	8.0	72.6
untreated		8.3	48.8	12.8	112.8

Weed seeds (0.3 tbl of seed per one-half flat) or nutsedge tubers (15 tubers per one-half flat) were planted in flats, covered with fabric, and irrigated to keep media moist. All fabrics completely suppressed emergence of sicklepod (*Cassia obtusifolia*) and small flower morningglory (*Jacquemontia tamnifolia*) seedlings. *Source:* Martin, Ponder, and Gilliam 1991.

growing roots down into media, and it also blocks weeds underneath the mulch from growing shoots (Table 86). In containers, a layer of organic mulch can stay drier than the potting mix surface, reducing germination and establishment of windblown seeds. This drier surface is especially pronounced with subsurface irrigation, but it also occurs in mulched containers with surface irrigation.

Mulch provides many cultural and environmental benefits in addition to controlling weeds. However, some of the effects of mulch can be undesirable, for example, too much organic mulch may lower soil temperature, delaying germination. Consider the particular characteristics of each material when selecting and managing mulch. Evaluate the prevailing site conditions (such as moisture, temperature, and reflected light) in comparison with the optimal conditions needed for that crop and select a mulch that improves those conditions in addition to controlling weeds.

Organic mulches usually lower soil temperatures, which can delay crop maturity by several days. Plastic mulch (except white plastic) generally increases soil temperature, which may shorten crop time to maturity. Clear plastic increases soil temperature more than black or other colored plastics. Gray, silver, and white reflective mulches delay colonization of young field-grown plants by certain insects. This repelling of insects is especially effective in reducing disease from insect-vectored viruses (see the chapter "Diseases").

Mulch conserves water by reducing evaporation from the soil surface. Mulching may require modification of the amount, frequency, and methods of irrigation to allow applied water to reach plant roots or to avoid excessively moist conditions in the rooting zone. Crops such as China aster and snapdragon do not tolerate fine organic mulch close to their stems, possibly because excess moisture promotes root and crown diseases. However, delphinium and Dutch iris grow more vigorously in organically mulched beds, possibly because of reduced root temperatures in warmer climates.

Bark, wood, and foliage mulches contain naturally occurring compounds, some of which (allelochemicals) may be harmful to young plants. Certain fresh organic mulches or degradation products from these are most likely to have phytotoxic allelochemicals. Avoid any potential phytotoxicity by composting the material or leaching it with several inches of water before use. When applied around containers or established plants, allelochemicals in mulch can be beneficial if they enhance weed control by inhibiting weed seed germination. This allelochemical weed control affect is largely undocumented and would not provide long-term control, in part because allelochemicals decompose and are leached away after several irrigations.

Synthetic fabric mulches. Synthetic mulches made from plastics are widely used as weed block mulches. Synthetic mulch can be very effective in annual or perennial crops when applied to bare soil around established plants, when transplants are placed into the soil through holes in the mulch, or when mulch is used on aisles or beneath containers and benches. Synthetic mulches are often covered with gravel or another mulch, either inorganic or organic. Covering the fabric protects it from degradation by UV light, holds the material down when conditions are windy, reduces tearing, covers a potentially slippery surface that can be hazardous, and improves aesthetics in locations where appearance is important.

Traditional black or clear polyethylene plastic mulches are increasingly being replaced with specially designed polypropylene or polyester geotextiles, also called landscape fabrics or weed barriers. A major advantage of these geotextiles is that most have some porosity that allows passage of air and water. To avoid excess humidity, shore flies, and growth of algae and moss, especially in greenhouses, use perforated polyethylene or water-permeable geotextiles that allow drainage.

Commercial geotextitles vary significantly in cost, performance, and special features. Depending on the product, some plastic mulches are impregnated with herbicide, incorporate compounds that resist degradation by UV light, or are designed to slowly decompose when exposed to light. Biodegradable plastics may avoid disposal problems. However, biodegradation has been inconsistent; decomposition greatly reduces the length of time products are effective in controlling weeds, and buried plastic remains in soil until it is brought to the surface and exposed to sunlight. Many geotextiles are currently not recyclable because of the type of plastic and presence of soil contamination. These plastics generally are disposed of in landfills.

Weeds outside this greenhouse are controlled in part by landscape fabric covering the embankment and a densely planted conifer hedgerow that shades soil and provides a barrier to windblown seeds.

Plastic mulch applied on planting beds can control weeds. This mulch also enhances crop growth by conserving moisture. Certain reflective mulches repel aphids, whiteflies, and some other insects during early stages of crop growth.

A special geotextile disk in the container on the left has prevented weed growth seen in the uncovered container on the right. Although their use is initially more expensive than other mulches, they can work well in drip-irrigated perennials.

Protecting plastic from degradation by UV light (either by covering it or using a product that incorporates UV protection chemicals, or both) greatly increases the life span of the mulch. Light-proof fabrics reduce the growth of weeds beneath the plastic better than clear, lightly colored, or thin plastics that allow passage of some light. Thicker fabrics are often more durable and better able to exclude all light. The method of manufacture also appears to affect fabric effectiveness. One study of polypropylene geotextiles found that woven fabrics and nonwoven spun-bound products generally prevented weed penetration better than most nonwoven meshed or nonwoven perforated fabrics (Table 86).

Before applying plastic mulch, improve soil drainage if necessary so that water will not puddle on the surface. Install any required subsurface infrastructure (such as irrigation pipes or utility conduits) and equipment that must penetrate the soil surface (such as roof support posts or the legs of permanent benches). As described in the section on solarization earlier in this chapter, apply plastic only to relatively flat, smooth surfaces free of debris and emerged weeds. Use care during application to protect the geotextile from tears or punctures. Keep workers and equipment off the plastic surface until it has been covered with an approximately 1-inch-thick (2.5-cm-thick) layer of gravel or another material that protects the plastic's surface.

Weeds will grow in soil that accumulates on top of fabric. Exclude windblown soil, avoid tracking in dirt, and prevent spilling of container mix. Prevent runoff water drainage into growing areas. Depending on the growing situation and the weed species present, other methods such as hand-weeding or herbicides may be necessary in combination with geotextiles to completely control all weeds.

Geotextile barrier disks. Geotextile disks can be placed on the potting mix surface to control weeds in containers. The disks are precut to fit the size of the container and have a slit to fit around the plant. Suppliers provide disks in several different sizes. The fabric's pliability allows some adjustment of disks to cover surfaces despite small variations in diameter among containers. Some disks are treated with herbicide to prevent surface rooting and weed seed germination. One study found that commercially available fabric disks treated with copper hydroxide controlled broadleaf weeds (common groundsel, creeping woodsorrel, and northern willow herb) in 5-gallon containers for at least 6 months in the nursery. Disks can last up to three years, so they may provide long-term control in container perennials or can be reused with subsequent annual crops.

Disadvantages include the labor required to apply container disks, and disks exposed to direct light can increase the temperature of media, affecting root health. This container heating may be undesirable in warm growing areas but could have a beneficial effect on container plants growing in cool areas. With overhead sprinkler irrigation, windblown seeds can germinate if they are washed into the fabric slit or edge that is not well-covered. Irrigating overhead can wash or float media onto the fabric and move seeds to the edges and center hole, allowing some weed growth. Disk barriers work best in drip-irrigated or subirrigated containers.

Organic mulches. Bark, compost, nut shells, sawdust, and straw are among the materials growers use as organic mulches. Organic mulch can be applied between and within rows of field-grown annuals or perennials, on top of container media, and on bare soil between containers. Carefully select materials, as some organics can be contaminated with seeds or other propagules of weeds. Certain organic mulches can be undesirably high in soluble salts unless they have been leached with several inches of water. Organic mulch can also increase populations of certain soil-dwelling pests, including earwigs, mice, slugs, and sowbugs. Although organic mulch initially prevents weed growth, it gradually breaks down and can become a substrate that promotes growth of windblown seeds. To provide long-term control, periodically cover mulch with additional mulch or stir or lightly cultivate mulch to dry it out and uproot weeds soon after weed seedlings emerge. In many situations, mulch composed of fine particles (such as well-composted, finished greenwaste) provides good weed control when applied as a layer about 2 to 3 inches (5–7.5 cm) thick. Bark chips and other coarse mulch particles generally are most effective when applied about 3 to 6 inches (7.5–15 cm) thick.

When mulch is applied to field-grown crops, decomposition is desirable if the mulch becomes incorporated during cultivation after harvest or before replanting. If mulch is worked into the soil before planting, the decomposing mulch will deplete soil nitrogen levels and temporarily retard crop growth unless nitrogen is also added to the soil. To avoid crop emergence problems in mulched fields, use transplants or plant transplants or seeds into a mulch-free strip on top of the planting row. Alternative labor-intensive methods are to plant seeds or transplants in planting tubes or sleeves that keep mulch away from the seedling's stem; or to cover transplants with inverted cups, apply mulch, then remove the cups, leaving a small mulch-free area around each seedling.

A layer ⅛ to 1½ inches (3–37 mm) thick of organic mulch such as pine bark, fir bark, or pecan shells covering the bare surface of containers can control broadleaf weeds such as common groundsel, creeping woodsorrel, and willow herb for at least 6 months as long as new weed seeds are not deposited onto the surface. Mulching containers is effective with subirrigation or top-irrigation. Subirrigating mulched containers can provide the best weed control. When using mulch and subirrigation in combination, regularly monitor moisture levels in the root zone and adjust irrigations as needed to prevent excessively wet conditions. In comparison with subirrigation, mulch depth and particle size are more critical when using top-irrigation. Mulch particles must be large enough to allow water to penetrate and surfaces to dry between irrigations, yet small enough to exclude light and prevent windblown seeds from falling into crevices between particles. If particles are too small, they may be moved by the wind, exposing bare surfaces that provide substrate for weed growth.

Cover Crops

Cover crops, also called smother crops or living mulches, are plants grown not for harvest but to provide other benefits such as suppressing weeds (Table 87). Cover crops prevent weed growth by covering the soil surface to exclude light and by outcompeting the weeds for water and nutrients. Cover crops in floriculture and nursery crops are primarily grown in nonproduction areas bordering crops, in fallow fields, and in rotation with the production crop.

In most of California cover crops can be grown any time of year when fields are unplanted for about 2 months or longer. They are usually grown during the winter in rotation with transplanted summer annual floral crops. Winter cover crops require little irrigation, and if fallow fields are left unmanaged they are prone to erosion, nutrient leaching, and extensive weed growth. Winter annual cover crops can be planted in late summer to fall and grown through the winter. In the spring, winter annual cover crops are typically killed or suppressed by mowing or sometimes by applying herbicides. Cover crops are often incorporated into the soil, but weed control benefits occur mostly during the fallow season if the cover crop is incorporated before planting the floral crop. If nitrogen-fixing leguminous cover crops are cultivated into the soil, they make about 50 to 150 pounds per acre (56–168 kg/ha) of nitrogen available to the subsequent crop.

A winter cover crop can be incorporated into the soil only along the planting strip if the cover crop is not likely to compete with the summer floral crop or cause management

Redwood bark chips covering the surface of this drip-irrigated container plant are an effective and attractive method of weed control.

CHERYL A. WILEN

The rice hulls covering these iris beds help control weeds and conserve moisture. A fine organic mulch such as this can be incorporated before replanting beds, improving soil organic matter content.

Table 87. Potential Advantages and Disadvantages of Cover Crops.

Advantages
- Effective weed control.
- Improved water penetration.
- Better traction for equipment.
- Increased populations of beneficial insects.
- Addition of organic matter and possibly nitrogen to soil.
- Reduced erosion.
- Reduced off-site movement of nutrients, herbicides, and other pesticides that might contaminate runoff water and silt.

Disadvantages
- Depletion of soil moisture with summer annual cover crops.
- Increased frost hazard when intercropped with production crops, especially with tree and vine crops.
- Increased populations of certain insect pests, such as armyworms, cutworms, and lygus bugs.
- Creates weed problems if the cover crop produces seed, competes with the production crop, or does not outcompete weeds.
- Temporary soil nitrogen depletion if incorporated into the soil, except with legumes.
- Increased management costs, which may be outweighed by the benefits.

problems such as producing seed. Cover crop residue can be removed from a strip along the seedling row, but this increases labor costs and eliminates weed suppression closest to young plants where it is needed the most. The summer flower crop can be transplanted in spring through the residue of a dead or dying cover crop that provides some weed control. Crops can also be direct-seeded through the cover crop residue, but seedling establishment may be relatively poor when direct-seeding through the denser crop residues that provide better weed control. Many mechanical planters are unable to penetrate a thick mulch, and transplanting equipment may need to be modified to penetrate it.

Manage cover crops to prevent potential problems and to avoid crop yield loss from competition (Table 88). Control cover crops before they flower and prevent them from producing seeds that become weeds in subsequent crops. To reduce their chance of becoming weeds, use cover crop species that produce little or no hard seed, such as bell or faba bean (*Vicia faba*), common vetch (*Vicia sativa*), field pea (*Pisum sativum*), and cereal grains.

Work with someone knowledgeable about your situation to help select cover crops. Cover crop selection depends on many factors, including soil type, environmental conditions, and the production crop to be grown. Most cover crops are either legumes or grasses. Cover crop mixes are often used partly because a single species cannot be expected to grow well every year. Winter annual cover crops include crimson, rose, and subterranean clovers (*Trifolium* spp.), medics (*Medicago* spp.), and vetches (*Vicia* spp.). Bur medic or bur clover (*Medicago polymorpha*) and *Trifolium* spp. clovers are often grown mixed together. Fall-planted oats (*Avena sativa*) or cereal rye, (*Secale cereale*), sometimes mixed with vetch, can also be good winter cover crops. These cereal grains can provide better weed control because they are more competitive than clovers and medics. However, grains do not fix nitrogen. Turfgrass (*Festuca* spp. and others) and summer annual grains such as sorghum or sudangrass (*Sorghum* spp.) can be good cover crops in areas bordering flower and nursery crops.

Before selecting a cover crop, consult crop host lists to identify what pests attack production crops and potential cover crops. Avoid cover crop species that host important

pests of both crops. Information sources on potential pests include the cover crops database at the UC SAREP World Wide Web site at www.sarep.ucdavis.edu/ccrop, the UC Davis nematology database at http://ucdnema.ucdavis.edu, and pest management manuals and crop production guides for clovers, grains, and turfgrass listed in the suggested reading section at the end of this book. Also consult *Cover Cropping in Vineyards* (Ingels et al. 1998), *Covercrops for California Agriculture* (Miller et al. 1989), and *Managing Cover Crops Profitably* (Bowman, Shirley, and Cramer 1998) for more information.

Hand-Weeding

Hand-pulling and manual hoeing of weeds are effective, widely used methods of weed control that have many advantages (Table 89). These hand-weeding techniques are usually used in combination with other practices. Hand-weeding may be the best option once weeds grow among nursery and greenhouse crops or when infested container plants are about to be shipped or moved into weed-free production areas. If only a few weeds are present, prompt hand-weeding may be the most efficient and economical control method. Direct each employee to pull scattered weeds when they see them. If crops are heavily infested or a high degree of weed control is needed, use close cultivation, herbicides, or other methods to lower weed populations followed by hand-weeding to increase control effectiveness and reduce the costs of hand-weeding (Table 90). Always remove weeds before flowering to prevent seed production.

Table 88. Methods to Minimize Competition Between Flower or Nursery Crops and Cover Crops.

- Grow cover crops in nonproduction areas, such as borders around growing areas and locations upwind of crops that otherwise would be a source of windblown seeds.
- Plant selectively, such as by cover cropping only in otherwise empty rows between the harvested crop.
- Select appropriate species, such as annual cover crops that die when the harvested crop starts growing and are not alternate hosts of important pests.
- Manage cover crops using timed irrigation, mowing, cultivation, selective herbicides, or a combination of methods that complement the IPM program.

Table 89. Advantages and Disadvantages of Hand-Hoeing and Hand-Pulling Weeds.

Advantages

- Provides versatile and selective weed control in situations where no other method is effective.
- Reduces losses due to weed competition.
- Prevents weed seed production, reducing future weed densities.
- Avoids creating herbicide-resistant weeds and controls herbicide-tolerant or resistant species.
- Creates a more attractive, less weedy crop.

Disadvantages

- Causes some damage to crop roots.
- Loss of some crop plants will occur.
- Effectiveness varies depending on the situation and the labor used.
- Often costs more than most other weed control practices.

Adapted from Dexter 1996.

Table 90. How to Estimate the Cost of Hand-Weeding or Thinning.

- Select a representative area of the crop, such as one-half of a field row or a specific number of square feet of growing area.
- Time how long it takes to hand-pull or hoe the weeds in that area.
- Include enough time to walk through the area and look for weeds.
- Multiply the time required to weed, walk, and look over the representative area by the total number of similar areas that need to be weeded.
- Multiply the total hours times the hourly cost of labor.

Common groundsel growing at the end of this row of snapdragon is an obvious candidate for hand-weeding. Unfortunately, the weed has been allowed to mature. Common groundsel's fluffy white heads produce seeds that are readily dispersed throughout the growing area by wind or fans.

The most feasible control method in many situations is hand-pulling weeds, such as this young prickly lettuce infesting a miniature rose container.

This shuffle or scuffle hoe is useful for controlling scattered weeds such as this common groundsel growing beneath a nursery bench.

A combination of hand-hoeing within rows and mechanical tilling between rows can efficiently control weeds in some field-grown crops.

Hand-pulling. The goal of hand-pulling is to pull up weed roots. Removing the aboveground part temporarily improves crop aesthetics, but established weeds often develop new shoots from the parts remaining underground. Irrigate the soil the day before hand-pulling to make it easier to remove roots. Instruct workers to grasp weeds firmly near their base, rock weeds back and forth several times to loosen roots, then steadily pull (don't jerk) weeds upwards. Place weeds into covered containers and dispose of them away from crops to remove any insects they contain, to prevent discarded weeds from rerooting in growing areas, and to eliminate any seeds.

Hoeing. Kill small weeds by hand-hoeing with tools that chop, cut, or scrape weeds. Hoe when weeds and the crop are young, the soil surface is relatively dry, and no rain is expected and no irrigation is planned for at least several days after hoeing. Plan to delay irrigation for at least 1 day after hoeing weeds. Leave weed roots and shoots to dry in the open area between rows unless conditions are expected to be wet. If the soil surface is moist, it is best to rake up weeds after hoeing to prevent them from rerooting and establishing new plants. Young broadleaf weeds are easily controlled by cutting them at the soil surface. Grasses often have their growing point just beneath the soil surface. Before hoeing grasses, hand-pull several of them and determine the depth of their crown (the point where roots and stems meet). Cut weeds at or just below their crown, which is often about ¼ inch (0.6 cm) below the surface.

Explain to workers that the goal of hoeing is to chop out or cut weed roots at or just below the soil surface. When using a hoe, chop no deeper than about 1 inch (25 mm) using a sharp blade, while minimizing soil disturbance. Scuffle hoes, also called shuffle or hula hoes, are used by scraping back and forth using a push-pull motion on the surface of dry soil to cut weeds off at their basal stem. Hoeing at the soil surface or no deeper than about 1 inch (25 mm) reduces the likelihood of injuring crop roots, minimizes damage to any protective layer of preemergence herbicide, and limits exposing new weed seeds to the surface for germination.

Evaluating hand-weeding and thinning. Hand-weeding is very effective. However, as with any other single control method, it is difficult to obtain optimal crop density and total elimination of weeds. A suggested evaluation criteria is that not over 1% of the original weeds should survive after a single hand-weeding. Skilled labor may do better than this with low weed densities in a small crop, or with low densities of weeds that have become taller than the crop canopy. A higher percentage of weeds will be missed with high weed populations, larger or denser crop plants, or weeds that resemble the crop. Growers may not be able to afford the labor cost of hand-weeding close to crop plants. Weeds very close to the crop stem probably cannot be hoed or pulled without damaging or removing the crop plant. This distance depends on soil conditions and the relative size and species of crops and weeds. Hand labor cannot be expected to remove dense weed populations and weeds close to the crop without a detrimental effect on the crop.

Evaluating the quality and relative value of hand-weeding can be complicated. Table 91 summarizes some reasons why hand-weeding may not meet grower expectations. Table 92 provides suggestions for reducing disputes that may arise between growers and hand laborers regarding the relative quality of the work performed and the fair price for work.

Cultivation

Cultivation kills weeds by burying, cutting, or scraping them. Tilling or cultivation are used in the field before planting, outside planting areas, and between crop rows.

Table 91. Reasons Why Hand-Weeding Results May Not Meet the Grower's Expectations.

- The production crop was less dense or of poorer quality than desired before weeding.
- Hand labor cannot find and remove 100% of the weeds in a field in a single operation.
- Hand removal of weeds results in some removal or injury of crop plants. Hand-weeding a field with a dense weed population can result in some crop damage.
- Some weeds may emerge after the weeding is done.
- Certain weed species are more difficult to control than others.
- Established perennial weeds regrow after top growth is removed.

Adapted partly from Dexter 1996.

Cultivation is most effective on annual weeds and seedlings (Table 93). Seedlings of certain perennials, such as johnsongrass and yellow nutsedge, can also be controlled if cultivation is properly timed or repeated, but only when no crop is present and the soil is dry. Cultivate when weeds and crops are small, because young weeds are more easily killed and late-season cultivation can disturb crop roots, reducing yields. Use shallow tilling and avoid deep plowing. Many seeds left near the soil surface are decomposed by microorganisms or eaten by birds, insects, and rodents. Buried seeds can remain viable for many years. As part of the soil seed bank, many of these weed seeds may eventually resurface and germinate. If the growing

Table 92. Suggestions for Reducing Disputes Between Growers and Hand-Weeding Laborers.

- Establish a block of weeded and thinned crop as an example before the labor starts work.
- Count crop and weed populations in the field before and after the hand-weeding or hand-thinning.
- Leave a small unweeded, unthinned check area for comparison.
- Make clear the expectations on final crop and final weed population before the labor begins.
- Have reasonable expectations after considering the starting weed and crop populations and the labor wages.

Adapted from Dexter 1996.

Table 93. Approximate Effectiveness of Cultivation or Mowing in Controlling Some Weed Species.

Common name	Effectiveness of method	
	Cultivation	Mowing
bermudagrass	good to fair	poor
bindweed, field	fair to poor	poor
bluegrass, annual	good	fair to poor
clover	good	poor
crabgrass	good	fair to poor
cudweed	good	poor
dock, curly	fair	poor
fieldcress, creeping	poor	poor
filaree	good	poor
groundsel, common	good	poor
knotweed	fair	poor
lettuce, prickly	good	fair
nutsedges	fair to poor	poor
oat, wild	good	fair
plantain	good	poor
ryegrass, annual	good	fair
sowthistle, annual	good	fair
willow herbs	good	poor

Control effectiveness is the approximate percentage of weeds that will be killed or prevented from setting seed by well-timed cultivation or mowing: good = 80–90%, fair = 60–79%, poor = <60%. Adapted from Molinar n.d.

area is infested with established perennial weeds, use other methods such as herbicides to control perennials before cultivating the soil. Cultivating perennials can spread their tubers or rhizomes to uninfested soils, causing new infestations.

Many weeds germinate during a certain time of the year and only under specific environmental conditions. Delaying planting and cultivating until after these weeds emerge helps deplete the weed seed bank and improves crop establishment. Cultivation between rows during early crop growth reduces weed competition until the crop canopy grows enough to shade out later-emerging weeds.

Row crop precision cultivators include various bed knives, rotary tiller cultivators, shield and spring tooth gangs, and cultivator knives. Because precision cultivation and herbicides usually do not eliminate all weeds, close cultivation in high-value flower crops is often followed by hand-weeding.

Weed Control Outside Growing Areas

Weeds growing upwind or adjacent to flower and nursery crops are an important source of weed contamination. Control weeds in these areas to eliminate weed seeds, diseases, and insect pests that can be carried into growing areas by equipment, people, water, and wind. Nearby perennial weeds may also able to grow underground into growing areas. Control weeds in nonproduction areas by mowing closely, cultivating, applying herbicides, mulching, managing turf or other cover crops to competitively exclude weeds, or with a combination of methods. Use fences, hedgerows, and screens to exclude or trap windblown weed seeds. Also work with neighbors, for example, by encouraging them to control weeds on their property and offering to help clean up surrounding weedy areas if they are a problem near your crops.

A vegetation-free border at least 6 feet (2 m) wide is often recommended around greenhouses and nurseries. Bare soil border areas can be covered with geotextile and a layer of gravel or other inorganic mulch, treated with preemergence herbicides, or both. Regularly remove any escaped weeds by hand-weeding, or use a postemergence herbicide if border areas can be efficiently sprayed without risk of phytotoxicity to nearby crops. Take care when using herbicides adjacent to greenhouses and other growing areas. Tightly close greenhouses before application, prevent drift, and chose equipment and herbicides carefully, for example, by avoiding herbicides that are likely to volatilize and move after application.

Mowing

Mow grass or weedy areas near fields throughout the growing season. Mow weeds closely and regularly prior to flowering to prevent seed head formation. Cultivation and mowing generally are more effective on annual weeds than perennial species (Table 93), but proper timing of cultivation or mowing can also suppress some perennials, such as johnsongrass.

Weed species that have flower heads below the level of the blade are not effectively controlled by mowing. Repeated mowing over several years or seasons without using other methods of weed control often favors the establishment of perennial low-growing grasses, which are very competitive for water and nutrients. Regular mowing of a well-selected and maintained turf provides effective weed control, as discussed in the cover crops section earlier in this chapter.

Screens and Hedgerows

Prevent waterborne or windblown seeds from entering irrigation systems and growing areas. Install and properly maintain weed seed barriers, such as fences or hedgerows bordering fields and nurseries, and filters on irrigation water intakes. Exclude windblown seeds by using floating row covers for field crops and screens for greenhouse openings.

Plastic or mesh screen fences with a grid size small enough to exclude windblown weed seeds can be placed just outside crop rows and nurseries on the sides of prevailing wind. Hedgerows or border crops of tall perennials (often flowering ornamentals) are planted by some growers to function as windbreaks to trap weed seeds. Hedges are aesthetically pleasing and also serve as visual barriers and living screens to reduce potential conflicts with neighbors concerned about dust, noise, and pesticide drift. Some growers are experimenting with border crops of insectary plants that can provide natural enemies with food and shelter and increase their fecundity, longevity, and ability to locate and kill pests. Avoid insectary plants or other nearby plantings that may be reservoirs of viruses or alternate hosts of other pests that can damage your crops. Consult publications such as *Pests of Landscape Trees and Shrubs* (Dreistadt 1994), *Insects that Feed on Trees and Shrubs* (Johnson and Lyon 1988), and *Diseases of Trees and Shrubs* (Sinclair, Lyon, and Johnson 1987) and compare that information to the chapter "Crop Tables" to identify alternate hosts of your pests.

Biological Control

Biological control uses predators, parasites, pathogens, and competitors to control pests. As discussed in the chapters "Insects, Mites, and Other Invertebrates" and "Diseases," these natural enemies can be very helpful. However, in cultivated areas where crops and organisms are frequently disturbed, biological control has had little impact on weed control.

Properly composting organic debris to kill weed seeds with heat generated by microorganisms could be considered a type of biological weed control. Biological control includes seed predators and pathogens that, in combination with shallow tilling or leaving seeds on the soil surface, can reduce weed seed survival. Instead of deep plowing, which buries seeds where they can survive for many years, leave seeds near the surface where they are more readily eaten by birds, insects, and rodents or are

Two introduced weevils (*Microlarinus* spp.) provide complete biological control of puncturevine in Hawaii and partial control in some areas of California. Weevil presence can be recognized by feeding scars (lighter patches on the stem and brownish areas on the green seed capsule) or by larvae, pupae, or frass in plant crowns, stems, or seed capsules (it may be necessary to dissect the plants to find these). An adult weevil emerged from the hole in this stem after feeding inside.

decomposed by microorganisms. Weeder geese are used in some field crops and nurseries because they eat grasses but leave almost all broadleaf crops alone. However, geese require intensive management, which makes them expensive and limits their use primarily to small-scale or organic farms.

Biological weed control has been most successful for specific problem weeds in uncultivated areas such as roadsides and rangelands. For example, two introduced *Microlarinus* species weevils help control puncturevine (*Tribulus terrestris*). This weed's spiny seed capsules injure people and puncture tires. The small grayish to brown weevils mine puncturevine seeds and stems, reducing weed reproduction and eventually killing the plants, retarding this weed's spread into growing areas. Increase the effectiveness of puncturevine biological control by avoiding application of broad-spectrum persistent insecticides around puncturevine. Prevent irrigation water from running off onto areas infested with puncturevine because the weevils provide much better control of puncturevine if the weeds are not irrigated. For more discussion of biological control, consult *Natural Enemies Handbook* (Flint and Dreistadt 1998).

Types of Weeds

Weeds are classified according to plant type (broadleaf, grass, or sedge) and life cycle (annual, biennial, or perennial). Flowers are used to definitively identify the species of plants. Because weeds should be controlled before they flower, the shape and arrangement of vegetative plant parts such as leaves, stems, and veins are among the key characteristics used to identify different types of weeds (Fig. 67).

Most broadleaf weeds have showy flowers and netlike veins in their leaves. Grasses and sedges resemble each other, but they are very different. Grass leaves have parallel veins

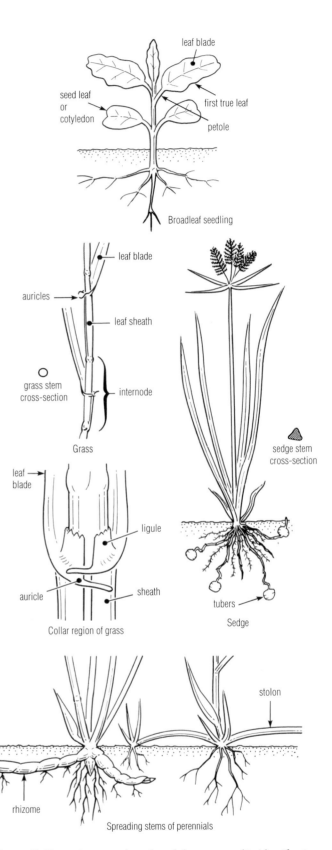

Figure 67. Vegetative parts of weeds and the terms used in identification. Note that not all sedges have tubers (sometimes called nutlets). For the most effective control, the species should be identified and control action taken before weeds mature beyond the seedling stage.

that are longer than they are wide, and the leaves alternate on each side of the stem; sedge leaves are joined to the stem in groups of three. Grass stems are hollow, rounded, and have nodes (joints) that are hard and closed; sedges have a solid stem that is triangular in cross-section.

This section describes and illustrates selected weeds common in California flower and nursery crops. Consult the other resources listed in the suggested reading for more detailed information, especially *Weeds of the West* (Whiston et al. 1991), *Grower's Weed Identification Handbook* (UC DANR 1998), and *The Jepson Manual of Higher Plants of California* (Hickman 1993).

ANNUAL WEEDS

Annual weeds complete their life cycle from germination through seed production and senescence in 12 months or less. Summer annuals germinate in late winter or spring and grow into summer or early fall. Under natural conditions, winter annuals germinate in fall or early winter and may grow through spring. However, along coastal California and in nurseries, winter annuals often germinate or grow during summer months.

Annual Grasses

Annual bluegrass, crabgrass, ryegrass, and wild oat are probably the most common annual grasses (family Poaceae, formerly Gramineae) infesting floricultural and nursery crops. Control annual grasses by cultivating, using good exclusion and sanitation, hand-weeding, applying herbicide, mulching, solarizing or steam pasteurizing growing media, and fumigating the soil.

Annual Broadleaf Weeds

About two dozen annual broadleaf species are relatively common weeds in flower and nursery crops (Table 76). Common groundsel, common purslane, cudweeds, mallows, and spurges are common species. Lesser seeded bittercress and willow herbs are increasingly important and relatively new pests. Cultivation, excluding seeds, flaming, hand-hoeing, hand-pulling, herbicides, mulching, soil fumigation, and solar or steam pasteurization of growing media are effective in controlling most annual broadleaf weeds.

Common Groundsel
Senecio vulgaris
Common groundsel is a winter annual that can cause problems any time of year in container nurseries, greenhouses, and coastal area fields. This member of the sunflower family (Asteraceae, formerly Compositae) produces yellow blossom clusters that open into flower disks about ¼ inch (6 mm) in diameter. Flowers develop into fluffy white seed heads with

Annual bluegrass (*Poa annua*) has light green, short, smooth leaf blades. Leaves are often folded at the tip, resembling the prow of a boat, especially on young plants. Seedlings such as this germinate in the fall or anytime where warm soil is frequently irrigated.

Annual bluegrass grows 3 to 12 inches (8–30 cm) tall at maturity. Its flower heads are branched with clusters of 3 to 6 flowers at the tip of each branch.

Large crabgrass (*Digitaria sanguinalis*) infesting this container is also a problem in fields. It has many branches at the base and spreads from roots growing at swollen joints in the stem. Large crabgrass grows best in the summer and dies off in cold weather.

Common groundsel cotyledons (seed leaves) are elongate and oval with a blunt, rounded tip. The first true leaves, also seen here, have shallow teeth. Older plants have deeply lobed, alternate leaves.

Cudweed seed leaves and first true leaves are covered with whitish to light gray woolly hairs. The first true leaves are smooth, entire, and taper gradually toward the base.

Large crabgrass flower heads look like bird claws. These inflorescences arise from two or more points along the stem, each point usually separated by about ⅛ to ¼ inch (3–6 mm). This differs from the similar-looking bermudagrass flower heads, which usually branch from a single point at the tip of the stem.

This common groundsel can be confused with other sunflowers or thistles, such as annual sowthistle and prickly lettuce. Common groundsel can be distinguished by the conspicuous black tips on the green bracts surrounding groundsel's yellow flower clusters (lower right).

Cudweed flower heads are crowded and densely arranged on the stem or at the base of leaf stalks. The fruit bear bristly, tuftlike projections that are shed at maturity.

very light seed that are easily spread by wind. Mature plants are about 2 to 3 feet (60–90 cm) tall.

Common groundsel seed germinate only in the top ½ inch (1.3 cm) of soil. Irrigation to germinate seed followed by shallow cultivation of seedlings just before planting provides some control. Control effectiveness is augmented by throwing a layer of dry soil or light mulch along the seed row during or immediately after cultivation. Applying certain herbicides, hand-hoeing, hand-puling, mulching, solarizing, and excluding windblown and waterborne seed are also effective.

Cudweeds
Gnaphalium spp.

Cudweeds are pests in fields and container nurseries. These members of the sunflower family are usually annuals, but some plants survive into a second year before maturing. Mature cudweed is sparsely branched, mostly erect, and 8 to 20 inches (20–50 cm) tall. Plants develop many dense tufts of long woolly hairs. Cudweeds can be controlled by cultivating, excluding windblown seed, flaming, hand-hoeing, hand-pulling, mulching, and applying certain herbicides as listed in Table 82.

The two seed leaves of little mallow are heart-shaped. True leaves often have a red spot at the base of the blade where the leaf joins the petiole.

Mature mallow forms dense bushes that trail along the ground or grow upright about 1 to 4 feet (30–120 cm) tall.

Little Mallow
Malva parviflora

Little mallow is one of several *Malva* species (family Malvaceae) that infest field-grown crops. Mallows are also called cheeseweeds because their fruit are disk shaped or button shaped with flattened lobes resembling an uncut block of cheese. True leaves are roundish and crinkled with wavy, shallow-toothed margins. Mature mallow develops a tough, deep taproot. Depending on location, little mallow is an annual, winter annual, or biennial. In addition to being a direct pest, mallows are hosts for thrips, impatiens necrotic spot virus, and tomato spotted wilt virus.

Cultivating, flaming, and hand-hoeing are effective against mallow during the seedling stage. Mallow is susceptible to solarization, but seed are not controlled by methyl bromide fumigation. Certain preemergence and postemergence herbicides can provide control; however, mallow often escapes preemergence herbicide application because its seed can persist for many years and germinate even though buried 1 to 2 inches (2.5–5 cm) deep.

Lesser-Seeded Bittercress
Cardamine oligosperma

Lesser-seeded bittercress is also called little bittercress or yellow bittercress. This annual member of the mustard family (Brassicaceae, formerly Cruciferae) infests container nurseries and fields and is especially problematic in greenhouses. Its light green seed leaves are round and $\frac{1}{25}$ to $\frac{1}{8}$ inch (1–3 mm) wide with relatively long stalks. True leaves occur mostly in rosettes around the basal stem. These variable leaves are elongate, lobbed, ovate, or round and range from about $\frac{1}{8}$ to $\frac{3}{5}$ inch (3–15 cm) long. Plants grow about 3 to 12 inches (7.5–30 cm) tall and have roots that grow up to 28 inches (71 cm) deep underground. Flowers mature into pods that can eject seed up to several feet. Seed stick to soil surfaces or become carried in irrigation water that is applied to crops.

Lesser-seeded bittercress produces small, white, inconspicuous flowers. Flowers develop into narrow, many-seeded pods about $\frac{1}{2}$ to $\frac{3}{4}$ inch (12–19 mm) long, such as those on the terminals of the weed growing in the lower left container.

Use good sanitation to avoid introducing lesser-seeded bittercress. Exclude windblown and waterborne seed. Manage irrigation and water runoff to minimize excessively moist soil surface conditions because seed germinate and plants thrive under cool, moist conditions. Hand-pull or hand-hoe plants before they mature. Solarization, mulch, and preemergence herbicides can provide control.

Common Purslane
Portulaca oleracea

Purslane (family Portulacaceae) infests fields and container nurseries. It forms a prostrate mat or grows up to 1 foot (0.3 m) tall and branches at the base and along the stems. Common purslane is an annual weed that grows rapidly in spring and summer. It thrives under dry conditions but also competes well in irrigated situations.

Cultivation and many herbicides control common purslane. Purslane plants are also controlled by hand-hoeing or hand-pulling, but if soil is moist plants should be removed

Common purslane seed leaves are elongate, smooth, and succulent with a reddish tinge. The first three true leaves, also seen here, have rounded tips that are broader than the leaf base.

Common purslane leaves and stems are very succulent and often tinged red. Small yellow flowers are borne singly or in clusters of two or three in stem axils or at the tips of stems. Flowers usually open only on sunny mornings.

The oval seed leaves on spotted spurge are bluish green, powdery or mealy on the upper surface, and have a reddish tinge underneath. The plant is named for the dark, reddish spots found in the middle of many leaves.

and disposed of away from crops. Until purslane has dried, plants can reestablish from cuttings or roots if the area receives rainfall or irrigation. If plants are not removed until after they flower, their seed are easily dislodged and left behind. Purslane seed are very tiny and are produced in abundance. Plants left uncontrolled until flowering can produce a heavy infestation.

Spotted Spurge
Chamaesyce (=Euphorbia) maculata

Spotted spurge is the major spurge species infesting California container nurseries, fields, and greenhouses. Of the five other spurges that can also be pests, creeping spurge (*Chamaesyce serpens*), and ground spurge (*C. prostrata*) are the most common. Spotted spurge is distinguished from other spurges (family Euphorbiaceae) by the distinctive reddish spot on most spotted spurge leaves. Spurges have milky, sticky sap; they are summer annuals with inconspicuous flowers.

Spotted spurge is a widely spreading, many-branched, low-growing, mat-forming summer annual. Leaves on mature plants grow opposite on short stalks.

Spotted spurge has tiny red and white flowers. Milky, sticky sap exuding from the broken stem is characteristic of plants in the family Euphorbiaceae.

Willow herbs, such as this *Epilobium ciliatum*, produce tiny seeds with silken white tufts, so seed are easily dispersed by wind.

Reduce spurge germination by covering seeds and growing media surface with a fine layer of mulch about 1 inch (2.5 cm) thick. Many preemergence herbicides also provide control. There are no selective herbicides that will control spurge once it is established. Hand-hoe or hand-pull established plants in growing areas before they produce seed.

Willow Herbs
Epilobium spp.
Northern willow herb (*Epilobium ciliatum*) and panicle-leaf willow herb, also called panicle willowweed (*E. brachycarpum =E. paniculatum*), are two similar-looking weeds that infest containers, field crops, and greenhouses. These members of the evening primrose family (Onagraceae) are also called fireweeds. These willow herbs are usually annuals that vary at maturity from about ½ to 6 feet (15–180 cm) tall. Their white, pink, or purplish flowers occur from about June through September.

Epilobium species are preferred hosts of black vine weevil. Chewed *Epilobium* leaves can indicate that weevils are present in growing areas and may need to be controlled to prevent larval feeding from damaging roots.

Control willow herbs before they flower or produce seed. Each seed is attached to a tuft of long white hairs, so seed are easily dispersed by wind. Reduce infestations from windblown seed by screening growing areas. Manage drainage and irrigation systems to prevent water puddles where windblown seed often collect and germinate. Cultivation, hand-weeding, soil solarization, and certain preemergence herbicides can control willow herbs. Flaming is effective on seedling or annual willow herbs. A 1-inch (2.5-cm) layer of coarse mulch or a fabric disk treated with copper hydroxide (Spin Out) placed on the potting mix surface can control northern willow herb for several months in nursery containers.

Northern willow herb develops tiny pinkish flowers on the end of short stalks. Each of these stalked flowers will mature into ½ inch (12 mm) long, brown seed pods.

PERENNIAL WEEDS

Perennial weeds live for more than 2 years. Most produce seeds, but they reproduce and persist with bulbs, rhizomes (underground stems), stolons (aboveground stems), or tubers as well as with seeds. Because of their persistent underground propagules, established perennials are the most difficult weeds to control. All perennials should be eliminated from growing areas before planting. Control often requires prolonged, repeated effort and a combination of methods such as cultivation, hand-hoeing, hand-pulling, and herbicides. The perennial weeds pictured here are bermudagrass, birdseye pearlwort, creeping fieldcress, creeping woodsorrel (also called oxalis), field bindweed, nutsedges, and white clover.

Bermudagrass
Cynodon dactylon
Bermudagrass is a container and field pest that forms a dense mat with spreading, branching stolons and rhizomes. Bermudagrass is drought tolerant but grows poorly in dense shade.

Use good sanitation to avoid introducing bermudagrass seed, rhizomes, or stolons. These propagules can contaminate partially decomposed compost, organic mulch, soil, mowers, and tools. Roots are easily killed when turned to the sun, so repeated cultivation provides control if soil is dry and not irrigated for about 1 week after each cultivation. Proper

These bermudagrass stems creeping along the ground (stolons) are a primary method of spread by this weed and certain other perennials.

The three to seven flowering spikes of each bermudagrass plant usually radiate from a single point at the tip of the stem. The similar flower spikes of large crabgrass usually radiate from two or more points on each stem.

This conspicuous ring or fringe of short, whitish hairs at the base of each blade distinguishes bermudagrass from other common grasses.

solarization controls bermudagrass. Several herbicides are effective if they are applied when bermudagrass is well-watered and growing actively, such as during bloom or soon after seed heads form.

Creeping Fieldcress
Rorippa sylvestris

This perennial mustard (family Brassicaceae) is a relatively new pest in containers, fields, and greenhouses in California. Creeping fieldcress is also called yellow fieldcress because of its profuse, bright yellow spring and summer blossoms. The stalks are 6 to 12 inches (15–30 cm) long, and each contains numerous flowers, each of which is $\frac{1}{5}$ to $\frac{1}{4}$ inch (5–6 mm) wide with 4 petals. Flowers mature into narrow pods that are $\frac{1}{2}$ inch (12 mm) long that produce relatively few seed.

Creeping fieldcress spreads primarily by rhizomes that grow up to 3 feet (90 cm) deep in the soil. These fine, white rhizomes are often spread as contaminants with the bulbs, tubers, or the root mass of ornamental crops arriving from other states. New plants readily develop from rhizome pieces as small as $\frac{3}{5}$ to $1\frac{1}{5}$ inches (1.5–3 cm) long.

A similar-looking species, R. palustris, is also found in California. This annual, biennial, or perennial grows up to about 32 inches (80 cm) tall, about twice the height of creeping fieldcress. Rorippa palustris usually has a single dominant, erect stem. The shorter stems of creeping fieldcress are either weakly erect or sprawling.

Because of its deep rhizomes, neither steaming nor fumigation eliminates creeping fieldcress from soils. Cultivation of established creeping fieldcress spreads infestations. Certain preemergence herbicides (isoxaben, oryzalin, pendimethalin, and trifluralin) suppress top growth, but buried rhizomes remain alive and produce new plants once the herbicide

Creeping fieldcress has bright, smooth, deep green leaves. Seed leaves are narrow with long stalks. True leaves are deeply lobed, resembling leaves of London rocket (Sisymbrium irio) another Brassicaceae.

degrades. Prevent infestations from spreading by using good sanitation measures, including physically removing rhizome pieces from bulbs, tubers, and root masses or destroying infested plants.

Creeping Woodsorrel
Oxalis corniculata

Creeping woodsorrel is the most important of several *Oxalis* species (family Oxalidaceae) weeds that infest container nurseries, greenhouses, and fields. Creeping woodsorrel prefers shady conditions and commonly grows in containers and beneath benches. It has yellow flowers and cloverlike leaves that grow from running rootstocks. Flowers mature into elongate green seed pods. Mature pods forcefully eject reddish seed, which can spread to containers and soil within several feet. Seed remain viable for months and germinate under a variety of environmental conditions. In greenhouses, seed are produced year-round. In addition to being a direct pest, *Oxalis* species host several whitefly species, which can move to attack ornamental crops.

Manage irrigation and runoff to minimize surface moisture, which favors creeping woodsorrel. Use cultivation, hand-hoeing, or hand-pulling to control young plants before they flower. Unless well-established plants are entirely removed, creeping woodsorrel can be a persistent problem because new plants can take root from remaining stolons. Solarization and several preemergence herbicides are effective (Table 82), but there are no selective postemergence herbicides for controlling creeping woodsorrel infestations in broadleaf crops.

Field Bindweed
Convolvulus arvensis

Field bindweed, also called perennial morningglory (family Convolvulaceae), is a pest of field-grown crops. Mature plants have twining stems up to 5 feet (1.5 m) long. Roots can grow 10 feet (3 m) deep or more and spread laterally for several feet. Flowers mature into roundish brown pods containing abundant seed, which can remain viable in soil for 20 years. Because of its extensive root system and persistent seed, established field bindweed infestations are very difficult to manage and require repeated control efforts.

Use good sanitation and water management to avoid spreading seed or root fragments in soil or surface water. Field bindweed is easily controlled by cultivating seedlings before they mature beyond the 5-leaf stage. Repeated cultivation at about 3-week intervals for more than 1 year can eventually control established infestations, but lack of persistent effort when cultivating simply spreads the weed. Soil fumigation does not kill seed or deeply buried roots.

Glyphosate provides control in noncrop areas. Multiple applications are often needed unless plants are seedlings. This translocated herbicide is generally most effective in combination with irrigation and cultivation. Disc infested

Seed leaves (nearest to the soil) and first true leaves of creeping woodsorrel.

Several elongate, pointed-tip seed pods of creeping woodsorrel can be seen infesting these orchid (*Phalaenopsis* sp.) containers.

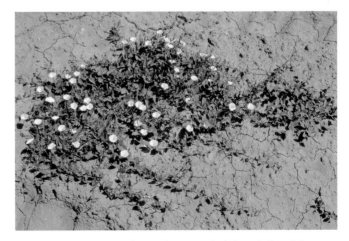

Field bindweed produces showy white to pinkish funnel-shaped flowers that open on sunny mornings.

A field bindweed seed leaf (bottom right) is square with an indented tip. True leaves vary greatly in shape but are often rounded with a blunted tip and shaped like an arrowhead. Petioles have a distinctly grooved upper surface.

areas, irrigate to stimulate regrowth, spray when regrowth has developed a few flowers, and cultivate again in about 3 to 4 weeks. Plants should be dust-free and growing vigorously when sprayed.

Nutsedges
Cyperus spp.

Nutsedges are a problem in field crops and containers. Although nutsedges are sometimes called nutgrass, they are true sedges (family Cyperaceae), with leaves that are V-shaped or triangular in cross-section growing from the base in sets of three. Grass stems are round and hollow, and the leaves grow alternately on opposite sides of the stem. Sedges have solid flower stems (Fig. 67). Yellow nutsedge (*Cyperus esculentus*) is the most common species. Purple nutsedge (*C. rotundus*) is also a problem.

Yellow and purple nutsedges produce tubers, which are incorrectly called *nuts* or *nutlets*. These tubers are produced on rhizomes (underground stems) that grow as deep as 8 to 14 inches (20–35 cm) below the soil surface. Nutsedges spread vegetatively from tubers, which often contaminate field soils and partially composted organic matter. It can be important to distinguish between purple and yellow nutsedge because certain herbicides differ in their efficacy against these weeds (Table 82).

Yellow nutsedge has light brown flowers and seed; purple nutsedge flowers have a reddish tinge and the seed are dark brown or black. Yellow nutsedge tubers are round, smooth, brown or black, and pleasant tasting, and only one tuber is formed at the end of a rhizome. Purple nutsedge tubers are covered with red or red-brown scales, are bitter tasting, and are formed in chains with several tubers on a single rhizome.

The best time to remove small nutsedge plants is before they develop more than five or six leaves. After this stage,

A yellow nutsedge seedling. Nutsedge leaves are V-shaped or triangular in cross section and grow from the base in sets of three.

A yellow nutsedge with light brown flowers.

Birdseye pearlwort *(Sagina procumbens)* infests greenhouses and containers. This sunflower (family Asteraceae, formerly Compositae) is a perennial or sometimes an annual weed. It forms bright green, prostrate mats. It has minute leaves, and is shown here developing tiny white flowers.

This white clover *(Trifolium repens)* can be a problem in field-grown flowers. It is a creeping perennial legume (family Fabaceae, formerly Leguminosae) with the typical three-leaflet clover leaf. White clover has a ball-shaped white or pinkish flower head. Mature plants have branching stems 4 to 12 inches (10–15 cm) long that grow prostrate and root at the joints. The first true leaves of seedlings (not shown) are round.

new tubers begin to form. Shallow cultivation, hand-pulling, or hoeing will kill seedlings. Continually removing shoots produced from tubers eventually depletes their energy. Most herbicides have limited or no effectiveness against nutsedges. Certain synthetic mulches can prevent nutsedge emergence (Table 86), and the underground propagules will eventually die if new shoots are unable to obtain sunlight.

Other Perennial Broadleaf Weeds
Other perennial broadleaf weeds include birdseye pearlwort *(Sagina procumbens)* and white clover *(Trifolium repens)*.

AQUATIC WEEDS

Algae, duckweeds, liverworts, and mosses are among the weeds that thrive where conditions are wet. Annual bluegrass, dallisgrass, nutsedges, and certain other weeds are also promoted by excessively damp conditions. The wet conditions favoring aquatic weeds also cause other problems. Certain invertebrate pests, including fungus gnats, shore flies, slugs, and snails cause damage only when conditions are damp. The excess humidity occurring under damp conditions also promotes development of foliar pathogens. Wet slippery conditions pose a worker safety hazard.

Control aquatic weeds and related problems by avoiding overwatering and minimizing irrigation and fertilizer runoff. Provide good drainage and minimize puddling water. Clean growing areas regularly to reduce dirt, as algae requires organic matter for growth. Take measures to reduce condensation and relative humidity, for example, by increasing ventilation and temperature.

Common duckweed *(Lemna minor)* growing beneath this propagation bench is favored by poor drainage and excess irrigation and fertilization.

Moss growing on the surface of this otherwise empty and apparently forgotten nursery container can spread by the spore capsules growing from the filamentous tubes visible here.

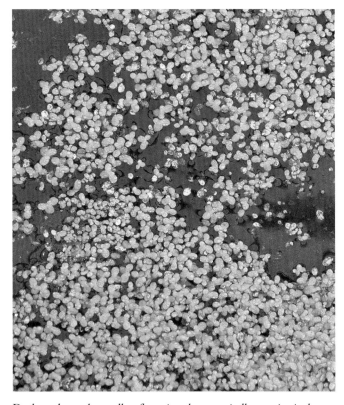

Duckweeds are the smallest flowering plants, typically growing in dense mats on wet surfaces.

A few materials are available for directly controlling certain aquatic weeds such as algae growing on surfaces. Algicides include hydrated lime, copper sulfate, potassium salts of fatty acids, and other registered materials. However, algaecides can be highly phytotoxic, often limiting their application to periods when crops are not present. Some counties may restrict growers' use of hydrated lime. Aquatic weed control in most growing situations must rely on cultural and environmental methods that reduce moisture.

Liverworts are lower plants with fleshy leaflike structures (thallus) that grow into mats. The umbrella-shaped stalks are male reproductive structures (archegonia). The female reproductive structures (gemma cups) are the suction cuplike protuberances on the thallus. Liverworts thrive in cool, moist, shaded soils and can be a problem in containers and greenhouses, especially in liner production. Blasting sand or pecan shells applied to the surface of container media can control liverwort.

Nematodes

Nematodes are tiny (usually microscopic) unsegmented roundworms. Except for foliar nematodes (*Aphelenchoides* spp.) that feed in leaves, pest nematodes feed on bulbs, roots, and basal stems. Root knot nematodes (*Meloidogyne* spp.) are the most prevalent nematodes attacking floricultural crops. Root-feeding nematodes in at least ten other genera infest a limited number of hosts, as listed in Table 94 and described briefly in the chapter "Crop Tables." Most soil-dwelling nematode species are sampled and managed using the same general techniques. Because growing media used in containers and greenhouses is usually pasteurized, soil-dwelling nematodes are primarily a problem in field soils.

Damage

Pest nematodes feed by inserting their entire body or only their spearlike mouthparts into plant tissue and consuming cell contents. This feeding directly injures or kills plant cells, disrupts nutrient and water flow between roots and aboveground parts, and can induce physiological changes in plant growth. Nematode damage symptoms that are visible aboveground include stunted growth, plant tip dieback, and foliage that is chlorotic, curled, wilted, or dropping prematurely. Similar decline symptoms can be caused by root or vascular wilt diseases, certain insects or mites, and a lack of proper cultural care, such as inappropriate irrigation or fertilization. Nematodes can also act in combination with other pests by creating wounds that provide entry for microorganisms. Certain nematodes vector pathogenic microorganisms.

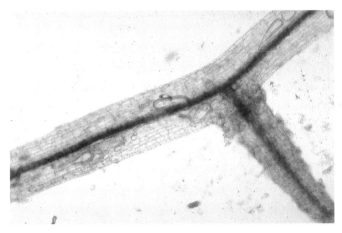

Adult root lesion nematodes (*Pratylenchus neglectus*) visible inside a root.

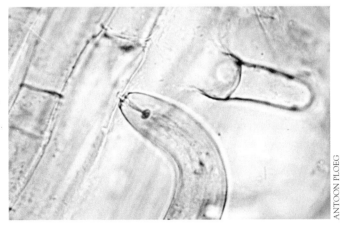

An adult root lesion nematode (*Pratylenchus penetrans*) is attached to the outside of a root by its mouthparts, which have punctured the cell wall to suck out root contents.

ANTOON PLOEG

Table 94. Some Floriculture Crops Attacked by Nematodes.

Common name	Nematode species		
	Root knot	Foliar	Other
African violet	●	●	
agapanthus	●		
ageratum		●	
amaryllis			stem and bulb
anemone		●	
anthurium	●	●	burrowing
aster	●	●	
azalea	●	●	stubby root, stunt
begonia	●	●	
bird of paradise	●		stem and bulb, spiral
calceolaria		●	
calendula	●		
calla	●		
camellia			spiral, stunt
carnation	●		ring, root lesion
cassia	●		
Christmas cactus			cactus cyst
chrysanthemum	●	●	root lesion
cyclamen		●	
daffodil		●	stem and bulb, root lesion
dahlia	●	●	root lesion
delphinium		●	
dieffenbachia	●		
doronicum		●	
everlasting	●		
ferns		●	
fig		●	
foxglove		●	
gardenia	●		
geranium		●	
gerbera	●		stem and bulb
gladiolus	●		stem and bulb, root lesion
gloxinia	●	●	
gypsophila	●		
hibiscus		●	
hydrangea	●	●	root lesion
impatiens	●	●	
iris	●	●	root lesion, stem and bulb
larkspur	●		
liatris	●		
lily	●	●	root lesion
Marguerite daisy	●		root lesion
narcissus		●	root lesion, stem and bulb
orchids		●	
pansy, violet		●	

Common name	Nematode species		
	Root knot	Foliar	Other
pelargonium		●	
peony	●		
philodendron	●		burrowing
phlox		●	stem and bulb
poinsettia	●		
primula		●	stem and bulb
protea	●		
rhododendron		●	spiral, stem and bulb, stubby root, stunt
rose	●		dagger, root lesion
rudbeckia		●	
safflower	●		
sage		●	
scabiosa		●	
Shasta daisy	●		
snapdragon	●	●	
statice	●	●	
sweet pea	●		
tagetes		●	
verbena	●	●	
veronica		●	
vinca	●		
zinnia	●	●	

KEY:

burrowing nematodes	*Rhadopholus* spp.
cactus cyst nematode	*Cactodera* (=*Heterodera*) *cacti*
dagger nematode	*Xiphinema index*
ring nematodes	*Criconemoides* spp.
root lesion nematodes	*Pratylenchus* spp.
spiral nematodes	*Heliocotylenchus* spp.
stem and bulb nematode	*Ditylenchus dipsaci*
stubby root nematodes	*Paratrichodorus*, *Trichodorus* spp.
stunt nematodes	*Tylenchorhynchus* spp.

Consult *Pests of Landscape Trees and Shrubs* (Dreistadt 1994) for the nematode susceptibility of woody ornamental plants.
Sources: Becker 1996; Dutky and Sindermann 1993; McKenry and Roberts 1985; Radewald, Shibuya, and Westerdahl n.d.

Identification and Biology

Nematodes usually lay eggs in the soil or in or on roots. Most nematodes develop through four juvenile stages. In warm, moist soil they can complete one generation in 3 to 6 weeks. With root knot nematodes and certain other species, only adult males and second-stage juveniles are mobile in soil or roots; the other juvenile stages and adult females are immobile (Fig. 68). Nematodes require moist environments to feed and reproduce. When conditions are adverse, such as cold temperatures, dry soils, or absence of host plants, some nematode species develop resistant stages that can persist for several years until conditions again become suitable for growth.

Root knot nematodes caused sparse floral crop growth in these uncultivated field rows, which then became heavily colonized by weeds.

Certain nematodes can vector plant pathogens. These notched, crumpled gladiolus leaf edges were caused by tobacco rattle virus vectored by stubby root nematodes (*Trichodorus* spp.).

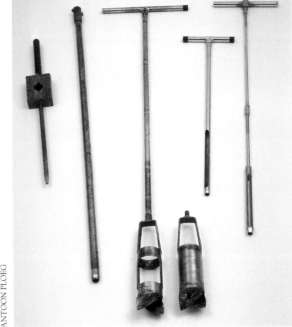

Soil sampling tools (from left): a two-piece Veihmeyer tube, soil augers, and two Oakfield soil tubes.

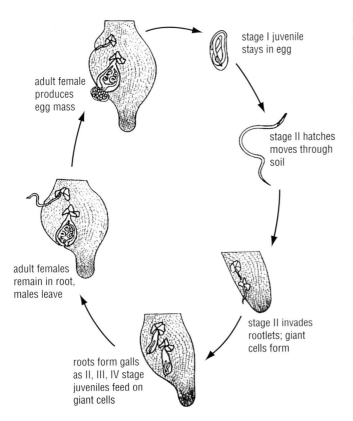

adult female produces egg mass

stage I juvenile stays in egg

stage II hatches moves through soil

adult females remain in root, males leave

roots form galls as II, III, IV stage juveniles feed on giant cells

stage II invades rootlets; giant cells form

Figure 68. Root knot nematodes spend most of their active life cycle in galls on roots. Second-stage larvae invade new sites, usually near root tips, causing root cells to grow into giant cells where nematodes feed. As feeding continues, the plant produces a gall around the infected area.

Their microscopic size, hidden feeding habits, easily confused symptoms, and sometimes subtle damage make it difficult to diagnose nematode infestations. If no other cause for unhealthy plants is obvious, remove plants from containers or dig them from the soil and examine roots for signs of nematodes. Ease the roots out of the soil gently so that the smaller feeder roots are not broken off. Nematode-infested roots may have lesions, dark spots, or a dirty appearance. Other signs of nematode infestation include root galls, an abnormally large number of shallow lateral roots, and plants that have fewer roots than normal.

Not all nematodes produce obvious symptoms on roots. Laboratory analysis of soil, plant roots, or both is typically necessary to confirm whether nematodes are present in sufficient numbers to be pests. Post-treatment laboratory testing indicates whether control actions were effective. Consider using laboratory tests before replanting in areas where nematodes have been a problem and after treating with a new or experimental method.

Most plant-feeding nematodes are less than $1/25$ inch (1 mm) long and can be seen clearly only with a microscope. Experts have historically identified nematodes based on surface or internal structures visible with a light or electron microscope. Computer programs now provide easy access to information for identifying problems based on nematode appearance, host crop, soil type, and the known distribution of pest nematodes. DNA analysis (such as polymerase chain reaction, PCR) and other molecular techniques (such as isoenzyme or protein electrophoresis) are being developed for reliably distinguishing nematode species.

Sampling Nematodes

The best time to sample for nematodes is when the previous crop is in the field. Nematodes are usually concentrated near plant roots, and plants with damage symptoms are available then for testing. Unless your laboratory recommends other procedures, the following general method can be used. Divide the field into areas of uniform plant growth and similar soil characteristics and cropping history. Take several soil subsamples from locations scattered throughout each uniform field area. Each subsample can be about 1 pint (0.5 l) of soil. Collect moist (not soggy) soil from the plant root zone or the upper 6 to 18 inches (15–45 cm) of soil if no crop is present. Thoroughly mix the subsamples to make a composite sample and send about 1 quart (about 1 l) of soil to be tested. Repeat this sampling procedure for each field area. If plants have symptoms, dig them up along with their roots and surrounding soil and place them in a bag for testing. Also bag separately at least one or two plants and soil sampled from a healthy part of the field and send them for testing.

Label each sample with field location, current crop, cropping history, crop injury observed, and your name, address, and phone number. Seal samples in plastic to prevent them from drying out and keep them cool at about 50° to 60°F (10° to 16°C) until material reaches the laboratory. Laboratories report sampling results as the genus of nematode found, the number of nematodes per unit of soil (usually per pint or liter), and the extraction efficiency. It is important to know the laboratory's method (and the method's efficiency) for extracting nematodes from soil. Certain methods are not adequate for identifying the presence of certain genera of pests; or certain tests provide only qualitative results, which tell you that nematodes are present but not whether they are abundant enough to be pests. See Table 32 for suggestions on submitting samples to a diagnostic laboratory.

Management

Sanitation, crop rotation, employing good cultural practices, and pasteurizing media are the most important strategies for preventing and managing most soil-dwelling nematodes. Soil amendments and biological controls may sometimes suppress nematode populations. Foliar nematodes discussed later in this chapter are managed differently than the soil-dwelling species discussed here.

Sanitation and Cultural Practices

Avoid introducing nematode-infested plants into growing areas. Use only good-quality stock from a reliable supplier. Nematode-free plants for certain crops can be obtained from participants in the California Certification Nursery program. Pasteurize growing media before planting. Do not transfer soil from around infested plants to healthy plants. Do not allow irrigation water from around infested plants to run off onto healthy plants, as this spreads nematodes.

Unless soil is treated first, do not plant susceptible crops in field soils where nematodes have previously been a problem. For example, do not replant the same plant genera into the old site; rotate crops by replanting with species or varieties more tolerant of, or resistant to, the specific nematodes present.

Provide crops with proper cultural care so that they are vigorous and better able to tolerate feeding by nematodes and other pests. More frequent irrigation of drought-stressed plants can reduce damage caused by root knot nematodes, but it does not reduce the population levels of nematodes. Consult the more detailed sanitation and cultural practices discussion in the chapter "Managing Pests in Flower and Nursery Crops."

Heat Pasteurization

Pasteurizing media with heat, such as steam, can control nematodes and other pests in container mix and greenhouse beds. Special tractor-drawn steam rakes are available (Fig. 21), but except for raised beds, steam is difficult to use in field soils. Heat generated by decomposer microorganisms during composting of container media can control certain nematodes (see the chapter "Diseases"), but preparing pathogen-free compost requires careful management and monitoring.

Solarization

Solarization before planting temporarily reduces nematode populations in the upper 12 inches (30 cm) of soil (Table 95). Solarization involves covering moist, bare soil or container mix with clear plastic for several weeks during hot weather, as discussed and illustrated in the chapter "Weeds." This technique reduces nematode damage to annual plants and may help young perennial plants become established before nematode populations increase. In some cases, incorporating amendments (such as compost or green manure) or applying lower than normal rates of fumigant pesticides in combination with solarization can provide better control than using any single method.

Table 95. Some Flower and Nursery Crop Nematodes Controlled by Solarization.

Common name	Scientific name
citrus	*Tylenchulus semipenetrans*
dagger	*Xiphinema* spp.
ring	*Criconemella* (=*Criconemoides*) *xenoplax*
root knot	*Meloidogyne hapla*
root knot	*Meloidogyne incognita*
root knot	*Meloidogyne javanica*
root lesion	*Pratylenchus* spp.
stem and bulb	*Ditylenchus dipsaci*

Sources: Stapleton and DeVay 1995; Stapleton, Ferguson, and McKenry 1998.

Solarizing container mix is an approved treatment method specified in the California Department of Food and Agriculture's Nursery Stock Nematode Control Program. The media must be in either polyethylene planting bags or piles no more than 12 inches (30 cm) high, and placed on polyethylene film, disinfected concrete, or some other surface that prevents contamination (Fig. 64). Be sure media is moist to near field capacity before covering media with a layer of clear plastic. Monitor and record temperatures at the bottom center of piles or bags to ensure that minimum temperatures of 158°F (70°C) are achieved for 30 minutes. Container mix solarization is illustrated and discussed further in the chapter "Weeds."

Fumigants

A soil fumigant can be used in certain situations to reduce nematode populations before planting. Before using a fumigant, be sure that nematodes or other soil pests are the cause of your problem by having a laboratory test performed or by having an expert examine your plants and soil. Consider alternatives before using a nematicide. Be sure the nematicide is registered for that crop or growing situation. Follow label directions strictly; improper application is not effective and may be hazardous. Postplant nematicides for use in soil around established plants may be available, but it is generally more effective to employ other controls and preventive measures before planting. For more information, read the fumigation discussion in the chapter "Diseases."

Hot Water Dips

Hot water dips can control nematodes and certain other pests infesting bulbs, corms, and rhizomes of crops such as amaryllis, daffodil, gladiolus, lily, and tulip (Table 8). The temperature and time needed to provide control depend on the nematode species and crop variety. Exceeding temperature or exposure limits can damage plants; insufficient temperatures or exposure time may not kill nematodes. Read the treatment of plants section in the chapter "Managing Pests in Flower and Nursery Crops," and consult an expert before beginning any large-scale treatments. A general recommendation is to presoak bulbs, corms, or rhizomes for 2 or 3 hours or overnight in 75°F (24°C) water containing a wetting agent before immersing them in 111°F (44°C) water for about 1½ hours. Cool plants immediately afterward with clean, cold water, then dry thoroughly in warm air or sunshine. Store material afterwards under cool, low-humidity conditions until plants are used.

Amendments and Biological Control

Although amendments and biological control agents reduce plant pathogenic nematodes in certain situations, control has been unreliable. The reasons for this variable effectiveness are not well known. To provide a basis for comparison, growers using amendments and biological controls should consider leaving several randomly selected areas of their fields untreated or treated with more conventional methods or both.

Soil amendments used for nematode control can be placed into four categories: inorganics, animal-based, plant-based, and microbial. Except for inorganics (such as ammonium sulfate fertilizer and powdered rock), nematode suppression from most amendments is at least partly the result of biological control. Animal-based amendments include chitin-containing crab shells and egg shells that apparently stimulate populations of soil-dwelling fungi that feed on chitin. Because chitin is a component of nematodes' outer integument, these chitin-feeding fungi also feed on nematodes. Incorporating animal manure, organic fertilizers, green crop debris, and compost increases the organic matter content of soil. This improves water and nutrient availability to plants, reduces plant stress, and can encourage greater numbers of nematode predators and parasites. However, organic amendments sometimes contain contaminants such as weed seeds, and their effectiveness is largely limited to the depth of material incorporation.

Barley, marigold, perennial rye, and certain legumes such as clover and vetch are planted as cover crops, trap crops, or crop rotations in some row crops. These plants may sometimes reduce populations of certain soil-dwelling plant-parasitic nematodes by producing chemicals that kill or repel nematodes, suppress nematode growth, stimulate premature egg hatch, or disrupt the attraction between nematodes seeking to mate. However, crops suppressive to one species of nematode often host other nematode species. Rotating certain marigold cultivars with crops such as lilies grown for bulb production has been somewhat successful in controlling nematodes. The marigolds must be left in the soil, either through cultivation or by mowing the tops and leaving the roots underground. However, this practice is generally not recommended, as phytotoxicity to lilies and other crops is often observed when they are grown in rotation after incorporating marigolds into the soil.

Some new biological pesticides (mycopesticides) contain nematode-killing microorganisms. These beneficial microorganisms include certain *Burkholderia* and *Pseudomonas* species bacteria and natural by-products of *Myrothecium* species fungi. At least one mycopesticide, *Myrothecium verrucaria* (Ditera), is registered for nematode control in California. Various microbial products not registered as pesticides are sold with the implication that these products can control nematodes. Because mycopesticides must be registered and labeled in accordance with pesticide regulations, the testing requirements and available information on mycopesticides is more extensive and reliable than information on largely unregulated soil amendments or inoculants.

Root Knot Nematodes

Root knot nematodes (*Meloidogyne* spp.), are probably the most common nematode species attacking field-grown ornamentals (Table 94). They cause galls or swellings on roots of many broadleaf plants. Severely infected roots may be attacked by a variety of decay- or disease-causing organisms, including crown gall and root rot fungi. Many weeds and nonfloral crops host root knot nematodes. Some infected plants, especially annual grasses, may exhibit no galls.

Root knot nematodes occur throughout California and most of the United States. Root knot nematodes can enter roots only during their larvae stage. The nematodes become immobile soon after entering roots and spend most of their active life cycle in galls on roots (Fig. 68). Root knot nematodes are most commonly a pest of plants grown in warm, sandy, irrigated soils. The particular *Meloidogyne* species present depends on seasonal temperature and rainfall. At least some *Meloidogyne* species also show host preferences, so cropping history can influence the species of root knot nematodes present.

To tentatively confirm an infestation, dig the plants up after they have grown for about 4 to 6 weeks in soil above 65°F (19°C). Wash or gently tap the soil from their roots and examine the roots for swellings and gnarled, restricted root growth. Cut open any galls and use a hand lens or binocular microscope to examine galls for the presence of pinhead-sized, shiny white females that look like tiny pearls.

Although beneficial nitrogen-fixing bacteria often form nodules on the roots of legumes such as cassia, sweet pea, and vinca, these nodules rub off roots easily, whereas galls caused by root knot nematodes are truly swellings on the roots. Also, a thumbnail can be pressed into a bacterial gall easily, but not into a root knot gall. To provide positive identification, collect galled roots and surrounding soil and send the material to a diagnostic laboratory. Consult Table 41 for a list of common causes of plant galls and suggestions for distinguishing among them.

Foliar Nematodes

Foliar nematodes, also called bud and leaf nematodes, prefer moderate temperatures and moist conditions. *Aphelenchoides fragariae* and *A. ritzemabosi* are the leaf-infesting nematodes that attack ornamental plants in California. Strawberries, ferns, tropical foliage plants, and vegetatively propagated ornamentals are important hosts of *A. fragariae*. *Aphelenchoides* species have been reported as attacking over 250 plant species in about 50 families, some of which are listed in Table 94. Foliar nematode damage in California occurs mostly in certain greenhouses and along coastal areas where ornamental hosts and strawberries are grown (Fig. 69).

Galls caused by a root knot nematode infestation.

Figure 69. Approximate distribution of the two most common foliar nematodes (*Aphelenchoides* spp.) in California. *Source:* McKenry and Roberts 1985.

Damage

Foliar nematodes cause vein-limited blotches and lesions on leaves. If young leaves or shoots are infested, they may remain undersized, become bushy or distorted, and produce little or no marketable foliage or flowers. Damage usually appears beginning in spring (or winter in coastal areas) and becomes most severe by summer.

Foliar nematode damage usually begins as yellowish leaf spots that eventually turn dark green to blackish brown. Discoloring typically starts near the leaf base and spreads outward. The lesions are often angular because nematodes in leaves are initially contained between the main veins. Because monocots have parallel veins, discoloring on them looks like streaks. Damaged foliage may become brittle or shrivel and then drop. Necrotic lesions on plants such as dahlia cause foliage to crumble into small pieces. On African violets, lesions form sunken areas between veins on the underside of leaves. Infested begonia foliage turns reddish or bronze.

Identification and Biology

Foliar nematode damage can be confused with damage caused by bacteria, fungi, viruses, nutrient deficiencies, or chemical injuries. Nematodes may interact with certain fungi or bacteria to cause severe foliar blight. Foliar nematodes are tiny, only $1/50$ to $1/25$ inch (0.5–1 mm) long, and must be identified by a specialist. To confirm an infestation, send symptomatic plants to a diagnostic laboratory staffed with a trained nematologist. When viewed under a 100× microscope, foliar nematodes are slender with a delicate stylet (spearlike mouthpart) and a relatively large median bulb (spherical esophagus cavity) in their anterior that occupies three-fourths or more the width of their body.

Growers can make an initial diagnosis by tearing symptomatic tissue into small pieces and placing it in a glass dish. Add just enough water to immerse the plant tissue, then cover the dish to reduce evaporation. After 24 hours, carefully examine the water under strong light using a 10× hand lens or, preferably, a binocular microscope providing higher magnification. Nematodes will appear as tiny strands moving in the water.

Foliar nematodes infest new plants by swimming up stems and along the surface of moist plant tissue. After entering leaves through stomata, females lay their eggs in intracellular leaf spaces. Foliar nematodes can mature from egg to adult in about 2 weeks, allowing many generations to develop during one growing season. Foliar nematodes can also live for a few months in soil or decomposing organic material by feeding on fungi. They typically overwinter in dormant buds, plant terminals, and on soil in dead leaves that drop from infested plants. In slowly drying leaf tissue, adults of A. ritzemabosi can enter a desiccated resting stage that allows them to survive for several years until moist conditions allow them to resume activity.

Management

Grow plants in soilless media or pasteurize media before use. Propagate only nematode-free stock. Foliar nematodes are typically introduced into growing areas in cuttings, seedlings, and other vegetative propagation material that may be asymptomatic. Take cuttings only from the tops of long, vigorous growth to reduce the likelihood that it is infested.

If the plants will tolerate heat without damage, cuttings can be disinfected by dipping them in hot water at 122°F (50°C) for 5 minutes or at 111°F (44°C) for 30 minutes. Foliar nematodes infesting Easter lilies may be controlled by dipping bulblets in 125°F (52°C) water for 10 minutes prior to planting. However, treatment at the same temperature for 20 minutes resulted in severe damage to the crop. Consult the section on heat treatment of plants in the chapter "Managing Pests in Flower and Nursery Crops" before using this method.

Employ good sanitation practices by removing plant debris, promptly disposing of all infested plants, and eliminating from around growing areas weeds (such as goldenrod, groundsel, and sneezeweed) that can host foliar nematodes. Avoid crowding plants and use irrigation methods other than overhead water to reduce the risk that foliar nematodes will spread throughout the crop by traveling in a water film on plant surfaces.

Crop Tables

These crop tables provide a symptom-based, crop-specific guide for diagnosing problems in floriculture and nurseries. They list damage symptoms, probable causes, and recommended controls for problems affecting over 120 flower and foliage crop genera or species. If the problem is discussed elsewhere in this manual, page numbers refer you to more information on identification, biology, and management of the pest. Crops are presented alphabetically by crop common name. Because plants often have several common names, consult the index to identify the name under which your crop is listed.

Excluded from these tables are common problems affecting most crops, such as too much or too little water. These problems are discussed in the chapter "Abiotic Disorders and Cultural Practices." Most woody ornamental crops are not included because those crop tables are provided in *Pests of Landscape Trees and Shrubs* (Dreistadt 1994), another University of California IPM publication. Producers of woody ornamental crops should use these two publications in combination. Nursery growers of commercial or home-garden fruit and vegetable crops should consult other appropriate publications, including *Pests of the Garden and Small Farm* (Flint 1998); UC IPM manuals for almonds, apples and pears, citrus, cole crops and lettuce, stone fruits, strawberries, tomatoes, and walnuts; or *UC IPM Pest Management Guidelines* for about 40 major crops.

Because of the broad scope of this publication and its California emphasis, and because new species of crops and pests are often introduced from elsewhere, some of the pests you may encounter may not be described or pictured here; consult other sources of information listed in the suggested reading and literature cited at the end of this manual. Some problems can be diagnosed reliably only by experts—do not hesitate to seek their help. Your Cooperative Extension advisor or consultants such as pest control advisers may be able to make an identification and diagnosis or direct you to professional diagnostic services.

What the problem looks like	Probable cause	Comments

AFRICAN BOXWOOD (Myrsine africana), Cape myrtle

What the problem looks like	Probable cause	Comments
Foliage darkens. Plants wilt, often die suddenly. Roots and stems brown or blackish and decayed.	**Root and crown rot,** *Phytophthora* spp. Fungi survive in media. Favored by wet, poorly drained soil. Not reported on *Myrsine* in California.	Don't overirrigate. Provide good drainage. Pasteurize media before planting. Dispose of infected plants. See pages 93–97.
Plants wilt and may die. Brown cankers form at base of petioles or on lower stems, which may rot and have white, cottony fungal growth.	**Crown and seedling rot,** *Rhizoctonia solani.* Fungus persists in media. Promoted by warm, moist conditions. Not reported on *Myrsine* in California.	Pasteurize media before planting. Don't overirrigate. Provide good drainage. See pages 93–98.
Plant has sticky honeydew and blackish sooty mold. Foliage may yellow from small insects on leaves or stems.	**Brown soft scale,** *Coccus hesperidum.* Oval, flat, or bulbous; yellow, orange, or brown insects (family Coccidae), less than ⅛ inch long.	See Scales, page 186.
Foliage yellows. Plant declines or dies back. Tan, yellowish, or white encrustations, usually on leaves.	**Oleander scale,** *Aspidiotus nerii.* Circular, flattened insects, less than ⅟16 inch long.	See Scales, page 186.
Plant has sticky honeydew and blackish sooty mold. Foliage may yellow.	**Barnacle scale,** *Ceroplastes cirripediformis.* Gray, waxy, globular insects; up to ⅕ inch long.	See Scales, page 186.
Plant has sticky honeydew, blackish sooty mold, and possibly cottony waxy material.	**Obscure mealybug,** *Pseudococcus affinis.* Grayish, oval, waxy insects; slow-moving, with marginal filaments.	See Mealybugs, page 183.
Foliage bleached, stippled. Dark varnishlike excrement on underside of leaves.	**Greenhouse thrips,** *Heliothrips haemorrhoidalis.* Tiny slender, black adults and yellowish nymphs.	See Thrips, page 161.
Foliage discolored, stippled, bleached, or reddened. May be fine webbing. Leaves may drop.	**Spider mites.** Tiny greenish, yellowish, or reddish insects; may have 2 dark spots.	See page 213.

AFRICAN VIOLET (Saintpaulia ionantha)

What the problem looks like	Probable cause	Comments
Leaves turn brown or black. Plants wilt, often die suddenly from center of plant out. Roots and stems brown or blackish, decayed.	**Root and crown rot,** *Phytophthora, Pythium* spp. Fungi survive in media and subirrigation mats. Favored by wet, poorly drained soil.	Don't overirrigate. Provide good drainage. Dispose of infected plants and media. Thoroughly disinfect containers. Use *Phytophthora*-resistant cultivars. See pages 93–97.
Plants wilt and may die. Brown cankers form at base of petioles or on lower stems, which may rot and have white, cottony fungal growth.	**Crown and seedling rot,** *Rhizoctonia solani.* Fungus persists in media. Promoted by warm, moist conditions.	Pasteurize media before planting. Don't overirrigate. Provide good drainage. See pages 93–98.
Leaves or petals have brown, water-soaked decay or spots. Dead tissue may have woolly gray growth (spores). Stems may be girdled, rot.	**Gray mold,** *Botrytis cinerea.* Fungus develops in crop debris or inactive tissue. Favored by high humidity at 70° to 77°F. Spores airborne.	Use good sanitation. Avoid overhead irrigation. Keep humidity low. Provide good air circulation. Don't crowd plants. See page 108.
Leaves have yellow to brown patches, lines, or ring spots; may brown, wilt, and die. Plants may be distorted or have stem lesions.	**Impatiens necrotic spot virus, Tobacco mosaic virus, Tomato spotted wilt virus.** Viruses spread by thrips, infect wide host range.	Rogue infected plants; cover and dispose of them away from crop. Control weeds. Control and exclude thrips. See page 121.
Leaves, petioles, or flowers have white powdery growth or lesions.	**Powdery mildew,** *Acrosporium* or *Oidium* sp. Free water not required for fungus infection. Use resistant cultivars in Ballet, Melodie, and Rhapsodie series: 'Allison,' 'Brilliant Eva,' 'Dolly,' 'Mitzi,' 'Pearl,' and 'Rachel.'	Provide good air circulation and adequate light. Consider applying fungicide to prevent. Sulfur can prevent but can damage flowers. See page 112.
Soft, brown stem rot near soil line. Foliage yellows and wilts. Leaves may have irregular water-soaked spots or lesions.	**Bacterial blight,** *Erwinia chrysanthemi.* Persists in media and infected seed and stock. Favored by wet or humid conditions. Avoid injuring plant, as disease infects wounds.	Keep foliage dry. Don't overwater. Provide good drainage. Use good sanitation; rogue infected and nearby plants. Plant resistant 'Apollo Pink,' 'Athena,' 'Roxanne,' or 'Butterfly.' See pages 100, 107.
Foliage has chlorotic mottling or light spots, looks like virus or leafminers. Common on plants with overhead irrigation.	**Ring spot.** Noninfectious disorder caused by overhead cold water or rapid temperature changes in the presence of light.	Provide proper growing conditions. Prevent rapid temperature changes. Avoid overhead irrigation; don't spray pesticides using cold water.
Leaves blotchy yellow, white, dark green, or brown; may distort. Damage develops progressively up from base. Plants stunted. Not common in California.	**Foliar nematodes,** *Aphelenchoides ritzemabosi, A. fragariae.* Tiny roundworms spread in plant debris and by vegetative propagation and splashing water.	Use uninfected stock plants. Remove plant debris. Avoid overhead irrigation; leaves must be wet for infection to occur. See page 265.

What the problem looks like	Probable cause	Comments
Foliage yellows or wilts. Knots or swellings on feeder roots and fleshy roots.	**Root knot nematode,** *Meloidogyne* spp. Tiny roundworms that prefer warm, sandy media. Many hosts.	Pasteurize or treat media before planting. Rogue affected plants. Prevent movement of contaminated water among plants. See page 265.
Foliage bleached, brittle; edges may be curled or ragged. Blossoms distort or discolor. Slow growth.	**Broad mite,** *Polyphagotarsonemus latus.* Translucent to dark green mites, $1/100$ inch long or smaller.	See page 217.
Foliage has brown, dead flecks. Foliage may be bleached, stippled, or reddish. Leaves may drop. Tiny mites on underside of leaves.	**Privet mite,** *Brevipalpus obovatus.* Tiny bright red adults with 2 darkened, eyelike spots on back.	A false spider mite that produces no webbing. Attacks many floral crops. See Mites, page 213.
Foliage blotched or dark streaked. Leaves or terminals distorted. Flowers small. Plants severely stunted. Buds darken or drop.	**Cyclamen mite,** *Phytonemus pallidus.* A pinkish orange mite (family Tarsonemidae), $1/100$ inch long or smaller.	See page 217.
Blossoms have irregular white or brown blotches. Blossoms or terminals may be distorted. Foliage may be distorted.	**Western flower thrips,** *Frankliniella occidentalis.* Tiny slender dark brown to yellowish insects.	See Thrips, page 161.
Leaf axils and undersides have cottony material (females and egg sacs). Foliage has sticky honeydew or blackish sooty mold. Foliage may yellow.	**Mealybugs,** including *Phenacoccus gossypii, Planococcus citri, Pseudococcus longispinus, Pseudococcus obscurus.* Slow-moving, oval, powdery insects with waxy marginal filaments.	See page 183.
Foliage has sticky honeydew, blackish sooty mold, or whitish cast skins. Foliage may yellow.	**Aphids.** Tiny pear-shaped insects, often green, yellowish, or blackish.	See page 179.

AGAPANTHUS *(Agapanthus africanus)*

Older foliage yellows. Plants may die. Bulbs soft and decayed.	**Root and crown rot,** *Phytophthora* spp. Fungi survive in media. Favored by wet, poorly drained soil.	Don't overirrigate. Provide good drainage. Dispose of infected plants and media. Reduce humidity during storage. See pages 93–97.
Crowns or stems decay; often soft, brown odorous rot at soil line. Leaf edges and stems may be discolored, soft, rotted.	**Soft rot,** *Erwinia carotovora.* Persists in media. Favored when wet. Avoid injuring plant; disease is secondary, infecting wounds.	Provide good drainage. Don't overwater. Use good sanitation; immediately discard infected plants and those nearby. See pages 100, 107.
Foliage has brown to yellow spots or blotches that may have dark or yellowish margins. Foliage may shrivel and drop.	**Leaf spot,** *Gloeosporium* sp. Spread by air or splashing water. Favored by prolonged wet conditions. Persist in plant debris.	Avoid wetting foliage. Use drip irrigation. Use good sanitation; promptly remove and dispose of debris and infected leaves. See pages 116–118.
Foliage or shoots chewed, ragged, or clipped. May be slimy or silvery trails on or around plants.	**Snails** and **Slugs,** including *Deroceras reticulatum, Helix aspersa, Milax gagates.* Slow-moving, slimy. May have external shell. Favored by moist, dark conditions.	See page 219.
Base of leaves has whitish, cottony material. Foliage may have sticky honeydew and blackish sooty mold. Foliage may yellow.	**Amaryllis mealybug** or **Lily bulb mealybug,** *Chorizococcus lounsburyi* or *Vryburgia amaryllidis.* Powdery gray insects, up to $1/8$ inch long. Colonies sometimes form a mat of whitish egg sacs, up to 2 inches long, around leaf bases.	See Mealybugs, page 183.

AGLAONEMA *(Aglaonema spp.)*, Chinese evergreen

Leaves may turn yellowish or darken. Plant may wilt and die. Roots and stem around soil dark and decayed.	**Pythium root rot,** *Pythium* spp.; **Rhizoctonia aerial blight,** *Rhizoctonia solani;* **Phytophthora leaf spot,** *Phytophthora* spp. Fungi promoted by wet, poorly drained soil.	Provide good drainage. Avoid excess irrigation and reduce watering if disease develops. See pages 93–98.
Plants yellow, wilt, and may die. Stems may have lesions and be dark and decayed at base.	**Fusarium stem rot,** *Fusarium solani.* Fungal disease spread in water or infested plants. Persists for years in soil. Not reported on *Aglaonema* in California.	Use pathogen-free stock. Pasteurize media before planting. Avoid overwatering. Avoid overhead irrigation. See pages 93–96.

What the problem looks like	Probable cause	Comments

AGLAONEMA (*Aglaonema* spp.), Chinese evergreen (continued)

What the problem looks like	Probable cause	Comments
Brown to black water-soaked spots or decay on leaves or stems near soil. Tissue may have tiny black to dark green spore-forming structures and white mycelia.	**Myrothecium leaf spot,** *Myrothecium roridum.* Spreads by waterborne spores. Infects through wounds. Favored by 70° to 81°F and excess nitrogen or salts.	Minimize plant wounds. Keep foliage dry. Use good sanitation. Avoid excess fertilization. Growing plants above 86°F may arrest or prevent disease.
Leaves have tan to brown circular spots or blotches. Plants turn slightly yellow, wilt. Crown and root tissue eventually may decay, causing plant to die.	**Anthracnose,** *Colletotrichum* spp. Fungi survive in crop debris. Spores spread by splashing water. Favored by wet weather and overhead irrigation.	Avoid overhead irrigation. Minimize wounding plants. Use good sanitation. Fungicide application may help to prevent problem. See pages 116–118.
Foliage yellows and wilts. Leaves may have spots, lesions, or rings that are irregular, water-soaked, or dark. Soft brown stem rot near soil line. Stems may collapse and die.	**Bacterial leaf spots,** *Erwinia carotovora, E. chrysanthemi, Pseudomonas cichorii.* Persist in media and infected stock, infect through wounds. Favored when wet.	Keep foliage dry. Use drip irrigation. Don't overwater. Provide good drainage. Use good sanitation; rogue infected and nearby plants. Avoid injuring plants. See pages 100, 107, 118.
Leaves have yellow, reddish, or brown spots up to ¼ inch in diameter; rarely on stems and petioles. Spots become larger, dark, angular blotches or wedges and may have distinct margins. Leaves and stem may wilt and die. Stem vascular tissue and roots may be black but not rotted.	**Bacterial leaf spot,** *Xanthomonas campestris* pv. *dieffenbachiae.* Spreads by splashing water and infected stock, debris, and equipment. Favored by 70° to 80°F, moist conditions, and rapid growth, such as from excess nitrogen.	Pasteurize media before planting. Avoid overhead water. Regularly inspect and rogue plants infected and those nearby. Isolate new plants; symptoms may not appear immediately. Use good sanitation. Some bactericides can be effective. See pages 107, 118.
Leaves have yellowish patterns, may distort severely. Veins may yellow. Plants grow slowly, are stunted.	**Dasheen mosaic virus.** Spread by aphids or mechanically in sap, such as through contaminated tools.	Use virus-free plants produced by tissue culture. Rogue infected plants. Pasteurize equipment to avoid mechanical spread. Control aphids. See Viruses, page 121.
Plant has sticky honeydew, blackish sooty mold, and possibly cottony waxy material.	**Mealybugs,** including Obscure mealybug, *Pseudococcus affinis.*	Grayish, oval, waxy, slow-moving insects with marginal filaments. See page 183.

ALSTROEMERIA (*Alstroemeria* spp.)

What the problem looks like	Probable cause	Comments
Plants wilt, often die suddenly. Roots and stem dark, decayed.	**Root rot,** *Pythium* sp. Fungi survive in soil. Favored by wet, poorly drained media.	Don't overirrigate. Provide good drainage. See pages 93–96.
Leaves and flower stalks have irregular, yellow to brownish blotches or chlorotic streaking. Blossoms are usually symptomless.	**Hippeastrum mosaic virus.** Aphid-vectored.	Rogue infected plants. Exclude or control aphids. See Viruses, page 121.
Foliage chlorotic or necrotic; streaked or mottled.	**Tomato spotted wilt virus.** Spread by thrips. Infects wide host range.	Rogue infected plants; cover and dispose of them away from crop. Control alternate hosts and vectors. See Viruses, page 121.
Plant has sticky honeydew and blackish sooty mold. Foliage may yellow. Tiny white mothlike adults present.	**Whiteflies,** including Silverleaf whitefly, *Bemisia argentifolii;* Sweetpotato whitefly, *Bemisia tabaci.* Nymphs and pupae flattened, oval, translucent, and greenish or yellow.	See page 170.
Terminals distorted. Foliage may have sticky honeydew, blackish sooty mold, and whitish cast skins.	**Aphids.** Tiny green (or other-colored) pear-shaped insects that suck plants juices.	See page 179.
Foliage discolored, stippled, brownish, or bleached, and may drop. Terminals may distort. May be fine webbing.	**Twospotted mite,** *Tetranychus urticae.* Tiny greenish, reddish, or yellowish mites; may have 2 dark spots.	See Mites, page 213.
Leaves have yellow or white blotches. Foliage may wilt, turn brown, and die.	**Harlequin bug,** *Murgantia histrionica.* Black and reddish stink bugs, up to ⅜ inch long.	Attacks many vegetable crops. Control host weeds in mustard family. See True Bugs, page 194.

ALYSSUM (*Alyssum, Lobularia* spp.), Sweet alyssum

What the problem looks like	Probable cause	Comments
Foliage pale and wilted. Plants stunted and may die. Knobby, spindlelike swellings on roots. Prevalent in soils where *Brassica* spp. crops have previously grown.	**Clubroot,** *Plasmodiophora brassicae.* A plasmodium microorganism. Propagules very persistent in media and infect roots, especially when wet. Soil pH of 7.2 or higher inhibits spore germination.	Plant only pathogen-free stock. Pasteurize media before planting. Don't grow cruciferous crops in soil where other infested plants in mustard family have grown, including certain weeds and crops such as broccoli and cabbage. Provide good drainage. Adjust pH if possible.

What the problem looks like	Probable cause	Comments
Foliage yellows and wilts, often on only one side. Plants stunted and may die. Roots dark and decayed. Young plants collapse and die.	**Root and crown rots,** *Pythium* spp., *Rhizoctonia solani*. Fungi persist in soil, spread in media and water. Favored by excess moisture and poor drainage.	Provide good drainage. Avoid excess irrigation and reduce watering if disease develops. See pages 93–98.
Petals have brown, decayed, water-soaked spots. Lower leaves rotted, may have woolly gray growth (spores). Stem may be girdled.	**Gray mold,** *Botrytis* sp. Fungus develops in plant debris. Favored by high humidity and 70° to 77°F.	Use good sanitation. Avoid overhead irrigation. Keep humidity low. Provide good air circulation. Don't crowd plants. See page 108.
Leaves have purplish red to dark brown, irregular, angular spots. Lower leaf surface covered with soft, fluffy fungal growth. Leaves yellow and drop.	**Downy mildew,** *Plasmopara* (=*Peronospora*) *pygmaea*. Spores produced only on living plants. Fungus persists as resistant oospores when conditions are dry. Favored by wet, humid conditions.	Provide good air circulation. Avoid overhead watering. Consider applying fungicide to protect foliage. See page 115.
Shoots short, swollen, flattened, or distorted. Secondary rot may infect shoot clumps, killing plant. Plants lack vigor.	**Fasciation,** cause often uncertain. May be viral, bacterial (e.g., *Rhodococcus fascians*), or genetic. Manage as bacterial and take additional measures.	Use pathogen-free stock. Avoid injuring base of plants, especially when wet. Keep base of plants dry. Dispose of infected plants. See page 121.
Plants severely stunted. Leaf terminals distorted, hardened. Buds deformed, discolored, and may drop.	**Cyclamen mite,** *Phytonemus pallidus*. A pinkish orange mite (family Tarsonemidae), $\frac{1}{100}$ inch long or smaller.	See page 217.
Foliage has small holes. Underside of leaves scraped, pitted, or mined. Terminals and buds may be chewed, stunting growth and reducing flowering. Plants may defoliate.	**Diamondback moth,** *Plutella xylostella*. Slender, pale green larvae, with scattered black hairs; rear prolegs form distinct V. Forms silken cocoons on foliage or debris. Gray to brown adult and mature larva about $\frac{1}{3}$ inch long. Attacks most Brassicaceae.	Exclude egg-laying moths with row covers. Apply *Bacillus thuringiensis* against larvae. *Trichogramma* parasite releases may be effective against eggs. See Caterpillars, page 203.

AMARYLLIS (*Amaryllis belladonna* or *Hippeastrum equestris*), Barbados lily, Belladonna lily, Naked-lady

Bulbs or basal stems decay. Soft, brown, odorous rot often at soil line. Leaf edges and stems may be discolored, soft, rotted.	**Soft rot,** *Erwinia* sp. Fungus persists in soil. Favored when wet. Disease is secondary, infecting wounds.	Avoid injuring bulbs or plants. Provide good drainage. Don't plant too deeply. Don't overwater. Use good sanitation; immediately discard infected plants and those nearby. See pages 100, 107.
Petals have brown, decayed, water-soaked spots. Lower leaves rotted, may have woolly gray growth (spores). Stem may be girdled.	**Gray mold,** *Botrytis cinerea*. Fungus develops in crop debris or inactive tissue. Favored by high humidity and 70° to 77°F. Spores airborne.	Use good sanitation. Avoid overhead irrigation. Keep humidity low. Provide good air circulation. Don't crowd plants. See page 108.
Roots and bulbs decay and may have irregular lesions. Stems may decay near soil line.	**Crown and root rots,** *Pythium* sp., *Rhizoctonia solani*. Fungi present in many soils. Infect bulbs through wounds. Favored by warm, moist conditions.	Avoid injuring plants or bulbs. Avoid deep planting. Don't overirrigate. Clean bulbs soon after digging, store them below 50°F. *Pythium*-labeled products may prevent. See pages 93–98.
Leaves discolor, wilt, stunt, or drop prematurely. Stems discolored, cankered, may ooze sap and die.	**Armillaria root rot,** *Armillaria mellea*. Present in many soils. Favored by warm, wet soil. Persists for years in infected roots.	Remove woody roots $\frac{1}{2}$ inch diameter or larger before planting. Pasteurize or air-dry soil well or avoid growing in fields previously planted with oaks or other susceptible woody plants. See page 99.
Lower leaves discolor or wilt. Basal stems rot. Plants collapse. May have white fungal mat and $\frac{1}{32}$- to $\frac{1}{8}$-inch, round, tan to brown sclerotia on decaying tissue and nearby soil.	**Southern blight** or **Crown rot,** *Sclerotium rolfsii*. Fungus survives in soil for 10 years. Spread in infected plants. Has wide host range.	Solarize or otherwise pasteurize soil before planting. Use pathogen-free stock. Fungicide applied around plant bases can prevent. See page 101.
Foliage or flower stalks have yellow, brown, or reddish streaks or mottling.	**Viruses,** including Hippeastrum mosaic (aphid-vectored), Tomato spotted wilt (thrips-vectored, many hosts).	Rogue infected plants; cover and dispose of them away from crop. Exclude or control insect vectors. See Viruses, page 121.
Leaves stunted, distorted; often swollen and thickened near base. Yellow to brown swellings in leaf centers and margins. May be discolored spots or blotches where stem joins bulb. Severely infected bulbs grow poorly and may rot.	**Stem and bulb nematode,** *Ditylenchus dipsaci*. Nematodes survive in infected bulbs and field debris for about 3 years. Also spread by infected water and equipment. Optimal temperature for infection and reproduction is 50° to 69°F.	Rogue infected plants and surrounding plants from field. Clean equipment well after working in diseased fields. Treating bulbs with hot water may control but may injure bulbs, causing stunted and deformed flowers. See page 265.

What the problem looks like	Probable cause	Comments

AMARYLLIS *(Amaryllis belladonna* or *Hippeastrum equestris)*, Barbados lily, Belladonna lily, Naked-lady (continued)

What the problem looks like	Probable cause	Comments
Flower stalks or leaves have red to brown spots or blotches; sometimes on bulb scales or flower buds. Infected stalks or leaves bent.	**Fire spot** or **Red spot,** *Stagonospora curtisii.* Fungal disease persists in dormant bulbs. Favored by moist, humid conditions.	Avoid injuring bulbs. Discard badly infected bulbs. Remove infected leaves and bulb scales. Avoid overwatering. Provide good drainage. Keep greenhouse humidity low. Provide adequate light and low temperatures during forcing.
Leaves or bulb scales have dark spots or otherwise discolored. Poor growth.	**Bulb scale mite,** *Steneotarsonemus laticeps.* Associated with injured or diseased bulbs.	Avoid injuring bulbs. Hot water immersion of bulbs can kill mites but may injure bulbs. See page 218.
Base of leaves has whitish, cottony material. Foliage may have sticky honeydew and blackish sooty mold. Foliage may yellow.	**Amaryllis mealybug** or **Lily bulb mealybug,** *Chorizococcus lounsburyi* or *Vryburgia amaryllidis;* **Citrus mealybug,** *Planococcus citri;* **Obscure mealybug,** *Pseudococcus affinis.* Powdery, gray insects, up to $\frac{1}{8}$ inch long. Colonies sometimes form a mat of whitish egg sacs, up to 2 inches long, around leaf bases.	See Mealybugs, page 183.
Blossoms have discolored blotches or streaks. Leaves or stems bleached, brownish, spotted, withered, or distorted. Buds turn brown and die. Stored bulbs may have sticky, scabby areas.	**Gladiolus thrips,** *Thrips simplex.* Slender, dark brown to shiny black adults; gray to whitish band at wing base. Nymphs and pupae yellow to orange. Feed hidden in leaf or bud sheaths, usually in groups.	See Thrips, page 161.
Foliage stippled, bleached, or blotched; may have varnishlike excrement.	**Banded greenhouse thrips,** *Hercinothrips femoralis.* Adult dark brown to yellowish, with three white bands on wings and dark brown basal segment on legs. Nymphs and pupae whitish to pale yellow. Sluggish thrips, usually in colonies; pupate on host or nearby on soil surface. Reportedly cannot survive outdoors overwinter in California and most other areas. Many hosts.	See Thrips, page 161.
Foliage discolored, stippled, bleached, or reddened. Leaves may have fine webbing and may drop.	**Twospotted spider mite,** *Tetranychus urticae.* Tiny green, yellowish, or red pests; may have 2 dark spots.	See Mites, page 213.
Flower buds may be mined. Petals, flower buds, terminals, or foliage chewed or scraped.	**Armyworms,** *Spodoptera* spp.; **Spotted cutworms,** *Xestia* spp. Greenish to brownish larvae, up to 2 inches long, with light stripes or spots.	Screen to exclude nocturnal moths. Avoid growing near other major hosts. *Bacillus thuringiensis* kills larvae. See Caterpillars, page 203.
Foliage yellow, stunted, producing no blooms. Bulbs feel soft and spongy; are hollowed and filled with brown excrement from wrinkled, gray, white, or brownish maggots boring inside.	**Bulb flies,** including Narcissus bulb fly, *Merodon equestris* and *Eumerus* spp. Adult is a hairy fly (family Syrphidae), black with gray to orange, resembles a bumble bee; hovers around blooming plants where eggs are laid. M. *equestris* adult and mature larva about $\frac{1}{2}$ inch long. *Eumerus* spp. smaller.	Inspect and discard spongy bulbs before planting. See page 200.

ANEMONE *(Anemone* spp.), Windflower

What the problem looks like	Probable cause	Comments
Petals have brown, decayed, water-soaked spots. Lower leaves rotted, may have woolly gray growth (spores). Stem may be girdled.	**Gray mold,** *Botrytis cinerea.* Fungus develops in crop debris or inactive tissue. Favored by high humidity and 70° to 77°F. Spores airborne.	Use good sanitation. Avoid overhead irrigation. Keep humidity low. Provide good air circulation. Don't crowd plants. See page 108.
Plants wilt, often die suddenly. Roots and stems dark, decayed.	**Root rot,** *Pythium* sp. Fungus survives in soil. Favored by wet, poorly drained media.	Don't overirrigate. Provide good drainage. See pages 93–96.
Leaves have purplish red to dark brown spots that are irregular and angular. Lower leaf surface covered with soft, fluffy fungal growth. Leaves yellow and drop.	**Downy mildew,** *Plasmopara* (=*Peronospora*) *pygmaea.* Spores produced only on living plants. Fungus persists in dead leaves when conditions are dry. Favored by moist, humid conditions.	Provide good air circulation. Avoid overhead watering. Consider applying fungicide to protect foliage. See page 115.
Plants wilt and collapse. Basal stem and tubers rotted. White cottony fungus growth may form on infected plant parts and soil. Tan or brown sclerotia about $\frac{1}{16}$ inch in diameter form on rotted tissue.	**Southern blight,** *Sclerotium rolfsii.* Sclerotia survive in soil, germinate there, and infect susceptible plants. No airborne spores are formed. Many hosts. Favored by high temperatures.	Avoid fields where disease has occurred or pasteurize soil before planting. Rogue all infected plants. Fungicide applied at base of plants may help to prevent. See page 101.

What the problem looks like	Probable cause	Comments
Cottony growth or large, black sclerotia inside stems. Stems become bleached, white, and girdled.	**Cottony rot**, *Sclerotinia sclerotiorum*. Airborne spores from infected media. Favored when wet.	Avoid overhead irrigation. Irrigate early in the day so plants dry. Remove and dispose of plant debris around growing area. See page 101.
Leaves have brown to orangish powdery pustules and yellowish spots. Leaves may yellow and drop.	**Rusts**, *Puccinia, Tranzschelia* spp. Fungi survive on living tissue. Spores are airborne. Favored by high humidity and water.	Avoid overhead irrigation. Water in morning. Provide good air circulation. Don't crowd plants. See page 119.
Leaves or stems have small circular to irregular, greenish, yellow, or brownish spots, sometimes with discolored border. Spots may be somewhat thickened; are evident on both sides of leaf.	**Leaf and Stem smut**, *Urocystis anemones*. Fungus survives on live plants and refuse. Spores borne on wind and rain. Favored by rain and overhead irrigation.	Avoid overhead irrigation. Use good sanitation; remove and dispose of plant refuse.
Cluster of yellow shoots, often on base of one side plant. Plant stunted. Flowers may be green and deformed.	**Aster yellows**. Phytoplasmalike organisms spread by leafhoppers. Wide host range.	Control weeds and leafhoppers near crop. Don't plant near weedy areas. See pages 129–130.
Leaves have yellow to brown patches or mottling; may die. Plants may be stunted or distorted and may die.	**Anemone mosaic virus, Tobacco necrosis virus, Tobacco ringspot virus, Tomato spotted wilt virus**. Some are spread by thrips and have a wide host range.	Rogue infected plants; cover and dispose of them away from crop. Control weeds and thrips. See page 121.
Buds killed or distorted. Blossoms may drop prematurely. Flowers may be deformed or discolored.	**Thrips**, including Pear thrips, *Taeniothrips inconsequens*. Tiny slender, dark brown, black, yellowish, or whitish insects.	See page 161.
Plant has sticky honeydew and blackish sooty mold. Foliage may yellow. Tiny white mothlike adults present.	**Whiteflies**. Nymphs and pupae flattened, oval, translucent, and greenish or yellow.	See page 170.
Foliage has sticky honeydew, blackish sooty mold, and whitish cast skins. Terminals and young leaves may curl or distort. Foliage may yellow.	**Aphids**, including Crescent-marked lily aphid, *Aulacorthum circumflexum* or *Myzus circumflexus*. Small pear-shaped insects, often green, yellow, reddish or blackish.	See page 179.
Leaves yellowish with dark green to brown, vein-limited, angular blotches that develop progressively up from base.	**Foliar nematodes**, *Aphelenchoides fragariae*. Tiny roundworms spread in plant debris by vegetative propagation, and by splashing water. Not common in California.	Use uninfected stock plants. Remove plant debris. Avoid overhead irrigation; leaves must be wet for infection to occur. See page 265.
Foliage chewed and webbed together with silk. Stems may be mined by larvae that wriggle vigorously when touched.	**Greenhouse leaftier**, *Udea rubigalis*. Larva yellowish green with three longitudinal green to white stripes. Adult reddish brown with black wavy lines on wings.	Adult and mature larva about ¾ inch long. Pyralidae moth has about 6 generations per year. Avoid growing floral hosts near celery, a major host. See Caterpillars, page 203.

ANIGOZANTHOS (*Anigozanthos* spp.), Kangaroo paw

Leaves have small reddish or yellowish spots or blotches. Foliage dries and drops.	**Leaf spot**, *Alternaria* sp. Favored by warm, humid conditions. Spread in air and splashing water.	Avoid overhead irrigation. Provide good air circulation; don't crowd plants. Rogue infected plants. Dispose of debris. See pages 116–118.
Foliage has dark spots. Leaf spots may have chlorotic margins or grayish centers. Dark spore masses may be visible on lesions. Leaves may die and drop.	**Ink spot**, *Drechslera* (=*Bipolaris*) *iridis*. Fungus survives in infected plant debris. Moist conditions and 68° to 77°F favor the disease.	Use good sanitation. Promptly dispose of infected plant debris.

ANTHURIUM (*Anthurium* spp.)

Leaves may turn yellowish or darken. Plant may wilt and die. Roots and stem around soil dark and decayed.	**Pythium root rot**, *Pythium* spp.; **Rhizoctonia aerial blight**, *Rhizoctonia solani*; **Phytophthora leaf spot**, *Phytophthora* spp. Fungi promoted by wet, poorly drained soil.	Provide good drainage. Avoid excess irrigation and reduce watering if disease develops. See pages 93–98.
Foliage yellows and wilts. Leaves may have brown, tan, reddish or dark spots, lesions, or rings that are irregular or water-soaked. Stems or flowers may spot. Soft brown stem rot near soil line. Stems may collapse and die.	**Bacterial leaf spot and blight**, *Erwinia carotovora, E. chrysanthemi, Pseudomonas cichorii, Xanthomonas campestris*. Persist in media and infected stock. Infect through wounds. Favored when wet.	Keep foliage dry. Use drip irrigation. Don't overwater. Provide good drainage. Use good sanitation; rogue infected and nearby plants. Don't crowd plantings. Avoid injuring plants. See pages 100, 107, 118.

What the problem looks like	Probable cause	Comments
ANTHURIUM (*Anthurium* spp.) (continued)		
Leaves or flower stalks have tan to brown circular spots or blotches. Plants turn slightly yellow, wilt, and may die. Crown tissues decay. Roots are not affected during early stages.	**Anthracnose,** *Colletotrichum gloeosporioides.* Fungus survives in infected plants and debris. Spores spread by splashing water. Favored by wet weather and overhead irrigation.	Avoid overhead irrigation. Minimize wounding plants. Fungicide application may help prevent problem. See pages 116–118.
Leaves have yellowish patterns, may distort severely. Veins may yellow. Plants grow slowly, are stunted.	**Dasheen mosaic virus.** Spread by aphids or mechanically in sap, such as through contaminated tools.	Use virus-free plants produced by tissue culture. Rogue infected plants. Pasteurize equipment to avoid mechanical spread. Control aphids. See Viruses, page 121.
Buds or flowers blacken, distort, or fail to develop.	**Chilling injury.** Noninfectious disorder resulting from exposure to cold to induce flowering.	Avoid prolonged cool conditions or excessively low temperatures.
Foliage yellows or wilts. Knots or swellings on feeder roots and fleshy roots.	**Root knot nematode,** *Meloidogyne* spp. Tiny roundworms; prefer warm, sandy soil. Many hosts.	Pasteurize or treat media before planting. Rogue affected plants. See page 265.
Foliage has sticky honeydew or blackish sooty mold. Foliage may yellow. Plant may grow slowly. Cottony egg sacs may be visible.	**Citrus mealybug,** *Planococcus citri;* **Longtailed mealybug,** *Pseudococcus longispinus.* Powdery gray insects, with waxy marginal filaments.	See Mealybugs, page 183.
Plant has sticky honeydew and blackish sooty mold. Foliage may yellow. Tiny, white, mothlike adults present.	**Whiteflies,** including Silverleaf whitefly, *Bemisia argentifolii;* Sweetpotato whitefly, *Bemisia tabaci.* Nymphs and pupae flattened, oval, translucent, and greenish or yellow.	See page 170.
Foliage or stems have blackish sooty mold. Plant may die back or decline.	**Brown soft scale,** *Coccus hesperidum;* **Long brown scale,** *Coccus longulus;* **Hemispherical scale,** *Saissetia coffeae;* **Nigra scale,** *Parasaissetia nigra.* Orange, black, or brown flattened to bulbous insects.	Outdoors, natural enemies may provide good control. See Scales, page 186.
Foliage turns yellow. Plant may decline or die back. Stems or leaves have gray, whitish, yellow, reddish, or brownish encrustations from small roundish to elongate insects.	**Armored scales,** including Chinese lepidosaphes scale, *Lepidosaphes chinensis;* Cyanophyllum scale, *Hemiberlesia cyanophylii;* Dictyosperum scale, *Chrysomphalus dictyospermi.* Colonies of circular, flat insects, less than $1/16$ inch long.	See Scales, page 186.
Foliage discolored, stippled, bleached, or reddened. Leaves may have fine webbing and may drop.	**False spider mites,** *Brevipalpus* spp.; **Twospotted spider mite,** *Tetranychus urticae.* Tiny greenish, yellowish, or red mites; may have 2 darker spots.	See Mites, page 213.
Flower bracts or spathes have pale streaks, stippling, or distortion.	**Thrips.** Tiny, slender, yellowish to dark brown insects. Adults have fringes or tiny hairs on wings.	See page 161.
Leaves yellowish; have dark green to brown, vein-limited bands or angular blotches that develop progressively up from older leaves.	**Foliar nematodes,** *Aphelenchoides fragariae.* Tiny roundworms spread in plant debris and by vegetative propagation and splashing water. Not common in California.	Use uninfected stock plants. Remove plant debris. Avoid overhead irrigation; leaves must be wet for infection to occur. See page 265.
ASPARAGUS FERN (*Asparagus setaceus*), Fern asparagus		
Plants yellow and wilt. Stem base black. Vascular tissue brownish. Roots may be dark but not rotted.	**Crown, root, and stem rot; Fusarium wilt,** *Fusarium* spp. Fungal disease spread by infected seed, water, or media. Persists for years in soil. Most severe in warm soil.	Use pathogen-free or fungicide-treated seed. Pasteurize media before planting or grow only once every 5 years on infested land. See pages 93–96, 104.
Plant stunted, yellow, or wilted. Stem rotted with brown cankers at soil line.	**Root and stem rot,** *Rhizoctonia* spp. Soilborne fungi favored by warm, moist conditions. Not reported on *Asparagus* in California.	Pasteurize media before planting. Practice good sanitation. Avoid overwatering and deep planting. See pages 93–98.
Petals have brown water-soaked spots. Lower leaves rotted and may have woolly gray growth (spores). Stem may be girdled.	**Gray mold,** *Botrytis cinerea.* Fungus develops in crop debris or inactive tissue. Favored by high humidity and 70° to 77°F. Spores airborne.	Use good sanitation. Avoid overhead irrigation. Keep humidity low. Provide good air circulation. Don't crowd plants. See page 108.
Leaves or stems have brown to yellow spots or or blotches. Spots may have dark or yellowish margins. Foliage may shrivel and drop.	**Leaf and stem spots, Blights,** including *Alternaria, Cercospora, Colletotrichum, Phyllosticta* spp. Spread by splashing water. Favored by prolonged wet conditions. Persist in plant debris. Only *Cercospora* is reported on *Asparagus* in California.	Avoid wetting foliage; use drip irrigation. Use good sanitation; promptly remove and dispose of debris and infected leaves. See Leaf Spots, pages 116–118.

What the problem looks like	Probable cause	Comments
Foliage yellows. Growth stunted.	**Noninfectious disorders.** Causes include prolonged cool temperature, iron or manganese deficiency, excess salts in media; or possibly root injury or root rot fungi.	Provide appropriate environmental conditions and use good cultural practices.
Foliage or blossoms have irregular white or brown blotches or stippling. Blossoms or terminals may distort or die. Growth may be stunted.	**Thrips.** Tiny slender dark brown to yellowish insects.	See page 161.
Foliage discolored, stippled, bleached, or reddened; may have fine webbing. Leaves may drop.	**Spider mites.** Tiny greenish, yellowish, or reddish pests; may have 2 dark spots.	See page 213.
Foliage turns yellow. Plant may decline or die back. Stems or leaves have tan to yellow encrustations.	**Oleander scale,** *Aspidiotus nerii.* Circular flat insects, less than $1/16$ inch long.	See Scales, page 186.
Plant has sticky honeydew, blackish sooty mold, and whitish cast skins. Foliage may yellow.	**Aphids.** Small pear-shaped insects, often green, yellowish, or blackish; often in colonies.	See page 179.
Sticky honeydew or blackish sooty mold on foliage. Foliage may wilt or yellow. Plant grows slowly.	**Mealybugs,** including Citrus mealybug, *Planococcus citri;* Longtailed mealybug, *Pseudococcus longispinus.* Powdery, gray insects with waxy marginal filaments.	See page 183.
Leaves and blossoms chewed (edges notched).	**Fuller rose beetle,** *Asynonychus godmani.* Adult pale brown weevil rarely seen, feeds at night. Larva whitish maggot, lives in soil, eats roots.	See Weevils, page 208.
Buds or leaves mined or chewed and may be webbed with silk.	**Omnivorous leaftier,** *Cnephasia longana.* Gray to brownish larvae and nocturnal moths, $1/2$ inch long. Larvae may have grayish stripes. Attacks strawberries and many other hosts. Common along central California coast. Has 1 generation per year outdoors.	See Caterpillars, page 203.
Foliage, buds, and stems chewed. Young plants clipped at base. Stocky moths present, attracted to lights at night, wings folded at rest.	**Variegated cutworm,** *Peridroma saucia.* Gray or brown larva with dark markings, row of yellow dots on back. Hides in soil during day.	Exclude moths, which fly to lights at night. Apply *Bacillus thuringiensis* to young larvae. Insecticide bait kills larvae. See Caterpillars, page 203.

ASTER (*Aster* spp.), CHINA ASTER (*Callistephus chinensis*)

What the problem looks like	Probable cause	Comments
Plants yellow and wilt, often on one side. Stem base black. Vascular tissue brownish. Seedlings die. Plants stunted. May be pink spore mass at soil level.	**Fusarium wilt,** *Fusarium oxysporum* f. sp. *callistephi.* Fungal disease spread by infected seed, water, or media. Persists for years in soil. Most severe in warm soil.	Use pathogen-free or fungicide-treated seed. Pasteurize media before planting or grow only once every 5 years on infested land. See page 104.
Plants yellow and wilt, often on one side. Similar to Fusarium wilt, but no basal pink spore mass. Vascular tissue darkens.	**Verticillium wilt,** *Verticillium dahliae.* Most severe during warm weather after cool weather. Uncommon on aster in California.	Pasteurize media or avoid planting in infested soil. See pages 104–106.
Plants wilt, often die suddenly. Roots and stem blackish, decayed.	**Root rot,** *Pythium, Phytophthora* spp. Fungi survive in soil, favored by wet, poorly drained media.	Don't overirrigate. Provide good drainage. Outdoors, plant in raised beds. See pages 93–97.
Outside of plant has cottony growth. Inside stems have large black sclerotia. Stems become bleached, white, and girdled.	**Cottony rot,** *Sclerotinia sclerotiorum.* Airborne spores from infected media, favored when humid, wet.	Avoid overhead irrigation. Irrigate early in the day so plants dry. Remove and dispose of plant debris around growing area. See page 101.
Lower leaves discolor and decay. Brown rot on stem at soil line. Plants die.	**Stem rot,** *Rhizoctonia solani.* Fungus favored by high temperatures. Spread by infected media or plant debris.	Pasteurize media or treat seedlings before planting. See page 93–98.
Petals have brown, decayed, water-soaked spots. Lower leaves rotted and may have woolly gray growth (spores). Stem may be girdled.	**Gray mold,** *Botrytis cinerea.* Fungus develops in crop debris or inactive tissue. Favored by high humidity and 70° to 77°F. Spores airborne.	Use good sanitation. Avoid overhead irrigation. Keep humidity low. Provide good air circulation. Don't crowd plants. See page 108.
White powdery growth, primarily on older leaves and stem.	**Powdery mildew,** *Erysiphe cichoracearum.* Free water not required for infection.	Provide good air circulation and adequate light. Consider applying fungicide to prevent. See page 112.

What the problem looks like	Probable cause	Comments

ASTER (*Aster* spp.), CHINA ASTER (*Callistephus chinensis*) (continued)

What the problem looks like	Probable cause	Comments
Leaf underside has orange, powdery pustules. Leaf upperside may have yellow spots. Leaves may discolor overall, dry, and die.	**Rusts,** *Coleosporium asterum, Puccinia* sp. Fungi favored by wet foliage.	Don't wet foliage. Use good sanitation. Sulfur, Bordeaux, and some synthetics can control. See page 119.
Irregular, circular, brown, yellow, red, or black spots on lower leaves. Leaves may die.	**Leaf spots,** including *Septoria* spp. Fungal spores are spread by water. Infection favored by wet foliage.	Plant where air circulation is good. Don't wet foliage or use overhead irrigation. See pages 116–118.
Leaves have chlorotic streaks, spots, mottling, or rings; sometimes also on petioles and flower stalks. Leaves may develop necrotic lesions. Plant may be stunted.	**Tomato spotted wilt virus.** Virus spread by thrips, infects wide host range.	Rogue infected plants; cover and dispose of them away from crop. Control weeds. Exclude or control thrips. See Viruses, page 121.
Cluster of yellow shoots grows from base of stunted plant, sometimes on one side. Flowers green, deformed.	**Aster yellows.** Phytoplasmalike organism, has wide host range and is spread by leafhoppers.	Control weeds and leafhoppers near crop. Don't plant near weedy areas. See pages 129–130.
Foliage distorted, discolored, stippled, or brown; may drop prematurely. Stems or leaves have pimplelike (egg-laying) punctures.	**Aster leafhopper,** *Macrosteles quadrilineatus.* Slender green or yellowish insects that suck plant sap and readily jump, fly, or crawl away sideways when disturbed. Leafhopper moves from infected weeds and vectors aster yellows.	Control weeds. See Leafhoppers, page 193.
Shoots short, swollen, flattened, or distorted. Secondary rot may infect shoot clumps, killing plant. Plants lack vigor.	**Fasciation,** cause often uncertain. May be viral, bacterial (e.g., *Rhodococcus fascians*), or genetic. Manage as bacterial and take additional measures.	Use pathogen-free stock. Avoid injuring base of plants, especially when wet. Keep base of plants dry. Dispose of infected plants. See page 121.
Shoots or blossoms blackened, dwarfed, discolored, or distorted. Leaf tips may wilt and die.	**Plant bugs,** *Lygus* spp. Brown, green, or yellowish bugs, up to ¼ inch long, that suck plant juices.	Control nearby weeds, from which bugs move. Exclude bugs from growing area. See True Bugs, page 194.
Foliage or blossoms have irregular white or brown blotches or stippling. Blossoms or terminals may distort. Growth may be stunted. Varnishlike excrement may be visible.	**Banded greenhouse thrips,** *Hercinothrips femoralis;* **Western flower thrips,** *Frankliniella occidentalis.* Tiny slender dark brown to yellowish insects.	See Thrips, page 161.
Foliage stippled, bleached, bronzed. Blackish excrement may be present.	**Chrysanthemum lace bug,** *Corythucha marmorata.* Black and white insects with some brown; up to ⅛ inch long.	Control goldenrod (*Solidago* spp.), alternate hosts, and nearby weeds. See True Bugs, page 194.
Foliage discolored, stippled, bleached, or reddened and may drop. Fine webbing may be present.	**Spider mites.** Tiny greenish, yellowish, or red mites; may have 2 dark spots.	See page 213.
Plant has sticky honeydew and blackish sooty mold. Foliage may yellow. Tiny, white, mothlike adults present.	**Iris whitefly,** *Aleyrodes spiraeoides;* **Greenhouse whitefly,** *Trialeurodes vaporariorum;* **Silverleaf** and **Sweetpotato whiteflies,** *Bemisia* spp. Nymphs and pupae flattened, oval, translucent, and greenish or yellow.	See Whiteflies, page 170.
Plant growth may be retarded from small insects infesting roots and possibly stems near soil.	**Aster or Erigeron root aphid,** *Aphis middletonii.* Small pear-shaped insects, light gray to dark green.	Infests many Asteraceae; control nearby weeds in this family. See Aphids, page 179.
Plant has sticky honeydew, blackish sooty mold, and whitish cast skins. Foliage may yellow.	**Aphids,** including *Aphis, Macrosiphum* spp. Pear-shaped, often green, yellowish, or black insects.	See page 179.
Foliage or stems have blackish sooty mold. Plant may wilt, decline, or die back.	**Black scale,** *Saissetia oleae.* Orange, black, or brown scale insects, flattened to bulbous.	See Scales, page 186.
Plant has sticky honeydew, blackish sooty mold, and elongated, whitish material (egg sacs). Insects on twigs or leaves.	**Cottony cushion scale,** *Icerya purchasi.* Females brown, orange, red, or yellow. Uncommon.	Natural enemies can provide good control. See Scales, page 186.
Winding tunnels in (mostly basal) leaves, may extend into petiole and stem. Leaves may turn white, wilt. Leaves have pale spots or punctures.	**Leafminers,** *Liriomyza huidobrensis, L. sativae, L. trifolii.* Small active flies, dark with yellow. Yellowish maggots bore in tissue.	Avoid planting aster near vegetable hosts of *L. huidobrensis:* beet, celery, pea, and spinach. See page 167.
Leaves and blossoms chewed (edges notched).	**Weevils,** including Cribrate weevil, *O. cribricollis.* Rarely seen adult weevils brown, black, to gray, feed at night. Larvae are whitish maggots that feed on roots.	See page 208.

What the problem looks like	Probable cause	Comments
Flowers, terminals, or foliage chewed or scraped. Leaves may be webbed with silk. Stems may be clipped near soil surface. Flower buds may be mined.	**Beet armyworm,** *Spodoptera exigua;* **Cabbage looper,** *Trichoplusia ni;* **Carnation leafroller,** *Platynota sultana;* **Corn earworm,** *Helicoverpa zea;* **Cutworms,** *Agrotis* spp.; **Omnivorous leaftier,** *Cnephasia longana.* Green to brownish larvae, up to 1½ inches long; may have light, longitudinal stripes.	Screen to exclude moths from growing areas. Avoid growing near other major hosts. *Bacillus thuringiensis* kills larvae. See Caterpillars, page 203.
Foliage chewed, may have lacy skeleton between veins. Blossoms chewed.	**Japanese beetle,** *Popillia japonica.* Shiny, metallic green, coppery beetles with whitish tufts of hair. Larvae are white grubs that chew roots, especially turf. Occurs in eastern U.S. Report to agricultural officials if found in western U.S.	In eastern U.S., apply *Bacillus popilliae,* parasitic nematodes, or other insecticide to soil and nearby turf in spring, before adults emerge. Spray foliage if adults present. See White Grubs, page 211.

AUCUBA (*Aucuba japonica*)

What the problem looks like	Probable cause	Comments
Foliage yellows and wilts, often on only one side of plant. Plant stunted. Roots darken and decay.	**Root and crown rot,** *Phytophthora* spp. Fungal disease favored by too much water and poor drainage.	See pages 93–97.
Foliage yellows and wilts, often only on one side of plant. Leaves dry and die from base of plant up. Plant may have brown vascular streaking.	**Verticillium wilt,** *Verticillium dahliae.* Fungus contaminates soil, cuttings, and root divisions. Favored by cool weather followed by hot conditions.	Use pathogen-free stock. Pasteurize media before planting. Avoid overwatering. See pages 104–106.
Leaves discolor, wilt, stunt, or drop prematurely. Stems discolored, cankered, may ooze sap and die.	**Armillaria root rot,** *Armillaria mellea.* Present in many soils. Favored by warm, wet soil. Persists for years in infected roots.	Remove woody roots ½ inch diameter or larger before planting. Pasteurize or air-dry soil well or avoid growing in fields previously planted with oaks or other susceptible woody plants. See page 99.
Petals have brown, water-soaked spots. Lower leaves rotted and may have woolly gray growth (spores). Stem may be girdled.	**Gray mold,** *Botrytis cinerea.* Fungus develops in crop debris or inactive tissue. Favored by high humidity and 70° to 77°F. Spores airborne.	Use good sanitation. Avoid overhead irrigation. Keep humidity low. Provide good air circulation. Don't crowd plants. See page 108.
Leaves blackened between veins. Upper plant affected first. Problem occurs mostly in warmer growing areas.	**Sunburn.** Excess light conditions can occur even under some shade cloths.	Reduce light with higher-percentage shade cloth. See page 62.
Leaf terminals and margins appear scorched, necrotic; plant dies back.	**Noninfectious disorders.** Excess salt, excess sun, or high pH.	Leach media. Check pH and adjust if needed. Provide shade.
Foliage turns yellow. Plant declines or dies back. Bark or leaves have tan, yellow, brown, gray, or reddish encrustations (colonies of circular flat insects, less than ⅟16 inch long).	**Bifasciculate scale,** *Chrysomphalus bifasciculatus;* **California red scale,** *Aonidiella aurantii;* **Greedy scale,** *Hemiberlesia rapax;* **Latania scale,** *H. lataniae;* **Oleander scale,** *Aspidiotus nerii.*	See Scales, page 186.
Foliage or stems have blackish sooty mold. Plant may wilt, decline, or die back.	**Black scale,** *Saissetia oleae;* **Brown soft scale,** *Coccus hesperidum.* Orange, yellow, black, or brown insects, flattened to bulbous.	See Scales, page 186.
Plants stunted, decline, may die. Powdery, waxy material may be visible on roots and around crown.	**Ground mealybug,** *Rhizoecus* spp. Small, slender, pale insects; may be lightly covered with powdery wax, but no marginal filaments.	See page 186.
Foliage has sticky honeydew or blackish sooty mold; may wilt or yellow. Plant grows slowly.	**Longtailed mealybug,** *Pseudococcus longispinus.* Powdery, gray insects with waxy marginal filaments. Unlike most mealybugs, no cottony egg sacs are produced.	See Mealybugs, page 183.

AZALEA, RHODODENDRON (*Rhododendron* spp.)

What the problem looks like	Probable cause	Comments
Foliage yellows and wilts, often on only one side. Plant stunted and may die. Stems or roots soft, dark, decayed. Stem may have girdling necrosis or canker near soil line. Young plants collapse and die.	**Damping-off,** *Rhizoctonia solani, Pythium* spp.; **Root rot and wilt,** *Phytophthora* spp.; **Cylindrocladium blight and root rot,** *Cylindrocladium scoparium.* Fungi persist in soil, spread in media or water. Favored by excess moisture and poor drainage.	Pasteurize media before planting. Use good sanitation. Provide good drainage. Avoid excess irrigation. Use drip irrigation where feasible. Reduce watering if disease develops. See pages 93–98.
Leaves discolor, wilt, stunt, or drop prematurely. Stems discolored, cankered, may ooze sap and die.	**Armillaria root rot,** *Armillaria mellea.* Present in many soils. Favored by warm, wet soil. Persists for years in infected roots.	Remove woody roots ½ inch diameter or larger before planting. Pasteurize or air-dry soil well or avoid growing in fields previously planted with oaks or other susceptible woody plants. See page 99.

What the problem looks like	Probable cause	Comments

AZALEA, RHODODENDRON (*Rhododendron* spp.) (continued)

What the problem looks like	Probable cause	Comments
Leaves have small reddish, tan, or yellowish spots or blotches. Spots may have discolored border. Foliage dries and drops.	**Cercospora leaf spot**, *Pseudocercospora handelii*; **Leaf scorch**, *Septoria azaleae*. Favored by warm, humid conditions. Spread in air and splashing water.	Avoid overhead irrigation. Provide good air circulation; don't crowd plants. Rogue infected plants. Dispose of debris. See Leaf Spots, pages 116–118.
Leaf underside has yellow to brownish pustules. Leaf upperside may spot. Foliage may yellow and drop prematurely.	**Chrysomyxa leaf rust**. *Chrysomyxa* spp. Fungal disease spread by splashing water.	Avoid overhead irrigation. Keep humidity low. Consider protecting foliage with fungicide. See Rusts, page 119.
Flowers have small, round, white or brown spots or larger blotches. Flowers collapse, become soft, and cling to leaves or stems. Small black sclerotia may appear on diseased tissue.	**Ovulinia petal blight**, *Ovulinia azaleae*. Fungus favored by cool, wet, or humid conditions. Spores spread by splashing water.	Don't overhead water. Remove and dispose of diseased blossoms. Fungicide may prevent damage if applied before wet conditions. Where practical, apply 4 inches of organic mulch under plants to reduce spore survival.
Petals have brown water-soaked spots. Lower leaves rotted and may have woolly gray growth (spores). Stem may be girdled.	**Botrytis petal blight**, *Botrytis cinerea*. Fungus develops in crop debris or inactive tissue. Favored by high humidity and 70° to 77°F. Spores airborne.	Use good sanitation. Avoid overhead irrigation. Keep humidity low. Provide good air circulation. Don't crowd plants. See page 108.
White, powdery growth or lesions primarily on older leaves and stem. Severely affected leaves dry and die.	**Powdery mildew**, *Erysiphe polygoni*, *Microsphaera penicillata*. Free water not required for infection.	Provide good air circulation and adequate light. Consider applying fungicide to prevent. See page 112.
Leaves have dark dead spots or ring patterns.	**Rhododendron necrotic leaf spot**. Viral disease transmissible by grafting.	Don't graft symptomatic plants. Replace plants if growth is not satisfactory. See Viruses, page 121.
Foliage yellows, wilts, may drop prematurely. Plants stunted, may die back. Roots may be distorted, galled, or have few rootlets.	**Nematodes**, including *Meloidogyne*, *Trichodorus*, *Tylenchorhynchus* spp. Microscopic roundworms that feed on roots.	See page 265.
New foliage yellow, except veins green.	**Iron deficiency**. Noninfectious disorder.	See pages 56–59.
Few or no flowers. Uneven flowering or asynchronous blossoming.	**Flower failure**. Causes include deficient light, improper temperatures, late pinching, and over crowding.	Provide proper growth conditions and good cultural care. Allow enough time between pinching shoots and dormancy-breaking treatments.
Plants defoliate. Most or all leaves drop.	**Leaf drop**. Causes include ethylene pollution, lack of water, low humidity, fertilizer injury, low light, excess air movement.	Provide proper growth and storage conditions and good cultural care.
Leaf partly or all thickened, distorted, and crisp. Blossoms distorted and discolored. White or pinkish spores cover infected tissue.	**Leaf and flower gall**, *Exobasidium vaccinii*. Fungus spread by air only during wet conditions.	Avoid overhead watering. Prune out and dispose of infected tissue. Cut and prune plants only when conditions and plant are dry. Remove dropped petals.
Plants severely stunted. Leaf terminals distorted, hardened. Buds deformed, discolored, and may drop.	**Cyclamen mite**, *Phytonemus pallidus*. A pinkish orange mite (family Tarsonemidae), 1/100 inch long or smaller.	See page 217.
Foliage bleached, brittle; edges may be curled or ragged. Blossoms distort or discolor. Slow growth.	**Broad mite**, *Polyphagotarsonemus latus*. Translucent to dark green insect, 1/100 inch long or smaller.	See page 217.
Brown, dead flecks in foliage, which may be bleached, stippled, or reddened. Leaves may drop. Fine webbing may be present. May be worse under dry conditions and on drought-stressed plants.	**Mites**, including Privet mite, *Brevipalpus obovatus*; Southern red mite, *Oligonychus ilicis*; Twospotted spider mite, *Tetranychus urticae*. Tiny green, yellow, or reddish pests; may have 2 darkened spots on back.	See page 213.
Leaves bleached, stippled, bronzed, or mottled. Leaf underside may have dark, varnishlike excrement. Foliage remains discolored until drops or is pruned off.	**Azalea lace bug**, *Stephanitis pyrioides*. Adults about 1/8 inch long with expanded, reticulated, or lace-like thorax and forewings. Nymphs dark and spiny. Favored by dry conditions. Several generations per year. Pest in eastern U.S.	Avoid planting in full sun, where azalea lace bugs cause more damage. Water plants adequately. Oil or soap applied to underside of leaves kills lace bugs. See True Bugs, page 194.
Foliage bleached, stippled. Leaf undersides have dark varnishlike excrement.	**Greenhouse thrips**, *Heliothrips haemorrhoidalis*. Tiny, slender, black adults and yellowish nymphs.	See page 161.
Foliage yellows. Plant declines or dies back. Leaves or stems have tan, yellowish, white, gray, or brown encrustation.	**Latania scale**, *Hemiberlesia lataniae*; **Oleander scale**, *Aspidiotus nerii*. Circular, flat scale insects less than 1/16 inch long.	See page 186.

What the problem looks like	Probable cause	Comments
Distorted terminals. Plant has whitish wax, usually around terminals and leaf axils. Plant may have sticky honeydew and blackish sooty mold.	**Woolly azalea scale,** *Eriococcus azaleae*. Female resembles mealybug, red to purplish, surrounded by or covered with whitish wax. Mature females about ⅛ inch long. Apparently only 1 generation per year, but all stages can be present at once.	See page 186.
Plant has sticky honeydew, blackish sooty mold, and possibly cottony waxy material.	**Citrus mealybug,** *Planococcus citri*; **Longtailed mealybug,** *Pseudococcus longispinus*; **Obscure mealybug,** *Pseudococcus affinis*. Grayish, oval, waxy, slow-moving insects with marginal filaments.	See Mealybugs, page 183.
Sticky honeydew and blackish sooty mold on plant. Foliage may yellow. Tiny, waxy, white, mothlike adults.	**Whiteflies,** including Azalea whitefly, *Pealius azaleae*; Greenhouse whitefly, *Trialeurodes vaporariorum*; Silverleaf whitefly, *Bemisia argentifolii*. Nymphs and pupae are oval, flattened, translucent, and yellowish.	See page 170.
Foliage has sticky honeydew, blackish sooty mold, and whitish cast skins. Foliage may yellow. New terminals may be distorted.	**Aphids,** including *Aphis citricola, A. gossypii, Illinoia azaleae, I. rhododendri*. Small pear-shaped insects, often green or yellowish.	See page 179.
Leaves brown, especially tips; mined in blotches, curled and tied with silk that may contain dark fecal pellets. Adult moths with bright yellow and purple markings.	**Azalea leafminer,** *Gracillaria* or *Caloptilia azaleella*. Greenish larvae up to ½ inch long; secretive, mine when young, feed externally as mature.	Control difficult. Exclude moths with screens. Clip and dispose of infested foliage. Apply oil for mature larvae, systemic insecticide for all stages. See page 167.
Leaves yellowish; have dark green or brown, vein-limited, angular blotches that develop progressively up from older leaves.	**Foliar nematodes,** *Aphelenchoides fragariae*. Tiny roundworms spread in plant debris and by vegetative propagation and splashing water. Not common in California.	Use uninfected stock plants. Remove plant debris. Avoid overhead irrigation; leaves must be wet for infection to occur. See page 265.
Leaves stunted, distorted, often swollen and thickened near base. Leaf centers and margins have yellow to brown swellings. Stems may have discolored spots or blotches. Plants grow poorly and may rot.	**Stem and bulb nematode,** *Ditylenchus dipsaci*. Nematodes survive in infected plants and plant debris, also spread by infected water and equipment. Optimal temperature for infection and reproduction is 50° to 69°F.	Rogue infected plants and surrounding plants from field. Clean equipment well after working in diseased fields. See page 265.
Chewed leaves (edges notched) and blossoms.	**Black vine weevil,** *Otiorhynchus sulcatus*; **Cribrate weevil,** *O. cribricollis*; **Fuller rose beetle,** *Asynonychus godmani*; **Woods weevil,** *Nemocestes incomptus*. Rarely seen adults brown, black, to gray snout beetles that feed at night. Larvae whitish maggots that feed on roots.	See page 208.
Dead, broken shoots and terminals. Leaves may be curled, scraped on underside, and yellow. Stems and roots mined by whitish larva, up to ¾ inch long.	**Azalea** or **Rhododendron stem borer,** *Oberea myops*. Adult beetle yellowish, ½ inch long, with 2 dark spots and long antennae. One generation requires 2 years. Cerambycidae occurs in eastern U.S., not California.	Provide good cultural care. Prune and dispose of swollen, infested shoots, which may have holes or exude frass.
Pale green to yellow foliage. Shoots may die and break. Sawdustlike frass on ground or on bark, which may have holes from boring by whitish larvae. Brownish pupal cast skins may protrude from bark; if empty, moths have emerged, inspect bark to determine when.	**Rhododendron borer,** *Synanthedon rhododendri*. Adult black and yellow, wasplike, clearwing moth, (family Sesiidae) ½ inch long. Occurs only in eastern U.S. Prefers stressed or injured plants.	Provide good cultural care and avoid making wounds. Pheromone trap and correctly identify adults. Spray persistent insecticide 1 to 2 weeks after catching first moth, repeat 3 weeks later if moths still caught. Nematodes injected into holes or sprayed on bark in spring/late summer may kill larvae.
Leaves or shoots chewed or scraped, foliage may be tied together with silk. Yellow, green, or pink larvae may have lengthwise stripes.	**Armyworms,** *Spodoptera* spp.; **Carnation leafroller,** *Platynota sultana*; **Omnivorous looper,** *Sabulodes aegrotata* or *S. caberata*. Adult moths tan to brownish.	See Caterpillars, page 203.
Buds, flowers, and foliage chewed. Yellowish or greenish caterpillars, with darker, longitudinal stripes.	**Corn earworm,** *Heliothis* or *Helicoverpa zea*. Tan to brownish moths with darker bands on wings.	Larva and nocturnal adult (family Noctuidae), up to 1½ inch long. See Caterpillars, page 203.
Leaves skeletonized. Foliage and stems may be chewed.	**Saltmarsh caterpillar,** *Estigmene acrea*. Larva up to 2 inches long with long hairs and orange, white, and black tufts.	Barriers stop migrating larvae. *Bacillus thuringiensis* kills young larvae. See Caterpillars, page 203.

What the problem looks like	Probable cause	Comments

BEGONIA (*Begonia* spp.)

What the problem looks like	Probable cause	Comments
Plant stunted, yellow, or wilted. Stem rotted with brown cankers at soil line. Seedlings wilt and die.	**Root and stem rot,** *Rhizoctonia solani.* Soilborne fungus favored by warm, moist conditions. Common in new plantings.	Pasteurize media before planting. Practice good sanitation. Avoid overwatering and deep planting. See pages 93–98.
Plants yellow, stunted, may die. Black, girdling lesions on stem near soil. Roots, stems, and leaves may decay. Seedlings wilt and die.	**Root, stem, and leaf rot,** *Pythium, Phytophthora* spp. Fungi spread in contaminated soil and water.	Solarize or otherwise pasteurize soil. Use pathogen-free water. See pages 93–97.
Plant wilts and dies. Basal stem rotted. Long, black sclerotia in and on stems. Cottony mycelia in and on stems if conditions are moist.	**Cottony rot,** *Sclerotinia sclerotiorum.* Fungus survives in soil as sclerotia, which may infect plants on contact. Favored by overhead irrigation and high humidity. Many hosts.	Avoid planting in infested media or pasteurize media before planting. Avoid overhead irrigation. Irrigate early in day so plants dry quickly. See page 101.
Foliage yellows and wilts. Plants grow slowly and die. Roots dark black and rotted. Stems below ground may develop dark cracks.	**Black root rot,** *Thielaviopsis basicola.* Spreads in water, media, and by infected plants. Fungus persists in infected media. Favored by cool, wet conditions.	Pasteurize media before planting. Avoid overwatering and splashing water. Provide good drainage. Allow soil to dry between watering. Rogue infected plants. Avoid high salts and high pH. See pages 95–99.
Leaves discolor, wilt, stunt, or drop prematurely. Stems discolored, cankered, may ooze sap and die.	**Armillaria root rot,** *Armillaria mellea.* Present in many soils. Favored by warm, wet soil. Persists for years in infected roots.	Remove woody roots ½ inch diameter or larger before planting. Pasteurize or air-dry soil well or avoid growing in fields previously planted with oaks or other susceptible woody plants. See page 99.
Leaf uppersides have wet, greasy spots. Later, white, powdery growth or dark, bruised-looking areas, primarily on older leaves and stem. Severely affected leaves dry, die.	**Powdery mildew,** *Erysiphe, Oidium* spp. May occur as small dark structures on old leaves. Free water not required for infection. Develop at 50° to 79°F.	Provide good air circulation and adequate light. Consider applying fungicide to prevent. Six days at 90°F may eliminate fungus. See page 112.
Petals or leaves have brown, water-soaked spots. Stems may be girdled. Foliage wilts. May be woolly gray growth (spores) on dead tissue.	**Gray mold,** *Botrytis cinerea.* Fungus develops in crop debris or inactive tissue. Favored by high humidity and 70° to 77°F. Spores airborne.	Use good sanitation. Avoid overhead irrigation. Keep humidity low. Provide good air circulation. Don't crowd plants. See page 108.
Brown to yellow spots or blotches, mostly on older leaves. Spots may have dark or yellowish margins. Foliage may shrivel and drop.	**Leaf spot,** *Phyllosticta* sp. Spread by air or splashing water. Favored by prolonged, cool, wet, conditions. Persists in plant debris.	Avoid wetting foliage. Use drip irrigation and raised benches. Use good sanitation; promptly remove and dispose of debris and infected leaves. See pages 116–118.
Leaves have irregular brown or black spots. Buds and stems may darken and die. Stems may have water-soaked lesions; pith becomes jellylike. Terminals may turn black and exude liquid drops. Stem may split or break. Plants may wilt.	**Bacterial blight,** *Erwinia chrysanthemi.* Occurs in plant debris. Favored by high humidity and 80° to 90°F. Spreads on infected tools, equipment, hands, and plants.	Use pathogen-free cuttings. Use good sanitation; regularly inspect crop and immediately dispose of any infected plants. See pages 100, 107.
Tubers, crowns, or stems decay; soft, brown, odorous rot often at soil line. Leaf edges and stems may be discolored, soft, rotted. Only affects tuberous begonias.	**Soft rot,** *Erwinia carotovora.* Persists in media. Wet conditions favor the bacteria. Avoid injuring plant; disease infects wounds.	Provide good drainage. Don't overwater. Use good sanitation; immediately discard infected plants and those nearby. See pages 100, 107.
Leaves have small, blisterlike lesions. Leaves have brown, translucent, or dead spots or blotches that may have yellow borders or be vein-limited. Leaves may drop. Lesions may be greasy or ooze. Plant may wilt and die.	**Bacterial leaf spot, Blight,** *Xanthomonas campestris* pv. *begoniae.* Bacteria spread by splashing water and contaminated equipment. Favored by high humidity. Non-Stop begonias are resistant.	Rogue infected plants. Use good sanitation. Avoid overhead irrigation. Provide good air circulation. Don't crowd plantings. Some Elatior begonias are especially susceptible. See pages 107, 118.
Leaves mottled, ring-spotted, discolored; may develop necrotic lesions. Leaf veins discolored. Foliage may distort, yellow, redden, wilt, and drop. Plants may stunt. Blossoms and stems may discolor.	**Cucumber mosaic virus** (aphid-vectored, attacks plants in over 40 families). **Impatiens necrotic spot virus, Tomato spotted wilt virus** (thrips-vectored, infect wide host range).	Rogue infected plants; cover and dispose of them away from crop. Control alternate hosts. Exclude or control insect vectors. See Viruses, page 121.
Leaves have dark green to brown, vein-limited bands or angular blotches. Leaves may yellow, wilt, and die. Affects older leaves first.	**Foliar nematodes,** *Aphelenchoides olesistis, A. fragariae.* Tiny roundworms spread in plant debris and by vegetative propagation and splashing water. Not common in California.	Use uninfected stock plants. Remove plant debris. Avoid overhead irrigation; leaves must be wet for infection to occur. See page 265.

What the problem looks like	Probable cause	Comments
Foliage yellows or wilts. Feeder roots and fleshy roots have knots or swellings.	**Root knot nematode,** *Meloidogyne* spp. Tiny roundworms that prefer warm, sandy soil. Many hosts.	Pasteurize or treat media before planting. Rogue infected plants. Plant only nonhosts in infested soil. See page 265.
Leaf undersides may have pimplelike blisters or water-soaked spots. Leaves appear corky, especially on underside. Foliage yellows, drops.	**Edema** or **Oedema.** Noninfectious disorder. Leaves accumulate excess water when soil is warm and moist and air is cool and moist.	True cause is not known. See page 41.
Flowers small, pale, late, or don't form.	**Flower failure.** Noninfectious disorder, may be caused by high temperatures.	Provide proper growing conditions.
Foliage hardened with reddish margins.	**Leaf hardening.** Can be caused by low temperatures with high light.	Provide proper growing conditions.
Internodes short; plants stunted. Foliage brownish. Leaf terminals distorted, hardened. Buds deformed, discolored, dry, and may drop.	**Cyclamen mite,** *Phytonemus pallidus.* A pinkish orange mite (family Tarsonemidae), $\frac{1}{100}$ inch long or smaller.	See page 217.
Leaves or petals streaked, flecked, or distorted. Stippled, bleached, or blotched foliage, may have dark varnishlike excrement.	**Banded greenhouse thrips,** *Hercinothrips femoralis;* **Greenhouse thrips,** *Heliothrips haemorrhoidalis.* Tiny, slender, black, dark brown, yellow, or whitish insects. Many hosts.	See page 161.
Foliage bleached, bronzed, or reddened and may be brittle or ragged. Blossoms may distort or discolor. Slow growth.	**Broad mite,** *Polyphagotarsonemus latus.* Translucent to dark green, $\frac{1}{100}$ inch long or smaller.	See page 217.
Foliage discolored, stippled, bleached, or reddened; may drop. Fine webbing may be present.	**Privet mite,** *Brevipalpus obovatus;* **Twospotted spider mite,** *Tetranychus urticae.* Greenish, yellowish, or red, tiny, may have 2 dark spots.	See Mites, page 213.
Foliage turns yellow. Plant declines or dies back. Bark has gray, brown, or tan encrustations.	**Greedy scale,** *Hemiberlesia rapax;* **Latania scale,** *H. lataniae.* Circular flattened insects, less than $\frac{1}{16}$ inch long.	See page 186.
Plant has sticky honeydew, blackish sooty mold. Plant may yellow, decline, or die back.	**Brown soft scale,** *Coccus hesperidum;* **Hemispherical scale,** *Saissetia coffeae;* **Long brown scale,** *Coccus longulus.* Orange, black, or brown, flattened to bulbous insects.	See page 186.
Plant has sticky honeydew, blackish sooty mold, and whitish cast skins. Foliage may curl or yellow.	**Aphids,** including Melon aphid, *Aphis gossypii.* Small pear-shaped insects, green, yellowish, or black.	See page 179.
Foliage has sticky honeydew and blackish sooty mold. Copious white waxy material present with certain species. Leaves may yellow and wither. Tiny, whitish, mothlike adult insects.	**Giant whitefly,** *Aleurodicus dugesii;* **Greenhouse whitefly,** *Trialeurodes vaporariorum;* **Silverleaf whitefly,** *Bemisia argentifolii;* **Sweetpotato whitefly,** *Bemisia tabaci.* Nymphs and pupae oval, flattened, translucent, and greenish or yellow.	See page 170.
Foliage has sticky honeydew and blackish sooty mold. Foliage may yellow. Cottony egg sacs may be present.	**Citrus mealybug,** *Planococcus citri;* **Longtailed mealybug,** *Pseudococcus longispinus;* **Obscure mealybug,** *Pseudococcus affinis.* Powdery gray insects with waxy marginal filaments.	See page 183.
Leaves have cottony mealybuglike egg sacs, $\frac{1}{3}$ inch long. Foliage has sticky honeydew and blackish sooty mold. Foliage may yellow.	**Greenhouse orthezia,** *Orthezia insignis.* Pale brown to dark green insect with two white rows on back and white bands along side. Usually not a pest in California.	Controls as for mealybugs or scales may be effective.
Foliage chewed and webbed together with silk. Disturbed larvae wriggle and drop on a thread. Eggs laid in overlapping mass like fish scales.	**Orange tortrix,** *Argyrotaenia citrana.* Larva whitish, head brown. Gray to brown moth. Both up to 1 inch long. Moth (family Tortricidae), often abundant near citrus orchards. Has many other hosts.	See Caterpillars, page 203.
Foliage chewed, scraped, and tied together with silk by greenish larva with dark head.	**Carnation leafroller,** *Platynota sultana.* Adults moths (family Tortricidae), brownish or tan with black, about 1 inch wide. Head has snoutlike projection.	See Caterpillars, page 203.

What the problem looks like	Probable cause	Comments

BEGONIA (*Begonia* spp.) (continued)

What the problem looks like	Probable cause	Comments
Leaves and blossoms chewed (edges notched).	**Black vine weevil,** *Otiorhynchus sulcatus;* **Fuller rose beetle,** *Asynonychus godmani.* Rarely seen adults brown, black, to gray snout beetles that feed at night. Larvae whitish maggots that feed on roots. Adult and mature larva about ³⁄₈ inch long.	See page 208.
Foliage yellows, wilts, and dies. Basal stem has holes or decay. Grayish larvae up to ³⁄₄ inch long, head dark, boring in plant.	**Crown borer,** *Opogona omoscopa.* Dark, brownish moth (family Tineidae), attracted to decaying tissue; probably a secondary pest.	Avoid wounding plants. Provide good cultural care. Avoid excess irrigation. Use good sanitation; remove debris and dying plants.
Leaves have winding tunnels. Leaves may have pale spots, punctures, turn white, wilt, and drop. Mines may extend into petiole and stem.	**Leafminers,** *Liriomyza* spp. Small active flies, usually black with yellow. Yellowish or whitish maggot bores in tissue.	See page 167.

BELLS-OF-IRELAND (*Moluccella laevis*), Shell flower

What the problem looks like	Probable cause	Comments
Foliage yellows and wilts. Plants stunted and may die. Basal stems or roots, soft, dark, and decayed.	**Root and crown rots.** Fungi persist in soil. Spread in water. Favored by excess moisture and poor drainage.	Pasteurize media before planting. Use good sanitation. Provide good drainage. Avoid excess irrigation. Use drip irrigation where feasible. Reduce watering if disease develops. See pages 93–96.

BIRD OF PARADISE (*Strelitzia* spp.)

What the problem looks like	Probable cause	Comments
Plants stunted. Foliage may yellow. Root system reduced, small roots rotted.	**Pythium root rot,** *Pythium* spp. Soilborne fungi. Spread in soil and water. Favored by excess moisture and poor drainage.	Provide good drainage. Avoid excess irrigation. See pages 93–96.
Leaves discolor, wilt, stunt, or drop prematurely. Stems discolored, cankered, may ooze sap and die.	**Armillaria root rot,** *Armillaria mellea.* Present in many soils. Favored by warm, wet soil. Persists for years in infected roots.	Remove woody roots ½ inch diameter or larger before planting. Pasteurize or air-dry soil well or avoid growing in fields previously planted with oaks or other susceptible woody plants. See page 99.
Leaves have irregular, black, tarlike spots, sometimes on stems and petioles. From underside of leaf, spots appear brown.	**Black leaf spot,** *Pseudomonas syringae.* Bacteria survive in crop debris, spread in splashing water. Disease favored by cool, wet weather.	Rotate field to a different crop. Remove old leaves and stems from perennial field plantings. Avoid overhead irrigation. See pages 107, 118.
Petals or leaves have brown, water-soaked spots or decay. Dead tissue may have woolly gray growth (spores). Stem may be girdled.	**Gray mold,** *Botrytis cinerea.* Fungus develops in crop debris or inactive tissue. Favored by high humidity and 70° to 77°F. Spores airborne.	Use good sanitation. Avoid overhead irrigation. Keep humidity low. Provide good air circulation. Don't crowd plants. See page 108.
Leaves or flowers have brown to yellow spots or blotches. Spots may have dark or yellowish margins. Foliage or flowers may shrivel and drop.	**Leaf and flower spots,** including *Alternaria, Cercospora, Colletotrichum, Curvularia, Phyllosticta* spp. Spread by air or splashing water. Favored by prolonged wet conditions. Persist in plant debris. Diseases occur in Florida, not reported in California.	Avoid wetting foliage; use drip irrigation. Use good sanitation; promptly remove and dispose of debris and infected leaves. See pages 116–118.
Leaves stunted, distorted, often swollen and thickened near base. Leaf centers and margins have yellow to brown swellings. May have discolored spots or blotches where stem joins bulb. Severely infected bulbs grow poorly and may rot.	**Stem and bulb nematode,** *Ditylenchus dipsaci.* Nematodes survive in infected bulbs and field debris for about 3 years. Also spread by infected water and equipment. Optimal temperature for infection and reproduction is 50° to 69°F.	Rogue infected plants and surrounding plants from field. Clean equipment well after working in diseased fields. Treating bulbs with hot water may control, but may injure bulbs, causing stunted and deformed flowers. See page 265.
Foliage has sticky honeydew and blackish sooty mold. Foliage may yellow. Plant may have cottony material (egg sacs).	**Citrus mealybug,** *Planococcus citri;* **Longtailed mealybug,** *Pseudococcus longispinus;* **Obscure mealybug,** *Pseudococcus affinis.* Powdery gray insects with waxy filaments.	See Mealybugs, page 183.
Foliage has sticky honeydew, blackish sooty mold. Copious white waxy material present with certain species. Leaves may yellow and wither. Tiny, whitish, mothlike adult insects.	**Greenhouse whitefly,** *Trialeurodes vaporariorum;* **Giant whitefly,** *Aleurodicus dugesii;* **Iris whitefly,** *Aleyrodes spiraeoides.* Nymphs and pupae are flattened, oval, and translucent to yellowish.	See page 170.

What the problem looks like	Probable cause	Comments
Foliage has sticky honeydew, blackish sooty mold, and whitish cast skins on. Foliage may yellow.	**Aphids.** Tiny pear-shaped insects, often green, yellowish, or blackish.	See page 179.
Foliage has sticky honeydew or blackish sooty mold. Foliage may yellow and plant may die back.	**Brown soft scale,** *Coccus hesperidum;* **Nigra scale,** *Parasaissetia nigra.* Orange, black, brown or yellow, flattened to bulbous, oval insects.	See Scales, page 186.
Foliage turns yellow. Plant declines or dies back. Stems or leaves have gray, brown, tan, reddish, or white encrustations from circular, flattened insects, less than ¹⁄₁₆ inch long.	**California red scale,** *Aonidiella aurantii;* **Cycad scale,** *Furchadiaspis zamiae;* **Dictyospernum scale,** *Chrysomphalus dictyospermi;* **Greedy scale,** *Hemiberlesia rapax;* **Latania scale,** *H. lataniae;* **Oleander scale,** *Aspidiotus nerii.*	See page 186.
Plants, brown, wilt, and may die from sucking by stink bugs.	**Harlequin bug,** *Murgantia histrionica* (family Pentatomidae). Black with red or orangish, up to ³⁄₈ inch long.	See True Bugs, page 194.
Plants stunted, decline, may die. Powdery waxy material may be visible on roots and around crown.	**Ground mealybug,** *Rhizoecus* spp. Small, slender, pale insects, may be lightly covered with powdery wax, but lack marginal filaments.	See page 186.
Foliage yellows, wilts, and dies. Basal stem has holes or decay. Grayish larva up to ³⁄₄ inch long, head dark, boring in plant.	**Crown borer,** *Opogona omoscopa.* Dark, brownish moth (family Tineidae), attracted to decaying tissue; probably a secondary pest.	Avoid wounding plants. Provide good cultural care. Avoid excess irrigation. Use good sanitation; remove debris and dying plants.

BORONIA (*Boronia* spp.)

What the problem looks like	Probable cause	Comments
Plants are stunted. Foliage chlorotic. Roots or basal stems dark and decayed.	**Root and crown rots,** *Phytophthora, Pythium, Rhizoctonia* spp. Fungi present in many soils. Favored by poor drainage and overwatering.	Provide excellent drainage and careful watering. Don't overirrigate, but prevent growing media from drying completely. See pages 93–98.
Leaves and branches yellow, wilted, and necrotic, often on one side of plant. Leaves dry and die from the base of plant up. Stems may have brown vascular streaking.	**Verticillium wilt,** *Verticillium* sp. Fungus contaminates soil, cuttings, and root divisions. Favored by cool weather followed by hot.	Use pathogen-free cuttings and resistant cultivars. Pasteurize media before planting. See pages 104–106.

BOUVARDIA (*Bouvardia* spp.)

What the problem looks like	Probable cause	Comments
Petals or leaves have brown, water-soaked spots or decay. Dead tissue may have woolly gray growth (spores). Stem may be girdled.	**Gray mold,** *Botrytis cinerea.* Fungus develops in crop debris or inactive tissue. Favored by high humidity and 70° to 77°F. Spores airborne.	Use good sanitation. Avoid overhead irrigation. Keep humidity low. Provide good air circulation. Don't crowd plants. See page 108.
Foliage discolored, stippled, brownish, or bleached, and may drop. Terminals may distort. Fine webbing may be present.	**Twospotted mite,** *Tetranychus urticae.* Tiny greenish, reddish, or yellowish mite, may have 2 dark spots.	See page 213.
Internodes short; plants stunted. Foliage brownish. Leaf terminals distorted, hardened. Buds deformed, discolored, dry, and may drop.	**Cyclamen mite,** *Phytonemus pallidus.* A pinkish orange mite (family Tarsonemidae), ¹⁄₁₀₀ inch long or smaller.	See page 217.
Foliage has cottony material (egg sacs), sticky honeydew, and blackish sooty mold. Foliage may yellow.	**Citrus mealybug,** *Planococcus citri.* Powdery gray insects, less than ¹⁄₄ inch long, with waxy filaments.	See page 183.
Foliage has sticky honeydew and blackish sooty mold. Copious white waxy material present with certain species. Leaves may yellow and wither. Tiny, whitish, mothlike adult insects.	**Greenhouse whitefly,** *Trialeurodes vaporariorum;* **Giant whitefly,** *Aleurodicus dugesii;* **Iris whitefly,** *Aleyrodes spiraeoides;* **Silverleaf whitefly,** *Bemisia argentifolii;* **Sweetpotato whitefly,** *Bemisia tabaci.* Nymphs and pupae are flattened, oval, and translucent to yellowish.	See Whiteflies, page 170.
Foliage turns yellow. Plant declines or dies back. Stems or leaves have gray, brown, tan, reddish, or white encrustations from circular, flattened insects, less than ¹⁄₁₆ inch long.	**Latania scale,** *Hemiberlesia lataniae;* **Oleander scale,** *Aspidiotus nerii.*	See page 186.

What the problem looks like	Probable cause	Comments
BROMELIADS (*Bromelia* spp. and others)		
Plants are stunted. Foliage chlorotic. Roots or basal stems dark and decayed.	**Root and crown rots,** *Phytophthora, Pythium, Rhizoctonia* spp. Fungi present in many soils. Favored by poor drainage and overwatering.	Provide excellent drainage; roots naturally grow in air, not in wet media. Don't overirrigate. See pages 93–98.
Leaves have brown to yellow, spots or blotches. Spots may have dark or yellowish margins. Foliage may shrivel, drop.	**Blights, Leaf spots,** including *Colletotrichum, Phyllosticta* spp. Persist in crop debris. Favored by prolonged wet conditions. Not reported on bromeliads in California.	Use good sanitation; promptly remove and dispose of debris and infected leaves. See Leaf Spots, pages 116–118.
Plant has sticky honeydew, blackish sooty mold, and cottony waxy material. Leaves may yellow or wither.	**Mealybugs.** Grayish, oval, waxy, slow-moving insects with marginal filaments.	See page 183.
CALENDULA (*Calendula officinalis*), Pot-marigold		
Plants stunted. Foliage chlorotic. Roots or basal stems dark and decayed.	**Root and crown rots,** *Pythium, Phytophthora* spp., *Rhizoctonia solani*. Fungi present in many soils. Favored by poor drainage, overwatering, and heavy rain.	Provide good drainage. Don't overirrigate. See pages 93–98.
Plants wilt and die. Basal stem rotted. Black sclerotia in and on stems. Cottony mycelia in and on stems if conditions are moist.	**Cottony rot,** *Sclerotinia sclerotiorum*. Fungus survives in soil as sclerotia, which may infect plants on contact. Favored by overhead irrigation and high humidity. Many hosts.	Pasteurize media before planting. Avoid overhead irrigation. Irrigate early in day so plants dry quickly. See page 101.
Plants wilt and collapse. Basal stem and roots rotted. White cottony fungus growth and tan or brown sclerotia (about 1/16 inch) may form on infected plant tissue and surrounding soil.	**Southern blight,** *Sclerotium rolfsii*. Sclerotia survive in soil, germinate, and infect susceptible plants. No airborne spores are formed. Many hosts. Favored by high temperatures.	Pasteurize media before planting. Fungicide applied at base of plants can help to prevent. See page 101.
Leaves and stems have white powdery growth. More common on older leaves and older plants.	**Powdery mildew,** *Sphaerotheca fuliginea, Erysiphe cichoracearum*. Fungal disease favored by moderate temperatures and shady locations, but may occur in full sun on lower leaves. Spores are windborne.	Rogue infected plants and dispose of plant debris. Plant at sunny location. Provide good air circulation; don't overcrowd plants. See page 112.
Petals or leaves have brown, water-soaked spots or decay. Dead tissue may have woolly gray growth (spores). Stem may be girdled.	**Gray mold,** *Botrytis cinerea*. Fungus develops in crop debris or inactive tissue. Favored by high humidity and 70° to 77°F. Spores airborne.	Use good sanitation. Avoid overhead irrigation. Provide good air circulation. Don't crowd plants. See page 108.
Leaves have circular to irregular, 1/4 to 1/2 inch diameter, greenish yellow or brownish spots, sometimes with discolored border. Spots may be somewhat thickened, are evident on both sides of leaf.	**Smut,** *Entyloma calendulae*. Fungus survives on live plants and refuse. Spores are windborne. Favored by rain and overhead irrigation.	Avoid overhead irrigation. Use good sanitation; remove and dispose of plant debris and infected plants.
Leaves have small reddish or yellowish spots or blotches. Foliage dries and drops.	**Leaf spots,** *Alternaria* sp., *Cercospora calendulae*. Favored by warm, humid conditions. Spread in air and splashing water.	Avoid overhead irrigation. Provide good air circulation; don't crowd plants. Rogue infected plants. Dispose of debris. See pages 116–118.
Leaves have brown to orangish powdery pustules and yellowish spots, may be on stems. Leaves may yellow and drop.	**Rusts,** *Coleosporium* sp., *Puccinia flaveriae* or *P. melampodii*. Fungi survive on living tissue. Spores are airborne. Favored by humid or wet conditions. *Puccinia* is in eastern U.S., not a problem in California.	Avoid overhead irrigation. Water in morning. Provide good air circulation. Don't crowd plants. See page 119.
Leaves, petioles, or flower stalks with yellow to white streaks, spots, or rings. Leaves or stems have necrotic lesions. Leaves mottled, distorted.	**Tomato spotted wilt virus.** Virus spread by thrips, infects wide host range. **Cucumber mosaic virus.** Spread by aphids, has many hosts.	Rogue infected plants, cover and dispose of them away from crop. Control alternate hosts and vectors. See Viruses, page 121.
Foliage chlorotic. Plant stunted. Spindly, upright yellow shoots and few or no flowers.	**Aster yellows.** Phytoplasmalike organism spread by leafhoppers. Not spread by seed, handling, aphids, or other insects. Many hosts.	Don't plant seed beds downwind from other hosts. Eliminate nearby weeds. Control leafhoppers. Rogue infected plants. See pages 129–130.
Foliage yellows or wilts. Feeder roots and fleshy roots have knots or swellings.	**Root knot nematode,** *Meloidogyne* spp. Tiny roundworms that feed on roots and prefer warm media. Many hosts.	Pasteurize or treat media before planting. Rogue affected plants. See page 265.
Flower seed coats injured, discolored, scabby. Thin-coated seed die. Flowers may be distorted from feeding by tiny, slender insects.	**Composite thrips,** *Microcephalothrips abdominalis*. Tiny dark brown adults, wings light brown. Entire life cycle spent in flowers, including debris.	Don't grow seed plants near other Asteraceae crops or weeds. Use good sanitation; remove debris before planting. See Thrips, page 161.

What the problem looks like	Probable cause	Comments
Shoots or blossoms blackened, dwarfed, discolored, or distorted. Leaf tips may wilt and die.	**Plant bugs,** *Lygus* spp. Brown, green, or yellowish bugs, up to $1/4$ inch long, suck plant juices.	Control nearby weeds, from which bugs move. Exclude bugs from growing area. See True Bugs, page 194.
Foliage has sticky honeydew, blackish sooty mold. Leaves yellow and wither. Tiny, whitish, mothlike adult insects.	**Whiteflies,** including Silverleaf whitefly, *Bemisia argentifolii*; Sweetpotato whitefly, *Bemisia tabaci*. Oval, flattened, yellow to greenish nymphs and pupae with few or no waxy filaments.	See page 170.
Flower stems or leaves have sticky honeydew, blackish sooty mold, and white cast skins from aphids.	**Brown ambrosia aphid,** *Uroleucon ambrosiae*. Brown to reddish aphid, larger than average size. Vectors viruses.	See page 179.
Leaves have winding tunnels. Heavily infested leaves may drop. Yellowish to white maggots in mines. Leaves may have pale leaf spots or adult punctures.	**Serpentine leafminer,** *Liriomyza trifolii*. Adults are tiny black and yellow flies.	See page 167.
Leaves skeletonized, chewed, or pitted and may drop. Foliage yellows or wilts due to damage by root-feeding larvae. Plant stunted.	**Flea beetles.** Adults shiny black, metallic, or pale beetles, $1/8$ inch long or less. Adults jump when disturbed but feed mostly at night. Larvae are pale soil-dwelling maggots.	See page 212.
Seedlings clipped. Leaves chewed, often between veins. Foliage yellows and wilts from slender, whitish larvae feeding on roots.	**Cucumber beetles,** *Acalymma*, *Diabrotica* spp. Greenish yellow adults with black heads and black spots or stripes. Have several generations per year.	Avoid growing near alternate host Cucurbitaceae crops. Control cucurbit weeds, where adults overwinter and feed. Exclude adults, especially from seedlings. See page 212.
Foliage and flower buds chewed. Green caterpillars, up to $1 1/2$ inches long, with white stripes.	**Cabbage looper,** *Trichoplusia ni*. Moths mottled brown and silver, about 1 inch wide.	See Caterpillars, page 203.
Leaves or shoots chewed and webbed. Terminals may be mined by larvae, causing plant to yellow and wilt.	**Plume moth,** *Anstenoptilia marmarodactyla*. Pale yellow to light green larvae. Small gray or brown moth (family Pterophoridae) with narrow wings.	See Caterpillars, page 203.

CALLA (*Zantedeschia* spp.), Calla lily

What the problem looks like	Probable cause	Comments
Foliage yellows and wilts. Stems may collapse and plants die. Roots and sometimes rhizomes or basal stems have lesions or odorless, soft, brown, decay.	**Root and crown rots,** *Pythium ultimum*, *Pythium* sp., *Phytophthora cryptogea*, *Phytophthora erythroseptica*, *Phytophthora* sp., *Rhizoctonia solani*. Fungi present in many soils, favored by moist conditions.	Pasteurize media before planting. Plant on raised beds. Avoid deep planting. Avoid injuring plants. Don't overirrigate. Provide good drainage. Clean rhizomes soon after digging, store them below 50°F. *Pythium*-labeled products may prevent. See pages 93–98.
Foliage yellows and wilts. Plants grow slowly and die. Roots and rhizomes dark black and rotted.	**Black root rot,** *Thielaviopsis basicola*. Spreads in water, soil, and by infected plants. Fungus persists in infected media. Favored by cool, wet conditions.	Pasteurize media before planting. Avoid overwatering and splashing water. Provide good drainage. Allow soil to dry between watering. Rogue infected plants. See pages 95–99.
Leaves discolor, wilt, stunt, or drop prematurely. Stems discolored, cankered, and die.	**Armillaria root rot,** *Armillaria mellea*. Present in many soils. Favored by warm, wet soil. Persists for years in infected roots.	Remove woody roots $1/2$ inch diameter or larger before planting. Pasteurize or air-dry soil well or avoid growing in fields previously planted with oaks or other susceptible woody plants. See page 99.
Lower leaves discolor or wilt. Basal stems rot. Plants collapse. May be white fungal mat and $1/32$ to $1/8$ inch, round, tan to brown sclerotia on decaying tissue and nearby soil.	**Southern blight** or **Crown rot,** *Sclerotium rolfsii*. Fungus survives in soil for 10 years. Spread in infected plants. Has wide host range.	Solarize where feasible or otherwise pasteurize soil before planting. Use pathogen-free stock. Fungicide applied around plant bases can prevent. See page 101.
Flowers, flower heads, lower leaves, or growing points have soft brown decay. Dead tissue may have woolly gray spore growth.	**Gray mold,** *Botrytis cinerea*. Fungus develops in crop debris or inactive tissue. Favored by high humidity and 70° to 77°F. Spores airborne.	Use good sanitation. Avoid overhead irrigation. Keep humidity low. Provide good air circulation. Don't crowd plants. See page 108.
Leaves have brown to yellow spots or blotches that may have dark or yellowish margins. Foliage may shrivel and drop.	**Leaf spots,** *Coniothecium* sp., *Phyllosticta* sp. Spread by air or splashing water. Favored by prolonged wet conditions. Persist in plant debris.	Avoid wetting foliage. Use drip irrigation. Use good sanitation; promptly remove and dispose of debris and infected leaves. See pages 116–118.

What the problem looks like	Probable cause	Comments
CALLA (*Zantedeschia* spp.), Calla lily (continued)		
Petals have tiny brownish lesions that may expand into large necrotic areas.	**Flower spot,** *Alternaria alternata.* Spreads by air and splashing water. Favored if wet or humid.	Avoid overhead irrigation. Keep blossoms dry or water in morning. Use good sanitation; fungus survives in plant debris. Some *Zantedeschia* cultivars appear to be resistant. See pages 116–118.
Rhizomes or stems decay; soft, odorous, brown rot often at soil line. Leaf edges and stems may be discolored, soft, rotted. Rhizomes become chalky.	**Soft rot,** *Erwinia aroidae, E. carotovora.* Persist in soil. Favored when wet. Avoid injuring plant; disease is secondary, infecting wounds.	Provide good drainage. Don't plant too deeply. Don't overwater. Use good sanitation; don't plant decayed rhizomes and immediately discard infected plants and those nearby. See pages 100, 107.
Leaves have yellowish patterns. Leaves may severely distort. Veins may yellow. Plants grow slowly, are stunted.	**Dasheen mosaic virus.** Spreads by aphids or mechanically in sap, such as through contaminated tools.	Use virus-free plants produced by heat treatment and tissue culture. Rogue infected plants. Pasteurize equipment and tools to avoid spread. Control aphids. See Viruses, page 121.
Leaves have chlorotic streaks, spots, mottling, or rings, sometimes also on petioles and flower stalks. Necrotic lesions may develop on leaves. Plants may be stunted.	**Impatiens necrotic spot virus, Tomato spotted wilt virus.** Spread by thrips; infect wide host range.	Rogue infected plants; cover and dispose of them away from crop. Control weeds. Exclude or control thrips. See pages 121–129.
Foliage yellows or wilts. Feeder roots and fleshy roots have knots or swellings.	**Root knot nematode,** *Meloidogyne* sp. Tiny roundworms that prefer warm, sandy soil. Many hosts.	Pasteurize or treat media before planting. Rogue affected plants. Plant nonhosts in infested soil at that site. See page 265.
Stems or flower stalks abnormally long.	**Stretching.** Noninfectious disorder caused by temperatures over about 85°F, especially during short day length.	Provide good care, high light, and moderate to cool temperatures.
Flowers or leaves abnormally shaped.	**Gibberellic acid dip toxicity.** Growth regulator use damage.	Provide proper growing conditions. Strictly follow growth regulator label directions.
Fleshy bulb scales have reddish brown discoloration. Roots, rhizomes, or basal stems rotted and infested with tiny, oval, white to brownish mites.	**Bulb mites,** *Rhizoglyphus* spp. Sluggish mites, look like eggs, may also be on stems and leaves. Secondary pests that prefer decayed tissue but may help fungi infect plants.	See page 218.
Foliage has sticky honeydew, blackish sooty mold, and white cast skins. Foliage may curl or yellow.	**Aphids,** including *Aulacorthum circumflexum, Myzus persicae.* Pear-shaped green or yellowish insects.	See page 179.
Foliage has sticky honeydew and blackish sooty mold. Plant may yellow or die back.	**Brown soft scale,** *Coccus hesperidum.* Small, yellow, orangish or brown, flattened, oval insects.	See page 186.
Foliage has sticky honeydew and blackish sooty mold. Foliage may yellow. Plant may grow slowly.	**Longtailed mealybug,** *Pseudococcus longispinus.* Powdery gray insects with waxy marginal filaments.	See page 183.
Foliage discolored, stippled, brownish, or bleached, and may drop. Terminals may distort. May be fine webbing.	**Twospotted mite,** *Tetranychus urticae.* Tiny greenish, reddish, or yellowish mites, may have 2 dark spots.	See page 213.
Foliage stippled, bleached, or blotched, has varnishlike excrement.	**Thrips,** including Greenhouse thrips, *Heliothrips haemorrhoidalis;* Banded greenhouse thrips, *Hercinothrips femoralis.* Adults black, dark brown, or yellowish insects. Nymphs and pupae whitish to pale yellow.	See page 161.
Blossoms and young leaves chewed by adult beetle. Larvae live in soil.	**Hoplia beetle,** *Hoplia callipyge.* Adult (family Scarabaeidae) about ¼ inch long, mostly reddish brown with silver, black or white. White larvae chew on roots. Nearby turf, alfalfa, and other hosts important in population densities.	Adults apparently prefer white and yellow blossoms; concentrate monitoring (look for adults and damage) and foliar spraying there. See White Grubs, page 211.
Buds, flowers, or leaves mined or chewed, may be webbed with silk.	**Omnivorous leaftier,** *Cnephasia longana.* Gray to brownish, ½ inch long larvae and nocturnal moths. Larvae may have grayish stripes. Attacks strawberries and many other hosts. Occurs in central California coast. Has 1 generation per year.	Time any spray for young larvae emerging from mines in spring. See Caterpillars, page 203.

What the problem looks like	Probable cause	Comments
CAMELLIA (*Camellia japonica*)		
Plants stunted. Foliage yellows, wilts, and dies. Roots and basal stems have dark brown decay. Stems girdled and collapse.	**Root and crown rot,** *Pythium* sp., *Phytophthora* spp., *Rhizoctonia solani.* Fungi present in some soils and surface waters. Favored by wet, poorly drained media.	Pasteurize or treat propagation and growing media. Avoid excess irrigation. Provide good drainage. See pages 93–98.
Leaves discolor, wilt, and drop prematurely. Plants stunted, then collapse. Roots dead. White fungal plaques grow beneath bark.	**Armillaria root rot,** *Armillaria mellea.* Present in many soils. Favored by warm, wet soil. Persists for years in infected roots.	Remove woody roots ½ inch diameter or larger before planting. Pasteurize or air-dry soil well or avoid growing in fields previously planted with oaks or other susceptible woody plants. See page 99.
Foliage yellows and wilts. Plants grow slowly and die. Roots dark black and rotted.	**Black root rot,** *Thielaviopsis basicola.* Spreads in water, media, and by infected plants. Fungus persists in infected media. Favored by cool, wet conditions.	Pasteurize media before planting. Avoid overwatering and splashing water. Provide good drainage. Allow soil to dry between watering. Rogue infected plants. Avoid high salts and high pH. See pages 95–99.
Branches wilt and die. Leaves darken and remain attached. Branches girdled by fungus entering wounds, including leaf scars.	**Dieback,** *Glomerella cingulata.* Fungus has many hosts, spread by splashing water. Favored by warm, wet conditions and plant injuries.	Avoid overwatering or stressing plants. Prune off and dispose of diseased tissue. Consider treating pruning wounds.
Small tan to brown spots on petals only. Petals rot. Flower veins accented. Infected flowers heavy and drop easily.	**Flower blight,** *Ciborinia camelliae.* Fungus survives for several years as sclerotia in soil. Fruiting bodies arise from sclerotia and forcibly eject infective spores. Promoted by wet conditions.	Avoid overhead irrigation. Pick up and dispose of fallen blossoms. Mulch soil 4 inches deep to promote decay of sclerotia. Soil can be fungicide treated.
Flowers have necrotic brown spots; woolly gray spores form if humidity is high. Flower rotted, but not as quickly as with *Ciborinia*.	**Gray mold,** *Botrytis cinerea.* Fungus develops in crop debris or inactive tissue. Favored by high humidity and 70° to 77°F. Spores airborne.	Avoid overhead watering. Remove and dispose of plant debris. Provide good air circulation. Don't crowd plants. See page 108.
Shoots yellow, wilt, and die back. Leaves, stems, and flowers may have tan to brown circular spots or blotches, and decay.	**Shoot dieback,** *Colletotrichum* spp. Fungi survive in crop debris. Spread by splashing water. Favored by wet conditions.	Avoid overhead irrigation. Maintain low humidity. Use good sanitation. See Leaf Spots, pages 116–118.
Leaves have irregular yellow mottling. Blossoms mottled white.	**Camellia yellow mottle virus.** Vector(s) unknown.	Can be introduced through grafting. Sometimes deliberately introduced to produce attractive variegation. See Viruses, page 121.
New foliage light green to yellow, especially at sunny sites.	**Light damage.** Noninfectious disorder caused by high-intensity light.	Provide good growing conditions and shading. See page 62.
Buds drop prematurely. Fewer flowers than normal.	**Bud blast.** Noninfectious disorder caused by poor cultural practices and poor growing conditions.	Provide appropriate irrigation and good drainage. Bud drop in spring is caused by poor cultural practices the previous summer and fall when buds developed.
Flower bud edge turns brown, then entire bud browns and drops. Petals turn brown or drop.	**Camellia bud mite,** *Cosetacus* or *Aceria camelliae.* Translucent to white eriophyids, ¹⁄₁₀₀ inch long, that infest inner surface of bud scales or petals.	See Gall Mites, page 219.
Leaf surface browns. Leaves have whitish encrustation from waxy cast skins and dead mites.	**Purple camellia mite,** *Calacarus adornatus;* **Yellow camellia rust mite,** *Acaphylla steinwedeni.* Minute eriophyid mites. Both species free-living, often occur together on leaves.	See Gall Mites, page 219.
Foliage discolored, stippled, or bleached, and may drop. Terminals may distort. Plant may have fine webbing.	**Spider mites,** including *Oligonychus ilicis;* Citrus red mite, *Panonychus citri.* Tiny greenish, reddish, or yellowish mites.	See page 213.
Foliage yellows or drops. Plants stunted. Twigs die back. Pale encrustations mostly on leaves.	**Camellia parlatoria scale,** *Parlatoria camelliae;* **Degenerate scale,** *Hemiberlesia degenerata.* Elongate to oval, gray, whitish, or yellowish armored scales.	See Scales, page 186.
Plant has elongate, slender, cottony material (egg sacs), may have sticky honeydew and blackish sooty mold.	**Cottony camellia scale,** *Pulvinaria floccifera.* Oval, flattened, yellow or brown insects and cottony eggs.	See Scales, page 186.
Sticky honeydew, blackish sooty mold, and cottony waxy material on plant.	**Longtailed mealybug;** *Pseudococcus longispinus;* **Obscure mealybug,** *Pseudococcus affinis.* Grayish, oval, waxy, and slow-moving, with marginal filaments.	See Mealybugs, page 183.

What the problem looks like	Probable cause	Comments
CAMELLIA *(Camellia japonica)* **(continued)**		
Foliage has sticky honeydew and blackish sooty mold. Leaves yellow and wither. Tiny, whitish, mothlike adult insects.	**Greenhouse whitefly,** *Trialeurodes vaporariorum.* Oval, flattened, yellow to greenish nymphs and pupae with waxy filaments.	See page 170.
Sticky honeydew and blackish sooty mold on foliage. Twigs or branches decline or die back.	**Black scale,** *Saissetia oleae;* **Brown soft scale,** *Coccus hesperidum;* **Hemispherical scale,** *Saissetia coffeae;* **Long brown scale,** *Coccus longulus.* Bulbous to flattened, black, brown, yellow, or orangish insects that suck plant sap.	See page 186.
Plant has sticky honeydew, blackish sooty mold and whitish cast skins. Foliage may yellow.	**Aphids,** including Black citrus aphid, *Toxoptera aurantii;* Green peach aphid, *Myzus persicae;* Melon aphid, *Aphis gossypii.* Small reddish brown, black, green, or yellowish insects.	See page 179.
Foliage turns yellow. Plant declines or dies back. Bark or leaves have gray, brown, tan, or white encrustations that are circular, flattened insects, less than ¹⁄₁₆ inch long.	**Cactus scale,** *Diaspis echinocacti;* **Dictyosperum scale,** *Chrysomphalus dictyospermi;* **Greedy scale,** *Hemiberlesia rapax;* **Latania scale,** *H. lataniae;* **Oleander scale,** *Aspidiotus nerii;* **Yellow scale,** *Aonidiella citrina.*	See page 186.
Foliage turns yellow. Plant declines or dies back. Bark has dark brown encrustations.	**Oystershell scale,** *Lepidosaphes ulmi.* Elongate to oval insects (family Diaspididae), often shaped like oyster shells, less than ¹⁄₁₆ inch long. Scale insects.	See Scales, page 186.
Leaves and blossoms chewed (edges notched).	**Black vine weevil,** *Otiorhynchus sulcatus;* **Fuller rose beetle,** *Asynonychus godmani.* Rarely seen adults brown, black, to gray snout beetles that feed at night. Larvae whitish maggots that feed on roots.	See Weevils, page 208.
Foliage chewed, may be webbed together with silk. Stems may be clipped. Yellow, green, pink whitish, or brownish caterpillars or their black frass pellets may be present.	**Caterpillars,** including Amorbia, *Amorbia cuneana;* Beet armyworm, *Spodoptera exigua;* Black orangeworm, *Holcocera iceryaeella;* Carnation leafroller, *Platynota sultana;* Omnivorous looper, *Sabulodes aegrotata* or *S. caberata;* Orange tortrix, *Argyrotaenia citrana.* Nocturnal moths. *Amorbia, Argyrotaenia, Platynota* (family Tortricidae) and *Holcocera* (Blastobasidae) may be common near citrus, an alternate host.	See page 203.
CANDYTUFT *(Iberis* **spp.)**		
Foliage yellows and wilts. Plant stunted, may collapse and die. Roots and basal stem brown and decayed.	**Root and stem rot,** *Phytophthora* sp., *Rhizoctonia solani.* Soilborne fungus favored by warm, moist conditions. Common in new plantings.	Pasteurize media before planting. Avoid overwatering and deep planting. See pages 93–98.
Foliage pale and wilted. Plants stunted and may die. Knobby, spindlelike swellings on roots. Prevalent in soils where *Brassica* spp. crops have previously grown.	**Clubroot,** *Plasmodiophora brassicae.* A plasmodium microorganism. Propagules very persistent in media and infect roots, especially when wet. Soil pH of 7.2 or higher inhibits spore germination.	Plant only pathogen-free stock. Pasteurize media before planting. Don't grow cruciferous crops in soil where other infested plants in mustard family have grown, including certain weeds and crops such as broccoli and cabbage. Provide good drainage. Adjust pH if possible.
Stems rotted. Flowers have brown spots, like gray mold. May be cottony fungal mass on decayed tissue and black sclerotia inside and outside of stems.	**Cottony rot,** *Sclerotinia sclerotiorum.* Fungal sclerotia in contaminated media produce airborne spores. Favored by high humidity.	Pasteurize media before planting. Use pathogen-free stock. Irrigate early in day so plants dry quickly. Use good sanitation; remove and dispose of debris and old plants. Keep humidity low. Provide good air circulation. See page 101.
Leaves have pale spots or white, pink, or brown pustules. Affects most cruciferous plants, but usually not lethal.	**White rust,** *Albugo candida.* Airborne spores spread only from living tissue. Plant must be wet for infection.	Avoid overhead sprinkling. Provide good air circulation. Prevent excess humidity. Dispose of infected plants.
Lesions or brown spots mostly on older leaves or stems. Foliage yellows and wilts. Plants may die.	**Stem cankers and dieback,** *Leptosphaeria* sp. Fungus infects mainly through wounds. Spread or promoted by rain, splashing water.	Avoid wounding plants. Provide proper cultural care and good growing conditions to keep them vigorous. Dispose of diseased plants.
Leaves have purplish red to dark brown, irregular, angular spots. Lower leaf surface covered with soft, fluffy fungal growth. Leaves yellow and drop.	**Downy mildew,** *Peronospora parasitica.* Spores produced only on living plants. Fungus persists as resistant oospores when conditions are dry. Favored by moist, humid conditions.	Provide good air circulation. Avoid overhead watering. Consider applying fungicide to protect foliage. See page 115.

What the problem looks like	Probable cause	Comments
Leaves and stems have white powdery patches. Basal leaves yellow, then brown and die. Flowers may be deformed. Uncommon on *Iberis*.	**Powdery mildew,** *Erysiphe polygoni*. Fungus survives on living plants. Favored by moderate temperatures, shade, and crowding.	Avoid overcrowding. Provide adequate light and good air circulation. See page 112.
Leaves or petals have purple, brown, or tan spots or blotches. Spots may have discolored border. May have stem lesions around stem base.	**Alternaria leaf and flower blight,** *Alternaria* sp. Spread by wind, splashing water, and in infected cuttings. Favored if wet or humid.	Avoid overhead irrigation. Keep foliage dry or water in morning. Use good sanitation; fungus survives in plant debris. See Leaf Spots, pages 116–118.
Foliage chlorotic. Plant stunted. Spindly, upright yellow shoots and few or no flowers.	**Aster yellows.** Phytoplasmalike organism spread by leafhoppers. Not spread by seed, handling, aphids, or other insects. Many hosts.	Don't plant downwind from other hosts. Eliminate nearby weeds. Exclude or control leafhoppers. Rogue infected plants. See pages 129–130.
Blossoms have irregular white or brown blotches. Blossoms or terminals may be distorted. Growth may be stunted.	**Western flower thrips,** *Frankliniella occidentalis*. Tiny, slender, dark brown to yellowish insects.	See page 161.
Foliage discolored, stippled, brownish, or bleached, and may drop. Terminals may distort. Plant may have fine webbing.	**Twospotted mite,** *Tetranychus urticae*. Tiny greenish, reddish, or yellowish mites, may have 2 dark spots.	See page 213.
Plants grow slowly. Waxy material on roots. Foliage may yellow.	**Root aphid,** *Pemphigus* sp. White to yellowish aphids, may be waxy covered, feed in colonies on roots.	See page 182.
Foliage has small holes. Leaf undersides scraped, pitted, or mined. Terminals and buds may be chewed, stunting growth and reducing flowering. Plants may defoliate. Attacks most Brassicaceae.	**Diamondback moth,** *Plutella xylostella*. Slender, pale green larvae with scattered black hairs; rear prolegs form distinct V. Forms silken cocoons on foliage, or debris where cocoons occur from insects that dropped and pupated, which can be disposed of. Gray to brown adult and mature larva about $\frac{1}{3}$ inch long.	Exclude egg-laying moths with row covers. Apply *Bacillus thuringiensis* to kill larvae. *Trichogramma* parasite releases may be effective against eggs. See Caterpillars, page 203.

CARNATION (*Dianthus caryophyllus*)

What the problem looks like	Probable cause	Comments
Leaves and stem yellow and wilt, often initially on one side of plant. Plants may brown and die. Stem vascular tissue discolored. 'Sim' cultivars very susceptible.	**Fusarium wilt,** *Fusarium oxysporum* f. sp. *dianthi*. Persists in soil. Infects through roots. Low pH may favor disease.	Plant in raised beds. Pasteurize media with heat before planting. Tarp pasteurized beds throughout production to exclude contamination. Use good sanitation. Sanitize irrigation systems. Use resistant cultivars. Avoid overwatering. Provide good drainage. See page 104.
Flower cut stubs die back, then main branches. Basal stems roots have reddish lesions and decay. Cutting bases often affected.	**Fusarium cutting rot,** *Fusarium roseum*, *Fusarium* spp. Persist in soil. Spread by air and in cuttings. Enter through wounds. Favored by wet, warm conditions.	Pasteurize media before planting. Avoid deep planting. Don't overwater. Provide good drainage. Don't overfertilize around harvest or after planting cuttings. See pages 93–96.
Foliage yellows and wilts, often on only one side. Plants stunted and may die. Roots dark and decayed. Young plants collapse and die.	**Pythium root rot,** *Pythium ultimum*, *Pythium* spp.; **Phytophthora wilt,** *Phytophthora* sp. Fungi persist in soil. Spread in media and water. Favored by excess moisture and poor drainage.	Provide good drainage. Avoid excess irrigation. See pages 93–97.
Plant stunted, yellow, or wilted. Stem rotted with brown cankers at soil line.	**Rhizoctonia stem rot,** *Rhizoctonia solani*. Soilborne fungus favored by warm, moist conditions. Common in new plantings.	Pasteurize media before planting. Practice good sanitation. Avoid overwatering and deep planting. See pages 93–98.
Stems girdled, bleached, and killed. May have brown to black seedlike sclerotia or cottony fungal mass on or inside infected stems.	**Sclerotinia flower rot,** *Sclerotinia sclerotiorum*. Fungal sclerotia in contaminated media produce airborne spores. Favored by high humidity.	Pasteurize media before planting. Use pathogen-free stock. Irrigate early in day so plants dry quickly. Use good sanitation; remove and dispose of debris and old plants. Keep humidity low. Provide good air circulation. See page 101.
Leaves discolor, wilt, stunt, or drop prematurely. Stems discolored, cankered, may ooze sap and die.	**Armillaria root rot,** *Armillaria mellea*. Present in many soils. Favored by warm, wet soil. Persists for years in infected roots.	Remove woody roots $\frac{1}{2}$ inch diameter or larger before planting. Pasteurize or air-dry soil well or avoid growing in fields previously planted with oaks or other susceptible woody plants. See page 99.
Lower leaves discolor or wilt. Basal stems rot. Plants collapse. May be white fungal mat and $\frac{1}{32}$ to $\frac{1}{8}$ inch, round, tan to brown sclerotia on decayed tissue and nearby media.	**Southern blight,** *Sclerotium rolfsii*. Fungus persists in media. Spreads in infected plants. Has wide host range. Favored by high temperatures.	Pasteurize media before planting. Use pathogen-free stock. Fungicide applied around plant bases can prevent. See page 101.

What the problem looks like	Probable cause	Comments
CARNATION *(Dianthus caryophyllus)* (continued)		
Foliage yellows, browns, or wilts. Plants stunted. Roots and basal stem black and rotted, may have tiny black sclerotia inside.	**Charcoal rot,** *Macrophomina phaseolina.* Persists in media. Favored by hot weather. Prefers seedlings and stressed plants.	Pasteurize media before planting. Avoid stressing plants; provide good cultural care.
Leaves and stems have small, oily, radiating or spider-weblike patterns due to dissolved cuticle.	**Greasy blotch,** *Zygophiala jamaicensis.* Favored by high humidity.	Provide good air circulation; keep humidity low.
Leaves, flowers, or stems have tan spots or blotches with purple margins. May have lesions around stem base.	**Alternaria blight,** *Alternaria dianthi, A. dianthicola.* Spread by wind, splashing water, and infected cuttings. Favored if 75° to 95°F and wet or humid.	Avoid overhead irrigation. Water in morning, so quicker drying; plant must be wet for fungal germination. Use good sanitation; fungi survive in plant debris.
Leaves, stems, or calyxes have sunken or irregular brown, yellow, or purplish blotches or spots. Spots may be angular; fungus spread is limited by veins.	**Septoria leaf spot,** *Septoria dianthi.* Fungus prefers wet, humid conditions. Spreads in splashing water.	Avoid overhead irrigation. Use good sanitation; rogue infected plants. See pages 116–118.
Leaves have yellowish brown, withered spots with purplish margins. Foliage has raised, circular, gray to brown lesions. May be greenish spores. Leaves may die, appear scorched.	**Fairy-ring leaf spot,** *Cladosporium* (=*Heterosporium*) *echinulatum.* Favored by cool, wet, humid conditions.	Avoid overhead watering; keep foliage dry. Limit cool temperatures. Use good sanitation; rogue infected plants. See pages 116–118.
Foliage dull, yellow, wilts, dries, and dies. Stem or entire plant wilts. Stem vascular tissue brownish or yellow and sticky. Most common on older plants.	**Bacterial wilt,** *Pseudomonas caryophylii.* Persists in soil, infects through wounds. Favored by 75° to 95°F and wet conditions.	Spread by contaminated water, soil, debris, equipment, or workers. Use good sanitation. Pasteurize media before planting. Use culture-indexed stock. Don't wound plants. See page 107.
Sepals, petals, or leaves have brown, water-soaked spots that wilt and rot. Dead tissue may have woolly gray growth (spores). Stem may be girdled.	**Gray mold,** *Botrytis cinerea.* Fungus develops in crop debris or inactive tissue. Favored by high humidity and 70° to 77°F. Spores airborne.	Use good sanitation. Keep humidity low during culture and in storage. Provide good air circulation. Don't crowd plants. See page 108.
Flower calyx or foliage has whitish powdery growth or lesions.	**Powdery mildew,** *Oidium dianthi.* A fungal disease.	Some fungicides applied at first signs of disease provide control. See page 112.
Leaves have purplish red to dark brown, irregular, angular spots. Lower leaf surface covered with soft, fluffy fungal growth. Leaves yellow and drop.	**Downy mildew,** *Peronospora dianthicola.* Spores produced only on living plants. Fungus persists as resistant oospores when conditions are dry. Favored by moist, humid conditions.	Provide good air circulation. Avoid overhead watering. Consider applying fungicide to protect foliage. See page 115.
Leaf margins pale green or red. Foliage may yellow and wilt. Stems may crack.	**Phialophora wilt,** *Phialophora cinerescens.* Fungal pathogen favored by cool soil temperatures.	Pasteurize media before planting. Plant only pathogen-free cuttings.
Sepals darken and decay. Flowers rot and drop. Sepals or leaves may be spotted.	**Calyx rot,** *Stemphylium botryosum* (=*Pleospora tarda*). Persists in infected plants and debris. Favored by warm, wet conditions, especially by overhead irrigation.	Don't use overhead irrigation. Keep humidity low. Use good sanitation; remove and dispose of debris. Fungicides can prevent.
Leaves have long, narrow, brownish lesions, yellow spots, or brownish pustules, sometimes on stems or buds. Leaves may curl, wither, and drop prematurely. Plants may be stunted.	**Rust,** *Uromyces dianthi* (=*U. caryophyllinus*). Spores spread by wind. Fungus survives only on living tissue; must be wet for infection.	Avoid overhead irrigation. Keep foliage dry or water in morning. Use good sanitation. Provide good air circulation. Avoid crowding plants. Use resistant cultivars. See page 119.
Leaves have brown, yellow, white, or reddish spots, blotches, flecks, rings, streaks, or mottling. Petals discolored in streaks or blotches. Plants stunted.	**Viruses,** including Carnation latent, Carnation mottle, Carnation necrotic fleck, Carnation ringspot, and Carnation streak viruses; Impatiens necrotic spot and Tomato spotted wilt viruses.	Use virus-free, culture-indexed stock. Control vectors. Use good sanitation; rogue infected plants. Depending on virus, spread by aphids, thrips, tools, equipment, or vegetatively. See page 121.
Shoots short, swollen, flattened, or distorted. Secondary rot may infect shoot clumps, killing plant. Plants lack vigor.	**Fasciation,** cause often uncertain. May be viral, bacterial (e.g., *Rhodococcus fascians*), or genetic. Manage as bacterial and take additional measures.	Use pathogen-free stock. Avoid injuring base of plants, especially when wet. Keep base of plants dry. Dispose of infected plants. See page 121.
Foliage yellows or wilts. Feeder and fleshy roots have knots or swellings.	**Root knot nematode,** *Meloidogyne* spp. Tiny roundworms that prefer warm, moist media. Many hosts.	Use nematode-free stock. Pasteurize or treat media before planting. Rogue affected plants. See page 265.

What the problem looks like	Probable cause	Comments
Plants stunted. Root cortex and deep tissues have necrotic lesions.	**Root lesion nematodes,** *Pratylenchus* spp. Nematodes survive in media as eggs, larvae, and adults.	Use nematode-free stock. Pasteurize media before planting. Rogue affected plants. See page 265.
Lower stem has distorted callus growth or gall. Plant stunted. Roots may be gnarled, stunted, or hairy with mostly small rootlets.	**Crown gall,** *Agrobacterium tumefaciens.* Bacteria persists in media, enters plant through wounds. Favored by rapid plant growth. Not reported on carnation in California.	Pasteurize media before planting. Inspect stock and use only if pathogen-free. Avoid wounding plants. Dip cuttings in *Agrobacterium tumefaciens* K-84 to prevent. See page 102.
Foliage blotched or dark streaked. Leaves or terminals distorted. Flowers small. Plants severely stunted. Buds darken or drop.	**Cyclamen mite,** *Phytonemus pallidus.* A pinkish orange mite (family Tarsonemidae), $1/100$ inch long or smaller.	See page 217.
Foliage turns yellow. Plant declines or dies back. Stems or leaves have tan to yellow encrustations.	**Oleander scale,** *Aspidiotus nerii.* Circular flat insects, less than $1/16$ inch long.	See Scales, page 186.
Foliage has sticky honeydew, blackish sooty mold, and whitish cast skins. Foliage may curl or yellow.	**Aphids,** including *Aphis fabae, Aulacorthum solani, Myzus persicae.* Tiny pear-shaped insects, often greenish, yellow, or blackish.	See page 179.
Foliage has sticky honeydew and blackish sooty mold. Foliage may yellow and drop.	**Brown soft scale,** *Coccus hesperidum.* Oval yellow, orange, or brown flat to bulbous insects.	See page 186.
Blossoms have irregular white or brown streaks or blotches. Blossoms or terminals may distort. Growth may be stunted.	**Western flower thrips,** *Frankliniella occidentalis.* Slender dark brown to yellowish insects, $1/16$ inch long or less.	See page 161.
Foliage discolored, stippled, bleached, or reddened, and may drop. Plant may have fine webbing.	**Twospotted spider mite,** *Tetranychus urticae.* Tiny greenish or yellowish mites with 2 darker spots.	See page 213.
Distorted, yellow, stunted shoots and buds. May be excess basal shoots. Shoots may appear dusty because they are covered with mites.	**Carnation bud mite,** *Aceria paradianthi.* Tiny eriophyid lives at leaf, shoot, and stem axils and in flower calyxes.	Plant only mite-free cuttings. Regularly inspect crop and rogue infested plants. See page 219.
Foliage, buds, and stems chewed. Young plants clipped at base. Stocky moths present, attracted to lights at night, wings folded at rest.	**Variegated cutworm,** *Peridroma saucia.* Gray or brown larvae with dark markings, row of yellow dots on back. Hides in soil during day.	Exclude moths, which fly to lights at night. Apply *Bacillus thuringiensis* to young larvae. Insecticide bait kills larvae. See page 203.
Flowers, terminals, or foliage chewed. Leaves may be webbed with silk. Flower buds may be mined. Caterpillars or their black frass pellets may be present.	**Caterpillars,** including Beet armyworm, *Spodoptera exigua;* Cabbage looper, *Trichoplusia ni;* Carnation leafroller, *Platynota sultana;* Tobacco budworm, *Helicoverpa virescens.* Nocturnal moths.	Screen to exclude moths from growing areas. Avoid growing near other major hosts. *Bacillus thuringiensis* kills larvae. See page 203.
Foliage chewed and webbed together with silk. Stems may be mined. Larvae wriggle vigorously when touched.	**Greenhouse leaftier,** *Udea rubigalis.* Larvae yellowish green with three longitudinal green to white stripes. Adult (family Pyralidae) reddish brown with black wavy lines on wings. Mature adult and larva about $3/4$ inch long. Has about 6 generations per year.	Avoid growing floral hosts near celery, a major host. See Caterpillars, page 203.
Foliage chewed, scraped, tied together with silk by greenish larvae with dark head.	**Carnation leafroller,** *Platynota sultana;* **Obliquebanded leafroller,** *Archips* or *Choristoneura rosaceana.* Adults moths (family Tortricidae) about 1 inch wide, brownish or tan with black. Heads have snoutlike projection.	See Caterpillars, page 203.
Buds, flowers, or leaves mined or chewed, may be webbed with silk.	**Omnivorous leaftier,** *Cnephasia longana.* Gray to brownish, $1/2$ inch long larvae and nocturnal moths. Larvae may have grayish stripes. Attacks strawberries and many other hosts. Occurs in central California coast. Has 1 generation per year.	Time any spray for young larvae emerging from mines in spring. See Caterpillars, page 203.
Leaves and blossoms chewed (edges notched).	**Fuller rose beetle,** *Asynonychus godmani.* Rarely seen adult pale brown weevil feeds at night. Larva whitish maggot, eats roots.	See Weevils, page 208.
Winding tunnels in (mostly basal) leaves, may extend into petiole and stem. Leaves may have pale spots and punctures; may whiten, wilt, and drop.	**Leafminers,** *Liriomyza huidobrensis, L. trifolii.* Small active flies, dark with yellow. Yellowish or whitish maggot bores in tissue.	See page 167.

What the problem looks like	Probable cause	Comments
CASSIA (*Cassia* spp.), Senna		
Plant stunted or yellows and wilts. Stem rotted at soil line.	**Rhizoctonia stem rot,** *Rhizoctonia solani.* Favored by warm, moist conditions. Dark fungal strands may be visible on soil with hand lens. Not reported on cassia in California.	Fungus persists in soil. Practice good sanitation. Avoid overwatering and deep planting. See pages 93–98.
Leaves have yellow or brown blotches or spots. Leaves may yellow, wilt, and die.	**Leaf spots, Blight,** *Alternaria, Cercospora, Phomopsis, Septoria* spp. Fungi promoted by wet conditions. Not reported on cassia in California.	Avoid overhead irrigation. Use good sanitation; rogue infected plants. See pages 116–118.
Foliage discolors, may turn brown and die. Leaf underside has powdery brownish pustules.	**Rusts,** including *Ravenelia* spp. Airborne spores spread only from living tissue. Plant must be wet for infection. Not reported on cassia in California.	Avoid overhead irrigation. Water in morning so foliage dries. Keep humidity low. See page 119.
White, powdery growth or lesions, primarily on older leaves and stem. Severely affected leaves dry and die.	**Powdery mildews,** *Erysiphe polygoni, Oidium* sp. Free water not required for fungal infection. Not reported on cassia in California.	Provide good air circulation and adequate light. If prior problem, consider applying fungicide to prevent. See page 112.
Leaves have water-soaked, yellow, or dark spots or blotches, often with distinct colored margins. Plant may wilt and die. Roots may be black but not rotted.	**Bacterial leaf spot, Blight,** *Xanthomonas campestris, Pseudomonas* sp. Spread by splashing water and infected stock, debris, and equipment. Favored by warm, moist conditions and rapid plant growth.	Plant only uninfected stock. Avoid overhead irrigation. Regularly inspect and rogue plants infected and those nearby. Use good sanitation. See pages 107, 118.
Foliage yellows or wilts. Feeder and fleshy roots have knots or swellings.	**Root knot nematode,** *Meloidogyne* sp. Tiny roundworms that prefer warm, sandy soil. Many hosts.	Pasteurize media before planting. Rogue affected plants. See page 265.
Foliage stippled or bleached. Terminals may distort.	**Thrips.** Tiny, slender, blackish or yellowish insects.	See page 161.
Foliage bleached or stippled. Terminals or leaves may distort.	**Eggplant lace bug,** *Gargaphia solani.* Brown and yellow true bug (family Tingidae), up to about ⅛ inch long. Adult has clear, bulbous, reticulated cover. Nymphs spiny. Attacks solanums, including eggplant, potato, and tomato.	See True Bugs, page 194.
Plant has sticky honeydew and blackish sooty mold. Foliage may yellow from small insects on leaves or stems.	**Brown soft scale,** *Coccus hesperidum.* Oval, flat or bulbous; yellow, orange, or brown insects, less than ⅛ inch long.	See Scales, page 186.
CELOSIA (*Celosia cristata, C. plumosa),* Cockscomb		
Foliage yellow, and wilted, possibly along leaf margins, often one side of plant. Leaves dry and die from the base of plant up. Stems may have brown vascular streaking.	**Verticillium wilt,** *Verticillium dahliae.* Fungus contaminates soil, cuttings, and root divisions. Favored by cool weather followed by hot.	Use pathogen-free cuttings and resistant cultivars. Pasteurize media before planting. See pages 104–106.
Plant stunted or yellows and wilts. Stem rotted at soil line. Dark fungal strands may be visible on soil with hand lens.	**Rhizoctonia stem rot,** *Rhizoctonia solani.* Soilborne fungus favored by warm, moist conditions.	Practice good sanitation. Avoid overwatering and deep planting. See pages 93–98.
Leaves have yellow or brown spots or blotches. Leaves may yellow, die.	**Leaf spots,** *Alternaria, Cercospora, Phyllosticta, Septoria* spp. Fungi promoted by wet conditions. Only *Septoria* is common on celosia in California.	See pages 116–118.
Blossoms or leaves have light streaks, blotches, or mottling. Flowers and foliage distorted. Plants may be stunted and die.	**Beet curly top virus.** Spread by leafhoppers. Infects many hosts.	Use virus-free stock. Control nearby weeds. Exclude or control leafhoppers. See Viruses, page 121.
Foliage chlorotic. Plant stunted. Spindly, upright yellow shoots and few or no flowers.	**Aster yellows.** Phytoplasmalike organism spread by leafhoppers. Not spread by seed, handling, aphids, or other insects. Many hosts.	Don't plant downwind from other hosts. Eliminate nearby weeds. Exclude or control leafhoppers. Rogue infected plants. See pages 129–130.
Foliage discolored, stippled, bleached, or reddened, and may drop. Plant may have fine webbing.	**Twospotted spider mite,** *Tetranychus urticae.* Tiny greenish or yellowish mites with 2 darker spots.	See page 213.
Foliage has sticky honeydew and blackish sooty mold. Leaves yellow and wither. Tiny, whitish, mothlike adults.	**Whiteflies,** including Silverleaf whitefly, *Bemisia argentifolii;* Sweetpotato whitefly, *Bemisia tabaci.* Oval, flattened, yellow to greenish nymphs.	See page 170.
Foliage has sticky honeydew, blackish sooty mold, and whitish cast skins. Terminal or young leaves may curl or yellow.	**Aphids,** including Green peach aphid, *Myzus persicae.* Small pear-shaped insects, often green, yellowish, or blackish.	See page 179.

What the problem looks like	Probable cause	Comments

CENTAUREA (Centaurea cyanus), Bachelors-buttons, Bluebottle, Cornflower

What the problem looks like	Probable cause	Comments
Plants wilt suddenly and die. Water-soaked cankers appear on stem near soil. Stem has cottony growth, later large, black sclerotia.	**Stem rot**, *Sclerotinia sclerotiorum*. Fungal sclerotia persist in soil. Favored by cool, moist conditions.	Avoid planting where disease has occurred. Many hosts, including vegetable crops. Avoid overwatering. Irrigate early in day so plants dry quickly. See page 101.
White, powdery growth, primarily on older leaves and stem. Severely affected leaves dry and die.	**Powdery mildew**, *Erysiphe cichoracearum*. Free water not required for infection.	Provide good air circulation and adequate light. Consider applying sulfur or other fungicide to prevent. See page 112.
Flowers, flower heads, lower leaves, or growing points have soft brown decay. Dead tissue may have woolly gray growth (spores).	**Gray mold**, *Botrytis cinerea*. Fungus develops in crop debris or inactive tissue. Favored by high humidity and 70° to 77°F. Spores airborne.	Use good sanitation. Avoid overhead irrigation. Keep humidity low. Provide good air circulation. Don't crowd plants. See page 108.
Foliage discolors. Leaf underside has powdery brownish pustules.	**Rust**, *Puccinia cyani*. Airborne spores spread only from living tissue. Plant must be wet for infection.	Avoid overhead irrigation. Water in morning so foliage dries. Keep humidity low. See page 119.
Foliage chlorotic. Plant stunted. Spindly, upright yellow shoots and few or no flowers.	**Aster yellows**. Phytoplasmalike organism spread by leafhoppers. Not spread by seed, handling, aphids, or other insects. Many hosts.	Don't plant seed beds downwind from other hosts. Eliminate nearby weeds. Control leafhoppers. Rogue infected plants. See pages 129–130.
Growth may be retarded from small insects infesting roots and possibly stems near soil.	**Aster or Erigeron root aphid**, *Aphis middletonii*. Small pear-shaped insects, light gray to dark green.	Infests many Asteraceae; control nearby weeds in this family. See page 182.
Foliage has sticky honeydew, blackish sooty mold, and whitish cast skins. Leaves may curl or pucker. Foliage may yellow.	**Aphids**, including Leaf curl plum aphid, *Aphis* or *Brachycaudus helichrysi*. Small pear-shaped insects, often green, reddish, yellowish, or blackish.	See page 179.
Foliage has sticky honeydew and blackish sooty mold. Leaves may yellow and wither. Tiny, whitish, mothlike adult insects.	**Whiteflies**, including Silverleaf whitefly, *Bemisia argentifolii*; Sweetpotato whitefly, *Bemisia tabaci*. Oval, flattened, yellow to greenish nymphs.	See page 170.
Blossoms have irregular white or brown blotches. Leaves may turn brown. Blossoms or terminals may be distorted. Growth may be stunted.	**Western flower thrips**, *Frankliniella occidentalis*. Slender dark brown to yellowish insects, $\frac{1}{16}$ inch long or less.	See Thrips, page 161.
Foliage chewed. May be dark frass present or beetle larvae that have only three pairs of true legs and no abdominal appendages.	**Leaf beetle**, *Glyptoscelis squamulata*. Adult oblong, metallic bronze to grayish beetle (family Chrysomelidae).	Exclude or control beetles. See page 212.
Buds, flowers, or leaves mined or chewed, may be webbed with silk.	**Omnivorous leaftier**, *Cnephasia longana*. Gray to brownish larvae and nocturnal moths, $\frac{1}{2}$ inch long. Larvae may have grayish stripes. Attacks strawberries and many other hosts. Occurs in central California coast. Has 1 generation per year.	Time any spray for young larvae emerging from mines in spring. See Caterpillars, page 203.

CHRISTMAS CACTUS (Schlumbergera bridgesii); THANKSGIVING CACTUS (S. truncata), holiday cactus, crab cactus

What the problem looks like	Probable cause	Comments
Stems wilt, yellow, and may drop. Crown, basal stem, or roots soft and decayed. Necrotic stem or leaf spots or blotches may develop if hot and humid.	**Root and crown rot**, *Pythium aphanidermatum*, *Pythium irregulare*, *Phytophthora parasitica*. Fungi favored by wet, poorly drained media.	Provide good drainage. Avoid overwatering. Fungicide application may be needed to prevent. 'Gold Charm' is highly susceptible to *P. parasitica*. See pages 93–97.
Basal stem or roots brown and rotted. Brown stem or leaf spots. Plant may yellow, wilt, and die.	**Fusarium rot**, *Fusarium oxysporum*. Spreads in contaminated media and stock. Favored by high relative humidity, 80°F or warmer, overwatering, and poorly drained media.	Pasteurize media before planting. Use pathogen-free plants. Provide good drainage. Don't overwater. Avoid high humidity. 'Gold Charm' is highly susceptible. 'Peach Parfait' and some other cultivars are resistant. See pages 93–96, 104.
Plant stunted or yellows and wilts. Stem rotted at soil line. Dark fungal strands may be visible on soil with hand lens.	**Rhizoctonia stem rot**, *Rhizoctonia solani*. Soilborne fungus favored by warm, moist conditions.	Practice good sanitation. Avoid overwatering and deep planting. See pages 93–98.
Leaves soft brown and decayed. Dark spore masses may be visible on lesions.	**Stem rot**, *Bipolaris* (=*Drechslera*) *cactivora*. Fungus persists in infected plants and debris. Favored by wet or humid conditions. Spores airborne.	Avoid excess humidity. Use good sanitation. 'Gold Charm' is highly susceptible. 'White Christmas' is resistant. Manage like similar pathogens discussed in Root and Crown Rots, pages 93–96.

What the problem looks like	Probable cause	Comments

CHRISTMAS CACTUS (Schlumbergera bridgesii); THANKSGIVING CACTUS (S. truncata), holiday cactus, crab cactus (continued)

What the problem looks like	Probable cause	Comments
Crowns or stems decay; soft, brown, odorous rot often at soil line. Leaf edges and stems may be discolored, soft, rotted.	**Soft rot**, *Erwinia carotovora*. Persists in media. Favored when wet.	Avoid injuring plant; disease is secondary, infecting wounds. Provide good drainage. Use good sanitation; immediately discard infected plants and those nearby. 'Gold Charm' is highly susceptible. 'White Christmas' is resistant. See pages 100, 107.
Petals have brown, water-soaked spots. Lower leaves rotted and may have woolly gray growth (spores). Stem may be girdled.	**Gray mold**, *Botrytis cinerea*. Fungus develops in crop debris or inactive tissue. Favored by high humidity and 70° to 77°F. Spores airborne.	Use good sanitation. Avoid wetting foliage. Keep humidity low. Provide good air circulation. Don't crowd plants. See page 108.
Vegetative parts drop from plants, often when shipped long distances.	**Shattering**. Caused by stress or ethylene exposure, especially during shipping.	Apply ethylene inhibitor 2 to 3 weeks before shipping. See page 67.
Branches or blossoms have sunken chlorotic lesions or dark green spots or streaks; may be distorted.	**Tomato spotted wilt virus**. Spread by thrips, not by tools. Some infected plants may be symptomless. Has many alternate hosts.	Use virus-free cuttings. Eliminate nearby weeds and other hosts. Control thrips in and around growing area. See page 121.
Plants may grow slowly, otherwise symptomless.	**Cactus x virus**. Not spread by insects or in seed. Mechanically spread during plant contact, by tools, or during propagation.	Rogue infected plants. See Viruses, page 121.
Stems wilted and yellowish or reddened. Plants stunted. Roots have tiny white or brown cysts.	**Cactus cyst nematode**, *Cactodera cacti*. Tiny roundworms live in root cysts. Spread in irrigation runoff water or if plants and containers close and often wet.	Pasteurize media before planting. Minimize contamination from irrigation runoff. Provide rapid drainage. Keep growing area relatively dry.
Blossoms have irregular white or brown streaks or blotches. Blossoms or terminals may distort. Growth may be stunted.	**Western flower thrips**, *Frankliniella occidentalis*. Slender dark brown to yellowish insects, $\frac{1}{16}$ inch long or less.	See page 161.
Plant grows slowly, yellows. Stems or leaves have whitish encrustations (scale colonies).	**Scales**, including Cactus scale, *Diaspis echinocacti*. Small, whitish, flattened, circular to elongate, immobile insects.	See page 186.
Plant has sticky honeydew, blackish sooty mold, and cottony waxy material.	**Mealybugs**. Grayish, oval, waxy, slow-moving insects with marginal filaments.	See page 183.

CHRYSANTHEMUM (Dendranthema grandiflora, Chrysanthemum morifolium), Mum

What the problem looks like	Probable cause	Comments
Foliage yellow and wilted, possibly only along leaf margins, often on only one side of plant. Leaves dry and die from the base of plant up and often remain attached and hang down against the stem. Stem may have dark vascular streaks. Symptoms commonly appear only after blossom buds have formed. Young, vigorous plants may be symptomless.	**Verticillium wilt**, *Verticillium dahliae*. Fungus contaminates soil, cuttings, and root divisions. Favored by cool weather followed by hot.	Pasteurize media before planting. Use pathogen-free cuttings. Most cultivars are resistant; avoid susceptible cultivars, including: 'Bright Golden Ann,' 'Echo,' 'Glowing Mandalay,' 'Mountain Peak,' 'Paragon,' 'Pert,' 'Puritan,' and 'Wedgewood.' See pages 104–106.
Foliage yellow, may be wilted and stunted overall. Plant looks water stressed. Often affects one side, toward which stem may curve. Foliage may brown and die. Vascular system becomes reddish brown.	**Fusarium wilt**, *Fusarium oxysporum* f. sp. *chrysanthemi* and f. sp. *tracheiphilum*. Fungi spread in contaminated soil and cuttings. Favored by high relative humidity, 80°F or warmer, overwatering, and poorly drained media.	Solarize or otherwise pasteurize soil. Use pathogen-free plants. Adjust soil pH to 6.5 to 7.0. Use nitrate nitrogen. Avoid highly susceptible cultivars: 'Bravo,' 'Cirbronze,' 'Illini Trophy,' 'Orange Bowl,' 'Royal Trophy,' 'Yellow Delaware.' See page 104.
Plants stunted. Black, girdling lesions on stem near soil.	**Pythium root rot**, *Pythium* spp. Fungi spread in contaminated soil or water. Favored by wet, poorly drained soil.	Solarize or otherwise pasteurize media. Use pathogen-free water. Provide good drainage. Don't overwater. See pages 93–96.
Plant stunted, yellow, or wilted. Stem rotted near soil, may have vascular streaks. Dark fungal strands may be visible on soil with hand lens.	**Rhizoctonia stem rot**, *Rhizoctonia solani*. Soilborne fungus favored by warm, moist conditions. Newly planted cuttings commonly infected.	Practice good sanitation. Avoid overwatering and deep planting. Treat base of transplants or soil before planting. See pages 93–98.
Lower leaves and stem rot. Petals have blackish rot beginning at center (or ray) florets, may extend into flower stalk. Foliage may distort or die on one side from stem infection below soil.	**Ray blight**, *Didymella ligulicola* (=*Ascochyta chrysanthemi*). Persists in plant debris. Spores spread in air and water. Favored by overhead irrigation and rain.	Use pathogen-free cuttings. Avoid wetting foliage. Keep flowers dry during production, storage, and shipping; symptoms may not appear until at market. Keep humidity low. Fungicides can protect foliage.

What the problem looks like	Probable cause	Comments
Center petals have small, necrotic, light to dark brown lesions. Lesions may grow and blossoms die.	**Ray speck,** *Stemphylium lycopersici.* Wet conditions and 60° to 85°F required for infection. Reportedly not found in California.	Don't overhead water. Keep plants dry. Provide good ventilation. Don't crowd plants. Rogue and dispose of infected plants.
Stems rotted. Flowers have brown spots, like gray mold. Decayed tissue may have cottony fungal mass. Inside and outside of stems may have black sclerotia.	**Sclerotinia rot,** *Sclerotinia sclerotiorum.* Fungal sclerotia persist in contaminated soil. Favored by high humidity.	Use good sanitation; remove and dispose of debris and old plants. Keep humidity low. Irrigate early in day so plants dry quickly. Provide good air circulation. See page 101.
Leaf underside has powdery brownish pustules, may be on stem. Leaf upperside has brown or yellow spots. Foliage may yellow and drop.	**Rust,** *Puccinia tanaceti* (=*P. chrysanthemi*). Airborne and water-splashed spores spread only from living tissue. Plant must be wet for infection. Uncommon; mostly a field disease.	Use resistant cultivars. Avoid wetting foliage. Keep humidity low. Fungicide can be applied when rust first appears. See page 119.
Leaf upperside has pale green, yellow, or white spots. Leaf underside has white, pink, or brown pustules.	**White rust,** *Puccinia horiana.* Survives only on living mum foliage. Foliage must be wet for airborne spores to germinate. Direct sunlight destroys spores. Mostly greenhouse problem; under eradication in California.	Quarantined pathogen. Regulations require that infected plants be destroyed to prevent disease establishment. See pages 119–120.
Older leaves and stem have white powdery growth and round spots, then larger blotches. Foliage may be deformed or puckered. Severely affected leaves dry and die.	**Powdery mildew,** *Erysiphe cichoracearum.* Free water not required for infection, but most severe at high humidity.	Provide good air circulation and keep humidity low. Provide adequate light. Consider applying sulfur or other fungicide to prevent. See page 112.
Petals or lower leaves have brown, water-soaked decay or spots. May be woolly gray growth (spores). Stem may be girdled. Flowers in storage or transit may rot entirely.	**Gray mold,** *Botrytis cinerea.* Fungus develops in crop debris or inactive tissue. Favored by high humidity and 70° to 77°F. Spores airborne.	Use good sanitation; remove debris and old plants. Keep humidity low. Provide good air circulation. Don't crowd plants. See page 108.
Leaves have sunken, circular to irregular or angular, brown, tan, or yellow spots or blotches. May develop from base of plant upward. Foliage may yellow and die.	**Septoria leaf spot,** *Septoria chrysanthemi.* Fungus prefers moist conditions. Spreads in splashing water.	Avoid overhead irrigation. Use good sanitation; rogue infected plants. See pages 116–118.
Leaves have tan to dark spots or blotches that may be bordered or ringed. Discoloring may follow leaf veins. Leaves may wilt and die.	**Bacterial leaf spot,** *Pseudomonas cichorii.* Spread by air and splashing water. Uncommon on mums in California.	Avoid overhead irrigation. Don't overwater or crowd plants. Use good sanitation. See page 107.
Leaves have irregular brown or black spots. Buds and stems may darken and die. Stems may have water-soaked lesions; pith becomes jellylike. Terminals may turn black and exude liquid drops. Stems may split or break. Plants may wilt.	**Bacterial blight,** *Erwinia chrysanthemi.* Survives in plant debris. Favored by surface moisture, high humidity, and 80° to 90°F. Spreads on infected tools, equipment, hands, and plants.	Pasteurize media. Use pathogen-free cuttings. Reduce humidity. Increase air circulation. Avoid wetting foliage. Use good sanitation; regularly inspect crop and immediately dispose of any infected plants. See pages 100, 107.
Pith near soil deteriorates and collapses in cuttings; collapse may extend up several internodes. Stem tissue brown. Plant grows slowly.	**Hollow stem,** *Erwinia carotovora.* Bacteria survive in undecomposed debris and symptomless mums. High temperatures and humidity favor it.	Use pathogen-free cuttings. Avoid susceptible 'Red Torch,' 'Tempo,' and 'Tempter.' Reduce humidity. Avoid using liquid dips. See pages 100, 107.
Cutting base, lower stem, or roots have distorted callus growth or gall; occasionally found on leaves. Plant stunted. Roots may be gnarled, stunted, or hairy with mostly small rootlets.	**Crown gall,** *Agrobacterium tumefaciens.* Bacteria persist in soil for years, enter plant through wounds. Favored by rapid plant growth.	Avoid wounding plants. Don't plant in infested soil for 3 years; plant nonhost species or solarize or otherwise pasteurize soil. Dip cuttings in *Agrobacterium tumefaciens* K-84 to prevent. See page 102.
Shoots short, swollen, flattened, or distorted. Secondary rot may infect shoot clumps, killing plant. Plants lack vigor.	**Fasciation,** *Rhodococcus fascians.* Other causes may include viruses or genetic disorder. Manage as bacterial and take additional measures.	Use pathogen-free stock. Avoid injuring base of plants, especially when wet. Keep base of plants dry. Dispose of infected plants. See page 121.
Foliage chlorotic. Plant stunted. Spindly, upright yellow shoots and few or no flowers.	**Aster yellows.** Phytoplasmalike organism spread by leafhoppers. Many hosts.	Don't plant cuttings downwind from other hosts. Eliminate nearby weeds. Control leafhoppers. Rogue infected plants. See pages 129–130.
Flowers distorted and small. Streaking or color break in red, bronze, and pink florets. Leaves usually symptomless.	**Aspermy,** Tomato aspermy virus. Spread by aphids, handling, and contaminated tools.	Use pathogen-free cuttings. Rogue infected plants. Control aphids. Serious if tomatoes are rotated with or grown near mums. See page Viruses, 121.

What the problem looks like	Probable cause	Comments
CHRYSANTHEMUM (*Dendranthema grandiflora, Chrysanthemum morifolium*), Mum (continued)		
Foliage mottled, then completely yellow. Looks like nutritional deficiency. Plants may be necrotic or dwarfed.	**Chrysanthemum chlorotic mottle viroid.** Causal agent spread by handling and contaminated tools. Symptoms may not appear under low light and below 70°F.	Use pathogen-free cuttings. Rogue infected plants. See page 121.
Plants stunted. Flowers small and blossom early. Foliage may be pale with young upright leaves.	**Chrysanthemum stunt viroid.** Easily transmitted by handling and contaminated tools. Not spread by aphids or thrips. Symptomless in some plants.	Obtain pathogen-free plants from an indexing program. Rogue infected plants. If present, pasteurize tools, equipment, and hands before moving between plants. See Viruses, page 121.
Leaves or stems have yellow to brown or bronze streaks, rings, spots, or mottling. Leaves or flowers stunted, distorted, or wilted. Stem necrosis. Leaves wilt and drop.	**Impatiens necrotic spot virus, Tomato spotted wilt virus.** Thrips-vectored. Many alternate hosts.	Use virus-free cuttings. Rogue infected plants immediately. Eliminate nearby weeds and other hosts. Exclude or control thrips. See page 121.
Leaves have mosaic mottling. Flowers, stems, and leaves dwarfed, crinkled, and distorted.	**Chrysanthemum mosaic virus.** Aphid-vectored.	Use virus-free cuttings. Rogue infected plants. Control aphids. See page 121.
Leaves yellowish. Leaves have dark green or brown, vein-limited, angular spots or blotches that develop progressively up from older leaves.	**Foliar nematodes,** *Aphelenchoides fragariae; A. ritzemabosi.* Tiny roundworms spread in plant debris and by vegetative propagation and splashing water. Not common in California.	Use uninfected stock plants. Remove plant debris. Avoid overhead irrigation; leaves must be wet for infection to occur. See page 265.
Foliage yellows or wilts. Feeder and fleshy roots have knots or swellings.	**Root knot nematode,** *Meloidogyne* spp. Tiny roundworms that prefer warm, sandy soil. Many hosts.	Pasteurize media before planting. Rogue affected plants. See page 265.
Plants grow slowly, are stunted. Leaves small.	**Noninfectious disorders,** including nitrogen deficiency, excess or deficient water, excess salts in media, and low temperatures or low light during vegetative growth.	Provide proper growing conditions and good cultural care.
Foliage yellows between veins.	**Interveinal chlorosis.** Causes include high media pH, high temperatures, and iron or manganese deficiency.	Provide proper growing conditions and good cultural care.
Inflorescence color break. Distorted, delayed, or no flowers.	**Noninfectious disorders.** Inappropriate light or temperatures.	Provide appropriate growing conditions.
Uneven blossoming. Few or no flowers. Flowers distorted. Petal color faded or white petals are pinkish.	**Flower failure.** Causes include improper light or excess temperature (heat delay) and poor air quality or pollutants.	Provide proper growing conditions and good cultural care.
Plants grow slowly. Foliage sparse or stunted.	**Poor growth.** Causes include poor drainage, overwatering, lack of light, excess or deficient nitrogen, and improper media pH.	Provide proper growing conditions and good cultural care.
Lack of many shoots for several weeks after terminals are pinched.	**Insufficient shoots.** Causes include insufficient nitrogen, nights too cool, air too dry, or pinching too hard (pinching into hard stems).	Provide proper growing conditions and good cultural care. Short nights promote vegetative growth; long nights induce flowering.
Plants small, internodes shorter than normal.	**Short plants.** Causes include excess growth retardant, insufficient nitrogen, lack of enough long days.	Provide proper growing conditions and good cultural care.
Plants too tall, internodes longer than normal.	**Tall plants.** Causes include too many long days, inadequate light intensity, overcrowding, high day temperatures with cold nights, or insufficient growth retardant.	Provide proper growing conditions and good cultural care.
Crown buds and vegetative shoots develop instead of inflorescences. Bract buds develop into oversized bracts.	**Improper bud development.** Causes include improper light photoperiod, uniformity, or intensity; improper covering or black cloth use; and poor air quality, such as from heater exhaust.	Provide proper growing conditions and environmental control.
Early blossoms. Flowers develop when plants are still short.	**Early blossoming.** Caused by too few short nights or too few interrupted nights after planting.	Provide night-interrupt lighting (light 10 pm to 2 am); natural spring light may be unsuitable.

What the problem looks like	Probable cause	Comments
Foliage has sticky honeydew, blackish sooty mold, and whitish cast skins. Leaves may cup or terminals may be distorted. Foliage may yellow.	**Aphids,** including *Acyrthosiphon pisum, Aphis gossypii, Brachycaudus helichrysi, Macrosiphum euphorbiae, Myzus persicae, Macrosiphoniella sanborni.* Small pear-shaped insects, often green, yellowish, or blackish.	See page 179.
Foliage or stems have blackish sooty mold. Plant may yellow, wilt, decline, or die back.	**Black scale,** *Saissetia oleae;* **Hemispherical scale,** *Saissetia coffeae.* Orange, black, or brown flattened to bulbous insects.	See page 186.
Plant has sticky honeydew, blackish sooty mold, and cottony waxy material.	**Mealybugs.** Grayish, oval, waxy, slow-moving insects with marginal filaments.	See page 183.
Leaves have cottony cylindrical egg sacs up to ⅓ inch long. Foliage has sticky honeydew and blackish sooty mold. Foliage may yellow.	**Greenhouse orthezia,** *Orthezia insignis.* Pale brown to dark green insect with two white rows on back and white bands along side. Usually not a pest in California. Has about 2 generations per year.	Controls for mealybugs or scales may be effective.
Foliage has sticky honeydew and blackish sooty mold. Leaves yellow and wither. Tiny, whitish, mothlike adult insects.	**Whiteflies,** including Silverleaf whitefly, *Bemisia argentifolii;* Sweetpotato whitefly, *Bemisia tabaci.* Nymphs oval, flattened, yellow to greenish.	See page 170.
Blossoms distorted; color streaked and broken. Terminals may be distorted. Growth may be stunted. Foliage may have dark, varnishlike fecal specks.	**Banded greenhouse thrips,** *Hercinothrips femoralis;* **Chrysanthemum thrips,** *Thrips nigropilosus;* **Greenhouse thrips,** *Heliothrips haemorrhoidalis;* **Western flower thrips,** *Frankliniella occidentalis.* Tiny, slender, dark brown to yellowish insects.	See Thrips, page 161.
Foliage blotched or dark streaked. Leaves or terminals distorted. Flowers small. Plants severely stunted. Buds darken or drop.	**Cyclamen mite,** *Phytonemus pallidus.* A pinkish orange mite (family Tarsonemidae), ¹⁄₁₀₀ inch long or smaller.	See page 217.
Foliage bleached, brittle, edges may be curled or ragged. Blossoms distort or discolor. Plant grows slowly.	**Broad mite,** *Polyphagotarsonemus latus.* Translucent to dark green, ¹⁄₁₀₀ inch long or smaller.	See page 217.
Foliage, terminals, buds, and petals may be discolored, bleached, or distorted. Plant may have fine webbing.	**Privet mite,** *Brevipalpus obovatus;* **Twospotted spider mite,** *Tetranychus urticae.* Tiny greenish, yellowish, or red mites, may have 2 dark spots.	See page 213.
Foliage distorted, discolored, stippled or brown; may drop prematurely. Stems or leaves have pimplelike (egg-laying) punctures.	**Leafhoppers.** Slender insects, often green or yellowish, that suck plant sap and readily jump, fly, or crawl away sideways when disturbed.	Control weeds; leafhoppers often move from weeds. Control of adults is difficult; insecticidal soap or oil can reduce nymph populations. See page 193.
Unusual branching, excess and short branches. Premature flower bud formation. Flowers distorted. Delayed or no flowers. Dead leaf patches. Leaf tips may wilt.	**Plant bugs,** *Lygus* spp. Brown, green, or yellowish bugs, up to ¼ inch long, suck plant juices.	Control nearby weeds, from which bugs move. Exclude bugs form growing area. See True Bugs, page 194.
Leaves and stems have cone-shaped to elongate galls. Leaves, stems, and possibly flowers are distorted or thickened and may die. Plant may be dwarfed and may not bloom.	**Chrysanthemum gall midge,** *Rhopalomyia chrysanthemi.* Tiny green, white, or orangish maggots mine tissue. Adults are slender, orangish, delicate flies. Have several generations per year.	Attacks only chrysanthemum. Plant only gall-free cuttings. Regularly inspect plants and clip and immediately dispose of galled tissue or entire plants, before pest becomes abundant. See page 202.
Foliage, buds, and stems chewed. Young plants clipped at base. Stocky moths present, attracted to lights at night, wings folded at rest.	**Variegated cutworm,** *Peridroma saucia.* Gray or brown larvae with dark markings, row of yellow dots on back. Hide in soil during day.	Exclude moths, which fly to lights at night. Apply *Bacillus thuringiensis* to young larvae. Insecticide bait kills larvae. See page 203.
Flower buds may be mined. Petals, flower buds, terminals, or foliage chewed or scraped. Leaves may be webbed with silk from greenish to brown larvae, up to 1½ inches long, with light stripes.	**Caterpillars,** including Beet armyworm, *Spodoptera exigua;* Cabbage looper, *Trichoplusia ni;* Tobacco budworm, *Helicoverpa virescens;* Corn earworm, *H. zea.* Omnivorous leaftier, *Cnephasia longana.*	Screen to exclude white, brownish, or grayish moths from growing areas. Avoid growing near other major hosts. *Bacillus thuringiensis* kills exposed-feeding larvae. See page 203.
Foliage chewed, often only on underside, and webbed together with silk. Stems may be mined. Adult and mature larva present, about ¾ inches long.	**Greenhouse leaftier,** *Udea rubigalis* (family Pyralidae). Larvae yellowish green with three longitudinal green to white stripes. Adult reddish brown with black wavy lines on wings. Has about 6 generations per year.	Avoid growing floral hosts near celery, a major host. Exclude night-flying moths from growing area. See page 203.

What the problem looks like	Probable cause	Comments

CHRYSANTHEMUM (*Dendranthema grandiflora, Chrysanthemum morifolium*), Mum (continued)

What the problem looks like	Probable cause	Comments
Leaves and blossoms chewed (edges notched).	**Black vine weevil,** *Otiorhynchus sulcatus;* **Fuller rose beetle,** *Asynonychus godmani.* Rarely seen adults brown, black, to gray snout beetles that feed at night. Larvae whitish maggots that feed on roots.	See page 208.
Leaves have light-colored, winding tunnels. Yellowish to white maggots in mines. Heavily infested leaves may drop. Leaves have pale spots or punctures from adult flies.	**Serpentine leafminer,** *Liriomyza trifolii;* **Pea leafminer,** *L. huidobrensis;* **Chrysanthemum leafminer,** *Chromatomyia syngenesiae. Liriomyza* adults are small, black and yellow flies; *Chromatomyia* are grayish and pupate in leaves, but otherwise are similar to *Liriomyza* spp.	See Leafminers, page 167.

CINERARIA (*Senecio cruentus*)

What the problem looks like	Probable cause	Comments
Plants stunted. Foliage yellows, wilts, and dies. Roots rotted. Basal stem of collapsed plants girdled, dark brown, rotted.	**Root and collar rot,** *Phytophthora* spp. Fungi persist in media and spread in water. Favored by wet, poorly drained media.	Pasteurize media before planting. Provide good drainage. Don't overwater. See pages 93–97.
Leaves yellow and drop. Plants stunted, may collapse. Roots brown and decayed.	**Root rot,** *Pythium ultimum.* Fungus present in many soils. Infects corms through wounds. Favored by warm, moist conditions.	Pasteurize media before planting. Provide good drainage. Avoid overwatering. See pages 93–96.
Foliage chlorotic. Basal stem dark and decayed. Seedlings wilt and decay.	**Collar rot,** *Rhizoctonia solani.* Fungus persists in media. Promoted by warm, moist conditions.	Pasteurize media before planting. Provide good drainage. Avoid overwatering. See pages 93–98.
Plant wilts and dies. Basal stem rotted. Black sclerotia in and on stems. Cottony mycelia in and on stems if conditions are moist.	**Stem rot,** *Sclerotinia sclerotiorum.* Fungus persists in media. Favored by overhead irrigation and high humidity. Many hosts.	Pasteurize media before planting. Avoid overhead irrigation. Irrigate early in day so plants dry quickly. See page 101.
Leaves have small brown, orangish, or purplish spots or larger patches. Foliage may shrivel and drop.	**Leaf spot,** *Alternaria cinerea.* Spread by air. Favored by prolonged, cool, wet, conditions. Persists in plant debris.	Avoid wetting foliage. Use good sanitation; promptly remove and dispose of debris and infected leaves. See pages 116–118.
Foliage yellow with downy gray growth (spores) on underside. Leaves roll downward.	**Downy mildew,** *Plasmopara halstedii.* Airborne spores. Favored by wet conditions and temperatures around 59°F.	Avoid overhead watering. Keep humidity low; provide good air circulation and don't crowd plants. See page 115.
Flowers, flower heads, lower leaves, or growing points have soft brown decay. Dead tissue may have woolly gray growth (spores).	**Gray mold,** *Botrytis cinerea.* Fungus develops in crop debris or inactive tissue. Favored by high humidity and 70° to 77°F. Spores airborne.	Use good sanitation. Avoid overhead irrigation. Keep humidity low. Provide good air circulation. Don't crowd plants. See page 108.
White, powdery growth, primarily on older leaves and stem. Severely affected leaves dry and die.	**Powdery mildew,** *Erysiphe cichoracearum, Sphaerotheca fuliginea.* Free water not required for fungus infection.	Provide good air circulation and adequate light. Don't crowd plants. See page 112.
Foliage or petals streaked.	**Streak virus.** Aphid-vectored. Carried in infected seed.	Use seed from virus-free plants. Exclude or control aphids. Rogue infected plants. See Viruses, page 121.
Brown, yellow or white spots, rings, or mottling on (often older) leaves, which may be distorted. Stems, petioles, or leaves have dark veins or streaks. Plants stunted.	**Impatiens necrotic spot virus, Tomato spotted wilt virus.** Spread by thrips, not by tools. Some infected plants may be symptomless. Have many alternate hosts.	Use seed from virus-free plants. Eliminate nearby weeds and other hosts. Exclude or control thrips in and around growing area. See page 121.
Blossoms have irregular white or brown streaks or blotches. Leaves may turn brown. Blossoms or terminals may distort. Growth	**Western flower thrips,** *Frankliniella occidentalis.* Slender dark brown to yellowish insects, 1/16 inch long or less.	See page 161.
Foliage discolored, stippled, or bleached, and may drop. Terminals may distort. Plant may have fine webbing.	**Spider mites.** Tiny greenish, reddish, or yellowish mites; may have 2 dark spots.	See page 213.
Foliage has sticky honeydew and blackish sooty mold. Leaves may yellow and wither. Tiny, whitish, mothlike adult insects.	**Greenhouse whitefly,** *Trialeurodes vaporariorum.* Nymphs oval, flattened, yellow to greenish.	See page 170.
Foliage has sticky honeydew and blackish sooty mold. Foliage may yellow. Plants may grow slowly.	**Longtailed mealybug,** *Pseudococcus longispinus.* Powdery gray insects with waxy marginal filaments.	See page 183.

What the problem looks like	Probable cause	Comments
Foliage has sticky honeydew, blackish sooty mold, and whitish cast skins. New terminals and leaves may distort or yellow.	**Aphids,** including *Aphis fabae, Aulacorthum circumflexum, A. solani, Macrosiphum euphorbiae, Myzus persicae.* Small pear-shaped insects, often green, yellow, or blackish.	See page 179.
Leaves have winding tunnels. Heavily infested leaves may drop. Yellowish to white maggots in mines. Leaves have pale spots or punctures from adult flies.	**Serpentine leafminer,** *Liriomyza trifolii;* **Chrysanthemum leafminer,** *Chromatomyia syngenesiae; Phytomyza atricornis.* Adults are tiny flies. *Liriomyza* adults are small and black and yellow. *Chromatomyia* are grayish and pupate in leaves. *Phytomyza* are uniformly blackish.	See Leafminers, page 167.
Flowers, terminals, or foliage chewed. Leaves may be webbed with silk. Flower buds may be mined.	**Beet armyworm,** *Spodoptera exigua;* **Cabbage looper,** *Trichoplusia ni.* Greenish larvae, up to 1½ inches long, with light, longitudinal stripes.	Exclude moths from growing areas. Avoid growing near other major hosts. *Bacillus thuringiensis* kills larvae. See page 203.
Foliage chewed and webbed together with silk. Disturbed larvae wriggle and drop on a thread. Eggs laid in overlapping mass like fish scales.	**Orange tortrix,** *Argyrotaenia citrana.* Larva whitish, head brown. Gray to brown moth (family Tortricidae), often abundant near citrus orchards. Has many other hosts. Both up to 1 inch long.	See page 203.
Foliage chewed and webbed with silk. Caterpillars, up to 1½ inches long, alternately banded yellowish green and dark purplish.	**Painted beauty,** *Vanessa virginiensis.* Butterfly mostly orange and brown, up to 2½ inches wide, white and blue spots.	Eliminate alternate host weeds, including thistles, mallow, and malva. *Bacillus thuringiensis* kills larvae. See page 203.
Foliage, buds, and stems chewed. Young plants clipped at base. Stocky moths present, attracted to lights at night, wings folded at rest.	**Variegated cutworm,** *Peridroma saucia.* Gray or brown larvae with dark markings, row of yellow dots on back. Hides in soil during day.	Exclude moths, which fly to lights at night. Apply *Bacillus thuringiensis* to young larvae. Insecticide bait kills larvae. See page 203.
Foliage chewed, often only on underside, and webbed together with silk. Stems may be mined. Adult moth and mature larva about ¾ inches long.	**Greenhouse leaftier,** *Udea rubigalis* (family Pyralidae). Larvae yellowish green with three longitudinal green to white stripes. Adult reddish brown with black wavy lines on wings. Has about 6 generations per year.	Avoid growing floral hosts near celery, a major host. Exclude night-flying moths from growing area. See page 203.

COLUMBINE (*Aquilegia* spp.)

Plants stunted. Foliage yellows, wilts, and dies. Roots and basal stems have dark brown decay. Stems girdled and collapse.	**Root and crown rot,** *Pythium* spp., *Rhizoctonia solani.* Fungi present in many soils. Favored by wet, poorly drained media. Not reported on columbine in California.	Pasteurize or treat media. Avoid excess irrigation. Provide good drainage. See pages 93–98.
Foliage yellow and wilted, possibly only along leaf margins, often on one side of plant. Leaves dry and die from the base of plant up. May be brown vascular streaking.	**Verticillium wilt,** *Verticillium albo-atrum.* Fungus contaminates soil, cuttings, and root divisions. Most columbines are resistant to more common *Verticillium dahliae.* Affects *Aquilegia chrysantha.*	Use pathogen-free cuttings. Pasteurize media before planting. Don't overwater. Provide good drainage. See Verticillium wilt, pages 104–106.
White, powdery growth, primarily on older leaves and stem. Severely affected leaves dry and die.	**Powdery mildew,** *Erysiphe* spp. Free water not required for fungus infection.	Provide good air circulation and adequate light. Consider applying fungicide to prevent. See page 112.
Foliage discolors. Leaf underside has powdery brownish pustules.	**Rust,** *Puccinia recondita.* Airborne spores spread only from living tissue. Plant must be wet for infection.	Avoid overhead irrigation. Water in morning so foliage dries. Keep humidity low. See page 119.
Leaves or stems have irregular brown, yellow, or purplish blotches or spots.	**Leaf spots,** including *Ascochyta aquilegiae, Cercospora aquilegiae, Septoria aquilegiae.* Fungi prefer wet, humid conditions. Spread in splashing water. Not reported on columbine in California.	Avoid overhead irrigation. Use good sanitation; rogue infected plants. See pages 116–118.
Few or no flowers.	**Flower failure.** Causes include insufficient chilling, chilling too soon, improper growth regulator use, insufficient light intensity, and too short of days.	Provide proper environmental conditions, especially appropriate temperature and light. Cultivars vary in response.
Leaves mottled, spotted, or ring-spotted. Petals may be spotted or streaked. Leaf veins may discolor. Foliage may distort, wilt, and drop. Plants may be stunted.	**Cucumber mosaic virus,** (aphid-vectored, attacks plants in over 40 families); **Tomato spotted wilt virus,** (thrips-vectored, infects wide host range).	Rogue infected plants; cover and dispose of them away from crop. Control alternate hosts. Exclude or control insect vectors. See Viruses, page 121.
Plants stunted, decline, may die. Powdery waxy material may be visible on roots and around crown.	**Ground mealybug,** *Rhizoecus falcifer.* Small, slender, pale insects, may have powdery covering but no marginal filaments.	See page 186.

What the problem looks like	Probable cause	Comments

COLUMBINE (*Aquilegia* spp.) (continued)

What the problem looks like	Probable cause	Comments
Foliage discolored, stippled, or bleached, and may drop. Plant may have fine webbing.	**Spider mites.** Tiny greenish, reddish, or yellowish mites; may have 2 dark spots.	See page 213.
Foliage has sticky honeydew and blackish sooty mold. Leaves yellow and wither. Tiny, whitish, mothlike adult insects.	**Greenhouse whitefly,** *Trialeurodes vaporariorum.* Oval, flattened, yellow to greenish nymphs and pupae with waxy filaments.	See page 170.
Foliage has sticky honeydew, blackish sooty mold, and whitish cast skins. Terminals and leaves may distort. Foliage may yellow.	**Aphids,** including Columbine aphid, *Kakimia essigi;* Crescent-marked lily aphid, *Aulacorthum circumflexum* or *Myzus circumflexus.* Small pear-shaped insects, often green, pinkish, yellowish, or blackish.	See page 179.
Leaves have blotch mines or winding tunnels due to pale larvae. Plants may be stunted. Leaves may drop.	**Columbine leafminers,** *Phytomyza* spp. Adults small black, metallic bluish, or dark brownish flies.	Picking infested leaves provides control where feasible. See Leafminers, page 167.
Foliage yellows and wilts. Stems die back. May be sawdustlike frass from pale young larvae boring in stems or petioles or from older larvae boring in crown and roots.	**Columbine borer,** *Papaipema purpurifascia.* Adult moth nocturnal (family Noctuidae), tan, yellow, and brown, about 1½ inches wide. Overwinters as eggs in litter and on soil near columbines.	Rogue and dispose of affected plants. Remove litter and scrape soil to destroy eggs in spring.
Foliage chewed or skeletonized and may be webbed together with silk. Stems may be clipped. Caterpillars or their dark frass may be present.	**Whitelined sphinx,** *Hyles lineata.* Adult nocturnal hawk moth (family Sphingidae), 2½ to 3½ inches, white and brown moth. Larva up to 3 inches long, green or blackish, with pale spots or lines. Attacks many fruit, vegetable, and flowering plants.	See Caterpillars, page 203.

CONEFLOWER (*Echinacea purpurea*), Purple coneflower

What the problem looks like	Probable cause	Comments
Leaves or stems have irregular brown, yellow, or purplish blotches or spots.	**Leaf spots,** including *Ascochyta, Cercospora, Phyllosticta, Septoria* spp. Fungi prefer wet, humid conditions. Spread in splashing water. Not reported on coneflower in California.	Avoid overhead irrigation. Use good sanitation; rogue infected plants. See pages 116–118.
Foliage yellows. Stems may wilt and die from boring by pale maggot.	**Stem miner,** *Melanagromyza* or *Agromyza* sp. Adult tiny dark fly.	See Leafminers, page 167.
Leaves or stems stippled, brown, distorted, or wilted. Buds may drop or develop only partially.	**Brown stink bug,** *Euschistus servus.* Shield-shaped bugs, brownish to blackish or green, lay barrel-shaped eggs in clusters.	Control nearby weeds. Exclude or control stink bugs. See True Bugs, page 194.
Foliage has sticky honeydew, blackish sooty mold, and whitish cast skins. Terminals and leaves may distort. Foliage may yellow.	**Aphids,** including Cornflower aphid, *Macrosiphum rudbeckiae.* Small pear-shaped insects, often brown, reddish, green, yellow, or black.	See page 179.
Foliage yellowish, reddish. Plant stunted. Spindly, upright, bunchy yellow shoots and flowers. Few or no flowers.	**Aster yellows.** Phytoplasmalike organism spread by leafhoppers. Not spread by seed, handling, aphids, or other insects. Many hosts.	Avoid planting downwind from other hosts. Eliminate nearby weeds. Exclude or control leafhoppers. Rogue infected plants. See pages 129–130.

COSMOS (*Cosmos* spp.)

What the problem looks like	Probable cause	Comments
White, powdery growth primarily on older leaves and stem. Foliage may yellow and die.	**Powdery mildew,** *Erysiphe cichoracearum, Oidium* sp. Free water not required for infection.	Provide good air circulation and adequate light. Consider applying fungicide to prevent. See page 112.
Foliage yellows and wilts. Stems may have lesions or cankers and dieback.	**Stem blight,** *Diaporthe stewartii.* Fungus infects through wounds, persists in infected tissue.	Use good sanitation. Avoid wounding plants and keep plants dry.
Foliage chlorotic. Plant stunted. Spindly, upright yellow shoots and few or no flowers.	**Aster yellows.** Phytoplasmalike organism spread by leafhoppers. Not spread by seed, handling, aphids, or other insects. Many hosts.	Avoid planting downwind from other hosts. Eliminate nearby weeds. Exclude or control leafhoppers. Rogue infected plants. See pages 129–130.
Leaves yellow, streaked, blotched, or mottled. Flowers and foliage may be distorted. Plants may be stunted.	**Beet curly top virus,** (leafhopper vectored); **Tomato spotted wilt virus,** (thrips-vectored). Many hosts.	Use virus-free stock. Rogue infected plants. Control nearby weeds. Exclude or control insect vectors. See Viruses, page 121.
Shoot tips wilt. Excess branching, often below wilted tips. Distorted, delayed, or no flowers. Leaves have dead patches.	**Plant bugs,** *Lygus* spp. Brown, green, or yellowish bugs, up to ¼ inch long, that suck plant juices.	Control nearby weeds, from which bugs move. Exclude bugs from growing area. See True Bugs, page 194.
Buds killed or distorted. Blossoms may drop early. Flowers may deform, discolor.	**Thrips.** Tiny slender dark brown, black, yellowish, or whitish insects.	See page 161.

What the problem looks like	Probable cause	Comments
Foliage may yellow. Plant growth may be retarded from small insects infesting roots or stems near soil.	**Aster or Erigeron root aphid,** *Aphis middletonii*. Small pear-shaped insects, light gray to dark green.	Infests many Asteraceae; control nearby weeds in this family. See page 182.
Foliage has sticky honeydew, blackish sooty mold, and whitish cast skins. Terminals and leaves may distort. Foliage may yellow.	**Aphids,** including Spirea aphid, *Aphis spiraecola*; Melon aphid, *Aphis gossypii*. Small pear-shaped insects, often green, yellowish, or blackish.	See page 179.

CROTON (*Codiaeum variegatum*)

What the problem looks like	Probable cause	Comments
Leaves have yellow spots that enlarge to become angular blotches or wedges that are brown or black, with yellow or raised margins. Leaves may appear water-soaked. Plant may wilt and die. Roots may be black but not rotted.	**Bacterial leaf spot and blight,** *Xanthomonas campestris*. Spreads by splashing water and infected stock, debris, and equipment. Favored by warm, moist conditions and rapid plant growth.	Inspect and plant only uninfected stock. Avoid overhead irrigation. Regularly inspect and rogue plants infected and those nearby. Use good sanitation. See pages 107, 118.
Leaves have purplish red to dark brown, irregular, angular spots. Lower leaf surface covered with soft, fluffy fungal growth. Leaves yellow and drop.	**Downy mildew,** *Bremia* sp. Spores produced only on living plants. Fungus persists as resistant oospores when conditions are dry. Favored by moist, humid conditions.	Provide good air circulation. Avoid overhead watering. Consider applying fungicide to protect foliage. See page 115.
Brown to yellow, spots or blotches, mostly on older leaves. Spots may have dark or yellowish margins. Foliage may shrivel and drop.	**Leaf spot,** *Mycocentrospora* sp. Spread by splashing water. Favored by prolonged cool, wet, conditions. Persists in plant debris.	Avoid wetting foliage. Use drip irrigation. Use good sanitation; promptly remove and dispose of debris and infected leaves. See pages 116–118.
Stems discolor and die. Stems may have cankers and cankers may exude sap. Uncommon disease.	**Canker and dieback,** *Botryosphaeria ribis*. Fungus attacks only weakened plants. Spreads in splashing water.	Rogue infected plants. Keep plants vigorous. Provide good cultural care, especially proper irrigation. See page 102.
Corky galls or distorted callus growth on lower stem or roots, sometimes on leaves. Plant stunted. Roots may be gnarled, stunted, or hairy with mostly small rootlets.	**Crown gall,** *Agrobacterium tumefaciens*. Bacteria persist in soil for years, enter plant through wounds. Favored by rapid plant growth.	Avoid wounding plants. Don't plant in infested soil for 3 years, plant nonhost species, or solarize or otherwise pasteurize soil. See page 102.
Stems elongated and thin. Foliage color dull, not vibrant.	**Inadequate light.** Noninfectious disorder.	Provide brighter light; plant also prefers warm, humid conditions.
Plant or media has creamy white, slimy, or crusty gray growth.	**Slime mold.** Generally harmless fungi. Feed on bacteria in debris. Favored by warm, moist conditions.	Rogue affected plants. Avoid excess irrigation, overhead watering, and excess humidity. Use good sanitation; clean up debris.
Foliage or woody parts have blackish sooty mold. Plant may die back and decline.	**Black scale,** *Saissetia oleae*; **Long brown scale,** *Coccus longulus*; **Hemispherical scale,** *Saissetia coffeae*; **Nigra scale,** *Parasaissetia nigra*. Orange, black, or brown, flattened to bulbous insects.	See Scales, page 186.
Foliage has sticky honeydew and blackish sooty mold. Foliage may yellow. May be cottony material (egg sacs) on plant.	**Citrus mealybug,** *Planococcus citri*; **Longtailed mealybug,** *Pseudococcus longispinus*. Powdery gray insects, with waxy filaments.	See page 183.
Plant has sticky honeydew, blackish sooty mold, and elongated, whitish material (egg sacs). Insects on twigs or leaves.	**Cottony cushion scale,** *Icerya purchasi*. Brown, orange, red, or yellow females live on twigs or leaves. Uncommon.	Natural enemies can provide good control. See page 186.
Foliage turns yellow. Plant declines or dies back. Stems have gray, brown, or tan encrustations.	**Latania scale,** *Hemiberlesia lataniae*. Circular flattened insects, less than 1/16 inch long.	See page 186.
Foliage turns yellow. Plant declines or dies back. Stems have dark encrustations.	**Purple scale,** *Lepidosaphes beckii*. Scale insects (family Diaspididae), often shaped like oyster shells, purple to brown, elongate to oval, less than 1/16 inch long.	See page 186.
Foliage discolored, bleached or stippled. Leaf underside has dark, varnishlike excrement.	**Dracaena thrips,** *Parthenothrips dracaenae*; **Greenhouse thrips,** *Heliothrips haemorrhoidalis*.	Tiny slender black, brown, or yellowish insects. See page 161.

What the problem looks like	Probable cause	Comments
CYCLAMEN (*Cyclamen* spp.)		
Leaves yellow, often beginning at base. Entire plant may yellow, wilt, and die. Basal stem and corm vascular tissue discolored, dark, but initially not soft.	**Fusarium wilt,** *Fusarium oxysporum* f. sp. *cyclaminis*. Fungus survives in soil for years; favored by warm, wet media.	Pasteurize media before planting. Use media pH of 6.0 or higher. Avoid ammonium fertilizers. See page 104.
Leaves may turn yellowish or darken. Plant may wilt and die. Roots and stem around soil dark and decayed.	**Root and crown rots,** *Phytophthora, Pythium* spp., *Rhizoctonia solani*. Fungi promoted by wet, poorly drained soil.	See pages 93–98.
Foliage yellows and wilts. Plants grow slowly and die. Roots or corms dark black and rotted. Stems below ground may develop dark cracks.	**Black root rot,** *Thielaviopsis basicola*. Spreads in water, media, and by infected plants. Fungus persists in infected media. Favored by cool, wet conditions.	Pasteurize media before planting. Avoid overwatering and splashing water. Provide good drainage. Allow soil to dry between watering. Rogue infected plants. Avoid high salts and high pH. See pages 95–99.
Roots, corms, and petioles rot. Corms have brown discoloration. Plants wilt.	**Corm rot,** *Cylindrocladium* spp. Spores spread in splashing water. Infects through leaves or roots. Not reported on cyclamen in California.	Pasteurize media before planting. Use good sanitation. Rogue infected plants. Avoid overhead water.
Flowers, flower heads, lower leaves, or growing points have soft brown decay. May be woolly gray growth (spores) on dead tissue.	**Gray mold,** *Botrytis cinerea*. Fungus develops in crop debris or inactive tissue. Favored by high humidity and 70° to 77°F. Spores airborne.	Use good sanitation. Avoid overhead irrigation. Keep humidity low. Provide good air circulation. Don't crowd plants. See page 108.
Leaves have pale green to yellowish circular spots with distinct margins. Foliage may yellow, shrivel, or drop.	**Gloeosporium leaf spot,** *Gloeosporium cyclaminis*. Spread by splashing water. Favored by prolonged wet conditions. Persists in plant debris.	Avoid wetting foliage; use drip irrigation. Use good sanitation; promptly remove and dispose of debris and infected leaves. See pages 116–118.
Leaves have yellowish to brownish spots, usually near margins. Foliage may yellow, shrivel, or drop.	**Phyllosticta leaf spot,** *Phyllosticta cyclaminis*. Spread by splashing water. Favored by prolonged wet conditions. Persists in plant debris.	Avoid wetting foliage; use drip irrigation. Use good sanitation; promptly remove and dispose of debris and infected leaves. See pages 116–118.
Leaves have red concentric spots that may turn gray with reddish border. Foliage may yellow, shrivel, or drop.	**Septoria leaf spot,** *Septoria cyclaminis*. Spread by splashing water. Favored by prolonged wet conditions. Persists in plant debris.	Avoid wetting foliage; use drip irrigation. Use good sanitation; promptly remove and dispose of debris and infected leaves. See pages 116–118.
Plants stunted. Leaves or corms may have circular to irregular yellow to brown spots or blotches. Flowers may develop below leaves.	**Stunt,** *Ramularia cyclaminicola*. Fungus spreads by air or on contaminated tools or stock. Persists in plant debris.	Avoid overhead watering. Use good sanitation; remove and dispose of debris and infected leaves. High media salts can also stunt plants.
Stem bases and sometimes crown are dark and decayed. Stems may fall over. Rotted tissue is odorous. Roots darken, turn soft and mushy. Most prevalent during warm, wet conditions.	**Bacterial soft rot,** *Erwinia carotovora*. Bacteria persist in plant debris, spread in water (e.g., plant-to-plant splashing), and infect through wounds.	Use only pathogen-free plants. Don't plant too deeply. Avoid high growing temperatures. Rogue infected plants. Avoid overwatering and injuring plants. Provide good drainage. See pages 100, 107.
Leaves have brown or yellow spots, mottling, or concentric rings. Stems and flowers may discolor or wilt. Plants distorted, stunted. Stems necrotic.	**Impatiens necrotic spot virus, Tomato spotted wilt virus.** Viruses spread by thrips, infect wide host range.	Rogue infected plants, cover and dispose of them away from crop. Control weeds. Control and exclude thrips. See page 121.
Buds discolor, distort, or drop. Few, small, or delayed flowers. Uneven blossoming.	**Bud blast, Flower failure.** Causes include improper light, temperature, fertilizer, irrigation, or poorly adapted cultivar for local conditions.	Provide appropriate cultural care and a good growing environment. Grow cultivars well adapted for that location and environment.
Plant tissue may be soft or wilted. Stem structure is weak. Stems may be elongated. Plants may grow slowly.	**Weak or soft growth.** Causes include high temperature, crowding, insufficient light, improper fertilization, excess media salts, excess growth regulator, disease.	Provide appropriate cultural care and good growing environment. Inspect for fungal diseases discussed above.
Plants too tall.	**Tall plants.** Causes include high temperature, insufficient light, overcrowding, excess irrigation.	Provide appropriate cultural care and good growing environment.
Foliage yellows. Plant growth may be slow.	**Yellowing.** Causes include improper irrigation, poor drainage, nutrient imbalance, excess light, disease, or lack of fluctuating temperature.	Provide appropriate cultural care and good growing environment. Inspect for fungal diseases discussed above.

What the problem looks like	Probable cause	Comments
Leaves yellowish. Leaves have dark green or brown, vein-limited, angular blotches that develop progressively up from older leaves.	**Foliar nematodes,** *Aphelenchoides fragariae.* Tiny roundworms spread in plant debris and by vegetative propagation and splashing water. Not common in California.	Use uninfected stock plants. Remove plant debris. Avoid overhead irrigation; leaves must be wet for infection to occur. See page 265.
Foliage turns yellow. Plant declines or dies back. Stems have gray, brown, or tan encrustations.	**Latania scale,** *Hemiberlesia lataniae.* Circular flattened insects, less than $\frac{1}{16}$ inch long.	See page 186.
Foliage has sticky honeydew and blackish sooty mold. Leaves yellow and wither. Tiny, whitish, mothlike adult insects.	**Silverleaf whitefly,** *Bemisia argentifolii,* **Sweetpotato whitefly,** *Bemisia tabaci.* Oval, flattened, yellow to greenish nymphs.	See Whiteflies, page 170.
Flowers distorted, color streaked or spotted. Foliage discolored, bleached, stippled, or distorted. Leaf underside may have dark, varnishlike excrement.	**Greenhouse thrips,** *Heliothrips haemorrhoidalis;* **Western flower thrips,** *Frankliniella occidentalis.* Tiny slender black, brownish, to yellowish insects.	See page 161.
Leaves curled or distorted. Leaves or flowers discolored, bronzed, or stiff. Buds deformed, discolored, may drop. Plants may be stunted.	**Cyclamen mite,** *Phytonemus pallidus.* A pinkish orange mite (family Tarsonemidae), $\frac{1}{100}$ inch long or smaller.	See page 217.
Foliage discolored, stippled, brownish, or bleached, and may drop. Terminals may distort. Plant may have fine webbing.	**Twospotted mite,** *Tetranychus urticae.* Tiny greenish, reddish, or yellowish mites; may have 2 dark spots.	See page 213.
Foliage has sticky honeydew, blackish sooty mold, and whitish cast skins. Terminals and young leaves may curl or distort. Foliage may yellow.	**Crescent-marked lily aphid,** *Aulacorthum circumflexum* or *Myzus circumflexum;* **Green peach aphid,** *Myzus persicae;* **Melon aphid,** *Aphis gossypii.*	Small pear-shaped insects, often green or yellowish. See Aphids, page 179.
Plants may wilt. Leaves and blossoms chewed (edges notched).	**Black vine weevil,** *Otiorhynchus sulcatus;* **Cribrate weevil,** *O. cribricollis;* **Fuller rose beetle,** *Asynonychus godmani;* **Vegetable weevil,** *Listroderes difficilis.* Rarely seen adults brown, black, to gray snout beetles that feed at night. Larvae whitish maggots that feed on roots. Adult and mature larva about $\frac{3}{8}$ inch long.	See page 208.
Foliage chewed, curled, or webbed together with silk. Plants may be defoliated.	**Leafrollers,** including Cyclamen leaf roller, *Clepsis busckana* or *C. fucana.*	See page 203.
Foliage chewed, may be webbed together with silk. Stems may be clipped. Caterpillars or their black frass pellets may be present.	**Amorbia,** *Amorbia cuneana;* **Armyworms,** *Spodoptera* spp.; **Carnation leafroller,** *Platynota sultana.* *Amorbia* and *Platynota* (family Tortricidae) may be common near citrus, an alternate host.	See Caterpillars, page 203.
Foliage yellows, wilts, and dies. Basal stem has holes or decay. Grayish larva up to $\frac{3}{4}$ inch long, head dark, boring in plant.	**Crown borer,** *Opogona omoscopa.* Dark, brownish moth (family Tineidae), attracted to decaying tissue, probably a secondary pest.	Avoid wounding plants. Provide good cultural care. Avoid excess irrigation. Use good sanitation; remove debris and dying plants.

DAFFODIL (*Narcissus* spp.)

Bulbs rot: first a wet rot, later bulbs are dry and woody. White fungal mat and $\frac{1}{32}$ to $\frac{1}{8}$ inch, round, tan to brown sclerotia occur on decaying bulbs and in soil.	**Crown rot,** *Sclerotium rolfsii.* Fungus survives in soil for 10 years. Spreads by infected bulbs. Has wide host range. Favored by high temperatures.	Avoid planting hosts in previously infected fields for 4 or more years. Deep plowing may help to control by burying sclerotia. Treat bulbs with hot water before planting. Fungicide applied at planting can help. See page 101.
Plants stunted. Leaves distorted and yellow. Plant dies. Few or no roots on bulbs. Entire bulb eventually rots. Bulb beneath outer scales reddish brown, decayed. White to pinkish fungus may be visible at base between scales. 'Carlton' and 'Golden Harvest' are susceptible. 'Toorak Gold,' 'Dutch Master,' and 'Hollywood' are moderately susceptible. Most prevalent in storage or shipping.	**Basal rot,** *Fusarium oxysporum* f. sp. *narcissi.* Fungus survives in soil for years; short rotations ineffective. Favored by warm soils and high levels of nitrogen fertilizer. Temperatures below 55°F limit disease. Applying potassium fertilizer may help to reduce damage. Dig carefully; avoid wounding bulbs.	Rotate previously infected soils out of daffodil for at least three years. Plant resistant 'St. Keverne' or moderately resistant 'Malvern City,' 'Rijnveld's Early Sensation,' 'White Lion,' 'Soleil d'Or,' or 'Dulcimer.' Hot water bulb treatment can reduce disease but may damage bulbs. Plant when soil is cool. Immediately dig and fungicide-dip bulbs from infected areas. Store bulbs below 64°F. See page 104.
Leaves discolor, wilt, stunt, or drop prematurely. Stems discolored, cankered, and die.	**Armillaria root rot,** *Armillaria mellea.* Present in many soils. Favored by warm, wet soil. Persists for years in infected roots.	Remove woody roots $\frac{1}{2}$ inch diameter or larger before planting. Pasteurize or air-dry soil well or avoid growing in fields previously planted with oaks or other susceptible woody plants. See page 99.

What the problem looks like	Probable cause	Comments

DAFFODIL (*Narcissus* spp.) (continued)

What the problem looks like	Probable cause	Comments
Leaves, flowers, or stems have soft brown decay or spots. Sprouts or stems may darken and rot near soil. Dead tissue may have woolly gray growth (spores).	**Blight, Gray mold,** *Botryotinia, Botrytis* spp. Fungi develop in plant debris. Favored by cool, humid conditions.	Use good sanitation. Avoid overhead irrigation. Keep humidity low. Provide good air circulation. Don't crowd plants. See page 108.
Leaves spotted, yellow, wilted, may die. Stems and roots may be cankered, soft, dark, or rotted. Cuttings may rot near base.	**Root rot,** *Cylindrocladium destructans.* Spores spread in splashing water. Infects through leaves or roots.	Pasteurize media before planting. Inspect and don't plant infected cuttings. Avoid overhead water. Use good sanitation.
Bulbs or basal stem ragged or decayed. Brown mycelia on infected tissue visible with a hand lens.	**Gray bulb rot,** *Rhizoctonia solani.* Soilborne fungus favored by wet conditions.	Provide good soil drainage. Plant in raised beds. Avoid excess irrigation. See pages 93–98.
Leaves yellow and die. Plants stunted, fail to bloom. Leaf bases or stems rotted near soil, tissue appears shredded. Many very small black sclerotia imbedded in dead tissue. Bulb lesions are dark brown, sunken, with raised margins.	**Dry rot,** *Stromatinia gladioli.* Attacks and survives in bulbs stored or in soil. Persists in infested soil for 10 or more years. Favored by cool, wet soil or humid storage.	Pasteurize or treat soil before planting. Don't grow in infested soil during cool weather. Use pathogen-free bulbs. Provide good soil drainage. Store bulbs at low humidity.
Plants yellow, wilt, and die or fail to emerge. Bulbs and below ground shoots covered with gray fungal mass. Infected parts contain gray or white mycelia and black sclerotia.	**Black slime,** *Sclerotinia bulborum.* Fungal sclerotia survive in soil for several years. Favored by cool weather.	Pasteurize soil before planting or don't grow hosts in that soil for 3 to 4 years after an infection. Hosts are hyacinth, iris, and daffodil. Bulbs can be dipped in fungicide to prevent disease.
Leaves or stems have powdery brownish pustules. Foliage may be spotted yellow or yellow overall. Leaves may dry and die.	**Rusts,** *Puccinia schracteri, Coleosporium narcissi.* Airborne spores spread only from living tissue. Plant must be wet for infection. Not a problem in California.	Avoid wetting foliage. Provide good air circulation. Keep humidity low and don't crowd plants. See page 119.
Leaf tips have yellow to brown lesions. Leaves have elongate, reddish brown spots. Small black pycnidia form in necrotic areas.	**Scorch,** *Stagonospora curtisii.* Fungus survives in the neck and between scales. Infects plants in Amaryllidaceae family. Spores spread by splashing water. Favored by mild, moist conditions.	Pasteurize media before planting. Hot water bulb treatment before planting can control but may injure bulbs or stunt flowers. Consider fungicide applications, beginning when first leaves emerge.
Brown, streaked lesions appear first on leaf tips. Leaves infected on inner edge may curl. Diseased tissue may have woolly gray growth (spores) and small black sclerotia, especially near soil. Stored bulbs rot.	**Smoulder,** *Sclerotinia* or *Botrytis narcissicola.* Fungus survives as sclerotia in infected bulbs in soil. Conidia (spores) are airborne. Favored by cool, wet weather.	Rotate planting site with other crops. Provide good drainage. Dig up bulbs early. Consider dipping bulbs in fungicide before planting or spraying plants with basic copper sulfate or other fungicide after planting.
Petals have water-soaked areas that brown and wither. Flowers attacked, then foliage. Small, elliptical, tan spots near leaf tips, followed by yellow streaking of leaves.	**White mold,** *Ramularia vallisumbrosae.* Fungus survives as sclerotia in dead leaves and on bulbs. Sclerotia germinate and produce conidia as leaves emerge. Favored by warm, moist conditions. Problem in Pacific Northwest.	Infects only daffodil; don't replant daffodil for 1 year in field where disease has occurred. Don't overwater. Provide good air circulation. Copper or other fungicides can protect foliage.
Crown, basal stems, bulbs, or foliage dark and decayed. Plants may wilt and die; may have odorous rot or gray to whitish mycelial growth with black spores.	**Soft rot,** *Erwinia carotovora, Rhizopus stolonifer.* Persist in plant debris and spread in water. *Erwinia* (a bacterium that causes odorous rot) and *Rhizopus* (a fungus that causes mycelial growth and black spores) most prevalent during warm, wet conditions.	Pasteurize media. Avoid wounding or weakening plants. Use good sanitation; dispose of dead and dying plants. Reduce humidity. Lower temperatures. Avoid overhead irrigation. See pages 100, 107.
Flowers or bulbs may be rotted. Plants may be stunted or lack flowers. Infected tissue may have bluish mold.	**Blue mold,** *Penicillium* sp. Bacteria infect through wounds. Problem during high humidity.	Avoid long storage and transport. Provide good ventilation and low humidity during storage. Examine bulbs and plant only if healthy. Avoid injuring plants. Bulbs can be dipped, but some *Penicillium* strains are resistant to certain materials. Don't overwater.
Foliage has brown, black, or yellowish streaks or blotches. Foliage may wilt and die.	**Bacterial streak,** *Pseudomonas* sp. Spread by splashing water and contaminated equipment. Favored by wet, humid conditions.	Use only bacteria-free stock. Rogue infected plants immediately. Avoid wetting foliage. Use drip irrigation. See pages 107, 118.
Leaves and flower stalk have narrow, dark green to purple streaks that later become white to yellow-white after flowering. Reduced bulb size and yield from premature senescence.	**Narcissus white streak virus,** Vectored by aphids. Affects only daffodil. Symptoms don't occur until air temperatures exceed 64°F.	Symptoms may be confused with bulb nematodes or bulb scale mites. Rogue infected plants. Exclude or control aphids. See Viruses, page 121.

What the problem looks like	Probable cause	Comments
Leaves and flower stalk have conspicuous light green to yellow streaks and mottling shortly after emergence. Leaf distortion and color-break of flowers may occur. Bulb yields are reduced.	**Narcissus yellow stripe virus.** Vectored by aphids. Affects only daffodil. Symptoms appear early in growing season.	Symptoms may be confused with bulb nematodes or bulb scale mites. Rogue infected plants. Exclude or control aphids. See Viruses, page 121.
Leaves yellowish. Leaves have dark green or brown, vein-limited, bands or blotches that develop progressively up from older leaves.	**Foliar nematodes,** *Aphelenchoides fragariae*. Tiny roundworms that spread in plant debris, vegetative propagation, and splashing water. Not common in California.	Use uninfected stock plants. Remove plant debris. Avoid overhead irrigation; leaves must be wet for infection to occur. See page 265.
Plants stunted. Root cortex and deep tissues have necrotic lesions.	**Root lesion nematode,** *Pratylenchus penetrans*. Microscopic roundworms survive in soil as eggs, larvae, and adults.	Pasteurize soil before planting. See page 265.
Leaves stunted, distorted, often swollen and thickened near base. Leaf centers and margins have yellow to brown swellings. May be discolored spots or blotches where stem joins bulb. Severely infected bulbs grow poorly and may rot.	**Stem and bulb nematode,** *Ditylenchus dipsaci*. Nematodes survive in infected bulbs and field debris for about 3 years. Also spread by infected water and equipment. Optimal temperature for infection and reproduction is 50° to 69°F.	Rogue infected plants and surrounding plants. Clean equipment well after working in diseased fields. Treating bulbs with hot water can control but may injure bulbs, causing stunted and deformed flowers. See page 265.
Few or no blooms. Flowers may be smaller than normal. Foliage appears healthy, but may be sparse.	**Bloom failure.** Cultural problem from overcrowding, excess shade, overheating, premature foliage removal, excess cooling during forcing, or undersized bulbs.	Provide proper environmental conditions and good cultural care.
Blossoms have irregular white or brown blotches. Leaves may turn brown. Blossoms or terminals may be distorted. Growth may be stunted.	**Western flower thrips,** *Frankliniella occidentalis*. Slender, dark brown to yellowish insects, 1/16 inch long or less.	See page 161.
Foliage has sticky honeydew, blackish sooty mold, and whitish cast skins. Foliage may yellow.	**Aphids,** including *Aulacorthum solani, Myzus persicae, Macrosiphum euphorbiae*. Small pear-shaped insects, often green, yellowish, or blackish.	See page 179.
Fleshy bulb scales or basal stems have reddish or yellowish brown discoloration. Bulbs rotted and infested with tiny, oval, white to brownish mites. Flowers stunted or distorted. Few flowers.	**Bulb mites,** *Rhizoglyphus* spp.; **Bulb scale mite,** *Steneotarsonemus laticeps*. Sluggish pale mites that look like tiny eggs on bulbs and basal stems; may also be on stems and leaves. Secondary pests that prefer decayed tissue but may help fungi infect plants. Symptoms may be confused with virus or bulb nematodes.	See page 218.
Foliage yellow, stunted, or produces no blooms. Bulbs feel soft and spongy, are hollowed and filled with brown excrement from wrinkled, gray, white, or brownish maggots boring inside.	**Bulb flies,** including Narcissus bulb fly, *Merodon equestris* and *Eumerus* spp. Adult hairy fly (family Syrphidae), black with gray to orange, resembles a bumble bee, hovers around blooming plants where eggs are laid. *M. equestris* adult and mature larva about 1/2 inch long, *Eumerus* spp. smaller.	Inspect and discard spongy bulbs before planting. See page 200.
Buds, flowers or leaves mined or chewed, may be webbed with silk.	**Omnivorous leaftier,** *Cnephasia longana*. Gray to brownish, 1/2 inch long larvae and nocturnal moths. Larvae may have grayish stripes. Attacks strawberries and many other hosts. Occurs in central California coast. Has 1 generation per year.	Time any spray for young larvae emerging from mines in spring. See Caterpillars, page 203.

DAHLIA (*Dahlia* spp.)

Basal leaves wilted and yellowish; one branch is often affected first. Vascular system discolored, dark. Plant dies, especially if young; older plants may be stunted.	**Wilt,** *Verticillium dahliae, Fusarium oxysporum*. Fungi persist in soil for years. *Verticillium* has wide host range, most severe during warm weather after cool period. *Fusarium* is host-specific, severe when soil is warm.	Grow plants where disease has not previously occurred. Solarize or otherwise pasteurize soil before planting. Rogue infected plants. See pages 104–106.
Foliage yellows and wilts, often on only one side. Plant stunted and may die. Roots dark and decayed. Young plants collapse and die.	**Root and crown rots,** *Pythium* spp., *Rhizoctonia* spp. Fungi persist in soil. Spread in media and water. Favored by excess moisture and poor drainage.	Provide good drainage. Avoid excess irrigation and reduce watering if disease develops. See pages 93–98.
Plants wilt suddenly and die. Water-soaked cankers appear on stem near soil. Cottony growth on stems, later large, black sclerotia, in stems. Roots may be black, rotted.	**Cottony rot,** *Sclerotinia sclerotiorum*. Fungal sclerotia in soil produce airborne spores. Favored by cool, moist conditions.	Avoid planting where disease has occurred. Many hosts, including vegetable crops. Avoid overwatering. Irrigate early in day so plants dry quickly. Consider protective fungicide. See page 101.
Foliage yellows, especially outer leaves. Soft rot of basal stem or roots. White mycelia and small, tan to reddish brown sclerotia may develop on infected tissue around soil.	**Southern wilt,** *Sclerotium rolfsii*. Sclerotia survive in soil. Disease favored by moist, poorly drained, 77° to 95°F soil. Many hosts.	Avoid planting in infested soil, or pasteurize soil before planting. Avoid excess irrigation. Consider fungicide drench to infected soil. See page 101.

What the problem looks like	Probable cause	Comments

DAHLIA (*Dahlia* spp.) (continued)

What the problem looks like	Probable cause	Comments
Leaves discolor, wilt, stunt, or drop prematurely. Stems discolored, cankered, and die.	**Armillaria root rot,** *Armillaria mellea.* Present in many soils. Favored by warm, wet soil. Persists for years in infected roots.	Remove woody roots ½ inch diameter or larger before planting. Pasteurize or air-dry soil well or avoid growing in fields previously planted with oaks or other susceptible woody plants. See page 99.
Tuberous roots rot in storage, develop dark brown, sunken areas. Tubers fail to produce or foliage wilts and dies.	**Storage rots,** *Botrytis cinerea, Erwinia carotovora, Fusarium* spp. Common when warm and humid.	Avoid injuring plants. Maintain low storage humidity and keep temperature at 40°F. See pages 93, 100, 107, 108.
Leaves have yellowish or tan, circular to irregular spots. Spots may have dark borders. Leaves may later brown, dry, and die.	**Smut,** *Entyloma dahliae.* Occurs in plant debris. Favored by wet weather.	Avoid overhead irrigation. Use good sanitation. Fungicide application may help to prevent.
Brown to yellow spots or blotches, mostly on older leaves. Spots may have dark or yellowish margins. Foliage may shrivel and drop.	**Leaf spots,** *Alternaria, Cercospora, Phyllosticta* spp. Spread by air or splashing water. Favored by prolonged, cool, wet, conditions. Persist in plant debris. Not reported on dahlia in California.	Avoid wetting foliage. Use drip irrigation. Use good sanitation; promptly remove and dispose of debris and infected leaves. See pages 116–118.
Leaves, flowers, or flower heads have soft brown decay or spots. Lower leaves or growing points may decay. Dead tissue may have woolly gray growth (spores).	**Gray mold,** *Botrytis cinerea.* Fungus develops in crop debris or inactive tissue. Favored by high humidity and 70° to 77°F. Spores airborne.	Use good sanitation. Avoid overhead irrigation. Keep humidity low. Provide good air circulation. Don't crowd plants. See page 108.
White, powdery growth, primarily on older leaves and stem. Severely affected leaves dry and die.	**Powdery mildew,** *Erysiphe cichoracearum.* Free water not required for fungus infection.	Provide good air circulation and adequate light. Consider applying sulfur or other fungicide to prevent. See page 112.
Leaf color irregular, pale adjacent to veins. Leaves may distort. Plants may have short internodes and be severely stunted. Flower color usually normal.	**Dahlia mosaic virus.** Spread by aphids or vegetatively by cuttings and roots. Virus almost symptomless in some cultivars.	Rogue infected plants. Control aphids. See page 121.
Older leaves have well-defined yellowish mottle, rings, wavy lines. Leaves spotted, chlorotic, distorted, or with discolored veins.	**Ringspot, Impatiens necrotic spot virus, Tomato spotted wilt virus.** Spread by thrips or vegetatively by cuttings and roots. Have many weed and crop hosts.	Virus-free stock may be created by taking small stem-tip cuttings from rapidly growing plants. Eliminate host weeds. Rogue infected plants. Control thrips. See page 121.
Leaves mildly mottled with little or no distortion.	**Cucumber mosaic virus.** Spread by aphids or vegetatively by cuttings and roots. Many hosts. Some dahlia are symptomless carriers.	Rogue infected plants. Control aphids. See page 121.
Stems and roots have growths or galls. Plants may grow slowly.	**Crown gall,** *Agrobacterium tumefaciens.* Bacteria persist in soil for years, enter plant through wounds. Favored by rapid plant growth.	Avoid wounding plants. Don't plant in infested soil for 3 years, plant nonhost species, or solarize or otherwise pasteurize soil. See page 102.
Foliage yellows or wilts. Feeder and fleshy roots have knots or swellings.	**Root knot nematode,** *Meloidogyne* spp. Tiny roundworms that prefer warm, sandy soil. Many hosts.	Pasteurize or treat soil before planting. Rogue affected plants. Plant nonhosts at that site. See page 265.
Leaves yellowish. Leaves have dark green or brown, vein-limited, angular blotches that develop progressively up from older leaves.	**Foliar nematodes,** *Aphelenchoides fragariae.* Tiny roundworms spread in plant debris and by vegetative propagation and splashing water. Not common in California.	Use uninfected stock plants. Remove plant debris. Avoid overhead irrigation; leaves must be wet for infection to occur. See page 265.
Foliage yellows and wilts. Plants may be stunted, fall over, or die from root-feeding beetles. Basal stems or leaves may be chewed.	**Carrot beetle,** *Ligyrus gibbosus.* Adults (family Scarabaeidae) reddish brown, ½ inch long, feed above and below ground. Larvae up to 1¼ inches long, white to bluish, head dark.	Attacks grains and vegetable crops, especially tubers. Exclude adults, which fly at night to lights. Eliminate decaying vegetation that harbors adults around plants. See page 211.
Foliage turns yellow. Plant declines or dies back. Stems or leaves have tan to yellow encrustations.	**Oleander scale,** *Aspidiotus nerii.* Circular flat insects, less than ¹⁄₁₆ inch long.	See Scales, page 186.
Foliage stippled, bleached, or blotched, has varnishlike excrement. Tiny slender black, dark brown, yellowish, or whitish insects.	**Greenhouse thrips,** *Heliothrips haemorrhoidalis;* **Banded greenhouse thrips,** *Hercinothrips femoralis;* **Western flower thrips,** *Frankliniella occidentalis.*	See Thrips, page 161.
Foliage discolored, stippled, or bleached, and may drop. Plant may have fine webbing.	**Spider mites.** Tiny greenish, reddish, or yellowish mites, may have 2 dark spots.	See page 213.
Foliage bleached, brittle; edges may be curled or ragged. Blossoms distort or discolor.	**Broad mite,** *Polyphagotarsonemus latus.* Translucent to dark green insects, ¹⁄₁₀₀ inch long or smaller.	See page 217.

What the problem looks like	Probable cause	Comments
Plants severely stunted. Leaf terminals distorted. Buds deformed, black, or discolored, and may drop.	**Cyclamen mite,** *Phytonemus pallidus.* A pinkish orange mite (family Tarsonemidae), $^{1}/_{100}$ inch long or smaller.	See page 217.
Shoots or blossoms blackened, dwarfed, discolored, or distorted. Leaf tips may wilt and die.	**Plant bugs,** *Lygus* spp. Brown, green, or yellowish bugs, up to $^{1}/_{4}$ inch long, that suck plant juices.	Control nearby weeds, from which bugs move. Exclude bugs from growing area. See True Bugs, page 194.
Foliage distorted, discolored, stippled, or brown. Foliage may drop prematurely. Stems or leaves have pimplelike (egg-laying) punctures.	**Leafhoppers.** Slender insects, often yellowish green, that suck plant sap and readily jump, fly, or crawl away sideways when disturbed.	Control weeds; leafhoppers often move from weeds. Control of adults is difficult; insecticidal soap or oil can reduce nymph populations. See page 193.
Plant has sticky honeydew and blackish sooty mold, and may have cottony waxy material.	**Obscure mealybug,** *Pseudococcus affinis.* Grayish, oval, waxy insects with marginal filaments.	See page 183.
Foliage has sticky honeydew and blackish sooty mold. Leaves may yellow and wither. Tiny, whitish, mothlike adult insects.	**Greenhouse whitefly,** *Trialeurodes vaporariorum.* Oval, flattened, yellow to greenish nymphs. Pupae have many long filaments.	See page 170.
Foliage has sticky honeydew, blackish sooty mold, and whitish cast skins. Foliage may curl or yellow.	**Aphids,** including *Aphis fabae, A. gossypii, Aulacorthum solani, Myzus persicae.* Small pear-shaped insects, often green, yellowish, or blackish.	See page 179.
Growth may be retarded from small insects infesting roots and possibly stems near soil.	**Aster or Erigeron root aphid,** *Aphis middletonii.* Small pear-shaped insects, light gray to dark green.	Infests many Asteraceae; control nearby weeds in this family. See page 182.
Foliage chewed and webbed together with silk. Stems may be mined. Larvae wriggle vigorously when touched.	**Greenhouse leaftier,** *Udea rubigalis.* Larvae yellowish green with three longitudinal green to white stripes. Adult reddish brown with black wavy lines on wings. Mature adult and larva about $^{3}/_{4}$ inches long. Pyralidae moth has about 6 generations per year.	Avoid growing floral hosts near celery, a major host. See page 203.
Foliage chewed by yellowish and black, very hairy caterpillars up to 2 inches long.	**Yellow woollybear,** *Spilosoma virginica.* Adult moth (family Arctiidae), white, yellowish, and brown with black wing markings. Overwinters in hairy cocoon. Has 2 generations per year.	See Caterpillars, page 203.
Winding tunnels in (mostly basal) leaves, may extend into petiole and stem. Leaves may have pale spots or punctures and may whiten, wilt, or drop.	**Leafminers,** *Liriomyza* spp. Small active flies, dark with yellow. Yellowish maggots bore in tissue.	See page 167.
Leaves, buds, or blossoms chewed. Stems clipped near soil. Plants discolor, wilt, or die.	**Black vine weevil,** *Otiorhynchus sulcatus;* **Vegetable weevil,** *Listroderes costirostris.* Dull gray, blackish, or brown snout beetles. *Listroderes* adults and green larvae feed on roots and at night feed above ground. *Otiorhynchus* adults feed on foliage; white maggots chew roots.	See Weevils, page 208.
Foliage chewed or skeletonized. Dark beetle larvae may be present, often in groups.	**Blue milkweed beetle,** *Chrysochus cobaltinus.* Adult beetle metallic green-blue, about $^{1}/_{3}$ inches long.	Control nearby milkweed (*Asclepias* spp.) and oleander (*Nerium oleander*), alternate hosts. See page 212.

DIEFFENBACHIA (*Dieffenbachia* spp.), Dumb cane

Leaves and stem yellow and wilt, often on only one side of plant. Plants may brown and die. Stem and root vascular tissue discolored.	**Fusarium stem rot,** *Fusarium solani.* Persists in soil. Infects through roots.	Pasteurize media before planting. Use good sanitation. Avoid overwatering. Provide good drainage. See pages 93–96.
Leaves may turn yellowish or darken. Plant may wilt and die. Roots and stem around soil dark and decayed.	**Pythium root rot,** *Pythium* spp.; **Rhizoctonia aerial blight,** *Rhizoctonia solani;* **Phytophthora leaf spot,** *Phytophthora* spp. Fungi promoted by wet, poorly drained soil.	Provide good drainage. Avoid excess irrigation and reduce watering if disease develops. See pages 93–98.
Leaves or stems near soil have brown to black water-soaked spots or decay. Tissue may have tiny black to dark green spore-forming structures and white mycelia.	**Myrothecium leaf spot,** *Myrothecium roridum.* Spreads by waterborne spores. Infects through wounds. Favored by 70° to 81°F and excess nitrogen or salts.	Minimize plant wounds. Keep foliage dry. Use good sanitation. Avoid excess fertilization. Growing plants above 86°F may arrest or prevent disease.
Leaves have tan to brown circular spots or blotches. Plants turn slightly yellow, wilt. Crown and root tissue eventually may decay, causing plant to die.	**Anthracnose,** *Colletotrichum* spp. Fungi survive in crop debris. Spores spread by splashing water. Favored by wet weather and overhead irrigation.	Avoid overhead irrigation. Minimize wounding plants. Use good sanitation. Fungicide application may help to prevent problem. See pages 116–118.

What the problem looks like	Probable cause	Comments

DIEFFENBACHIA (*Dieffenbachia* spp.), Dumb cane (continued)

What the problem looks like	Probable cause	Comments
Foliage yellows and wilts. Leaves may have irregular water-soaked to dark spots, lesions, or rings. Soft, brown, stem rot near soil line. Stems may collapse and die.	**Bacterial leaf spots**, *Erwinia carotovora*, *E. chrysanthemi*, *Pseudomonas cichorii*. Persist in media and infected stock, infect through wounds, and are favored when wet.	Keep foliage dry. Use drip irrigation. Don't overwater. Provide good drainage. Use good sanitation; rogue infected and nearby plants. Avoid injuring plants. See pages 100, 107.
Leaves have yellow, reddish, or brown spots up to ¼ inch in diameter; rarely on stems and petioles. Spots become larger, dark, angular blotches or wedges, may have distinct margins. Leaves and stem may wilt and die. Stem vascular tissue and roots may be black but not rotted.	**Bacterial leaf spot**, *Xanthomonas campestris* pv. *dieffenbachiae*. Spreads by splashing water, infected stock, debris, and equipment. Favored by 70° to 80°F, moist conditions, and rapid growth, such as from excess nitrogen.	Pasteurize media before planting. Avoid overhead water. Regularly inspect and rogue plants infected and those nearby. Isolate new plants; symptoms may not appear immediately. Use good sanitation. Some bactericides can be effective. See pages 107, 118.
Leaves have yellowish patterns. Leaves may severely distort. Veins may yellow. Plants grow slowly, are stunted.	**Dasheen mosaic virus**. Spread by aphids or mechanically in sap, such as through contaminated tools.	Use virus-free plants produced by tissue culture. Rogue infected plants. Pasteurize equipment to avoid mechanical spread. Control aphids. See Viruses, page 121.
Stems darken and develop cankers at bases; affected branches turn tan, wilt, and die. Leaves may discolor and distort. Plants may be stunted.	**Tomato spotted wilt virus**. Spread by thrips. Many hosts.	Rogue infected plants. Control nearby weeds. Exclude or control thrips. See page 121.
Plants stunted. Root cortex and deep tissues have necrotic lesions.	**Lesion nematodes**, *Pratylenchus* spp. Nematodes survive in soil as eggs, larvae, and adults.	Pasteurize growing media before planting. See page 265.
Leaf tips and margins brittle and brown or brown with yellow margin. Leaves wilt, yellow, and may die and drop.	**Salt damage**. Noninfectious disorder due to poor water quality, improper pH, or excess fertilization.	Leach media with low-salt water. Avoid overfertilization. Check media pH; if low, adjust to 6 to 7. Trim out damaged tissue. See page 47.
Foliage yellows or browns between veins. Older or light-colored foliage is most affected.	**Sunburn**. Noninfectious disorder from improper light. Inadequate water can contribute to problem.	Shade variegated or light-colored varieties. Avoid abrupt change from dim to bright conditions. Provide adequate irrigation. See page 62.
Stems elongated and thin. Foliage yellows, browns, wilts, and drops, beginning with older leaves. Plants stunted or grow slowly.	**Insufficient light**. Noninfectious disorder from inadequate light. Dieffenbachia requires more light than most other foliage plants.	Provide more light, but gradually if growing area has been dim. Cut and reroot terminal stems if lower leaves all dropped. Provide adequate water.
Leaves have irregular white or brown blotches or stippling. Terminals may be distorted.	**Thrips**. Slender dark brown to yellowish insects, ¹⁄₁₆ inch long or less.	See page 161.
Foliage discolored, stippled, or bleached, and may drop. Terminals may distort. Plant may have fine webbing.	**Spider mites**. Tiny greenish, reddish, or yellowish mites, may have 2 dark spots.	See page 213.
Foliage has sticky honeydew, blackish sooty mold, and white cast skins. Terminals and leaves may distort.	**Aphids**. Small pear-shaped insects, often green, black, yellow, or pinkish. Commonly in colonies on new terminals.	See page 179.
Plant has sticky honeydew, blackish sooty mold, and cottony waxy material.	**Citrus mealybug**, *Planococcus citri*; **Obscure mealybug**, *Pseudococcus affinis*. Grayish, oval, waxy insects with marginal filaments.	See page 183.

DIOSMA (*Diosma*, *Coleonema* spp.), Breath of heaven

What the problem looks like	Probable cause	Comments
Leaves yellow or wilt then darken and die. Leaf bases and roots may be soft, dark, and rotted. Plants die.	**Root and crown rot**, *Phytophthora* sp. Favored by wet, poorly drained media. Persists in soil.	Plant only disease-free stock. Plant only where drainage is excellent. Avoid overwatering. Pasteurize soil before planting or avoid growing in fields where this has been a problem. See pages 93–97.

DRACAENA (*Dracaena* spp.), Corn plant, Dragon tree

What the problem looks like	Probable cause	Comments
Foliage yellows and wilts, often on only one side. Plant stunted and may die. Roots dark and decayed. Young plants collapse and die.	**Phytophthora stem rot**, *Phytophthora* spp. Fungi persist in soil. Spread in media and water. Favored by excess moisture and poor drainage.	Provide good drainage. Avoid excess irrigation and reduce watering if disease develops. See pages 93–97.
Leaves and stem yellow or brown, wilt, and may die. Foliage may have yellow to brownish spots or blotches. Stem and root vascular tissue discolored.	**Fusarium leaf spot**, *Fusarium moniliforme*. Persists in soil. Infects through roots.	Pasteurize media before planting. Use good sanitation. Avoid overwatering. Provide good drainage. See pages 93–96.

What the problem looks like	Probable cause	Comments
Leaves have tan to brown circular spots or blotches. Leaf tips die. Plants turn slightly yellow, wilt. Crown and root tissue eventually may decay, causing plant to die.	**Anthracnose,** *Glomerella cingulata.* Fungus survives in crop debris. Spores spread by splashing water. Favored by wet conditions and overhead irrigation.	Avoid overhead irrigation. Minimize wounding plants. Use good sanitation. Fungicide application may help to prevent problem. See pages 116–118.
Foliage yellows and wilts. Leaves may have irregular water-soaked spots or lesions. Soft, brown, odorous stem rot near soil line. Stems may collapse and die.	**Bacterial leaf spot, Erwinia blight,** *Erwinia carotovora, E. chrysanthemi.* Persist in media and infected stock. Favored when wet. Avoid injuring plant, as bacteria infect wounds.	Keep foliage dry. Use drip irrigation. Don't overwater. Provide good drainage. Use good sanitation; rogue infected and nearby plants. Avoid injuring plants. See pages 100, 107.
Leaves have soft brown decay or spots. Lower leaves or growing points may decay. Dead tissue may have woolly gray growth (spores).	**Gray mold,** *Botrytis cinerea.* Fungus develops in crop debris or inactive tissue. Favored by high humidity and 70° to 77°F. Spores airborne.	Use good sanitation. Avoid overhead irrigation. Keep humidity low. Provide good air circulation. Don't crowd plants. See page 108.
Leaf tips and margins brittle and brown or brown with yellow margin. Foliage may yellow and die.	**Salt damage.** Noninfectious disorder due to poor water quality, improper pH, or excess fertilization.	Leach media with low salt water. Avoid overfertilization. Check pH and adjust if necessary. Trim out damaged tissue. See page 47.
Foliage stippled, bleached, or blotched, may have varnishlike excrement. Terminals may distort. Growth may be stunted.	**Banded greenhouse thrips,** *Hercinothrips femoralis;* **Dracaena thrips,** *Parthenothrips dracaenae.* Tiny, slender, dark brown to yellowish insects.	See Thrips, page 161.
Foliage discolored, stippled, or bleached. Terminals may distort. Plant may have fine webbing.	**Spider mites.** Tiny greenish, reddish, or yellowish mites; may have 2 dark spots.	See page 213.
Foliage has sticky honeydew and blackish sooty mold. Foliage may yellow. Plants may grow slowly.	**Mealybugs,** including Longtailed mealybug, *Pseudococcus longispinus.* Powdery gray insects with waxy marginal filaments.	See page 183.
Plants stunted, decline, may die. Powdery waxy material may be visible on roots and around crown.	**Ground mealybug,** *Rhizoecus falcifer.* Small, slender, pale insects; may have powdery wax covering but no marginal filaments.	See page 186.
Leaves and blossoms chewed (edges notched).	**Fuller rose beetle,** *Asynonychus godmani.* Rarely seen brownish adults feed at night. Whitish maggots (larvae) live in soil, eat roots.	See page 208.

ENGLISH DAISY *(Bellis perennis)*

What the problem looks like	Probable cause	Comments
Leaves and stem yellow and wilt, often on only one side of plant. Plants may brown and die. Stem vascular tissue discolored.	**Fusarium wilt,** *Fusarium oxysporum.* Persists in soil. Infects through roots.	Pasteurize media before planting. Use good sanitation. Avoid overwatering. Provide good drainage. See page 104.
Brown to yellow spots or blotches, mostly on older leaves. Spots may have dark or yellowish margins. Foliage may shrivel, drop.	**Leaf spot,** *Phyllosticta* sp. Spreads by air or splashing water. Favored by prolonged wet conditions. Persists in plant debris.	Avoid wetting foliage. Use drip irrigation. Use good sanitation; promptly remove and dispose of debris and infected leaves. See pages 116–118.
Blossoms have irregular white or brown blotches. Leaves may turn brown. Blossoms or terminals may be distorted. Growth may be stunted.	**Western flower thrips,** *Frankliniella occidentalis.* Slender dark brown to yellowish insects, $\frac{1}{16}$ inch long or less.	See page 161.
Foliage has sticky honeydew and blackish sooty mold. Leaves yellow and wither. Tiny, whitish, mothlike adult insects.	**Greenhouse whitefly,** *Trialeurodes vaporariorum.* Yellowish, oval, flattened nymphs and pupae.	See page 170.
Leaves chewed, may be rolled or tied together with silk. Yellow, green, or pink larvae with yellow, green, or black lengthwise stripes.	**Omnivorous looper,** *Sabulodes aegrotata* or *S. caberata.* Adult moth (family Geometridae) tan to brownish with wavy black band across middle of wings. Mature larva and nocturnal adult up to about $1\frac{1}{2}$ inches long. Oval eggs laid in clusters.	See page 203.
Leaves have winding tunnels. Heavily infested leaves may drop. Yellowish to pale maggots in mines. Leaves have pale spots or punctures.	**Serpentine leafminer,** *Liriomyza trifolii.* Adults are tiny black and yellow flies.	See page 167.

What the problem looks like	Probable cause	Comments
EUCALYPTUS (*Eucalyptus* spp.), Gum		
Leaves discolor, wilt, stunt, or drop prematurely. Discolored bark or cankers may ooze sap. Branches or plant dies.	**Root and crown rots,** *Phytophthora* spp. Fungal diseases often promoted by moist soil.	See pages 93–97.
Leaves discolor, wilt, stunt, or drop prematurely. Stems discolored, cankered, and die.	**Armillaria root rot,** *Armillaria mellea.* Present in many soils. Favored by warm, wet soil. Persists for years in infected roots.	Remove woody roots ½ inch diameter or larger before planting. Pasteurize or air-dry soil well or avoid growing in fields previously planted with oaks or other susceptible woody plants. See page 99.
Seedlings yellow, wilt, and collapse. Stem rotted at soil line. Dark fungal strands may be visible on soil with hand lens.	**Rhizoctonia stem rot,** *Rhizoctonia solani.* Soilborne fungus favored by warm, moist conditions.	Pasteurize media before planting. Practice good sanitation. Avoid overwatering and deep planting. See pages 93–98.
Seedlings have soft brown, tan, or gray spots or decay. Seedlings wilt and die. Dead tissue has woolly gray growth (spores).	**Seedling blight,** *Botrytis* spp. Fungi develop in plant debris. Favored by wet, humid conditions.	Use good sanitation. Avoid overhead irrigation. Keep humidity low. Provide good air circulation. Don't crowd plants. See pages 93–96, 108.
Wood rotted. Spore-forming bodies, commonly mushroom- or seashell-shaped, may be present.	**Wood decay,** *Ganoderma, Laetiporus, Phellinus, Trametes* spp. Airborne spores infect through wounds.	Avoid wounding wood. When making cuts, use good technique to facilitate wound closure.
Brown to yellow spots or blotches, mostly on older leaves. Spots may have dark or yellowish margins. Foliage may shrivel, drop. Twigs may die back.	**Leaf spots,** *Colletotrichum, Didymosphaeria, Macrophoma, Monochaetia, Mycosphaerella, Phyllosticta, Septosporium* spp. Persist in crop debris. Favored by prolonged wet conditions.	Spread by air or splashing water. Avoid wetting foliage. Use drip irrigation. Use good sanitation; promptly remove and dispose of debris and infected leaves. See pages 116–118.
Foliage discolors. Branches have cankers and die back.	**Canker and dieback,** *Botryosphaeria dothidea.* Fungus spreads by splashing water.	Provide good cultural care, especially appropriate irrigation. Use drip irrigation. See page 102.
Leaf underside has pimplelike blisters or water-soaked spots. Leaves brown, harden, appear corky, especially on underside. Foliage yellows, drops.	**Edema** or **Oedema.** Noninfectious disease. Leaves accumulate excess water when soil is warm and moist and air is cool and moist. Exact cause unknown.	Irrigate only in morning. Avoid irrigation if cool and cloudy. Provide good air circulation. Keep humidity low. Provide good drainage. See page 41.
New shoots distorted, covered with whitish, waxy strands or tiny cones. Foliage covered with sticky honeydew and blackish sooty mold. Adults look like tiny cicadas. Pairs mating tail-to-tail look like grayish moth.	**Psyllids,** including Blue gum psyllid, *Ctenarytaina eucalypti;* Eucalyptus psyllid, *Blastopsylla occidentalis;* Red gum lerp psyllid, *Glycaspis brimblecombei.* Tiny gray, green, or orange aphidlike insects that suck plant sap. Tiny pale yellow to cream-colored eggs are laid in bud or leaf axils or openly on leaves. Red gum lerp psyllid produces conelike coverings (lerps), resembling armored scales.	Promoted by succulent plant growth; reducing fertilizer and irrigation reduces populations. Insecticidal soap, oil, or other insecticide may temporarily control. An introduced parasite, *Psyllaephagus pilosus,* provides good control of blue gum psyllid in many areas unless disrupted.
Foliage has sticky honeydew, blackish sooty mold, and white cast skins. Terminals and leaves may distort.	**Cowpea aphid,** *Aphis craccivora;* **Potato aphid,** *Macrosiphum euphorbiae.* Small black, grayish, green or pinkish insects, often in colonies on new terminals.	See Aphids, page 179.
Foliage has sticky honeydew and blackish sooty mold. Copious white waxy material present with certain species. Leaves may yellow and wither. Tiny, whitish, mothlike adult insects.	**Bandedwinged whitefly,** *Trialeurodes abutilonea;* **Giant whitefly,** *Aleurodicus dugesii;* **Woolly whitefly,** *Aleurothrixus floccosus.* Oval or flattened yellow, greenish, or brownish nymphs. Tiny adults are whitish, mothlike.	See Whiteflies, page 170.
Leaves skeletonized between veins or chewed or notched at edge. Buds chewed and die back; terminals regrow as stubby tufts or witches' brooms.	**Eucalyptus snout beetle,** *Gonipterus scutellatus;* **Australian tortoise beetle** or leaf beetle, *Trachymela sloanei.* Yellowish or green larvae and brownish or green adults chew foliage. Dark fecal chain often trail weevil larvae.	*Eucalyptus pulverulenta* and some other eucalyptus reportedly are not attacked. Provide good cultural care. Avoid spraying eucalyptus with broad-spectrum insecticide that may disrupt the introduced egg parasite *Anaphes nitens* (Mymaridae) which provides good biological control of snout beetle.
Foliage chewed and webbed together with silk. Disturbed larvae wriggle and drop on a thread. Eggs laid in overlapping mass like fish scales.	**Orange tortrix,** *Argyrotaenia citrana.* Larva whitish, head brown. Adult gray to brown moth (family Tortricidae) often abundant near citrus orchards. Both up to 1 inch long. Has many other hosts.	See page 203.

What the problem looks like	Probable cause	Comments
Leaves chewed, may be rolled or tied together with silk. Yellow, green, or pink larvae with yellow, green, or black lengthwise stripes.	**Omnivorous looper,** *Sabulodes aegrotata* or *S. caberata.* Adult moth (family Geometridae) tan to brownish with wavy black band across middle of wings. Mature larva and nocturnal adult, up to about 1½ inches long. Oval eggs laid in clusters.	See page 203.
Foliage yellows and wilts. Trunk or limbs dying. Broad galleries under bark from boring by whitish larvae up to 1½ inches long.	**Eucalyptus longhorned borers,** *Phoracantha recurva, P. semipunctata.* Adults banded blackish, tan, and reddish brown, about 1 inch long.	Prune dead limbs. Remove and dispose of all dead eucalyptus wood. Provide good cultural care, especially adequate irrigation. Insecticides are not effective.

EURYOPS (*Euryops* spp.)

Foliage yellows and wilts. Plant stunted and may die. Roots dark and decayed. Young plants collapse and die.	**Root and crown rot,** *Phytophthora* sp. Fungus persists in soil. Spread in media and water. Favored by excess moisture and poor drainage.	Provide good drainage. Avoid excess irrigation and reduce watering if disease develops. See pages 93–97.
Leaves discolor, wilt, stunt, or drop prematurely. Stems discolored, cankered, and die.	**Armillaria root rot,** *Armillaria mellea.* Present in many soils. Favored by warm, wet soil. Persists for years in infected roots.	Remove woody roots ½ inch diameter or larger before planting. Pasteurize or air-dry soil well or avoid growing in fields previously planted with oaks or other susceptible woody plants. See page 99.

EVERLASTING (*Helipterum roseum*)

Leaves have yellow to brown blotches, spots, or streaks. Foliage may die. Plant may be distorted and stunted.	**Tomato spotted wilt virus.** Spread by thrips. Has many crop and weed hosts.	Rogue infected plants. Exclude or control thrips. See page 121.
Foliage yellows or wilts. Feeder and fleshy roots have knots or swellings.	**Root knot nematodes,** *Meloidogyne* spp. Tiny roundworms that prefer warm, sandy soil. Many hosts.	Pasteurize media before planting. Rogue affected plants. See page 265.

EXACUM (*Exacum affine*), German violet

Leaves yellow, wither, and drop, beginning with basal leaves. Plants stunted. Vascular tissue brownish.	**Fusarium wilt,** *Fusarium* sp. Fungus persists in soil for years. A problem during warm weather.	Pasteurize media before planting. See page 104.
Stems have dark decay or sunken cankers. Vascular tissue may be soft and rotted. Stems wilt or die.	**Basal stem rot,** *Nectria haematococca.* Fungus spreads in wind and splashing water.	Avoid overhead irrigation. Rogue infected plants.
Plant grows slowly, may wilt and collapse. Roots dark, water-soaked, decayed.	**Root rot,** *Pythium ultimum.* Fungus persists in media. Favored by warm, moist conditions.	Avoid overwatering. Provide good drainage. See pages 93–96.
Leaves or flowers have soft brown to gray spots or decay. Cankers may form at stem base. Plants may wilt. Dead tissue may have woolly gray growth (spores).	**Gray mold,** *Botrytis cinerea.* Fungus develops in crop debris or inactive tissue. Favored by high humidity and 70° to 77°F. Spores airborne.	Use good sanitation. Avoid overhead irrigation. Keep humidity low. Provide good air circulation. Don't crowd plants. See page 108.
Stems darken and develop lesions at bases. Leaves wilted, discolored, ring spotted, or distorted. Plants may be stunted. Symptoms may appear bacterialike.	**Impatiens necrotic spot virus, Tomato spotted wilt virus.** Spread by thrips. Many hosts.	Control nearby weeds. Exclude and control thrips. Rogue infected plants. See page 121.
Young terminals and upper leaves wilt and die.	**Calcium deficiency.** Noninfectious disorder.	Check, and if necessary adjust, pH. Provide proper nutrition.
Plant has sticky honeydew and blackish sooty mold. Foliage may yellow. Tiny, white, mothlike adults present.	**Whiteflies.** Flattened, oval, translucent to yellowish nymphs and pupae.	See page 170.
Plant has sticky honeydew, blackish sooty mold, and possibly cottony waxy material.	**Mealybugs.** Grayish, oval, waxy insects with marginal filaments.	See page 183.
Tips yellow and distort. Buds fail to open.	**Broad mites.** Tiny mites most common on upper plant parts.	See page 217.
New growth dark and distorted. Buds deformed, black and discolored, and may drop. Plants severely stunted.	**Cyclamen mite,** *Phytonemus pallidus.* A pinkish orange mite (family Tarsonemidae), ¹⁄₁₀₀ inch long or smaller.	See page 217.
Petals or foliage discolored, streaked, stippled, or distorted.	**Thrips.** Tiny, slender, blackish to yellowish insects.	See page 161.

What the problem looks like	Probable cause	Comments

FICUS (*Ficus* spp.), Fig, Indian laurel, Laurel fig

What the problem looks like	Probable cause	Comments
Foliage yellows and wilts, often on only one side of plant. Plant stunted and may die. Roots dark and decayed. Young plants collapse and die.	**Root and crown rots,** *Pythium, Phytophthora, Rhizoctonia* spp. Fungi persist in soil. Spread in media and water. Favored by excess moisture and poor drainage.	Provide good drainage. Avoid excess irrigation and reduce watering if disease develops. See pages 93–98.
Leaves discolor, wilt, stunt, or drop prematurely. Stems discolored, cankered, and die.	**Armillaria root rot,** *Armillaria mellea.* Present in many soils. Favored by warm, wet soil. Persists for years in infected roots.	Remove woody roots ½ inch diameter or larger before planting. Pasteurize or air-dry soil well or avoid growing in fields previously planted with oaks or other susceptible woody plants. See page 99.
Brown to black water-soaked spots or decay on stems near soil or on leaves. Tissue may have tiny, black to dark green, spore-forming structures and white mycelia.	**Myrothecium rot** or **Crown rot,** *Myrothecium roridum.* Spreads by waterborne spores. Infects through wounds. Favored by 70° to 81°F and excess nitrogen.	Minimize plant wounds. Keep foliage dry. Use good sanitation. Avoid excess fertilization. Growing plants above 86°F may arrest or prevent disease.
Leaves have yellowish green spots, mottling, or bands. Foliage may yellow or somewhat distort. Plants may be stunted.	**Fig mosaic virus.** Vectored by mites.	Use good sanitation. Rogue affected plants. Control or exclude mites. See Viruses, page 121.
Brown to yellow spots or blotches, mostly on older leaves. Spots may have dark or yellowish margins. Foliage may shrivel and drop.	**Leaf spots.** Caused by many different fungi. Spread by splashing water. Favored by wet conditions. Persist in crop debris.	Avoid wetting foliage. Use drip irrigation. Use good sanitation; promptly remove and dispose of debris and infected leaves. See pages 116–118.
Leaf undersides may have pimplelike blisters or water-soaked spots. Leaves brown or appear corky, especially on undersides. Foliage yellows, drops.	**Edema** or **Oedema.** Noninfectious disorder. Leaves accumulate excess water when soil is warm and moist and air is cool and moist. Exact cause is unknown.	Irrigate only in morning. Avoid irrigation if cool and cloudy. Provide good air circulation Keep humidity low. Provide good drainage. See page 41.
Leaves drop. Dropped leaves may be yellow or a healthy-looking green.	**Noninfectious disorders.** Causes include excess or deficient water, inadequate light, and rapid environmental changes.	Keep soil below surface moist, but not soggy. Provide good drainage. Grow where well lit. Prevent great fluctuations in temperature or light. Avoid drafty areas.
Leaf tips and margins or entire leaf brittle and brown, dull green, or yellow. Foliage may die and drop.	**Salt damage.** Noninfectious disorder due to poor water quality, improper pH, or excess fertilization.	Leach media with low salt water. Avoid overfertilization. Check pH and adjust if necessary. Trim out damaged tissue. See page 47.
Sticky honeydew and blackish sooty mold on plant. Foliage may yellow. Tiny, waxy, white mothlike adults present.	**Whiteflies,** including Greenhouse whitefly, *Trialeurodes vaporariorum;* Silverleaf whitefly, *Bemisia argentifolii.*	See page 170.
Sticky honeydew, blackish sooty mold, and may be cottony waxy material on plant.	**Mealybugs,** including Citrus mealybug, *Planococcus citri;* Longtailed mealybug, *Pseudococcus longispinus.* Grayish, oval, waxy insects with marginal filaments.	See page 183.
Plant has sticky honeydew and blackish sooty mold. Foliage may yellow. Leaves and twigs have white to brownish encrustations (insects).	**Wax scales,** *Ceroplastes* spp. Mature female soft scales are about ⅕ inch long. Spread as tiny yellowish crawlers.	See Scales, page 186.
Foliage discolored, bleached, or stippled. Leaf underside has dark varnishlike excrement.	**Greenhouse thrips,** *Heliothrips haemorrhoidalis.* Tiny slender black, dark brown, to yellowish insects.	See page 161.
Terminal leaves have curling (galling) and purple pitting.	**Cuban laurel thrips,** Slender, black adults or yellow nymphs about ⅛ inch long. All stages occur year round in curled leaves; populations are highest from October through December. In California, problem mostly in southern parts of state. Also problem in Hawaii and Gulf Coast States.	*Ficus microcarpa* (=*F. nitida, F. retusa*) is preferred. Conserve *Macrotracheliella nigra* (a minute pirate bug) and green lacewing predators. Prune and dispose of infested terminals during winter; overwintering thrips cannot survive outside of galls.
Leaves with warty blisters, which may have circular insect emergence holes. Foliage yellows drops prematurely.	**Ficus gall wasp,** *Josephiella microcarpae.* Pale larvae feed in leaves. Adults are tiny, dark wasps.	Remove infested leaves. Attacks only *F. microcarpa;* growing other *Ficus* spp. avoids problem. Systemic insecticides may control it.

FORGET-ME-NOT (*Myosotis* spp.)

What the problem looks like	Probable cause	Comments
Plant wilts and dies. Basal stem rotted. Black sclerotia in and on stems. Cottony mycelium in and on stems if conditions are moist.	**Cottony rot,** *Sclerotinia sclerotiorum.* Fungus survives in media as sclerotia. Favored by overhead irrigation and high humidity. Many hosts. Not reported on *Myosotis* in California.	Pasteurize media before planting. Avoid overhead irrigation. Irrigate early in day so plants dry quickly. Consider fungicide application to base and lower foliage of plants. See page 101.

What the problem looks like	Probable cause	Comments
Leaves, flowers, or stems have soft brown decay or spots. Sprouts or stems may darken and rot near soil. Dead tissue may have woolly gray growth (spores).	**Gray mold,** *Botrytis cinerea.* Fungus develops in plant debris. Favored by high humidity and 70° to 77°F.	Use good sanitation. Avoid overhead irrigation. Keep humidity low. Provide good air circulation. Don't crowd plants. See page 108.
Leaves have purplish red to dark brown irregular and angular spots. Lower leaf surface covered with soft, fluffy fungal growth. Leaves yellow and drop.	**Downy mildew,** *Peronospora myosotidis.* Spores produced only on living plants. Fungus persists as resistant oospores when conditions are dry. Favored by moist, humid conditions. Not reported on *Myosotis* in California.	Provide good air circulation. Avoid overhead watering. Consider applying fungicide to protect foliage. See page 115.
White, powdery growth, mostly on older leaves and stems. Foliage may dry and die.	**Powdery mildew,** *Erysiphe cichoracearum.* Free water not required for infection.	Provide good air circulation and adequate light. Don't crowd plants. Consider applying sulfur or other fungicide to prevent. See page 112.
Powdery, brownish pustules on leaf underside and may be on stem. Leaf upperside has brown or yellow spots. Foliage may yellow and drop.	**Rust,** *Puccinia* spp. Airborne spores spread only from living tissue. Plant must be wet for infection. Not reported on *Myosotis* in California.	Avoid wetting foliage; spreads in splashing water. Keep humidity low. Rogue infected plants. See page 119.
Leaves have yellow to brown blotches, spots, or streaks. Foliage may die. Plant may be distorted and stunted.	**Tomato spotted wilt virus.** Spread by thrips. Has may crop and weed hosts.	Eliminate nearby weeds. Exclude or control thrips. Rogue infected plants. See page 121.
Foliage chewed and webbed with silk. Caterpillars up to 1½ inches long, alternately banded yellowish green and dark purplish.	**Painted beauty,** *Vanessa virginiensis.* Butterfly mostly orange and brown, up to 2½ inches wide, with white and blue spots.	Eliminate alternate host weeds, including thistles, mallow, and malva. *Bacillus thuringiensis* kills larvae. See Caterpillars, page 203.

FORSYTHIA (*Forsythia* spp.)

Foliage yellows and wilts, often on only one side. Plant stunted and may die. Roots dark and decayed. Young plants collapse and die.	**Root and crown rots,** *Phytophthora* spp. Fungi persist in soil. Spread in media and water. Favored by excess moisture and poor drainage. Not reported on forsythia in California.	Pasteurize media before planting. Provide good drainage. Avoid excess irrigation and reduce watering if disease develops. See pages 93–97.
Brown to yellow, spots or blotches, mostly on older leaves. Spots may have dark or yellowish margins. Foliage may shrivel and drop.	**Leaf spots, Blight,** *Alternaria, Colletotrichum, Phyllosticta* spp. Spread by splashing water. Favored by prolonged, wet, conditions. Persist in plant debris. Not reported on forsythia in California.	Avoid wetting foliage. Use drip irrigation. Use good sanitation; promptly remove and dispose of debris and infected leaves. See pages 116–118.

FOXGLOVE (*Digitalis* spp.)

Leaf veins yellow beginning with basal leaves, then entire leaf yellows, withers, and drops. Plants stunted. Vascular tissue brownish.	**Fusarium wilt,** *Fusarium* sp. Fungus persists in soil for years and can be carried in corms. A problem during warm weather.	Pasteurize media before planting. See pages 93–96.
Foliage yellows. Soft rot of basal stem or roots. White mycelium and small, tan to reddish brown sclerotia may develop on infected tissue around soil.	**Southern wilt,** *Sclerotium rolfsii.* Sclerotia survive in soil. Fungal disease favored by moist, poorly drained, 77° to 95°F soil. Many hosts. Not reported on foxglove in California.	Avoid planting in infested soil, or pasteurize soil before planting. Avoid excess irrigation. See page 101.
Brown to yellow spots or blotches, mostly on older leaves. Spots may have dark or yellowish margins. Foliage may shrivel and drop.	**Leaf spots, Blight,** *Colletotrichum, Phyllosticta, Ramularia* spp. Spread by splashing water. Favored by prolonged, wet, conditions. Persist in plant debris. Not reported on foxglove in California.	Avoid wetting foliage. Use drip irrigation. Use good sanitation; promptly remove and dispose of debris and infected leaves. See pages 116–118.
Foliage discolored, stippled, or bleached, and may drop. Terminals may distort. Plant may have fine webbing.	**Spider mites.** Tiny greenish, reddish, or yellowish mites, may have 2 dark spots.	See page 213.
Plant has sticky honeydew and blackish sooty mold, and may have cottony waxy material.	**Mealybugs.** Grayish, oval, waxy insects with marginal filaments.	See page 183.
Plant has blackish sooty mold, sticky honeydew, and whitish cast skins. Leaves may curl or yellow.	**Aphids.** Small pear-shaped insects, often green, yellow, or blackish.	See page 179.
Foliage chewed. Larvae up to 1½ inches long, dark green or black, spiny, with orange or yellow.	**Buckeye,** *Junonia coenia.* Butterfly mostly brown with orange and 1 or 2 eyespots on each wing.	Exclude moths from growing area. Use good sanitation; remove infested plants. Apply *Bacillus thuringiensis* to young larvae. See Caterpillars, page 203.

What the problem looks like	Probable cause	Comments
FREESIA *(Freesia × hybrida)*		
Leaves yellow, often beginning at base, then entire leaf yellows, withers, and drops. Plants stunted. Corm vascular tissue brownish.	**Fusarium wilt,** *Fusarium* spp. Fungi persist in soil for years and can be carried in corms. A problem during warm weather.	Pasteurize media before planting. See pages 93–96.
Foliage yellows and wilts. Stem rotted at soil line. Corms may be dark and decayed.	**Root and stem rot,** *Rhizoctonia* sp. Soilborne fungus favored by warm, moist conditions.	Pasteurize media before planting. Practice good sanitation. Avoid overwatering and deep planting. See pages 93–98.
Corms or stems decay; soft, brown, odorous rot often at soil line. Leaf edges and stems may be discolored, soft, rotted.	**Bacterial soft rot,** *Erwinia* sp. Persists in media. Favored when wet.	Avoid injuring plant; disease is secondary, infecting wounds. Provide good drainage. Don't overwater. Use good sanitation; immediately discard infected plants and those nearby. See pages 100, 107.
Leaves yellow and die. Plants stunted, fail to bloom. Corms, roots, and basal stems and leaves decay. Dead tissue may be imbedded with small black sclerotia.	**Dry rot,** *Stromatinia gladioli.* Persists in plant debris or in soil. Persists in infested soil for 10 or more years. Favored by cool, wet conditions.	Pasteurize or treat soil before planting. Use pathogen-free plants. Avoid overwatering. Provide good soil drainage.
Leaves have brown spots or elongate blotches or streaks. Leaf tips may turn brown. Older leaves affected first. Reduced flowering.	**Leaf scorch.** Noninfectious disorder, may be caused by fluoride toxicity, which can develop in low pH media.	Provide proper cultural care. Avoid superphosphate, fluoridated water, and fluoride-containing materials. Consider increasing media pH.
Leaves mottled yellow and distorted. Plants chlorotic, stunted, or killed.	**Viruses,** including Bean yellow mosaic, Cucumber mosaic. Spread by aphids. Carried in infected corms and seed.	Use virus-free plants. Rogue infected plants. Control aphids. Oil spray temporarily reduces aphid virus transmission in some crops. See page 121.
Flower buds fail to develop and drop. Fewer flowers than normal.	**Bud blast.** Caused by low light and/or high temperatures during rapid flower development.	Provide appropriate growing conditions and good cultural care.
Blossoms have irregular white or brown blotches. Leaves may turn brown. Blossoms or terminals may be distorted. Growth may be stunted.	**Western flower thrips,** *Frankliniella occidentalis.* Slender dark brown to yellowish insects, $\frac{1}{16}$ inch long or less.	See page 161.
Plant has blackish sooty mold, sticky honeydew, and whitish cast skins. Leaves may curl or yellow.	**Aphids,** including Green peach aphid, *Myzus persicae.* Small pear-shaped insects, often green, yellow, or blackish.	See page 179.
May be poor growth from corms, young shoots distorted, plants stunted. Aphids under leaf sheaths, on stems near soil, and beneath outer scales of corms stored or in the field; occasionally on flowers.	**Tulip bulb aphid,** *Dysaphis tulipae.* Small pear-shaped insect, yellow, pink, gray, or green; waxy covered. Easily overlooked; usually causes direct damage only to stored corms. Vectors viral disease in lily and tulip. Other hosts include gladiolus and lily.	See page 182.
Corms discolored brownish, rotted, infested with tiny, oval, white to brownish mites.	**Bulb mites,** *Rhizoglyphus* spp. Sluggish mites, look like eggs, may also be on stems and leaves. Secondary pests that prefer decayed tissue but may help fungi to infect plants.	See page 218.
FUCHSIA *(Fuchsia* spp.)		
Foliage fades, yellows, browns, and wilts, often on one side of plant. Branches and entire plant may die.	**Verticillium wilt,** *Verticillium dahliae.* Fungus persists in soil, infects through roots.	See pages 104–106.
Foliage yellows and wilts. Plants grow slowly and die. Roots dark black and rotted.	**Black root rot,** *Thielaviopsis basicola.* Spreads in water, soil, and by infected plants. Fungus persists in infected media. Favored by cool, wet conditions. High pH may favor disease.	Pasteurize media before planting. Avoid overwatering. Provide good drainage. Allow soil to dry between watering. Rogue infected plants. Avoid high salts and high pH. See pages 95–99.
Foliage yellows and wilts, often on only one side of plant. Plant stunted and may die. Roots and basal stems dark and decayed. Young plants collapse and die.	**Root and crown rots,** *Phytophthora, Pythium, Rhizoctonia* spp. Fungi persist in soil. Spread in media and water. Favored by excess moisture and poor drainage.	Provide good drainage. Avoid excess irrigation and reduce watering if disease develops. See pages 93–98.
Leaves discolor, wilt, stunt, or drop prematurely. Stems discolored, cankered, and die.	**Armillaria root rot,** *Armillaria mellea.* Present in many soils. Favored by warm, wet soil. Persists for years in infected roots.	Remove woody roots $\frac{1}{2}$ inch diameter or larger before planting. Pasteurize or air-dry soil well or avoid growing in fields previously planted with oaks or other susceptible woody plants. See page 99.

What the problem looks like	Probable cause	Comments
Flowers decay. Plants may be stunted or lack flowers. Bluish mold may grow on infected tissue.	**Blue mold,** *Penicillium* sp. Bacteria infect through wounds. Problem during high humidity. Provide good ventilation and low humidity during storage.	Plant only healthy stock. Avoid injuring plants. Cuttings can be dipped, but some *Penicillium* strains are resistant to certain materials. Don't overwater.
Leaves or flowers have soft brown decay. Stem may be dark or cankered. Plant may wilt. Dead tissue may have woolly gray growth (spores).	**Gray mold,** *Botrytis cinerea.* Fungus develops in crop debris or inactive tissue. Favored by high humidity and 70° to 77°F. Spores airborne.	Use good sanitation. Avoid overhead irrigation. Keep humidity low. Provide good air circulation. Don't crowd plants. See page 108.
Leaf underside has orangish pustules. Leaves spotted; spots may be tan with dark border. Leaves may drop.	**Fuchsia rust,** *Pucciniastrum epilobii.* Fungus requires wet conditions to develop.	Avoid overhead irrigation. Keep foliage dry. Improve air circulation. See Rusts, page 119.
Leaves mottled yellow and distorted. Leaves or flowers with dark streaks, spots, or concentric rings. Plant distorted, stunted, or killed.	**Bean yellow mosaic virus, Cucumber mosaic virus.** Spread by aphids or infected cuttings. Bean yellow mosaic can persist in seed. **Tomato spotted wilt virus.** Thrips-vectored.	Use virus-free plants. Rogue infected plants. Exclude or control vectors. Oil spray reduces aphid virus transmission in some crops. See Viruses, page 121.
Plants stunted, decline, may die. Powdery waxy material may be visible on roots and around crown.	**Ground mealybug,** *Rhizoecus* spp. Small, slender, pale insects, may be lightly covered with powdery wax, but have no marginal filaments.	See page 183.
New growth dark and distorted. Buds deformed, black and discolored, and may drop. Plants severely stunted.	**Cyclamen mite,** *Phytonemus pallidus.* A pinkish orange mite (family Tarsonemidae), $\frac{1}{100}$ inch long or smaller.	See page 217.
Shoots, leaves, and sometimes blossoms thickened, distorted, or galled. Plant stunted.	**Fuchsia gall mite,** *Aculops fuchsiae.* Microscopic wormlike eriophyid mite.	Grow resistant species or cultivars. Prune or pinch off infested tips; follow with two miticide applications if severe. See page 219.
Foliage has brown, dead flecks. Foliage may be bleached, stippled, reddened. Leaves may drop. May be fine webbing.	**Mites,** including Privet mite, *Brevipalpus obovatus*; Twospotted spider mite, *Tetranychus urticae.* Tiny green, yellow, or red; may have 2 darkened spots on back. *B. obovatus* is a false spider mite, which produces no webbing. Both species attack many floral crops.	See page 213.
Foliage turns yellow. Plant declines or dies back. Stems or leaves have gray, brown, reddish, or tan encrustations.	**California red scale,** *Aonidiella aurantii*; **Greedy scale,** *Hemiberlesia rapax*; **Latania scale,** *H. lataniae.* Circular flattened insects less than $\frac{1}{16}$ inch long.	See page 186.
Foliage discolored, bleached, or stippled. Leaf underside has dark varnishlike excrement.	**Greenhouse thrips,** *Heliothrips haemorrhoidalis.* Tiny slender black, dark brown, to yellowish insects.	See page 161.
Foliage has sticky honeydew and blackish sooty mold. Copious white waxy material present with certain species. Leaves may yellow and wither. Tiny, whitish, mothlike adult insects.	**Bandedwinged whitefly,** *Trialeurodes abutilonea*; **Giant whitefly,** *Aleurodicus dugesii*; **Greenhouse whitefly,** *Trialeurodes vaporariorum*; **Iris whitefly,** *Aleyrodes spiraeoides.* Flattened, oval, translucent to yellowish nymphs and pupae.	See Whiteflies, page 170.
May have cottony material (egg sacs) on foliage and sometimes around crown or on roots. Foliage has sticky honeydew and blackish sooty mold. Foliage may yellow.	**Citrus mealybug,** *Planococcus citri*; **Longtailed mealybug,** *Pseudococcus longispinus*; **Mexican mealybug,** *Phenacoccus gossypii.* Powdery gray insects with waxy filaments.	See page 183.
Leaves have cottony cylindrical egg sacs up to $\frac{1}{3}$ inch long. Foliage has sticky honeydew and blackish sooty mold. Foliage may yellow.	**Greenhouse orthezia,** *Orthezia insignis.* Pale brown to dark green insect with two white rows on back and white bands along side. Usually not a pest in California. Has about 2 generations per year.	Controls for mealybugs or scales may be effective.
Foliage has sticky honeydew, blackish sooty mold, and whitish cast skins. Leaves or terminals may curl or distort. Foliage may yellow.	**Aphids,** including Crescent-marked lily aphid, *Aulacorthum circumflexum*; Green peach aphid, *Myzus persicae*; Potato aphid, *Macrosiphum euphorbiae.* Small green, yellowish, or pinkish pear-shaped insects.	See page 179.

What the problem looks like	Probable cause	Comments

FUCHSIA (*Fuchsia* spp.) (continued)

What the problem looks like	Probable cause	Comments
Foliage or woody parts have blackish sooty mold. Plant may decline and die back.	**Black scale**, *Saissetia oleae*; **Nigra scale**, *Parasaissetia nigra*. Orange, black, or brown insects, flattened to bulbous.	See Scales, page 186.
Foliage chewed or skeletonized and may be webbed together with silk. Stems may be clipped. Caterpillars or their dark frass may be present.	**Carnation leafroller**, *Platynota sultana*; **Cotton square borer**, *Strymon melinus*; **Saltmarsh caterpillar**, *Estigmene acrea*; **Whitelined sphinx**, *Hyles lineata*.	See Caterpillars, page 203.

GARDENIA (*Gardenia jasminoides*)

What the problem looks like	Probable cause	Comments
Plant yellows and dies back. Sunken or decayed stem lesions that girdle stems or trunks. Yellowish tissue beneath bark. Lower stems enlarged.	**Collar canker**, *Phomopsis gardeniae*, *Phoma* spp. Fungi invade through wounds. Prefer stressed plants.	Minimize wounding plants. Provide good care to minimize stress. Fungicide can be effective.
Foliage yellows and wilts, often on only one side of plant. Plant stunted and may die. Roots dark and decayed. Young plants collapse and die.	**Root and crown rots**, *Phytophthora*, *Rhizoctonia* spp. Fungi persist in soil. Spread in media and water. Favored by excess moisture and poor drainage.	Provide good drainage. Avoid excess irrigation and reduce watering if disease develops. See pages 93–98.
Leaves discolor, wilt, stunt, or drop prematurely. Stems discolored, cankered, and die.	**Armillaria root rot**, *Armillaria mellea*. Present in many soils. Favored by warm, wet soil. Persists for years in infected roots.	Remove woody roots ½ inch diameter or larger before planting. Pasteurize or air-dry soil well or avoid growing in fields previously planted with oaks or other susceptible woody plants. See page 99.
Leaves, stems, and petioles have yellow to brown spots up to ¼ inch in diameter. Spots become larger, dark, angular blotches or wedges, may have yellow margins. Leaves and stem may wilt and die. Stem vascular tissue and roots may be black but not rotted.	**Leaf spot**, *Xanthomonas campestris* pv. *maculifoliigardeniae*. Spreads by splashing water, infected stock, debris, and equipment. Favored by 70° to 80°F, moist conditions, and rapid growth, such as from excess nitrogen.	Pasteurize media before planting. Inspect and isolate new plants; symptoms may not appear immediately. Avoid overhead water. Regularly inspect and rogue plants infected and those nearby. Use good sanitation. See page 118.
Leaves have dark, irregular spots. Plants may decline and die. Underside of leaves has black or white fungal growths.	**Myrothecium leaf spot**, *Myrothecium roridum*. Fungal disease, most prevalent in greenhouses. Infects through wounds when tissue is wet.	Minimize plant wounds. Keep foliage dry. Use good sanitation. Avoid excess fertilization. Growing plants above 86°F may arrest or prevent disease.
Flowers, flower heads, lower leaves, or growing points have soft brown decay. Dead tissue may have woolly gray growth (spores).	**Gray mold**, *Botrytis cinerea*. Fungus develops in crop debris or inactive tissue. Favored by high humidity and 70° to 77°F. Spores airborne.	Use good sanitation. Avoid overhead irrigation. Keep humidity low. Provide good air circulation. Don't crowd plants. See page 108.
Foliage yellows or wilts. Feeder and fleshy roots have knots or swellings.	**Root knot nematode**, *Meloidogyne* spp. Tiny roundworms that prefer warm, sandy soil. Many hosts.	Pasteurize media before planting. Rogue affected plants. See page 265.
Young foliage yellow, except for veins.	**Iron deficiency**. Noninfectious disorder associated with cool soil temperatures.	Maintain adequate soil temperature, pH, and iron levels. Provide proper light. See pages 56–59.
Buds drop prematurely. Fewer flowers than normal.	**Bud blast**. Noninfectious disorder caused by poor cultural practices and poor growing conditions.	Provide appropriate irrigation and good drainage. Bud drop in spring is caused by poor cultural practices the previous summer and fall, when buds developed.
Blossoms have discolored blotches or streaks. Foliage stippled, bleached, or blotched; has varnishlike excrement.	**Banded greenhouse thrips**, *Hercinothrips femoralis*; **Western flower thrips**, *Frankliniella occidentalis*. Tiny slender dark brown to yellowish adults. Nymphs and pupae whitish to pale yellow.	See Thrips, page 161.
Foliage discolored, stippled, or bleached, and may drop. Terminals may distort. Plant may have fine webbing.	**Spider mites**. Tiny greenish, reddish, or yellowish mites, may have 2 dark spots.	See page 213.
Plant has blackish sooty mold, sticky honeydew, and whitish cast skins. Leaves may curl or yellow.	**Aphids**, including Green peach aphid, *Myzus persicae*; Melon aphid; *Aphis gossypii*. Small pear-shaped insects, often green, yellow, or blackish.	See page 179.
Foliage has sticky honeydew and blackish sooty mold. Foliage may yellow. Plant may die back.	**Black scale**, *Saissetia oleae*; **Hemispherical scale**, *S. coffeae*; **Brown soft scale**, *Coccus hesperidum*. Small yellow, orangish, brown, or black oval insects; flattened to bulbous.	See page 186.

What the problem looks like	Probable cause	Comments
Foliage has sticky honeydew and blackish sooty mold. Leaves may yellow and wither. Tiny, whitish, mothlike adult insects. Tiny, flattened, oval, yellow to greenish insects.	**Bayberry whitefly,** *Parabemisia myricae;* **Citrus whitefly,** *Dialeurodes citri;* **Greenhouse whitefly,** *Trialeurodes vaporariorum;* **Silverleaf whitefly,** *Bemisia argentifolii;* **Sweetpotato whitefly,** *Bemisia tabaci. P. myricae,* a former pest of avocado and citrus, is now under complete biological control.	Conserve natural enemies. See Whiteflies, page 170.
Plant has sticky honeydew and blackish sooty mold, and may have cottony waxy material.	**Citrus mealybug,** *Planococcus citri;* **Longtailed mealybug,** *Pseudococcus longispinus;* **Obscure mealybug,** *P. affinis.* Grayish, oval, waxy insects with marginal filaments.	See Mealybugs, page 183.
Plant has sticky honeydew and blackish sooty mold. Elongated, whitish material (egg sacs) present. Insects on twigs or leaves.	**Cottony cushion scale,** *Icerya purchasi.* Females brown, orange, red, or yellow.	Natural enemies can provide good control. Uncommon. See page 186.
Cottony cylindrical egg sacs, up to ⅓ inch long, on leaves. Foliage has sticky honeydew and blackish sooty mold. Foliage may yellow.	**Greenhouse orthezia,** *Orthezia insignis.* Pale brown to dark green insect with two white rows on back and white bands along side.	Usually not a pest in California. Has about 2 generations per year. Controls for mealybugs or scales may be effective.
Plant has sticky honeydew and blackish sooty mold. Plant grows slowly. Foliage may yellow.	**Pyriform scale,** *Protopulvinaria pyriformis.* Triangular, ⅛ inch long, brown, yellow, or mottled red. May be small white egg sac. Common in Florida and southern California.	See Scales, page 186.
Leaves and blossoms chewed (edges notched).	**Black vine weevil,** *Otiorhynchus sulcatus;* **Cribrate weevil,** *O. cribricollis;* **Fuller rose beetle,** *Asynonychus godmani.* Rarely seen adults brown, black, to gray snout beetles that feed at night. Larvae whitish maggots that feed on roots.	See page 208.
Leaves chewed, may be tied together with silk.	**Leafrollers,** including Orange tortrix, Fruittree leafroller, Omnivorous looper.	See page 203.
Foliage, buds, and stems chewed. Young plants clipped at base. Stocky moths present attracted to lights at night, wings folded at rest.	**Variegated cutworm,** *Peridroma saucia.* Gray or brown larva with dark markings, row of yellow dots on back. Hides in soil during day.	Exclude moths, which fly to lights at night. Apply *Bacillus thuringiensis* to young larvae. Insecticide bait kills larvae. See page 203.

GERANIUM (*Pelargonium* spp.)

What the problem looks like	Probable cause	Comments
Leaves, stems, and petioles have yellow to brown spots up to ¼ inch in diameter. Spots become larger, dark, angular blotches or wedges and may have yellow margins. Leaves and stem may wilt and die. Stem vascular tissue and roots may be black but not rotted.	**Bacterial leaf spot and blight,** *Xanthomonas campestris* pv. *pelargonii.* Spreads by splashing water, infected stock, debris, and equipment. Favored by 70° to 80°F, moist conditions, and rapid growth, such as from excess nitrogen. Affects only geranium; often the most important disease of geranium.	Use only culture-indexed stock. Pasteurize media before planting. Inspect and isolate new plants and cuttings, as symptoms may not appear immediately. Avoid overhead water. Regularly inspect and rogue plants infected and those nearby. Use good sanitation. 'Hardy' and 'Regal' geraniums are less susceptible, but can be a source of inoculum infecting ivy and zonal geraniums. See pages 107, 118.
Leaves have black, brown, or dark green spots or wedges, may have yellow borders. Spots may be sunken and dry. Foliage may wilt and die.	**Bacterial leaf spot,** *Pseudomonas cichorii.* Spreads by splashing water and contaminated equipment. Favored by wet, humid conditions.	Use only pathogen-free stock. Rogue infected plants immediately. Avoid wetting foliage. Use drip irrigation. Use raised benches. Copper bactericides help prevent disease. See page 107.
Dark red or brown spots, mostly on older leaves. Spots may have red or yellowish margins and distinct borders. Foliage may darken, shrivel, and drop. Only on 'Martha Washington' cultivar.	**Alternaria leaf spot,** *Alternaria alternata.* Spread by air or splashing water. Favored by prolonged, cool, wet, conditions. Persists in plant debris.	Avoid wetting foliage. Use drip irrigation and raised benches. Use good sanitation; promptly remove and dispose of debris and infected leaves. See pages 116–118.
Leaves and stems have yellow to dark spots or concentric rings, up to ½ inch in diameter, that may merge into larger blotches. Reddish brown pustules, mostly on underside of leaves. Leaves yellow and drop. Affects only *P. hortorum.*	**Geranium rust,** *Puccinia pelargonii-zonalis.* Spreads by air and splashing water. Spores germinate at about 60° to 70°F. Favored by wet conditions. Can spread rapidly, but plant usually survives.	Plant only uninfected stock. Avoid overhead watering. Don't crowd plants. Use good sanitation. Rogue or treat plants before sporulation. See Rusts, page 119.
Flowers, leaves, or stems have soft brown spots or decay; may yellow and wilt. Dead tissue may have woolly gray growths.	**Gray mold,** *Botrytis cinerea.* Fungus develops in crop debris or inactive tissue. Favored by high humidity and 70° to 77°F. Spores airborne.	Use good sanitation. Avoid overhead irrigation. Keep humidity low. Provide good air circulation. Don't crowd plants. See page 108.

What the problem looks like	Probable cause	Comments

GERANIUM (*Pelargonium* spp.) (continued)

What the problem looks like	Probable cause	Comments
Leaves yellow, brown, and wilt, often on only one side of plant. Growth stunted. Plant may die.	**Verticillium wilt,** *Verticillium dahliae, V. albo-atrum.* Persist in soil for years.	Use only culture-indexed stock. Pasteurize media before planting. See pages 104–106.
Leaves yellow, wilt, and die. Stems may soften and blacken near soil. Roots or basal stems black and decayed. Plant dies.	**Blackleg, Root and stem rot,** *Pythium, Phytophthora, Rhizoctonia* spp. Favored by wet soil and poor drainage.	Plant pathogen-free stock in pasteurized media. Provide good drainage. Avoid overirrigation. See pages 93–98.
Foliage yellows and wilts. Plants grow slowly and die. Roots dark black and rotted. Stems below ground may develop dark cracks.	**Black root rot,** *Thielaviopsis basicola.* Spreads in water, media, and by infected plants. Fungus persists in infected media. Favored by cool, wet conditions.	Pasteurize media before planting. Avoid overwatering and splashing water. Provide good drainage. Allow soil to dry between watering. Rogue infected plants. Avoid high salts and high pH. See pages 95–99.
Leaves discolor, wilt, stunt, or drop prematurely. Stems discolored, cankered, and die.	**Armillaria root rot,** *Armillaria mellea.* Present in many soils. Favored by warm, wet soil. Persists for years in infected roots.	Remove woody roots ½ inch diameter or larger before planting. Pasteurize or air-dry soil well or avoid growing in fields previously planted with oaks or other susceptible woody plants. See page 99.
Stem has spherical galls, usually near plant base. Heavily infected plants become stunted.	**Crown gall,** *Agrobacterium tumefaciens.* Spreads in soil and survives in soil for many years. Has wide host range.	Propagate from and plant disease-free plants. Avoid wounding plants, especially when wet. Dip or spray cuttings with *Agrobacterium tumefaciens* K-84 immediately after any wounding. See page 102.
Shoots short, swollen, flattened, or distorted. Secondary rot may infect shoot clumps, killing plant. Plants lack vigor.	**Fasciation,** cause often uncertain. May be viral, bacterial (e.g., *Rhodococcus fascians*), or genetic. Manage as bacterial and take additional measures.	Use pathogen-free stock. Avoid injuring base of plants, especially when wet. Keep base of plants dry. Dispose of infected plants. See page 121.
Leaves have chlorotic to black spots, rings, mottling, lines, or vein clearing. Leaves may curl. Plants stunted. Reduced flowering. Flowers may discolor, streak, or distort.	**Virus,** including Cucumber mosaic, Curly top, Impatiens necrotic spot, Pelargonium flower break, Tobacco mosaic, Tobacco ringspot, and Tomato spotted wilt viruses.	Use culture-indexed stock. Rogue infected plants. See page 121.
Leaves yellowish. Leaves have dark green or brown, vein-limited, angular blotches that develop progressively up from older leaves.	**Foliar nematodes,** *Aphelenchoides fragariae.* Tiny roundworms spread in plant debris, vegetative propagation, and splashing water. Not common in California.	Use uninfected stock plants. Remove plant debris. Avoid overhead irrigation; leaves must be wet for infection to occur. See page 265.
Leaf underside may have pimplelike blisters or water-soaked spots. Leaves brown, harden, appear corky, especially on underside. Foliage yellows, drops.	**Edema** or **Oedema.** Noninfectious disease. Leaves accumulate excess water when soil is warm and moist and air is cool and moist. Exact cause unknown. Common problem on ivy geranium.	Irrigate only in morning. Avoid irrigation if cool and cloudy. Provide good air circulation Keep humidity low. Provide good drainage. Low media pH or high levels of nitrogen may help to prevent. See page 41.
Leaves have scattered brown flecks. Foliage yellow, margins necrotic.	**Iron** or **Manganese toxicity.** Noninfectious disorder.	Provide acidic media. Fertilize appropriately. Use good quality water. See pages 56–59.
Foliage yellows or browns; may discolor more along margins or between veins.	**Yellowing.** Caused by excess heat and/or high light.	Provide good growing conditions; cool or shade plants. Grow heat-tolerant cultivars in hot areas.
Petals drop prematurely.	**Petal shatter.** Caused by excess ethylene, poor air quality, prolonged storage or shipping, and late harvest or shipping. Petal drop tendency may be inherent to certain varieties.	Provide good ventilation. Remove decaying plant debris. Lower temperatures around flowering. Ship before full flowering. Consider using a preservative containing an antiethylene agent. See page 67.
New growth dark and distorted. Buds deformed, black, and discolored, and may drop. Plants severely stunted.	**Cyclamen mite,** *Phytonemus pallidus.* A pinkish orange mite (family Tarsonemidae), ⅟₁₀₀ inch long or smaller.	See page 217.

What the problem looks like	Probable cause	Comments
Flowers, terminals, or foliage chewed. Leaves may be webbed with silk. Flower buds may be mined. Few blossoms. Black frass or excrement from caterpillars. Young plants may be clipped at base from cutworm larvae hiding in soil during day.	**Caterpillars,** including Beet armyworm, *Spodoptera exigua;* Cabbage looper, *Trichoplusia ni;* Geranium or Tobacco budworm, *Helicoverpa virescens;* Bollworm, *H. zea;* Obliquebanded leafroller, *Archips* or *Choristoneura rosaceana;* Omnivorous leaftier, *Cnephasia longana;* Variegated cutworm, *Peridroma saucia.* Greenish to brownish larvae, 1 to 1½ inches long at maturity, may have longitudinal stripes.	Exclude moths, which fly to lights at night. Apply *Bacillus thuringiensis* to young larvae. Insecticide bait kills cutworm caterpillars. Ivy geranium, *P. peltatum,* is resistant to *H. virescens* in comparison with susceptible standard types (*P. hortorum*). See page 203.
Buds or terminal leaves chewed. Stems may be mined. Black frass on leaves.	**Geranium plume moth,** *Platyptilia* or *Amblyptilia pica.* Adults narrow-winged, tan to black and white; adults and caterpillars up to 1 inch long.	Exclude moths from growing area. Use good sanitation; remove infested plants. Apply *Bacillus thuringiensis* to young larvae.
Leaves and blossoms chewed (edges notched).	**Fuller rose beetle,** *Asynonychus godmani.* Rarely seen brownish adults feed at night. Whitish maggots (larvae) live in soil, feed on roots.	See page 208.
Foliage has sticky honeydew, blackish sooty mold, and whitish cast skins. Foliage may curl or yellow.	**Aphids,** including *Aphis gossypii, Myzus persicae, Macrosiphum* spp. Small pear-shaped insects, often green, yellowish, or blackish.	See page 179.
Foliage has sticky honeydew and blackish sooty mold. Copious white waxy material present with certain species. Leaves may yellow and wither. Tiny, whitish, mothlike adult insects.	**Bandedwinged whitefly,** *Trialeurodes abutilonea;* **Giant whitefly,** *Aleurodicus dugesii;* **Greenhouse whitefly,** *Trialeurodes vaporariorum;* **Sweetpotato whitefly,** *Bemisia tabaci.* Oval, flattened, yellow to greenish nymphs.	See Whiteflies, page 170.
Plant has sticky honeydew, blackish sooty mold, and elongated, whitish material (egg sacs). Insects on twigs or leaves.	**Cottony cushion scale,** *Icerya purchasi.* Brown, orange, red, or yellow females live on twigs or leaves.	Natural enemies can provide good control. Uncommon. See page 186.
Foliage has cottony material; sometimes around crown or on roots. Foliage has sticky honeydew and blackish sooty mold. Foliage may yellow.	**Citrus mealybug,** *Planococcus citri;* **Mexican mealybug,** *Phenacoccus gossypii.* Oval, powdery female with short filaments produces long white egg sac.	See Mealybugs, page 183.
Foliage discolored, stippled, bleached, or reddened, and may drop. Plant may have fine webbing.	**Twospotted spider mite,** *Tetranychus urticae.* Tiny greenish or yellowish mites with 2 darker spots.	See page 213.
Petals or leaves have irregular silver, white, or brown streaks or blotches. Blossoms or terminals may distort. Growth may be stunted.	**Western flower thrips,** *Frankliniella occidentalis.* Slender dark brown to yellowish insects, ⅟16 inch long or less.	See page 161.

GERBERA (*Gerbera jamesonii*), Barberton daisy, Gerbera daisy, Transvaal daisy

Plant wilts and dies. Basal stem rotted. Black sclerotia in and on stems. Cottony mycelia in and on stems if conditions are moist.	**Cottony rot,** *Sclerotinia sclerotiorum.* Fungus survives in media as sclerotia. Favored by overhead irrigation and high humidity. Many hosts.	Solarize or otherwise pasteurize media before planting. Avoid overhead irrigation. Irrigate early in day so plants dry quickly. Consider fungicide application to base and lower foliage of plants. See page 101.
Foliage yellows and wilts. Plants grow slowly and die. Roots dark black and rotted.	**Black root rot,** *Thielaviopsis basicola.* Spreads in water, media, and by infected plants. Fungus persists in media. Favored by cool, wet conditions.	Pasteurize media before planting. Avoid overwatering and splashing water. Provide good drainage. Allow soil to dry between watering. Rogue infected plants. Avoid high salts and high pH. See pages 95–99.
Foliage wilted and yellow, often on only one side of plant. Plants grow slowly. Crown and roots appear healthy, unlike with *Thielaviopsis.*	**Verticillium wilt,** *Verticillium dahliae.* Persists in media. Many hosts. Fungus invades plants during cool weather, plugging water-conducting tissue, causing symptoms when plant is water stressed, usually in early summer.	Pasteurize media before planting. Provide appropriate irrigation. See pages 104–106.
Leaves may turn yellowish or darken. Plant may wilt and die. Stem around soil and roots rotted.	**Root, Crown, and Stem rots,** *Phytophthora, Pythium* spp., *Rhizoctonia solani.* Fungi promoted by wet, poorly drained soil.	See pages 93–98.
Flowers, flower heads, or lower leaves have soft brown rotted spots or blotches. Terminals decay. Dead tissue may have woolly gray growth (spores).	**Gray mold,** *Botrytis cinerea.* Fungus develops in crop debris or inactive tissue. Favored by high humidity and 70° to 77°F. Spores airborne.	Use good sanitation. Avoid overhead irrigation. Keep humidity low. Provide good air circulation. Don't crowd plants. See page 108.

What the problem looks like	Probable cause	Comments
GERBERA (*Gerbera jamesonii*), Barberton daisy, Gerbera daisy, Transvaal daisy (continued)		
Leaf underside has pale spots or white or pink pustules.	**White rust,** *Albugo tragopogonis.* Airborne spores spread only from living tissue. Plant must be wet for infection. Not established in the United States; if suspected, report to agriculture officials.	Plant only pathogen-free stock. Inspect new plants. Quarantined disease; by regulation infected plants in U.S. must be destroyed.
Brown to yellow spots or blotches, mostly on older leaves. Spots may have dark or yellowish margins. Foliage may shrivel, drop.	**Leaf spots,** including *Alternaria gerberae, Ascochyta gerberae.* Spread by air or splashing water. Favored by prolonged wet conditions. Persist in plant debris.	Avoid wetting foliage. Use drip irrigation and raised benches. Use good sanitation; promptly remove and dispose of debris and infected leaves. See pages 116–118.
Leaves have brown to tan spots or blotches. Discoloring may follow leaf veins. Leaves may wilt and die.	**Bacterial leaf spot and blight,** *Pseudomonas cichorii.* Spreads by air and splashing water.	Avoid overhead irrigation. Don't overwater. Don't crowd plants. Use good sanitation. See page 107.
Yellow spots or lesions, then white, powdery growth, primarily on older leaves and stem. Leaves may dry and die.	**Powdery mildew,** *Erysiphe cichoracearum.* Free water not required for infection. A common problem.	Provide good air circulation and adequate light. Consider applying fungicide to prevent. See page 112.
Leaves have yellow to brown spots, blotches, or streaks. Foliage may die. Plant may be distorted and stunted.	**Tomato spotted wilt virus.** Spread by thrips. Has may crop and weed hosts.	Rogue infected plants. Exclude and control thrips. See page 121.
New foliage yellow, except for green veins. Leaves may be stunted.	**Iron deficiency.** Noninfectious disorder. Nutrient deficiency or pH problem.	See pages 56–59.
Leaves stunted, distorted, often swollen and thickened near base. Leaf centers and margins have yellow to brown swellings. May have discolored spots or blotches where stem joins roots, which may rot.	**Stem and bulb nematode,** *Ditylenchus dipsaci.* Nematodes survive in infected basel stems and field debris for about 3 years. Also spread by infected water and equipment. Optimal temperature for infection and reproduction is 50° to 69°F.	Rogue infected plants and surrounding plants from field. Clean equipment well after working in diseased fields. See page 265.
Foliage discolored, stippled, or bleached, and may drop. Terminals may distort. May be fine webbing.	**Privet mite,** *Brevipalpus obovatus;* **Twospotted spider mite,** *Tetranychus urticae.* Greenish, yellowish, or red, tiny, may have 2 dark spots.	See page 213.
Foliage bleached, brittle; edges may be curled or ragged. Blossoms distort or discolor. Plant grows slowly.	**Broad mite,** *Polyphagotarsonemus latus.* Translucent to dark green, 1/100 inch long or smaller.	See page 217.
Petals streaked. Flower buds drop prematurely or are deformed. Fewer, distorted, or discolored flowers.	**Mold or Pollen mite,** *Tyrophagus putrescentiae.* Whitish mite (family Acaridae), about 1/50 inch long, feeds in buds under pollen cap. Mites associated with damage but not confirmed as cause.	See Mites, page 213.
New growth dark and distorted. Buds deformed, black and discolored, and may drop. Plants severely stunted.	**Cyclamen mite,** *Phytonemus pallidus.* A pinkish orange mite (family Tarsonemidae), 1/100 inch long or smaller.	See page 217.
Petals have irregular white or brown streaks or blotches. Leaves may turn brown. Blossoms or terminals may be distorted. Growth may be stunted.	**Western flower thrips,** *Frankliniella occidentalis.* Slender dark brown to yellowish insects, 1/16 inch long or less.	See page 161.
Foliage has sticky honeydew and blackish sooty mold. Leaves yellow and wither. Tiny, whitish, mothlike adult insects.	**Greenhouse whitefly,** *Trialeurodes vaporariorum;* **Silverleaf whitefly,** *Bemisia argentifolii;* **Sweetpotato whitefly,** *Bemisia tabaci.* Yellowish, oval, flattened nymphs and pupae.	See Whiteflies, page 170.
Foliage has sticky honeydew, blackish sooty mold, and whitish cast skins. Foliage may curl or yellow.	**Aphids.** Small pear-shaped insects, often green, yellowish, or blackish.	See page 179.
Leaves have winding tunnels or blotches. Heavily infested leaves may drop. Leaves have pale spots or punctures from adult flies. Yellowish to white maggots in mines.	**Leafminers,** including Serpentine leafminer, *Liriomyza trifolii.* Adults are tiny, active, black flies with yellow. Major problem in production.	See page 167.

What the problem looks like	Probable cause	Comments
GLADIOLUS (*Gladiolus* spp.)		
Leaves yellow progressively, often beginning on one side of the plant. Leaves may turn downward and die. Florets distorted. Brownish to black rot of corms in ground or storage, begins in core and basal plate then extends upward through vascular strands into leaf bases.	**Fusarium yellows,** *Fusarium oxysporum* f. sp. *gladioli.* Occurs in diseased underground stems (corms) and persists for years in infested soil. Cultivars vary in susceptibility. Infection without obvious symptoms is common. Favored by wet soil above 70°F. Disease may be less severe if soil pH is 6.6 to 7 and 80–90% of nitrogen is in nitrate form.	Pasteurize soil before planting, grow where infestation has not occurred, or rotate out of gladiolus for 4 years after any infestation. Use resistant cultivars or pathogen-free corms. Rogue infected plants. Dig and handle corms carefully to avoid injuring them. Treat with hot water and cure corms immediately after digging to eliminate fungus. See page 104.
Leaves yellow and die. Plants stunted, fail to bloom. Leaf sheaths rot near soil; rotted tissue appears shredded. Many very small black sclerotia imbedded in dead tissue. Corm lesions are dark brown and sunken with raised margins.	**Dry rot,** *Stromatinia gladioli.* Attacks and survives in corms stored or in soil. Persists in infested soil for 10 or more years. Favored by cool, wet soil or humid storage.	Pasteurize or treat soil before planting. Don't grow in infested soil during cool weather. Use pathogen-free corms or treat with hot water and cure corms to eliminate fungus from stock. Provide good soil drainage. Store at low humidity.
Foliage yellowing, especially outer leaves. Soft rot of basal stem or roots. White mycelia and small, tan to reddish brown sclerotia may develop on infected tissue around soil.	**Southern wilt,** *Sclerotium rolfsii.* Sclerotia survive in soil. Disease favored by moist, poorly drained, 77° to 95°F soil. Many hosts.	Avoid planting in infested soil, or pasteurize soil before planting. Avoid excess irrigation. Consider fungicide drench to infected soil. See page 101.
Corms don't produce or foliage yellows and wilts. Firm brown rot on stored corms; if moist, greenish blue mass (spores) develops over rotted tissue.	**Penicillium corm rot,** *Penicillium gladioli.* Occurs on corms and gladiolus debris in storage. Rot develops rapidly in high humidity.	Dig and handle corms carefully to avoid damage. Store corms under low humidity. Destroy infected corms or treat with hot water and cure corms to eliminate disease from stock.
Leaves have tiny pale to brownish spots or larger blotches. Petals have brown water-soaked spots. Infections may penetrate from basal stem to corm. Corms may continue to decay in cold storage. Decayed tissue may have woolly gray spores. Corms and roots have black, seedlike sclerotia.	**Botrytis disease** or **Neck rot,** *Botrytis gladiolorum, B. cinerea.* Occur on corms and gladiolus debris. Spores are airborne. Favored by moist conditions and 50° to 70°F. Especially severe in coastal California, where fungicide applications are probably necessary to prevent disease.	Treat with hot water and cure corms immediately after harvest to eliminate fungus from stock. Consider applying fungicide to foliage and treat flower spikes after harvest before packing. Incorporate deeply or remove and dispose of old plants and plant debris. See pages 93–96, 108.
Stem below ground and husks appear shredded. Brown mycelia on infected tissue visible with a hand lens.	**Rhizoctonia neck rot,** *Rhizoctonia solani.* Common soilborne fungus with many hosts. Favored by warm, wet conditions.	Provide good soil drainage. Plant in raised beds. Avoid excess irrigation. Fungicide sprays or dipping corms can control. See pages 93–98.
Corms have brown to black, irregular or round, sunken spots with shiny brittle, varnishlike bacterial exudate on surface. Leaf bases have red or brown specks.	**Scab,** *Pseudomonas gladioli.* Occurs on corms. Persists in soil refuse for 2 years. Favored by poorly drained, wet, warm soils. Heavy nitrogen fertilization encourages.	Rotate planting site at least every 3 years. Provide good soil drainage. Don't overirrigate or overfertilize. Control chewing insects in soil that injure corms.
Leaves, stems, or petals have tan to brown spots. Leaves may yellow. Corms may rot, especially in cormel stock. Flower stalks may rot.	**Curvularia leaf spot,** *Curvularia lunata, C. trifolii.* Persist in soil several years. Attack young leaves when warm and wet or humid.	Pasteurize media before planting. Use good sanitation. Avoid overhead irrigation.
Leaves have yellowish, circular to irregular spots. Leaves later turn brown, dry, and die.	**Smut,** *Urocystis gladiolicola.* Occurs in plant debris. Favored by wet weather. Rare in California.	Avoid overhead irrigation. Use good sanitation. Fungicide application may help to prevent.
Green tissue has small round or angular yellow spots with red dot in center (some cultivars develop large spots).	**Stemphylium leaf spot,** *Stemphylium* spp. Persist in gladiolus foliage and refuse. Favored by warm, wet conditions, especially by sprinklers and rain.	Don't use overhead irrigation. Remove and dispose of gladiolus refuse, plow refuse under, or rotate plantings so gladiolus are not grown in same spot 2 years in a row. Fungicides can prevent.
Leaves have sunken, irregular blotches. Spots may be angular, because fungus is vein-limited.	**Septoria leaf spot,** *Septoria gladioli.* Uncommon on gladiolus in California.	Avoid overhead irrigation. Rogue infected plants. See pages 116–118.
Many thin, weak, yellowish leaves; flower spikes distorted and blossoms may remain green, all from corms infected the previous season. Corms mature early and are small. Roots stunted from current-season infection.	**Aster yellows, Grassy top.** Phytoplasma spread by leafhoppers. Has many alternate hosts.	Rogue infected plants. Control nearby weeds and leafhoppers. See pages 129–130.
Leaves have yellow or whitish ring patterns and blotches.	**Tobacco ringspot virus.** Spread by nematodes and mechanically in tools.	Pasteurize soil before planting. Rogue infected plants. Control nematodes.

What the problem looks like	Probable cause	Comments
GLADIOLUS (*Gladiolus* spp.) (continued)		
Petals have white or pale blotches, streaks, or flecks. Leaves may have faint yellow streaking. Common in most gladiolus cultivars.	**Bean yellow mosaic virus** or **Mild mosaic**. Spread by aphids and mechanically by tools. Legume hosts include bean, peas, and vetch.	Plant only pathogen-free stock grown in isolated area. Plant away from legume alternate hosts. Control aphids. See page 121.
Leaves have white streaking or flecking. Petals have white blotches or color break. Flowers sometimes fail to open.	**White break,** Cucumber mosaic virus. Spread by aphids and mechanically by tools. Cucurbit hosts include melons, cucumber, and squash.	Plant away from cucurbit alternate hosts. Rogue infected plants at flowering time or as soon as symptoms appear. Control aphids. See page 121.
Flowers have white blotches. Flowers open poorly and may shrivel.	**White break**. Spread in infected corms. Other possible vector(s) and specific microorganism unknown.	Propagate from pathogen-free plants grown in isolated area. Rogue infected plants at flowering time or as soon as symptoms appear.
Leaves have yellow to brown spots, blotches, or streaks. Foliage may die. Plant may be distorted and stunted.	**Gladiolus mosaic virus** (vector unknown); **Tomato spotted wilt virus** (spread by thrips, has may crop and weed hosts).	Eliminate nearby weeds. Exclude or control thrips. Rogue infected plants. See page 121.
Plants stunted and produce short spikes.	**Stunt**. Viruslike cause unknown.	If a problem, avoid commonly infected cultivars: 'Chamouny,' 'Spic and Span,' 'Elizabeth the Queen.'
Foliage yellows or wilts. Feeder and fleshy roots have knots or swellings.	**Root knot nematode,** *Meloidogyne* spp. Tiny roundworms that prefer warm, sandy soil. Many hosts.	Pasteurize, treat soil before planting, or plant only nonhosts at that site. Treat corms with hot water before planting. Rogue infected plants. See page 265.
Bulbs discolored, brownish red, rotted; infested with tiny, oval, white to brownish mites.	**Bulb mites,** *Rhizoglyphus* spp. Sluggish mites may look like tiny eggs. Feed mostly on bulbs but may also be on stems and leaves. Secondary pests that prefer decayed tissue but may help fungi infect plants.	See page 218.
Petals streaked. Flower buds drop prematurely or are deformed. Fewer, distorted, or discolored flowers.	**Mold or Pollen mite,** *Tyrophagus putrescentiae*. Whitish mite (family Acaridae), about $\frac{1}{50}$ inch long mite. Feeds under pollen cap. May infest corms in storage. Mites associated with damage but not confirmed as cause of damage.	See Mites, page 213.
Shoots or blossoms blackened, dwarfed, discolored, or distorted. Leaf tips may wilt and die.	**Plant bugs,** *Lygus* spp. Brown, green, or yellowish bugs, up to $\frac{1}{4}$ inch long that suck plant juices.	Control nearby weeds, from which bugs move. Exclude bugs from growing area. See True Bugs, page 194.
Foliage has sticky honeydew and blackish sooty mold. Copious white waxy material present with certain species. Leaves may yellow and wither. Tiny, whitish, mothlike adult insects.	**Giant whitefly,** *Aleurodicus dugesii*; **Greenhouse whitefly,** *Trialeurodes vaporariorum*; **Iris whitefly,** *Aleyrodes spiraeoides*. Flattened, oval, translucent to yellowish nymphs and pupae.	See Whiteflies, page 170.
Plant has sticky honeydew, blackish sooty mold, and cottony waxy material.	**Obscure mealybug,** *Pseudococcus affinis*. Grayish, oval, waxy, slow-moving insects with marginal filaments.	See Mealybugs, page 183.
May grow poorly from corms and produce stunted plants. Young shoots distorted. Aphids present under leaf sheaths and on stems near soil and under outer scales of corms stored or in the field.	**Tulip bulb aphid,** *Dysaphis tulipae*. Small pear-shaped yellow, pink, gray, or green, waxy insects. Easily overlooked; usually causes direct damage only to stored corms.	Vectors viral disease in lily and tulip. Other hosts include iris and freesia. See page 182.
Blossoms have discolored blotches or streaks. Leaves, stems, and flower spikes bleached, brownish, spotted, withered, or distorted. Buds turn brown and die. Stored corms have sticky, scabby areas.	**Gladiolus thrips,** *Thrips simplex*. Slender, dark brown to shiny black adults with gray to whitish band at wing base. Nymphs and pupae yellow to orange. Feed hidden within leaf or bud sheaths, usually in groups. Overwinter and develop on stored corms.	Plant only thrips-free corms. Storing corms at 35° to 40°F for at least 4 months kills thrips but don't freeze corms. Heat treatment as for disease may provide control. See Thrips, page 161.
Blossoms have discolored blotches or streaks. Foliage stippled, bleached, or blotched; has varnishlike excrement.	**Banded greenhouse thrips,** *Hercinothrips femoralis*; **Western flower thrips,** *Frankliniella occidentalis*. Tiny, slender, dark brown to yellowish adults. Nymphs and pupae whitish to pale yellow.	See Thrips, page 161.
Foliage discolored, stippled, or bleached, and may drop. Terminals may distort. Plant may have fine webbing.	**Spider mites**. Tiny greenish, reddish, or yellowish mites; may have 2 dark spots.	See page 213.

What the problem looks like	Probable cause	Comments
Foliage yellows. Plant declines or dies back. Bark has gray, brown, or tan encrustations.	**Latania scale,** *Hemiberlesia lataniae.* Circular to flattened insects, less than $\frac{1}{16}$ inch long.	See page 186.
Buds, flowers, and foliage chewed. Yellowish or greenish caterpillars, with darker, longitudinal stripes.	**Corn earworm,** *Heliothis* or *Helicoverpa zea.* Tan to brownish moths (family Noctuidae) with darker bands on wings. Larva and nocturnal adult up to $1\frac{1}{2}$ inch long.	See page 203.
Flowers, terminals, or foliage chewed. Leaves may be webbed with silk. Flower buds may be mined.	**Armyworms,** *Spodoptera* spp.; **Cabbage looper,** *Trichoplusia ni;* **Omnivorous leaftier,** *Cnephasia longana.* Gray, brownish, or greenish larvae, $\frac{1}{2}$ to $1\frac{1}{2}$ inches long when mature.	Exclude nocturnal moths from growing areas. Avoid growing near other major hosts. *Bacillus thuringiensis* kills exposed-feeding larvae. See page 203.

GLOXINIA *(Sinningia speciosa)*

Plants stunted. Foliage may yellow. Root system reduced, small roots rotted.	**Root rot,** *Pythium* spp. Persist in media. Spread by spores in media and water. Favored by excess moisture and poor drainage.	Provide good drainage. Avoid excess irrigation. See pages 93–96.
Foliage yellows or turns brown. Leaves or entire plant may wilt and die. Crown tissue and roots discolored, soft, wet, decayed. Foliar symptoms similar to TSWV.	**Root, crown, and stem rots,** *Phytophthora cryptogea, P. nicotianae.* Fungi persist in media. Favored by wet conditions.	Pasteurize media before planting. Provide good drainage. Don't moisture-stress or overwater plants. See pages 93–97.
Tubers or stems near soil infected with sunken, dark lesions that are dry first then become a soft and wet decay.	**Crown and tuber rot,** *Rhizoctonia solani.* Fungus persists in media. Favored by warm, wet conditions.	Pasteurize media before planting. Avoid deep planting. Consider basal fungicide spray before or after planting. See pages 93–98.
Brown to black water-soaked spots or decay on stems near soil or on leaves. Tissue may have tiny, black to dark green, spore-forming structures and white mycelia.	**Myrothecium rot** or **Crown rot,** *Myrothecium roridum.* Spreads by waterborne spores. Infects through wounds. Favored by 70° to 81°F and excess nitrogen.	Minimize plant wounds. Keep foliage dry. Use good sanitation. Avoid excess fertilization. Growing plants above 86°F may arrest or prevent disease.
Plants wilt and collapse. Basal stem, roots, or tubers rotted. Rotted tissue and soil may have white cottony fungus growth and tan or brown sclerotia (about $\frac{1}{16}$ inch diameter).	**Southern blight,** *Sclerotium rolfsii.* Sclerotia persist in media, germinate there, and infect susceptible plants. No airborne spores are formed. Many hosts.	Pasteurize potentially infected media before planting. Fungicide applied at base of plants may help to prevent. See page 101.
Flowers or flower head have soft brown decay. Lower leaves and growing points may decay. Dead tissue has woolly gray growth (spores).	**Gray mold,** *Botrytis cinerea.* Fungus develops in crop debris or inactive tissue. Favored by high humidity and 70° to 77°F. Spores airborne.	Use good sanitation. Avoid overhead irrigation. Keep humidity low. Provide good air circulation. Don't crowd plants. See page 108.
Petals discolor and wilt; may be covered with cottony growth. Stems may become bleached, white, and girdled.	**Cottony rot** and **Flower blight,** *Sclerotinia sclerotiorum.* Airborne spores from soil. Favored by wet conditions. Infects only flowers.	Avoid overhead irrigation. Irrigate early in day so plants dry quickly. Remove and dispose of plant debris around growing area. See page 101.
Brown to tan blotches, rings, or streaks on leaves. Young plants may die. Plant distorted, stunted. Necrotic stems. Symptoms similar to *Phytophthora.*	**Impatiens necrotic spot virus, Tomato spotted wilt virus.** Spread by thrips. Have many crop and weed hosts.	Use only virus-free plants. Exclude and control thrips. See page 121.
Leaves yellow, brown, or become necrotic. Discoloring often vein-limited, then progresses to entire leaf, often beginning with older leaves.	**Foliar nematodes,** *Aphelenchoides* spp. Tiny roundworms spread in plant debris, vegetative propagation, and splashing water. Not common in California.	Use uninfected stock plants. Remove plant debris. Avoid overhead irrigation; leaves must be wet for infection to occur. See page 265.
Plant has sticky honeydew, blackish sooty mold, and cottony waxy material.	**Citrus mealybug,** *Planococcus citri;* **Obscure mealybug,** *Pseudococcus affinis.* Grayish, oval, waxy, slow-moving insects with marginal filaments.	See Mealybugs, page 183.
Foliage has sticky honeydew and blackish sooty mold. Leaves may yellow and wither. Tiny, whitish, mothlike adult insects.	**Greenhouse whitefly,** *Trialeurodes vaporariorum.* Yellowish, oval, flattened nymphs and pupae.	See page 170.
Foliage has sticky honeydew, blackish sooty mold, and whitish cast skins. Foliage may yellow. Foliage or flowers may distort.	**Aphids,** including Green peach aphid, *Myzus persicae.* Small pear-shaped insects, often green, yellowish, or blackish.	See page 179.
Flowers silvery or with bleached streaks. Blossoms distorted, color broken or streaked. Leaves or terminals may be distorted.	**Western flower thrips,** *Frankliniella occidentalis;* **Chrysanthemum thrips,** *Thrips nigropilosus.* Tiny slender dark brown to yellowish insects. *T. nigropilosus* has X-shaped flecks on front part of body, *F. occidentalis* does not.	See page 161.

What the problem looks like	Probable cause	Comments

GLOXINIA (*Sinningia speciosa*) (continued)

What the problem looks like	Probable cause	Comments
Foliage reddish brown and hardened, especially in center of leaves. Plants severely stunted. Leaf terminals distorted. Buds deformed, discolored, and may drop.	**Cyclamen mite**, *Phytonemus pallidus*. A pinkish orange mite (family Tarsonemidae), $1/100$ inch long or smaller.	See page 217.
Flowers, terminals, or foliage chewed. Leaves may be webbed with silk. Flower buds may be mined.	**Beet armyworm**, *Spodoptera exigua*; **Western yellowstriped armyworm**, *S. praefica*; **Cabbage looper**, *Trichoplusia ni*. Greenish larvae, up to $1\frac{1}{2}$ inches long, with light, longitudinal stripes. S. *praefica* larvae are black on top, reddish below, with yellow stripes.	Exclude moths from growing areas. Avoid growing near other major hosts. *Bacillus thuringiensis* kills larvae. See page 203.
Leaves and blossoms chewed (edges notched).	**Black vine weevil**, *Otiorhynchus sulcatus*. Rarely seen adults brown, black, to gray snout beetles that feed at night. Larvae whitish maggots that feed on roots.	See page 208.

GODETIA (*Clarkia, Godetia* spp.)

What the problem looks like	Probable cause	Comments
Leaves turn yellow or brown. Plants wilt, often suddenly. Roots and stems brown or blackish, decayed. Seedlings may wilt and die.	**Root and stem rot**, *Phytophthora*, *Pythium* spp. Fungi persist in soil. Favored by wet, poorly drained soil.	Pasteurize soil before planting. Don't overirrigate. Provide good drainage; plant in raised beds. See pages 93–97.
Leaves yellow and wilt, usually beginning with basal leaves. Plants stunted. Basal stems decayed. Vascular tissue brownish.	**Wilt, Stem rot**, *Fusarium* sp. Fungus persists in soil for years. A problem during warm weather.	Pasteurize soil before planting. See pages 93–96.
Foliage wilted and yellow, often on only one side of plant. Crown and roots appear healthy, unlike with *Phytophthora*.	**Verticillium wilt**, *Verticillium albo-atrum*, *V. dahliae*. Soilborne fungi with wide host range. Fungi invade plants during cool weather, plugging water-conducting tissue, causing symptoms when plant is water-stressed, usually in early summer.	Use pathogen-free stock. Pasteurize soil before planting. Avoid planting sites that have grown susceptible weeds or crops, including chrysanthemum, nightshade, strawberries, and tomato. See pages 104–106.
Leaves have purplish red to dark brown irregular, angular spots. Lower leaf surface covered with soft, fluffy fungal growth. Leaves yellow and drop.	**Downy mildew**, *Peronospora arthurii*. Spores produced only on living plants. Fungus persists as resistant oospores when conditions are dry. Favored by moist, humid conditions.	Provide good air circulation. Avoid overhead watering. Consider applying fungicide to protect foliage. See page 115.
White, powdery growth, mostly on older leaves and stems. Foliage may dry and die.	**Powdery mildew**, *Erysiphe cichoracearum*. Free water not required for infection.	Provide good air circulation and adequate light. Don't crowd plants. Consider applying sulfur or other fungicide to prevent. See page 112.
Leaves have brown to orangish powdery pustules and yellowish spots. Leaves may yellow and drop.	**Rusts**, *Puccinia* spp. Fungi survive on living tissue. Spores are airborne. Favored by humid or wet conditions.	Avoid overhead irrigation. Water in morning. Provide good air circulation. Don't crowd plants. See page 119.
Leaves have yellow to brown blotches, spots, or streaks. Foliage may die. Plant may be distorted and stunted.	**Tomato spotted wilt virus**. Spread by thrips. Has may crop and weed hosts.	Rogue infected plants. Exclude or control thrips. See page 121.
Foliage chlorotic. Plant stunted. Spindly, upright yellow shoots and few or no flowers.	**Aster yellows phytoplasma**. Spread by leafhoppers. Not spread by seed, handling, aphids, or other insects. Many hosts.	Don't plant seed beds downwind from other hosts. Eliminate nearby weeds. Control leafhoppers. Rogue infected plants. See pages 129–130.
Leaves have pale green to light yellow blotches or spots, usually on upper surface of older foliage.	**Water spots**. Noninfectious disorder caused by sprinkling with cold water or rapid temperature change.	Avoid overhead irrigation, especially with cold water. Use drip irrigation. Prevent rapid temperature changes.
Plants fail to blossom. Leaves may turn dark green and stems may elongate.	**Flower failure**. Noninfectious disorder from insufficient light or improper cultural care.	Grow where well lit. Provide proper cultural care, especially appropriate irrigation.
Blossoms or leaves have irregular white or brown blotches or streaks. Blossoms or terminals may be distorted. Growth may be stunted.	**Thrips**. Slender dark brown to yellowish insects, $1/16$ inch long or less.	See page 161.
Foliage has sticky honeydew, blackish sooty mold, and/or whitish cast skins. Foliage may yellow.	**Aphids**. Tiny pear-shaped insects, often green, yellowish, or black.	See page 179.

What the problem looks like	Probable cause	Comments

GYPSOPHILA (*Gypsophila paniculata*), Baby's breath

What the problem looks like	Probable cause	Comments
Leaves wilt and turn light green. Entire plant may collapse and die. Crown tissue discolored, soft, wet, decayed. Secondary bacteria cause diseased tissue to putrefy.	**Root and crown rot,** *Phytophthora parasitica*, *Pythium* spp. Soilborne fungi present in many fields. Favored by 90°F and wet conditions.	Solarize or otherwise pasteurize soil before planting. Provide good drainage. Plant in raised beds. Don't moisture-stress or overwater plants. Soil drench with fungicide can help to prevent. See pages 93–97.
Soft, wet decay of seedlings and propagation plants. Leaves turn gray-green. Roots are rotted and plants are stunted in the field.	**Root rot,** *Pythium* spp. Fungi favored by poorly drained, wet soil. *P. aphanidermatum* favored when hot, *P. ultimum* favored by cooler temperatures.	Fungi present in many soils. Pasteurize soil before planting. Provide good drainage. Plant in raised beds. Don't overwater. See pages 93–96.
Stems infected at or just beneath soil. Sunken, dark lesions are dry first, then become a soft and wet decay.	**Stem rot,** *Rhizoctonia solani*. Fungus occurs in many soils. Favored by warm, wet conditions and deep planting.	Pasteurize soil before planting. Avoid deep planting. Consider basal fungicide spray after planting. See pages 93–98.
Cottony growth or large, black sclerotia inside stems. Stems become bleached, white, and girdled.	**Cottony rot,** *Sclerotinia sclerotiorum*. Persists in infested soil. Favored by wet conditions.	Avoid overhead irrigation. Irrigate early in day so plants dry quickly. Remove and dispose of plant debris around growing area. See page 101.
Foliage yellows or wilts. Feeder and fleshy roots have knots or swellings.	**Root knot nematode,** *Meloidogyne* sp. Tiny roundworms that prefer warm, sandy soil. Many hosts.	Pasteurize or treat soil before planting. Rogue affected plants. Plant nonhosts at that site. See page 265.
Shoots short, swollen, flattened, or distorted. Secondary rot may infect shoot clumps, killing plant. Plants lack vigor.	**Fasciation,** cause often uncertain. May be viral, bacterial (e.g., *Rhodococcus fascians*), or genetic. Manage as bacterial and take additional measures.	Use pathogen-free stock. Avoid injuring base of plants, especially when wet. Keep base of plants dry. Dispose of infected plants. See page 121.
Flowers, flower heads, lower leaves, or growing points have soft brown decay. Dead tissue may have woolly gray growth (spores).	**Flower blight,** *Alternaria* sp., *Botrytis cinerea*. Fungi develop in crop debris or inactive tissue. Favored by high humidity, splashing water. Spores airborne.	Use good sanitation. Avoid overhead irrigation. Provide good air circulation. Don't crowd plants. See pages 108, 116–118.
Basal stem has soft, rotted galls. Leaves or stems have brown or black streaks, spots, or lesions. Tissue may darken, soften, and decay. Plant may grow slowly, wilt, die.	**Bacteria streak,** *Erwinia herbicola*. Occurs in plant debris. Spread by infected equipment, hands, and plants. Favored by high humidity and 80° to 90°F.	Reduce humidity and improve air circulation; don't crowd plants. Use good sanitation; regularly inspect crop and immediately dispose of any infected plants. See pages 100, 107.
Stems and roots have growths or galls. Plants may grow slowly.	**Crown gall,** *Agrobacterium tumefaciens*, *A. gypsophilae*. Bacteria persist in soil, enter plant through wounds. Favored by rapid plant growth.	Avoid wounding plants. Don't plant in infested soil for 3 years, plant nonhost species, or solarize or otherwise pasteurize soil. See page 102.
Flowers revert to green leafy tissue. Spindly, upright yellow shoots and no flowers produced on plants infected the previous year.	**Aster yellows phytoplasma.** Spreads by leafhoppers. Not spread by seed, handling, aphids, or other insects. Many hosts.	Don't plant seed beds downwind from other hosts. Eliminate nearby weeds. Control leafhoppers. Rogue infected plants. See pages 129–130.
Yellow to brown leaf blotches, spots, or streaks. Foliage may die. Plant may be distorted and stunted.	**Tomato spotted wilt virus.** Spread by thrips. Has many crop and weed hosts.	Rogue infected plants. Exclude or control thrips. See page 121.
Blossoms have irregular white or brown blotches. Leaves may turn brown. Blossoms or terminals may be distorted. Growth may be stunted.	**Western flower thrips,** *Frankliniella occidentalis*. Slender dark brown to yellowish insects, $\frac{1}{16}$ inch long or less.	See page 161.
Foliage discolored, stippled, brownish, or bleached, and may drop. Terminals may distort. Plant may have fine webbing.	**Twospotted mite,** *Tetranychus urticae*. Tiny greenish, reddish, or yellowish mites, may have 2 dark spots.	See page 213.
Foliage has sticky honeydew, blackish sooty mold, and whitish cast skins. Foliage may yellow.	**Aphids.** Tiny pear-shaped insects, often green, yellowish, or black.	See page 179.

What the problem looks like	Probable cause	Comments

GYPSOPHILA (*Gypsophila paniculata*), Baby's breath (continued)

What the problem looks like	Probable cause	Comments
Foliage, terminals, or petals chewed. Leaves may be webbed with silk. Flower buds may be mined.	**Beet armyworm,** *Spodoptera exigua;* **Cabbage looper,** *Trichoplusia ni;* **Corn earworm,** *Helicoverpa zea.* Greenish to yellowish larvae, up to 1½ inches long; may have longitudinal stripes. Tan to brownish moths with darker bands on wings. *H. zea* larvae and adults of all these species are nocturnal.	See Caterpillars, page 203.
Foliage yellows, wilts, and dies. Basal stem has holes or decay. Grayish larva up to ¾ inch long, head dark, boring in plant.	**Crown borer,** *Opogona omoscopa.* Dark, brownish moth (family Tineidae) attracted to decaying tissue. Probably a secondary pest.	Avoid wounding plants. Provide good cultural care. Avoid excess irrigation. Use good sanitation; remove debris and dying plants.
Winding tunnels in (mostly basal) leaves, may extend into petiole and stem. Leaves may have pale spots and punctures and whiten, wilt, and drop.	**Leafminers,** *Liriomyza huidobrensis, L. trifolii.* Small active flies, dark with yellow. Yellowish or whitish maggot bores in tissue.	See page 167.

HEATHER, HEATH (*Calluna vulgaris, Erica* spp.)

What the problem looks like	Probable cause	Comments
Foliage yellows, wilts, and may drop prematurely. Plants stunted and usually die, often suddenly. Roots dead. Base of stem dark, partly or completely girdled. Discolored bark may ooze sap.	**Root and crown rot,** *Phytophthora cinnamomi, Rhizoctonia* spp. Soilborne fungi also survive in infected plants. Favored by wet, poorly drained soil. Some *Erica* are resistant.	Pasteurize media before planting. Provide good drainage. Don't overwater. Avoid introducing infected plants. Use pathogen-free stock; take cuttings from high on mother plant. See pages 93–98.
Foliage becomes grayish, yellow, and wilts. Plants stunted and eventually may die. Roots brown, necrotic.	**Cylindrocladium root and crown rot,** *Cylindrocladium pauciramosum.* Spores spread in splashing water. Fungus infects through leaves or roots.	Rogue affected plants. Pasteurize media and sterilize containers before planting. Plant only pathogen-free stock. Use good sanitation. Avoid overhead water.
Plants stunt, wilt, and collapse. Roots dead. White fungal plaques beneath bark.	**Armillaria root rot,** *Armillaria mellea.* Present in many soils. Favored by wet soil. Persists for years in infected roots. Unlike *Phytophthora, Armillaria* produces the white fungal plaques and is uncommon.	Remove woody roots ½ inch diameter or larger before planting. Pasteurize or air-dry soil well or avoid growing in fields previously planted with oaks or other susceptible woody plants. See page 99.
Foliage wilted and yellowed, often on only one side of plant. Crown and roots appear healthy. *Erica australis* and *E. persoluta* are affected.	**Verticillium wilt,** *Verticillium dahliae.* Soilborne fungus with wide host range. Fungus invades plants during cool weather, plugging water-conducting tissue, causing symptoms when plant is water-stressed, usually in early summer. Unlike with *Phytophthora,* crown and roots appear healthy.	Plant only pathogen-free stock. Pasteurize soil before planting. Avoid planting sites that have grown susceptible weeds or crops, including chrysanthemum, nightshade, strawberries, and tomato. See pages 104–106.
Foliage yellows, may turn almost white, especially new growth. Terminals may die. Plants stunted.	**Iron deficiency.** Most common in high-pH soils with low organic content.	Acidify soil. Increase soil organic matter. Spray plants monthly during new growth with 6–8 lb ferrous sulfate per 100–150 gal water per acre. See pages 56–59.
Leaves have powdery orange pustules. Leaves usually yellow and drop. Infects *Erica hirtiflora* and *E. persoluta* var. *alba.*	**Rust,** *Uredo ericae.* Spores from foliage may be carried for miles by wind. Favored by low temperatures, dew, and rain.	Avoid overhead irrigation. Sulfur applied every 10–14 days during rainy weather can prevent infection but may damage foliage if weather is hot or excessive rates are applied. See page 119.
Shoot tips turn reddish, then yellow, brown, and drop. Plants may be stunted and bushy; growth may be twisted or crooked from side buds developing into new terminals after successive tip killing.	**Powdery mildew,** *Erysiphe polygoni.* Fungus develops on living tissue, favored by moderate temperatures, shade, and poor air circulation. *Erica persoluta* is affected.	Provide good air circulation. Avoid shady planting sites. Disease prevented by sulfur applied beginning in spring and after each irrigation, but may damage foliage and flowers if applied when it is hot or at excess rates. See page 112.
Foliage discolored, stippled, brownish, or bleached, and may drop. Terminals may distort. Plant may have fine webbing.	**Twospotted mite,** *Tetranychus urticae.* Tiny greenish, reddish, or yellowish mites; may have 2 dark spots.	See page 213.
Foliage yellows. Plant declines or dies back. Bark or leaves have gray, brown, tan, or yellow encrustations (colonies of scales).	**Greedy scale,** *Hemiberlesia rapax;* **Oleander scale,** *Aspidiotus nerii;* **Oystershell scale,** *Lepidosaphes ulmi.* Circular flat or elongate to oval insects, less than 1/16 inch long.	See Scales, page 186.

What the problem looks like	Probable cause	Comments
Buds, flowers, or leaves mined or chewed, may be webbed with silk.	**Omnivorous leaftier,** *Cnephasia longana*. Gray to brownish, ½ inch long larvae and nocturnal moths. Larvae may have grayish stripes. Attacks strawberries and many other hosts. Has 1 generation per year. Occurs in central California coast.	Time any spray for young larvae emerging from mines in spring. See Caterpillars, page 203.
Leaves and blossoms chewed (edges notched). Whitish maggots present in soil.	**Black vine weevil,** *Otiorhynchus sulcatus*. Rarely seen adults brown, black, to gray snout beetles that feed at night. Larvae whitish maggots that feed on roots.	See page 208.

HIBISCUS (*Hibiscus* spp.)

What the problem looks like	Probable cause	Comments
Leaves yellow. Plant grows slowly. Plants wilt and die. Roots and stem near soil dark and decayed.	**Root, crown, and stem rot,** *Pythium, Phytophthora* spp. Fungi persist in soil. Favored by wet, poorly drained media.	Pasteurize media before planting. Don't overirrigate. Provide good drainage. See pages 93–97.
Leaves discolor, wilt, stunt, or drop prematurely. Stems discolored, cankered, and die. White mycelial growth beneath bark.	**Armillaria root rot,** *Armillaria mellea*. Present in many soils. Favored by warm, wet soil. Persists for years in infected roots.	Remove woody roots ½ inch diameter or larger before planting. Pasteurize or air-dry soil well or avoid growing in fields previously planted with oaks or other susceptible woody plants. See page 99.
Flowers or flower head have soft brown decay. Lower leaves, growing points may decay. Dead tissue has woolly gray growth (spores).	**Gray mold,** *Botrytis cinerea*. Fungus develops in crop debris or inactive tissue. Favored by high humidity and 70° to 77°F. Spores airborne.	Use good sanitation. Avoid overhead irrigation. Keep humidity low. Provide good air circulation. Don't crowd plants. See page 108.
Brown to yellow spots or blotches, mostly on older leaves. Spots may have dark or yellowish margins. Foliage may shrivel, drop.	**Leaf spots,** including *Cercospora* spp. Spread by air or splashing water. Favored by prolonged wet conditions. Persist in plant debris. Uncommon on hibiscus in western U.S.	Avoid wetting foliage. Use drip irrigation and raised benches. Use good sanitation; promptly remove and dispose of debris and infected leaves. See pages 116–118.
Stem blackens and rots. Foliage may discolor, distort, or die, possibly on one side of plant, from stem infection below soil.	**Stem rot,** *Mycosphaerella* sp. Fungus persists in plant debris. Spores spread in air and water. Favored by overhead irrigation and rain.	Use pathogen-free stock. Avoid wetting foliage. Keep humidity low. Use good sanitation. Fungicides may prevent disease. See pages 93–96.
Stems have dark, sunken cankers, may be surrounded by callus tissue. Vascular tissue may be soft and rotted. Stems break or wilt and die.	**Nectria canker,** *Nectria* spp. Fungi spread in wind, splashing water. Infect many woody ornamental and fruit tree hosts. Not reported on hibiscus in western U.S.	Avoid overhead irrigation. Prune out and dispose of infected tissue or entire plant. Fungicide, such as Bordeaux mixture applied to deciduous perennials after leaf drop, can help to control.
Leaves have dark, angular spots or blotches, may have reddish margin or yellow border. Foliage may yellow and drop.	**Bacteria leaf spots,** *Pseudomonas, Xanthomonas* spp. Spread by air and splashing water.	Avoid overhead irrigation. Don't overwater. Don't crowd plants. Use good sanitation. Excess fertilizer may reduce *Xanthomonas* damage. See pages 107, 118.
Veins pale. Foliage may have yellow mottling or mosaic. Plants may be stunted.	**Malva vein clearing virus.** Aphid-vectored.	Rogue infected plants. Exclude or control aphids. See Viruses, page 121.
Leaves yellowish. Dark green or brown, vein-limited, angular blotches on leaves, developing progressively up from older leaves.	**Foliar nematodes,** *Aphelenchoides fragariae*. Tiny roundworms spread in plant debris, vegetative propagation, and splashing water. Not common in California.	Use uninfected stock plants. Remove plant debris. Avoid overhead irrigation; leaves must be wet for infection to occur. See page 265.
Leaves bleached, stippled, may turn brown and drop. Terminals may be distorted. Plant may have fine webbing.	**Privet mite,** *Brevipalpus obovatus;* **Twospotted spider mite,** *Tetranychus urticae*. Greenish, yellowish, or red, tiny, may have 2 dark spots.	See page 213.
Sticky honeydew, blackish sooty mold, and whitish cast skins on foliage. Foliage may yellow.	**Aphids,** including Melon aphid, *Aphis gossypii*. Tiny, pear-shaped often green, yellowish, or black.	See page 179.
Sticky honeydew and blackish sooty mold on plant. Foliage may yellow from small insects, on leaves or stems.	**Black scale,** *Saissetia oleae;* **Brown soft scale,** *Coccus hesperidum;* **Nigra scale,** *Parasaissetia nigra*. Insects (family Coccidae) mostly immobile.	Oval, flat, or bulbous, yellow, orange, brown, or black insects, less than ⅜ inches long. See page 186.
Foliage has sticky honeydew and blackish sooty mold. Copious white waxy material present with certain species. Leaves may yellow and wither. Tiny, whitish, mothlike adult insects.	**Bandedwinged whitefly,** *Trialeurodes abutilonea;* **Giant whitefly,** *Aleurodicus dugesii;* **Greenhouse whitefly,** *Trialeurodes vaporariorum;* **Nesting whitefly,** *Paraleyrodes minei;* **Silverleaf whitefly,** *Bemisia argentifolii*.	Nymphs and pupae flattened, oval, translucent, and greenish or yellow. See page 170.

What the problem looks like	Probable cause	Comments
HIBISCUS (*Hibiscus* spp.) (continued)		
Plant grows slowly. Foliage yellows or wilts from mealybugs attacking roots or crown area.	**Solanum mealybug,** *Phenacoccus solani.* Powdery, waxy covered, up to ⅛ inch long, marginal filaments short or absent.	See page 183.
Foliage turns yellow. Plant decline or dieback. Gray, yellow, or orange encrustations mostly on bark.	**San Jose scale,** *Quadraspidiotus perniciosus.* Circular, flattened insects, less than 1⁄16 inch long.	See page 186.
Leaves and blossoms chewed (edges notched).	**Fuller rose beetle,** *Asynonychus godmani.* Brownish adults feed at night. Whitish maggots (larvae) in soil.	See page 208.
Flower buds, petals, or leaves discolored, deformed, or drop prematurely. Reduced flowering.	**Stink bugs.** Shield-shaped, green to brownish bugs. Eggs barrel-shaped and laid in clusters.	Control nearby weeds. Exclude or control stink bugs. See True Bugs, page 194.
HYACINTH (*Hyacinthus orientalis*)		
Flowers or bulbs may be rotted. Plants may be stunted or lack flowers. Blue mold may grow on infected tissue.	**Blue mold,** *Penicillium* spp. Bacteria infect through wounds. Problem during high humidity. Avoid long storage and transport. Provide good ventilation and low humidity during storage.	Examine bulbs and plant only if healthy. Avoid injuring plants. Bulbs can be dipped, but don't use thiabendazole or benzimidazole when resistant *Penicillium* strains are present. Don't overwater.
Bulbs don't produce or flowers develop poorly. Bulbs rot. Flower stalks rot near soil and fall over. Odorous decay.	**Soft rot,** *Erwinia carotovora.* Bacteria occur in soil or infected bulbs. Favored when wet.	Store bulbs under cool, dry conditions. Avoid injuring plant; disease infects through wounds. Don't plant infected bulbs. Don't overwater. See pages 100, 107.
Plants yellow, wilt, and die or fail to emerge. Bulbs and belowground shoots covered with gray fungus mass. Infected parts contain gray or white mycelia and black sclerotia.	**Black slime,** *Sclerotinia bulborum.* Fungal sclerotia survive in soil for several years. Favored by cool weather.	Don't grow hyacinth, iris, or narcissus in that soil for 3 to 4 years after an infection. Bulbs can be dipped in fungicide. See page 101.
Red to brown spots or blotches on stems or leaves, sometimes on flower buds. Tissue may rot.	**Leaf spot and rot,** *Stagonospora* sp. Fungal disease favored by moist, humid conditions.	Use good sanitation. Avoid wounding plants. Avoid overwatering. Provide good drainage. See pages 116–118.
Yellow to brown spots up to ¼ inch in diameter on leaves, stems and petioles. Spots become larger, dark, angular blotches or wedges, may have yellow margins. Leaves and stem may wilt and die. Stem vascular tissue and roots may be black, but not rotted.	**Leaf spot, Blight,** *Xanthomonas* sp. Spreads by splashing water, infected stock, debris, and equipment. Favored by 70° to 80°F, moist conditions, and rapid growth, such as from excess nitrogen.	Pasteurize media before planting. Inspect and isolate new plants; symptoms may not appear immediately. Avoid overhead water. Regularly inspect and rogue plants infected and those nearby. Use good sanitation. See pages 107, 118.
Bulbs discolored reddish brown, rotted, infested with tiny, oval, white to brownish mites.	**Bulb mites,** *Rhizoglyphus* spp. Sluggish mites, look like tiny eggs, may also be on stems and leaves.	Secondary pests, prefer decayed tissue, but may help fungi to infect plants. See page 218.
Flower stems very short; poor stalk emergence. Flowers abnormally small. Common when temperatures exceed 70°F during emergence.	**Short stems.** Noninfectious disorder caused by warm temperatures during early growth and/or inadequate chilling.	Adequately chill bulbs before planting. Keep temperatures cool or plant at a site that is cool during flower stalk emergence.
Foliage yellow stunted, producing no blooms. Bulbs feel soft and spongy, are hollowed, filled with brown excrement from wrinkled, gray, white, or brownish maggots (family Syrphidae), boring inside.	**Bulb flies,** including Narcissus bulb fly, *Merodon equestris* and *Eumerus* spp. Adult hairy fly, black with gray to orange, bumble beelike, hovers around blooming plants, where eggs are laid.	*M. equestris* adult and mature larva about ½ inch long are primary pest. *Eumerus* spp. smaller. Inspect and discard spongy bulbs before planting. See page 200.
Foliage has sticky honeydew and blackish sooty mold. Foliage may yellow or plant may die back.	**Brown soft scale,** *Coccus hesperidum.* Small yellow, brown, or orangish, flattened, oval insects.	See Scales, page 186.
Foliage has sticky honeydew, blackish sooty mold, and whitish cast skins. Foliage may yellow.	**Aphids.** Pear-shaped insects, often green, yellowish, or blackish.	See page 179.

What the problem looks like	Probable cause	Comments

HYDRANGEA (*Hydrangea* spp.)

What the problem looks like	Probable cause	Comments
Plants stunted. Root system reduced, small roots rotted.	**Pythium root rot,** *Pythium* spp. Soilborne fungi. Spread by spores in soil and water. Favored by excess moisture and poor drainage.	Avoid poorly drained soils. Plant in raised beds. Avoid excess irrigation and reduce watering if disease develops. See pages 93–96.
Plant is stunted or yellows and wilts. Stem rotted at soil line. Roots dark and decayed. Dark fungal strands may be visible on soil with hand lens.	**Rhizoctonia root and stem rot,** *Rhizoctonia solani.* Soilborne fungus favored by warm, moist conditions.	Practice good sanitation. Avoid overwatering and deep planting. Provide good drainage. See pages 93–98.
Plants wilt and collapse. Basal stem and roots rotted. White cottony fungus growth and tan or brown sclerotia (about ¹⁄₁₆ inch) may form on infected plant parts and in soil.	**Southern blight,** *Sclerotium rolfsii.* Sclerotia survive in soil, germinate there, and infect susceptible plants. No airborne spores are formed. Many hosts.	Avoid or pasteurize potentially infected media before planting. Fungicide applied at base of plants may help to prevent. See page 101.
Leaves discolor, wilt, stunt, or drop prematurely. Stems discolored, cankered, and die. White mycelial growths beneath bark.	**Armillaria root rot,** *Armillaria mellea.* Present in many soils. Favored by warm, wet soil. Persists for years in infected roots.	Remove woody roots ½ inch diameter or larger before planting. Pasteurize or air-dry soil well or avoid growing in fields previously planted with oaks or other susceptible woody plants. See page 99.
Brown to yellow spots or blotches on leaves. Spots may have dark or yellowish margins. Foliage may shrivel and drop.	**Leaf spots,** including *Cercospora hydrangeae,* *Phyllosticta hydrangeae, Septoria hydrangeae.* Spread by air or splashing water. Favored by prolonged, cool, wet, conditions. Persist in plant debris. Not reported on hydrangea in California.	Avoid wetting foliage. Use drip irrigation and raised benches. Use good sanitation; promptly remove and dispose of debris and infected leaves. See pages 116–118.
Brown to orangish, powdery pustules and yellowish spots on leaves. Leaves may yellow and drop.	**Rust,** *Pucciniastrum hydrangeae.* Fungi survive on living tissue. Spores are airborne. Favored by high humidity and water.	Avoid overhead irrigation. Water in morning. Provide good air circulation. Don't crowd plants. See page 119.
Soft, brown decay on flowers, buds, or leaves. Buds rot in storage. May be woolly gray growth (spores) on dead tissue.	**Gray mold,** *Botrytis cinerea.* Fungus develops in crop debris or inactive tissue. Favored by high humidity and 70° to 77°F. Spores airborne.	Use good sanitation. Avoid overhead irrigation. Keep humidity low and provide good air circulation, especially in storage. Don't crowd plants. See page 108.
White powdery patches on leaves and stems. Brown patches may be on upper surface of leaves. Basal leaves may yellow, then, and die. Flowers may be deformed or spotted.	**Powdery mildew,** *Erysiphe polygoni.* Fungus survives on living plants. Spores spread by splashing water. Favored by moderate temperatures, shade, and crowding.	Avoid overcrowding. Provide adequate light and good air circulation. See page 112.
Slow plant growth. Leaf veins yellow. Foliage bunchy. Flowers green. Flower buds dwarfed, dead, or produce excess vegetative growth.	**Virescence.** Phytoplasmalike organism. Symptoms may appear only when forcing inflorescence development.	Carefully identify and rogue out infected plants. Certain varieties (e.g., Stafford, Rose Supreme) are more susceptible and first indicate pathogen presence.
Yellow to brown leaf blotches, spots, or streaks. Foliage may die. Plant may be distorted and stunted.	**Tomato spotted wilt virus.** Spread by thrips. Has may crop and weed hosts.	Rogue infected plants. Exclude or control thrips. See page 121.
Leaves distorted, crinkled, or rolled. Yellow or brown spots or rings in foliage. Fewer flowers. Plants dwarfed, most often in winter.	**Hydrangea ringspot virus.** Vector unknown.	Rogue plants performing unsatisfactorily. See Viruses, page 121.
Leaves yellowish. Dark green or brown, vein-limited, bands or blotches on leaves, develop progressively up from older leaves.	**Foliar nematodes,** *Aphelenchoides* spp. Tiny roundworms spread in plant debris, vegetative propagation, and splashing water. Not common in California.	Use uninfected stock plants. Remove plant debris. Avoid overhead irrigation; leaves must be wet for infection to occur. See page 265.
Plants are stunted. Foliage may yellow. May be swellings, galls, or lesions on roots. Rootlets sparse.	**Nematodes,** *Meloidogyne, Pratylenchus* spp. Nematodes persist in soil. Most severe problem in sandy soils.	Pasteurize media before planting. See page 265.
New growth chlorotic, except for green veins. Plants may be stunted.	**Iron deficiency.** Noninfectious disorder.	See pages 56–59.
Foliage has sticky honeydew, blackish sooty mold, and whitish cast skins. Foliage may yellow.	**Aphids,** including *Aphis gossypii, Aulacorthum circumflexum, Myzus persicae.* Pear-shaped, often green or yellowish insects.	See page 179.
Foliage has sticky honeydew and blackish sooty mold. Copious white waxy material present with certain species. Leaves may yellow and wither. Tiny, whitish, mothlike adult insect.	**Giant whitefly,** *Aleurodicus dugesii;* **Greenhouse whitefly,** *Trialeurodes vaporariorum;* **Silverleaf whitefly,** *Bemisia argentifolii;* **Sweetpotato whitefly,** *Bemisia tabaci.*	Nymphs and pupae flattened, oval, translucent, and greenish or yellow. See Whiteflies, page 170.

What the problem looks like	Probable cause	Comments

HYDRANGEA (*Hydrangea* spp.) (continued)

What the problem looks like	Probable cause	Comments
Elongate, slender, cottony material (egg sacs) on plant. May be sticky honeydew and blackish sooty mold.	**Cottony hydrangea scale,** *Pulvinaria hydrangeae.* Oval, flattened, yellow or brown insects and cottony eggs.	See page 186.
Foliage turns yellow. Decline or dieback of plant. Dark brown encrustations on bark.	**Oystershell scale,** *Lepidosaphes ulmi.* Elongate to oval insects, less than $1/16$ inch long.	Scale insects (family Diaspididae), often shaped like oyster shells. See Scales, page 186.
Unusual branching. Premature flower bud formation. Distorted flowers. Delayed or no flowers. Dead leaf patches. Leaf tips may wilt.	**Plant bugs,** *Lygus* spp. Brown, green, or yellowish bugs, up to $1/4$ inch long, suck plant juices.	Control nearby weeds, from which bugs move. Exclude bugs from growing area. See True Bugs, page 194.
Stippled, bleached, or blotched foliage with varnishlike excrement.	**Banded greenhouse thrips,** *Hercinothrips femoralis.* Adult dark brown to yellowish, with three white bands on wings and dark brown basal segment on legs. Nymphs and pupae whitish to pale yellow.	Sluggish thrips, usually in colonies; pupate on host or nearby on soil surface. Reportedly cannot survive outdoors overwinter in California and most other areas. Many hosts. See Thrips, page 161.
Leaves bleached, stippled, may turn brown and drop. Terminals may be distorted. Plant may have fine webbing.	**Spider mites,** *Tetranychus* spp. Tiny often green, pink, or red pests; may have 2 dark spots.	See page 213.
Foliage chewed and webbed together with silk. Stems may be mined. Larvae wriggle vigorously when touched.	**Greenhouse leaftier,** *Udea rubigalis.* Larvae yellowish green with three longitudinal green to white stripes. Adult reddish brown with black wavy lines on wings. Mature adult and larva about $3/4$ inches long. Has about 6 generations per year.	Avoid growing floral hosts near celery, a major host. See page 203.

IMPATIENS (*Impatiens wallerana*), New Guinea impatiens

What the problem looks like	Probable cause	Comments
Leaves yellow and drop. Plants stunted, may collapse. Stem near soil and roots may have brown lesions and rot.	**Root, crown, and stem rot,** *Rhizoctonia solani,* *Pythium* spp. Fungi prefer wet, poorly drained soil. Spread in media and water.	Pasteurize media before planting. Rogue infected plants. Provide good drainage. Avoid excess irrigation. See pages 93–98.
Foliage fades, yellows, browns, and wilts, often on one side of plant. Branches and entire plant may die.	**Verticillium wilt,** *Verticillium dahliae.* Fungus persists in soil, infects through roots.	See pages 104–106.
Foliage yellows and wilts. Plant grows slowly and die. Roots dark, black, and rotted.	**Black root rot,** *Thielaviopsis basicola.* Spreads in water, soil, and by infected plants. Fungus persists in infected media. Favored by cool, wet conditions.	Pasteurize media before planting. Avoid overwatering and splashing water. Provide good drainage. Allow soil to dry between watering. Rogue infected plants. Avoid high salts and high pH. See pages 95–99.
Foliage yellows, especially outer leaves. Soft rot of basal stem or roots. White mycelia and small, tan to reddish brown sclerotia may develop on tissue and in soil.	**Southern wilt,** *Sclerotium rolfsii.* Sclerotia survive in soil. Disease favored by moist, poorly drained, 77° to 95°F soil. Not reported on impatiens in California.	Pasteurize media before planting. Avoid excess irrigation. Consider fungicide drench to infected soil. See page 101.
Petals, lower leaves, or growing points have soft brown decay or spots. Dead tissue may have woolly gray growth (spores).	**Gray mold,** *Botrytis cinerea.* Fungus develops in crop debris or inactive tissue. Favored by high humidity and 70° to 77°F. Spores airborne.	Use good sanitation. Avoid overhead irrigation. Keep humidity low. Provide good air circulation. Don't crowd plants. See page 108.
Leaves have brown to yellow spots or blotches. Spots may have dark or yellowish margins. Foliage may shrivel and drop.	**Leaf spots,** *Cercospora, Phyllosticta, Ramularia, Septoria* spp. Spread by air or splashing water. Favored by prolonged wet conditions. Persist in plant debris. Not reported on impatiens in California.	Avoid wetting foliage. Use drip irrigation and raised benches. Use good sanitation; promptly remove and dispose of debris and infected leaves. See pages 116–118.
Leaves have brown to blackish spots or blotches that may have tan center or reddish margin.	**Bacteria leaf spot,** *Pseudomonas syringae.* Spread by air and splashing water.	Avoid overhead irrigation. Don't overwater. Don't crowd plants. Use good sanitation. See page 107.
Terminals near soil proliferate and basal shoots are stunted and distorted. Plants lack vigor.	**Fasciation,** cause often uncertain. May be viral, bacterial (e.g., *Rhodococcus fascians*), or genetic. Manage as bacterial and take additional measures.	Use pathogen-free stock. Avoid injuring base of plants, especially when wet. Keep base of plants dry. Dispose of infected plants. See page 121.
Plants don't produce or flowers develop poorly. Plants rot. Flower stalks rot near soil and fall over. Odorous decay.	**Soft rot,** *Erwinia carotovora.* Bacteria occur in soil or infected plants. Favored when wet.	Avoid injuring plant; disease infects through wounds. Don't plant infected stock. Don't overwater. See pages 100, 107.

What the problem looks like	Probable cause	Comments
Leaves have concentric ring spots or blotches, often tan to brown with black margins. Leaves may be distorted, blistered, or pinched. Midveins may darken or turn black. Stem may have dark necrosis. Plants may be stunted and may die.	**Impatiens necrotic spot virus, Tomato spotted wilt virus.** Spread by thrips. Many hosts. Impatiens is highly susceptible, being readily infected and quickly exhibiting symptoms.	Control nearby weeds and grasses. Control thrips. Impatiens is used as indicator host of INSV and TSWV presence in other plants; place uninfected impatiens with other hosts and thrips and observe if symptoms develop. See page 121.
Leaves yellowish. Leaves have dark green or brown vein-limited angular blotches that develop progressively up from older leaves.	**Foliar nematodes,** *Aphelenchoides fragariae.* Tiny roundworms spread in plant debris, vegetative propagation, and splashing water. Not common in California.	Use uninfected stock plants. Remove plant debris. Avoid overhead irrigation; leaves must be wet for infection to occur. See page 265.
Foliage yellows or wilts. Plants stunted. Feeder and fleshy roots have knots or swellings.	**Root knot nematode,** *Meloidogyne* spp. Tiny roundworms that prefer warm, sandy soil. Many hosts.	Pasteurize media before planting. Rogue affected plants. Use good sanitation. See page 265.
Foliage pale green or yellowish, may turn brown and drop.	**Sunburn.** Noninfectious disorder caused by excess light, insufficient water.	Provide appropriate light and water. See page 62.
Poor growth. Roots long and thin with few or unhealthy root hairs.	**Hypoxic roots.** Noninfectious disorder from excess water and inadequate nutrient uptake.	Avoid overwatering. Provide good drainage and appropriate fertilization.
Blossoms have irregular white or brown blotches. Leaves may turn brown. Blossoms or terminals may be distorted. Growth may be stunted.	**Western flower thrips,** *Frankliniella occidentalis.* Slender dark brown to yellowish insects, $\frac{1}{16}$ inch long or less.	See page 161.
Foliage and possibly blossoms, bleached, bronzed, or distorted. Plant stunted and may die.	**Broad mite,** *Polyphagotarsonemus latus.* Translucent to dark green, $\frac{1}{100}$ inch long or smaller.	See page 217.
Foliage discolored (stippled, bleached, or reddened) and may drop. Plant may have fine webbing.	**Twospotted spider mite,** *Tetranychus urticae.* Tiny greenish or yellowish mites with 2 darker spots.	See page 213.
Plants stunted. Leaf terminals curled, distorted. Buds deform, blacken, or discolor, and may drop.	**Cyclamen mite,** *Phytonemus pallidus.* A pinkish orange mite (family Tarsonemidae), $\frac{1}{100}$ inch long or smaller.	See page 217.
Foliage has sticky honeydew, blackish sooty mold, and whitish cast skins. Foliage may curl or yellow.	**Aphids,** including Melon aphid, *Aphis gossypii.* Small pear-shaped insects, often green, pink, yellowish, or blackish.	See page 179.
Plant has sticky honeydew and blackish sooty mold. Foliage may yellow. Tiny, white, mothlike adults present.	**Whiteflies,** including **Greenhouse whitefly,** *Trialeurodes vaporariorum.* Nymphs and pupae flattened, oval, translucent, and greenish or yellow.	See page 170.
Leaves have winding tunnels. Heavily infested leaves may drop. Leaves have pale spots or punctures from adult flies. Yellowish to white maggots in leaf mines.	**Serpentine leafminer,** *Liriomyza trifolii.* Adults are tiny, active, black and yellow flies.	See Leafminers, page 167.
Leaves and blossoms chewed (edges notched). Larva whitish maggot that lives in soil and feeds on roots.	**Black vine weevil,** *Otiorhynchus sulcatus.* Rarely seen adults brown, black, to gray snout beetles that feed at night. Larvae whitish maggots that feed on roots.	See Weevils, page 208.

IRIS (*Iris* spp.), Dutch iris, Bulbous and Rhizomatous iris

Foliage yellows and wilts. Plants stunted. Root system reduced. Roots and basal stems dark and decayed.	**Root and crown rots,** *Pythium irregulare,* *Phytophthora cryptogea, Rhizoctonia solani.* Fungi spread in soil and water. Favored by excess moisture and poor drainage.	Provide good drainage. Avoid deep planting. Avoid excess irrigation and reduce watering if disease develops. See pages 93–98.
Outer leaves yellowing, then all foliage. Bulbs, rhizomes, or leaf bases have soft rot. White mycelia and small, tan to reddish brown sclerotia present on bulbs and in soil.	**Southern wilt or blight** or **Crown rot,** *Sclerotium rolfsii.* Sclerotia survive in soil. Spread by infected bulbs and movement of contaminated soil. Disease favored by moist, poorly drained, 77° to 95°F soil. Many hosts.	Avoid planting in infested soil. Pasteurize soil before planting. Kill fungus by treating rhizomes with 122°F hot water before planting. Avoid excess irrigation. Consider fungicide drench to infected soil. See page 101.
Foliage yellows and wilts. Roots decay. Plants die suddenly. White mycelial growth on infected tissue and nearby soil. May be dark crust on roots or crown.	**Dematophora root rot,** *Rosellinia necatrix.* Fungus favored by mild, wet conditions. Infects primarily through healthy roots growing near infested plants. Affects most fruit and nut trees and vines. White fungal patches are much smaller than with *Armillaria.*	Infected tissue sealed in moist container produces white fluff within several days. Pasteurize media before planting. Remove infected plants. Avoid excess irrigation. See page 100.

What the problem looks like	Probable cause	Comments

IRIS (*Iris* spp.), Dutch iris, Bulbous and Rhizomatous iris (continued)

What the problem looks like	Probable cause	Comments
Bulbs or stems decay; soft, brown, odorous rot often at soil line. Leaf edges and stems may be discolored, soft, rotted.	**Bacterial soft rot,** *Erwinia* sp. Persists in media. Favored when wet. Disease is secondary, infecting wounds.	Avoid injuring plant. Provide good drainage. Don't overwater. Use good sanitation; immediately discard infected plants and those nearby. See pages 100, 107.
Bulbs or basal stem ragged or decayed. Brown mycelia on infected tissue visible with a hand lens.	**Gray bulb rot,** *Rhizoctonia tuliparum.* Soilborne fungus favored by wet conditions.	Provide good soil drainage. Plant in raised beds. Avoid excess irrigation. See pages 93–98.
Rhizomes decay, may be covered with woolly grayish growth (fungal spores).	**Botrytis rhizome rot,** *Botrytis convoluta.* Fungal disease prefers cool, moist conditions. Not a common cause of rhizome decay in California.	Provide good drainage, plant in raised beds. Avoid excess irrigation. Avoid excessively cool growing conditions.
Plants yellow, wilt, and die or fail to emerge. Bulbs and belowground shoots covered with gray fungus mass. Infected parts contain gray or white mycelia and black sclerotia.	**Black slime,** *Sclerotinia bulborum.* Fungal sclerotia survive in soil for several years. Favored by cool weather.	Don't grow hyacinth, iris, or narcissus in that soil for 3 to 4 years after an infection. Bulbs can be dipped in fungicide. See page 101.
Plants are stunted, discolored, lack flowers, and die prematurely.	**Blue mold,** *Penicillium* spp. Bacteria only infect through wounds caused by insects, harvesting, sunburn, etc. Late or early digging favors disease.	Examine bulbs and plant only if healthy. Avoid very early or very late digging. Prevent injuries. Heat-cure bulbs rapidly, within 5 days of digging. Provide good ventilation during storage. Bulbs can be dipped, but don't use thiabendazole or benzimidazole when resistant *Penicillium* strains are present.
Foliage has dark, reddish brown, elongated spots with chlorotic margins, mostly on older leaves. Spots on older leaves have gray centers. Dark spore masses may be visible on lesions. Fungus may be severe on plants not dug for 2 years.	**Ink spot,** *Drechslera* or *Bipolaris iridis.* Fungus survives in infected bulbs and plant debris. Moist conditions and 68° to 77°F favor the disease.	Dig bulbs every year. Incorporate plant debris into soil. Plant iris in same soil only 1 year out of every three.
Flowers, flower heads, lower leaves, or growing points have soft brown decay. Dead tissue may have woolly gray growth (spores).	**Gray mold,** *Botrytis cinerea.* Fungus develops in crop debris or inactive tissue. Favored by high humidity and 70° to 77°F. Spores airborne.	Use good sanitation. Avoid overhead irrigation. Keep humidity low. Provide good air circulation. Don't crowd plants. See page 108.
Bulbs brown to black and decayed. Bulbs fail to produce or plants are stunted, wilted, stems rot, and plants die.	**Black storage molds,** *Rhizopus* sp., *Aspergillus* sp. Persist in infected tissue. Spread by airborne spores. Infect through wounds. Favored by high humidity, warm temperatures.	Store bulbs under low humidity and cool temperatures. Avoid wounding bulbs. Use good sanitation; dispose of infected bulbs and dying plants.
Oval to elongate spots, often on leaf near tip. Spots reddish brown, surrounded by yellow or red border, may begin as yellowish flecks. Center of old spots turns gray. Leaves may die back. Flower buds, stems, and bulbs may be infected. May be greenish spores.	**Fire** or **Leaf spot,** *Heterosporium gracile,* *Mycosphaerella* (=*Didymellina*) *macrospora.* Fungal spores survive on living and dead leaves, spread by air. Disease favored by 50° to 70°F and wet conditions.	Dig bulbs annually. Remove and dispose of diseased tissue, from which fungus spreads. Consider cutting off infected parts of leaves. Consider fungicide application to foliage during wet weather. See pages 116–118.
Central leaves wither and die back, beginning at tips. Leaves may turn reddish brown. Root cortical tissue rotted, leaving only central water-conducting and other tubelike tissues. Rhizomes remain firm.	**Scorch.** Cause unknown, possibly due to root rot fungi or bacteria. Affects rhizomatous iris. Disease favored by moist soil, at least 60°F.	No sure method of control; sometimes replanting without treatment yields unaffected plants. Thoroughly clean, dry, then dip stock in registered disinfectant before replanting.
Both sides of leaf have pale green to yellow spots. Leaves have brown to orangish powdery pustules. Leaves may drop prematurely. Cultivars vary greatly in susceptibility.	**Rust,** *Puccinia iridis.* Fungus survives on living iris tissue. Spores are airborne. Favored by high humidity, rain, and overhead irrigation.	Avoid cultivars that have been especially susceptible, such as 'Blue Ribbon.' Avoid overhead irrigation. Water so foliage dries within a few hours. Provide good air circulation. See page 119.
Elongated, water-soaked lesions or spots on leaves near base or on flower stems. Leaves may yellow and die.	**Bacterial blight or spot,** *Xanthomonas campestris* pv. *tardicrescens.* Bacteria survive in infected tissue and crop residue. Favored by moist conditions. Infects through wounds. Uncommon on iris in California.	Avoid overhead irrigation. Don't overwater or crowd plants. Use good sanitation. Avoid injuring plants. See pages 107, 118.
Leaves mottled. Foliage may be distorted. Plants may be stunted.	**Cucumber mosaic virus.** Spread by aphids or vegetatively by cuttings and roots. Many hosts.	Rogue infected plants. Exclude or control aphids. See Viruses, page 121.
Foliage mildly mottled. Growth may be somewhat retarded.	**Iris mild mosaic virus.** Vector unknown.	Rogue and don't propagate infected plants. See Viruses, page 121.

What the problem looks like	Probable cause	Comments
Foliage has light and dark green mottling and yellow stippling, especially on young leaves. Plants may be stunted. Affects bulbous and rhizomatous iris.	**Mosaic virus, Iris virus 1**. Spread by aphids. Affects iris family (Iridaceae) plants; *I. germanica* and its hybrids are only slightly stunted, may be unaffected.	Rogue infected plants. Exclude or control aphids. Consider avoiding Oncocyclus iris, *I. susiana*, which is severely damaged. See page 121.
Leaves have dark streaks, spots, or slits. Leaf edges may appear ragged. Leaf bases may rot. Rhizomes may have holes and rot.	**Iris borer,** *Macronoctua onusta*. Pink larvae, up to 2 inches long, bore in leaves, then stalks and rhizomes. Adult nocturnal, brownish moth (family Saturniidae). Not reported in western U.S.	Dispose of debris, where moth overwinters as eggs. Dispose of infested rhizomes. If feasible, kill larvae in spring by squeezing infested leaves near damage.
Foliage yellows and wilts. Plants may be stunted, fall over, or die from root-feeding beetles. Basal stems or leaves may be chewed.	**Carrot beetle,** *Ligyrus gibbosus*. Adults (family Scarabaeidae) reddish brown, ½ inch long, feed above and below ground. Larvae up to 1¼ inches long, white to bluish, head dark. Attacks grains and vegetable crops, especially tubers.	Exclude adults, which fly at night to lights. Eliminate decaying vegetation that harbors adults around plants. See page 211.
Plant has sticky honeydew and blackish sooty mold. Foliage yellows. Tiny, white, mothlike adults present with 2 dark spots on each wing.	**Iris whitefly,** *Aleyrodes spiraeoides*. Flattened, oval, translucent to yellowish pupae, without filaments. Confused with silverleaf and sweetpotato whitefly, except adults leave much more white wax on plants when laying eggs.	See page 170.
Foliage has sticky honeydew, blackish sooty mold, and whitish cast skins. Foliage may yellow. Young terminal growth may distort.	**Aphids,** including *Aulacorthum solani, Macrosiphum euphorbiae, Myzus persicae, Sitobion avenae*. Small pear-shaped insects, often green, pink, yellowish, or blackish.	See page 179.
May be poor growth from bulbs or rhizomes. Plants stunted. Young shoots distorted. Aphids under leaf sheaths and on stems near soil, and on rhizomes and bulbs stored or in the field.	**Iris root aphid** or **Tulip bulb aphid,** *Dysaphis tulipae*. Small pear-shaped insect, yellow, pink, gray, or green; waxy covered. Easily overlooked. Usually causes direct damage only to stored bulbs.	Vectors virus in lily and tulip. Other hosts include freesia and gladiolus. See page 182.
Foliage yellow, stunted, producing no blooms. Bulbs feel soft and spongy, are hollowed and filled with brown excrement from wrinkled, gray, white, or brownish maggots boring inside.	**Lesser bulb flies,** *Eumerus* spp. Adult (family Syrphidae) hairy fly, black with gray to orange, resembles a bumble bee, hovers around blooming plants. Adult may be confused with species that have aphid-predaceous larvae. Adult and mature larva about ¼ inch long. Usually secondary pest attacking damaged bulbs.	Avoid injuring bulbs. Inspect and discard spongy bulbs before planting. See Bulb flies, page 200.
Leaves yellowish. Leaves have dark green or brown vein-limited bands or blotches that develop progressively up from older leaves.	**Foliar nematodes,** *Aphelenchoides fragariae*. Tiny roundworms spread in plant debris, vegetative propagation, and splashing water. Not common on iris in California.	Use uninfected stock plants. Remove plant debris. Avoid overhead irrigation; leaves must be wet for infection to occur. See page 265.
Blossoms discolored with blotches or streaks. Leaves, stems, or flower spikes bleached, brownish, spotted, withered, or distorted. Buds turn brown and die. Stored corms have sticky, scabby areas.	**Gladiolus thrips,** *Thrips simplex*. Slender dark brown to shiny black adults; gray to whitish band at wing base. Nymphs and pupae yellow to orange. Feed hidden within leaf or bud sheaths, usually in groups. Overwinter and develop on stored corms.	Plant only thrips-free corms. Storing corms at 35° to 40°F for at least 4 months kills thrips; don't freeze corms. Heat treatment as for disease may also control. See Thrips, page 161.
Blossoms have discolored blotches or streaks. Foliage stippled, bleached, or blotched; has varnishlike excrement.	**Western flower thrips,** *Frankliniella occidentalis*. Tiny, slender, dark brown to yellowish adults. Nymphs and pupae whitish to pale yellow.	See Thrips, page 161.
Foliage discolored or distorted. Plant may have fine webbing, which can reduce pollination and seed yield.	**Twospotted spider mite,** *Tetranychus urticae*. Tiny greenish or yellowish mites with 2 darker spots.	See page 213.
Leaves chewed, may be rolled or tied together with silk. Yellow, green, or pink larvae present with yellow, green, or black lengthwise stripes.	**Omnivorous looper,** *Sabulodes aegrotata* or *S. caberata*. Adult moth (family Geometridae) tan to brownish, with wavy black band across middle of wings. Mature larva and nocturnal adult up to about 1½ inches long. Oval eggs laid in clusters.	See page 203.
Buds, flowers or leaves mined or chewed, may be webbed with silk.	**Omnivorous leaftier,** *Cnephasia longana*. Gray to brownish, ½ inch long larvae and nocturnal moths. Larva may have grayish stripes. Attacks strawberries and many other hosts. Occurs in central California coast. Has 1 generation per year.	Time any spray for young larvae emerging from mines in spring. See Caterpillars, page 203.

What the problem looks like	Probable cause	Comments
IVY (*Hedera* spp.)		
Leaves have yellow, brown, or black blotches. Spots usually angular and vein-limited where veins are large, round where veins are absent. Dark spots may have yellow halos. Spots may appear greasy, water-soaked. Leaves may drop.	**Bacterial leaf spot.** *Xanthomonas campestris* pv. *hederae*. Bacteria spread by water. Favored by cool, wet weather. 'Brokamp,' 'Hahn Variegated,' 'Green Feather,' and 'Ivalace' are most susceptible English ivy.	Avoid overhead irrigation. Don't overwater or crowd plants. Use good sanitation. Propagate from clean mother plants. High nutrition (N, P, K) may reduce severity. Plant resistant English ivy: 'California,' 'Eva,' 'Gold Dust,' 'Perfection,' and 'Sweet Heart.' See page 118.
Leaves have tan to dark spots or blotches that may have discolored borders or rings. Discoloring may follow leaf veins. Leaves may wilt, die, drop.	**Bacterial leaf spot and blight,** *Pseudomonas cichorii.* Spread by air and splashing water.	Avoid overhead irrigation. Don't overwater or crowd plants. Use good sanitation. See page 107.
Foliage yellows. Plants wilt and die, often suddenly. Roots and stem near soil dark, decayed, girdled by lesions. Leaves have large dark spots.	**Root, crown, and stem rot,** *Pythium, Phytophthora* spp. Fungi survive in soil, favored by wet, poorly drained media.	Don't overirrigate. Provide good drainage. See pages 93–97.
Leaves have brown to yellow spots or blotches. Spots may have dark or yellowish margins. Foliage may shrivel and drop. Some of these fungi may spot stems or rot stems and roots.	**Leaf spots or blight, Anthracnose,** *Alternaria, Colletotrichum, Phyllosticta* spp. Spread by air or splashing water. Wet conditions favor. Persist in crop debris. *Colletotrichum* has white spore masses and dark setae visible with a hand lens. *Phyllosticta* has dark pycnidia (black specks) and lacks white spore masses and dark setae. Spots often less angular and have less of a chlorotic halo than with *Xanthomonas*.	Propagate from clean mother plants. Avoid wetting foliage. Use drip irrigation and raised benches. Use good sanitation; promptly remove and dispose of debris and infected leaves. Consider 'Gold Dust' and 'Shamrock,' which are less susceptible to *Colletotrichum.* See pages 116–118.
Discolored spots between veins. Large spots chlorotic, then tan or brown.	**Sunburn.** Noninfectious disorder, appears during or after high temperatures.	See page 62.
Leaf underside may have pimplelike blisters or water-soaked spots. Leaves brown, harden, appear corky, especially on underside. Foliage yellows, drops.	**Edema or Oedema.** Noninfectious disease. Leaves accumulate excess water when soil is warm and moist and air is cool and moist. Exact cause unknown.	Irrigate only in morning. Avoid irrigation if cool and cloudy. Provide good air circulation. Keep humidity low. Provide good drainage. See page 41.
Foliage and possibly blossoms bleached, bronzed, or distorted. New growth and plant stunted.	**Broad mite,** *Polyphagotarsonemus latus.* Translucent to dark green, $\frac{1}{100}$ inch long or smaller.	See page 217.
Reddish brown hardened foliage, especially in center of leaves. Plants severely stunted. Leaf terminals distorted. Buds deformed, discolored, and may drop.	**Cyclamen mite,** *Phytonemus pallidus.* A pinkish orange mite (family Tarsonemidae), $\frac{1}{100}$ inch long or smaller.	See page 217.
Foliage discolored, stippled, or bleached, and may drop. Terminals may distort. Plant may have fine webbing.	**Privet mite,** *Brevipalpus obovatus;* **Twospotted spider mite,** *Tetranychus urticae.* Greenish, yellowish, or red, tiny; may have 2 dark spots.	See page 213.
Plant has sticky honeydew and blackish sooty mold. Plant grows slowly. Foliage may yellow.	**Pyriform scale,** *Protopulvinaria pyriformis.* Triangular, $\frac{1}{8}$ inch long, brown, yellow, or mottled red. May be small white egg sac. Common in Florida and southern California.	See Scales, page 186.
Foliage yellows. Plant declines or dies back. Bark or leaves have gray, brown, tan, or yellow encrustations from colonies of circular, flat insects, less than $\frac{1}{16}$ inch long.	**Dictyosperum scale,** *Chrysomphalus dictyospermi;* **Greedy scale,** *Hemiberlesia rapax;* **Latania scale,** *H. lataniae;* **Oleander scale,** *Aspidiotus nerii;* **Yellow scale,** *Aonidiella citrina.*	See page 186.
Plant has sticky honeydew and blackish sooty mold. Foliage may yellow from small insects on leaves or stems.	**Nigra scale,** *Parasaissetia nigra;* **Brown soft scale,** *Coccus hesperidum.* Oval, flat or convex, yellow, orange, brown, or black insects (family Coccidae), less than $\frac{3}{8}$ inches long.	See page 186.
Plant has sticky honeydew, blackish sooty mold, and whitish cast skins. Foliage may yellow from aphids sucking sap.	**Aphids,** including Bean aphid, *Aphis fabae;* Green peach aphid, *Myzus persicae;* Ivy aphid, *Aphis hederae.* Small pear-shaped insects, often green, yellowish, or blackish.	See page 179.
Plant has cottony material (egg sacs), sticky honeydew, and blackish sooty mold. Foliage may yellow.	**Grape mealybug,** *Pseudococcus maritimus.* Oval, soft, powdery, waxy covered insects, up to $\frac{1}{8}$ inch long.	See page 183.

What the problem looks like	Probable cause	Comments
Foliage has sticky honeydew and blackish sooty mold. Leaves may yellow and wither. Tiny, whitish, mothlike adult insects.	**Whiteflies,** including Citrus whitefly, *Dialeurodes citri*. Oval, flattened, translucent, yellow to greenish nymphs and pupae.	See page 170.
Leaves chewed; may be rolled or tied together with silk. Yellow, green, or pink larvae with yellow, green, or black lengthwise stripes.	**Omnivorous looper,** *Sabulodes aegrotata* or *S. caberata*. Adult moth (family Geometridae) tan to brownish, with wavy black band across middle of wings. Mature larva and nocturnal adult up to about $1\frac{1}{2}$ inches long. Oval eggs laid in clusters.	See page 203.
Foliage or shoots chewed, ragged, or clipped. May be slimy or silvery trails on or around plants.	**Snails,** including *Helix aspersa*. Have spiraled shell and move slowly on slimy, muscular foot.	Snails are favored by moist, dark conditions. See page 219.

IXIA (*Ixia* spp.), African corn lily

What the problem looks like	Probable cause	Comments
Brownish to black rot of corms in ground or storage. Corms may fail to produce. Plants may grow poorly. Leaves may yellow, distort, wilt, and die. Basal stem may rot.	**Corm rots,** *Fusarium oxysporum* f. sp. *gladioli*, *Sclerotium* spp. Occur in diseased underground stems (corms). Persist for years in infested soil. May be favored by wet soil, excess nitrogen, and wounding corms.	Pasteurize soil before planting or plant where disease has not occurred. Plant only pathogen-free corms. Rogue infected plants. Dig and handle corms carefully to avoid injuring them. Grow nonhost crops for 4 years to reduce *Fusarium*. See pages 101, 104.
Irregular light lines or mottling of foliage. Plants may be stunted.	**Ixia mosaic virus**. Aphid-vectored.	Rogue infected plants. Control aphids. See page 121.
Foliage has sticky honeydew, blackish sooty mold, and whitish cast skins. Foliage may curl or yellow.	**Aphids,** including Green peach aphid, *Myzus persicae*. Small pear-shaped insects, often green, yellow, or blackish.	See page 179.

KALANCHOE (*Kalanchoe blossfeldiana*)

What the problem looks like	Probable cause	Comments
Foliage yellows and wilts. Shoots blacken. Stem lesions appear around soil line. Crowns wet and decayed. Plants brown, shrivel, and die.	**Root and crown rot,** *Phytophthora*, *Rhizoctonia* spp. Favored by wet conditions, such as heavy rain, overirrigation, and poor drainage.	Pasteurize media before planting. Provide good drainage. Don't overwater. See pages 93–98.
Brown to black water-soaked spots or decay on stems near soil or on leaves. Infected tissue may have tiny black spore-forming structures and white mycelia.	**Stem rot,** *Myrothecium roridum*. Spreads by airborne spores. Infects through wounds. Favored by 70° to 81°F and excess nitrogen and salts.	Minimize plant wounds. Keep foliage dry. Use good sanitation. Avoid excess fertilization. Growing plants above 86°F may arrest or prevent disease.
Foliage yellows and wilts. Plants grow slowly and die. Roots dark black and rotted.	**Black root rot,** *Thielaviopsis basicola*. Spreads in water, media, and by infected plants. Fungus persists in media. Favored by cool, wet conditions.	Pasteurize media before planting. Avoid overwatering and splashing water. Provide good drainage. Allow soil to dry between watering. Rogue infected plants. Avoid high salts and high pH. See pages 95–98.
Leaves or stems have brown, tan, or white spots or lesions. Lesions may have yellow borders. Foliage may yellow, shrivel, or drop.	**Leaf spots,** including *Stemphylium*, *Cercospora* spp. Spread by air or splashing water. Favored by wet conditions. Persist in debris. Not reported on kalanchoe in California.	Avoid wetting foliage. Use drip irrigation and raised benches. Use good sanitation; promptly remove and dispose of debris and infected leaves. See pages 116–118.
Leaves have grayish powdery growth; may curl, bronze, stunt, or die.	**Powdery mildew,** *Sphaerotheca fuliginea*. Cool temperatures and high humidity favor fungus.	Provide adequate heat and good ventilation. Grow thicker, darker-leafed cultivars, which appear to be more resistant. See page 112.
Stems and leaves have soft brown decay or spots; may also be on petals and terminals. Dead tissue may have woolly gray growth (spores).	**Gray mold,** *Botrytis cinerea*. Fungus develops in crop debris or inactive tissue. Favored by high humidity and 70° to 77°F. Spores airborne.	Use good sanitation. Avoid overhead irrigation. Keep humidity low. Provide good air circulation. Don't crowd plants. See page 108.
Leaves have dark concentric ring spots or blotches. Leaves may be distorted. Stem necrosis. Plants may be stunted and may die.	**Impatiens necrotic spot virus**. Spread by thrips.	Control nearby weeds. Exclude or control thrips. Rogue infected plants. See Viruses, page 121.
Mild mosaic or pale blotching of foliage.	**Kalanchoe virus 1**. Vector unknown.	See Viruses, page 121.
Few, late, or no flowers or flower buds.	**Flower failure**. Dark period too warm or short. Insufficient day light intensity.	Provide proper growing conditions, including at least 40 days with 12-hour nights at about 60°F and about 4500 foot-candles during 72°F days.

What the problem looks like	Probable cause	Comments

KALANCHOE (*Kalanchoe blossfeldiana*) (continued)

What the problem looks like	Probable cause	Comments
Leaves have pimplelike blisters or water-soaked spots. Leaves brown, harden, and appear corky, especially on underside. Foliage yellows, drops.	**Edema** or **Oedema**. Noninfectious disease. Leaves accumulate excess water when soil is warm and moist and air is cool and moist. Exact cause unknown.	Irrigate only in morning. Avoid irrigation if cool and cloudy. Provide good air circulation. Keep humidity low. Provide good drainage. Low media pH or high nitrogen levels may help to prevent. See page 41.
Plants severely stunted. Leaf terminals distorted. Buds deform, blacken or discolor, and may drop.	**Cyclamen mite,** *Phytonemus pallidus*. A pinkish orange mite (family Tarsonemidae), 1/100 inch long or smaller.	See page 217.
Foliage has sticky honeydew, blackish sooty mold, and white cast skins. Foliage may curl or yellow.	**Aphids,** including Melon aphid, *Aphis gossypii;* Green peach aphid, *Myzus persicae*. Small pear-shaped insects, often green to pinkish.	See page 179.
Foliage has sticky honeydew and blackish sooty mold. Foliage may yellow. Plant may die back.	**Brown soft scale,** *Coccus hesperidum*. Small yellow, brown, or orangish flattened, oval insects.	See page 186.
Foliage has sticky honeydew and blackish sooty mold. Leaves may yellow, distort, or wither. Tiny, whitish, mothlike adult insects.	**Whiteflies.** Nymphs and pupae flattened, oval, translucent, and greenish or yellow.	See page 170.
Cottony material (egg sacs), Foliage has sticky honeydew and blackish sooty mold. Foliage may yellow.	**Citrus mealybug,** *Planococcus citri*. Powdery gray insects with waxy marginal filaments, often sheltered at base of petioles and in axils.	See page 183.
Flowers, terminals, or foliage chewed. Leaves may be webbed with silk. Flower buds may be mined.	**Cabbage looper,** *Trichoplusia ni*. Greenish larvae, up to 1½ inches long, with light, longitudinal stripes.	Exclude moths from growing areas. Avoid growing near other major hosts. *Bacillus thuringiensis* kills larvae. See page 203.
Foliage, buds, and stems chewed. Young plants clipped at base. Stocky moths present, attracted to lights at night, wings folded at rest.	**Variegated cutworm,** *Peridroma saucia*. Gray or brown larvae with dark markings, row of yellow dots on back. Hide in soil during day.	Exclude moths, which fly to lights at night. Apply *Bacillus thuringiensis* to larvae. Insecticide bait kills caterpillars. See page 203.

LARKSPUR (*Consolida, Delphinium* spp.)

What the problem looks like	Probable cause	Comments
Plants stunted, yellowish. Roots decayed. Lower stems or crown sometimes rot.	**Root rots,** *Pythium, Phytophthora* spp. Fungi occur in most soils. Spread in water. Favored by wet, poorly drained soil.	Improve drainage. Plant in raised beds. Don't overirrigate. See pages 93–97.
Stem bases and sometimes crown are black and rotted. Stems may fall over. Rotted tissue is odorous. Most prevalent during warm, wet conditions.	**Soft crown rot** or **Blackleg,** *Erwinia carotovora*. Bacteria persist in plant debris, spread in water, and infect through wounds. Seed may be infected.	Pasteurize media used for seedlings. Avoid overhead irrigation, especially after flower spikes elongate. Plant on raised beds. Avoid wetting corms. See pages 100, 107.
Plants wilt suddenly and die. Water-soaked cankers appear on stem near soil. Stems have cottony growth, later large, black sclerotia.	**Cottony rot,** *Sclerotinia sclerotiorum*. Fungal sclerotia in soil produce airborne spores. Favored by cool, moist conditions. Many hosts, including vegetable crops.	Avoid planting where disease has occurred. Avoid overwatering. Irrigate early in day so plants dry quickly. Consider protective fungicide. See page 101.
Foliage yellows, especially outer leaves. Soft rot of basal stem or roots. White mycelia and small, tan to reddish brown sclerotia may develop on tissue around soil.	**Southern wilt,** *Sclerotium rolfsii*. Sclerotia survive in soil. Disease favored by moist, poorly drained, 77° to 95°F soil. Many hosts.	Avoid planting in infested soil, or pasteurize soil before planting. Avoid excess irrigation. Consider fungicide drench to infected soil. See page 101.
Flowers, flower heads, lower leaves, or growing points have soft brown decay. Dead tissue may have woolly gray growth (spores).	**Gray mold,** *Botrytis cinerea*. Fungus develops in crop debris or inactive tissue. Favored by high humidity and 70° to 77°F. Spores airborne.	Use good sanitation. Avoid overhead irrigation. Keep humidity low. Provide good air circulation. Don't crowd plants. See page 108.
Basal leaves wilted and yellowish; often, one branch is affected first. Vascular system has dark discoloration. Plant dies.	**Wilt,** *Verticillium dahliae, Fusarium oxysporum* f. sp. *delphinii*. Fungi persist in soil for years. *Verticillium* has wide host range, most severe during warm weather after cool period. *Fusarium* is host-specific, severe when soil is warm.	Grow plants where disease has not previously occurred. Pasteurize soil before planting. Rogue infected plants. See pages 104–106.
Seedlings wilt and collapse. Dark decay on stems near soil.	**Root rot,** *Rhizoctonia solani, Pythium* spp. Persist in soil. Favored by wet soil and poor drainage.	See pages 93–98.

What the problem looks like	Probable cause	Comments
Roots, basal stems, or flower stalks near soil are decayed. Few or no flowers. Decay odorous.	**Soft rot,** *Erwinia carotovora.* Bacteria occur in soil or infected plants. Favored when wet.	Use pathogen-free stock. Avoid injuring plant. Use good sanitation. Don't overwater. See pages 100, 107.
Brown to black stem cankers, often on base of older plants, may girdle stem; tops die and break. Dead tissue has tiny black pycnidia (black specks).	**Diplodia disease,** *Diplodia delphinii.* Fungus survives in crown of infected, living plants and in delphinium debris. Splashing water spreads spores.	Don't replant delphinium for 2 or more years where disease has occurred. Plant in raised beds. Remove plant debris and old stems. Avoid overhead irrigation.
Irregular, black, tarlike spots on leaves, sometimes on stems and petioles. From underside of leaf, spots appear brown. Disease favored by cool, wet weather.	**Black leaf spot,** *Pseudomonas syringae* pv. *delphinii.* Bacteria survive in delphinium debris from previous crop, spread in splashing water.	Rotate field to a different crop. Remove old leaves and stems from perennial field plantings. Avoid overhead irrigation. See page 107.
Leaves have brown, red, tan or yellow spots or blotches on. Foliage may yellow and die.	**Leaf spots,** *Cercospora delphinii* (not reported on larkspur in California), *Ascochyta aquilegiae,* *Ramularia delphinii.* Prefer wet conditions.	Avoid overhead irrigation. Keep humidity low. Employ good sanitation. See pages 116–118.
White powdery patches on leaves and stems. Basal leaves yellow, then brown and die. Flowers may be deformed.	**Powdery mildew,** *Erysiphe polygoni, Sphaerotheca humuli, S. macularis.* Fungi survive on living plants. Spores spread by splashing water. Favored by moderate temperatures, shade, and crowding. Common problem on this crop.	Avoid overcrowding. Provide adequate light and good air circulation. Consider applying foliar fungicide. See page 112.
Flowers revert to green leafy tissue. Spindly, upright yellow shoots and no flowers produced on plants infected the previous year.	**Aster yellows phytoplasma.** Spread by leafhoppers. Not spread by seed, handling, aphids, or other insects. Many hosts.	Don't plant seed beds downwind from delphinium or celery fields. Eliminate nearby weeds. Control leafhoppers. Rogue infected plants. See pages 129–130.
Leaves blotched, mottled, spotted, or streaked. Plant may be distorted and stunted. Foliage may die.	**Viruses,** including cucumber mosaic virus (aphid-vectored) and tomato spotted wilt (thrips-vectored), which have may hosts.	Use virus-free plants. Exclude and control insects. Rogue infected plants. See page 121.
Stem and leaf underside have powdery, brownish pustules. Foliage may yellow.	**Rust,** *Puccinia* spp. Airborne spores spread only from living tissue. Plant must be wet for infection. Mostly a field disease. Common problem on this crop.	Use resistant cultivars. Avoid wetting foliage. Keep humidity low. Fungicide can be applied when rust first appears. See page 119.
Leaves have white or yellowish circular to irregular spots. Leaves later turn brown, dry, and die.	**Leaf smut,** *Entyloma winteri, Urocystis sorosporioides.* Occur in plant debris. Favored by wet conditions.	Avoid overhead irrigation. Use good sanitation. Fungicide application may help to prevent.
Shoots short, swollen, flattened or distorted. Secondary rot may infect shoot clumps, killing plant. Plants lack vigor.	**Fasciation,** cause often uncertain. May be viral, bacterial (e.g., *Rhodococcus fascians*), or genetic. Manage as bacterial and take additional measures.	Use pathogen-free stock. Avoid injuring base of plants, especially when wet. Keep base of plants dry. Dispose of infected plants. See page 121.
Foliage yellows or wilts. Feeder and fleshy roots have knots or swellings.	**Root knot nematode,** *Meloidogyne* spp. Tiny roundworms, prefer warm, sandy soil. Many hosts.	Pasteurize or treat soil before planting. Rogue affected plants. Plant nonhosts at that site. See page 265.
Buds black, discolored, deformed, and may drop. Terminals distorted. Plants severely stunted.	**Cyclamen mite,** *Phytonemus pallidus.* A pinkish orange mite (family Tarsonemidae), $\frac{1}{100}$ inch long or smaller.	See page 217.
Foliage discolored, stippled, or bleached, and may drop. Terminals may distort. Plant may have fine webbing.	**Spider mites.** Tiny greenish, reddish, or yellowish mites; may have 2 dark spots.	See page 213.
Plant has blackish sooty mold, sticky honeydew, and whitish cast skins. Foliage may distort or yellow.	**Aphids,** including Green peach aphid, *Myzus persicae.*	Small pear-shaped insects, often green, yellow, or blackish. See page 179.
Flowers, terminals, or foliage chewed. Leaves may be webbed with silk. Flower buds may be mined.	**Bilobed looper,** *Autographa biloba;* **Cabbage looper,** *Trichoplusia ni.* Green or brown larvae, up to $1\frac{1}{2}$ inches long, with pale and dark or pale, longitudinal stripes. Adult moths brown and silver, 1 inch long.	Screen to exclude moths from growing areas. Avoid growing near other major hosts. *Bacillus thuringiensis* kills larvae. See page 203.

What the problem looks like	Probable cause	Comments

LEATHERLEAF FERN (*Dryopteris erythrosora*), wood fern

What the problem looks like	Probable cause	Comments
Fronds galled, blistered, curled, or distorted. Leaves may discolor. Plants may defoliate if severe. Only young tissue is susceptible to infection, which may not become apparent until later growth.	**Leaf galls,** *Taphrina* spp. Fungi persist on infected plants. Spores airborne. Infect only when bud development or new growth coincides with cool weather, high humidity, and wet foliage.	Avoid overhead irrigation. Keep humidity low; don't crowd plants. Use good sanitation; rogue infected plants. Fungicide applied after buds swell can provide control.
Fronds have powdery, colorless pustules. Leaves may be yellow spotted, dry, and drop.	**Rusts,** *Milesina* spp. Fungi survive on living tissue. Spores are airborne. Favored by high humidity and water. In Oregon and eastern U.S.; not reported on ferns in California.	Avoid overhead irrigation. Water in morning. Provide good air circulation. Don't crowd plants. See page 119.
Fronds have circular to irregular, yellow to brown spots, blotches, or water-soaked decay. Foliage may yellow and drop or die.	**Leaf spots,** *Cercospora, Colletotrichum, Cylindrocladium, Phoma* spp. Fungi persist in plant debris. Spread by splashing water. Not reported on ferns in California.	Avoid overhead watering. Use good sanitation, promptly remove and dispose of debris and infected leaves. See pages 116–118.
Foliage or woody parts have blackish sooty mold. Plant may yellow, decline, or die back.	**Hemispherical scale,** *Saissetia coffeae.* Orange, black, or brown, flattened to bulbous insects.	See page 186.
Foliage has sticky honeydew and blackish sooty mold. Foliage may yellow.	**Longtailed mealybug,** *Pseudococcus longispinus.* Powdery gray insects with waxy marginal filaments.	See page 183.

LEPTOSPERMUM (*Leptospermum* spp.), Tea tree

What the problem looks like	Probable cause	Comments
Plant declines and eventually dies. White fungal plaques develop between bark and wood.	**Armillaria root rot,** *Armillaria mellea.* Persists for many years in infected roots in soil. May be introduced on infected plants or in compost that contains woody material. Favored by warm, moist soil.	Remove all woody roots ½ inch diameter or larger before planting. Pasteurize or air-dry soil well before planting. See page 99.
Foliage yellows or turns brown. Leaves or entire plant may wilt and die. Crown tissue and roots discolored, soft, wet, decayed.	**Root and crown rots,** *Phytophthora* spp. Fungi persist in media. Favored by wet conditions.	Pasteurize media before planting. Provide good drainage. Don't moisture-stress or overwater plants. See pages 93–97.

LIATRIS (*Liatris* spp.), Gay-feather

What the problem looks like	Probable cause	Comments
Foliage wilts and yellows, often first on one side of plant. Corm vascular tissue discolored. No apparent decay during early stages.	**Verticillium wilt,** *Verticillium albo-atrum.* Soilborne fungus. Plugs water-conducting tissue, causing symptoms when plant is water-stressed.	Pasteurize media before planting. Provide appropriate irrigation. See pages 104–106.
Leaves have circular to irregular, yellow to brown spots or blotches. Foliage may yellow and drop or die.	**Leaf spots,** *Phyllosticta liatridis, Septoria liatridis.* Fungi spread by splashing water, persist in plant debris. Not reported on *Liatris* in California.	Avoid overhead watering. Use good sanitation, promptly remove and dispose of debris and infected leaves. See pages 116–118.
Leaves have brown to orangish powdery pustules and yellowish spots. Leaves may yellow and drop.	**Rusts,** *Coleosporium laciniariae, Puccinia poarum.* Fungi survive on living tissue. Spores are airborne. Favored by high humidity and water. Not reported on *Liatris* in California.	Avoid overhead irrigation. Water in morning. Provide good air circulation. Don't crowd plants. See page 119.
Plants are stunted. Foliage may yellow. Roots have swellings or galls. Few tiny rootlets.	**Root knot nematode,** *Meloidogyne* spp. Nematodes persist in soil as eggs. Most severe in warm, sandy soils.	Pasteurize soil before planting. See Nematodes, page 265.
Stem abnormally flat and distorted. Bushy, stunted growth.	**Fasciation,** cause often uncertain. May be viral, bacterial (e.g., *Rhodococcus fascians*), or genetic. Manage as bacterial and take additional measures.	Use pathogen-free stock. Avoid injuring base of plants, especially when wet. Keep base of plants dry. Dispose of infected plants. See page 121.
Foliage has sticky honeydew, blackish sooty mold, and white cast skins. Foliage may curl or yellow.	**Aphids.** Small pear-shaped insects, often green, yellowish, or blackish.	See page 179.

LILY (*Lilium* spp.), Asiatic lilies, Easter lily, Oriental lilies

What the problem looks like	Probable cause	Comments
Plants yellow, stunted, wilted. Leaves have brown, dead patches. Flower buds may wither, not open. Bulbs and roots may rot. Stems may canker. Seedlings may damp off.	**Root, bulb, and stem rots,** *Fusarium oxysporum* f. sp. *lilii,* *Phytophthora, Pythium* spp., *Rhizoctonia solani.* Fungi favored by wet, poorly drained soil.	Pasteurize media before planting. Avoid overwatering. Provide good drainage. See pages 93–98.
Bulb scales, bulbs, and sometimes stems are brown or black and decayed.	**Scale rots,** *Colletotrichum* spp. Fungi favored by prolonged wet conditions. Persist in crop debris.	Avoid excess irrigation. Provide good drainage. Use good sanitation; promptly remove and dispose of debris and infected leaves.

What the problem looks like	Probable cause	Comments
Bulb decay in storage.	**Bulb rots,** *Rhizopus stolonifer, Penicillium* spp. Persist in infected crop debris. Favored by high humidity. Spores airborne and spread in water.	Store bulbs under cool, low-humidity conditions. Regularly inspect and dispose of infected bulbs.
Leaves have brown to orangish powdery pustules or yellowish blotches. Leaves may drop.	**Rusts,** *Uromyces* spp. Survive on living tissue. Spores are airborne. Favored by high humidity, rain, and overhead irrigation.	Avoid overhead irrigation. Water in morning so foliage dries. Keep humidity low. See page 119.
Brown, tan, or white spots or lesions on leaves or stems. Lesions may have yellow borders. Foliage may yellow, shrivel, drop.	**Leaf spots,** *Cercospora, Cercosporella, Heterosporium, Ramularia* spp. Spread splashing water. Favored by wet conditions. Persist in debris. Not reported on lily in California.	Avoid wetting foliage. Use drip irrigation and raised beds. Use good sanitation; promptly remove and dispose of debris and infected leaves. See pages 116–118.
Petals, flower heads, or leaves have soft tan to brown decay or spots. Foliage may wilt. Dead tissue may have woolly gray growth.	**Gray mold,** *Botrytis* spp. Fungi develop in plant debris. Favored by high humidity.	Use good sanitation. Avoid overhead irrigation. Keep humidity low. Provide good air circulation. Don't crowd plants. See page 108.
Petals have small brown spots. Plant wilts and dies. Basal stem rotted. Black sclerotia in and on stems. Cottony mycelia in and on stems if conditions are moist.	**Cottony rot,** *Sclerotinia sclerotiorum.* Fungus survives in soil as sclerotia that may infect plants on contact. Favored by overhead irrigation and high humidity. Many hosts. Not reported on lily in California.	Pasteurize media before planting. Avoid overhead irrigation. Irrigate early in day so plants dry quickly. See page 101.
Leaves have many pale flecks or discolored mottling or streaks. Foliage distorted. Stunted growth. Flowers streaked, may not fully open. Terminals may be tufted.	**Viruses,** including Cucumber mosaic, Lily mottle, Lily streak, Lily symptomless, Rosette, Tomato spotted wilt (thrips-vectored), and Tulip breaking viruses. Persist in infected bulbs. Most are vectored by aphids.	Use only virus-free corms. Rogue infected plants. Exclude or control insect vectors. Increased starting temperatures and increased humidity may reduce symptoms from some viruses. See page 121.
Leaves yellowish. Leaves have dark green or brown, vein-limited, bands or blotches that develop progressively up from older leaves. Plant may have dense, bunchy growth.	**Foliar nematodes,** *Aphelenchoides fragariae, A. olesistis.* Tiny roundworms spread in plant debris, vegetative propagation, and splashing water. Not common in California.	Use uninfected stock plants. Remove plant debris. Avoid overhead irrigation; leaves must be wet for infection to occur. See page 265.
Plants are stunted. Foliage may yellow. Swellings or galls on roots. Few tiny rootlets.	**Root knot nematode,** *Meloidogyne* spp. Nematodes persist in soil. Most severe in warm, sandy soils.	Pasteurize soil before planting. See page 265.
Leaf edges have brown, crescent-shaped or elongate blotches. Leaf tips may brown. Older leaves affected first. 'Ace' and 'Croft' are highly susceptible.	**Leaf scorch.** Noninfectious disorder, may be caused by fluoride toxicity, which can develop in low-pH media. 'Nellie White' cultivars are resistant.	Provide proper cultural care. Avoid superphosphate or other fluoride-containing materials. Consider increasing media pH to about 6.8 to 7.2.
Bulbs die; if they sprout, growth is slow with few, late, or no flowers.	**Bulb failure.** Apparently due to poor storage conditions, including low oxygen, excess carbon dioxide, low bulb moisture, or freezing.	Use only quality bulbs stored under appropriate conditions.
Foliage yellows rapidly or gradually from plant bottom; often starts at bud initiation.	**Yellowing.** Causes include root diseases or noninfectious disorders, such as poor growing conditions, inadequate cultural care, or damage from use of plant growth regulators.	Avoid excessive drying, root rot, or insufficient nitrogen. Avoid late high-temperature forcing or late use of growth regulator. Avoid long storage or shipping of plants.
Buds stop growing and shrivel starting at base, then turn brown. Buds may drop; small scars remain among bractlike leaves where buds normally appear.	**Bud blast** or **Bud abortion.** Noninfectious disorder, common from high-temperature forcing. Water stress, root injury, high salts in media, or growth retardant application apparently contribute to the problem.	Avoid temperatures that are too high after bud initiation. Provide adequate irrigation, humidity, light, and good care. Avoid root injuries or root rot. Avoid excess cold storage.
Foliage yellows and wilts. Plants may be stunted, fall over, or die from root-feeding beetles. Basal stems or leaves may be chewed.	**Carrot beetle,** *Ligyrus gibbosus.* Adult beetles (family Scarabaeidae) reddish brown, ½ inch long, feed above and below ground. Larvae up to 1¼ inches long, white to bluish, head dark.	Attacks grains and vegetable crops, especially tubers. Exclude adults, which fly at night to lights. Eliminate decaying vegetation that harbors adults around plants. See White Grubs, page 211.
Foliage has sticky honeydew and blackish sooty mold. Leaves may yellow and wither. Tiny, whitish, mothlike adult insects.	**Greenhouse whitefly,** *Trialeurodes vaporariorum.* Oval, flattened, yellow to greenish nymphs. Pupae have many long filaments.	See page 170.
Foliage has sticky honeydew, blackish sooty mold, and whitish cast skins. Foliage may curl or yellow.	**Aphids,** including *Aphis fabae, A. gossypii, Aulacorthum circumflexum A. solani, Macrosiphum euphorbiae, Myzus persicae, Rhopalosiphum nymphaeae.*	Small pear-shaped insects, often green, yellowish, or blackish. See page 179.

What the problem looks like	Probable cause	Comments
LILY (*Lilium* spp.), Asiatic lilies, Easter lily, Oriental lilies (continued)		
Poor growth from bulbs. Plants stunted. Young shoots distorted. Aphids under leaf sheaths, on stems near soil, and under scales of stored bulbs and bulbs in the field.	**Tulip bulb aphid,** *Dysaphis tulipae.* Small pear-shaped yellow, pink, gray, or green insects, waxy covered. Easily overlooked; usually cause direct damage only to stored bulbs. Vectors persistent lily symptomless virus. Has other hosts, including freesia, gladiolus, iris, and especially tulip where it vectors nonpersistent tulip breaking virus.	See page 182.
Bulbs discolored reddish brown, rotted, and infested with tiny, oval, white to brownish mites.	**Bulb mites,** *Rhizoglyphus* spp. Sluggish mites that look like tiny eggs; may also be on stems, leaves. Secondary pests that prefer decayed tissue but may help fungi infect plants.	See page 218.
Blossoms have discolored blotches or streaks. Foliage stippled, bleached, or blotched, may have dark, varnishlike excrement.	**Banded greenhouse thrips,** *Hercinothrips femoralis;* **Western flower thrips,** *Frankliniella occidentalis.*	Tiny, slender, dark brown to yellowish adults. Nymphs and pupae whitish to pale yellow. See Thrips, page 161.
Bulb scale surface injured, rusty brown, somewhat sunken. Tiny slender insects feeding on bulbs.	**Lily bulb thrips,** *Liothrips vaneeckei.* Adult glossy black, wings silvery white. Nymphs and pupae salmon pink. Feeds and spends entire life cycle only on outer bulb scales near base; usually not a serious problem.	See page 161.
Foliage yellow, stunted, produces no blooms. Bulbs feel soft and spongy, are hollowed and filled with brown excrement from wrinkled, gray, white, or brownish maggots, boring inside.	**Bulb flies,** including Narcissus bulb fly, *Merodon equestris* and *Eumerus* spp. Adult hairy fly (family Syrphidae), black with gray to orange, like bumble bee, hovers around blooming plants, where eggs are laid. M. *equestris* adult and mature larva about ½ inch long; *Eumerus* spp. smaller.	Inspect and discard spongy bulbs before planting. See page 200.
Leaves bleached, stippled, may turn brown and drop. Plant may have fine silk.	**Spider mites,** *Tetranychus* spp. Tiny green, yellow, pink, or red pests.	See page 213.
Foliage yellows. Plant declines or dies back. Bark or leaves have yellow to brownish encrustations.	**Dictyosperum scale,** *Chrysomphalus dictyospermi.* Colonies of circular, flat insects, less than ⅟16 inch long.	See page 186.
Seedlings clipped. Leaves chewed, often between veins. Foliage yellows and wilts from slender, whitish larvae feeding on roots.	**Cucumber beetles,** *Acalymma, Diabrotica* spp. Greenish yellow adults with black heads and black spots or stripes. Have several generations per year.	Avoid growing near alternate host Cucurbitaceae crops. Control cucurbit weeds, where adults overwinter and feed. Exclude adults, especially from seedlings. See page 212.
Leaves and blossoms chewed (edges notched). Foliage may yellow and wilt from whitish maggots feeding on roots.	**Black vine weevil,** *Otiorhynchus sulcatus;* **Fuller rose beetle,** *Asynonychus godmani.* Rarely seen adults brown, black, to gray snout beetles that feed at night. Larvae whitish maggots that feed on roots.	See Weevils, page 208.
Leaves have winding tunnels. Heavily infested leaves may drop. Leaves have pale spots or punctures from adult flies. Yellowish to white maggots in mines.	**Leafminer,** *Liriomyza* sp. Adults are tiny, active, black and yellow flies.	See page 167.
LILY, NERINE (*Nerine* spp.), Lily		
Leaf tips have yellow to brown lesions. Leaves have elongate, reddish brown spots. Small, black pycnidia (black specks) form in necrotic areas.	**Scorch** or **Red spot,** *Stagonospora curtisii.* Fungus persists on infected plants. Infects plants in Amaryllidaceae family. Spores spread by splashing water. Favored by mild, moist conditions.	Pasteurize media before planting. Treating bulbs with hot water before planting can control but may injure bulbs or stunt flowers. Consider fungicide applications, beginning when first leaves emerge.
LISIANTHUS (*Lisianthus russellianus* or *Eustoma grandiflora*), Texas bluebell		
Basal stem or roots brown, wet, and rotted. Foliage may yellow, discolor brownish, wilt, and die. Seedlings may wilt and collapse.	**Root and stem rot,** *Fusarium, Phytophthora, Pythium, Rhizoctonia* spp. Spread in contaminated media and stock. Favored by high relative humidity, warm temperatures, overwatering, and poorly drained media.	Pasteurize media before planting. Use pathogen-free plants. Provide good drainage. Don't overwater. Avoid high humidity. See pages 93–98.
Flowers or leaves have soft brown decay or spots. Stems may have cankers. Plants may wilt. Dead tissue may have woolly gray growth (spores).	**Gray mold,** *Botrytis cinerea.* Fungus develops in crop debris or inactive tissue. Favored by high humidity and 70° to 77°F. Spores airborne.	Use good sanitation. Avoid overhead irrigation. Keep humidity low. Provide good air circulation. Don't crowd plants. See page 108.

What the problem looks like	Probable cause	Comments
Yellow lesions on leaves and stems. White, powdery growth, primarily on older leaves and stem. Severely affected leaves may become twisted, bent, dry, and die.	**Powdery mildew,** *Leveillula* (=*Oidiopsis*) *taurica.* Free water not required for infection.	Use good sanitation. Provide good air circulation and adequate light. Consider applying sulfur or other fungicide to prevent. See page 112.
Brown to yellow spots or blotches, mostly on older leaves. Spots may have dark or yellowish margins. Foliage may shrivel, drop.	**Leaf spots,** including *Cercospora eustomae.* Spread by air or splashing water. Favored by prolonged, cool, wet, conditions. Persist in plant debris.	Avoid wetting foliage. Use drip irrigation and raised benches. Use good sanitation; promptly remove and dispose of debris and infected leaves. See pages 116–118.
Terminal growth yellow with brown, dead areas. Foliage yellow, spotted or streaked, may drop. Stems necrotic.	**Impatiens necrotic spot virus, Tomato spotted wilt virus.** Spread by thrips. Have many crop and weed hosts.	Eliminate nearby weeds. Exclude or control thrips. Rogue infected plants. See page 121.
Plants are yellow, stunted. Roots have numerous small swellings or galls. Few tiny rootlets.	**Root knot nematode,** *Meloidogyne* sp. Nematodes persists in soil as eggs. Most severe problem in warm, sandy soils.	Pasteurize soil before planting. See page 265.
Blossoms have irregular white or brown blotches. Leaves may turn brown. Blossoms or terminals may be distorted. Growth may be stunted.	**Western flower thrips,** *Frankliniella occidentalis.* Slender dark brown to yellowish insects, $^1/_{16}$ inch long or less.	See page 161.
Foliage discolored, stippled, bleached, or reddened, and may drop. Plant may have fine webbing.	**Spider mites.** Tiny pests, often greenish, yellowish, or reddish; may have 2 dark spots.	See page 213.
Foliage has sticky honeydew, blackish sooty mold, and white cast skins. Foliage may curl or yellow.	**Aphids.** Tiny pear-shaped insects, often green, yellowish, or blackish.	See page 179.
Plant has sticky honeydew and blackish sooty mold. Foliage may yellow. New growth may distort or wilt.	**Greenhouse whitefly,** *Trialeurodes vaporariorum;* **Silverleaf whitefly,** *Bemisia argentifolii.* Nymphs and pupae flattened, oval, translucent, and greenish or yellow. Adults tiny, waxy, white, and mothlike.	See page 170.
Leaves have winding tunnels. Heavily infested leaves may drop. Leaves have pale spots or punctures from adult flies. Yellowish to white maggots in mines.	**Leafminers,** *Liriomyza* spp. Adults are tiny, active, black and yellow flies.	See page 167.
Foliage, terminals, or petals chewed. Leaves may be webbed with silk. Flower buds may be mined.	**Beet armyworm,** *Spodoptera exigua.* Greenish larvae, up to $1^3/_8$ inches long, with light, longitudinal stripes.	Exclude moths. Apply *Bacillus thuringiensis* to young larvae. See page 203.

MARGUERITE DAISY (*Chrysanthemum frutescens*)

What the problem looks like	Probable cause	Comments
Plant wilts and dies. Basal stem rotted. Black sclerotia in and on stems. Cottony mycelia in and on stems if conditions are moist.	**Cottony rot,** *Sclerotinia sclerotiorum.* Fungus survives in soil as sclerotia that may infect plants on contact. Favored by overhead irrigation and high humidity. Many hosts, including carrots, celery, and lettuce.	Avoid planting in infested fields or pasteurize soil before planting. Avoid overhead irrigation. Irrigate early in day so plants dry quickly. Consider fungicide application to base and lower foliage of plants. See page 101.
Foliage wilted or yellow. Plants stunted. Root system reduced, small roots rotted.	**Root and crown rot,** *Rhizoctonia solani, Pythium* spp. Soilborne fungi. Spread by spores in soil and water. Favored by excess moisture and poor drainage.	Pasteurize media before planting. Provide good drainage. Plant in raised beds. Avoid excess irrigation and reduce watering if disease develops. See pages 93–98.
Plants wilt and collapse. Basal stem and roots rotted. White cottony fungus growth or tan or brown sclerotia (about $^1/_{16}$ inch) may form on plant parts or soil.	**Southern blight,** *Sclerotium rolfsii.* Sclerotia survive in soil. No airborne spores are formed. Many hosts. Favored by high temperatures.	Avoid fields where disease has occurred or pasteurize soil before planting. Fungicide applied at base of plants can help prevent. See page 101.
Plants yellow and wilt, often first on one side of plant. Vascular tissue darkens.	**Verticillium wilt,** *Verticillium dahliae.* Most severe during warm weather after cool weather.	Pasteurize soil or avoid planting in soil where disease has occurred. See pages 104–106.
Flowers or leaves have soft brown decay or spots. May be stem cankers. Plants may wilt. Dead tissue may have woolly gray growth (spores).	**Gray mold,** *Botrytis cinerea.* Fungus develops in crop debris or inactive tissue. Favored by high humidity and 70° to 77°F. Spores airborne.	Use good sanitation. Avoid overhead irrigation. Keep humidity low. Provide good air circulation. Don't crowd plants. See page 108.
White, powdery growth, primarily on older leaves and stem. Severely affected leaves dry and die.	**Powdery mildew,** *Erysiphe cichoracearum.* Free water not required for infection.	Provide good air circulation and adequate light. Consider applying sulfur or other fungicide to prevent. See page 112.

What the problem looks like	Probable cause	Comments
MARGUERITE DAISY (Chrysanthemum frutescens) (continued)		
Leaves or stems have yellow to brown streaks, rings, spots, or mottling. Leaves or flowers stunted, distorted, or wilted.	**Viruses,** including Beet curly top (leafhopper-vectored); Chrysanthemum mosaic (aphid-vectored).	Use virus-free cuttings. Rogue infected plants immediately. Eliminate nearby weeds and other hosts. Exclude or control insect vectors. See page 121.
Flowers revert to green leafy tissue. Spindly, upright yellow shoots and no flowers produced on plants infected the previous year.	**Aster yellows phytoplasma.** Spread by leafhoppers. Not spread by seed, handling, aphids, or other insects. Many hosts.	Don't plant seed beds downwind from delphinium, celery, or other hosts. Eliminate nearby weeds. Control leafhoppers. Rogue infected plants. See pages 129–130.
Bulbs do not produce or flowers develop poorly. Bulbs rot. Flower stalks rot near soil and fall over. Odorous decay.	**Soft rot,** *Erwinia carotovora.* Bacteria occur in soil or infected bulbs. Favored when wet.	Store bulbs under cool, dry conditions. Avoid injuring plant; disease infects through wounds. Don't plant infected bulbs. Don't overwater. See pages 100, 107.
Shoots short, swollen, flattened or distorted. Secondary rot may infect shoot clumps, killing plant. Plants lack vigor.	**Fasciation,** cause often uncertain. May be viral, bacterial (e.g., *Rhodococcus fascians*), or genetic. Manage as bacterial and take additional measures.	Use pathogen-free stock. Avoid injuring base of plants, especially when wet. Keep base of plants dry. Dispose of infected plants. See page 121.
Stem has spherical galls, usually near plant base. Heavily infected plants become stunted.	**Crown gall,** *Agrobacterium tumefaciens.* Spreads in soil and survives in soil for many years. Has wide host range.	Propagate from and plant disease-free plants. Avoid wounding plants, especially when wet. Dip or spray cuttings with *Agrobacterium tumefaciens* K-84 immediately after any wounding. See page 102.
Plants are stunted. Roots have swellings or galls. Few tiny rootlets.	**Root knot nematode,** *Meloidogyne hapla.* Nematodes persists in soil as eggs. Most severe problem in warm, sandy soils.	Pasteurize soil before planting. See page 265.
Plants stunted. Necrotic lesions in root cortex and deep tissues.	**Root lesion nematodes,** *Pratylenchus* spp. Nematodes survive in soil as eggs, larvae, and adults.	Pasteurize soil before planting. See page 265.
Foliage has sticky honeydew, blackish sooty mold, and whitish cast skins. Leaves may curl or pucker. Foliage may yellow.	**Aphids,** including Leaf curl plum aphid, *Aphis* or *Brachycaudus helichrysi.* Small pear-shaped insects, often green, reddish, yellowish, or blackish.	See page 179.
Plants stunted, decline, may die. Powdery waxy material may be visible on roots and around crown.	**Ground mealybug,** *Rhizoecus* spp. Small, slender, pale insects, may be lightly covered with powdery wax, but no marginal filaments.	See page 183.
Foliage discolored, stippled, bleached, or reddened, and may drop. Plant may have fine webbing.	**Spider mites.** Tiny pests, often greenish, yellowish, or reddish; may have 2 dark spots.	See page 213.
Plants severely stunted. Leaf terminals distorted. Buds deform, blacken, or discolor, and may drop.	**Cyclamen mite,** *Phytonemus pallidus.* A pinkish orange mite (family Tarsonemidae), $\frac{1}{100}$ inch long or smaller.	See page 217.
Blossoms have irregular white or brown blotches. Blossoms or terminals may be distorted. Plant growth and seed production may be reduced.	**Western flower thrips,** *Frankliniella occidentalis.* Tiny slender dark brown to yellowish insects.	See page 161.
Leaves have winding tunnels. Heavily infested leaves may drop. Yellowish to white maggots in mines. Leaves may have pale spots or punctures from adult flies.	**Serpentine leafminer,** *Liriomyza trifolii;* **Chrysanthemum leafminer,** *Chromatomyia syngenesiae. Liriomyza* adults are small, grayish or black and yellow flies.	See Leafminers, page 167.
Buds, flowers, or leaves mined or chewed; may be webbed with silk.	**Omnivorous leaftier,** *Cnephasia longana.* Gray to brownish, $\frac{1}{2}$ inch long larvae and nocturnal moths. Larvae may have grayish stripes. Attacks strawberries and many other hosts. Occurs in central California coast. Has 1 generation per year.	Time any spray for young larvae emerging from mines in spring. See Caterpillars, page 203.
MARIGOLD (Tagetes spp.)		
Foliage yellows. Plants wilt and die, often suddenly. Roots and stem near soil may be cankered, dark, and decayed.	**Root, crown, and stem rot,** *Fusarium, Pythium, Phytophthora* spp. Fungi survive in soil, favored by wet, poorly drained media.	Pasteurize media before planting. Don't overirrigate. Provide good drainage. See pages 93–96.
Foliage fades, yellows, browns, and wilts, often on one side of plant. Branches and entire plant may die.	**Verticillium wilt,** *Verticillium dahliae.* Fungus persists in soil, infects through roots.	See pages 104–106.

What the problem looks like	Probable cause	Comments
Plants wilt and die. Cottony growth in or on stems if conditions are moist. Large, black sclerotia on or inside stems.	**Cottony rot,** *Sclerotinia sclerotiorum.* Fungal sclerotia in soil infect by direct contact with plants. Not common on marigold in western U.S.	Avoid planting in previously infested fields or pasteurize media before planting. Many hosts. Favored by wet conditions. Irrigate early in day so plants dry quickly. See page 101.
Stems or roots have growths or galls, typically around previously injured tissue. Roots may be gnarled, stunted, or hairy due to mostly small roots or rootlets.	**Crown gall,** *Agrobacterium tumefaciens.* Spreads in water, survives in soil, infects through wounds. Galls favored by rapid plant growth.	See page 102.
Flowers or leaves have soft brown decay or spots. May be stem cankers. Plants may wilt. Dead tissue may have woolly gray growth (spores).	**Gray mold,** *Botrytis cinerea.* Fungus develops in crop debris or inactive tissue. Favored by high humidity and 70° to 77°F. Spores airborne.	Use good sanitation. Avoid overhead irrigation. Keep humidity low. Provide good air circulation. Don't crowd plants. See page 108.
Brown to yellow spots or blotches, mostly on older leaves. Spots may have dark or yellowish margins. Petals or foliage may shrivel and drop. May be stem cankers.	**Leaf spots,** *Alternaria, Ascochyta, Cercospora, Phyllosticta* spp. Spread by air or splashing water. Favored by cool, wet conditions. Persist in debris. Only *Alternaria* is reported on marigold in California.	Avoid wetting foliage. Use drip irrigation and raised benches. Use good sanitation; promptly remove and dispose of debris and infected leaves. See pages 116–118.
Spindly, upright yellow shoots. Few or no flowers. Plants stunted. Flowers revert to green leafy tissue.	**Aster yellows phytoplasma.** Spread by leafhoppers. Not spread by seed, handling, aphids, or other insects. Many hosts.	Avoid planting near other hosts. Eliminate nearby weeds. Exclude or control leafhoppers. Rogue infected plants. See pages 129–130.
Yellow to brown leaf blotches, spots, or streaks. Foliage may die. Plant may be distorted and stunted.	**Tomato spotted wilt virus.** Spread by thrips. Has many crop and weed hosts	Eliminate nearby weeds. Exclude or control thrips. Rogue infected plants. See page 121.
Blossoms have irregular white or brown blotches. Blossoms or terminals may be distorted. Plant growth and seed production may be reduced.	**Western flower thrips,** *Frankliniella occidentalis.* Tiny, slender, dark brown to yellowish insects.	See Thrips, page 161.
Flower seed coats injured, discolored, scabby. Thin-coated seed die. Flowers may be distorted from feeding by tiny, slender insects.	**Composite thrips,** *Microcephalothrips abdominalis.* Tiny dark brown adults, wings light brown. Entire life cycle spent in flowers, including debris.	Don't grow seed plants near other Asteraceae crops or weeds. Use good sanitation; remove debris from seedbeds before planting. See Thrips, page 161.
Foliage discolored or distorted. Plant may have fine webbing, which can reduce pollination and seed yield.	**Twospotted spider mite,** *Tetranychus urticae.* Tiny greenish or yellowish mites with 2 darker spots.	See page 213.
Foliage has sticky honeydew and blackish sooty mold. Leaves may yellow and wither. Tiny, whitish, mothlike adult insects.	**Greenhouse whitefly,** *Trialeurodes vaporariorum;* **Silverleaf whitefly,** *Bemisia argentifolii;* **Sweetpotato whitefly,** *Bemisia tabaci.* Oval, flattened, yellow to greenish nymphs.	See Whiteflies, page 170.
Foliage has sticky honeydew, blackish sooty mold, and whitish cast skins. Foliage may yellow. Flowers and seed reduced. Plants stunted.	**Aphids,** including Melon aphid, *Aphis gossypii;* Green peach aphid, *Myzus persicae.* Small pear-shaped insects, often green, yellowish, or black.	See page 179.
Leaves have winding tunnels. Leaves may drop. Plants stunted. Flower and seed production reduced. Young plants may die. Pale leaf spots or punctures from adult flies. Yellowish to white maggots in mines.	**Serpentine leafminer,** *Liriomyza trifolii.* Adults are tiny, active, black and yellow flies.	See page 167.
Flowers, terminals, or foliage chewed. Leaves may be webbed with silk. Flower buds and heads may be mined. May be dark frass from caterpillars.	**Beet armyworm,** *Spodoptera exigua;* **Cabbage looper,** *Trichoplusia ni;* **Orange tortrix,** *Argyrotaenia citrana;* **Sunflower moth,** *Homoeosoma electellum;* **Tobacco budworm,** *Helicoverpa virescens.*	Exclude moths from growing areas. Avoid growing near other major hosts. *Bacillus thuringiensis* kills exposed-feeding larvae. See Caterpillars, page 203.

NASTURTIUM (*Tropaeolum* spp.)

What the problem looks like	Probable cause	Comments
Circular to irregular, yellow to brown spots or blotches on leaves. Foliage may yellow and die.	**Leaf spots,** including *Cercospora, Phyllosticta, Pleospora* spp. Spread by splashing water or contaminated tools or stock. Persist in plant debris. Not reported on nasturtium in California.	Avoid overhead watering. Use good sanitation; promptly remove and dispose of debris and infected leaves. See pages 116–118.
Shoots short, swollen, flattened, or distorted. Secondary rot may infect shoot clumps, killing plant. Plants lack vigor.	**Fasciation,** cause often uncertain. May be viral, bacterial (e.g., *Rhodococcus fascians*), or genetic. Manage as bacterial and take additional measures.	Use pathogen-free stock. Avoid injuring base of plants, especially when wet. Keep base of plants dry. Dispose of infected plants. See page 121.

What the problem looks like	Probable cause	Comments
NASTURTIUM (*Tropaeolum* spp.) (continued)		
Leaves have pale mottling, mosaic, or rings. Foliage may be crinkled, cupped, or deformed. Veins may turn pale. Petals may be streaked or spotted. Plants may be stunted.	**Viruses,** including Cucumber mosaic (aphid-vectored), Nasturtium mosaic (aphid-vectored), Tomato spotted wilt (thrips-vectored), Turnip mosaic (aphid-vectored).	Eliminate nearby weeds. Exclude or control aphids and thrips. Rogue infected plants. See page 121.
Spindly, upright yellow shoots. Few or no flowers. Flowers revert to green leafy tissue.	**Aster yellows phytoplasma.** Spread by leafhoppers. Not spread by seed, handling, aphids, or other insects. Many hosts.	Avoid planting near other hosts. Eliminate nearby weeds. Exclude or control leafhoppers. Rogue infected plants. See pages 129–130.
Foliage pale and wilted. Plants stunted and may die. Knobby, spindlelike swellings on roots. Prevalent in soils where *Brassica* spp. crops have previously grown.	**Clubroot,** *Plasmodiophora brassicae.* A plasmodium microorganism. Propagules very persistent in media and infect roots, especially when wet. Soil pH of 7.2 or higher inhibits spore germination.	Plant only pathogen-free stock. Pasteurize media before planting. Don't grow cruciferous crops in soil where other infested plants in mustard family have grown, including certain weeds and crops such as broccoli and cabbage. Provide good drainage. Adjust pH if possible.
Foliage discolored, stippled, brownish, or bleached, and may drop. Terminals may distort. Plant may have fine webbing.	**Twospotted mite,** *Tetranychus urticae.* Tiny greenish, reddish, or yellowish mites; may have 2 dark spots.	See page 213.
Foliage distorted, discolored, stippled, or brown. Foliage may drop prematurely. Stems and leaves have pimplelike (egg-laying) punctures.	**Leafhoppers.** Slender insects, often yellowish green, that suck plant sap and readily jump, fly, or crawl away sideways when disturbed.	Control weeds; leafhoppers often move from weeds. Control of adults is difficult; insecticidal soap or oil can reduce nymph populations. See page 193.
Foliage has sticky honeydew and blackish sooty mold. Copious white waxy material present with certain species. Leaves may yellow and wither. Tiny, whitish, mothlike adult insects.	**Giant whitefly,** *Aleurodicus dugesii;* **Greenhouse whitefly,** *Trialeurodes vaporariorum.* Nymphs and pupae flattened, oval, translucent, and greenish or yellow.	See Whiteflies, page 170.
Foliage has sticky honeydew, blackish sooty mold, and whitish cast skins. Foliage may curl or yellow.	**Aphids,** including *Aphis fabae, A. gossypii, Myzus persicae.* Tiny pear-shaped insects, often green, yellowish, reddish, or blackish.	See page 179.
Foliage chewed and webbed together with silk. Stems may be mined. Larvae wriggle vigorously when touched.	**Greenhouse leaftier,** *Udea rubigalis.* Larvae yellowish green with three longitudinal green to white stripes. Adult reddish brown with black wavy lines on wings. Mature adult and larva about ¾ inches long. Has about 6 generations per year.	Avoid growing floral hosts near celery, a major host. See page 203.
Foliage chewed, no webbing. Green caterpillars, up to 1 inch long.	**Imported cabbageworm,** *Pieris rapae.* Adult white or yellowish moth with one or two black dots on wings. Attacks Brassicaceae.	Avoid growing near Brassicaceae crops and control weeds in that family. See page 203.
ORCHID, CATTLEYA (*Cattleya* spp.)		
Shoots, crown, roots, leaves, or stems infected with dark, wet rot, then plant dies. Seedlings wilt and die.	**Black rot, Seedling damping-off,** *Pythium* spp. Persist in media. Spread in media and water. Favored by wet media and poor drainage.	Pasteurize media before planting. Provide good drainage. Don't overwater. See pages 93–96.
Flowers, flower heads, lower leaves, or growing points have soft brown decay. Dead tissue may have woolly gray growth (spores).	**Gray mold,** *Botrytis cinerea.* Fungus develops in crop debris or inactive tissue. Favored by high humidity and 70° to 77°F. Spores airborne.	Use good sanitation. Avoid overhead irrigation. Keep humidity low. Provide good air circulation. Don't crowd plants. See page 108.
Leaves have pale to dark elongate spots or blotches. Foliage may yellow, shrivel, or drop.	**Leaf spot,** *Gloeosporium* spp. Spread by splashing water. Favored by prolonged wet conditions. Persist in plant debris.	Avoid wetting foliage; use drip irrigation. Use good sanitation; promptly remove and dispose of debris and infected leaves. See pages 116–118.
Soft, brown, stem rot near soil line. Foliage yellows and wilts. Leaves may have irregular water-soaked spots or lesions. Odorous rot.	**Bacterial soft rot or blight,** *Erwinia chrysanthemi.* Persists in media and infected stock. Favored when wet. Avoid injuring plant, as disease infects wounds.	Keep foliage dry. Don't overwater. Provide good drainage. Use good sanitation; rogue infected and nearby plants. See pages 100, 107.
Bulbs don't produce or flowers develop poorly. Bulbs rot. Flower stalks rot near soil and fall over. Odorous decay.	**Soft rot,** *Erwinia carotovora.* Bacteria occur in soil or infected bulbs. Favored when wet.	Store bulbs under cool, dry conditions. Avoid injuring plant; disease infects through wounds. Don't plant infected bulbs. Don't overwater. See pages 100, 107.
Leaves have tan to dark spots or blotches that may have discolored borders or rings. Discoloring may follow leaf veins. Leaves may wilt, die, drop.	**Bacterial leaf spot and blight,** *Pseudomonas cattleyae.* Spread by air and splashing water.	Avoid overhead irrigation. Don't overwater or crowd plants. Use good sanitation. See page 107.

What the problem looks like	Probable cause	Comments
Flowers or leaves have chlorotic or necrotic streaks, blotches, or mosaic patterns. Flowers may be distorted. Growth may be stunted.	**Viruses,** including Cymbidium mosaic, Odontoglossum ringspot. Persist in infected plants. Spread in cuttings, tools, and equipment during propagation. May spread in pollen.	Rogue infected plants immediately. Learn proper handling to avoid spread, such as sterilizing tools before moving between plants. See page 121.
Leaves yellowish. Leaves have dark green or brown, vein-limited bands or blotches that develop progressively up from older leaves.	**Foliar nematodes,** *Aphelenchoides fragariae.* Tiny roundworms spread in plant debris, vegetative propagation, and splashing water. Not common on orchid in California.	Use uninfected stock plants. Remove plant debris. Avoid overhead irrigation; leaves must be wet for infection to occur. See page 265.
Plant has sticky honeydew and blackish sooty mold. New growth distorted. Foliage may yellow.	**Orchid soft scale,** *Coccus pseudohesperidum.* Oval, flattened, brown or black with yellowish margin. May be some whitish wax.	See Scales, page 186.
Foliage or stems has blackish sooty mold. Plant may wilt, decline, and die back.	**Black scale,** *Saissetia oleae.* Orange, black, or brown flattened to bulbous insects.	See Scales, page 186.
Plant has sticky honeydew and blackish sooty mold. Foliage may yellow.	**Tessellated scale,** *Eucalymnatus tessellatus.* Looks like brown soft scale, except larger and dark brown, with mosaic of pale lines on back.	See Scales, page 186.
Leaves yellow, may die. Cottony mass (male scales) or whitish encrustations on stems or leaves.	**Boisduval scale,** *Diaspis boisduvalii.* Small, white, elongate to oval insects with tiny nipple.	See Scales, page 186.
Foliage has sticky honeydew, blackish sooty mold, and copious white waxy material. Leaves may yellow, wither, and drop.	**Giant whitefly,** *Aleurodicus dugesii.* Adults are tiny, whitish, mothlike insects. Nymphs and pupae flattened, oval, translucent, and greenish or yellow.	See Whiteflies, page 170.
Foliage turns yellow and is infested with immobile, dark, waxy-fringed insects.	**Fringed orchid aphid,** *Cerataphis orchidearum.* Flattened, oval, dark reddish to black, scalelike insect with dense, white waxy fringe.	Also referred to (mistakenly) as C. *lataniae,* latania aphid. See Aphids, page 179.
Foliage has cottony material (egg sacs), sticky honeydew, and blackish sooty mold. Foliage may yellow.	**Citrus mealybug,** *Planococcus citri.* Powdery gray insects with waxy marginal filaments.	See Mealybugs, page 183.
Buds don't bloom. Small white maggots feeding in cavities in bulbs or stem swellings.	**Orchidfly** or **Cattleyafly,** *Eurytoma orchidearum.* Adult is a slender, shiny black wasp, 1/6 inch long. Females oviposit mostly in basal shoots. Larvae feed and pupate within plant tissue.	Plant only uninfested stock. Destroy infested plants. Squeeze infested tissue or puncture cavities with a needle to kill larva if feasible.
Petals have discolored streaks or blotches. Flowers or shoots may distort. Foliage may be bleached or bronzed.	**Orchid thrips,** *Anaphothrips* or *Chaetanaphothrips orchidii;* **Western flower thrips,** *Frankliniella occidentalis.* Adult yellowish to brown.	See page 161.
Foliage discolored, stippled, bleached, or reddened, and may drop. Plant may have fine webbing.	**Twospotted spider mite,** *Tetranychus urticae.* Tiny greenish or yellowish mites with 2 darker spots.	See page 213.
Flower buds drop prematurely or are deformed. Fewer, distorted, or discolored flowers.	**Mold** or **Pollen mite,** *Tyrophagus putrescentiae.* Whitish mite (family Acaridae), about 1/50 inch long, feeds under pollen cap. Can prevent pollination or damage unopened blossoms.	See Mites, page 213.
Leaves and blossoms chewed and notched. Plant yellows or is stunted from root damage by larvae.	**Weevils.** Rarely seen adults brownish, gray, or blackish snout beetles, feed at night. Larvae whitish maggots, eat roots.	See page 208.

ORCHID, CYMBIDIUM (*Cymbidium* spp.)

What the problem looks like	Probable cause	Comments
Leaves yellow, often beginning at base. Entire plant may yellow, wilt, and die. Basal stem, bulbs, or roots rotted. Vascular tissue discolored, dark.	**Bulb and Root rot,** *Fusarium oxysporum.* Fungus survives in soil for years; favored by warm, wet media.	See pages 93–96.
Plants stunted, yellowish. Roots decayed. Lower stems or crown may rot.	**Root and crown rots,** *Phytophthora, Rhizoctonia* spp. Fungi occur in most soils. Spread in water. Favored by wet, poorly drained soil.	Improve drainage. Plant in raised beds. Don't overirrigate. See pages 93–98.
Foliage yellows and wilts. Plants grow slowly and die. Roots dark black and rotted.	**Black root rot,** *Thielaviopsis basicola.* Spreads in water, soil, and by infected plants. Fungus persists in infected media. Favored by cool, wet conditions.	Pasteurize media before planting. Avoid overwatering and splashing water. Provide good drainage. Allow soil to dry between watering. Rogue infected plants. Avoid high salts and high pH. See pages 95–98.

What the problem looks like	Probable cause	Comments

ORCHID, CYMBIDIUM (*Cymbidium* spp.) (continued)

What the problem looks like	Probable cause	Comments
Foliage yellowing, especially outer leaves. Soft rot of basal stem or roots. White mycelia and small, tan to reddish brown sclerotia may develop on tissue and soil.	**Southern wilt,** *Sclerotium rolfsii.* Sclerotia survive in soil. Disease favored by moist, poorly drained, 77° to 95°F soil. Many hosts.	Pasteurize media before planting. Avoid excess irrigation. Consider fungicide drench if problem has been severe. See page 101.
Flowers, flower heads, lower leaves, or terminals have brown decay or spots. Dead tissue may have woolly gray growth (spores).	**Gray mold,** *Botrytis cinerea.* Fungus develops in crop debris or inactive tissue. Favored by high humidity and 70° to 77°F. Spores airborne.	Use good sanitation. Avoid overhead irrigation. Keep humidity low. Provide good air circulation. Don't crowd plants. See page 108.
Leaves have brown to yellow spots or blotches. Spots may have dark or yellowish margins. Foliage may shrivel and drop. Leaves, stems, or roots may rot.	**Leaf spots, Blight.** *Colletotrichum, Glomerella* spp. Spread by air or splashing water. Favored by prolonged wet conditions. Persist in crop debris.	Avoid wetting foliage. Use drip irrigation and raised benches. Use good sanitation; promptly remove and dispose of debris and infected leaves. See pages 116–118.
Stem bases (and sometimes crown) are black and rotted. Stems may fall over. Rotted tissue is odorous. Most prevalent during warm, wet conditions.	**Soft rot.** *Erwinia cypripedii.* Bacteria persist in plant debris, spread in water, and infect through wounds.	Pasteurize media used for seedlings. Use good sanitation. Avoid overhead irrigation. Provide good drainage. See pages 100, 107.
Leaves have tan to dark spots or blotches that may have discolored borders or rings. Discoloring may follow leaf veins. Leaves may wilt, die, drop.	**Bacterial leaf spot and blight,** *Pseudomonas catteleyae.* Spreads by air and splashing water.	Avoid overhead irrigation. Don't overwater or crowd plants. Use good sanitation. See page 107.
Leaves have diamond-shaped yellow, brown, or purple mottling or spots. Leaves or flowers may have pale rings or streaks.	**Viruses,** including Cymbidium mosaic, Impatiens necrotic spot, Odontoglossum ring spot, Tomato spotted wilt. Persist in infected plants. Spread in cuttings on tools and equipment during propagation. May spread in pollen.	Rogue infected plants immediately. Learn proper handling to avoid spread, such as sterilizing tools before moving between plants. See page 121.
Leaves yellowish. Leaves have dark green or brown, vein-limited bands or blotches that develop progressively up from older leaves.	**Foliar nematodes,** *Aphelenchoides fragariae.* Tiny roundworms that spread in plant debris, vegetative propagation, and splashing water. Not common in California.	Use uninfected stock plants. Remove plant debris. Avoid overhead irrigation; leaves must be wet for infection to occur. See page 265.
Plant has sticky honeydew and blackish sooty mold. New growth distorted.	**Orchid soft scale,** *Coccus pseudohesperidum.* Oval, flattened, brown or black with yellowish margin. May be some whitish wax on insects, on plants, or on both.	See Scales, page 186.
Leaves yellow, may die. Stems or leaves have cottony mass (male scales) or whitish encrustations.	**Boisduval scale,** *Diaspis boisduvalii.* Small, white, elongate to oval insects with tiny nipple.	See Scales, page 186.
Foliage yellowish. Stems or leaves encrusted with tiny hard insects.	**Cymbidium scale,** *Lepidosaphes machili.* Elongate, oystershell-like, purplish to brownish insects.	See Scales, page 186.
Foliage or stems have blackish sooty mold. Plant may wilt, decline, and die back.	**Black scale,** *Saissetia oleae.* Orange, black, or brown flattened to bulbous insects.	See page 186.
Plant has sticky honeydew and blackish sooty mold. Foliage may yellow.	**Tessellated scale,** *Eucalymnatus tessellatus.* Looks like brown soft scale, except larger and dark brown, with mosaic of pale lines on back.	See Scales, page 186.
Foliage yellows. Plant declines or dies back. Tan, yellowish, or white encrustations, usually on leaves.	**Oleander scale,** *Aspidiotus nerii.* Circular flattened insects, less than $\frac{1}{16}$ inch long.	See page 186.
Foliage has sticky honeydew, blackish sooty mold, and copious white waxy material. Leaves may yellow, wither, and drop.	**Giant whitefly,** *Aleurodicus dugesii.* Adults are tiny, whitish, mothlike insects. Nymphs and pupae flattened, oval, translucent, and greenish or yellow.	See Whiteflies, page 170.
Foliage yellows, is infested with immobile, dark, waxy-fringed insects.	**Fringed orchid aphid,** *Cerataphis orchidearum.* Flattened, oval, dark reddish to black, scalelike insect with dense, white waxy fringe.	Also referred to (mistakenly) as C. *lataniae,* latania aphid. See Aphids, page 179.
Foliage has sticky honeydew, blackish sooty mold, and white cast skins. Foliage may curl or yellow.	**Aphids,** including Bean aphid, *Aphis fabae.* Small pear-shaped insects, often green, yellow, or blackish.	See page 179.
Foliage discolored, stippled, bleached, or reddened, and may drop. Plant may have fine webbing.	**Twospotted spider mite,** *Tetranychus urticae.* Tiny greenish or yellowish mites with 2 darker spots.	See page 213.

What the problem looks like	Probable cause	Comments
Blossoms discolored, streaked, or blotched. Foliage bleached or stippled. Blossoms or terminals may distort. Growth may be stunted.	**Dracaena thrips,** *Parthenothrips dracaenae.* Tiny slender dark brown to yellowish insects.	See page 161.
Leaves, stems, or buds mined or chewed. Larvae often a secondary pest, feeding in decayed or injured tissue or plant debris.	**Leafminer,** *Pyroderces badia* (family Cosmopterigidae). Larva is pinkish with darker head; adult moth is brown to tan. Both are ³⁄₈ inch long or less.	Provide good cultural care. Avoid injuring plants and use good sanitation. See Leafminers, page 167.

ORCHID, PHALAENOPSIS (*Phalaenopsis* spp.), Moth orchid

Leaves yellow, often beginning at base. Entire plant may yellow, wilt, and die. Basal stem or roots rotted. Vascular tissue discolored, dark.	**Root rot,** *Fusarium oxysporum.* Fungus survives in soil for years; favored by warm, wet media.	See pages 93–96, 104.
Flowers, flower heads, lower leaves, or terminals have brown decay or spots. Dead tissue may have woolly gray growth (spores).	**Gray mold,** *Botrytis cinerea.* Fungus develops in crop debris or inactive tissue. Favored by high humidity and 70° to 77°F. Spores airborne.	Use good sanitation. Avoid overhead irrigation. Keep humidity low. Provide good air circulation. Don't crowd plants. See page 108.
Leaves have tan to dark spots or blotches that may have discolored borders or rings. Discoloring may follow leaf veins. Leaves may wilt, die, drop.	**Bacterial leaf spot and blight,** *Pseudomonas cattleyae.* Spreads by air and splashing water.	Avoid overhead irrigation. Don't overwater or crowd plants. Use good sanitation. See page 107.
Few or no flowers. Roots, basal stems, or flower stalks near soil are decayed. Decay odorous.	**Soft rot,** *Erwinia carotovora.* Bacteria occur in soil or infected plants. Favored when wet.	Pasteurize media before planting. Use pathogen-free stock. Avoid injuring plant. Use good sanitation. Don't overwater. See pages 100, 107.
Petals or leaves streaked, mottled, blotched, or distorted. Growth stunted.	**Viruses,** including Cymbidium mosaic, Odontoglossum ringspot. Persist in infected plants. Spread in cuttings, tools, and equipment during propagation. May spread in pollen. Impatiens necrotic spot virus, spread by thrips.	Use only virus-free plants. Rogue infected plants immediately. Learn proper handling to avoid spread, such as sterilizing tools before moving between plants. See page 121.
Upper surface of leaves has discolored, deep pits. Leaves may bleach or yellow.	**Phalaenopsis mite,** *Tenuipalpus pacificus.* Tiny flattened yellowish or reddish specks. A false spider mite.	See Mites, page 213.
Foliage has sticky honeydew, blackish sooty mold, and copious white waxy material. Leaves may yellow, wither, and drop.	**Giant whitefly,** *Aleurodicus dugesii.* Adults are tiny, whitish, mothlike insects. Nymphs and pupae flattened, oval, translucent, and greenish or yellow.	See Whiteflies, page 170.

PANSY (*Viola wittrockiana*), VIOLET (*Viola* spp.)

Leaves yellow or wilt. Roots and basal stems discolored, dark, and decayed. Plants grow slowly, then die.	**Root and stem rot,** *Pythium* spp. *Rhizoctonia solani, Thielaviopsis basicola.* Soilborne fungi. Spread in media, water, and infected plants. Favored by moist conditions.	Pasteurize media before planting. Avoid overwatering and splashing water. Provide good drainage. Allow soil to dry between watering. Rogue infected plants. See pages 93–99.
Plants wilt suddenly and die. Water-soaked cankers appear on stem near soil. Stems have cottony growth, later large, black sclerotia.	**Cottony rot,** *Sclerotinia sclerotiorum.* Fungal sclerotia in soil produce airborne spores. Favored by cool, moist conditions.	Avoid planting where disease has occurred. Many hosts, including vegetable crops. Avoid overwatering. Irrigate early in day so plants dry quickly. Consider protective fungicide. See page 101.
Foliage yellowing, especially outer leaves. Basal stem or roots has soft rot. White mycelia and small, tan to reddish brown sclerotia may develop on tissue and soil.	**Southern wilt,** *Sclerotium rolfsii.* Sclerotia survive in soil. Disease favored by moist, poorly drained, 77° to 95°F soil. Many hosts.	Pasteurize media before planting. Avoid excess irrigation. Consider fungicide drench if problem has been severe. See page 101.
Leafy shoots rotting at base; shoots wilt and fall over. Dead tissue may have woolly gray fungus growth (spores). Flower buds, and sometimes leaves, darken and wither.	**Gray mold,** *Botrytis cinerea, B. paeoniae.* Fungi survive on plant debris and as sclerotia in soil. Favored by wet weather and injury to tissues.	Provide good drainage. Avoid overwatering. Avoid injuring plants. Use good sanitation; rogue and dispose of infected plants. See page 108.
Leaves and stems have white powdery patches. Basal leaves yellow, then brown and die. Flowers may be deformed.	**Powdery mildew,** *Sphaerotheca* spp. Fungi survive on living plants. Spores spread by splashing water. Favored by moderate temperatures, shade, and crowding.	Avoid overcrowding. Provide adequate light and good air circulation. Consider applying foliar fungicide. See page 112.
Leaves have purplish red to dark brown irregular, angular spots. Lower leaf surface covered with soft, fluffy fungal growth. Leaves yellow and drop.	**Downy mildew,** *Peronospora violae.* Spores produced only on living plants. Fungus persists as resistant oospores when conditions are dry. Favored by moist, humid conditions.	Provide good air circulation. Avoid overhead watering. Consider applying fungicide to protect foliage. See page 115.

What the problem looks like	Probable cause	Comments

PANSY (*Viola wittrockiana*), VIOLET (*Viola* spp.) (continued)

What the problem looks like	Probable cause	Comments
Leaves have brown to orangish powdery pustules and yellowish spots. Leaves may yellow overall and drop prematurely.	**Rusts,** *Puccinia, Urocystis* spp. Fungi survive on living tissue. Spores are airborne. Favored by high humidity, rain, and overhead irrigation.	Avoid overhead irrigation. Water in morning. Provide good air circulation. Don't crowd plants. See page 119.
Leaves have circular to irregular, yellow to brown spots, blotches, or bull's-eye discoloring. Foliage may yellow and drop or die.	**Leaf spots,** including *Alternaria, Cercospora* spp. Fungi spread by splashing water. Persist in plant debris.	Avoid overhead watering. Use good sanitation; promptly remove and dispose of debris and infected leaves. See pages 116–118.
Blossoms or leaves have light streaks, blotches, or mottling. Flowers and foliage distorted. Leaf veins may become pale. Plants may be stunted and die.	**Viruses,** including Alfalfa mosaic (aphid-vectored), Beet curly top (leafhopper-vectored), Pansy flower breaking virus (aphid-vectored).	Use only seed from virus-free plants. Exclude or control insect vectors. Avoid growing near alternate hosts. See page 121.
Leaves yellowish. Leaves have dark green to brown, vein-limited, angular blotches that develop progressively up from base.	**Foliar nematodes,** *Aphelenchoides ritzemabosi, A. fragariae.* Tiny roundworms spread in plant debris, vegetative propagation, and splashing water. Not common on pansy in California.	Use uninfected stock plants. Remove plant debris. Avoid overhead irrigation; leaves must be wet for infection to occur. See page 265.
Foliage crinkled, deformed, and distorted.	**Improper light.** Noninfectious disorder from excess light during seedling stage.	Provide proper light, appropriate shading, and good cultural care.
Elongated, spindly, weak stems.	**Stem elongation.** Noninfectious disorder from insufficient light, improper fertilization, warm nights.	Provide adequate light and appropriate fertilization and temperatures.
Leaves are small, foliage sparse. Stems long and spindly. Flowers few and small.	**Poor growth.** Problems caused by old age, inadequate light, or failure to remove old flowers.	Provide a good growing environment and appropriate cultural care.
Foliage yellows, plant may decline. Crown has pale yellowish, soft, waxy-covered insects, also may be on roots or foliage. Plant may have honeydew or blackish sooty mold.	**Mealybugs.** Powdery gray insects. May or may not have short marginal filaments. May or may not have cottony egg sacs.	See page 183.
Foliage has sticky honeydew, blackish sooty mold, and whitish cast skins. Foliage may yellow.	**Aphids,** including *Acyrthosiphon pisum, Aphis gossypii, Aulacorthum circumflexum, Neotoxoptera* or *Micromyzus violae, Myzus persicae.*	Small pear-shaped insects, often green, whitish, yellow, dark reddish, or brownish. See page 179.
Plant has sticky honeydew and blackish sooty mold. Yellowish foliage. Tiny, white, mothlike adults.	**Greenhouse whitefly,** *Trialeurodes vaporariorum;* **Iris whitefly,** *Aleyrodes spiraeoides.* Flattened, oval, translucent to yellowish nymphs and pupae; *A. spiraeoides* has 2 dark spots on each wing. Adult *A. spiraeoides* leave much white wax on plants when egg laying, and pupae have few or no filaments; *T. vaporariorum* pupae have many long filaments and leave little egg-laying wax.	See page 170.
Foliage discolored, stippled, bleached, or reddened, and may drop. Plant may have fine webbing.	**Privet mite,** *Brevipalpus obovatus;* **Twospotted spider mite,** *Tetranychus urticae.* Tiny greenish, yellowish, or red, insects, may have 2 dark spots.	See page 213.
Leaves chewed between veins. No apparent insects; black, 1/16 inch long, oblong adults feed at night.	**Potato flea beetle,** *Epitrix cucumeris.* White maggots chew roots. Many hosts.	See page 212.
Foliage chewed by gray and black caterpillar, up to 2 inches long, with black and orange bristles.	**Coronis fritillary,** *Speyeria coronis.* Orange butterfly, up to 2 3/4 inches wide, wavy black marks. Silver spots on underside of wings.	Exclude butterflies from plants. *Bacillus thuringiensis* kills young larvae. See page 203.
Leaves chewed; may be rolled or tied together with silk. Yellow, green, or pink larvae with yellow, green, or black lengthwise stripes.	**Omnivorous looper,** *Sabulodes aegrotata* or *S. caberata.* Adult moth (family Geometridae) tan to brownish, with wavy black band across middle of wings. Mature larva and nocturnal adult up to about 1 1/2 inches long. Oval eggs laid in clusters.	See page 203.
Foliage, buds, and stems chewed. Young plants clipped at base. Stocky moths present, attracted to lights at night, wings folded at rest.	**Cutworms,** including Variegated cutworm, *Peridroma saucia.* Gray or brown larva with dark markings, dots. Hides in soil during day.	Exclude moths, which fly to lights at night. Apply *Bacillus thuringiensis* to young larvae. Insecticide bait kills caterpillars. See page 203.
Foliage chewed and webbed together with silk. Stems may be mined. Larvae wriggle vigorously when touched.	**Greenhouse leaftier,** *Udea rubigalis.* Larvae yellowish green with three longitudinal green to white stripes. Adult reddish brown with black wavy lines on wings. Mature adult and larva about 3/4 inches long. Has about 6 generations per year.	Avoid growing floral hosts near celery, a major host. See page 203.

What the problem looks like	Probable cause	Comments
Buds, flowers, or leaves mined or chewed, may be webbed with silk.	**Omnivorous leaftier,** *Cnephasia longana.* Gray to brownish, ½ inch long larvae and nocturnal moths. Larvae may have grayish stripes. Attacks strawberries and many other hosts. Occurs in central California coast. Has 1 generation per year.	Time any spray for young larvae emerging from mines in spring. See Caterpillars, page 203.
Leaves have small holes from young larvae chewing on underside. Leaf margins chewed from older larvae that feed at night.	**Violet sawfly,** *Ametastegia pallipes.* Wasplike adult (family Tenthredinidae) black with yellow. Larva dark green with pale spots and black head. Adult and mature larva about ¼ long. Eggs, laid in leaf underside, cause small leaf blister.	Plant only uninfested stock. Exclude adult sawflies. Inspect crop regularly for damage. Foliar insecticide application may be needed if larvae are abundant.
Leaves edges rolled, curled. Growth stunted from orangish maggots feeding in curled leaf tissue.	**Violet gall midge,** *Prodiplosis violicola.* Adults delicate, mosquitolike, with long slender legs and antennae.	Rogue infested plants. Treat media to control pupating larvae. Rotate crop to another site and avoid planting the same untreated soil repeatedly. See page 202.

PEONY (*Paeonia* spp.)

What the problem looks like	Probable cause	Comments
Foliage yellows and wilts. Young shoots, basal stems, and roots darken and die. Basal stems or roots may have lesions.	**Root and crown rots,** *Phytophthora cactorum, Rhizoctonia solani, Thielaviopsis basicola.* Favored by wet conditions. Spread in infested media and water.	Pasteurize media before planting. Provide good drainage. Avoid deep planting. Don't overwater. Consider basal fungicide spray or drench. See pages 93–99.
Plants wilt at flowering, but basal stems are not rotted. Water-conducting tissue (xylem) in stems is discolored. Infected plants may appear to recover, but symptoms will reoccur the following year.	**Verticillium wilt,** *Verticillium dahliae.* Fungus survives in soil for many years as microsclerotia. Favored by cool, rainy weather and hot weather at flowering. Many hosts.	Avoid planting where susceptible crops (e.g., chrysanthemums, cotton, strawberries, tomatoes) have been grown. Pasteurize soil before planting. Don't propagate plants exhibiting even the slightest symptoms. See pages 104–106.
Plant declines and eventually dies. White fungal plaques may develop in roots.	**Armillaria root rot,** *Armillaria mellea.* Persists for many years in infected wood in soil. May be introduced on infected plants or in compost that contains woody material. Favored by warm, moist soil.	Remove all woody roots ½ inch diameter or larger in soil before planting. Pasteurize or air-dry media well before planting. See page 99.
Plants wilt suddenly and die. Water-soaked cankers appear on stem near soil. Stems have cottony growth, later black sclerotia.	**Cottony rot,** *Sclerotinia sclerotiorum.* Fungal sclerotia in soil produce airborne spores. Favored by cool, moist conditions.	Avoid planting where disease has occurred. Many hosts, including vegetable crops. Avoid overwatering. Irrigate early in day so plants dry quickly. Consider protective fungicide. See page 101.
Foliage yellows and wilts. Roots decay. Plants die suddenly. Small patches of white mycelial growth on infected tissue and nearby soil. Roots or crown may have dark crust.	**Dematophora root rot,** *Rosellinia necatrix.* Fungus favored by mild, wet conditions. White fungal patches are much smaller than with *Armillaria.* Infects primarily through healthy roots growing near infested plants. Affects most fruit and nut trees and vines.	Infected tissue sealed in moist container produces white fluff within several days. Pasteurize media before planting. Remove infected plants. Avoid excess irrigation. See page 100.
Petals or leaves have dark water-soaked spots. Flower buds darken and wither. Leafy shoots rot at base. Plants wilt. Dead tissue may have woolly gray fungus growth.	**Gray mold,** *Botrytis cinerea, B. paeoniae.* Fungi survive on plant debris and as sclerotia in soil. Favored by wet weather and injury to tissues.	Provide good drainage; plant in raised beds. Remove or (where permitted) burn old growth in fall. Cut stalks below ground level. See page 108.
Shoot tips turn reddish, then yellow, brown, and drop. Plants may be stunted and bushy; growth may be twisted or crooked from side buds developing into new terminals after successive tip killing.	**Powdery mildew,** *Erysiphe polygoni.* Fungus develops on living tissue, favored by moderate temperatures, shade, and poor air circulation.	Provide good air circulation. Avoid shady planting sites. Disease prevented by fungicide application. See page 112.
Leaves have small red, tan, or yellowish spots or lesions. Foliage may dry and drop.	**Cercospora leaf spot,** *Cercospora paeoniae.* Favored by warm, humid conditions. Spread in air and splashing water. Not reported on peony in California.	Avoid overhead irrigation. Provide good air circulation; don't crowd plants. Rogue infected plants. Dispose of debris. See pages 116–118.
Leaves have tiny oval leaf spots, ⅟₅₀ to ⅕ inch in diameter. Larger spots penetrate through leaf, merging to give leaf an irregular, blotchy appearance. Upper surface of spots purple, lower surface is dull brown.	**Leaf blotch,** *Cladosporium paeoniae.* Fungus survives on infected peony debris and probably on infected scales of crown buds. Favored by rainy weather in spring.	Remove or (where permitted) burn plant debris in the fall. Avoid overhead watering. Consider protecting foliage in spring with fungicide applied as soon as green shoots appear.
Leaves have distinct yellow mottle and chlorotic rings, may have small necrotic spots. Growth may be reduced, but usually not obvious.	**Peony ringspot virus.** Virus is systemic in infected plants and can be transmitted mechanically. Natural transmission is not known.	Rogue infected plants. Don't propagate from infected stock. Pasteurize tools after working with infected plants. See page 121.

What the problem looks like	Probable cause	Comments

PEONY (*Paeonia* spp.) (continued)

What the problem looks like	Probable cause	Comments
Leaves have yellow to brown blotches, spots, or streaks. Foliage may die. Plant may be distorted and stunted.	**Tomato spotted wilt virus.** Spread by thrips. Has may crop and weed hosts.	Eliminate nearby weeds. Exclude or control thrips. Rogue infected plants. See page 121.
Plants dwarfed with many spindly shoots that fail to form flowers. Roots may be irregularly swollen on affected plants. Disease slowly spreads throughout planting, suggesting a soilborne vector.	**Le Moine disease.** Cause unknown. Plants are systemically infected and don't recover.	Destroy infected plants. Consider sterilizing soil and replanting peony in a different location.
Growths or galls form on stems or roots, typically around previously injured tissue. Roots may be gnarled, stunted, or hairy due to mostly small roots or rootlets.	**Crown gall,** *Agrobacterium tumefaciens.* Spreads in water, survives in soil, infects through wounds. Galls favored by rapid plant growth.	See page 102.
No flower buds produced or buds fail to develop into flowers.	**Bloom failure.** Causes include improper planting depth, insufficient fertilizer, excess shade, overcrowding, immaturity, and lack of chilling.	Plant properly at a suitable site and provide appropriate cultural care.
Foliage yellows. Plant growth stunted. Roots or basal stems rotted and infested with tiny, oval, white to brownish mites.	**Bulb mites,** *Rhizoglyphus* spp. Sluggish, pale mites, may look like tiny eggs. Secondary pests that prefer decayed tissue but may help fungi infect plants.	See page 218.
Blossoms or leaves have pale to brown blotches. Blossoms or terminals may distort. Growth may be stunted.	**Flower thrips,** *Frankliniella* spp. Tiny slender dark brown to yellowish insects.	See Thrips, page 161.
Foliage yellows. Plant declines or dies back. Bark has dark brown encrustations.	**Oystershell scale,** *Lepidosaphes ulmi.* Elongate to oval scale insects (family Diaspididae), less than $1/16$ inch long, often shaped like tiny oyster shells.	See Scales, page 186.
Foliage has cottony material (egg sacs), sticky honeydew, and blackish sooty mold. Foliage may yellow.	**Citrus mealybug,** *Planococcus citri.* Powdery gray insects with waxy marginal filaments.	See Mealybugs, page 183.

PETUNIA (*Petunia* × *hybrida*)

What the problem looks like	Probable cause	Comments
Foliage yellows or whitens. Plants wilt and die, often suddenly. Roots and stem blackish, decayed.	**Crown and root rot,** *Pythium, Phytophthora, Rhizoctonia* spp. Fungi survive in soil. Favored by wet, poorly drained soil.	Don't overirrigate. Provide good drainage. See pages 93–98.
Foliage fades, yellows, browns, and wilts, often on one side of plant. Stems or entire plant may die.	**Verticillium wilt,** *Verticillium dahliae.* Fungus persists in soil, infects through roots.	See pages 104–106.
Lower leaves yellow. Roots discolored, dark brown to black, lacking hairs, decayed but without distinct odor. Plants grow slowly and die.	**Black root rot,** *Thielaviopsis basicola.* Fungi persist in soil. Favored by wet, poorly drained media below 62°F. Excess fertilizer may favor disease.	Pasteurize media before planting. Avoid overwatering and splashing water. Provide good drainage. Allow soil to dry between watering. Rogue infected plants. See pages 95–99.
Plants wilt suddenly and die. Water-soaked cankers appear on stem near soil. Stems have cottony growth, later large, black sclerotia.	**Cottony rot,** *Sclerotinia sclerotiorum.* Fungal sclerotia in soil produce airborne spores. Favored by cool, moist conditions. Many hosts, including vegetable crops.	Avoid planting where disease has occurred. Avoid overwatering. Irrigate early in day so plants dry quickly. Consider protective fungicide. See page 101.
Foliage spotted. Roots, basal stems, or petioles may have dark lesions or decay.	**Leaf spot,** *Mycocentrospora acerina.* Fungus persists in media. Infects thorough wounds. Favored by cool, moist conditions. Uncommon on petunia.	Pasteurize media before planting. Avoid wounding plants. Use good sanitation. Rogue infected plants.
Flowers, lower leaves, or leaf tips have brown or gray decayed spots. Dead tissue may have woolly gray growth (spores).	**Gray mold,** *Botrytis cinerea.* Fungus develops in crop debris or inactive tissue. Favored by high humidity and 70° to 77°F. Spores airborne.	Use good sanitation. Avoid overhead irrigation. Keep humidity low. Provide good air circulation. Don't crowd plants. See page 108.
Leaves, petioles, or flowers have white powdery growth or lesions. Foliage yellows, may brown and die.	**Powdery mildew,** *Oidium* sp. Free water not required for fungus infection.	Provide good air circulation and adequate light. If previously a problem, consider applying fungicide to prevent. See page 112.
Plant or media has creamy white, slimy, or crusty gray growth.	**Slime mold.** Generally harmless but ugly, favored by warm, humid, moist conditions.	Avoid excess irrigation, overhead watering, and excess humidity.

What the problem looks like	Probable cause	Comments
Shoots short, swollen, flattened, or distorted. Secondary rot may infect shoot clumps, killing plant. Plants lack vigor.	**Fasciation,** cause often uncertain. May be viral, bacterial (e.g., *Rhodococcus fascians*), or genetic. Manage as bacterial and take additional measures.	Use pathogen-free stock. Avoid injuring base of plants, especially when wet. Keep base of plants dry. Dispose of infected plants. See page 121.
Foliage chlorotic. Plant stunted. Spindly, upright yellow shoots and few or no flowers.	**Aster yellows phytoplasma.** Spread by leafhoppers. Not spread by seed, handling, aphids, or other insects. Many hosts.	Don't plant seed beds downwind from other hosts. Eliminate nearby weeds. Control leafhoppers. Rogue infected plants. See pages 129–130.
Leaves have yellow to brown mottling or spotting.	**Petunia mosaic virus.** Vector(s) unknown.	See Viruses, page 121.
Leaves cupped. Plants stunted. Numerous secondary shoots. Veins have roughened appearance.	**Beet curly top virus.** Leafhopper-vectored. Many hosts.	Rogue infected plants. Exclude or control leafhoppers. See Viruses, page 121.
Infected leaves have pale to brown spots, necrotic lesions, or lines.	**Impatiens necrotic spot virus, Tomato spotted wilt virus.** Spread by thrips. Many hosts. Virus not systemic in petunias.	Rogue infected plants. Control nearby weeds. Exclude or control thrips. See page 121.
Poor plant growth; tissue weak and soft.	**Floppy growth.** Noninfectious disorder from overwatering and excess fertilization and ammonium.	Provide good care. Avoid excess water and fertilizer. Use low ammonium fertilizer.
New growth chlorotic, except for green veins.	**Iron deficiency.** Noninfectious disorder.	See pages 56–59.
Leaves have white scars that may have black margins. Blossoms have irregular white or brown blotches. Blossoms or terminals may be distorted. Growth may be stunted.	**Western flower thrips,** *Frankliniella occidentalis*. Tiny slender dark brown to yellowish insects.	See Thrips, page 161.
Plants severely stunted. Leaf terminals distorted. Buds deform, blacken or discolor, and may drop.	**Cyclamen mite,** *Phytonemus pallidus*. A pinkish orange mite (family Tarsonemidae), $\frac{1}{100}$ inch long or smaller.	See page 217.
Foliage discolored, stippled, bleached, or reddened, and may distort or drop. Plant may have fine webbing.	**Spider mites.** Tiny greenish, red, or yellowish mites, often with 2 darker spots.	See page 213.
Leaves have winding tunnels; also pale spots or punctures from adults. Leaves may drop. Plants stunted. Young plants may die. Yellowish to white maggots in mines.	**Serpentine leafminer,** *Liriomyza trifolii*. Adults are tiny, active, black and yellow flies.	See Leafminers, page 167.
Buds mined. Buds, petals, and leaves chewed. Few blossoms. Dark excrement from green to brown caterpillars, up to 1½ inches long, with dark lengthwise stripes.	**Petunia** or **Tobacco budworm,** *Heliothis* or *Helicoverpa virescens*. Young black caterpillars hatch from eggs laid on leaves by brown and gray moth. Adults fly to lights.	Screen moths out of growing areas. Apply *Bacillus thuringiensis* to kill young caterpillars. Avoid growing near other major hosts. See page 203.
Foliage, buds, and stems chewed. Young plants clipped at base. Stocky moths present, attracted to lights at night, wings folded at rest.	**Variegated cutworm,** *Peridroma saucia*. Gray or brown larva with dark markings, row of yellow dots on back. Hides in soil during day.	Exclude moths. Apply *Bacillus thuringiensis* to young larvae. Insecticide bait kills caterpillars. See page 203.

PHILODENDRON (*Philodendron* spp.)

What the problem looks like	Probable cause	Comments
Leaves may turn yellowish or darken. Plant may wilt and die. Roots and stem around soil dark and decayed.	**Pythium root rot,** *Pythium* spp.; **Rhizoctonia aerial blight,** *Rhizoctonia solani*; **Phytophthora leaf spot,** *Phytophthora* spp. Fungi promoted by wet, poorly drained soil.	Provide good drainage. Avoid excess irrigation and reduce watering if disease develops. See pages 93–98.
Brown to black water-soaked spots or decay on leaves or stems near soil. Tissue may have tiny, black to dark green, spore-forming structures and white mycelia.	**Myrothecium leaf spot,** *Myrothecium roridum*. Spreads by waterborne spores. Infects through wounds. Favored by 70° to 81°F and excess nitrogen or salts.	Minimize plant wounds. Keep foliage dry. Use good sanitation. Avoid excess fertilization. Growing plants above 86°F may arrest or prevent disease.
Leaves have tan to brown circular spots or blotches. Crown and root tissue eventually may decay, causing plant to die.	**Anthracnose,** *Colletotrichum* spp. Fungi survive in crop debris. Favored by wet weather and overhead irrigation.	Avoid overhead irrigation. Minimize wounding plants. Use good sanitation. Fungicide application may help to prevent problem. See pages 116–118.
Foliage yellows and wilts. Leaves may have irregular water-soaked to dark spots, lesions, or rings. Soft, brown, stem rot near soil line. Stems may collapse and die.	**Bacterial leaf spots,** *Erwinia carotovora, E. chrysanthemi, Pseudomonas cichorii*. Persist in media and infected stock, infect through wounds, and are favored when wet.	Keep foliage dry. Use drip irrigation. Don't overwater. Provide good drainage. Use good sanitation; rogue infected and nearby plants. Avoid injuring plants. See pages 100, 107.

What the problem looks like	Probable cause	Comments

PHILODENDRON (*Philodendron* spp.) (continued)

What the problem looks like	Probable cause	Comments
Leaves have yellow, reddish, or brown spots up to ¼ inch in diameter, rarely on stems and petioles. Spots become larger, dark, angular blotches or wedges, may have distinct margins. Leaves and stem may wilt and die. Stem vascular tissue and roots may be black, but not rotted.	**Leaf spot,** *Xanthomonas campestris* pv. *dieffenbachiae.* Bacteria spreads by splashing water, infected stock, debris, and equipment. Favored by 70° to 80°F, moist conditions, and rapid growth, such as from excess nitrogen.	Pasteurize media before planting. Avoid overhead water. Regularly inspect and rogue plants infected and those nearby. Isolate new plants; symptoms may not appear immediately. Use good sanitation. Some bactericides can be effective. See page 118.
Leaves have yellowish patterns; may severely distort. Veins may yellow. Plants grow slowly, are stunted.	**Dasheen mosaic virus.** Spread by aphids or mechanically in sap, such as through contaminated tools.	Use virus-free plants. Rogue infected plants. Pasteurize equipment to avoid mechanical spread. Exclude or control aphids. See Viruses, page 121.
Leaf tips and margins brittle and brown or brown with yellow margin. Foliage may yellow and die.	**Salt damage.** Noninfectious disorder due to poor water quality, improper pH, or excess fertilization.	Leach media with low salt water. Avoid overfertilization. Check pH and adjust if necessary. Trim out damaged tissue. See page 46.
Foliage discolored, stippled, bleached, or reddened; may distort or drop. Plant may have fine webbing.	**Spider mites.** Tiny greenish, red, or yellowish mites, often with 2 darker spots.	See page 213.
Leaves or shoots distorted or have discolored blotches.	**Thrips.** Tiny slender dark brown to yellowish insects.	See page 161.
Plant has sticky honeydew and blackish sooty mold, may have cottony waxy material. Foliage may yellow. Plant may grow slowly.	**Mealybugs,** including Citrus mealybug, *Planococcus citri.* Grayish, oval, waxy, slow-moving, with marginal filaments.	See page 183.

POINSETTIA (*Poinsettia* or *Euphorbia pulcherrima*), Christmas-flower

What the problem looks like	Probable cause	Comments
Plants stunted. Foliage may yellow, curl, wilt, and die if severe. Root system reduced, may be rotted. May be dark stem lesions or cankers near soil.	**Root and stem rot,** *Fusarium, Phytophthora, Pythium* spp. Soilborne fungi spread in media and contaminated water. Favored by wet, poorly drained soil.	Provide good drainage. Don't overirrigate. Reduce irrigation if symptoms develop. See pages 93–96.
Brown stem rot or canker near soil. Stems girdled. Leaves may spot, yellow, or brown, wilt, and drop. May be brown fungal strands visible with a hand lens. Common during propagation or soon after transplanting.	**Root and stem rot, Leaf spot,** *Rhizoctonia solani.* Soilborne fungus spread in media and contaminated water and plants. Favored by warm, moist media.	See pages 93–98.
Plant declines and eventually dies. Roots may have white fungal plaques.	**Armillaria root rot,** *Armillaria mellea.* Persists for many years in infected wood in soil. May be introduced on infected plants or with compost that contains woody material. Favored by warm, moist soil.	Remove all woody roots ½ inch diameter or larger in soil before planting. Pasteurize or air-dry media well before planting. See page 99.
Plant wilts and dies. Basal stem rotted. Black sclerotia in and on stems. Cottony mycelia in and on stems if conditions are moist.	**Cottony rot,** *Sclerotinia sclerotiorum.* Fungus survives in soil as sclerotia that may infect plants on contact. Favored by overhead irrigation and high humidity. Many hosts, including carrots, celery, and lettuce.	Avoid planting in infested fields or pasteurize soil before planting. Avoid overhead irrigation. Irrigate early in day so plants dry quickly. Consider fungicide application to base and lower foliage of plants. See page 101.
Foliage and stems soft, mushy, brown, and rotted. Leaves may have gray to whitish mycelial growth with black spores. Cuttings or older plants may wilt and die. Most common during propagation.	**Rhizopus soft rot,** *Rhizopus stolonifer.* Spores airborne and spread in water. Disease requires 75° to 95°F and over 75% relative humidity. Survives in plant debris.	Avoid wounding or weakening plants, which disease requires. Use good sanitation; dispose of dead and dying plants. Reduce humidity. Lower temperatures.
Soft, often odorous, rot, usually at basal end of cuttings. Common problem during propagation.	**Bacterial stem rot,** *Erwinia chrysanthemi, E. carotovora.* Bacteria spread in dead plants, equipment, and contaminated hands.	Use good sanitation in harvest and propagation. Avoid cutting dips. Provide good drainage. Avoid wounding plants. Prevent high temperature stress. See pages 100, 107.
Stems have black, elongated, water-soaked streaks. Leaves have dark blotches. Stem tips bend or drop.	**Bacterial canker,** *Curtobacterium flaccumfaciens* pv. *poinsettia, Corynebacterium poinsettia, Clavibacter poinsettiae.*	Rogue infected plants. Reduce humidity and temperatures. Avoid excess irrigation. Avoid wetting foliage.
Flowers, leaves, or stems have soft tan to brown decay or spots. Infected red bracts darken. Dead tissue may have brown stem cankers or woolly gray growth (spores). Most common during propagation and when finishing crops.	**Gray mold,** *Botrytis cinerea.* Fungus develops in crop debris or inactive tissue. Favored by high humidity and 70° to 77°F. Spores airborne.	Use good sanitation. Avoid overhead irrigation. Keep humidity low. Provide good air circulation, especially at night. Don't crowd plants. See page 108.

What the problem looks like	Probable cause	Comments
Leaves or stems have brown, tan, or white lesions that are often raised and may have yellow borders. Foliage may yellow, shrivel, drop.	**Leaf spots, Scab, Anthracnose**, *Alternaria, Cercospora* spp., *Sphaceloma poinsettiae*. Spread by air or splashing water. Favored by wet conditions. Persist in debris. Not common on poinsettia in California.	Avoid wetting foliage. Use drip irrigation and raised benches. Use good sanitation; promptly remove and dispose of debris and infected leaves. See pages 116–118.
Leaves have brown to orangish powdery pustules and yellowish spots. Leaves may yellow and drop.	**Rusts**, including *Melampsora, Uromyces* spp. Fungi survive on living tissue. Spores are airborne. Favored by high humidity and water.	Avoid overhead irrigation. Water in morning. Provide good air circulation. Don't crowd plants. See page 119.
Powdery white growth, somewhat circular, on underside of (usually older) leaves and sometimes on stems or bracts. Yellow spot on upper leaf surface. May be more common during finishing crop. Look for yellow spots or powdery growth when scouting whiteflies.	**Powdery mildew**, *Erysiphe* or *Microsphaera euphorbiae, Oidium* sp. Infection can increase rapidly from low infection levels even when bracts are showing color. Favored by 68° to 78°F. A short period above 86°F anytime each day limits sporulation and disease.	Apply controls early in production cycle. Inspect 4 to 8 fully expanded leaves, especially undersides, on about 1 out of every 10 to 30 plants each week. If active powdery mildew (fluffy colonies not laying flat on plant surface) is found, inspect all nearby plants. Pick off and bag infected leaves at an early stage and consider immediate fungicide treatment. Some systemics provide control. Soap provides temporary control. Isolate susceptible cultivars to facilitate management. See page 112.
Bracts have pale mosaic and distortion. Bracts may fail to develop color.	**Poinsettia mosaic virus**. Vector(s) unknown.	See Viruses, page 121.
Plants are stunted, grow slowly. Roots have swellings or galls.	**Root knot nematode**, *Meloidogyne* sp. Tiny roundworms feed on roots.	Pasteurize soil before planting. See page 265.
Interveinal chlorosis of older leaves.	**Magnesium deficiency**. Noninfectious disorder.	See page 56.
Leaf margins necrotic, starting with older leaves then moving up plant.	**Boron toxicity**. Noninfectious disorder caused by poor water quality.	Regularly monitor water quality. Use high-quality water. If boron is high in irrigation water, maintain media pH higher than 6.5 and regularly leach media. See page 56.
Crinkling and cupping of young leaves. Growth chlorotic, stunted.	**Calcium deficiency**. Noninfectious disorder.	Avoid low pH. Prevent imbalances of other nutrients, such as magnesium. Provide good care to keep growth vigorous. Apply calcium fertilizer and alkaline fertilizers.
Bract edges blacken and appear burned, usually on plants late in production cycle. May be confused with gray mold, which may also be present and aggravate symptoms. Stressed plants most affected.	**Bract necrosis**. Noninfectious disorder, usually associated with excess soft tissue growth late in production. Appears to be aggravated by high temperatures, excess fertilization, and excess soluble salts.	Avoid excess fertilization and irrigation, especially on older plants. Monitor and if needed adjust soluble salts. Reduce or stop fertilization during last 2 weeks of crop. Increase air flow, reduce humidity for older plants.
Black streaks on stems. Leaf veins black. Leaves drop prematurely.	**Disinfectant injury**. Plant injured by chlorine bleach disinfectant, sodium hypochloride.	Rinse disinfected containers, benches, and capillary mats thoroughly before they contact cuttings.
Leaves distorted. Leaf margins may appear pinched. Leaf tips may appear to have been cut off.	**Puckered leaves**. Noninfectious disorder of variable and uncertain causes, including nutrient deficiency, chemical burn, drying tissue, and excess light, heat, or air movement.	Prevent stress, provide good care and growing conditions, especially during establishment. Keep humidity low at night. Mist or syringe foliage until roots establish. Provide shade. Avoid rapid temperature changes.
True flowers drop from center of bract before flowers mature. Plants appear overmature. Most serious under high forcing temperatures, low light, and/or water stress.	**Cyathia drop**. Noninfectious disorder, most pronounced on plants underdeveloped late in production.	Provide for adequate early growth, especially enough light, warmth, and water. Avoid high forcing temperatures, especially under low light late in production. Avoid high EC and excess fertilization, especially late in production.
Leaves have whitish blotches. Plant distorted by latex that exuded and hardened, restricting later tissue growth. 'Paul Mikkelsen' and its sports are most susceptible.	**Latex eruption, Crud**. Noninfectious disorder, apparently from improper environment and inadequate care. Most cultivars are not highly susceptible.	Provide good drainage. Avoid excess irrigation. Prevent high humidity, especially at night. Prevent rapid temperature change. Avoid injuries.

What the problem looks like	Probable cause	Comments

POINSETTIA (*Poinsettia* or *Euphorbia pulcherrima*), Christmas-flower (continued)

What the problem looks like	Probable cause	Comments
Leaf tissue breakdown between veins on either side of bract midrib. Develops during flowering. 'Annette Hegg' cultivars most susceptible.	**Bilateral bract spots.** Noninfectious disorder, apparently from high or rapidly changing humidity or high temperatures, especially at night.	Avoid high temperatures and humidity, especially at night. Don't overfertilize, especially late in production cycle.
Stem branches produced at growing tips. True stem growth has stopped.	**Stem splitting.** Caused by excess night length, heavy shading, early shoot pinching, and/or old plants.	Provide adequate day length. Avoid heavily shaded stems. Discard early pinched shoots.
Bracts, leaves, or terminals streaked, blotched, brown, or distorted. Growth may be stunted.	**Western flower thrips,** *Frankliniella occidentalis.* Slender dark brown to yellowish insects, $\frac{1}{16}$ inch long or less.	See Thrips, page 161.
Foliage discolored, stippled, bleached, or reddened, may distort or drop. Plant may have fine webbing.	**Spider mites.** Tiny greenish, red, or yellowish mites, often with 2 darker spots.	See page 213.
Foliage yellows. Plant declines or dies back. Tan, yellowish, or white encrustations, usually on leaves.	**Oleander scale,** *Aspidiotus nerii.* Circular flattened insects, less than $\frac{1}{16}$ inch long.	See Scales, page 186.
Foliage has sticky honeydew and blackish sooty mold. Copious white waxy material present with certain species. Leaves may yellow and wither. Tiny, whitish, mothlike adult insects.	**Bandedwinged whitefly,** *Trialeurodes abutilonea;* **Giant whitefly,** *Aleurodicus dugesii;* **Greenhouse whitefly,** *Trialeurodes vaporariorum;* **Silverleaf whitefly,** *Bemisia argentifolii;* **Sweetpotato whitefly,** *B. tabaci.* Oval, flattened, yellow to greenish nymphs and pupae on underside of leaves.	Susceptibility varies: 'Angelika White' was least preferred and 'Freedom Red' was most susceptible to *B. argentifolii* in a study also including 'Celebrate 2,' 'Lilo Red,' 'Red Sails,' and 'Supjibi Red.' Less fertilizer and calcium nitrate may reduce populations; excess fertilizer and ammonium nitrate may promote populations. See Whiteflies, page 170.
Foliage has sticky honeydew, blackish sooty mold, and whitish cast skins on. Foliage may yellow. New terminals may be distorted.	**Aphids.** Small pear-shaped insects, often green, yellowish, or blackish, that suck plant sap.	See page 179.
Foliage has sticky honeydew and blackish sooty mold. Plant may die back.	**Brown soft scale,** *Coccus hesperidum;* **Hemispherical scale,** *Saissetia coffeae.* Small flattened, oval insects, yellow, orangish, or brown.	See Scales, page 186.
Foliage has sticky honeydew and blackish sooty mold. Foliage may yellow or wilt. Plant may have cottony material (egg sacs).	**Citrus mealybug,** *Planococcus citri;* **Longtailed mealybug,** *Pseudococcus longispinus.* Powdery gray insects with waxy marginal filaments.	See Mealybugs, page 183.
Plant has sticky honeydew, blackish sooty mold, and elongated, whitish material (egg sacs). Insects on twigs or leaves.	**Cottony cushion scale,** *Icerya purchasi.* Females brown, orange, red, or yellow.	Natural enemies can provide good control. Uncommon. See page 186.
Leaves chewed; may be rolled or tied together with silk. Yellow, green, or pink larvae with yellow, green, or black lengthwise stripes.	**Omnivorous looper,** *Sabulodes aegrotata* or *S. caberata.* Adult moth (family Geometridae) tan to brownish, with wavy black band across middle of wings. Mature larva and nocturnal adult up to about $1\frac{1}{2}$ inches long. Oval eggs laid in clusters.	See page 203.

POPPY (*Papaver* spp.)

What the problem looks like	Probable cause	Comments
Leaves yellow, wilt, and die or drop, followed by death of one or more shoots. Stems may be brown or purple. May affect only one side of plant.	**Verticillium wilt,** *Verticillium* sp. Persists in soil for many years and may go undetected in stock plants. Symptoms most severe in warm weather after cool conditions. Uncommon on poppy.	Pasteurize soil before planting. use pathogen-free stock. 'Manetti' rootstock is resistant to most *Verticillium* strains. See pages 104–106.
Plant is stunted or yellows and wilts. Stem rotted at soil line. Plant may have dark fungal strands visible with a hand lens.	**Rhizoctonia root and stem rot,** *Rhizoctonia solani.* Soilborne fungus favored by warm, moist conditions.	Practice good sanitation. Avoid overwatering and deep planting. See pages 93–98.
Plant wilts and dies. Basal stem rotted. Black sclerotia in and on stems. Cottony mycelia in and on stems if conditions are moist.	**Cottony rot,** *Sclerotinia sclerotiorum.* Fungus survives in soil as sclerotia that may infect plants on contact. Favored by overhead irrigation and high humidity. Many hosts including carrots, celery, and lettuce.	Avoid planting in infested fields, or pasteurize soil before planting. Avoid overhead irrigation. Irrigate early in day so plants dry quickly. Consider fungicide application to base and lower foliage of plants. See page 101.
White powdery patches on leaves and stems. Basal leaves yellow, may brown and die. Flowers may be deformed.	**Powdery mildew,** *Erysiphe polygoni.* Fungus survives on living plants. Spores airborne. Favored by moderate temperatures, shade, and crowding.	Avoid overcrowding. Provide adequate light and good air circulation. See page 112.

What the problem looks like	Probable cause	Comments
Leaves purplish red to dark brown with irregular, angular spots. Lower leaf surface covered with soft, fluffy fungal growth. Leaves yellow and drop.	**Downy mildew.** Spores produced only on living plants. Fungus persists as resistant oospores when conditions are dry. Favored by moist, humid conditions.	Provide good air circulation. Avoid overhead watering. Consider applying fungicide to protect foliage. See page 115.
Flowers or leaves have soft brown decay or spots. Growing points may decay. Dead tissue may have woolly gray growth (spores).	**Gray mold,** *Botrytis cinerea*. Fungus develops in crop debris or inactive tissue. Favored by high humidity and 70° to 77°F. Spores airborne.	Use good sanitation. Avoid overhead irrigation. Keep humidity low. Provide good air circulation. Don't crowd plants. See page 108.
Brown to yellow spots or blotches, mostly on older leaves. Spots may have dark or yellowish margins. Foliage may shrivel and drop.	**Leaf spots,** *Cercospora, Septoria* spp. Spread by air or splashing water. Favored by wet conditions. Persist in plant debris. Not reported on poppy in California.	Avoid wetting foliage. Use drip irrigation and raised benches. Use good sanitation; promptly remove and dispose of debris and infected leaves. See pages 116–118.
Leaves with circular to irregular greenish, yellow, or brownish spots, sometimes with discolored border. Spots evident on both sides of leaf, which may brown, dry, and die.	**Leaf smut,** *Entyloma fuscum*. Fungus survives on live plants and refuse. Spores borne on wind and rain. Favored by wet foliage and overhead irrigation. Not reported on poppy in western U.S.	Avoid overhead irrigation. Use good sanitation; remove and dispose of plant refuse.
Leaves have yellow to brownish spots or streaks, often along veins. Foliage yellows. Plants may die.	**Tomato spotted wilt virus.** Spread by thrips. Many hosts.	Eliminate nearby weeds. Exclude or control thrips. Rogue infected plants. See page 121.
Plant has sticky honeydew, blackish sooty mold, and whitish cast skins. Foliage may yellow. New growth may be distorted.	**Aphids,** including *Aphis fabae, A. gossypii, Myzus persicae*. Small pear-shaped insects, often green, yellowish, or blackish.	See page 179.
Plant has frothy, whitish material. Terminals may distort.	**Spittlebugs.** Immature bugs live in frothy material. Usually harmless to plants.	Eliminate nearby weeds and other alternate hosts. Wash from crop with forceful spray of water. Many insecticides provide control.
Shoots or blossoms blackened, dwarfed, discolored, or distorted. Leaf tips may wilt and die.	**Plant bugs,** *Lygus* spp. Brown, green, or yellowish bugs, up to ¼ inch long, that suck plant juices.	Control nearby weeds, from which bugs move. Exclude bugs from growing area. See True Bugs, page 194.

POUCH FLOWER (*Calceolaria* spp.)

What the problem looks like	Probable cause	Comments
Foliage yellows. Plants wilt and die, often suddenly. Roots and stem near soil dark and decayed.	**Root, crown, and stem rot,** *Pythium, Phytophthora* spp. Fungi survive in soil; favored by wet, poorly drained media.	Don't overirrigate. Provide good drainage. See pages 93–97.
Plants wilt and die. Cottony growth in or on stems if conditions are moist. Large, black sclerotia on or inside stems.	**Cottony rot,** *Sclerotinia sclerotiorum*. Fungal sclerotia in soil infect by direct contact with plants. Many hosts. Favored by wet conditions.	Pasteurize media before planting. Avoid overirrigation. Irrigate early in day so plants dry quickly. Provide good drainage. See page 101.
Foliage yellows, wilts, may drop. Shoots may darken and die. May affect only one side of plant. Vascular tissue may darken.	**Verticillium wilt,** *Verticillium* sp. Persists in media. Symptoms most severe in warm weather after cool conditions. Not reported on pouch flower in California.	Pasteurize media before planting. See pages 104–106.
Brown to black water-soaked spots or decay on stems near soil or on leaves. Tissue may have tiny, black to dark green, spore-forming structures and white mycelia.	**Myrothecium rot** or **Crown rot,** *Myrothecium roridum*. Spreads by waterborne spores. Infects through wounds. Favored by 70° to 81°F and excess nitrogen and salts.	Minimize plant wounds. Keep foliage dry. Use good sanitation. Avoid excess fertilization. Growing plants above 86°F may arrest or prevent disease.
Flowers or flower head have soft brown decay. Lower leaves, growing points may decay. Dead tissue has woolly gray growth (spores).	**Gray mold,** *Botrytis cinerea*. Fungus develops in crop debris or inactive tissue. Favored by high humidity and 70° to 77°F. Spores airborne.	Use good sanitation. Avoid overhead irrigation. Keep humidity low. Provide good air circulation. Don't crowd plants. See page 108.
Flowers or leaves have yellow, brown, or reddish mottling or rings on, mostly on older leaves of younger plants. Plants stunted.	**Impatiens necrotic spot virus, Tomato spotted wilt virus.** Thrips-vectored.	Control nearby weeds. Exclude or control thrips. Rogue infected plants. See page 121.
Plants severely stunted. Leaf terminals distorted. Buds deform, blacken or discolor, and may drop.	**Cyclamen mite,** *Phytonemus pallidus*. A pinkish orange mite (family Tarsonemidae), ¹⁄₁₀₀ inch long or smaller.	See page 217.
Foliage discolored, bleached, or reddened. Foliage may be distorted and may drop. Plant may have fine webbing.	**Spider mites.** Tiny greenish, yellowish, or reddish mites; may have 2 dark spots on back.	See page 213.

What the problem looks like	Probable cause	Comments

POUCH FLOWER (*Calceolaria* spp.) (continued)

What the problem looks like	Probable cause	Comments
Foliage has sticky honeydew and blackish sooty mold. Leaves yellow and wither. Tiny, whitish, mothlike adult insects.	**Whiteflies,** including Silverleaf whitefly, *Bemisia argentifolii*; Sweetpotato whitefly, *B. tabaci*. Oval, flattened, yellow to greenish nymphs.	See page 170.
Plant has sticky honeydew, blackish sooty mold, and whitish cast skins. Foliage may yellow. New growth may be distorted.	**Aphids.** Colonies of small pear-shaped insects, often green, yellowish, or blackish.	See page 179.
Leaves have winding tunnels; may drop. Plants stunted. Flower and seed production reduced. Young plants may die. Yellowish to white maggots in mines.	**Leafminers,** *Liriomyza* spp. Adults are tiny, active, black and yellow flies.	See page 167.

PRIMROSE (*Primula* spp.)

What the problem looks like	Probable cause	Comments
Leaves yellow, wilt, or die. Leaf bases and roots may be soft, dark and rotted. Plants die.	**Root and crown rot,** *Pythium* spp. Favored by wet, poorly drained media. Long persistence in soil.	See pages 93–96.
Foliage yellows and wilts. Plants grow slowly and die. Roots dark black and rotted. Stems below ground may develop dark cracks.	**Black root rot,** *Thielaviopsis basicola*. Spreads in water, media, and by infected plants. Fungus persists in infected media. Favored by cool, wet conditions.	Pasteurize media before planting. Avoid overwatering and splashing water. Provide good drainage. Allow soil to dry between watering. Rogue infected plants. Avoid high salts and high pH. See pages 95–99.
Brown to orangish powdery pustules and yellowish spots on leaves. Leaves may yellow and drop.	**Rusts,** including *Uromyces apiosporus*. Fungi survive on living tissue. Spores airborne. Favored by high humidity and wet plants.	Avoid overhead irrigation. Water in morning. Provide good air circulation. Don't crowd plants. See page 119.
Flowers, flower heads, lower leaves, or growing points have soft brown decay. Dead tissue may have woolly gray growth (spores).	**Gray mold,** *Botrytis cinerea*. Fungus develops in crop debris or inactive tissue. Favored by high humidity and 70° to 77°F. Spores airborne.	Use good sanitation. Avoid overhead irrigation. Keep humidity low. Provide good air circulation. Don't crowd plants. See page 108.
Leaves have circular to irregular or angular yellow to brown spots or blotches. Foliage may yellow and die. Does not kill plant.	**Leaf spot,** *Ramularia primulae*. Fungus spreads in air or contaminated tools or stock. Persists in plant debris.	Avoid overhead watering. Use good sanitation; promptly remove and dispose of debris and infected leaves. See pages 116–118.
Leaves have brown to blackish spots or blotches that may have tan center or reddish margin.	**Bacteria leaf spot,** *Pseudomonas syringae*. Spread by air and splashing water.	Avoid overhead irrigation. Don't overwater. Don't crowd plants. Use good sanitation. See page 107.
Spindly, upright yellow shoots. Few or no flowers. Flowers revert to green leafy tissue.	**Aster yellows phytoplasma.** Spread by leafhoppers. Not spread by seed, handling, aphids, or other insects. Many hosts.	Don't plant downwind from other hosts. Eliminate nearby weeds. Control leafhoppers. Rogue infected plants. See pages 129–130.
Leaves have yellow to brown spots, streaks, or ringspots, often along veins. Foliage yellows. Plant distorted, stunted, and may die.	**Impatiens necrotic spot virus, Tomato spotted wilt virus.** Spread by thrips. Many hosts.	Control nearby weeds. Exclude or control thrips. See page 121.
Leaves have pale mottling. Foliage yellow, crinkled, or curled. Pale streaks or mottling in petals. Plants may be stunted.	**Primula mosaic virus.** Vector unknown.	See Viruses, page 121.
Shoots short, swollen, flattened, or distorted. Secondary rot may infect shoot clumps, killing plant. Plants lack vigor.	**Fasciation,** cause often uncertain. May be viral, bacterial (e.g., *Rhodococcus fascians*), or genetic. Manage as bacterial and take additional measures.	Use pathogen-free stock. Avoid injuring base of plants, especially when wet. Keep base of plants dry. Dispose of infected plants. See page 121.
Young foliage pale green or yellow, except for green veins. Older leaves remain green. If severe, new grown stunted and whitish.	**Iron deficiency.** Noninfectious disorder.	See pages 56–59.
Blossoms have irregular white or brown blotches or streaks. Blossoms or terminals may bleach or distort. Underside of leaves may have dark varnishlike excrement.	**Greenhouse thrips,** *Heliothrips haemorrhoidalis*. Tiny slender black, dark brown, to yellowish insects.	See page 161.
Foliage discolored, stippled, brownish, or bleached, and may drop. Terminals may distort. Plant may have fine webbing.	**Twospotted mite,** *Tetranychus urticae*. Tiny greenish, reddish, or yellowish mites, may have 2 dark spots.	See page 213.

What the problem looks like	Probable cause	Comments
Foliage has sticky honeydew and blackish sooty mold. Leaves yellow and wither. Tiny, whitish, mothlike adult insects.	**Greenhouse whitefly,** *Trialeurodes vaporariorum.* Oval, flattened, yellow to greenish nymphs.	See page 170.
Foliage has sticky honeydew and blackish sooty mold. Foliage may yellow or wilt. Plant may have cottony material (egg sacs).	**Longtailed mealybug,** *Pseudococcus longispinus;* **Obscure mealybug,** *Pseudococcus affinis.* Powdery gray insects with waxy marginal filaments.	See Mealybugs, page 183.
Foliage has sticky honeydew, blackish sooty mold, and whitish cast skins. Foliage may yellow. New terminals may be distorted.	**Aphids,** including *Aphis craccivora, Myzus persicae.* Small pear-shaped insects, often green or yellowish.	See page 179.
Foliage, buds, and stems chewed. Young plants clipped at base. Stocky moths present, attracted to lights at night, wings folded at rest.	**Black cutworm,** *Agrotis ipsilon.* Gray or brown larva with faint, light, longitudinal stripes. Hides in soil during day.	Exclude moths, which fly to lights at night. Apply *Bacillus thuringiensis* to young larvae. Insecticide bait kills larvae. See page 203.
Foliage, terminals, or petals chewed. Leaves may be webbed with silk. Flower buds may be mined.	**Beet armyworm,** *Spodoptera exigua.* Greenish larvae, up to ⅜ inches long, with light, longitudinal stripes.	Exclude moths. Apply *Bacillus thuringiensis* to young larvae. See page 203.
Leaves have winding tunnels and pale leaf spots or punctures from adult flies. Leaves may drop. Plants stunted. Flower and seed production reduced. Young plants may die. Yellowish to white maggots in mines.	**Serpentine leafminer,** *Liriomyza trifolii.* Adults are tiny, active, black and yellow flies.	See page 167.
Leaves and blossoms chewed (edges notched). Foliage may yellow and wilt from whitish maggots feeding on roots. Growth may be stunted.	**Black vine weevil,** *Otiorhynchus sulcatus;* **Fuller rose beetle,** *Asynonychus godmani.* Rarely seen adults brown, black, to gray snout beetles that feed at night. Larvae whitish maggots that feed on roots.	See Weevils, page 208.

PROTEA (*Protea* spp.); BANKSIA (*Banksia* spp.); PINCUSHION (*Leucospermum* spp.); SILVER TREE (*Leucadendron* spp.)

Leaves yellow or wilt then darken and die. Leaf bases and roots may be soft, dark, and rotted. Plants die.	**Root and crown rots,** *Phytophthora, Rhizoctonia* spp. Favored by wet, poorly drained media. Persist in soil. Common problem.	Plant only disease-free stock. Plant only where drainage is excellent. Avoid overwatering. Pasteurize soil before planting or avoid growing in fields where these have been a problem. See pages 93–98.
Flowers, flower heads, lower leaves, or terminals have brown decay or spots. Dead tissue may have woolly gray growth (spores).	**Gray mold,** *Botrytis cinerea.* Fungus develops in crop debris or inactive tissue. Favored by high humidity and 70° to 77°F. Spores airborne.	Use good sanitation. Avoid overhead irrigation. Keep humidity low during production and shipping. Provide good air circulation. Don't crowd plants. See page 108.
Leaves or stems have discolored lesions that may have distinct borders. Foliage may yellow, shrivel, drop. Terminals die back. Seedlings die.	**Leaf spots, Anthracnose,** including *Colletotrichum, Leptosphaeria, Mycosphaerella* spp. Spread by splashing water. Favored by wet conditions. Persist in debris. Not reported on proteas in California.	Avoid wetting foliage. Use drip irrigation. Use good sanitation; promptly remove and dispose of debris and infected leaves. See pages 116–118.
Stems or terminals discolor and die. Stems may have cankers.	**Canker and dieback,** *Botryosphaeria* spp. Fungi attack only weakened plants. Spread in splashing water. Not reported on proteas in California.	Rogue infected plants. Keep plants vigorous. Provide good cultural care, especially proper irrigation. See page 102.
Leaves blacken or turn brown after harvest. Vase life short. *Protea eximia* (*P. latifolia*) is especially sensitive. Exposing cut flowers to darkness accelerates blackening (this can be used by growers to identify less-sensitive clones for propagation).	**Leaf blackening.** Noninfectious disorder apparently caused by carbohydrate translocation from leaves to inflorescence. Standard floral preservatives don't help to prevent unless they contain about 0.5 to 1.0% sugar.	Harvest during cool part of day. Keep flowers refrigerated. Don't store flowers in the dark. Store harvested flowers in sucrose. Use vase solution containing 0.5 to 1.0% sucrose (½ to 3 tbl of table sugar per gallon of water). Alternatively, remove inflorescence or girdle flower stem.
Foliage yellows. Young shoots die. Plants are stunted, grow slowly. Roots have swellings or galls.	**Root knot nematode,** *Meloidogyne* sp. Tiny roundworms feed on roots.	Pasteurize soil before planting. See page 265.
Foliage yellows, beginning with older leaves.	**Nitrogen deficiency.** Noninfectious disorder.	Provide small amounts of nitrogen. See pages 56–59.

What the problem looks like	Probable cause	Comments

What the problem looks like	Probable cause	Comments
New growth chlorotic, except for green veins.	**Iron deficiency.** Noninfectious disorder.	See pages 56–59.
Blossoms blotched or irregularly colored. Blossoms or terminals may be distorted. Plant growth and seed production may be reduced.	**Thrips.** Tiny slender dark brown to yellowish insects.	See page 161.
Foliage discolored (stippled, bleached, or reddened) and may drop. Plant may have fine webbing.	**Spider mites.** Tiny greenish or yellowish mites, often with 2 darker spots.	See page 213.
Foliage yellows. Plant declines or dies back. Stems or leaves have gray, brown, or tan encrustations.	**Latania scale,** *Hemiberlesia lataniae*. Circular flattened insects, less than $\frac{1}{16}$ inch long.	See Scales, page 186.
Leaves and blossoms chewed (edges notched).	**Fuller rose beetle,** *Asynonychus godmani*. Rarely seen adult is a pale brown weevil that feeds at night. Larva is a whitish maggot that lives in soil and eats roots.	See Weevils, page 208.

QUEEN ANNE'S LACE (Daucus carota), Wild carrot; BISHOP'S FLOWER (Ammi majus), Queen Anne's Lace

What the problem looks like	Probable cause	Comments
Leaves yellow, wilt, or die. Leaf bases, stems, and roots may be soft, dark, and rotted. Plants die. Seedlings wilt and die.	**Root, crown, and stem rots,** *Phytophthora, Pythium, Rhizoctonia*, spp. Favored by wet, poorly drained soil. Persist in media.	See pages 93–98.
Plants wilt and collapse. Basal stem and tubers rotted. White cottony fungus growth and tiny tan or brown sclerotia may form on decayed plant tissue and in soil.	**Southern blight,** *Sclerotium rolfsii*. Sclerotia survive in soil. No airborne spores are formed. Many hosts.	Pasteurize media before planting. Rogue all infected plants. Fungicide applied at base of plants may help to prevent. See page 101.
Black mold on tubers in storage or the field. Tubers don't produce. Foliage and stems soft, mushy, brown, and rotted. Plant may wilt and die. Tubers, foliage, or stems may have gray to whitish mycelial growth with black spores.	**Tuber rot,** *Rhizopus* spp. Spores airborne and spread in water. Persists in plant debris. Favored by warm and humid or wet conditions.	Avoid wounding or weakening plants. Provide good drainage. Use good sanitation; dispose of dead and dying plants. Reduce humidity and lower temperatures during storage and shipping.
Basal stem or roots or both are scabby or have a wet rot, or are both scabby and wet rotted. Plant may yellow, wilt, and die.	**Root and stem rot,** *Fusarium* sp. Spreads in contaminated media and stock. Favored by high relative humidity, warm temperatures, overwatering, and poorly drained media. Not common on *Daucus* in California.	Pasteurize media before planting. Use pathogen-free plants. Provide good drainage. Don't overwater. Avoid high humidity. See pages 93–96.
Foliage darkens, wilts, and dies. Black lesions on base of petiole, and possibly leaves, may extend down to roots. Crown blackened.	**Black root rot,** *Alternaria radicina*. Favored by cool, wet, conditions. Spores persist in soil.	Use pathogen-free seed. Use good sanitation. Avoid excess irrigation. Provide good drainage. Crop rotation reduces inoculum buildup, but some spores persist up to 5 years. Deep plowing buries spores and reduces inoculum.
Dark brown to black necrotic lesions along margins of leaves and petioles. Older foliage damaged first. Foliage scorched, blackened, or dried out. Oblong conidia spores visible with a hand lens as black specks on leaves and petioles.	**Leaf blight,** *Alternaria dauci*. Fungal pathogen favored by warm, moist conditions. Spread in splashing water. Persists in plant debris. Can be carried in seed.	Avoid wetting foliage. Use drip irrigation. Use good sanitation; promptly remove and dispose of debris and infected leaves. Some fungicides provide control. See Leaf Spots, pages 116–118.
Leaves and petioles have circular, light brown lesions. Foliage necrotic, scorched, or dried out.	**Early blight,** *Cercospora carotae*. Fungus favored by cool, moist conditions. Spread in splashing water. Persists in crop debris.	Lesions are lighter and more round than with *Alternaria*. Very thin, colorless threadlike spores (versus black for *Alternaria*) are visible in lesions if viewed under a microscope. Control as with *Alternaria*. See pages 116–118.
Leaves have brownish lesions with yellow margins. Sticky, clear ooze or dry, crusty flakes from lesions on flower stalks.	**Bacterial leaf blight,** *Xanthomonas campestris* pv. *carotate*. Can be carried in seed.	Use pathogen-free seed and good sanitation. Copper fungicides provide some control. See pages 107, 118.

What the problem looks like	Probable cause	Comments
White powdery mat on upper surface of older leaves. Foliage yellows.	**Powdery mildew**. Fungus favored when humidity is high and temperature are 55° to 89°F for several continuous hours.	Sulfur fungicides can control. See page 112.
Foliage chlorotic. Plant stunted. Shoots sparse or spindly, upright, and yellowish.	**Aster yellows phytoplasma**. Spread by leafhoppers. Not spread by seed, handling, aphids, or other insects. Many hosts.	Eliminate nearby weeds. Exclude or control leafhoppers. Rogue infected plants. See pages 129–130.
Leaves mottled yellow. Plants stunted and may die.	**Viruses,** including Carrot motley dwarf and Celery mosaic, both aphid-vectored.	Avoid planting near other hosts. Control weed alternate hosts of celery mosaic, especially poison hemlock, *Conium maculatum*. Exclude or control aphids. See page 121.
Foliage distorted, discolored, stippled, or brown; may drop prematurely. Stems and leaves have pimplelike (egg-laying) punctures.	**Leafhoppers**. Slender insects, often yellowish green, that suck plant sap and readily jump, fly, or crawl away sideways when disturbed.	Control weeds; leafhoppers often move from weeds. Control of adults is difficult; insecticidal soap or oil can reduce nymph populations. See page 193.
Stems or leaves have irregular streaks or blotches. Terminals may be distorted. Growth may be stunted.	**Thrips**. Slender dark brown to yellowish insects, $\frac{1}{16}$ inch long or less.	See page 161.
Foliage has sticky honeydew, blackish sooty mold, and whitish cast skins. Foliage may distort or yellow.	**Aphids,** including *Aphis fabae, A. helianthi, A. gossypii, Aphis* or *Brachycaudus helichrysi, Myzus persicae*. Tiny pear-shaped insects, often greenish, yellow, or blackish.	See page 179.
May be poor growth from bulbs and stunted plants. Young shoots distorted. Aphids under leaf sheaths, on stems near soil, and under bulb scales and in crevices of bulbs stored or in the field.	**Tulip bulb aphid,** *Dysaphis tulipae*. Small, pear shaped, waxy insects, often yellow, pink, gray, or green. Easily overlooked. Usually causes direct damage only in storage. Vectors nonpersistent tulip breaking virus. Has other hosts, especially iris, where it vectors persistent lily symptomless virus.	See page 182.
Foliage yellows and wilts. Plant may die back from brownish maggots boring in basal stem and roots.	**Carrot rust fly,** *Psila rosae*. Adult fly (family Psilidae) $\frac{1}{8}$ inch long, dark with yellow head, legs and sparse body hairs. Pupates in soil. Can have several generations per year. Attacks carrot, celery, and parsnips.	Rotate crop into uninfested soil. Where a problem, a soil drench can be applied when adults are common in yellow sticky traps.
Leaves skeletonized, chewed, and may drop. Foliage yellows or wilts due to damage by root-feeding larvae. Plant stunted.	**Flea beetles,** *Epitrix, Systena* spp. Adults shiny black, metallic, or pale beetles, $\frac{1}{8}$ inch long or less. Adults jump when disturbed, but feed mostly at night. Larvae are pale, soil-dwelling maggots.	See page 212.
Foliage yellows and wilts. Plants may be stunted, fall over, or die from root-feeding beetles. Basal stems or leaves may be chewed.	**Carrot beetle,** *Ligyrus gibbosus*. Adult beetles (family Scarabaeidae) reddish brown, $\frac{1}{2}$ inch long, feed above and below ground. Larvae up to $1\frac{1}{4}$ inches long, white to bluish, head dark. Attacks grains and vegetable crops, especially tubers.	Exclude adults, which fly at night to lights. Eliminate decaying vegetation that harbors adults around plants. See White Grubs, page 211.
Foliage, buds, and stems chewed. Young plants clipped at base. Stocky moths present, attracted to lights at night, wings folded at rest.	**Cutworms,** *Agrotis* spp. Whitish, gray, or brown larva with faint, light, longitudinal stripes. Hides in soil during day.	Exclude moths, which fly to lights. Apply *Bacillus thuringiensis* to young larvae. Insecticide bait kills larvae. See Caterpillars, page 203.
Foliage chewed by yellowish and black, very hairy caterpillars up to 2 inches long.	**Yellow woollybear,** *Spilosoma virginica*. Adult moth (family Arctiidae) white, yellowish, and brown with black wing markings. Overwinters in hairy cocoon. Has 2 generations per year.	See Caterpillars, page 203.
Shoots and leaves chewed by larvae, up to $1\frac{1}{2}$ inches long, mottled brown to greenish with yellow and black spots.	**Anise swallowtail,** *Papilio zelicaon*. Adult colorful butterfly (family Papilionidae), up to 3 inches wide, mostly black and yellow banded with orange and blue. Feeds mostly on anise (sweet fennel), sometimes chews citrus, celery, parsley, and parsnips.	Exclude adults or apply *Bacillus thuringiensis* for larvae. See Caterpillars, page 203.

What the problem looks like	Probable cause	Comments

RANUNCULUS (*Ranunculus* spp.), Buttercup

What the problem looks like	Probable cause	Comments
Foliage yellows and wilts. Plants stunted. Root system reduced. Roots or basal stem decayed.	**Root rot,** *Pythium* spp., *Rhizoctonia solani*. Soilborne fungi. Spread in soil and water. Favored by excess moisture and poor drainage.	Provide good drainage. Avoid excess irrigation. See pages 93–98.
Plant wilts and dies. Basal stem rotted. Long black sclerotia in and on stems. Cottony mycelia in and on stems if conditions are moist.	**Cottony rot,** *Sclerotinia sclerotiorum*. Fungus survives in soil as sclerotia that may infect plants on contact. Favored by overhead irrigation and high humidity. Many hosts.	Pasteurize media before planting. Avoid overhead irrigation. Irrigate early in day so plants dry quickly. See page 101.
Plants wilt and collapse. Basal stem and roots rotted. White cottony fungus growth may form on infected plant parts and soil. Tan or brown sclerotia (about $\frac{1}{16}$ inch long) form on rotted tissue.	**Southern blight,** *Sclerotium rolfsii*. Sclerotia survive in soil, germinate, and remain there, where they infect susceptible plants. No airborne spores are formed. Many hosts.	Pasteurize media before planting. Fungicide applied at base of plants can help to prevent. See page 101.
Leaves have purplish red to dark brown irregular, angular spots. Lower leaf surface covered with soft, fluffy fungal growth. Leaves yellow and drop.	**Downy mildew,** *Peronospora* spp. Spores produced only on living plants. Fungus persists as resistant oospores when conditions are dry. Favored by moist, humid conditions.	Provide good air circulation. Avoid overhead watering. Consider applying fungicide to protect foliage. See page 115.
Petals or leaves have brown, water-soaked spots or decay. Dead tissue may have woolly gray growth (spores). Stem may be girdled.	**Gray mold,** *Botrytis cinerea*. Fungus develops in crop debris or inactive tissue. Favored by high humidity and 70° to 77°F. Spores airborne.	Use good sanitation. Avoid overhead irrigation. Keep humidity low. Provide good air circulation. Don't crowd plants. See page 108.
Leaves have brown to orangish powdery pustules and yellowish spots. Leaves may yellow and drop.	**Rusts,** *Puccinia, Uromyces* spp. Fungi survive on living tissue. Spores are airborne. Favored by high humidity and wet plants.	Avoid overhead irrigation. Water in morning. Provide good air circulation. Don't crowd plants. See page 119.
Leaves and stems have white powdery patches. Basal leaves yellow, then brown and die. Flowers may be deformed.	**Powdery mildew,** *Erysiphe polygoni*. Fungus survives on living plants. Favored by moderate temperatures, shade, and crowding.	Avoid overcrowding. Provide adequate light and good air circulation. See page 112.
Leaves or stems have small, circular to irregular, greenish, yellow, or brownish spots, sometimes with discolored border. Spots may be somewhat thickened, are evident on both sides of leaf.	**Smut,** *Entyloma, Urocystis* spp. Fungi survive on live plants and refuse. Spores borne on wind and rain. Favored by rain and overhead irrigation. Not common in California.	Avoid overhead irrigation. Use good sanitation; remove and dispose of plant refuse.
Leaves have yellow or brownish spots or blotches. Foliage may yellow and drop prematurely.	**Leaf spots,** including *Ramularia* spp. Spread by air and splashing water. Prefer warm and moist environment.	Avoid overhead irrigation. Use good sanitation. Don't crowd plants. See pages 116–118.
Leaves and stems have pinpoint to large irregular necrotic lesions. Leaves may have yellow margins. Leaves die and drop. Young plants may wilt and collapse. Root tubers necrotic.	**Bacterial blight,** *Xanthomonas campestris*. Bacteria carried in seed, tubers, and plant debris; spread by water. Favored by cool, wet weather. Symptoms may be confused with those of other causes, like tomato spotted wilt virus.	Use bacteria-free stock if available or disinfect seed before planting. Pasteurize media before planting. Avoid wetting foliage; use drip irrigation. Use good sanitation. See pages 107, 118.
Leaves have yellow to brown blotches, spots, ringspots, or streaks. Stem necrosis. Foliage yellows, may die. Plant may be distorted and stunted.	**Tomato spotted wilt virus.** Spread by thrips. Has many crop and weed hosts. Symptoms may be confused with those of other causes, like bacterial blight.	Eliminate nearby weeds. Exclude or control thrips. Rogue infected plants. See page 121.
Leaves mottled yellow or pale green. Plants may be stunted. Flowers may be small and streaked.	**Ranunculus mosaic virus.** Persists in tubers. Vectored by aphids.	Discard infected plants. Use only seed from virus-free plants. Control aphids. See page 121.
Foliage chlorotic. Plant stunted. Spindly, upright yellow shoots and few or no flowers.	**Aster yellows phytoplasma.** Spread by leafhoppers. Not spread by seed, handling, aphids, or other insects. Many hosts.	Don't plant seed beds downwind from other hosts. Eliminate nearby weeds. Control leafhoppers. Rogue infected plants. See pages 129–130.
Blossoms have irregular blotches or streaks. Leaves may turn brown. Blossoms or terminals may be distorted. Growth may be stunted.	**Flower thrips,** *Frankliniella* spp. Slender, dark brown to yellowish insects, $\frac{1}{16}$ inch long or less.	See Thrips, page 161.
Foliage has sticky honeydew, blackish sooty mold, and whitish cast skins. Foliage may yellow.	**Aphids,** including Foxglove aphid, *Acyrthosiphon solani*; Green peach aphid, *Myzus persicae*; Waterlily aphid, *Rhopalosiphum nymphaeae*.	Tiny pear-shaped insects, often green, dark brown, or blackish. See page 179.
Plant growth may be retarded from small insects infesting roots and maybe stems near soil.	**Aster or Erigeron root aphid,** *Aphis middletonii*. Small pear-shaped insects, light gray to dark green. Infests many Asteraceae; control nearby weeds in this family.	See page 182.

What the problem looks like	Probable cause	Comments
RHAMNUS (*Rhamnus* spp.), Coffeeberry, Redberry		
Leaves have small brown spots on upperside and large dark pustules on underside.	**Rust,** *Puccinia coronata.* Airborne spores spread only from living tissue. Favored by wet or humid conditions.	Avoid wetting foliage. Keep humidity low. Don't crowd plants. Use good sanitation. See page 119.
Leaves or fruit have dark spots that are scabby or velvety.	**Scab,** *Venturia rhamni.* Fungal disease promoted by rain, overhead irrigation.	Avoid overhead irrigation or irrigate early in day so foliage dries quickly. Remove and dispose of fallen leaves, especially in fall. Sulfur applied about weekly when rainy can prevent.
Brown to yellow spots or blotches, mostly on older leaves. Spots may have dark or yellowish margins. Foliage may shrivel and drop.	**Leaf spots,** *Cylindrosporium, Septoria* spp. Spread by air or splashing water. Favored by wet conditions. Persist in plant debris.	Avoid wetting foliage. Use drip irrigation. Use good sanitation; promptly remove and dispose of crop debris and infected leaves. See pages 116–118.
Plant declines and eventually dies. Roots may have white fungal plaques.	**Armillaria root rot,** *Armillaria mellea.* Persists for many years in infected wood in soil. May be introduced on infected plants or with compost if it contains woody material. Favored by warm, moist soil.	Remove all woody roots ½ inch diameter or larger in soil before planting. Pasteurize or air-dry media well before planting. See page 99.
Plant has sticky honeydew and blackish sooty mold. Foliage may yellow or distort from small insects, on leaves or stems.	**Black scale,** *Saissetia oleae;* **Brown soft scale,** *Coccus hesperidum;* **European fruit lecanium,** *Parthenolecanium corni;* **Nigra scale,** *Parasaissetia nigra.* Oval, flat or convex, yellow, orange, brown, or black insects (family Coccidae), less than ⅜ inch long.	See page 186.
Foliage turns yellow. Plant declines or dies back. Bark has dark brown encrustations.	**Oystershell scale,** *Lepidosaphes ulmi.* Elongate to oval scale insects (family Diaspididae), often shaped like oyster shells, less than ¹⁄₁₆ inch long.	See Scales, page 186.
Foliage turns yellow. Plant declines or dies back. Gray, tan, white, brown, or orangish encrustations on bark or leaves.	**Greedy scale,** *Hemiberlesia rapax;* **Oleander scale,** *Aspidiotus nerii.* Circular to flattened insects, less than ¹⁄₁₆ inch long.	See Scales, page 186.
ROSE (*Rosa* spp.)		
Leaves drop, one or more shoots may die. May affect only one side of plant. Red flowered buds may turn blue and fail to open; leaves and green stem tissues may become mottled.	**Verticillium wilt,** *Verticillium albo-atrum, V. dahliae.* Persist in soil for many years and may go undetected in budwood. Symptoms most severe in warm weather after cool conditions.	Pasteurize soil before planting. Use pathogen-free stock. Manetti rootstock is resistant to most Verticillium wilt strains. See pages 104–106.
Plant declines and eventually dies. White fungal plaques develop between bark and wood.	**Armillaria root rot,** *Armillaria mellea.* Persists for many years in infected wood in soil. May be introduced on infected plants or with compost if it contains woody material. Favored by warm, moist soil.	Remove all woody roots ½ inch diameter or larger (in which disease persists) before planting. Pasteurize or air-dry soil well before planting. See page 99.
Plants stunted, may wilt and die if severe. Root system reduced; small roots rotted.	**Root and stem rot,** *Pythium* spp. Soilborne fungi spread with soil and water. Favored by wet, poorly drained soil.	Provide good drainage. Don't overirrigate. See pages 93–96.
Stem has brownish cankers, sometimes with grayish centers. Dead tissue has small, black, spore-forming fungal pycnidia.	**Stem cankers and dieback,** *Leptosphaeria cornothyrium, Coniothyrium fuckelii, Botryosphaeria dothidea, Cryptosporella umbrina.* Fungi infect mainly through wounds. Spread or promoted by rain, splashing water.	Provide plants with proper cultural care and good growing conditions to keep them vigorous. Prune off and dispose of diseased tissue; otherwise avoid wounding plants. When pruning, cut back to a node. See page 102.
Cuttings rot near base. Stems and roots soft, dark, rotted. Stem has cankers. Leaves spotted, yellow, wilt, may die.	**Crown canker, Cutting rot,** *Cylindrocladium scoparium.* Spores spread in splashing water. Infect through leaves or roots.	Pasteurize media before planting. Inspect and don't plant infected cuttings. Avoid overhead water. Use good sanitation.
Flower petals spotted. Buds rot. Twigs die back. Canes have cankers. Decayed tissue has woolly gray growth (spores).	**Gray mold,** *Botrytis cinerea.* Fungus develops in crop debris or inactive tissue. Favored by high humidity and 70° to 77°F. Spores airborne.	See page 108.
Purplish red to dark brown irregular, angular spots on leaves. Lower leaf surface covered with soft, fluffy fungal growth. Leaves yellow and drop. Newer growth more susceptible than old.	**Downy mildew,** *Peronospora sparsa.* Spores produced only on living plants. Fungus persists as resistant oospores on dead leaves when conditions are dry. Favored by moist, humid conditions.	Provide good air circulation. Avoid overhead watering. Suppressed by temperatures over 82°F. Consider applying fungicide to protect foliage. Sulfur commonly used. See page 115.

What the problem looks like	Probable cause	Comments

ROSE (*Rosa* spp.) (continued)

What the problem looks like	Probable cause	Comments
Leaves, stems, and flower buds have white to gray powdery growth. Leaves distorted and discolored. Cultivars vary greatly in susceptibility.	**Powdery mildew,** *Sphaerotheca pannosa* var. *rosae.* Survives on living tissue and in infected buds. Favored by 60° to 80°F and relative humidity at night of 90% or more.	Consider planting resistant varieties where powdery mildew has been a problem. Provide full sun and good air circulation. Consider protecting foliage with sulfur or other fungicide. See page 112.
Leaves and other green tissue have small orange pustules. Plants may defoliate. Cultivars vary greatly in susceptibility.	**Rust,** *Phragmidium* spp. Survive on living leaves and stems. Spread by airborne spores. Favored by cool, moist weather.	Consider planting resistant varieties where rust has been a problem. Avoid overhead irrigation. Consider protecting foliage with fungicide. See page 119.
Leaves have small reddish, tan, or yellowish spots or blotches. Spots may have discolored border. Foliage dries and drops.	**Cercospora leaf spot,** *Cercospora, Pseudocercospora* spp. Favored by warm, humid conditions. Spread in air and splashing water.	Avoid overhead irrigation. Provide good air circulation; don't crowd plants. Rogue infected plants. Dispose of debris. See pages 116–118.
Black spots with fringed margins on succulent stems and upper surface of leaves. May be yellow around spots. Plants may defoliate.	**Black spot,** *Diplocarpon rosae.* Survives on living and dead leaves and on infected stems. Waterborne spores spread by splashing water.	Avoid overhead irrigation. Remove, incorporate into soil, or (where permitted) burn infected fallen leaves and prunings.
Petals darken, especially at tips and along margins.	**Petal blackening.** Noninfectious disorder related to calcium deficiency. Can occur despite adequate available calcium.	Provide proper nutrition. Check for imbalances of other nutrients. Provide appropriate pH. Encourage good root growth, which can enhance nutrient uptake.
Variable leaf yellowing, ranging from conspicuous yellow blotches, intricate rings, and lines to overall chlorosis. Plants may be somewhat stunted.	**Prunus necrotic ringspot virus.** Carried in living plants and spread by grafting and budding; not spread by insects. Symptoms appear at moderate to low temperatures; infected plants developing at high temperatures may be symptomless.	Use only virus-free stock or heat-treat mother plants before taking cuttings. Exposing plants to 100°F for 4 weeks inactivates virus in most cuttings taken from the heat-treated mother plant. See page 121.
Leaves curl downward. Canes die back. Leaves fall from new shoots, which are typically pointed with a broad base.	**Rose leaf curl.** Probably a virus. Carried in living plants and spread by grafting and budding; not spread by insects or by other natural means.	Use only virus-free stock. Rogue infected plants. No known treatment. See Viruses, page 121.
Leaves of hybrid tea varieties have green mosaic and fine line pattern. *Rosa multiflora* 'Burr' is severely stunted, with small, deformed leaflets with distinct mottling and wrinkling. Symptomless or inconspicuous in some cultivars, especially floribunda roses.	**Rose ring pattern.** Probably a virus. Carried in living plants and spread by grafting and budding; not spread by insects or other natural means.	Use only virus-free stock or heat-treat mother plants before taking cuttings as described above for prunus necrotic ringspot. See Viruses, page 121.
Foliage has brownish rings. Veins have brown bands. Stems have water-soaked ring patterns.	**Rose streak virus.** Vector(s) unknown. Carried in buds and spread by grafting.	See Viruses, page 121.
Short internodes. Excess side shoots. Foliage bright red or necrosis between veins.	**Rosette virus.** Vectored by eriophyid mites.	See Viruses, page 121.
Leaves in spring are balled or curved and have conspicuously lighter veins and grow on very short shoots. Symptoms tend to disappear later in season.	**Rose spring dwarf.** Probably not a virus. Carried in living plants and spread by grafting and budding; not spread by insects or otherwise naturally.	Use only cuttings from symptom-free mother plants. Rogue infected plants; no other known treatment.
Leaves yellow. Growth stunted. Roots may be smaller, darker than on healthy plants. Symptoms on rose roots often are not obvious to the naked eye.	**Root lesion nematode,** *Pratylenchus* sp. Nematodes survive in media as eggs, larvae, and adults.	Use nematode-free stock. Pasteurize media before planting. Rogue affected plants. See page 265.
Plants stunted, grow slowly. Roots have swellings or galls.	**Dagger nematode,** *Xiphinema diversicaudatum, X. index;* **Root knot nematodes,** *Meloidogyne* spp. Microscopic roundworms.	Pasteurize soil before planting. *Xiphinema* spp. can vector plant viruses. See page 265.
Blossoms have irregular white or brown streaks or blotches. Leaves may turn brown. Blossoms or terminals may be distorted. Flower buds may die. Growth may be stunted.	**Western flower thrips,** *Frankliniella occidentalis.* Slender, dark brown to yellowish insects, 1/16 inch long or less.	Remove old blossoms; because of frequent harvest, thrips lack time to complete development in rose buds if good sanitation is used. See Thrips, page 161.

What the problem looks like	Probable cause	Comments
Foliage discolored (stippled, bleached, or reddened) and may drop. Plant may have fine webbing.	**Spider mites,** *Tetranychus* spp. Tiny greenish or yellowish mites, may have 2 darker spots on back.	Regularly inspect leaves for mites; field-grown roses tolerate at least 40% of leaves infested with mites without yield loss. See page 213.
Foliage has sticky honeydew, blackish sooty mold, and whitish cast skins. Foliage may yellow.	**Aphids,** including *Macrosiphum euphorbiae, M. rosae, Wahlgreniella nervata.* Small pear-shaped insects, often green, pink, or reddish.	See page 179.
Foliage has sticky honeydew and blackish sooty mold. Leaves yellow and wither. Tiny, whitish, mothlike adult insects.	**Greenhouse whitefly,** *Trialeurodes vaporariorum;* **Silverleaf whitefly,** *Bemisia argentifolii;* **Sweetpotato whitefly,** *B. tabaci.*	Oval, flattened, yellow to greenish nymphs. See Whiteflies, page 170.
Foliage has cottony material (egg sacs), sticky honeydew, and blackish sooty mold. Foliage may yellow.	**Mealybugs,** including Citrus mealybug, *Planococcus citri.* Powdery gray insects with waxy marginal filaments.	See page 183.
Plant has sticky honeydew and blackish sooty mold. Foliage may yellow from small insects, on leaves or stems.	**Black scale,** *Saissetia oleae;* **Brown soft scale,** *Coccus hesperidum;* **European fruit lecanium,** *Parthenolecanium corni;* **Nigra scale,** *Parasaissetia nigra.* Oval, flat or convex, yellow, orange, brown, or black insects (family Coccidae), less than ³⁄₈ inch long.	See page 186.
Foliage yellows. Plant declines or dies back. Gray, brown, tan, yellow, or white encrustations mostly on canes, may be on leaves.	**California red scale,** *Aonidiella aurantii;* **Greedy scale,** *Hemiberlesia rapax;* **Latania scale,** *H. lataniae;* **Rose scale,** *Aulacaspis rosae;* **San Jose scale,** *Quadraspidiotus perniciosus.* Colonies of oval to circular, flat insects (family Diaspididae), less than ¹⁄₁₆ inch long.	See page 186.
Stem or roots have growths or galls; typically around previously injured tissue. Roots may be gnarled, stunted, or hairy due to mostly small roots or rootlets.	**Crown gall,** *Agrobacterium tumefaciens.* Bacteria spread in water, survive in soil, infect through wounds. Galls favored by rapid plant growth.	See page 102.
Leaves chewed, may be rolled or tied together with silk. Yellow, green, or pink larvae with yellow, green, or black lengthwise stripes.	**Omnivorous looper,** *Sabulodes aegrotata* or *S. caberata.* Adult moth (family Geometridae) tan to brownish, with wavy black band across middle of wings. Mature larva and nocturnal adult, up to about 1½ inches long. Oval eggs laid in clusters.	See page 203.
Foliage chewed and webbed together with silk. Disturbed larvae wriggle and drop on a thread. Eggs laid in overlapping mass like fish scales.	**Orange tortrix,** *Argyrotaenia citrana* (family Tortricidae). Larva whitish, head brown. Gray to brown moth. Both up to 1 inch long. Moth is often abundant near citrus orchards. Has many other hosts.	See page 203.
Buds, flowers or leaves mined or chewed, may be webbed with silk.	**Omnivorous leaftier,** *Cnephasia longana.* Larvae and nocturnal moths gray to brownish, ½ inch long. Larvae may have grayish stripes. Attacks strawberries and many other hosts. Occurs in central California coast. Has 1 generation per year.	Time any spray for young larvae emerging from mines in spring. See Caterpillars, page 203.
Foliage chewed and webbed together with silk. Stems may be mined. Larvae wriggle vigorously when touched.	**Greenhouse leaftier,** *Udea rubigalis.* Larvae yellowish green with three longitudinal green to white stripes. Adult reddish brown with black wavy lines on wings. Mature adult and larva about ¾ inches long. Has about 6 generations per year.	Avoid growing floral hosts near celery, a major host. See page 203.
Foliage, terminals, or petals chewed. Leaves may be webbed with silk. Flower buds may be mined.	**Beet armyworm,** *Spodoptera exigua;* **Corn earworm,** *Heliothis* or *Helicoverpa zea;* **Green fruitworms,** *Amphipyra, Grapholitha,* and *Orthosia* spp. Greenish larvae up to 1³⁄₈ inches long, may have light, longitudinal stripes. Tan to brownish nocturnal moths, may have darker bands on wings.	*Bacillus thuringiensis* kills larvae. See page 203.
Margins of leaves or petals have semicircular holes.	**Leafcutting bees,** *Megachile* spp. About ½ inch long, robust, grayish bees. They are important pollinators; avoid killing them. Bees line their nests with cut plant parts.	No effective nonchemical controls known.

What the problem looks like	Probable cause	Comments
ROSE (*Rosa* spp.) (continued)		
Underside of leaves skeletonized, scraped. Holes chewed in leaves.	**Bristly roseslug,** *Cladius difformis.* Shiny black to pale green, bristly larvae, up to ⅝ inch long.	Crop can tolerate substantial foliar feeding if not on marketed plant parts. Inspect crop regularly for damage. Many foliar insecticides can provide control if needed.
Leaves and blossoms chewed (edges notched).	**Fuller rose beetle,** *Asynonychus godmani.* Rarely seen adult pale brown weevil feeds at night. Larvae whitish maggots that feed on roots.	See page 208.
Holes punched in flowers and canes. Blossoms ragged, chewed. Buds wilt and die. Fewer flowers than normal. Terminals may die back.	**Rose curculio,** *Merhynchites* or *Rhynchites bicolor.* Red to black snout beetle, ¼ inch long. Small, white larvae chew in flower buds. Has 1 generation per year. Larvae pupate and overwinter in soil.	Insecticides or soil nematodes may kill. Use good sanitation; larvae develop in dying and dropped buds and blossoms.
Blossoms chewed, especially white and yellow flowers, by adult beetle. Larvae in soil apparently not important.	**Hoplia beetle,** *Hoplia callipyge.* Adult beetle (family Scarabaeidae) about ¼ inch long, mostly reddish brown with silver, black or white. Whitish larvae eat roots.	Nearby turf, alfalfa, and other hosts important in population densities. See page 211.
Lacy skeleton of foliage chewed between veins. Blossoms chewed. Shiny, metallic green and coppery beetles with whitish tufts of hair.	**Japanese beetle,** *Popillia japonica.* Larvae are white grubs that chew roots, especially turf. Occurs in eastern U.S. Report to agricultural officials if found in western U.S.	In eastern U.S., apply *Bacillus popilliae* or parasitic nematodes to soil and nearby turf in spring, before adults emerge. Spray foliage if adults present. See page 211.
Tips of canes wilt and die back. Spiral girdling in canes by sawfly larvae.	**Raspberry horntail,** *Hartigia cressoni.* Larva segmented, up to 1 inch long, bores in canes. Adult sawfly black and yellow, wasplike.	Inspect canes regularly. Prune off and dispose of canes just below discolored, egg-laying incision and pronounced swelling from boring larva.
Decline or death of canes or entire plant. Whitish larvae, up to ¾ inch long, tunneling in canes.	**Flatheaded appletree borer,** *Chrysobothris femorata;* **Pacific flatheaded borer,** *C. mali.* Bullet-shaped adult, bronze, gray, green to blue, often metallic. Beetles (family Buprestidae), are attracted to injured or stressed woody plants.	Keep plants vigorous. Prune out infested canes. Dispose of all prunings.
SAFFLOWER (*Carthamus tinctorius*), False saffron		
Plants stunted. Foliage yellows, may wilt and drop. Roots or basal stems appear water-soaked, dark, and decayed.	**Root and stem rot,** *Phytophthora, Rhizoctonia* spp. Fungi present in many soils and persist there. Favored by poor drainage and overwatering.	Pasteurize media before planting. Provide good drainage. Don't overirrigate. See pages 93–98.
Plant yellows, wilts, and dies, often first on one side of plant. Roots or basal stem vascular tissue dark.	**Fusarium wilt,** *Fusarium oxysporum.* Spreads in contaminated media and infected seed. Favored by high relative humidity, overwatering, and poorly drained media.	Pasteurize media before planting or avoid frequent replanting of infested soil. Use pathogen-free seed. Provide good drainage. Don't overwater. See page 104.
Yellow and wilted foliage, may be just along leaf margins. Irregular yellow then brown leaf blotches. Leaves die from plant base up. May be brown vascular streaking.	**Verticillium wilt,** *Verticillium dahliae.* Fungus persists in media and contaminated stock. Infects through roots.	Pasteurize media before planting. Use pathogen-free seed. See pages 104–106.
Plant wilts and dies. Basal stem rotted. Black sclerotia in or on stems. Cottony mycelia in and on stems if conditions are moist. Roots usually not discolored or rotted during early stages.	**Cottony rot,** *Sclerotinia sclerotiorum.* Fungus survives in soil as sclerotia that may infect plants on contact. Favored by overhead irrigation and high humidity. Many hosts.	Avoid planting in previously infested soil or pasteurize media before planting. Avoid overhead irrigation. Irrigate early in day so plants dry quickly. See page 101.
Flower heads dead and yellow. Flower heads, petals, leaves, or stems have soft brown decay or spots; may wilt and die. Dead tissue may have woolly gray growth.	**Gray mold,** *Botrytis cinerea.* Fungus develops in crop debris or inactive tissue. Favored by high humidity and 70° to 77°F. Spores airborne.	Use good sanitation. Avoid overhead irrigation. Keep humidity low. Provide good air circulation. Don't crowd plants. See page 108.
Leaves have white powdery growth. Foliage may yellow, dry, and die. More common in greenhouse than in the field.	**Powdery mildew,** *Erysiphe, Oidium* spp. Persist in infected tissue. Free water not required for infection.	Provide good air circulation and adequate light. Don't crowd plants. See page 112.
Leaves have brown to orangish powdery pustules. Leaves may yellow, brown, or drop prematurely.	**Rust,** *Puccinia calcitrapae.* Fungus survives on living tissue. Spores are airborne. Favored by high humidity, rain, and overhead irrigation.	Avoid overhead irrigation. Water in morning. Provide good air circulation. Don't crowd plants. See page 119.

What the problem looks like	Probable cause	Comments
Leaves have circular to irregular yellow to brown spots or blotches. Foliage may yellow and die.	**Leaf spots,** *Alternaria, Cercospora, Septoria* spp. Spread by splashing water or contaminated tools or stock. Persist in plant debris. Only *Alternaria* is reported on safflower in California.	Avoid overhead watering. Use good sanitation; promptly remove and dispose of debris and infected leaves. See pages 116–118.
Leaves have brown to blackish spots or blotches that may have tan center or reddish margin. Dark lesions on stems or petioles.	**Bacteria leaf spot,** *Pseudomonas syringae.* Spread by air and splashing water. Problem during prolonged, cool weather.	Avoid overhead irrigation. Don't overwater. Don't crowd plants. Use good sanitation. Rotate fields into nonhost crops for 1 to 2 years. See page 107.
Leaves or flower bracts mottled, yellow, and distorted. Leaf veins may turn pale. Plants may be stunted.	**Viruses,** including Alfalfa mosaic (aphid-vectored, carried in seed), Cucumber mosaic (aphid-vectored), Lettuce mosaic (aphid-vectored, carried in seed, transmitted mechanically), and Turnip mosaic (aphid-vectored).	Use only virus-free seed. Rogue infected plants. Exclude or control aphids. See Viruses, page 121.
Plants stunted. Roots have swellings or galls.	**Root knot nematodes,** *Meloidogyne* spp. Nematodes survive in soil as eggs. Usually most severe in sandy soils in warm climates. Not common on safflower.	Pasteurize soil before planting. See page 265.
Buds darken, turn upright, and may drop. Flower bracts or leaves may discolor or distort.	**Western flower thrips,** *Frankliniella occidentalis.* Tiny slender yellow or orangish insects. Tend to attack smaller buds than lygus bugs, which cause similar damage.	See Thrips, page 161.
Buds discolor and drop. Flower head may darken and distort. Delayed or no flowering. Leaves may have discolored patches.	**Plant bugs,** *Lygus* spp. Brown, green, or yellowish bugs, up to ¼ inch long, suck plant juices. Thrips can cause similar damage.	Control nearby weeds, from which bugs move. Exclude bugs from growing area. See True Bugs, page 194.
Foliage has sticky honeydew, blackish sooty mold, and whitish cast skins. Foliage may yellow.	**Aphids,** including *Acyrthosiphon solani, Aphis gossypii, Myzus persicae, Rhopalosiphum nymphaeae, Uroleucon* spp. Tiny pear-shaped insects, often green, dark brown, yellowish or blackish.	See page 179.

SAGE (*Salvia* spp.)

Foliage yellow and wilted, possibly just along leaf margins, often on one side of the plant. Leaves dry and die from the base of plant up. May be brown vascular streaking.	**Verticillium wilt,** *Verticillium dahliae.* Fungus persists in media and contaminated stock. Infects through roots.	Pasteurize media before planting. Use pathogen-free stock. See pages 104–106.
White powdery growth, round spots, then larger blotches, on older leaves and stem. Foliage may be deformed or puckered. Severely affected leaves dry and die.	**Powdery mildew,** *Erysiphe cichoracearum.* Free water not required for infection, but most severe at high humidity.	Provide good air circulation and keep humidity low. Provide adequate light. Consider applying fungicide to prevent. See page 112.
Leaves have purplish red to dark brown, irregular, angular spots. Lower leaf surface covered with soft, fluffy fungal growth. Leaves yellow and drop.	**Downy mildew,** *Peronospora* spp. Spores produced only on living plants. Fungus persists as resistant oospores when conditions are dry. Favored by moist, humid conditions.	Provide good air circulation. Avoid overhead watering. Consider applying fungicide to protect foliage. See page 115.
Leaves have circular to irregular or angular yellow to brown spots or blotches. Foliage may yellow and die. Does not kill plant.	**Leaf spot,** *Ramularia* sp. Fungus spread in air or contaminated tools or stock. Persists in plant debris.	Avoid overhead watering. Use good sanitation, promptly remove and dispose of debris and infected. leaves. See pages 116–118.
Leaves have light green, brown, or yellow spots. Leaf underside has powdery, dark brownish pustules, possibly on stems.	**Rust,** *Puccinia* spp. Airborne spores spread only from living tissue. Plant must be wet for infection.	Avoid wetting foliage. Keep humidity low. Don't crowd plants. Use good sanitation. See page 119.
Spindly, upright yellow shoots. Few or no flowers. Flowers revert to green leafy tissue.	**Aster yellows phytoplasma.** Spread by leafhoppers. Not spread by seed, handling, aphids, or other insects. Many hosts.	Don't plant downwind from other hosts. Eliminate nearby weeds. Control leafhoppers. Rogue infected plants. See pages 129–130.
Leaves have yellow to brown spots or streaks, often along veins. Foliage yellows. Plants may die.	**Tomato spotted wilt virus.** Spread by thrips. Many hosts.	Control nearby weeds. Exclude or control thrips. See Viruses, page 121.

What the problem looks like	Probable cause	Comments

SAGE (*Salvia* spp.) (continued)

What the problem looks like	Probable cause	Comments
Leaves yellowish. Leaves have dark green or brown, vein-limited, angular blotches that develop progressively up from older leaves.	**Foliar nematodes,** *Aphelenchoides fragariae.* Tiny roundworms spread in plant debris, vegetative propagation, and splashing water. Not common in California.	Use uninfected stock plants. Remove plant debris. Avoid overhead irrigation; leaves must be wet for infection to occur. See page 265.
Leaves dark grayish. Leaf veins appear thick and protruding. Mostly affects early plugs when cool.	**Dark gray cast.** Noninfectious disorder from excess salts or ammonium in growing media.	Reduce fertilization or use fertilizers low in ammonium.
Poor growth. Roots stunted with few root hairs. Foliage may discolor.	**Poor roots.** Noninfectious disorder from excess water, improper nutrients.	Avoid overwatering. Provide appropriate fertilization.
Foliage has blackish sooty mold, sticky honeydew, and whitish cast skins.	**Aphids,** including bean aphid, *Aphis fabae.* Small pear-shaped insects, often green, brown, yellow, or green.	See page 179.
Frothy, whitish material on plant.	**Spittlebugs,** including *Clastoptera* sp. Immature bugs live in frothy material. Usually harmless to plants.	Wash from plants with forceful spray of water. Many insecticides provide control.
Foliage has sticky honeydew and blackish sooty mold. Leaves may yellow, distort, or wither. Tiny, whitish, mothlike adult insects.	**Greenhouse whitefly,** *Trialeurodes vaporariorum;* **Silverleaf whitefly,** *Bemisia argentifolii;* **Sweetpotato whitefly,** *Bemisia tabaci.* Nymphs and pupae flattened, oval, translucent, and greenish or yellow.	See page 170.
Leaves stippled or bleached. Leaf underside has specks of varnishlike excrement.	**Thrips.** Tiny, slender, blackish or orangish insects.	See page 161.
Shoots or blossoms blackened, dwarfed, discolored, or distorted. Leaf tips may wilt and die.	**Plant bugs,** *Lygus* spp. Brown, green, or yellowish bugs, up to ¼ inch long, that suck plant juices.	Control nearby weeds, from which bugs move. Exclude bugs from growing area. See True Bugs, page 194.
Foliage chewed. Plants may defoliate.	**Leaf beetle,** *Trirhabda* sp. Adults are green to black. Pupae overwinter in soil.	Usually does not kill established plants. See page 212.
Leaves have winding tunnels. Leaves have pale spots or punctures from adults flies. Leaves may drop. Plants stunted. Young plants may die. Yellowish to white maggots in mines.	**Serpentine leafminer,** *Liriomyza trifolii.* Adults are tiny, active, black and yellow flies.	See page 167.

SAPONARIA (*Saponaria* spp.), Soapwort

What the problem looks like	Probable cause	Comments
Leaves have black, brown, to tan spots or blotches, often with yellow border. Foliage may yellow and drop.	**Leaf spots,** including *Alternaria saponariae.* Fungi spread by splashing water. Favored by wet conditions.	Avoid wetting foliage. Use drip irrigation. Use good sanitation; promptly remove and dispose of debris and infected leaves. See pages 116–118.
Leaves have yellow to brown blotches, spots, or streaks. Necrotic areas may have red halos. Foliage may die. Plant may be distorted and stunted.	**Tomato spotted wilt virus.** Spread by thrips. Has may crop and weed hosts.	Eliminate nearby weeds. Exclude or control thrips. Rogue infected plants. See page 121.

SCABIOSA (*Scabiosa* spp.), Mourning-bride, Pincushion flower

What the problem looks like	Probable cause	Comments
Leaves yellow, wilt, or die. Leaf bases and roots may be soft, dark, and rotted.	**Root and stem rots,** *Pythium* sp. Favored by wet, poorly drained media. Persists in soil. Not reported on *Scabiosa* in California.	Pasteurize media before planting. Plant only where drainage is good. Avoid overwatering. See pages 93–96.
Plants wilt and die. Cottony growth in or on stems if conditions are moist. Black sclerotia on or inside stems.	**Cottony rot,** *Sclerotinia sclerotiorum.* Fungal sclerotia in soil infect by direct contact with plants. Many hosts, including carrots, celery, and lettuce. Favored by wet conditions. Not reported on *Scabiosa* in California.	Avoid planting in previously infested fields, or pasteurize soil before planting. Avoid overhead irrigation. Irrigate early in day so plants dry quickly. See page 101.
Leaves or stems have whitish powdery growth. Older infected leaves yellow and wither. Heavily infected plants are stunted and may die.	**Powdery mildew,** *Erysiphe polygoni.* Fungus produces abundant airborne spores. Moisture not necessary and is detrimental to germination and infection. Favored by moderate temperatures.	Use good sanitation; remove and dispose of plant debris. Sulfur or other fungicide can provide control. See page 112.
Leaves have yellow or brown mosaic, mottling, or spotting. Veins may turn pale. Plants may be stunted or distorted.	**Viruses,** including Teasel mosaic (aphid-vectored), Tomato spotted wilt (thrips-vectored).	Rogue infected plants. Exclude or control insect vectors and alternate hosts. See Viruses, page 121.

What the problem looks like	Probable cause	Comments
Foliage chlorotic. Plant stunted. Spindly, upright yellow shoots and few or no flowers.	**Aster yellows phytoplasma**. Spread by leafhoppers. Not spread by seed, handling, aphids, or other insects. Many hosts.	Avoid planting downwind from other hosts. Eliminate nearby weeds. Exclude or control leafhoppers. Rogue infected plants. See pages 129–130.
Foliage stippled or discolored. Terminals may distort.	**Leafhoppers**. Small, elongate, active insects, often greenish, yellow, or brightly colored.	See page 193.
Foliage, buds, or terminals stippled, discolored, or distorted.	**Thrips**. Tiny, slender, dark brown to yellowish adults and nymphs.	See page 161.
Foliage discolored, bleached, blackened, or reddened, and may drop. Plant may have fine webbing.	**Twospotted spider mite,** *Tetranychus urticae.* Tiny greenish or yellowish mites, may have 2 dark spots.	See page 213.
Leaves and blossoms chewed (edges notched).	**Fuller rose beetle,** *Asynonychus godmani.* Rarely seen adult pale brown weevil feeds at night. Larva whitish maggot, lives in soil and eats roots.	See Weevils, page 208.

SCHEFFLERA (*Schefflera* spp.)

What the problem looks like	Probable cause	Comments
Leaves yellow, wilt, or die. Leaf bases and roots may be soft, dark, and rotted. Plants die.	**Root, crown, and stem rots,** *Pythium, Rhizoctonia* spp. Favored by wet, poorly drained media. Persist in soil. Not reported on schefflera in California.	Pasteurize media before planting. Plant only where drainage is good. Avoid overwatering. See pages 93–98.
Leaves have black, brown, to tan spots or blotches, often with yellow border. Foliage may yellow and drop.	**Leaf spots,** *Cercospora, Alternaria* spp. Fungi spread by splashing water. Favored by wet conditions. Not reported on schefflera in California.	Avoid wetting foliage. Use drip irrigation and raised benches. Use good sanitation; promptly remove and dispose of debris and infected leaves. See pages 116–118.
Leaves have brown, yellow, or translucent spots that may have yellow margins. Stems or flowers may spot. Plants may wilt. Leaves may drop.	**Bacterial leaf spots,** *Pseudomonas cichorii, Xanthomonas campestris.* Bacteria spread by splashing water and contaminated equipment. Favored by high humidity. Not reported on schefflera in California.	Avoid overhead irrigation. Use good sanitation; rogue infected plants. Provide good air circulation. Don't crowd plantings. See pages 107, 118.
Leaves have yellow or brown ring spots, patches, or streaks. Stems may be streaked. Plants may be distorted or stunted and may die.	**Tomato spotted wilt virus**. Spread by thrips. Many hosts.	Control nearby weeds. Exclude or control thrips. Rogue infected plants. See page 121.
Foliage turns yellow. Plant declines or dies back. Bark has gray, brown, or tan encrustations.	**Latania scale,** *Hemiberlesia lataniae.* Circular, flattened insects, less than 1/16 inch long.	See page 186.
Foliage has sticky honeydew, blackish sooty mold, and white cast skins. Foliage may yellow. New terminals may be distorted.	**Aphids**. Small pear-shaped insects, often green, yellowish, or blackish.	See page 179.
Foliage has sticky honeydew and blackish sooty mold. Copious white waxy material present with certain species. Leaves may yellow and wither. Tiny, whitish, mothlike adult insects.	**Whiteflies,** including Citrus whitefly, *Dialeurodes citri*; Giant whitefly, *Aleurodicus dugesii.* Tiny, whitish, mothlike adult insects. Nymphs and pupae flattened, oval, translucent, and greenish or yellow.	See page 170.
Foliage has sticky honeydew and blackish sooty mold. May be cottony waxy material on plant. Foliage may yellow. Plant may grow slowly.	**Citrus mealybug,** *Planococcus citri;* **Obscure mealybug,** *Pseudococcus affinis.* Grayish, oval, waxy, slow-moving insects with marginal filaments.	See Mealybugs, page 183.
Plants severely stunted. Leaf terminals distorted. Buds deform, blacken, or discolor, and may drop.	**Cyclamen mite,** *Phytonemus pallidus.* A pinkish orange mite (family Tarsonemidae), 1/100 inch long or smaller.	See page 217.
Foliage stippled, bleached, or blotched, may have varnishlike excrement.	**Thrips,** including Banded greenhouse thrips, *Hercinothrips femoralis.* Tiny, slender, dark brown, whitish, or yellowish adults and nymphs.	See page 161.
Foliage discolored, bleached, blackened, or reddened, and may drop. Plant may have fine webbing.	**Twospotted spider mite,** *Tetranychus urticae.* Tiny greenish or yellowish mites, may have 2 dark spots.	See page 213.
Flowers, terminals or foliage chewed. Leaves may be webbed with silk. Flower buds may be mined.	**Armyworm,** *Spodoptera* sp. Greenish larvae, up to 1½ inches long, with light, longitudinal stripes.	Exclude moths from growing areas. Avoid growing near other major hosts. *Bacillus thuringiensis* kills larvae. See page 203.

What the problem looks like	Probable cause	Comments

SHASTA DAISY (*Chrysanthemum maximum*), Daisy

What the problem looks like	Probable cause	Comments
Foliage yellow and wilted, possibly just along leaf margins, often on one side of plant. Leaves dry and die from the base of plant up. Stems may have brown vascular streaking.	**Verticillium wilt,** *Verticillium dahliae*. Fungus persists in media and contaminated stock. Infects through roots.	Pasteurize media before planting. Use pathogen-free stock. See pages 104–106.
Plants stunted, may wilt and die if severe. Root system reduced; small roots rotted.	**Root rot,** *Pythium* spp. Soilborne fungi spread with soil and water. Favored by wet, poorly drained soil.	Avoid poorly drained soil. Plant in raised beds. Don't overirrigate. Reduce irrigation if symptoms develop. See pages 93–96.
Plants wilt and die. Cottony growth in or on stems if conditions are moist. Black sclerotia on or inside stems.	**Cottony rot,** *Sclerotinia sclerotiorum*. Fungal sclerotia in soil infect by direct contact with plants. Many hosts, including carrots, celery, and lettuce. Favored by wet conditions. Not reported on Shasta daisy in California.	Avoid planting in previously infested fields, or pasteurize soil before planting. Avoid overhead irrigation. Irrigate early in day so plants dry quickly. See page 101.
Plants stunted. Swellings or galls on roots.	**Root knot nematode,** *Meloidogyne hapla*. Nematode survives in soil as eggs. Usually most severe in sandy soils in warm climates.	Pasteurize soil before planting. See page 265.
Plants stunted, decline, may die. Powdery waxy material may be visible on roots and around crown.	**Ground mealybug,** *Rhizoecus* spp. Small, slender, pale insects that may be lightly covered with powdery wax but lack marginal filaments.	See page 186.
Shoots short, swollen, flattened, or distorted. Secondary rot may infect shoot clumps, killing plant. Plants lack vigor.	**Fasciation,** cause often uncertain. May be viral, bacterial (e.g., *Rhodococcus fascians*), or genetic. Manage as bacterial and take additional measures.	Use pathogen-free stock. Avoid injuring base of plants, especially when wet. Keep base of plants dry. Dispose of infected plants. See page 121.
Lower leaves wilted, stunted, chlorotic, or necrotic, often on one side of plant. Symptoms often appear with onset of flowering.	**Acremonium wilt,** *Acremonium strictum*. Soilborne fungus also carried in infected plants. Many hosts, including weeds. Symptoms more severe if plants stressed by excess soil moisture.	Plant pathogen-free stock. Pasteurize soil before planting. Provide good drainage, plant on raised beds.
Leaves have brown circular to irregular spots. Heavily infected leaves yellow and die. Minute black fungal pycnidia (specks) are visible as dots in center of infected spots.	**Leaf spot,** *Septoria leucanthemi*. Fungus survives in infected plants and debris. Spores spread by splashing water.	Rotate land for 2 years. Plant pathogen-free stock. Avoid overhead irrigation. Keep out of crop when wet. See pages 116–118.
Shoots or blossoms blackened, dwarfed, discolored, or distorted. Excess short shoots. Leaf tips may wilt and die.	**Plant bugs,** *Lygus* spp. Brown, green, or yellowish bugs, up to ¼ inch long, suck plant juices.	Control nearby weeds, from which bugs move. Exclude bugs from growing area. See True Bugs, page 194.
Plant has sticky honeydew, blackish sooty mold, and white cast skins. Foliage may yellow or distort.	**Aphids.** Small pear-shaped insects, color variable, but often green.	See page 179.
Leaves have winding tunnels. Heavily infested leaves may drop. Pale leaf spots or punctures from adult flies. Yellowish to white maggots in mines.	**Chrysanthemum leafminer,** *Chromatomyia syngenesiae*; **Serpentine leafminer,** *Liriomyza trifolii*. *Liriomyza* adults are small, grayish or black and yellow flies.	See Leafminers, page 167.
Foliage chewed. Plant may have silk webbing from young larvae. Caterpillars blackish, up to 1½ inches long, with orange compound spines.	**Chalcedon checkerspot,** *Occidryas* or *Euphydryas chalcedona*. Adult black or orange, 2 inches wide, with many tan, reddish, or yellow spots.	Exclude moths. Apply *Bacillus thuringiensis* to kill young larvae. See Caterpillars, page 203.
Buds, flowers or leaves mined or chewed, may be webbed with silk.	**Omnivorous leaftier,** *Cnephasia longana*. Gray to brownish, ½ inch long larvae and nocturnal moths. Larvae may have grayish stripes. Attacks strawberries and many other hosts. Occurs in central California coast. Has 1 generation per year.	Time any spray for young larvae emerging from mines in spring. See Caterpillars, page 203.

SMILAX (*Asparagus asparagoides*)

What the problem looks like	Probable cause	Comments
Leaves have pale green, yellowish, or dark elongate spots or blotches. Foliage may yellow, shrivel, or drop.	**Anthracnose,** *Gloeosporium* sp. Spread by air or splashing water. Favored by prolonged wet conditions. Persists in plant debris. Not reported on smilax in California.	Avoid wetting foliage; use drip irrigation. Use good sanitation; promptly remove and dispose of debris and infected leaves. See pages 116–118.
Foliage discolored, stippled, bleached, or reddened, and may drop. Plant may have fine webbing.	**Twospotted spider mite,** *Tetranychus urticae*. Tiny greenish or yellowish mites with 2 darker spots.	See page 213.
Foliage has sticky honeydew and blackish sooty mold. Leaves may yellow and wither. Tiny, whitish, mothlike adult insects.	**Whiteflies,** including Citrus whitefly, *Dialeurodes citri*; Greenhouse whitefly, *Trialeurodes vaporariorum*. Oval, flattened, yellow to greenish nymphs. *T. vaporariorum* pupae have many, long, marginal filaments.	See page 170.

What the problem looks like	Probable cause	Comments
Leaves may have cottony white material (egg sacs), sticky honeydew, or black sooty mold; may yellow. Plant may be stunted.	**Mealybugs,** including Citrus mealybug, *Planococcus citri;* Longtailed mealybug, *Pseudococcus longispinus.* Elongate, slow-moving, powdery insects with waxy fringe.	See page 183.
Foliage has sticky honeydew, blackish sooty mold, and whitish cast skins. Foliage may yellow. New terminals may be distorted.	**Aphids,** including *Aphis craccivora, Myzus persicae.* Small pear-shaped insects, often green, yellowish, or black.	See page 179.
Foliage or woody parts have blackish sooty mold. Plant may wilt, decline, and die back.	**Scales,** including Nigra scale, *Parasaissetia nigra.* Orange, black, or brown, flattened to bulbous insects.	See page 186.
Foliage, buds, and stems chewed. Young plants clipped at base. Stocky moths present, attracted to lights at night, wings folded at rest.	**Variegated cutworm,** *Peridroma saucia.* Gray or brown larva with dark markings, row of yellow dots on back. Hides in soil during day.	Exclude moths, which fly to lights at night. Apply *Bacillus thuringiensis* to young larvae. Insecticide bait kills caterpillars. See page 203.

SNAPDRAGON (*Antirrhinum majus*)

What the problem looks like	Probable cause	Comments
Foliage gray or yellowish. Plant grows slowly, may suddenly wilt and die. Seed don't sprout or seedlings wilt and decay near soil.	**Collar and root rot,** *Phytophthora, Pythium* spp., *Rhizoctonia solani.* Fungi present in most soils. Promoted by warm moist conditions.	Pasteurize media before planting. Avoid deep planting. Don't overirrigate. Provide good drainage. See pages 93–98.
Plant wilts and collapses. Basal stem and roots rotted. White cottony fungus growth and tiny tan or brown sclerotia may form on decayed plant tissue and in soil.	**Southern blight,** *Sclerotium rolfsii.* Sclerotia survive in soil. No airborne spores are formed. Many hosts.	Pasteurize media before planting. Rogue all infected plants. Fungicide applied at base of plants may help to prevent. See page 101.
Foliage discolors and wilts. Cottony growth or large, black sclerotia inside stems. Stems become bleached, white, and girdled.	**Cottony rot,** *Sclerotinia sclerotiorum.* Airborne spores from infected soil, favored when wet.	Remove and dispose of plant debris around growing area. Avoid overhead irrigation. Irrigate early in day so plants dry quickly. See page 101.
Foliage yellows, wilts, may drop. Shoots may darken and die. May affect only one side of plant. Vascular tissue may darken.	**Verticillium wilt,** *Verticillium dahliae, V. albo-atrum.* Persist in media. Symptoms most severe in warm weather after cool conditions.	Snapdragons can appear completely healthy until blossoms develop; then the foliage can suddenly wilt completely. Pasteurize media before planting. See pages 104–106.
Foliage yellows and wilts. Plants grow slowly and die. Roots dark black and rotted. Stems below ground may develop dark cracks.	**Black root rot,** *Thielaviopsis basicola* or *Chalara elegans.* Spreads in water, media, and by infected plants. Fungus persists in infected media. Favored by cool, wet conditions. Not reported on snapdragon in California.	Pasteurize media before planting. Avoid overwatering and splashing water. Provide good drainage. Allow soil to dry between watering. Rogue infected plants. Avoid high salts and high pH. See pages 95–99.
Leaves have tan, brown, or black blotches or spots; may curl and die. Stems may canker. Plants may wilt and die.	**Stem rot,** *Phyllosticta antirrhini.* Persists in plant debris. Favored by warm, wet, humid conditions.	Use good sanitation; promptly dispose of all debris and rogue infected plants. Avoid overhead irrigation.
Brown to yellow spots or blotches, mostly on older leaves. Spots may have dark or yellowish margins. Foliage may shrivel and drop.	**Leaf spots,** including *Phyllosticta* spp. Spread by air or splashing water. Favored by prolonged, cool, wet, conditions. Persist in plant debris.	Avoid wetting foliage. Use drip irrigation and raised benches. Use good sanitation; promptly remove and dispose of debris and infected leaves. See pages 116–118.
Petals or leaves have soft brown decay or spots. Terminals may die back. Stems may have dark cankers. Plants may wilt. Dead tissue may have woolly gray growth.	**Gray mold,** *Botrytis cinerea.* Fungus develops in crop debris or inactive tissue. Favored by high humidity and 70° to 77°F. Spores airborne.	Use good sanitation. Avoid overhead irrigation. Keep humidity low. Provide good air circulation. Don't crowd plants. See page 108.
Foliage yellow, with downy gray growth (spores) on underside. Leaves may curl downward, distort, wilt, and die. Seedlings often severely stunted and may die.	**Downy mildew,** *Peronospora antirrhini.* Airborne spores. Favored by wet, cool conditions. Fungus can be systemic.	Avoid overhead irrigation. Don't overwater. See page 115.
Leaves have whitish powdery growth, possibly on stems. Older infected leaves may yellow, wither. Heavily infected plants stunted.	**Powdery mildew,** *Oidium* sp. Fungus produces abundant airborne spores. Moisture not necessary for germination and infection.	Provide good air circulation and adequate light. Sulfur or other fungicides can prevent. See page 112.
Leaves have yellowish spots and reddish brown pustules; may also be on petioles or calyx. Leaves may dry and die.	**Rust,** *Puccinia antirrhini.* Fungus survives only on living tissue and seed. Spores spread in air. Favored by cool, crowded, wet, humid conditions. Favored by humid, 50° to 55°F nights and 70° to 75°F days.	Avoid overhead irrigation. Water early in day so foliage dries. Remove or incorporate all dead plant material after harvest, before replanting. See page 119.

What the problem looks like	Probable cause	Comments

SNAPDRAGON *(Antirrhinum majus)* (continued)

What the problem looks like	Probable cause	Comments
Stems or leaves have elliptical sunken white, brown, or reddish spots or lesions. Plants turn slightly yellow, wilt, and may die. Crown tissues decays. Roots are not affected during early stages.	**Anthracnose,** *Colletotrichum gloeosporioides* or *C. antirrhini.* Fungus survives in infected plants and debris. Spores spread by splashing water. Favored by wet weather and overhead irrigation. Not reported on snapdragon in California.	Avoid overhead irrigation. Keep plants dry. Sulfur, Bordeaux mixture, or other fungicides can control but may damage blossoms. See pages 116–118.
Leaves have small, tan, red or yellow lesions or larger blotches. Plants may wilt, darken, and die.	**Leaf spot** or **Blight,** *Cercospora antirrhini.* Fungal spores are airborne. Favored by warm, moist conditions. Not reported on snapdragon in California.	Avoid overhead irrigation. Keep humidity low; provide good air circulation. See pages 116–118.
Leaves have brown to blackish spots or blotches that may have tan center or reddish margin.	**Bacterial leaf spot,** *Pseudomonas syringae.* Spread by air and splashing water.	Avoid overhead irrigation. Don't overwater. Don't crowd plants. Use good sanitation. Grow nonhost crops in soil for 1 to 2 years. See page 107.
Foliage chlorotic. Plant stunted. Spindly, upright yellow shoots and few or no flowers.	**Aster yellows phytoplasma.** Spread by leafhoppers. Not spread by seed, handling, aphids, or other insects. Many hosts. Not reported on snapdragon in California.	Don't plant seed beds downwind from other hosts. Eliminate nearby weeds. Control leafhoppers. Rogue infected plants. See pages 129–130.
Leaves mottled, spotted, or ring-spotted. Petals may be spotted or streaked. Leaf veins may discolor. Foliage may distort, wilt, or drop. Stems necrotic. Plants stunted.	**Viruses,** including Cucumber mosaic (aphid-vectored, attacks plants in over 40 families); Impatiens necrotic spot, Tomato spotted wilt (thrips-vectored, many hosts).	Rogue infected plants; cover and dispose of them away from crop. Control alternate hosts. Exclude or control insect vectors. See Viruses, page 121.
Foliage yellows, may be somewhat stunted. Common production problem.	**Nutritional disorder.** Causes include improper pH, poor water quality, inadequate drainage, or inappropriate fertilization.	Monitor and provide proper pH and good water quality. Provide good drainage. Fertilize and irrigate appropriately.
Florets drop prematurely.	**Shattering.** Caused by excess ethylene or other air pollutants.	Provide adequate air circulation and good quality air. Using an anti-ethylene agent may help. See page 67.
Distorted callus growth or gall on lower stem or on roots. Plant stunted. Roots may be gnarled, stunted, or hairy with mostly small rootlets.	**Crown gall,** *Agrobacterium tumefaciens.* Bacteria persist in soil, enter plant through wounds. Favored by rapid plant growth.	Pasteurize media before planting. Inspect stock and use only if pathogen-free. Avoid wounding plants. See page 102.
Plants are stunted. Swellings or galls on roots.	**Root knot nematode,** *Meloidogyne* sp. Nematode survives in soil as eggs. Usually most severe in sandy soils in warm climates.	Pasteurize media before planting. See page 265.
Foliage has sticky honeydew, blackish sooty mold, and whitish cast skins. Foliage may yellow. New terminals may be distorted.	**Aphids,** including *Aphis gossypii, Myzus persicae.* Small, pear-shaped, insects, often green, yellowish, or blackish.	See page 179.
Foliage has sticky honeydew and blackish sooty mold. Leaves may yellow and wither. Tiny, whitish, mothlike adult insects.	**Whiteflies.** Oval, flattened, yellow to greenish nymphs and pupae.	See page 170.
Leaves may have cottony white material (egg sacs), sticky honeydew, or black sooty mold. Leaves may yellow. Plant may be stunted.	**Mealybugs.** Elongate, slow-moving, powdery insects with waxy fringe.	See page 183.
Foliage discolored, stippled, bleached, or reddened, and may drop. Plant may have fine webbing.	**Twospotted spider mite,** *Tetranychus urticae.* Tiny greenish or yellowish mites with 2 darker spots.	See page 213.
Plants severely stunted. Leaf terminals distorted. Buds deform, blacken, or discolor, and may drop.	**Cyclamen mite,** *Phytonemus pallidus.* A pinkish orange mite (family Tarsonemidae), $\frac{1}{100}$ inch long or smaller.	See page 217.
Buds or terminal leaves chewed. Stems may be mined. Leaves may have black frass.	**Snapdragon plume moth,** *Platyptilia* or *Stenoptilodes antirrhina.* Caterpillars and narrow-winged tan adults up to 1 inch long.	Exclude moths from growing area. Use good sanitation; remove infested plants. Apply *Bacillus thuringiensis* when young larvae are feeding exposed. See Caterpillars, page 203.
Foliage chewed. Larvae up to 1½ inches long, dark green or black, spiny, with orange or yellow.	**Buckeye,** *Junonia coenia.* Butterfly mostly brown with orange and 1 or 2 eyespots on each wing.	Exclude moths from growing area. Use good sanitation; remove infested plants. Apply *Bacillus thuringiensis* to young larvae. See Caterpillars, page 203.

What the problem looks like	Probable cause	Comments
Foliage, buds, and stems chewed. Young plants clipped at base. Stocky moths present, attracted to lights at night, wings folded at rest.	**Variegated cutworm,** *Peridroma saucia.* Gray or brown larva with dark markings, row of yellow dots on back. Hides in soil during day.	Exclude moths, which fly to lights at night. Apply *Bacillus thuringiensis* to young larvae. Insecticide bait kills caterpillars. See Caterpillars, page 203.
Flowers, terminals, or foliage chewed. Buds may be mined.	**Cabbage looper,** *Trichoplusia ni.* Greenish larvae, up to 1½ inches long, with light, longitudinal stripes.	Exclude moths from growing areas. Avoid growing near other major hosts. *Bacillus thuringiensis* kills larvae. See Caterpillars, page 203.
Foliage chewed, often only on underside, and webbed together with silk. Stems may be mined. Adult moth and mature larva present, about ¾ inches long.	**Greenhouse leaftier,** *Udea rubigalis.* Larvae (family Pyralidae) yellowish green with three longitudinal green to white stripes. Adult reddish brown with black wavy lines on wings. Has about 6 generations per year.	Avoid growing near celery, a major host. Exclude night-flying moths from growing area. See Caterpillars, page 203.
Winding leaf tunnels. Leaves have pale spots or punctures from adult flies. Leaves may drop. Plants stunted. Fewer flowers. Young plants die. Yellowish to white maggots in mines.	**Serpentine leafminer,** *Liriomyza trifolii.* Adults are tiny, active, black and yellow flies.	See page 167.

SOLIDAGO (*Solidago* spp.), Goldenrod

What the problem looks like	Probable cause	Comments
Foliage yellows and wilts. Stems may have lesions and die back.	**Stem blights,** *Diaporthe* spp. Fungi infect through wounds, persist in infected tissue. Not reported on goldenrod in California.	Use good sanitation. Avoid wounding plants and keep plants dry.
Whitish powdery growth on leaves or stems. Older infected leaves yellow and wither. Heavily infected plants are stunted and may die.	**Powdery mildews,** *Erysiphe* spp. Fungi produce abundant airborne spores. Moisture not necessary and is detrimental to germination and infection. Favored by moderate temperatures. Not reported on goldenrod in California.	Use good sanitation; remove and dispose of plant debris. See page 112.
Leaves have brown to orangish powdery pustules and yellowish spots. Leaves may yellow or brown and drop.	**Rusts,** *Coleosporium, Puccinia, Uromyces* spp. Fungi survive on living tissue. Spores are airborne. Favored by high humidity and wet plants. Not reported on goldenrod in California.	Avoid overhead irrigation. Water in morning. Don't crowd plants. Provide good air circulation. Use good sanitation. See page 119.
Leaves have brown to yellow spots or blotches that may have dark or yellowish margins. Foliage may shrivel and drop.	**Leaf spots,** including *Cercospora, Phyllosticta, Ramularia, Septoria* spp. Spread by air or splashing water. Favored by wet conditions. Persist in plant debris. Not reported on goldenrod in California.	Avoid wetting foliage. Use drip irrigation and raised benches. Use good sanitation; promptly remove and dispose of debris and infected leaves. See pages 116–118.
Foliage stippled, bleached, bronzed. May be blackish excrement.	**Chrysanthemum lace bug,** *Corythucha marmorata.* Black and white with brown, up to ⅛ inches long.	See True Bugs, page 194.
Leaves have dead patches. Leaf tips may wilt. Unusual branching. Premature flower bud formation. Distorted flowers. Delayed or no flowers.	**Plant bugs,** *Lygus* spp. Brown, green, or yellowish bugs, up to ¼ inch long, suck plant juices.	Control nearby weeds, from which bugs move. Exclude bugs from growing area. See True Bugs, page 194.
Leaves or stems stippled, brown, distorted, or wilted. Buds may drop or develop only partially.	**Brown stink bug,** *Euschistus servus.* Shield-shaped bugs, brownish to blackish or green that lay barrel-shaped eggs in clusters.	Control nearby weeds. Exclude or control stink bugs. See True Bugs, page 194.
Foliage yellows. Plant declines or dies back. Stems or leaves have gray, brown, or tan encrustations.	**Latania scale,** *Hemiberlesia lataniae.* Circular flattened insects, less than 1/16 inch long.	See Scales, page 186.
Terminals die back due to numerous punctures or slits in stems from treehopper egg laying.	**Buffalo treehopper,** *Stictocephala bisonia.* Elongate, green and yellow insects, up to 3/16 inches long. Suck plant juices.	Control nearby weeds it may infest. Exclude treehoppers. Broad-spectrum insecticides may provide control.
Foliage has sticky honeydew and blackish sooty mold. Plant may die back.	**Brown soft scale,** *Coccus hesperidum.* Small flattened, oval insects that are yellow, orangish, or brown.	See Scales, page 186.
Foliage has sticky honeydew, blackish sooty mold, and whitish cast skins on. Leaves may curl or pucker. Foliage may yellow.	**Aphids,** including Cornflower aphid, *Macrosiphum rudbeckiae*; Leaf curl plum aphid, *Aphis* or *Brachycaudus helichrysi.* Small pear-shaped insects, often green, reddish, yellowish, or blackish.	See page 179.
Plant has sticky honeydew and blackish sooty mold. Elongated, whitish material (egg sacs) present. Insects on twigs or leaves.	**Cottony cushion scale,** *Icerya purchasi.* Females brown, orange, red, or yellow. Uncommon.	Natural enemies can provide good control. See Scales, page 186.
Foliage yellows. Stems may wilt and die from boring by pale maggot.	**Leaf and stem miners,** including *Agromyza* sp. Adults are tiny flies, often blackish.	See page 167.

What the problem looks like	Probable cause	Comments

SOLIDAGO (*Solidago* spp.), Goldenrod (continued)

What the problem looks like	Probable cause	Comments
Foliage chewed. Plants may defoliate from chewing by blackish larvae.	**Leaf beetles,** including *Trirhabda* spp. Adults often green, yellow, or blackish. Pupae overwinter in soil.	See page 212.
Foliage chewed and webbed together with silk. Disturbed larvae wriggle and drop on a thread. Eggs laid in overlapping mass like fish scales.	**Orange tortrix,** *Argyrotaenia citrana.* Larva whitish, head brown. Gray to brown moth (family Tortricidae), often abundant near citrus orchards. Larva and moth up to 1 inch long. Has many other hosts.	See Caterpillars, page 203.

SPATHIPHYLLUM (*Spathiphyllum* spp.)

What the problem looks like	Probable cause	Comments
Leaves may yellow or darken. Plant may wilt and die. Roots and stem around soil dark and decayed.	**Pythium root rot,** *Pythium* spp.; **Rhizoctonia aerial blight,** *Rhizoctonia solani;* **Phytophthora leaf spot,** *Phytophthora* spp. Fungi promoted by wet, poorly drained soil.	Provide good drainage. Avoid excess irrigation and reduce watering if disease develops. See pages 93–98.
Brown to black water-soaked spots or decay on leaves or stems near soil. Tissue may have tiny, black to dark green, spore-forming structures and white mycelia.	**Myrothecium leaf spot,** *Myrothecium roridum.* Spreads by waterborne spores. Infects through wounds. Favored by 70° to 81°F and excess nitrogen or salts.	Minimize plant wounds. Keep foliage dry. Use good sanitation. Avoid excess fertilization. Growing plants above 86°F may arrest or prevent disease.
Foliage yellows and wilts. Leaves may have irregular water-soaked to dark spots, lesions, or rings. Soft, brown, stem rot near soil line. Stems may collapse and die.	**Soft rot,** *Erwinia carotovora, Pseudomonas* spp. (bacteria), *Acremonium* sp. (fungus). Persist in media and infected stock, infect through wounds, and are favored when wet.	Keep foliage dry. Use drip irrigation. Don't overwater. Provide good drainage. Use good sanitation; rogue infected and nearby plants. Avoid injuring plants. See pages 93–96, 100, 107.
Lower leaves spot, yellow, and wilt. Roots, petioles and corms soft, dark and rotted. Seedlings die.	**Cylindrocladium petiole and root rot,** *Cylindrocladium spathiphylii.* Spores spread in splashing water. Fungus infects through leaves or roots. Not reported on spathiphyllum in California.	Pasteurize media before planting. Avoid overhead water. Use good sanitation. Inspect plants and rogue those infected.
Leaf tips and possibly margins brown or brown with yellow margin. Foliage may yellow and die.	**Salt damage.** Noninfectious disorder due to poor water quality, excess fertilization, or insufficient water.	Leach media with low salt water. Avoid overfertilization. Provide proper irrigation. Trim out damaged tissue. See page 47.

STAR OF BETHLEHEM (*Ornithogalum arabicum*)

What the problem looks like	Probable cause	Comments
Plants wilt and collapse. Basal stem or bulbs rot. White cottony fungus growth or tiny, tan or brown sclerotia may form on rotted tissue and soil.	**Southern blight,** *Sclerotium rolfsii.* Sclerotia survive in soil, germinate there, and infect susceptible plants. No airborne spores are formed. Many hosts.	Avoid fields where disease has occurred or pasteurize soil before planting. Rogue all infected plants. See page 101.
Brown to yellow spots or blotches, mostly on older leaves. Spots may have dark or yellowish margins. Foliage may shrivel, drop.	**Leaf spots,** *Mycosphaerella ornithogali, Septoria ornithogali.* Spread by air or splashing water. Favored by cool, wet, conditions. Persist in plant debris.	Avoid wetting foliage. Use drip irrigation. Use good sanitation; promptly remove and dispose of debris and infected leaves. See pages 116–118.
Foliage has irregular light lines or mottling. Plants may be stunted. Foliage may distort.	**Ornithogalum mosaic virus.** Aphid-vectored.	Use virus-free bulbs. Exclude or control aphids. Rogue infected plants. See Viruses, page 121.
Blossoms or leaves have pale to brown blotches. Blossoms or terminals may distort. Growth may be stunted.	**Thrips.** Tiny, slender, dark brown to yellowish insects.	See page 161.
Foliage has sticky honeydew, blackish sooty mold, and whitish cast skins. Foliage may yellow.	**Aphids,** including Green peach aphid, *Myzus persicae.* Small pear-shaped insects, often green, yellow, or blackish.	See page 179.

STATICE (*Limonium* spp.)

What the problem looks like	Probable cause	Comments
Leaves have small dull red lesions that enlarge up to ⅔ inch and become tan and membranous, with reddish borders.	**Cercospora leaf spot,** *Cercospora insulana.* Fungal spores are airborne. Favored by warm, moist conditions.	See Leaf Spots, pages 116–118.
Leaves or stems have brownish pustules and yellow spots. Foliage may yellow, wither, and drop. Plants may be stunted.	**Rust,** *Uromyces* spp. Spores spread by wind, splashing water. Fungi survive only on living tissue; must be wet for infection.	Avoid overhead irrigation. Water in morning, so foliage dries. Use good sanitation. Provide good air circulation; don't crowd plants. See page 119.

What the problem looks like	Probable cause	Comments
Leaves, stems, flowers, and crowns may rot. Seedlings or older plants may die. Flower stubs remaining after flower harvest are especially susceptible. Dead tissue may have woolly gray growth (spores).	**Gray mold,** *Botrytis cinerea.* Fungus develops in crop debris or inactive tissue. Favored by high humidity and 70° to 77°F. Spores airborne.	Remove plant debris or incorporate debris into soil soon after harvest. Avoid overhead irrigation, especially when flowers are present. See page 108.
Plants stunted. Lower leaves yellow, wilt, and dry.	**Verticillium wilt,** *Verticillium dahliae, V. albo-atrum.* Fungi persist in soil as microsclerotia. Many hosts. *Verticillium dahlia* is not reported on statice in California.	Pasteurize soil before planting. Heat treat or otherwise pasteurize media used for growing transplants. See pages 104–106.
Plants wilt and collapse. Basal stem rots. White cottony fungus growth and tiny, tan or brown sclerotia may form on plants or media.	**Southern blight,** *Sclerotium rolfsii.* Sclerotia survive in media, germinate there, and infect susceptible plants. No airborne spores are formed. Many hosts. Not reported on statice in California.	Avoid fields where disease has occurred or pasteurize media before planting. Rogue all infected plants. See page 101.
Lower leaves die back. Plants collapse.	**Bacterial blight,** *Corynebacterium* sp. Bacteria spread in plant debris and water. Favored by cool, wet weather.	Avoid overhead irrigation. Keep foliage dry. Provide good air circulation. Don't crowd plant. Use good sanitation; remove and dispose of plant debris.
Plants turn slightly yellow and wilt. Crown tissues decays. Plant may die. Roots are not affected during early stages. Leaves, stems, and flowers may be spotted.	**Anthracnose,** *Colletotrichum gloeosporioides.* Fungus survives in infected plants and debris. Spores spread by splashing water. Favored by wet weather and overhead irrigation. Not reported on statice in California.	Avoid overhead irrigation. fungicide application may prevent, but may cause flowers to blacken. Consider avoiding 'Gold Coast,' which is highly susceptible. Plant blue and white cultivars, which are more tolerant. See pages 116–118.
Leaves or stems have whitish powdery growth. Older infected leaves yellow and wither. Heavily infected plants are stunted and may die.	**Powdery mildew,** *Erysiphe polygoni.* Fungus produces abundant airborne spores. Moisture not necessary and is detrimental to germination and infection. Favored by moderate temperatures. Not reported on statice in California.	Use good sanitation; remove and dispose of plant debris. See page 112.
Leaves have light green, yellow, or brownish irregular blotches. Lower leaf surface has gray to purplish, fuzzy fungal growth. Leaves turn brown, wilt, and die.	**Downy mildew,** *Peronospora statices.* Spores produced only on living plants. Fungus persists as resistant oospores on dead leaves when conditions are dry. Favored by moist, humid conditions.	Provide good air circulation. Keep humidity low. Keep foliage dry. Avoid overhead watering. Consider applying fungicide to protect foliage. See page 115.
Soft, brown, stem rot near soil line. Foliage yellows and wilts. Leaves may have irregular water-soaked spots or lesions. Odorous rot.	**Bacterial soft rot or blight,** *Erwinia chrysanthemi.* Persists in media and infected stock. Favored when wet. Avoid injuring plant, as disease infects wounds.	Keep foliage dry. Don't overwater. Provide good drainage. Use good sanitation; rogue infected and nearby plants. See pages 100, 107.
Basal stem or roots near soil darken and decay. Leaves may yellow, wilt, and die.	**Bacterial crown rot,** *Pseudomonas* sp. Spreads by air and splashing water. Not reported on statice in California.	Avoid overhead irrigation. Don't overwater. Don't crowd plants. Use good sanitation.
Leaves have light and dark green mosaic pattern. Plants stunted. Leaves may be distorted or necrotic. Infected young plants often die.	**Viruses,** including Tomato spotted wilt (thrips-vectored), Turnip mosaic virus (aphid-vectored, common in many Brassicaceae weeds).	Eliminate nearby weeds. Exclude or control aphids insect vectors. Rogue infected plants. See page 121.
Spindly, upright yellow shoots. Flowers are few, small, distorted, green, or may fail to open. Leaves reddish on basal rosette of mature plants.	**Yellows,** Phytoplasma and phytoplasmalike organisms spread by leafhoppers. Many hosts.	Don't plant downwind from other hosts. Eliminate nearby weeds. Exclude or control leafhoppers. Rogue infected plants. See pages 129–130.
Plants stunted. Swellings or galls on roots.	**Root knot nematode,** *Meloidogyne* spp. Tiny roundworms feed on roots.	Pasteurize soil before planting. See page 265.
Blossoms have irregular white or brown blotches or streaks. Blossoms or terminals may bleach or distort. Underside of leaves may have dark, varnishlike excrement.	**Greenhouse thrips,** *Heliothrips haemorrhoidalis.* Tiny, slender, black, dark brown to yellowish insects.	See page 161.
Foliage, terminals, or petals chewed. Leaves may be webbed with silk. Flower buds may be mined.	**Beet armyworm,** *Spodoptera exigua.* Greenish larvae, up to 1⅜ inches long, with light, longitudinal stripes.	Exclude moths. *Bacillus thuringiensis* kills larvae. See Caterpillars, page 203.
Foliage yellows, wilts, and dies. Basal stem has holes or decay. Grayish larva up to ¾ inch long, head dark, boring in plant.	**Crown borer,** *Opogona omoscopa.* Dark, brownish moth (family Tineidae), attracted to decaying tissue, probably a secondary pest.	Avoid wounding plants. Provide good cultural care. Avoid excess irrigation. Use good sanitation; remove debris and dying plants.
Dried flowers in storage chewed and webbed together with dirty silk by white, greenish, to pinkish larvae.	**Indianmeal moth,** *Plodia interpunctella.* Mature larva and grayish white to reddish brown adult moth are about ½ inch long.	Infests many stored and dried foods. Use good sanitation; dispose of debris and infested plants where moths live. Exclude moths.

What the problem looks like	Probable cause	Comments

STEPHANOTIS (*Stephanotis floribunda*), Madagascar jasmine

What the problem looks like	Probable cause	Comments
Leaves discolor, wilt, or drop. Brown root rot. Stem rot or canker near soil.	**Crown and root rot,** *Rhizoctonia* sp. Soilborne fungus spreads in media and contaminated water and plants. Favored by warm, moist soil. Not reported on stephanotis in California.	See pages 93–98.
Flowers or flower head have soft brown decay. Leaves or terminals may decay. Dead tissue may have woolly gray growth (spores).	**Flower blight,** *Botrytis* sp. Fungus develops in plant debris. Favored by wet or high humidity conditions. Not reported on stephanotis in California.	Use good sanitation. Avoid overhead irrigation. Keep humidity low. Provide good air circulation. Don't crowd plants. See page 108.
Stems wilt and die, may be cankered or girdled. Leaves darken and often remain attached after dying.	**Dieback,** *Glomerella cingulata*. Spreads by splashing water. Favored by warm, wet conditions and plant injuries. Many hosts. Not reported on stephanotis in California.	Avoid overwatering or stressing plants. Use good sanitation; rogue infected plants. Minimize injuries to plants.
Leaves have white powdery growth. Foliage may dry and die.	**Powdery mildew,** *Oidium* sp. Persists in infected tissue. Free water not required for infection. Not reported on stephanotis in California.	Provide good air circulation and adequate light. Don't crowd plants. See page 112.
Leaves have yellow to brown ring patterns or spots. Foliage may yellow. Plants may stunt or die.	**Impatiens necrotic spot, Tomato spotted wilt virus.** Spread by thrips. Many hosts.	Control nearby weeds. Exclude or control thrips. Rogue infected plants. See page 121.
Leaves may have cottony white material (egg sacs), sticky honeydew, or black sooty mold. Leaves may yellow. Plants may be stunted.	**Citrus mealybug,** *Planococcus citri*; **Ground mealybug,** *Rhizoecus falcifer*; **Longtailed mealybug,** *Pseudococcus longispinus*. Elongate, slow insects on foliage or in soil. *R. falcifer* feeds on roots and crown, makes little wax. *P. citri* and *P. longispinus* live on foliage and stems, have waxy fringes.	See page 183.
Foliage or stems has sticky honeydew or blackish sooty mold. Plant may yellow, decline, or die back.	**Scales,** including Hemispherical scale, *Saissetia coffeae*. Orange, black, or brown flattened to bulbous insects.	See page 186.

STOCK (*Matthiola* spp.), Gilliflower

What the problem looks like	Probable cause	Comments
Basal leaves yellow and drop. Leaf scars blackened. Stems yellow. Stem cankers, first soft and water-soaked, become dark and sunken. Vascular system blackish. Plants collapse. Roots may appear girdled and dieback. Young plants wilt and collapse.	**Bacterial blight,** *Xanthomonas campestris* pv. *incanae*. Bacteria spread in seed and plant debris; persist in soil for 2 years. Spread by water. Favored by cool, wet weather.	Use only seed grown from seed treated in 122° to 131°F water for 10 min. Grow *Matthiola* spp. in that soil only once every 3 years. See pages 107, 118.
Stem bases and sometimes crown are black and rotted. Stems may fall over. Rotted tissue is odorous. Most prevalent during warm, wet conditions.	**Soft crown rot,** *Erwinia carotovora*. Bacteria persist in plant debris, spread in water, and infect through wounds. Seed may be infected.	Pasteurize media used for seedlings. Provide good drainage. Avoid overhead irrigation. See pages 100, 107.
Brown stem rot at soil line, later becomes a sunken, dry canker. Brown fungal strands visible with a hand lens. Stems girdled. Seedlings damp off.	**Foot rot** or **Wire stem,** *Rhizoctonia solani*. Soilborne fungus favored by warm, moist soil.	Pasteurize soil before planting. Provide good drainage; plant in raised beds. Don't overwater. See pages 93–98.
Plants wilt or suddenly collapse. Roots and crown decay. Seedlings damp off.	**Water mold root rot,** *Phytophthora, Pythium* spp. Fungi persist in soil. Favored by wet, poorly drained soil.	Provide good drainage; plant on raised beds. Avoid excess irrigation. Consider treating seed before planting. See pages 93–97.
Girdling stem infection. Stems turn chalky white. Cottony masses or large, black fungal sclerotia grow inside stems.	**Cottony rot,** *Sclerotinia sclerotiorum*. Survives as fungal sclerotia in soil that infect plants on contact. Favored by cool, moist conditions. Many hosts.	Pasteurize soil before planting or avoid planting where disease has occurred, infects many vegetable crops. Avoid overhead irrigation. Irrigate early in day so plants dry quickly. Consider fungicide application to foliage. See page 101.
Flowers, flower heads, lower leaves, or growing points have soft brown decay. Dead tissue may have woolly gray growth (spores).	**Gray mold,** *Botrytis cinerea*. Fungus develops in crop debris or inactive tissue. Favored by high humidity and 70° to 77°F. Spores airborne.	Use good sanitation. Avoid overhead irrigation. Keep humidity low. Provide good air circulation. Don't crowd plants. See page 108.
Foliage yellows and wilts. Leaves die and dry up, progressively upward from base of plant. Vascular tissue darkens.	**Verticillium wilt,** *Verticillium albo-atrum*. Fungal microsclerotia persist in soil for many years. Symptoms most severe during warm weather after a cool period.	Pasteurize soil or avoid planting in fields where disease has occurred. See pages 104–106.

What the problem looks like	Probable cause	Comments
Beginning with basal leaves, leaf veins yellow, then entire leaf yellows, withers, and drops. Plants stunted. Vascular tissue brownish. Seed pods turn light yellow.	**Fusarium wilt,** *Fusarium oxysporum* f. sp. *mathioli.* Fungus seedborne and in soil, where it persists for years. A problem during warm weather.	Important in seed fields; pasteurize soil before planting seed crops. Usually not important in cut flowers grown in cool, coastal areas, especially during winter. See page 104.
Foliage pale and wilted. Plants stunted and may die. Knobby, spindlelike swellings on roots. Prevalent in soils where *Brassica* spp. crops have previously grown.	**Clubroot,** *Plasmodiophora brassicae.* A plasmodium microorganism. Propagules very persistent in media and infect roots, especially when wet. Soil pH of 7.2 or higher inhibits spore germination.	Plant only pathogen-free stock. Pasteurize media before planting. Don't grow cruciferous crops in soil where other infested plants in mustard family have grown, including certain weeds and crops such as broccoli and cabbage. Provide good drainage. Adjust pH if possible.
Leaves have round to elongate, concentric brown spots covered with black, powdery spores. Spots small at first, then enlarge turning grayish green with water-soaked margins.	**Leaf spot,** *Alternaria raphani.* Fungus develops in stock, debris, and plants in mustard (Brassicaceae) family. Airborne spores. Favored by wet weather.	Remove all plant debris and plow plants under immediately after harvest. See pages 116–118.
Leaves have yellow to brown ring spots, streaks, or mottling. Plants may be stunted or distorted. Blossoms may be spotted or streaked. Veins may clear. Symptoms vary with stock variety.	**Viruses,** including Beet curly top (leafhopper-vector), Tomato spotted wilt (thrips-vectored), Turnip mosaic (aphid-vectored). Not seedborne.	Eliminate nearby weeds. Exclude or control insect vectors. Rogue infected plants. See page 121.
Spindly, upright yellow shoots. Few or no flowers. Flowers revert to green leafy tissue.	**Aster yellows phytoplasma.** Spread by leafhoppers. Not spread by seed, handling, aphids, or other insects. Many hosts.	Don't plant downwind from other hosts. Eliminate nearby weeds. Exclude or control leafhoppers. Rogue infected plants. See pages 129–130.
Foliage has sticky honeydew, blackish sooty mold, and whitish cast skins. Foliage may distort or yellow.	**Aphids,** including *Aphis gossypii, Brevicoryne brassicae, Myzus persicae.* Tiny pear-shaped insects, often greenish, yellowish, or blackish.	See page 179.
Foliage has small holes. Underside of leaves scraped, pitted, or mined. Terminals and buds may be chewed, stunting growth, reducing flowering. Plants may defoliate.	**Diamondback moth,** *Plutella xylostella.* Slender, pale green larvae, with scattered black hairs; rear prolegs form distinct V. Forms silken cocoons on foliage or debris, which can be disposed of. Gray to brown adult and mature larva about ⅓ inch long. Attacks most Brassicaceae.	Exclude egg-laying moths with row covers. Apply *Bacillus thuringiensis* to kill larvae. *Trichogramma* parasite releases may be effective against eggs. See page 203.
Foliage skeletonized, holey, or chewed. Plants may be defoliated by adult beetles that jump when disturbed, but feed mostly at night.	**Western striped flea beetle,** *Phyllotreta ramosa.* Adult shiny black beetle, about 1/12 inch long, with yellowish white wing markings.	See page 212.

STRAWFLOWER (*Helichrysum bracteatum*)

What the problem looks like	Probable cause	Comments
Lower leaves wilted and yellow, usually on one side of plant. Vascular tissue discolored. Many hosts, including weeds, crops and ornamentals.	**Verticillium wilt,** *Verticillium dahliae, V. albo-atrum.* Fungi survive for years in soil. Favored by cool spring, with symptoms most obvious during hot weather at flowering.	Avoid planting in fields known to be infested. Pasteurize soil before planting. See pages 104–106.
Foliage yellow, with downy, whitish growth (spores) on underside. Leaves roll downward.	**Downy mildew,** *Plasmopara halstedii.* Airborne spores. Favored by wet weather and temperatures around 59°F.	Avoid overhead watering. See page 115.
Plants appear bleached, may wilt and die quickly. Stems may turn chalky white and be girdled. Cottony masses or large, black fungal sclerotia inside infected stems.	**Cottony rot,** *Sclerotinia sclerotiorum.* Survives as fungal sclerotia in soil that infect plants on contact. Favored by humid, wet conditions. Many hosts, including many vegetable crops.	Pasteurize soil before planting or avoid planting where disease has occurred. Avoid overhead irrigation. Irrigate early in day so plants dry quickly. Consider fungicide application to foliage. See page 101.
Plants stunted, distorted, and yellow, frequently on one side of plant. Flowers may develop as all-green tissue.	**Aster yellows phytoplasma.** Spread by leafhoppers. Many hosts, including weeds.	Control weeds in and nearby crops. Leafhopper control may help. See pages 129–130.
Foliage stippled or discolored. Terminals may distort.	**Leafhoppers.** Small, elongate, active insects, often greenish or brightly colored.	See page 193.
Shoots or blossoms blackened, dwarfed, discolored, or distorted. Leaf tips may wilt and die.	**Plant bugs,** *Lygus* spp. Brown, green, or yellowish bugs, up to ¼ inch long, that suck plant juices.	Control nearby weeds, from which bugs move. Exclude bugs from growing area. See True Bugs, page 194.
Buds, flowers or leaves mined or chewed, may be webbed with silk.	**Omnivorous leaftier,** *Cnephasia longana.* Gray to brownish larvae and nocturnal moths, ½ inch long. Larvae may have grayish stripes. Attacks strawberries and many other hosts. Occurs in central California coast. Has 1 generation per year.	Time any spray for young larvae emerging from mines in spring. See Caterpillars, page 203.

What the problem looks like	Probable cause	Comments
SUNFLOWER (*Helianthus* spp.)		
Plants stunted. Foliage yellows, may wilt and drop. Roots or basal stems dark and decayed.	**Root and stem rot,** *Phytophthora* spp. Fungi present in many soils and persist there. Favored by poor drainage and overwatering.	Pasteurize media before planting. Provide good drainage. Don't overirrigate. See pages 93–97.
Plant wilts and dies. Basal stem rotted. Black sclerotia in or on stems. Cottony mycelia in and on stems if conditions are moist.	**Cottony rot,** *Sclerotinia sclerotiorum*. Fungus survives in soil as sclerotia that may infect plants on contact. Favored by overhead irrigation and high humidity. Many hosts.	Avoid planting in previously infested soil or pasteurize media before planting. Avoid overhead irrigation. Irrigate early in day so plants dry quickly. See page 101.
Foliage yellowing, especially outer leaves. Basal stem or roots have soft rot. White mycelia and small, tan to reddish brown sclerotia may develop on infected tissue around soil.	**Southern wilt,** *Sclerotium rolfsii*. Sclerotia survive in soil. Disease favored by moist, poorly drained, 77° to 95°F media.	Pasteurize media before planting. Provide good drainage. Avoid excess irrigation. See page 101.
Foliage yellows, browns, or wilts. Plants stunted. Roots and basal stem black and rotted, may have tiny black sclerotia inside.	**Charcoal rot,** *Macrophomina phaseolina*. Persists in media. Favored by hot weather. Prefers seedlings and stressed plants.	Pasteurize media before planting. Avoid stressing plants; provide good cultural care.
Flower heads, petals, leaves, or stems have soft brown decay or spots and may wilt and die. Dead tissue may have woolly gray growth (spores).	**Gray mold,** *Botrytis cinerea*. Fungus develops in crop debris or inactive tissue. Favored by high humidity and 70° to 77°F. Spores airborne.	Use good sanitation. Avoid overhead irrigation. Keep humidity low. Provide good air circulation. Don't crowd plants. See page 108.
Leaves have white powdery growth. Foliage may dry and die.	**Powdery mildew,** *Erysiphe cichoracearum*. Persists in infected tissue. Free water not required for infection.	Provide good air circulation and adequate light. Don't crowd plants. See page 112.
Seedlings stunted and may die. Leaves have dark, irregular spots or blotches. Lower leaf surface covered with soft, fluffy grayish to white fungal growth. Leaves yellow and drop.	**Downy mildew,** *Plasmopara halstedii*. Spores produced only on living plants. Fungus persists as resistant oospores on dead leaves when conditions are dry. Favored by moist, humid conditions. Fungus can be seedborne and infection may become systemic in seedlings.	Plant resistant cultivars if available. Provide good air circulation. Avoid overhead watering. Consider applying fungicide to protect foliage. See page 115.
Leaves have circular to irregular yellow to brown spots or blotches. Foliage may yellow and die.	**Leaf spots,** *Alternaria, Cercospora, Septoria* spp. Spread by splashing water or contaminated tools or stock. Persist in plant debris. Not reported on sunflower in California.	Avoid overhead watering. Use good sanitation, promptly remove and dispose of debris and infected leaves. See pages 116–118.
Leaves have circular to irregular, brownish, greenish yellow, or pale spots, ¼ to ½ inch diameter, sometimes with discolored border. Spots may be somewhat thickened and are evident on both sides of leaf. Leaves may later turn brown, dry, and die.	**Smut,** *Entyloma calendulae*. Fungus survives on live plants and in plant debris. Spores are windborne. Favored by rain and overhead irrigation.	Avoid planting sunflower repeatedly in the same soil. Rotate soil to other crops. Avoid overhead irrigation. Use good sanitation; remove and dispose of plant debris and infected plants.
Flower heads, dark, decayed, sometimes in wedge shape. Infected tissue may be covered with gray to whitish mycelial growth. Entire flower head may die.	**Head rot,** *Rhizopus oryzae*. Fungus infects through wounds, such as moth larval feeding damage. Infection promoted by warm, humid conditions. Spores airborne and spread in water. Survives in plant debris.	Avoid wounding or weakening plants. Use good sanitation; dispose of dead and dying plants. Reduce humidity. Avoid overhead irrigation. Control seed-feeding insects.
Leaves have brown to orangish powdery pustules and yellowish spots. Leaves may yellow or brown and drop.	**Rusts,** *Coleosporium, Puccinia helianthi, Uromyces* sp. Fungi survive on living tissue. Spores are airborne. Favored by high humidity and wet plants.	Avoid overhead irrigation. Water in morning. Don't crowd plants. Provide good air circulation. Use good sanitation. See page 119.
Foliage chlorotic. Plant stunted. Spindly, upright yellow shoots and few or no flowers.	**Aster yellows phytoplasma.** Spread by leafhoppers. Not spread by seed, handling, aphids, or other insects. Many hosts.	Don't plant downwind from other hosts. Eliminate nearby weeds. Exclude or control leafhoppers. Rogue infected plants. See pages 129–130.
Foliage yellow, often more evident on older leaves. Plants stunted. Older leaves may be necrotic.	**Nitrogen deficiency.** Noninfectious disorder.	Provide adequate nitrogen, especially before floret initiation. See pages 56–59.
Growth stunted. Lower leaves may have yellowish to dark gray blotches or spots.	**Phosphorus deficiency.** Noninfectious. If severe, symptoms similar to *Alternaria* and *Septoria*.	May be more severe in absence of symbiotic mycorrhizae. Provide adequate nutrition.

What the problem looks like	Probable cause	Comments
Plants fall over. Problem when soil is often wet.	**Lodging.** Noninfectious disorder during wet conditions or caused by excess irrigation or frequent, shallow watering.	Provide good drainage and soil aeration. Avoid overwatering. Provide infrequent deep irrigation instead of frequent, light sprinklings. Plant seed at proper depth.
Plants fall over. Foliage yellows and wilts. Plants stunted and die from pale maggots boring in stalks.	**Sunflower stem weevil,** *Cylindrocopturus adspersus.* Adult beetle, about $\frac{1}{8}$ inch long, dark brown with light spots. Overwinters as larvae in lower stalks and crowns.	Consider delayed planting; many beetles will emerge and die before laying eggs. Rotate fields with other crops. Deeply incorporate or remove and dispose of debris. Parasites help to control; avoid broad-spectrum insecticides.
Flowers, terminals, or foliage chewed. Leaves may be webbed with silk. Flower buds, heads, and seeds may be mined. May be dark frass from caterpillars.	**Sunflower moth,** *Homoeosoma electellum.* Larvae up to 1 inch long, body tan or reddish with dark and light longitudinal stripes. Adult grayish moth with wing span about $\frac{3}{4}$ inch long. Has 2 generations per year.	Parasites help to control; avoid broad-spectrum insecticides. See Caterpillars, page 203.
Foliage yellows and wilts. Plants may be stunted, fall over, or die from root-feeding beetles. Basal stems or leaves may be chewed.	**Carrot beetle,** *Ligyrus gibbosus.* Adult beetles (family Scarabaeidae) reddish brown, $\frac{1}{2}$ inch long, feed above and below ground. Larvae up to $1\frac{1}{4}$ inches long, white to bluish, head dark. Attacks grains and vegetable crops, especially tubers.	Exclude adults, which fly at night to lights. Eliminate decaying vegetation that harbors adults around plants. See White Grubs, page 211.
Blossoms have irregular blotches or streaks. Leaves may turn brown. Blossoms or terminals may be distorted. Growth may be stunted.	**Flower thrips,** *Frankliniella* spp. Slender dark brown to yellowish insects, $\frac{1}{16}$ inch long or less.	See Thrips, page 161.
Foliage discolored, stippled, bleached, or reddened. Leaves may bend, distort, or drop. Plant may have fine webbing.	**Spider mites.** Tiny greenish, red, or yellowish mites, often with 2 darker spots. Mites may first be observed around where leaves are bending.	See page 213.
Foliage stippled or discolored. Terminals may distort.	**Leafhoppers.** Small, elongate, active insects, often greenish or brightly colored.	See page 193.
Leaves have yellow or white stippling or blotches. Foliage may wilt, turn brown, and die. Flowers buds may drop or flowers may be deformed or develop only partially.	**Stink bugs,** including Harlequin bug, *Murgantia histrionica.* Shield-shaped bugs, green to brownish (or black and red if M. *histrionica*). Eggs barrel-shaped in clusters and often attacked by parasites.	Control weeds. Avoid planting near alternate hosts (family Brassicaceae) or plant crucifers in early spring as a trap crop. After fall harvest, treat or destroy infested crucifers in a manner that does not cause bugs to move. See True Bugs, page 194.
Shoots or blossoms blackened, dwarfed, discolored, or distorted. Leaf tips may wilt and die.	**Plant bugs,** *Lygus* spp. Brown, green, or yellowish bugs, up to $\frac{1}{4}$ inch long, that suck plant juices.	Control nearby weeds, from which bugs move. Exclude bugs from growing area. See True Bugs, page 194.
Foliage has sticky honeydew, blackish sooty mold, and whitish cast skins. Foliage may yellow.	**Aphids,** including *Aphis gossypii, Aphis helianthi, Macrosiphum* spp. Small pear-shaped insects, often green, yellowish, or blackish.	See page 179.
Leaves chewed, often between veins. Seedlings may be clipped. Plants stunted. Foliage yellows and wilts from slender, whitish root-feeding larvae of beetles that have several generation per year.	**Leaf beetles,** including Cucumber beetles, *Acalymma, Diabrotica* spp. Greenish yellow adults with black heads and black spots or stripes. Flea beetles, *Epitrix* spp., adults shiny green to dark brown or black.	Control nearby weeds, where adults overwinter and feed. Avoid growing near alternate hosts. Exclude adults, especially from seedlings. If sprayed, systemics are more effective. See page 212.
Buds, flowers, and foliage chewed. Yellowish or greenish caterpillars present, with darker, longitudinal stripes.	**Corn earworm,** *Heliothis* or *Helicoverpa zea.* Tan to brownish moths (family Noctuidae) with darker bands on wings. Larva and nocturnal adult up to $1\frac{1}{2}$ inch long.	See page 203.
Leaves chewed; edges rolled or tied together with silk by pale green, black-headed larvae.	**Obliquebanded leafroller,** *Archips* or *Choristoneura rosaceana.* Reddish brown moth (family Tortricidae), about 1 inch wide, with wavy dark lines on wings. Moth has snoutlike projection.	See Caterpillars, page 203.
Foliage chewed and webbed with silk. Caterpillars present, up to $1\frac{1}{2}$ inches long, alternately banded yellowish green and dark purplish.	**Painted beauty,** *Vanessa virginiensis.* Butterfly mostly orange and brown, up to $2\frac{1}{2}$ inches wide, with white and blue spots.	Eliminate alternate host weeds, including thistles, mallow, and malva. *Bacillus thuringiensis* kills larvae. See Caterpillars, page 203.
Foliage chewed by yellowish and black, very hairy caterpillars up to 2 inches long.	**Yellow woollybear,** *Spilosoma virginica.* Adult moth (family Arctiidae), white, yellowish, and brown with black wing markings. Overwinters in hairy cocoon. Has 2 generations per year.	See Caterpillars, page 203.

What the problem looks like	Probable cause	Comments
SWEET PEA (*Lathyrus odoratus*)		
Poor growth. Seedlings may die. Roots rotted and have black lesions.	**Black root rot,** *Thielaviopsis basicola* or *Chalara elegans*. Soilborne fungus. Favored by cool, wet soil and any stress that weakens plant.	Pasteurize media before planting. Provide good soil drainage; plant in raised beds. Avoid excess irrigation and overfertilization. Rogue infected plants. See pages 95–99.
Lower leaves yellow, wilt, then die. Flower heads may drop. Discolored streaks inside stems. Plants stunted. Root system reduced, small roots rotted. Seedlings don't emerge. Seed rot in soil.	**Root and crown rot, Damping-off, Seed decay,** *Rhizoctonia solani, Fusarium, Pythium* spp. Fungi persist in soil and crop debris. Spread in soil and water. Favored by excess moisture and poor drainage.	Pasteurize media before planting. Provide good drainage; plant in raised beds. Use fungicide-treated seed. Avoid excess irrigation. See pages 93–98.
Lower leaves and stem rot. Petals have blackish rot, may extend into flower stalk. Foliage may distort or die.	**Ascochyta blight,** *Ascochyta lathyri*. Persists in plant debris. Spores spread in air and water. Favored by overhead irrigation and rain.	Use pathogen-free stock. Avoid wetting foliage. Keep flowers dry during production and shipping. Keep humidity low. Fungicides can protect foliage.
Plants wilt and die. Cottony growth in or on stems if conditions are moist. Black sclerotia on stems.	**Cottony rot,** *Sclerotinia sclerotiorum*. Fungal sclerotia in media infect by direct contact with plants. Favored by wet conditions. Not reported on sweet pea in California.	Pasteurize soil before planting. Many hosts. Favored by wet conditions. Avoid overhead irrigation. Irrigate early in day so plants dry quickly. See page 101.
Leaves and stems have whitish powdery growth. Older infected leaves yellow and wither. Heavily infected plants are stunted.	**Powdery mildew,** *Erysiphe polygoni*. Fungus produces abundant airborne spores. Moisture not necessary and is detrimental to germination and infection. Favored by moderate temperatures.	Use good sanitation; remove and dispose of plant debris. provide good air circulation. Common production problem. See page 112.
Leaves have dark, irregular spots or blotches. Lower leaf surface covered with soft, fluffy fungal growth. Leaves yellow and drop.	**Downy mildew,** *Peronospora viciae*. Spores produced only on living plants. Fungus persists as resistant oospores on dead leaves when conditions are dry. Favored by moist, humid conditions.	Provide good air circulation. Avoid overhead watering. Consider applying fungicide to protect foliage. See page 115.
Leaves or stems have brownish pustules and yellow spots. Foliage may yellow, wither, and drop. Plants may be stunted.	**Rust,** *Uromyces fabae*. Spores spread by wind, splashing water. Fungus survives only on living tissue; must be wet for infection.	Avoid overhead irrigation. Water in morning so foliage dries. Use good sanitation. Provide good air circulation; don't crowd plants. See page 119.
Leaves have large irregular or circular tan spots without definite margins. Lower leaves affected first. Infected leaves often drop.	**Ramularia leaf spot,** *Ramularia deusta*. Affects only sweet pea. Survives in sweet pea refuse. Favored by wet conditions.	Rotate with other crops every other year. Remove or incorporate plant debris. See Leaf Spots, pages 116–118.
Stems or leaves darken, wilt, and die. Leaves often remain attached after dying.	**Anthracnose,** *Glomerella cingulata*. Fungus spread by splashing water. Favored by warm, wet conditions and plant injuries. Many hosts. Not reported on sweet pea in California.	Avoid overwatering or stressing plants. Use good sanitation; rogue infected plants. See pages 116–118.
Leaves or stems have brown or black streaks, spots, or lesions. Tissue may darken, soften, and decay. Plant may grow slowly, wilt, die.	**Bacterial streak,** *Erwinia herbicola*. Occurs in plant debris. Spread by infected equipment, hands, and plants. Favored by high humidity and 80° to 90°F. Not reported on sweet pea in California.	Reduce humidity and improve air circulation; don't crowd plants. Use good sanitation; regularly inspect crop and immediately dispose of any infected plants. See pages 100, 107.
Shoots short, swollen, and flattened or distorted. Secondary rot may infect shoot clumps, killing plant. Plants lack vigor.	**Fasciation,** cause often uncertain. May be viral, bacterial (e.g., *Rhodococcus fascians*), or genetic. Manage as bacterial and take additional measures.	Use pathogen-free stock. Avoid injuring base of plants, especially when wet. Keep base of plants dry. Dispose of infected plants. See page 121.
Reddish brown streaks on stems. Leaves have circular spots, first yellow, then turning brown. Plants may die.	**Tomato spotted wilt virus**. Spread by thrips. Many hosts.	Control nearby weeds. Exclude or control thrips. Rogue infected plants. See page 121.
Leaves and sometimes blossoms have mottled, yellowish, and dark green areas or scattered, translucent, or windowlike areas. Leaves may be stunted, distorted, crumbly.	**Viruses,** including Pea enation mosaic, Pea mosaic, Pea virus 1. Spread by aphids. Hosts include many legumes.	Avoid planting near other legumes. Control nearby weeds, especially legumes. Exclude or control aphids. See page 121.
Plants stunted, grow slowly. Swellings or galls on roots.	**Root knot nematode,** *Meloidogyne* sp. Tiny roundworms feed on roots.	Pasteurize soil before planting. See page 265.
Foliage has sticky honeydew, blackish sooty mold, and whitish cast skins. Foliage may yellow.	**Aphids,** including *Aphis fabae, Aulacorthum solani, Macrosiphum euphorbiae, Myzus persicae*. Small pear-shaped insects, often green, yellowish, or blackish.	See page 179.
Foliage discolored, stippled, bleached, or reddened, and may drop. Plant may have fine webbing.	**Twospotted spider mite,** *Tetranychus urticae*. Tiny greenish or yellowish mites with 2 darker spots.	See page 213.

What the problem looks like	Probable cause	Comments
Irregular blotches or streaks on blossoms. Leaves may turn brown. Blossoms or terminals may be distorted. Growth may be stunted.	**Western flower thrips,** *Frankliniella occidentalis.* Slender, dark brown to yellowish insects, $\frac{1}{16}$ inch long or less.	See page 161.
Foliage, buds, and stems chewed. Young plants clipped at base. Stocky moths present, attracted to lights at night, wings folded at rest.	**Variegated cutworm,** *Peridroma saucia.* Gray or brown larva with dark markings, row of yellow dots on back. Hides in soil during day.	Exclude moths, which fly to lights at night. Apply *Bacillus thuringiensis* to young larvae. Insecticide bait kills caterpillars. See page 203.
Leaves have winding tunnels. Pale leaf spots or punctures from adults. Leaves may drop. Plants stunted. Flower and seed production reduced. Young plants may die. Yellowish to white maggots in mines.	**Serpentine leafminer,** *Liriomyza trifolii.* Adults are tiny, active, black and yellow flies.	See page 167.

SWEET WILLIAM (*Dianthus barbatus*)

What the problem looks like	Probable cause	Comments
New growth yellowish. Plants stunted. Leaves point downward, instead of up as in healthy plants. Leaves gradually yellow and die. Stem and root vascular system brown.	**Fusarium wilt,** *Fusarium oxysporum* f. sp. *barbati* or *dianthi.* Fungal chlamydospores survive in soil for many years. Favored by warm soils and high air temperatures.	Grow seedlings in heat-treated or otherwise pasteurized media. Pasteurize soil before planting. See page 104.
Plants stunted. Foliage may yellow and wilt. Root system reduced, small roots rotted.	**Root rot,** *Pythium ultimum.* Persists in media. Spreads in water. Favored by excess moisture and poor drainage.	Pasteurize media before planting. Provide good drainage. Avoid excess irrigation. See pages 93–96.
Plant is stunted or yellows and wilts. Stem rotted at soil line. Dark fungal strands on plant material may be visible with hand lens.	**Rhizoctonia stem rot,** *Rhizoctonia solani.* Soilborne fungus favored by warm, moist conditions.	Practice good sanitation. Avoid overwatering and deep planting. See pages 93–98.
Foliage yellowing, especially outer leaves. Basal stem or roots have soft rot. White mycelia and small, tan to reddish brown sclerotia may develop on infected tissue around soil.	**Southern wilt,** *Sclerotium rolfsii.* Sclerotia survive in soil. Disease favored by moist, poorly drained, 77° to 95°F media. Not reported on sweet William in California.	Pasteurize media before planting. Provide good drainage. Avoid excess irrigation. See page 101.
Flower heads, petals, leaves, or stems have soft brown decay or spots; may wilt and die. Dead tissue may have woolly gray growth (spores).	**Gray mold,** *Botrytis cinerea.* Fungus develops in crop debris or inactive tissue. Favored by high humidity and 70° to 77°F. Spores airborne.	Use good sanitation. Avoid overhead irrigation. Keep humidity low. Provide good air circulation. Don't crowd plants. See page 108.
Leaves with yellowish brown withered spots surrounded by purplish margin. Entire leaves and stem eventually become necrotic.	**Leaf spot,** *Cladosporium* (=*Heterosporium*) *echinulatum* or *Mycosphaerella dianthi.* Fungus survives in *Dianthus* debris. Spores airborne. Favored by wet weather and overhead irrigation.	Avoid overhead irrigation. Limit cool temperatures. Use good sanitation; rogue infected plants. See pages 116–118.
Leaves, stems, or calyxes have sunken irregular to angular (vein-limited) brown, yellow, or purplish blotches or spots.	**Septoria leaf spot,** *Septoria dianthi.* Fungus prefers wet, humid conditions. Spreads in splashing water. Not reported on sweet William in California.	Avoid overhead irrigation. Use good sanitation; rogue infected plants. See pages 116–118.
Leaves or stems have brownish pustules and possibly yellow spots. Foliage may yellow, wither, drop. Plants may be stunted.	**Rust,** *Uromyces caryophyllinus, U. dianthi, Puccinia arenariae.* Spores spread by wind, splashing water. Fungi survive only on living tissue; must be wet for infection. Not reported on sweet William in California.	Avoid overhead irrigation. Water in morning, so foliage dries. Use good sanitation; rogue infected plants. Provide good air circulation; don't crowd plants. See page 119.
Flowers and possibly leaves may darken, become spotted, dry, and die. Infected tissue has blackish powdery growth (spores).	**Anther smut,** *Ustilago violacea.* Fungus survives on live plants and refuse. Spores are airborne and insect-spread. Favored by wet plants and overhead irrigation. Not reported on sweet William in California.	Use pathogen-free or treated seed. Keep flowers and foliage dry; avoid overhead irrigation and water early in day. Use good sanitation; remove and dispose of plant refuse.
Shorted internodes. Excess, chlorotic secondary shoots. Flowers dwarfed. Petals reduced in number.	**Beet curly top virus.** Leafhopper-vectored. Many hosts.	Rogue infected plants. Exclude or control leafhoppers. See Viruses, page 121.
Foliage chlorotic. Plant stunted. Spindly, upright yellow shoots and few or no flowers.	**Aster yellows phytoplasma.** Spread by leafhoppers. Not spread by seed, handling, aphids, or other insects. Many hosts.	Don't plant downwind from other hosts. Eliminate nearby weeds. Exclude or control leafhoppers. Rogue infected plants. See pages 129–130.
Foliage has sticky honeydew, blackish sooty mold, and whitish cast skins. Foliage may yellow.	**Aphids,** including *Aphis fabae, Aulacorthum solani, Myzus persicae.* Tiny pear-shaped insects, often greenish, yellow, or blackish.	See page 179.
Foliage discolored (stippled, bleached, or reddened) and may drop. Plant may have fine webbing.	**Twospotted spider mite,** *Tetranychus urticae.* Tiny greenish or yellowish mites with 2 darker spots.	See page 213.

What the problem looks like	Probable cause	Comments
SWEET WILLIAM *(Dianthus barbatus)* (continued)		
Winding tunnels in (mostly basal) leaves, may extend into petiole and stem. Leaves may have pale spots, punctures, whiten, wilt, and drop.	**Leafminers,** *Liriomyza huidobrensis, L. trifolii.* Small active flies, dark with yellow. Yellowish or whitish maggot bores in tissue.	See page 167.
Buds, flowers or leaves mined or chewed, may be webbed with silk.	**Omnivorous leaftier,** *Cnephasia longana.* Gray to brownish, ½ inch long larvae and nocturnal moths. Larvae may have grayish stripes. Attacks strawberries and many other hosts. Occurs in central California coast. Has 1 generation per year.	Time any spray for young larvae emerging from mines in spring. See Caterpillars, page 203.
TIGRIDIA *(Tigridia pavonia),* **Tiger flower, Mexican shell flower**		
Leaves yellow progressively, often beginning on one side of plant. Leaves may turn downward and die. Florets distorted. Brownish to black rot of bulbs in ground or storage that begins in core and basal plate, then extends upward through vascular strands into leaf bases.	**Fusarium yellows,** *Fusarium oxysporum* f. sp. *gladioli.* Occurs in diseased bulbs and persists for years in infested soil. Favored by wet soil and temperatures above 70°F. Disease may be less severe if soil pH is 6.6 to 7 and 80 to 90% of nitrogen is in nitrate form.	Pasteurize soil before planting or rotate out of susceptible crops at that site for 4 years after infestation. Rogue infected plants. Dig and handle bulbs carefully to avoid injuring them. Store bulbs under cool, low-humidity conditions. See page 104.
Foliage discolored, stippled, bleached, or reddened. Leaves may bend, distort, or drop. Plant may have fine webbing.	**Spider mites.** Tiny greenish, red, or yellowish mites, often with 2 darker spots. Mites may first be observed around where leaves are bending.	See page 213.
TUBEROSE *(Polianthes tuberosa)*		
Petals or leaves have brown to tan soft decay, spots, or blotches. Stem and roots may rot. Foliage may wither and die. Dead tissue may have woolly gray growth (spores).	**Gray mold,** *Botrytis elliptica, Botrytis* spp. Fungi develop in plant debris. Favored by wet conditions and high humidity.	Use good sanitation. Avoid overhead irrigation. Keep humidity low. Provide good air circulation. Don't crowd plants. See page 108.
Foliage may yellow and wilt. Plants stunted and may die. Roots or stem at soil line rotted.	**Root and crown rot,** *Pythium, Rhizoctonia* spp. Persist in soil. Spread in water. Favored by excess moisture and poor drainage. Not reported on tuberose in California.	Pasteurize media before planting. Provide good drainage. Avoid excess irrigation. Avoid deep planting. See pages 93–98.
Foliage yellows, especially outer leaves. Soft rot of basal stem or roots. White mycelia and small, tan to reddish brown sclerotia may develop on infected tissue around soil.	**Southern wilt,** *Sclerotium rolfsii.* Sclerotia survive in soil. Disease favored by moist, poorly drained, 77° to 95°F media. Not reported on tuberose in California.	Pasteurize media before planting. Provide good drainage. Avoid excess irrigation. See page 101.
Leaves and sometimes stems have brown to yellow spots or blotches. Spots may have dark or yellowish margins. Foliage may shrivel, drop.	**Leaf spots,** including *Cercospora, Curvularia, Helminthosporium* spp. Spread by air or splashing water. Favored by prolonged wet conditions. Persist in plant debris. Not reported on tuberose in California.	Avoid wetting foliage. Use drip irrigation and raised benches. Use good sanitation; promptly remove and dispose of debris and infected leaves. See pages 116–118.
Foliage discolored, stippled, bleached, or reddened. Leaves may bend, distort, or drop. Plant may have fine webbing.	**Spider mites.** Tiny greenish, red, or yellowish mites, often with 2 darker spots. Mites may first be observed around where leaves are bending.	See page 213.
TULIP *(Tulipa* **spp.)**		
Foliage turns red or yellow. Plants wilt and die, often suddenly. Stem and bulbs soft, dark, decayed.	**Bulb, root, and stem rot,** *Fusarium, Pythium, Phytophthora, Rhizoctonia* spp. Fungi persist in soil, favored by wet, poorly drained soil.	Don't overirrigate. Avoid poorly drained soil. Plant in raised beds. See pages 93–98.
Bulbs or stems decay; soft, brown, odorous rot, often at soil line. Leaf edges and stems may be discolored, soft, and rotted.	**Bacterial soft rot,** *Erwinia* sp. Persists in media. Favored when wet. Avoid injuring plant; disease is secondary, infecting wounds.	Provide good drainage. Don't overwater. Use good sanitation; immediately discard infected plants and those nearby. See pages 100, 107.
Foliage yellows, especially outer leaves. Soft rot of basal stem or roots. White mycelia and small, tan to reddish brown sclerotia may develop on infected tissue around soil.	**Southern wilt,** *Sclerotium rolfsii.* Sclerotia survive in soil. Disease favored by moist, poorly drained, 77° to 95°F media.	Pasteurize media before planting. Provide good drainage. Avoid excess irrigation. See page 101.
Petals or leaves have brown to tan soft decay, spots, or blotches. Stem and roots may rot. Foliage may wither and die. Dead tissue may have woolly gray growth (spores).	**Gray mold,** *Botrytis tulipae, B. cinerea.* Fungi develop in plant debris. Favored by high humidity and 70° to 77°F.	Use good sanitation. Avoid overhead irrigation. Keep humidity low. Provide good air circulation. Don't crowd plants. See page 108.
Flower stems very short. Flowers may be small and bloom at soil level. Foliage looks healthy.	**Short stems.** Caused by excess temperature during early growth and/or inadequate bulb chilling.	Plant at appropriate site. Control temperature where feasible. Chill bulbs adequately before planting.

What the problem looks like	Probable cause	Comments
Bulbs produce little or no growth. If foliage develops, it may appear normal, but flower buds fail to develop or don't bloom.	**Bloom or Sprouting failure.** Causes include small or old bulbs, inadequate chilling, too little fertilizer, and removing foliage too soon.	Plant at good site. Use quality bulbs. Provide appropriate cultural care.
Flowers irregularly streaked, spotted, or mottled. Foliage may be streaked. Plants may be stunted.	**Viruses,** including nonpersistent tulip breaking virus. Some tulip viruses are aphid-vectored. Pink and white petal blotching and streaking resulting from infection by tulip breaking virus may be considered aesthetically desirable.	Use virus-free bulbs. Control aphids. See Viruses, page 121.
Foliage has sticky honeydew, blackish sooty mold, and whitish cast skins. Foliage may distort or yellow.	**Aphids,** including *Aphis fabae, A. gossypii, Aulacorthum solani, Myzus persicae.* Tiny pear-shaped insects, often greenish, yellow, or blackish.	See page 179.
May be poor growth from bulbs and stunted plants. Young shoots distorted. Aphids under leaf sheaths, on stems near soil, and under bulb scales and in crevices of bulbs stored or in the field.	**Tulip bulb aphid,** *Dysaphis tulipae.* Small pear-shaped insects, often yellow, pink, gray, or green; waxy covered. Easily overlooked, usually cause direct damage only in storage.	Aphid vectors nonpersistent tulip breaking virus. Has other hosts, especially iris, where it vectors persistent lily symptomless virus. See page 182.
Foliage yellow, stunted, producing no blooms. Bulbs feel soft and spongy, are hollowed and filled with brown excrement from wrinkled, gray, white, or brownish maggots, boring inside.	**Bulb flies,** including Narcissus bulb fly, *Merodon equestris* and *Eumerus* spp. Adult hairy fly (family Syrphidae), black with gray to orange, resembles a bumble bee, hovers around blooming plants, where eggs are laid. Adult and mature larva of *M. equestris* are about ½ inch long; *Eumerus* spp. are smaller.	Inspect and discard spongy bulbs before planting. See page 200.
Bulbs discolored reddish brown, rotted, and infested with tiny, oval, white to brownish mites.	**Bulb mites,** *Rhizoglyphus* spp. Sluggish mites, look like tiny eggs, may also be on stems and leaves. Secondary pests, prefer decayed tissue, but may help fungi to infect plants.	See page 218.
Foliage discolored, stippled, bleached, or reddened, and may drop. Plant may have fine webbing.	**Privet mite,** *Brevipalpus obovatus;* **Twospotted spider mite,** *Tetranychus urticae.* Greenish, yellowish, or red; tiny and may have 2 dark spots.	See page 213.
Buds, flowers, or leaves mined or chewed, may be webbed with silk.	**Omnivorous leaftier,** *Cnephasia longana.* Gray to brownish, ½ inch long larvae and nocturnal moths. Larvae may have grayish stripes. Attacks strawberries and many other hosts. Occurs in central California coast. Has 1 generation per year.	Time any spray for young larvae emerging from mines in spring. See Caterpillars, page 203.

VERBENA (*Verbena* spp.)

What the problem looks like	Probable cause	Comments
Foliage may yellow and wilt. Plants stunted and may die. Roots or stem at soil line rotted.	**Root and crown rot,** *Rhizoctonia solani, Phytophthora* sp. Persist in soil. Spread in water. Favored by excess moisture and poor drainage.	Pasteurize media before planting. Provide good drainage. Avoid excess irrigation. Avoid deep planting. See pages 93–98.
Foliage yellows and wilts. Plants grow slowly and die. Roots dark black and rotted. Stems below ground may develop dark cracks.	**Black root rot,** *Thielaviopsis basicola.* Spreads in water, media, and by infected plants. Fungus persists in infected media. Favored by cool, wet conditions.	Pasteurize media before planting. Avoid overwatering and splashing water. Provide good drainage. Allow soil to dry between watering. Rogue infected plants. Avoid high salts and high pH. See pages 95–99.
Leaves have brown to purple blotches. Stems and leaves have white powdery growth. Severely affected leaves may yellow, wither, and die.	**Powdery mildew,** *Erysiphe cichoracearum.* Occurs as small dark structures on old leaves. Free water not required for infection.	Use good sanitation; remove debris and infected leaves. Provide good air circulation and adequate light. Don't crowd plants. See page 112.
Leaves have sunken, irregular to angular (vein-limited), brown, yellow, or purplish blotches or spots.	**Leaf spot,** *Septoria verbenae.* Fungus prefers wet, humid conditions. Spreads in splashing water.	Avoid overhead irrigation. Use good sanitation; rogue infected plants. See pages 116–118.
Foliage has brown to yellow streaks or spots, sometimes on stems or flowers. Plants may yellow, distort, stunt and die.	**Tomato spotted wilt virus.** Spread by thrips. Many hosts. Not reported on verbena in California.	Eliminate nearby weeds. Exclude or control thrips. Rogue infected plants. See page 121.
Foliage has sticky honeydew, blackish sooty mold, and whitish cast skins. Foliage may distort or yellow.	**Aphids,** including *Aphis gossypii, Myzus persicae.* Tiny pear-shaped insects, often green, yellowish, or blackish.	See page 179.
Foliage has sticky honeydew and blackish sooty mold. Leaves may yellow or wither. Tiny, whitish, mothlike adult insects present.	**Greenhouse whitefly,** *Trialeurodes vaporariorum.* Oval, flattened, yellow to greenish nymphs.	Major pest on this crop. See Whiteflies, page 170.

What the problem looks like	Probable cause	Comments
VERBENA (*Verbena* spp.) (continued)		
Leaves have cottony, mealybuglike egg sacs, ⅓ inch long. Foliage has sticky honeydew and blackish sooty mold. Leaves may yellow.	**Greenhouse orthezia,** *Orthezia insignis*. Pale brown to dark green insect with two white rows on back and white bands along side. Usually not a pest in California.	Controls for mealybugs or scales may be effective.
Plant has sticky honeydew and blackish sooty mold. Elongated, whitish material (egg sacs) present. Insects on twigs or leaves.	**Cottony cushion scale,** *Icerya purchasi*. Females brown, orange, red, or yellow.	Natural enemies can provide good control. Uncommon. See page 186.
Blossoms have irregular white or brown blotches or streaks. Blossoms or terminals may bleach or distort. May be dark, varnishlike excrement on underside of leaves.	**Greenhouse thrips,** *Heliothrips haemorrhoidalis*; **Western flower thrips,** *Frankliniella occidentalis*. Tiny slender black, dark brown, to yellowish insects.	See page 161.
Foliage discolored, stippled, bleached, or reddened, and may drop. Plant may have fine webbing.	**Twospotted spider mite,** *Tetranychus urticae*. Tiny green, yellowish, or red mites; may have 2 dark spots.	See page 213.
Plants severely stunted. Leaf terminals distorted. Buds deform, blacken or discolor, and may drop.	**Cyclamen mite,** *Phytonemus pallidus*. A pinkish orange mite (family Tarsonemidae), ⅟₁₀₀ inch long or smaller.	See page 217.
Shoots or blossoms blackened, dwarfed, discolored, or distorted. Leaf tips may wilt and die.	**Plant bugs,** *Lygus* spp. Brown, green, or yellowish bugs, up to ¼ inch long, that suck plant juices.	Control nearby weeds, from which bugs move. Exclude bugs from growing area. See True Bugs, page 194.
Leaves have winding tunnels and pale spots or punctures. Heavily infested leaves may drop. Yellowish to white maggots in mines.	**Serpentine leafminer,** *Liriomyza trifolii*. Adults are tiny black and yellow flies.	See page 167.
Leaves chewed; may be rolled or tied together with silk. Yellow, green, or pink larvae present with yellow, green, or black lengthwise stripes.	**Omnivorous looper,** *Sabulodes aegrotata* or *S. caberata*. Adult moth (family Geometridae) tan to brownish, with wavy black band across middle of wings. Mature larva and nocturnal adult up to about 1½ inches long. Oval eggs laid in clusters.	See Caterpillars, page 203.
Leaves chewed; edges rolled or tied together with silk by pale green, black-headed larvae.	**Obliquebanded leafroller,** *Archips* or *Choristoneura rosaceana*. Reddish brown moth (family Tortricidae), about 1 inch wide, with wavy dark lines on wings; has snoutlike projection.	See Caterpillars, page 203.
Flower stalks have cylindrical swellings, about ⅓ inch long, each made by a pale larva.	**Verbena stem gall midge,** *Neolasioptera verbenae*. Adult is a slender, delicate fly.	Regularly inspect plants and clip and immediately dispose of galled tissue or entire plants, before pest becomes abundant. Treat media to control pupating larvae. Rotate crop to another site and avoid planting the same untreated soil repeatedly. See page 202.
VINCA (*Vinca* or *Catharanthus roseus*), Myrtle, Periwinkle		
Shoots, leaves, and stems yellow or blacken and wilt. Stems may blacken, have cankers. Plants grow slowly and may die. Roots dark, decayed. Seedlings may damp off.	**Root, stem and crown rot,** *Phytophthora*, *Rhizoctonia* spp., *Thielaviopsis basicola*. Fungal diseases promoted by excess moisture and poor drainage. Common production problem.	Pasteurize media before planting. Avoid overwatering. Provide good drainage. See pages 93–99.
Foliage fades, yellows, browns, and wilts, often on one side of plant. Stem xylem has reddish discoloration. Stems or entire plant may die.	**Verticillium wilt,** *Verticillium dahliae*, *V. albo-atrum*. Persist in soil, infect through roots.	See pages 104–106.
Foliage yellows, especially outer leaves. Soft rot of basal stem or roots. White mycelia and small, tan to reddish brown sclerotia may develop on tissue and in soil.	**Southern wilt,** *Sclerotium rolfsii*. Sclerotia survive in soil. Disease favored by moist, poorly drained, 77° to 95°F soil. Not reported on vinca in California.	Pasteurize media before planting. Avoid excess irrigation. Consider fungicide drench to infected soil. See page 101.
Leaves have brown to yellow spots or blotches. Spots may have dark or yellowish margins. Foliage may shrivel and drop. Stems may have spots or rot.	**Leaf spots,** *Alternaria*, *Phyllosticta*, *Septoria* spp. Spread by air or splashing water. Favored by wet conditions. Persist in plant debris. Uncommon on vinca in western U.S.; not reported on vinca in California.	Avoid wetting foliage. Use drip irrigation and raised benches. Use good sanitation; promptly remove and dispose of debris and infected leaves. See pages 116–118.
Stems yellow, wilt, blacken, and die. Shoots and runners have sunken or decayed lesions that girdle stems or trunks. Stems may enlarge. Leaf spots possible.	**Stem rot,** *Phoma exigua*. Fungus invades through wounds. Spreads in water. Favored by high soil moisture. Prefers stressed plants.	Inspect stock and use only if pathogen-free. Avoid overhead watering or reduce frequency. Provide good drainage. Fungicide can be effective.

What the problem looks like	Probable cause	Comments
Petals or leaves streaked, mottled, blotched, ring-spotted, or distorted. Internodes may be short. Plants may be stunted.	**Viruses,** including Cucumber mosaic (aphid-vectored), Necrotic ringspot (vector unknown), Prune dwarf (carried in infected seed), Tomato spotted wilt (thrips-vectored).	Use virus-free seed. Exclude or control insect vectors; many viruses also spread mechanically or are carried in infected plants. See page 121.
Flowers revert to green leafy tissue. Plants infected the previous year produce spindly, upright yellow shoots and no flowers.	**Aster yellows phytoplasma.** Spread by leafhoppers. Not spread by seed, handling, aphids, or other insects. Many hosts, including delphinium and celery.	Don't plant seed beds downwind from hosts. Eliminate nearby weeds. Control leafhoppers. Rogue infected plants. See pages 129–130.
New growth chlorotic, except for green veins.	**Iron deficiency.** Noninfectious disorder.	See pages 56–59.
Foliage discolored, stippled, bleached, or reddened; may distort or drop. Plant may have fine webbing.	**Spider mites.** Tiny greenish, red, or yellowish mites, often with 2 darker spots.	See page 213.
Foliage yellows. Plant declines or dies back. Stems or leaves have gray, tan, white, or purplish encrustations.	**Greedy scale,** *Hemiberlesia rapax;* **Oleander scale,** *Aspidiotus nerii;* **Oystershell scale,** *Lepidosaphes ulmi.* Circular to elongate, flattened armored scale insects (family Diaspididae), less than 1/16 inch long.	See Scales, page 186.
Foliage or stems have blackish sooty mold. Plant may wilt, decline, or die back.	**Black scale,** *Saissetia oleae.* Orange, black, or brown, flattened to bulbous insects.	See Scales, page 186.
Foliage has sticky honeydew and blackish sooty mold. Leaves yellow and wither. Tiny, whitish, mothlike adult insects present.	**Whiteflies,** including Citrus whitefly, *Dialeurodes citri;* Silverleaf whitefly, *Bemisia argentifolii;* Sweetpotato whitefly, *B. tabaci.* Oval, flattened, yellow to greenish nymphs.	See page 170.
Foliage has sticky honeydew, blackish sooty mold, and whitish cast skins. Foliage may yellow.	**Aphids,** including *Aphis* or *Brachycaudus helichrysi, Aulacorthum circumflexum, Myzus persicae.* Pear-shaped insects, often green, yellowish, or blackish.	See page 179.
Leaves and blossoms chewed (edges notched).	**Fuller rose beetle,** *Asynonychus godmani.* Rarely seen adult pale brown weevil feeds at night. Larvae (whitish maggots) live in soil and eat roots.	See Weevils, page 208.

WATSONIA (*Watsonia* spp.)

Plants stunted, wilted, and collapse. Roots dead. Infected tissue may have white fungal plaques.	**Armillaria root rot,** *Armillaria mellea.* Present in many soils. Persists for years in infected roots.	Remove woody roots 1/2 inch diameter or larger before planting. Pasteurize or air-dry soil well or avoid growing in fields previously planted with oaks or other susceptible woody plants. See page 99.
Irregular light lines or mottling of foliage. Plants may be stunted.	**Watsonia mosaic virus.** Aphid-vectored.	Rogue infected plants. Control aphids. See Viruses, page 121.
Foliage has sticky honeydew, blackish sooty mold, and whitish cast skins. Foliage may distort or yellow.	**Aphids,** including Green peach aphid, *Myzus persicae.* Small pear-shaped insects, often green, yellow, or blackish.	See page 179.
Buds, flowers, or leaves mined or chewed; may be webbed with silk.	**Omnivorous leaftier,** *Cnephasia longana.* Gray to brownish larvae and nocturnal moths, 1/2 inch long. Larvae may have grayish stripes. Attacks strawberries and many other hosts. Occurs in central California coast. Has 1 generation per year.	Time any spray for young larvae emerging from mines in spring. See Caterpillars, page 203.

WAXFLOWER (*Chamaelaucium uncinatum*), Geraldton waxflower, Geraldton wax

Foliage yellows. Plant grows slowly and may suddenly wilt and die. Roots and basal stems dark and decayed.	**Collar and Root rot,** *Phytophthora, Pythium* spp., *Rhizoctonia solani.* Fungi present in most soils. Promoted by moist conditions.	Pasteurize media before planting. Avoid deep planting. Don't overirrigate. Provide good drainage. See pages 93–98.
Flower heads and foliage sticky and covered with nectar or sooty mold. Foliage difficult to harvest and unattractive.	**Excess nectar.** Lack of bees and other pollinators that normally collect nectar; bees may have been killed by residue of persistent insecticides applied to kill gall wasps.	Avoid applying pesticides for gall wasps or other insects. Wash foliage prior to sale.
Leaves and terminals have small green swellings or galls. Foliage distorted.	**Gall wasp,** *Oncastichus goughi.* Tiny, black, delicate wasps (family Eulophidae). Has several generations per year, most abundant in fall. Larvae feed inside galls.	Plant less susceptible 'Lady Stephanie.' Avoid susceptible 'White.' Dispose of galled plant debris. If registered insecticide available, monitor adults with yellow sticky traps to time any applications.

What the problem looks like	Probable cause	Comments
YARROW (*Achillea* spp.)		
Leaves have brown to orangish powdery pustules and yellowish spots. Leaves may yellow and drop.	**Rust,** *Puccinia cnici-oleracei.* Fungus survives on living tissue. Spores are airborne. Favored by high humidity and water.	Avoid overhead irrigation. Water in morning. Provide good air circulation. Don't crowd plants. See page 119.
Foliage has grayish powdery growth. Leaves may yellow and die.	**Powdery mildew,** *Erysiphe, Oidium* spp. Fungi prefer shade, poor air circulation. Not reported on yarrow in California.	Avoid overcrowding plants. Provide good air circulation and adequate sun. See page 112.
Leaves have circular to irregular yellow to brown spots or blotches. Foliage may yellow and die.	**Leaf spots,** including *Alternaria, Cercospora, Septoria* spp. Spread by splashing water or contaminated tools or stock. Persist in plant debris. Not reported on yarrow in California.	Avoid overhead watering. Use good sanitation, promptly remove and dispose of debris and infected leaves. See pages 116–118.
Leaves have white powdery spots or blotches. Infected tissue may turn greenish, yellow, or brownish or become dry and die.	**Leaf smut,** *Entyloma compositarum.* Fungus survives on live plants and refuse. Spores borne on wind and rain. Favored by wet foliage and overhead irrigation.	Avoid overhead irrigation. Use good sanitation; remove and dispose of plant refuse. Avoid repeatedly replanting the same soil with susceptible crops.
Lower stem or roots have distorted callus growth or galls. Plant stunted. Roots may be gnarled, stunted, or hairy with mostly small rootlets.	**Crown gall,** *Agrobacterium tumefaciens.* Bacteria persist in soil, enter plant through wounds. Favored by rapid plant growth.	Pasteurize media before planting. Inspect stock and use only if pathogen-free. Avoid wounding plants. See page 102.
Flower stems or leaves have sticky honeydew, blackish sooty mold, and white cast skins. Foliage may yellow or distort.	**Aphids,** including Brown ambrosia aphid, *Uroleucon ambrosiae.* Large brown to red aphids; others species often green, yellow, or blackish.	See page 179.
Leaves or stem discolored or distorted.	**Thrips.** Tiny slender blackish or orangish insects.	See page 161.
Leaves have cottony, mealybuglike egg sacs, ⅓ inch long. Foliage has sticky honeydew and blackish sooty mold. Foliage may yellow.	**Greenhouse orthezia,** *Orthezia insignis.* Pale brown to dark green insect with two white rows on back and white bands along side.	Usually not a pest in California. Controls for mealybugs or scales may be effective.
Plant has sticky honeydew and blackish sooty mold. Elongated, whitish material (egg sacs) present. Insects on twigs or leaves.	**Cottony cushion scale,** *Icerya purchasi.* Females brown, orange, red, or yellow.	Natural enemies can provide good control. Uncommon. See page 186.
Leaves have dead patches. Leaf tips may wilt. Unusual branching. Premature flower bud formation. Distorted flowers. Delayed or no flowers.	**Plant bugs,** *Lygus* spp. Brown, green, or yellowish bugs, up to ¼ inch long, that suck plant juices.	Control nearby weeds, from which bugs move. Exclude bugs from growing area. See page 194.
ZINNIA (*Zinnia* spp.)		
Girdling stem infection. Stems turn chalky white. Cottony masses or large, black fungal sclerotia inside stems.	**Cottony rot,** *Sclerotinia sclerotiorum.* Survives as fungal sclerotia in soil. Infects plants on contact. Favored by cool, moist conditions. Many hosts, including vegetable crops.	Pasteurize soil before planting or avoid planting where disease has occurred. Avoid overhead irrigation. Irrigate early in day so plants dry quickly. Consider fungicide application to foliage. See page 101.
Leaves or blossoms have soft brown decay, spots, or blotches. Stems may have cankers. Plants may wilt. Dead tissue may be covered with woolly gray spores.	**Gray mold,** *Botrytis cinerea.* Fungus develops in crop debris or inactive tissue. Favored by high humidity and 70° to 77°F. Spores airborne.	Use good sanitation. Avoid overhead irrigation. Keep humidity low. Provide good air circulation. Don't crowd plants. See page 108.
White, powdery growth, primarily on older leaves and stem. Severely affected leaves dry and die.	**Powdery mildew,** *Erysiphe cichoracearum.* Occurs as small dark structures on old leaves. Free water not required for infection. Not common in western U.S.	Provide good air circulation and adequate light. Consider applying sulfur or other fungicide to prevent. See page 112.
Leaves or blossoms have tan to dark spots or blotches that may have yellow or dark margins. Leaves or blossoms may wilt and die. Stems may have cankers.	**Leaf spot and blight,** *Alternaria* spp. Promoted by wet conditions, high humidity. Spread by wind and splashing water.	Avoid overhead irrigation. Provide good air circulation; don't crowd plants. Dispose of debris and infected plants. See pages 116–118.
Brown to yellow spots or blotches, mostly on older leaves. Spots may have dark or yellowish margins. Foliage may shrivel and drop.	**Leaf spot,** *Phyllosticta zinniae.* Spreads by splashing water. Favored by prolonged, cool, wet, conditions. Persists in plant debris.	Avoid wetting foliage. Use drip irrigation. Use good sanitation; promptly remove and dispose of debris and infected leaves. See pages 116–118.

What the problem looks like	Probable cause	Comments
Basal leaves yellow and drop. Leaf scars blackened. Stems yellow. Stem cankers, first soft and water-soaked, become dark and sunken. Vascular system blackish. Young plants wilt and collapse.	**Bacterial blight**, *Xanthomonas campestris* pv. *zinniae*. Bacteria spread in seed and plant debris; persist in soil for 2 years. Spread by water. Favored by cool, wet weather.	Pasteurize media before planting. Use bacteria-free seed or surface disinfect seed before planting. Avoid wetting foliage; use drip irrigation. Use good sanitation. See pages 107, 118.
Short internodes. Excess, chlorotic secondary shoots. Flowers dwarfed. Petals reduced in number.	**Beet curly top virus**. Leafhopper-vectored. Many hosts.	Rogue infected plants. Exclude or control leafhoppers. See Viruses, page 121.
Foliage has fine mottling. Chlorotic areas near base of leaves. Veins may turn pale.	**Nasturtium mosaic virus**. Aphid-vectored.	Rogue infected plants. Exclude or control aphids. See Viruses, page 121.
Flowers deformed. Petals spotted or streaked. Plants may be stunted.	**Tomato spotted wilt virus**. Thrips-vectored. Many hosts.	Rogue infected plants. Exclude or control thrips. See page 121.
Flower seed coats injured, discolored, scabby. Thin-coated seed die. Flowers may be distorted from feeding by tiny, slender insects.	**Composite thrips**, *Microcephalothrips abdominalis*. Tiny, dark brown adults, wings light brown. Entire life cycle spent in flowers, including debris.	Don't grow seed plants near other Asteraceae crops or weeds. Use good sanitation; remove debris from seedbeds before planting. See Thrips, page 161.
Foliage discolored (bleached or reddened). Foliage may be distorted and may drop. Plant may have fine webbing.	**Spider mites**. Tiny greenish, yellowish, or reddish pests, may have 2 dark spots on back.	See page 213.
Foliage bleached, brittle; edges may be curled or ragged. Blossoms distort or discolor.	**Broad mite**, *Polyphagotarsonemus latus*. Translucent to dark green, $\frac{1}{100}$ inch long or smaller.	See page 217.
Shoots or blossoms blackened, dwarfed, discolored, or distorted. Leaf tips may wilt and die.	**Plant bugs**, *Lygus* spp. Brown, green, or yellowish bugs, up to $\frac{1}{4}$ inch long, that suck plant juices.	Control nearby weeds, from which bugs move. Exclude bugs from growing area. See True Bugs, page 194.
Plant has sticky honeydew and blackish sooty mold. Foliage may yellow. Tiny, white, mothlike adults present.	**Greenhouse whitefly**, *Trialeurodes vaporariorum*; **Silverleaf whitefly**, *Bemisia argentifolii*; **Sweetpotato whitefly**, *Bemisia tabaci*. Nymphs and pupae flattened, oval, translucent, and greenish or yellow.	See page 170.
Foliage has sticky honeydew, black sooty mold, and white cast skins; may yellow.	**Aphids**, including *Aphis fabae*. Small pear-shaped insects, often green, yellowish, or blackish.	See page 179.
Leaves have winding tunnels and pale spots or punctures. Heavily infested leaves may drop. Yellowish to white maggots in mines.	**Leafminers**, *Liriomyza* spp. Adults are tiny black and yellow flies.	See page 167.

Resources

Organizations

Many private organizations, government agencies, trade associations, and universities can assist flower and nursery crop managers.

American Floral Endowment
11 Glen-Ed Professional Park
Glen Carbon, IL 62034
(618) 692-0045
http://www.endowment.org

Association of Natural Bio-Control Producers
10202 Cowan Heights Dr.
Santa Ana, CA 92705
(714) 544-8295
www.anbp.org

Association of Specialty Cut Flower Growers
P.O. Box 268
Oberlin, OH 44074
(440) 774-2887

Bedding Plants Foundation, Inc.
P.O. Box 27241
Lansing, MI 48909
(517) 333-4617
www.bpfi.org

Bedding Plants International
525 S.W. 5th St., Suite A
Des Moines, IA 50309-4501
www.itag.org/bpi/welcome.html

California Association of Nurserymen (CAN)
3947 Lennane Drive, Suite 150
Sacramento, CA 95834-1957
(916) 928-3900
www.can-online.org

California Cut Flower Commission
73 Hangar Way
Watsonville, CA 95076
(831) 728-7333
www.ccfc.org

California Ornamental Research Federation (CORF)
710 West Clay Street
Ukiah, CA 95482
(707) 462-2425
http://envhort.ucdavis.edu/CE/CORF

Department of Pesticide Regulation
State of California
830 K Street
Sacramento, CA 95814-3510
(916) 445-4300
www.cdpr.ca.gov

Ohio Florists' Association
2130 Stella Court, Suite 200
Columbus, OH 43215-1033
(614) 487-1117
www.ofa.org

Oregon Association of Nurserymen
2780 S.E. Harrison, Suite 102
Milwaukie, OR 97222
(800) 342-6401

Professional Plant Growers Association (PPGA)
P.O. Box 27517
Lansing, MI 48909-0517
(800) 647-7742

Roses, Inc.
P.O. Box 99
1152 Haslett Rd.
Haslett, MI 48840
(800) 968-ROSE
www.rosesinc.org

Society of American Florists (SAF)
1601 Duke St.
Alexandria, VA 22314
(800) 336-4743
www.safnow.org

Publications

Many scientific journals, private organizations, government agencies, and universities regularly publish current information on flower and nursery crop production and pest management.

American Nurseryman
American Nurseryman Publishing Company
77 W. Washington St.
Suite 2100
Chicago, IL 60602
(312) 782-5505

CORF News
California Ornamental Research Foundation
(See Organizations, above)

Digger Magazine
Oregon Association of Nurserymen
(See Organizations, above)

Greenhouse Grower Magazine
Meister Publishing Company
37733 Euclid Ave.
Willoughby, OH 44094-5992
(440) 942-2000

Greenhouse Management and Production
Branch-Smith Publishing
P.O. Box 1868
Fort Worth, TX 76101
(817) 882-4120

Grower Talks
Ball Publishing
335 North River Street
Batavia, IL 60510
(630) 208-9080
www.growertalks.com

Growing Points
Department of Environmental Horticulture
University of California
One Shields Ave.
Davis, CA 95616-3560
http://envhort.ucdavis.edu

Nursery Management and Production
Branch-Smith Publishing
P.O. Box 1868
Fort Worth, TX 76101
(817) 882-4120

Plant Notes
UC Cooperative Extension
625 Miramontes, Suite 200
Half Moon Bay, CA 94019

World Wide Web Sites

The World Wide Web portion of the Internet is a vast source of information on crop production and pest management. Among the many resources available online through the Web are color photographs of crop damage, pests, and natural enemies; information on biology; management recommendations; decision-making models; and communication with pest control experts and practitioners. Although any printed list of online sites is immediately out of date, some relevant sites and their online address or (URL) at the time of this printing include:

Agdia plant pathogen diagnostic testing
www.agdia.com

California Department of Pesticide Regulation
www.cdpr.ca.gov

California Department of Water Resources
wwwdpla.water.ca.gov/cgi-bin/index or

California Integrated Waste Management Board
composting information
www.ciwmb.ca.gov/organics

Colorado State Cooperative Extension
www.colostate.edu

Commercial Biological-based Producers
www.nal.usda.gov/bic/Misc_pubs/bioprod.html

Cornell University Floriculture & Ornamental Horticulture
www.cals.cornell.edu/dept/flori

Database of IPM Resources
www.ippc.orst.edu

Extension Toxicology Network
http://ace.orst.edu/info/extoxnet

HortFYI horticulture and greenhouse website links
www.hortfyi.com

HortWorld—Horticulture, Pests and Diseases
www.hortworld.com

Insect Parasitic Nematodes
http://www2.oardc.ohio-state.edu/nematodes

Insecticide Resistance Action Committee
http://ipmwww.ncsu.edu/orgs/IRAC

Integrated Pest Management, New Zealand
www.crop.cri.nz

Internet IPM Resources on Ornamentals (Consortium for
International Crop Protection)
www.ippc.orst.edu

Iowa State Entomology Index of Internet Resources
www.ent.iastate.edu

IPM Information System, Canada
http://pupux1.env.gov.bc.ca

Michigan State University Entomology IPM Information
www.ent.msu.edu

Midwest Biological Control News
www.entomology.wisc.edu/mbcn/mbcn.html

National IPM Network—Western Region
www.colostate.edu

Nurserymen News
www.agnr.umd.edu/users/ipmnet/nmnwpage.htm

Ohio State Factsheet (database for all university sites)
www.hcs.ohio-state.edu

Pennsylvania State University Cooperative Extension
Plant Disease Facts
www.cas.psu.edu/docs/CASDEPT/PLANT/ext/fact.html

PestWeb (pest control industry website)
www.pestweb.com

Plant Pathology Internet Guide Book
www.scisoc.org/ppigb

Radcliffe's IPM World Textbook
http://ipmworld.umn.edu

Suppliers of Beneficial Organisms in North America
www.cdpr.ca.gov/docs/ipminov/bensuppl.htm

Texas A&M Horticulture Program
http://aggie-horticulture.tamu.edu

University of California Ornamental Horticulture
Research & Information Center
http://ohric.ucdavis.edu

University of California Statewide Integrated
Pest Management Project
www.ipm.ucdavis.edu

University of Florida
http://edis.ifas.ufl.edu

University of Missouri XPLOR—Extension Publications
Library on Request
http://muextension.missouri.edu

Suppliers

Certain industry publications, industry- and university-sponsored World Wide Web sites, and sponsors of trade fairs provide regularly updated buyers' guides or lists of manufacturers and suppliers. Also consult the organizations, publications, and World Wide Web sites listed in the resources for more current information on IPM product suppliers.

Environmental Monitoring and Control

Argus Control Systems
1281 Johnston Road
Rock, BC
Canada V4B 3Y9
(604) 538-3531
www.argus-controls.com

Micro Grow Greenhouse Systems
26111 Ynez Road, Suite C-4
Temecula, CA 92591
(909) 695-7280
www.microgrow.com

Onset Computer Corporation
P.O. Box 3450
Pocasset, MA 02559-3450
(800) 564-4377
www.onsetcomp.com

Priva Computers
3468 South Service Road
Vineland Station, Ontario L0R 2E0
Canada
(905) 562-7351
www.priva.ca

Q-COM Corporation
17782 Cowan Ave.
Irvine, CA 92614
(800) 833-9123
www.qcom-controls.com

ROTEM Computerized Controllers
23 Efal St.
P.O.B. 3392
Kiriat Arie Petach-Tikva 49511
Israel
www.rotem.com/rotem.htm

Starcom Computer Corp.
19515 Northcreek Parkway, Suite 220
Bothell, WA 98011
(425) 486-6464
www.starcomsoft.com

Stuppy Greenhouse Manufacturing
P.O. Box 12456
Kansas City, MO 64116
(800) 733-5025
www.stuppy.com

System USA, Inc.
P.O. Box 777, 512 Casserly Road
Watsonville, CA 95077
(831) 722-1188
www.systemusa.com

Wadsworth Control Systems
5541 Marshall Street
Arvada, CO 80005
(800) 821-5829

Insect Exclusion Screens

Baycor Products Group (Kontrol)
2170 Satellite Boulevard, Suite 350
Duluth, GA 30097-4074
(770) 689-2623
www.baycor.com

DuraGreen Marketing (Durascreen)
(See Ultraviolet Films, below)

Green-Tek (NoThrips, AntiVirus, Insecta)
407 North Main Street
Edgerton, WI 53534
(608) 884-9454
(800) 747-6440
www.green-tek.com/grnhouse.html

Green Thumb Group (BugBed, Bug Shield)
3380 Venard Rd.
Downers Grove, IL 60515
(800) 240-3371

L. S. Americas (Econet)
1813 Associates Ln.
Charlotte, NC 28217
(800) 742-3391
www.lsamericas.com

PAK Unlimited, Inc.
1 Suncrest Ave.
Collinsville, IL 62234
(770) 448-1917

Reemay, Inc.
70 Old Hickory Blvd.
Old Hickory, TN 37138
(800) 284-2780
www.reemay.com

Synthetic Industries (Lumite)
309 LaFayette Road
Chickamauga, GA 30707
(706) 375-3121
www.sind.com

Monitoring Equipment

BioQuip Products
17803 LaSalle Ave.
Gardena, CA 90248-3602
(310) 324-0620

Donegan Optical Company (Optivisor)
16549 West 108th St.
Lenexa, KS 86286
(913) 492-2500

Forestry Suppliers, Inc.
P. O. Box 8397
Jackson, MS 39284-8397
(601) 354-3565
www.forestry-suppliers.com

Gempler's
P.O. Box 270
Mt. Horeb, WI 53527
(800) 382-8473

Great Lakes IPM
10220 Church Road, NE
Vestaburg, MI 48891
(517) 268-5693

IPM Laboratories, Inc.
Main Street
Locke, NY 13092-0300
(315) 497-2063
www.ipmlabs.com

Phero Tech, Inc.
7572 Progress Way
Delta, British Columbia V4G 1E9
Canada
(800) 665-0076
www.pherotech.com

Praxis
P.O. Box 360
Allegan, MI 49010
(616) 673-2793

Seabright Laboratories
4067 Watts Street
Emeryville, CA 94608-3604
(800) 284-7363
www.seabrightlabs.com

The Tanglefoot Co.
314 Straight Ave., SW
Grand Rapids, MI 49504
(616) 459-4139

Trece, Inc.
1143 Madison Avenue
Salinas, CA 93907
(831) 758-0204
www.trece.com

Whitmire Micro-Gen
3568 Tree Court Ind. Blvd.
St. Louis, MO 63122
(800) 777-8570
www.wmmg.com

Reflective Mulch and Ultraviolet (UV) Absorbing Films

Adcock Manufacturing Corp.
1550 W. 132nd Street
Gardena, CA 90249
(310) 532-4350
(800) 523-2625
www.adcockmfg.com

AEP Industries
125 Phillips Avenue
South Hackensack, NJ 07606
(800) 999-2374
www.aepinc.com
info@aepinc.com

Blake Enterprises
344 E. Dinuba Avenue
Reedley, CA 93654
(559) 638-3631
www.bcag.net

Klerk's Plastic Products Manufacturing Inc.
Highway 9 S.
P.O. Box 368
Richburg, SC 29729
(803) 789-4000
sales@klerks.com

Polyon Barkai
972-6-387387
Israel
polyon@inter.net.il

Sonoco
North Second Street
Hartsville, SC 29550
(843) 383-3203
www.sonoco.com

Suggested Reading

This suggested reading list is organized by topic and includes publications useful for flower and nursery crop production and pest management.

Biological Control

Ball Identification Guide to Greenhouse Pests and Beneficials. 1998. S. Gill and J. Sanderson. Ball, Batavia, IL.

Biological Control of Plant Diseases, Progress and Challenges for the Future. 1992. E. C. Tjamos, G. C. Papavizas, and R. J. Cook, eds. Plenum Press, New York.

Biological Pest Control: The Glasshouse Experience. 1985. N. W. Hussey and N. Scopes, eds. Cornell University Press, Ithaca, NY.

A Grower's Guide to Using Biological Control for Silverleaf Whitefly on Poinsettia in the Northeastern United States. n. d. M. S. Hoddle, R. Van Driesche, S. Roy, T. Smith, M. Mazzola, P. Lopes, and J. Sanderson. University of Massachusetts, Amherst.

Knowing and Recognizing the Biology of Glasshouse Pests and Their Natural Enemies. 1992. M. Malais and W. J. Ravensberg. Koppert Biological Systems, Berkel en Rodenrijs, Netherlands.

Life Stages of California Red Scale and Its Parasitoids. 1995. L. D. Forster, R. F. Luck, and E. E. Grafton-Cardwell. Univ. Calif. Div. Agric. Nat. Res. Publ. 21529. Oakland.

Natural Enemies Are Your Allies. 1990. M. L. Flint and J. C. Clark. Poster. Univ. Calif. Div. Agric. Nat. Res. Publ. 21497. Oakland.

Natural Enemies Handbook: The Illustrated Guide To Biological Pest Control. 1998. M. L. Flint and S. H. Dreistadt. Univ. Calif. Div. Agric. Nat. Res. Publ. 3386. Oakland.

The Trichogramma Manual: A Guide to the Use of Trichogramma for Biological Control with Special Reference to Augmentative Releases of Control of Bollworm and Budworm in Cotton. 1998. A. Knutson. Texas Agricultural Extension Service B-6071. Dallas.

Toward predictable biological control of Liriomyza trifolii (Diptera: Agromyzidae) infesting greenhouse cut chrysanthemum. 1993. K. M. Heinz, L. Nunney, and M. P. Parrella. *Environ. Entomol.* 22: 1217–1233.

Composting

Compost Production and Utilization: A Growers' Guide. 1995. M. Van Horn. Univ. Calif. Div. Agric. Nat. Res. Publ. 21514. Oakland.

On-farm Composting Handbook. 1992. R. Rynk, ed. North Regional Agric. Engineering Ser. Coop. Exten. NRAES-54. Ithaca, NY.

Cover Crops

Cover Cropping in Vineyards. 1998. C. A. Ingels, R. L. Bugg, G. T. McGourty, and L. P. Christensen, eds. Univ. Calif. Div. Agric. Nat. Res. Publ. 3338. Oakland.

Covercrops for California Agriculture. 1989. P. R. Miller, W. L. Graves, W. A. Williams, and B. A. Madison. Univ. Calif. Div. Agric. Nat. Res. Publ. 21471. Oakland.

Diseases of Forage Legumes in Alabama. 1993. D. J. Collins. Auburn University, AL. www.acesag.auburn.edu

Integrated Pest Management for Small Grains. 1990. University of California Statewide Integrated Pest Management Project. Univ. Calif. Div. Agric. Nat. Res. Publ. 3340. Oakland.

Managing Cover Crops Profitably. 1998. G. Bowman, C. Shirley, and C. Cramer. U. S. Dept. Agric. Sustainable Agriculture Research and Education Program. Beltsville, MD.

Ohio Agronomy Guide: 13th ed. 1996. J. Beuerlein, D. Eckert, D. Jeffers, J. Johnson, P. Lipps, M. Loux, E. McCoy, W. Schmidt, M. Sulc, P. Sutton, P. Thomison, J. Undersood, M. Watson, and H. Willson. Ohio State Univ. Bull. 472. www.ag.ohio-state.edu/~ohioline

Red Clover. 1993. H. N. Wheaton. University of Missouri. Agric. Publ. G04638. http://muextension.missouri.edu

UC IPM Pest Management Guidelines: Turfgrass. 2000. Univ. Calif. Div. Agric. Nat. Res. Publ. 3365-T. Oakland.

Cultural Practices

A Grower's Guide to Water, Media, and Nutrition for Greenhouse Crops. 1996. D. W. Reed, ed. Ball, Batavia, IL.

Ball Redbook. 1991. V. Ball, ed. Ball, West Chicago, IL.

The Container Tree Nursery Manual, Volumes 1 to 7. 1989. T. D. Landis et al., eds. U. S. Department of Agriculture Forest Service. Agriculture Handbook 674. Washington, D.C.

Determining Daily Reference Evapotranspiration (Eto). 1987. R. L. Snyder, W. O. Pruitt, and D. A. Shaw. Univ. Calif. Div. Agric. Nat. Res. Leaflet 21426. Oakland.

Evapotranspiration and Irrigation Water Requirements. 1990. M. E. Jensen, R. D. Burman, and R. G. Allen, eds. American Society of Civil Engineers. New York.

Fertigation. 1995. C. Burt, K. O'Connor, and T. Ruehr. California Polytechnic State University Irrigation and Research Center. San Luis Obispo.

Florist Crop Production and Marketing. 1949. K. Post. Cornell University. Orange Judd, New York, NY.

Herbaceous Ornamental Plants. 1980. S. M. Still. Stipes Publishing, Champaign, IL.

The U.C. System For Producing Healthy Container-grown Plants Through The Use Of Clean Soil, Clean Stock, And Sanitation. 1957. K. F. Baker, ed. Univ. Calif. Div. Agric. Sci. Agric. Exp. Sta. Manual 23. Oakland. Reprinted 1985 by the Australian Nurserymen's Association.

Tropical Foliage Plants: A Grower's Guide. 1998. L. P. Griffith. Ball, Batavia, IL.

Water Quality: Its Effects on Ornamental Plants. 1985. D. S. Farnham, R. F. Hasek, and J. L. Paul. Univ. Calif. Div. Agric. Nat. Res. Leaflet 2995. Oakland.

Western Fertilizer Handbook Horticulture Edition. 1990. A. E. Ludwick, K. B. Campbell, R. D. Johnson, L. J. McClain, R. M. Milaway, S. L. Purcell, I. L. Phillips, D. W. Rush, and J. A. Waters, eds. Interstate, Danville, IL.

Diseases

Ball Field Guide to Diseases of Greenhouse Ornamentals. 1992. M. Daughtrey and A. R. Chase. Ball, West Chicago, IL.

Ball Pest and Disease Manual: Disease, Insect, and Mite Control on Flower and Foliage Crops. 2d ed. 1997. C. C. Powell and R. K. Lindquist. Ball, Batavia, IL.

Compendium of Chrysanthemum Diseases. 1997. R. K. Horst and P. E. Nelson, eds. APS Press, St. Paul, MN.

Compendium of Flowering Potted Plant Diseases. 1995. M. L. Daughtrey, R. L. Wick, and J. L. Peterson. APS Press, St. Paul, MN.

Compendium of Ornamental Foliage Plant Diseases. 1987. A. R. Chase. APS Press. St. Paul, MN.

Compendium of Rhododendron and Azalea Diseases. 1986. D. L. Coyier and M. K. Roane, eds. APS Press, St. Paul, MN.

Compendium of Rose Diseases. 1983. R. K. Horst. APS Press, St. Paul, MN.

Diseases and Disorders of Plants in Florida. 1994. S. A. Alfieri, K. R. Langdon, J. W. Kimbrough, N. E. El-Gholl, and C. Wehlburg. Florida Department of Agricultural and Consumer Services Bulletin 14. Gainesville.

Diseases of Annuals and Perennials: A Ball Guide. 1995. A. R. Chase, M. L. Daughtrey, and G. W. Stone. Ball, Batavia, IL.

Diseases of Safflower. 1964. Q. L. Holdeman and W. O. McCartney. California Department of Agriculture, Sacramento.

Diseases of Trees and Shrubs. 1987. W. A. Sinclair, H. H. Lyon, and W. T. Johnson. Cornell University Press, Ithaca, NY.

Foliage Plant Diseases Diagnosis and Control. 1997. A. R. Chase. APS Press, St. Paul, MN.

Easy On-Site Tests for Fungi and Viruses in Nurseries and Greenhouses. 1997. J. N. Kabashima, J. D. MacDonald, S. H. Dreistadt, and D. E. Ullman. University of California DANR Publication 8002. Available only online at: http://danrcs.ucdavis.edu

Managing Disease in Greenhouse Crops. 1992. W. R. Jarvis. APS Press, St. Paul, MN.

Plant Pathology. 4th ed. 1997. G. N. Agrios. Academic Press, San Diego, CA.

Plants Resistant or Susceptible to Verticillium Wilt. 1981. A. H. McCain, R. D. Raabe, and S. Wilhelm. Univ. Calif. Div. Agric. Nat. Res. Leaflet 2703. Oakland.

Resistance or Susceptibility of Certain Plants to Armillaria Root Rot. 1979. R. D. Raabe. Univ. Calif. Div. Agric. Nat. Res. Publ. Leaflet 2591. Oakland.

UC IPM Pest Management Guidelines: Floriculture and Ornamental Nurseries: Diseases. 1998. M. Grebus, R. Raabe, C. Wilen, and A. McCain. Univ. Calif. Div. Agric. Nat. Res. Publ. 3392. Oakland.

Vegetable Crop Diseases. 1981. G. R. Dixon. AVI Publishing Co., Westport, CT.

Insects, Mites, and Other Invertebrates

Ants of California with Color Pictures, A Key to the Most Common and/or Economically Important. 1987. P. Haney, P. A. Phillips, and R. Wagner. Univ. Calif. Div. Agric. Nat. Res. Leaflet 21433. Oakland.

Controlling Insects on Flowers. 1962. F. F. Smith. U. S. Department of Agriculture Bulletin 237. Washington, D.C.

The development of sampling strategies for larvae of *Liriomyza trifolii* in chrysanthemum. 1986. V. P. Jones and M. P. Parrella. *Environ. Entomol.* 15: 268–273.

Farmfacts: Organic Crop Management: Insect Management. K. Foster. 1996. Government of Saskatchewan. http://www.agr.gov.sk.ca/saf

Identification of Insects and Related Pests of Horticultural Plants. 1991. R. K. Lindquist. Ohio Florists' Association, Columbus, OH.

Insect Screening for Greenhouses. 1994. D. S. Ross and S. A. Gill. Dept. Agric. Engineering Facts 186. University of Maryland, College Park, MD.

Insects that Feed on Trees and Shrubs. 1988. W. T. Johnson and H. H. Lyon. Cornell University Press. Ithaca, NY.

The Scale Insects of California Part 1: The Soft Scales. R. J. Gill. 1988. California Department of Food and Agriculture, Sacramento.

Scale Insects of California Part 2: The Minor Families. R. J. Gill. 1993. California Department of Food and Agriculture, Sacramento.

Scale Insects of California Part 3: The Armored Scales. R. J. Gill. 1997. California Department of Food and Agriculture, Sacramento.

Screens deny specific pests entry to greenhouses. 1994. J. A. Bethke, R. A. Redak, and T. D. Paine. *Calif. Agric.* 48(3): 37–40.

Sticky trap monitoring of insect pests. 1998. S. H. Dreistadt, J. P. Newman, and K. L. Robb. Univ. Calif. Div. Agric. Nat. Res. Publ 21572. Oakland.

UC IPM Pest Management Guidelines: Floriculture and Ornamental Nurseries: Insects and Mites. 2000. K. L. Robb, H. Costa, J. Bethke, R. Cowles, and M. P. Parrella. Univ. Calif. Div. Agric. Nat. Res. Publ. 3392. Oakland.

Integrated Pest Management

Ball Pest and Disease Manual. 1992. C. C. Powell and R. K. Lindquist. Ball, West Chicago, IL.

Biological and integrated pest control in greenhouses. 1988. C. van Lenteren and J. Woets. *Ann. Rev. Entomol.* 33: 239–269.

Insect and Disease Management on Ornamentals, Proceedings for the 11th Conference. 1995. A. Bishop, M. Hausbeck, and R. Lindquist, eds. Society of American Florists, Alexandria, Va.

Insect and Disease Management on Ornamentals, Proceedings for the 12th Conference. 1996. M. Daughtrey and J. Hall, eds. Society of American Florists, Alexandria, VA.

Insect and Disease Management on Ornamentals, Proceedings for the 14th Conference. 1998. J. Hall and K. Robb, eds. Society of American Florists, Alexandria, VA.

Insect and Disease Management on Ornamentals, Proceedings for the 15th Conference. 1999. K. M. Heinz, ed. Society of American Florists, Alexandria, VA.

Integrated Pest Management for Almonds. 1985. University of California Statewide Integrated Pest Management Project. Univ. Calif. Div. Agric. Nat. Res. Publ. 3308. Oakland.

Integrated Pest Management for Bedding Plants: A Scouting and Pest Management Guide. 2000. C. Casey, ed. Cornell Univ. Coop. Ext. IPM No. 407. Ithaca, NY.

Integrated Pest Management for Citrus. 2d ed. 1991. University of California Statewide Integrated Pest Management Project. Univ. Calif. Div. Agric. Nat. Res. Publ. 3303. Oakland.

Pests of Landscape Trees and Shrubs. 1994. S. H. Dreistadt. Univ. Calif. Div. Agric. Nat. Res. Publ. 3359. Oakland.

Pests of the Garden and Small Farm. 2d ed. 1998. M. L. Flint. Univ. Calif. Div. Agric. Nat. Res. Publ. 3332. Oakland.

Recommendations for the Integrated Management of Greenhouse Florist Crops. Revised annually. Cornell University Cooperative Extension, Ithaca, NY.

Scouting Programs for Ornamental Crops. 1997. J. Newman and A. Mayers. Univ. Calif. Coop. Ext. Ornamentals & Row Crop Pest Management Project. IPM Information Series 8. Santa Maria, CA.

Nematodes

Phytonematology Study Guide. 1985. M. V. McKenry and P. A. Phillips. Univ. Calif. Div. Agric. Nat. Res. Publ. 4059. Oakland.

Pesticides

Managing Insects and Mites with Spray Oils. 1991. N. A. Davidson, J. E. Dibble, M. L. Flint, P. J. Marer, and A. Guye. Univ. Calif. Div. Agric. Nat. Res. Publ. 3347. Oakland.

Pesticide Safety: A Reference Manual For Growers. 1997. P. J. O'Connor-Marer. Univ. Calif. Div. Agric. Nat. Res. Publ. 3383. Oakland.

Pesticides: Theory and Application. 1983. G. W. Ware. Freeman, San Francisco.

The Safe and Effective Use of Pesticides. 2d ed. 1999. P. J. O'Connor-Marer. Univ. Calif. Div. Agric. Nat. Res. Publ. 3324. Oakland.

UC IPM Pest Management Guidelines: Floriculture and Ornamental Nurseries: 2000. Univ. Calif. Div. Agric. Nat. Res. Publ. 3392. Oakland.

Solarization

Soil solarization: a natural mechanism of integrated pest management. 1995. J. J. Stapleton and J. E. DeVay. In *Novel Approaches to Integrated pest Management*, R. Reuveni, ed. Lewis Publishers, Boca Raton, FL.

Soil Solarization: A Nonpesticidal Method for Controlling Diseases, Nematodes, and Weeds. 1997. C. L. Elmore, J. J. Stapleton, C. E. Bell, and J. E. DeVay. Univ. Calif. Div. Agric. Nat. Res. Leaflet 21377. Oakland.

Spanish-Language Materials

Como crear un programa de monitoreo de plagas en cultivos ornamentales. n.d. J. Newman, K. Robb, S. Tjosvold, A. King, P. Phillips, and M. Guerena. Unpublished.

Diccionario de floricultura Ball: Ball Floriculture Dictionary: English-Spanish with Spanish Definitions. 1995. V. Hoyos de Martens and M. L. Nydia Palms de Villareal. Ball, Batavia, IL.

El Manejo integrado de los insectos, acaros y enfermedades en los cultivos ornamentales. 1994. C. C. Powell and R. K. Lindquist. Ball, Batavia, IL.

Insectos y otras plagas de las flores y plantas de follaje. 1996. J. R. Baker. Hortitecnia Ltda., Bogotá, Columbia.

La Seguridad en el manejo de pesticidas: Manual de referencia para aplicadores privados. 1999. P. J. O'Connor-Marer. Univ. Calif. Div. Agric. Nat. Res. Publ. Publ. 3394. Oakland.

Un Programa de exploración para cultivos ornamentales. 1997. M. Guerena, J. Newman, P. Phillips, and D. Phillips. Univ. Calif. Coop. Ext. Ornamentals & Row Crop Pest Management Project. IPM Information Series 10. Santa Maria, CA.

Weeds

Grower's Weed Identification Handbook. 1998. B. B. Fischer et al., eds. Univ. Calif. Div. Agric. Nat. Res. Publ. 4030. Oakland.

Growers Weed Management Guide. 1993. H. H. Kempen. Thompson, Fresno, CA.

Herbicide Handbook: 7th ed. 1994. W. H. Ahrens, ed. Weed Science Society of America, Champaign, IL.

The Jepson Manual of Higher Plants of California. 1993. J. C. Hickman, ed. Univ. Calif. Press, Berkeley.

UC IPM Pest Management Guidelines: Floriculture and Ornamental Nurseries: Weeds. 2000. C. L. Elmore and C. Wilen. Univ. Calif. Div. Agric. Nat. Res. Publ. 3392. Oakland.

Weeds of the West. 1991. T. D. Whiston, L. C. Burrill, S. A. Dewey, D. W. Cudney, B. E. Nelson, R. D. Lee, and R. Parker. Western Society of Weed Science and University of Wyoming, Laramie, WY.

Weed management in landscape and nursery plantings. 1997. J. F. Derr, J. C. Neal, L. J. Kuhns, R. J. Smeda, L. A. Weston, C. Elmore, C. A. Wilen, J. Ahrens, A. Senesac, and T. Mervosh. In *Weed Management in Horticultural Crops*, M. E. McGiffen, ed. American Society for Horticultural Science. Alexandria, VA.

Literature Cited

These publications are cited in figures and tables as the sources of information and illustrations.

Agrios, G. N. 1997. *Plant Pathology*. 4th ed. San Diego: Academic Press.

Ahrens, W. H., ed. 1994. *Herbicide Handbook: 7th ed*. Champaign, IL: Weed Science Society of America.

Anonymous 1998. *Classification of Herbicides According to Mode of Action*. Herbicide Resistance Action Committee. http://ipmwww.ncsu.edu/HRAC

Anonymous. 1952. *The Yearbook of Agriculture: Insects*. Washington, D.C.: U. S. Dept. Agric.

Anonymous. 1990. *Western Fertilizer Handbook: Horticulture Edition*. Danville, IL: Interstate.

Antonelli, A. L., and R. L. Campbell. 1986. *Root Weevil Control on Rhododendrons*. Pullman: Washington State Univ. Exten. Bull. 0970.

Bailey, D. A. 1996. Alkalinity, pH, and Acidification. In D. W. Reed, ed. *A Grower's Guide to Water, Media, and Nutrition for Greenhouse Crops*. Batavia, IL: Ball. 69-91.

Baker, K. F., and C. N. Roistacher. 1957a. Heat treatment of soil. In *The U.C. System For Producing Healthy Container-grown Plants Through The Use Of Clean Soil, Clean Stock, And Sanitation*, K. F. Baker, ed. Oakland: Univ. Calif. Div. Agric. Sci. Agric. Exp. Sta. Manual 23.

———. 1957b. Equipment for heat treatment of soil. In *The U.C. System For Producing Healthy Container-grown Plants Through The Use Of Clean Soil, Clean Stock, And Sanitation*, K. F. Baker, ed. Oakland: Univ. Calif. Div. Agric. Sci. Agric. Exp. Sta. Manual 23.

Becker, J. O. 1996. Know your worms: foliar nematodes. *Co-Hort* 2.4. Riverside: Univ. Calif. Coop. Exten. and Dept. Botany and Plant Sciences.

Bethke, J. A., and T. D. Paine. 1991. Screen hole size and barriers for exclusion of insect pests of glasshouse crops. *J. Entomol. Sci*. 26: 169–177.

Bethke, J. A., R. A. Redak, and T. D. Paine. 1994. Screens deny specific pests entry to greenhouses. *Calif. Agric*. 48(3): 37–40.

Burt, C., K. O'Connor, and T. Ruehr. 1995. *Fertigation*. San Luis Obispo: California Polytechnic State University Irrigation and Research Center.

Costello, L. R., C. S. Koehler, and W. W. Allen. 1987. *Fuchsia Gall Mite*. Oakland: Univ. Calif. Div. Agric. Nat. Res. Publ. 7179.

Cudney, D., ed. n.d. Weed susceptibility chart. Riverside: University of California. Unpublished.

Davidson, N. A., J. E. Dibble, M. L. Flint, P. J. Mayers, and A. Guye. 1991. *Managing Insects and Mites with Spray Oils*. Oakland: Univ. Calif. Div. Agric. Nat. Res. Publ. 3347.

de Jager, C. M., R. P. T. Butìt, P. G. L. Klinkhamer, and E. Van Der Meijden. 1995. Chemical characteristics of chrysanthemum cause resistance to *Frankliniella occidentalis* (Thysanoptera: Thripidae). *J. Econ. Entomol*. 88: 1746–1753.

Derr, J. F., J. C. Neal, L. J. Kuhns, R. J. Smeda, L. A. Weston, C. Elmore, C. A. Wilen, J. Ahrens, A. Senesac, and T. Mervosh. 1997. Weed management in landscape and nursery plantings. In *Weed Management in Horticultural Crops*, M. E. McGiffen, ed. Alexandria, VA: American Society for Horticultural Science.

Dexter, A. G. 1996. *Weed Control Guide for Sugarbeet*. Sugarbeet Research and Extension Report. Vol. 27: 3–30. Crookston, MN: University of Minnesota.

Doucette, C. F. 1959. The Narcissus Bulb Fly. USDA Leaflet 444.

Dreistadt, S. H. 1994. *Pests of Landscape Trees and Shrubs: An Integrated Pest Management Guide*. Oakland: Univ. Calif. Div. Agric. Nat. Res. Publ. 3359.

———. 1997. *Fungus Gnats, Shore Flies, Moth Flies, and March Flies*. Oakland: Univ. Calif. Div. Agric. Nat. Res. Publ. 7448.

Dreistadt, S. H., and M. L. Flint. 1996. Melon aphid (Homoptera: Aphididae) control by inundative convergent lady beetle (Coleoptera: Coccinellidae) release on chrysanthemum. *Environ. Entomol*. 25: 688–697.

Drost, Y. C., J. C. van Lenteren, and H. J. W. van Roermund. 1998. Life-history parameters of different biotypes of *Bemisia tabaci* (Hemiptera: Aleyrodidae) in relation to temperature and host plant: a selective review. *Bull. Entomol. Res*. 88: 219–229.

Dutky, E. M., and A. B. Sindermann. 1993. Learn to diagnose foliar nematodes. *Grower Talks* 56(11): 63, 65, 67.

Easterbrook, M. A. 1992. The possibilities for control of two-spotted spider mite *Tetranychus urticae* on field-grown strawberries in the UK by predatory mites. *Biocontrol Sci. Tech*. 2: 235–245.

Ehler, L. E., and M. G. Kimsey. 1995. Ecology and management of *Mindarus kinseyi* Voegtlin (Aphidoidia: Mindaridae) on white-fir seedlings at a California nursery. *Hilgardia* 62: 1–62.

Elmore, C. L., J. J. Stapleton, C. E. Bell, and J. E. DeVay. 1997. *Soil Solarization: A Nonpesticidal Method for Controlling Diseases, Nematodes, and Weeds.* Oakland: Univ. Calif. Div. Agric. Nat. Res. Leaflet 21377.

Enkegaard, A. 1993. The poinsettia strain of the cotton whitefly, *Bemisia tabaci* (Homoptera: Aleyrodidae), biological and demographic parameters on poinsettia (*Euphorbia pulcherrima*) in relation to temperature. *Bull. Entomol. Res.* 83: 535–546.

Evans, R. 1998. The development and properties of container soils: Making a good mix. *Growing Points* 2(1): 1–4.

Fan, Y., and F. L. Petitt. 1994. Biological control of broad mite, *Polyphagotarsonemus latus* (Banks), by *Neoseiulus barkeri* Hughes on pepper. *Biol. Control* 4: 390–395.

Farnham, D. S., R. F. Hasek, and J. L. Paul. 1985. *Water Quality: Its Effects on Ornamental Plants.* Oakland: Univ. Calif. Div. Agric. Nat. Res. Leaflet 2995.

Flint, M. L. 1995. *Whiteflies in California: A Resource for Cooperative Extension.* Davis: Univ. Calif. IPM Publ. 19.

Flint, M. L., S. H. Dreistadt, J. Rentner, and M. P. Parrella. 1995. Lady beetle release controls aphids on potted plants. *Calif. Agric.* 49(2): 5–8.

Gorham, J. R., ed. 1991. Insect and Mite Pests in Food: An Illustrated Key. Washington, D.C.: U. S. Dept. Agric. Handb. 655.

Grebus, M. E., and C. A. Wilen. 1996. Compost manual. Univ. Calif. Riverside. Unpublished.

Hara, A. H., W. T. Nishijima, J. D. Hansen, B. C. Bushe, and T. Y. Hata. 1990. Reduced pesticide use in an IPM program for anthurium. *J. Econ. Entomol.* 83: 1531–1534.

Hausbeck, M. K., and S. P. Pennypacker. 1991. Influence of grower activity and disease incidence on concentrations of airborne conidia of *Botrytis cinerea* among geranium stock plants. *Plant Dis.* 75: 1236-1243.

Heinz, K. M., J. R. Brazzle, C. H. Picket, E. T. Natwick, J. M. Nelson, and M. P. Parrella. 1994. Predatory beetle may suppress silverleaf whitefly. *Calif. Agric.* 48(2): 35–40.

Heinz, K. M., L. Nunney, and M. P. Parrella. 1993. Toward predictable biological control of *Liriomyza trifolii* (Diptera: Agromyzidae) infesting greenhouse cut chrysanthemum. *Environ. Entomol.* 22: 1217–1233.

Hoelmer, K. A., L. S. Osborne, and R. K. Yokomi. 1993. Reproduction and feeding behavior of *Delphastus pusillus* (Coleoptera: Coccinellidae), a predator of *Bemisia tabaci* (Homoptera: Aleyrodidae). *J. Econ. Entomol.* 86: 322–329.

Horst, R. K. 1985. *Compendium of Rose Diseases.* St. Paul: APS Press.

Hunt, W. C. 1995. Rethinking spray technology. *Greenhouse Grower* 13(8): 135–138.

Kabashima, J., D. K. Giles, and M. P. Parrella. 1995. Electrostatic sprayers improve pesticide efficiency in greenhouses. *Cal. Agric.* 49(4): 31–35.

Kabashima, J. N., J. D. MacDonald, S. H. Dreistadt, and D. E. Ullman. 1997. *Easy On-Site Tests for Fungi and Viruses in Nurseries and Greenhouses.* Oakland: Univ. Calif. Div. Agric. Nat. Res. Publ. 8002.

Karlik, J. F., P. B. Goodell, and G. W. Osteen. 1995. Improved mite sampling may reduce acaricide use in roses. *Calif. Agric.* 49(3): 38–40.

Kaya, H. K. 1993. Contemporary issues in biological control with entomopathogenic nematodes. Taipei City, Taiwan: Food and Fertilizer Technology Center Exten. Bull. 375.

Kempen, H. H. 1993. *Growers Weed Management Guide.* Fresno, CA: Thompson.

Koehler, C. S., W. W. Allen, and L. R. Costello. 1985. Fuchsia gall mite management. *Calif. Agric.* 39(7, 8): 10–12.

Kono, T., and C. S. Papp. 1977. *Handbook of Agricultural Pests: Aphids, Thrips, Mites, Snails, and Slugs.* Sacramento: Calif. Depart. Food Agric.

Landis, T. D., R. W. Tinus, S. E. McDonald, and J. P. Barnett. 1990. *Containers and Growing Media.* Vol. 2, *The Container Nursery Manual.* United States Depart. Agric. Handb. 674.

Leith, H., D. Burger, P. Kiehl, S. Tjosvold, and G. Vogel. 1990. Reduce runoff from your potted crops by watering based on soil moisture. *Grower Talks* 54(5): 24–26, 28, 31–32.

Malais, M., and W. J. Ravensberg. 1992. *Knowing and Recognizing the Biology of Glasshouse Pests and Their Natural Enemies.* Berkel en Rodenrijs, Netherlands: Koppert Biological Systems.

Martin, C. A., H. G. Ponder, and C. H. Gilliam. 1991. Evaluation of landscape fabrics in suppressing growth of weed species. *J. Environ. Hort.* 9: 38–40.

McKenry, M. V., and P. A. Roberts. 1985. *Phytonematology study guide.* Oakland: Univ. Calif. Div. Agric. Nat. Res. Publ. 4045.

McKenzie, H. L. 1935. *Life History and Control of the Gladiolus Thrips in California.* Calif. Agric. Exp. Sta. Circ. 337: 1–16.

Molinar, R. H. n.d. Weed control in field-grown flowers and bulbs. Hayward, CA: Univ. Calif. Coop. Exten. Unpublished.

Moorman, G. W. 1990a. *Phytotoxicity.* State Park: Penn. State Univ. Coop. Ext. Plant Disease Facts. http://www.cas.psu.edu/docs/CASDEPT/PLANT/ext/phytotox.html

Moorman, G. W. 1990b. *Soil Treatments to Control Soil-borne Pests.* State Park: Penn. State Univ. Coop. Ext. Plant Disease Facts. http://www.cas.psu.edu/docs/CASDEPT/PLANT/ext/soiltrt.html

Nelson, P. V. 1991. *Greenhouse Operation and Management.* Englewood Cliffs, NJ: Prentice Hall.

Newman, J., and A. Mayers. 1997. *Scouting Programs For Ornamental Crops*. Santa Maria: Univ. Calif. Coop. Ext. Ornamentals & Row Crop Pest Management Project. IPM Information Series 8.

Newman, J., K. Robb, S. Tjosvold, and A. King. n.d. How to set up a scouting program on ornamental crops. University of California Cooperative Extension Ventura, San Diego, Monterey, and San Mateo Counties. Unpublished.

Osborne, L. S., and A. R. Chase. 1985. Relative susceptibility of twelve cultivars of *Hedera helix* to two-spotted spider mite and Xanthomonas leaf spot. *HortScience* 20: 269–271.

Osborne, L. S., L. E. Ehler, and J. R. Nechols. 1985. *Biological control of twospotted spider mite in greenhouses*. Gainesville: Univ. Florida Agric. Exp. Sta. Bull. 853.

Parrella, M. P., and B. C. Murphy. n.d. Development and implementation of a reduced-risk pest management strategy in fresh cut roses. Unpublished.

Peterson, A. 1960. *Larvae of Insects*. Part 2. Ann Arbor, MI: Edwards Brothers.

Peterson, J. C. 1982. *Effects of pH upon Nutrient Availability In a Commercial Soilless Root Medium Utilized for Floral Crop Production*. Ohio Agr. Res. and Devel. Center Res. Cir. 268: 16–19

Price, J. F., A. W. Englehard, A. J. Overman, V. W. Yingst, and M. K. Iverson. 1980. Integrated pest management demonstrations for commercial gypsophila. *Proc. Fla. State Hort. Soc.* 93: 187–190.

Quayle, H. J. 1932. *The Biology and Control of Citrus Insects and Mites*. Berkeley: Univ. Calif. Agric. Exper. Sta. Bull. 542.

———. 1938. Insects of Citrus and Other Subtropical Fruits. Ithaca, NY: Comstock.

Radewald, J. D., F. Shibuya, and B. D. Westerdahl. n.d. Ornamental plant-nematode associations currently recognized in California. Univ. Calif. Unpublished.

Redak, R. A., and J. A. Bethke. 1995. Detection and seasonal occurrence of gall-forming wasps (Hymenoptera: Eulophidae) on Geraldton wax plant. *J. Econ. Entomol.* 88: 387–392.

Retzinger, E. J., and C. Mallory-Smith. 1997. Classification of herbicides by site of action for weed resistance management strategies. *Weed Technology* 11: 384–393.

Robb, K. L. 1989. Analysis of *Frankliniella occidentalis* (Pergande) as a pest of floricultural crops in California greenhouses. Univ. Calif. Riverside Ph.D. dissertation.

Schuch, U. K., R. A. Redak, and J. Bethke. 1996. Cultural practices and chrysanthemum: How fertilizer, irrigation, and cultivar choice affect plant growth and insect pests. *Univ. of Calif. Coop. Ext. Co-Hort* 2(4): 9–10.

Smitley, D. R., P. Ferretti, W. H. Carlson, S. Newport, and T. Davis. 1994. How to avoid insecticide phytotoxicity. *Greenhouse Grower* 12(4): 57–64.

Stapleton, J. J., and J. E. DeVay. 1995. Soil solarization: A natural mechanism of integrated pest management. In R. Reuveni, ed. *Novel Approaches to Integrated Pest Management*. Boca Raton, FL: Lewis Publ. 309–322.

Stapleton, J., L. Ferguson, and M. McKenry. 1998. Using solarization to disinfect soil for containerized production. *Univ. Calif. Kearney Agric. Ctr. Plant Protection Qtr.* 8(1 & 2): 7–9.

Stary, P. 1993. Alternative host and parasitoid in first method in aphid pest management in glasshouses. *J. Appl. Ent.* 16:187–191.

Truog, E. 1948. Lime in relation to availability of plant nutrients. *Soil Science* 65: 1–7.

UCDANR. 1996. *Growers' Weed Identification Handbook*. Oakland: Univ. Calif. Div. Agric. Nat. Res. Publ. 4030.

UCIPM. 1991. *Integrated Pest Management for Citrus*. 2d ed. Oakland: Univ. Calif. Div. Agric. Nat. Res. Publ. 3303.

Ullman, D. E., J. L. Sherwood, and T. L. German. 1997. Thrips as vectors of plant pathogens. In T. Lewis, ed. *Thrips as Crop Pests*. Wallingford, UK: CABI. 539–565.

Van Dijken, F. R., M. T. A. Dik, B. Gebala, J. De Jong, and C. Mollema. 1994. Western flower thrips (Thysanoptera: Thripidae) effects on chrysanthemum cultivars: plant growth and leaf scarring in nonflowering plants. *J. Econ. Entomol.* 87: 1312–1317.

van Roermund, H. J. W., and J. C. van Lenteren. 1992. Life-history parameters of the greenhouse whitefly, *Trialeurodes vaporariorum* and the parasitoid *Encarsia formosa*. Wageningen, Netherlands: Wageningen Agricultural University Papers 92-3: 1–147.

Weller, S. C. 1997. Herbicide use and mode of action. In M. E. McGriffen, ed. *Weed Management in Horticultural Crops*. Alexandria, VA: American Society for Horticultural Science. 74–115.

Whitson, T. D., L. C. Burrill, S. A. Dewey, D. W. Cudney, B. E. Nelson, R. D. Lee, and R. Parker. 1991. *Weeds of the West*. Jackson, WY: University of Wyoming. Available as UC DANR Publication 3350.

Yang, J., and C. S. Sandof. 1995. Variegation in *Coleus blumei* and life history of citrus mealybug (Homoptera: Pseudococcidae). *Environ. Entomol.* 24: 1650–1655.

Yoder Brothers. 1988. Leafminer susceptibility ratings. Parrish, Fl. Unpublished.

Index

Major topic discussions are indicated by page numbers in bold type. *Photographs* and *illustrations* are indicated by page numbers in italic type. Most pests and disorders listed in the chapter "Crop Tables" are not indexed here; consult "Crop Tables" for the known pests of each flower crop and the page numbers referring you to more information.

abamectin (Avid), 156, 157, 165, 176
abiotic disorders. *See also* nutrients, disorders
air pollution and, **68**
biotic diseases distinguished from, 42
bud problems of camellia, 7, **293**
carbon dioxide and, **66–67**
chilling injury, 64, 65
containers and, 54
protection from, 65, 82–83
symptoms, 64–65
containers/container spacing, **54**, **63–64**
cultural practices and, **41–68**
defined, 41
disinfectant injury, 80, 359
drainage and, 88
edema, 41, 42, 117
environmental controls for, 32
ethylene, **67**
fertilization and, **54–56**
irrigation-related, **41–47**
leaf scorch, light-related, 7, **62–63**
monitoring methods, 11, 12–13
physical and mechanical injury, **66**, 66
phytotoxicity, 37, **60–61**, 61, 243, *243*
preventing, 6–7, 11
salt damage, **47–52**
shattering, *62*
sunburn/sunscald, **62–63**
symptoms, 41
temperature-related, **64–66**
ventilation problems, **64**
water quality and, **47–52**
abutilon, ornamental viral effects, 122
Acalymma spp. (cucumber beetles), **212**, *212*, 291, 346

acaricides, 156, 158, 215–16
Aceria paradianthi (carnation bud mite), 214, 297
Achillea spp. (yarrow), **390**
acidity, of irrigation water, 47–48, 50–51
Acremonium strictum (wilt), Shasta daisy, 374
Acrosporium spp. (powdery mildew), 274
Aculops fuchsiae (fuchsia gall mite), 33, 214, **219**, *219*, 321
Acyrthosiphon pisum (pea aphid), 140
aeration
of field soils, 23
of growing media, 32, 52, **53**, *53*
of irrigation water, 47
aeroponics systems, 47, 86
African boxwood (*Myrsine africana*), 172, **274**
African corn lily. *See* ixia
African violet, **274–75**
chilling injury, 64
nematodes, 266
pathogen susceptibility, 33
Verticillium wilt, 106
agapanthus, **275**
freezing injury, 65
nematodes, 266
ageratum
methyl bromide sensitive, 79
Verticillium wilt, 106
aglaonema, **275–76**
Agrobacterium radiobacter. *See Agrobacterium tumefaciens*, K-84 strain
Agrobacterium tumefaciens (crown gall), **102–4**
biological controls, 91, 94
identification and biology, 102–3
K-84 strain, 91, 94, *103*
management methods, 104
rotation/fallowing control, 89
symptoms, 102, *103*
Agrotis, 283, 365
ipsilon (black cutworm), 140, 205, 363
air pollution, **68**, 117
Albugo (white rust)
candida, 294
tragopogonis, 326
Aleurodicus dugesii (giant whitefly), 175, **178–79**, *179*, 333, 335, 360
Aleurothrixus floccosus (woolly whitefly), 179
Aleyrodes spiraeoides (iris whitefly), *171*, 173, *175*

algae, as weeds, *82*, 229, 245, 263–64
alkalinity, of irrigation water, 48, 51–52, *52*
allelopathic compounds
in compost, 78
in mulches, 247
alstroemeria, **276**
Alternaria (leaf and flower spots; blight), **117–18**
alternata, 292, 323
anigozanthos, 279
bishop's flower, 364
calendula, 290
calla, 292
candytuft, 295
carnation, 296
cassia, 298
cinerea, 304
dahlia, 312
damping-off, 93
dauci, 364
deep plowing and, 89
dianthi, dianthicola, 296
forsythia, 319
geranium, 323
gypsophila, 331
marigold, 349
poinsettia, 359
Queen Anne's lace, 364
radicina, 364
rotation/fallowing control, 89
safflower, 371
schefflera, 373
stock, 381
sunflower, 382
ultraviolet-absorbing films and, 83
vinca, 388
zinnia, 390
alternative crops, 31–33, 80
Althea rosea, Verticillium wilt, 106
alyssum, **276–77**
methyl bromide sensitive, 79
Verticillium wilt, 106
Amaranthus spp. *See* pigweeds
amaryllis, 29, **277–78**
heat treatment, 29
nematodes, 266
Amblyptilia pica. *See Platyptilia pica*
Amblyseius. *See Iphiseius*; *Neoseiulus*
Ametastegia pallipes (violet sawfly), 355
Ammi majus. *See* bishop's flower
ammonia toxicity
and heat treatment of media, 54

symptoms, 57, 58
Ampelomyces quisqualis (AQ-10), 90, 94, 115
Amphipyra spp. (green fruitworms), 204, 369
anemone, **278–79**
nematodes, 266
Verticillium wilt, 106
anigozanthos, **279**
anther smut, sweet William, 385
anthracnose, **116–18**
thresholds, anthurium, 23, 280
symptoms, 117, *118*
anthurium, **279–80**
control action guidelines for, 23
nematodes, 266
whiteflies, 172
antibiotics, 107–8, 119
Antirrhinum majus. *See* snapdragon
antitranspirants, 92, 115
ants (Formicidae), **191–93**
Argentine, 192
California harvester, 193
damage caused by, 191, *192*
honey, *192*
identification and biology, 191, 193
as insect predators, 147–48
management methods, 191–92
red imported fire, 192–93
southern fire, *192*
sticky material barriers, 145
termites distinguished from, *191*
Aonidiella aurantii (California red scale), 140, *187*, 187–88, *190*
Aphelenchoides (foliar nematodes), **271–72**, *271*
crop hosts, 266–67
fragariae, 274, 302, 354
as cause of leaf spots, 117
dispersal mechanisms, 28
olesistis, 286, 345
ritzemabosi, 274, 302, 354
aphidlions. *See* lacewings, green
Aphidius (aphid parasites), 181–82, *183*
Aphidoletes aphidimyza (aphid predator), 154, *181*, **181–82**
distinguished from fungus gnats, 196
aphids (Aphididae), **179–83**

aster or erigeron root, 182–83
crop hosts, 282, 299, 307, 313, 366
biological controls, 181–82, *183*
cabbage, 140
cotton. *See* aphids, melon
cultural controls, 180
damage caused by, 179
degree-day monitoring, 140
as disease vectors, 90, 123, 133
fertilizers and, 24
fringed orchid, on orchids, 351, 352
green peach, 140, 143, *180*
identification and biology, *135*, 179
insecticides for, 156, 181
iris root, 182–83, 339
life stages, *132*
management methods, 180–82
melon, *135*, 140, 143, 179, *180*
metamorphosis, *132*
monitoring, 180
natural enemies of, *146*, *147*, 149, 151, *151*, *152*
pea, 140
on rose, 22–23, 25, 36, 369
screening to exclude, 143
sooty molds and, 180
susceptibility, chrysanthemum, 33, 303
tulip bulb, 29, **182–83**, 328, 339, 387
woolly, 103
Aphis
gossypii (melon aphid), *135*, 140, 143, 179, *180*
middletonii, 181, 282, 299, 307, 313, 366
Aphytis (scale parasites)
lingnanensis, 189
melinus, 140, 189–90
Apiognomonia veneta, (sycamore anthracnose), *118*
Aquilegia spp. *See* columbine
Argyrotaenia citrana, 349
Armillaria root rot (*Armillaria mellea*), **99–100**
crop rotation to control, 88
identification and biology, 99
management methods, 99–100
symptoms, 99, *99*
armyworms
beet, *203*, 204, 205